D1568560

FOUNDATIONS OF ALGORITHMS

FOUNDATIONS OF ALGORITHMS

USING C++ PSEUDOCODE

SECOND EDITION

Richard E. Neapolitan
Kumarss Naimipour
Northeastern Illinois University

Jones and Bartlett Publishers
Sudbury, Massachusetts

Boston   London   Singapore

Editorial, Sales, and Customer Service Offices

Jones and Bartlett Publishers
40 Tall Pine Drive
Sudbury, MA 01776
(508) 443-5000
info@jbpub.com
http://www.jbpub.com

Jones and Bartlett Publishers International
Barb House, Barb Mews
London W6 7PA
UK

Library of Congress Cataloging-in-Publication Data

Neapolitan, Richard E.
    Foundations of algorithms : with C++ pseudocode / Richard E. Neapolitan, Kumarss Naimipour. —2nd ed.
        p.   cm.
    Includes index.
    ISBN 0-7637-0620-5
    1. Algorithms.   2. Constructive mathematics.   3. Computational complexity.
I. Naimipour, Kumarss.   II. Title.
QA9.58.N43   1997
005.1—dc21   97-28337
                                                                   CIP

Printed in the United States of America
00 99 98   10 9 8 7 6 5 4 3 2

Preface to the Second Edition

Other than correcting errors found in the first edition, the purpose of this second edition is to present algorithms using a C++ like pseudocode. Even though by the time we wrote this text, C and C++ had become the dominant programming languages, we chose a Pascal-like pseudocode because that language was designed specifically to be a teaching language for algorithms. We felt that students would more readily understand algorithms shown in the English-like notation of Pascal rather than the sometimes cryptic notation of C++. However, when students, who had seen only C or C++ in their earlier courses, arrived in our algorithms course, we realized that this is not the case. We learned that these students 'thought' in the C++ language when developing algorithms, and therefore they communicated most easily using that language. We found, for example, that it is most natural for students, versed only in C++, to interpret "&&" to mean "and." Indeed, we noticed that students (and then ourselves) began showing algorithms on the board using pseudocode that looked more like C++ than Pascal. The Pascal-like pseudocode in the text had become a burden rather than an asset. We therefore made the change to C++ in accordance with our primary objective to present analysis of algorithms as accessibly as possible.

As in the first edition, we still use pseudocode and not actual C++ code. The presentation of complex algorithms using all the details of any programming language would only cloud the students' understanding of the algorithms. Furthermore, the pseudocode should be understandable to someone versed in any high-level language, which means it should avoid details specific to any one language as much as possible. Significant deviations from C++ are discussed on pages 4-7 of the text.

We thank Cella Neapolitan for providing the photo of the chess board that appears on the cover of this edition. We also thank all those professors who pointed out errors in the first edition and who had kind words regarding our text. Again, please address and further comments/corrections to Rich Neapolitan, reneapol@gamut.neiu.edu.

R.N.
K.N.

Preface

This text is about designing algorithms, complexity analysis of algorithms, and computational complexity (analysis of problems). It does not cover other types of analyses, such as analysis of correctness. Our motivation for writing this book was our inability to find a text that rigorously discusses complexity analysis of algorithms, yet is accessible to computer science students at mainstream universities such as Northeastern Illinois University. The majority of Northeastern's students have not studied calculus, which means that they are not comfortable with abstract mathematics and mathematical notation. The existing texts that we know of use notation that is fine for a mathematically sophisticated student, but is a bit terse for our student body.

To make our text more accessible, we do the following:

1. assume that the student's mathematics background includes only college algebra and discrete structures;
2. use more English description than is ordinarily used to explain mathematical concepts;
3. give more detail in formal proofs than is usually done;
4. provide many examples.

Because the vast majority of complexity analysis requires only a knowledge of finite mathematics, in most of our discussions we are able to assume only a background in college algebra and discrete structures. That is, for the most part, we do not find it necessary to rely on any concepts learned only in a calculus course. Often students without a calculus background are not yet comfortable with mathematical notation. Therefore, wherever possible, we introduce mathematical concepts (such as "big O") using more English description and less notation than is ordinarily used. It is no mean task finding the right mix of these two—a certain amount of notation is necessary to make a presentation lucid, whereas too much vexes many students. Judging from students' responses, we have found a good mix.

This is not to say that we cheat on mathematical rigor. We provide formal proofs for all our results. However, we give more detail in the presentation of these proofs than is usually done, and we provide a great number of examples. By seeing concrete cases, students can often more easily grasp a theoretical concept. Therefore, if students who do not have strong mathematical backgrounds are willing to put forth sufficient effort, they should be able to follow the mathematical arguments and thereby gain a deeper grasp of the subject matter. Furthermore, we do include material that requires knowledge of calculus (such as the use of limits to determine order and proofs of some theorems). However, students do not need to master this material to understand the rest of the text. Material that requires calculus is marked with a ☻ symbol in the table of contents and in the margin of the text; material that is inherently more difficult than most of the text but that requires no extra mathematical background is marked with a ❖ symbol.

Prerequisites

As mentioned previously, we assume that the student's background in mathematics includes only finite mathematics. The actual mathematics that is required is reviewed in Appendix A. For computer science background, we assume that the student has taken a data structures course. Therefore, material that typically appears in a data structures text is not presented here.

Chapter Contents

For the most part, we have organized this text by technique used to solve problems, rather than by application area. We feel that this organization makes the field of algorithm design and analysis appear more coherent. Furthermore, students can more readily establish a repertoire of techniques that they can investigate as possible ways to solve a new problem. The chapter contents are as follows:

- **Chapter 1** is an introduction to the design and analysis of algorithms. It includes both an intuitive and formal introduction to the concept of order.

- **Chapter 2** covers the divide-and-conquer approach to designing algorithms.

- **Chapter 3** presents the dynamic programming design method. We discuss when dynamic programming should be used instead of divide-and-conquer.

- **Chapter 4** discusses the greedy approach and ends with a comparison of the dynamic programming and greedy approaches to solving optimization problems.

- **Chapters 5** and **6** cover backtracking and branch-and-bound algorithms respectively.

- In **Chapter 7** we switch from analyzing algorithms to computational complexity, which is the analysis of problems. We introduce computational complexity by analyzing the Sorting Problem. We chose that problem because of its importance, because there are such a large variety of sorting algorithms, and, most significantly, because there are sorting algorithms that perform about as well as the lower bound for the Sorting Problem (as far as algorithms that sort only by comparisons of keys). After comparing sorting algorithms, we analyze the problem of sorting by comparisons of keys. The chapter ends with Radix Sort, which is a sorting algorithm that does not sort by comparing keys.

- In **Chapter 8** we further illustrate computational complexity by analyzing the Searching Problem. We analyze both the problem of searching for a key in a list and the Selection Problem, which is the problem of finding the kth-smallest key in a list.

- **Chapter 9** is devoted to intractability and the theory of *NP*. To keep our text accessible yet rigorous, we give a more complete discussion of this material than is usually given in an algorithms text. We start out by explicitly drawing the distinction between problems for which polynomial-time algorithms have been found, problems that have been proven to be intractable, and problems that have not been proven to be intractable but for which polynomial-time algorithms have never been found. We then discuss the sets *P* and *NP*, *NP*-complete problems, complementary problems, *NP*-hard problems, *NP*-easy problems, and *NP*-equivalent problems. We have found that students are often left confused if they do not explicitly see the relationships among these sets. We end the chapter with a discussion of approximation algorithms.

- **Chapter 10** includes a brief introduction to parallel architectures and parallel algorithms.

- **Appendix A** reviews the mathematics that is necessary for understanding the text. **Appendix B** covers techniques for solving recurrences. The results in Appendix B are used in our analyses of divide-and-conquer algorithms in Chapter 2. **Appendix C** presents a disjoint set data structure that is needed to implement two algorithms in Chapter 4.

Pedagogy

To motivate the student, we begin each chapter with a story that relates to the material in the chapter. In addition, we use many examples and end the chapters with ample exercises, which are grouped by section. Following the section exercises are supplementary exercises that are often more challenging.

To show that there is more than one way to attack a problem, we solve some problems using more than one technique. For example, we solve the Traveling Salesperson Problem using dynamic programming, branch-and-bound, and an approximation algorithm. We solve the 0-1 Knapsack Problem using dynamic programming, backtracking, and branch-and-bound. To further integrate the material, we present a theme that spans several chapters, concerning a salesperson named Nancy who is looking for an optimal tour for her sales route.

Course Outlines

We have used the manuscript several times in a one-semester algorithms course that meets three hours per week. The prerequisites include courses in college algebra, discrete structures, and data structures. In an ideal situation, the students remember the material in the mathematics prerequisites sufficiently well for them to be able to review Appendixes A and B on their own. However, we have found it necessary to review most of the material in these appendixes. Given this need, we cover the material in the following order:

Appendix A: All
Chapter 1: All
Appendix B: All
Chapter 2: Sections 2.1–2.5, 2.8
Chapter 3: Sections 3.1–3.4, 3.6

Chapter 4: Sections 4.1, 4.2, 4.4
Chapter 5: Sections 5.1, 5.2, 5.4, 5.6, 5.7
Chapter 6: Sections 6.1, 6.2
Chapter 7: Sections 7.1–7.5, 7.7, 7.8.1, 7.8.2, 7.9
Chapter 8: Sections 8.1.1, 8.5.1, 8.5.2
Chapter 9: Brief introduction to the concepts.

Chapters 2–6 contain several sections each solving a problem using the design method presented in the chapter. We cover the ones of most interest to us, but you are free to choose any of the sections.

If your students are able to review the appendixes on their own, you should be able to cover all of Chapter 9. Although you still may not be able to cover any of Chapter 10, this material is quite accessible once students have studied the first nine chapters. Interested students should be able to read it independently.

Acknowledgments

We would like to thank all those individuals who have read this manuscript and provided many useful suggestions. In particular, we thank our colleagues William Bultman, Jack Hade, Mary and Jim Kenevan, Stuart Kurtz, Don La Budde, and Miguel Vian, all of whom quite readily and thoroughly reviewed whatever was asked of them. We further thank D. C. Heath's reviewers, who made this a far better text through their insightful critiques. Many of them certainly did a much more thorough job than we would have expected. They include David D. Berry, Xavier University; David W. Boyd, Valdosta State University; Vladimir Drobot, San Jose State University; Dan Hirschberg, University of California at Irvine; Raghu Karinthi, West Virginia University; C. Donald La Budde, Northeastern Illinois University; Y. Daniel Liang, Indiana Purdue University at Fort Wayne; David Magagnosc, Drexel University; Robert J. McGlinn, Southern Illinois University at Carbondale; Laurie C. Murphy, University of Mississippi; Paul D. Phillips, Mount Mercy College; H. Norton Riley, California State Polytechnic University, Pomona; Majid Sarrafzadeh, Northwestern University; Cliff Shaffer, Virginia Polytechnical Institute and State University; Nancy Van Cleave, Texas Tech University; and William L. Ziegler, State University of New York, Binghamton.

Errors

There are sure to be some errors in the first edition of an endeavor of this magnitude. If you find any errors or have any suggestions for improvements, we would certainly like to hear from you. Please send your comments to Rich Neapolitan, Computer Science Department, Northeastern Illinois University, 5500 N. St. Louis, Chicago, Illinois 60625. E-mail:reneapol@gamut.neiu.edu. Thanks.

R. N.
K. N.

Contents

CHAPTER 1

Algorithms: Efficiency, Analysis, and Order

*T*his text is about techniques for solving problems using a computer. By "technique," we do not mean a programming style or a programming language but rather the approach or methodology used to solve a problem. For example, suppose Barney Beagle wants to find the name "Collie, Colleen" in the phone book. One approach is to check each name in sequence, starting with the first name, until "Collie, Colleen" is located. No one, however, searches for a name this way. Instead, Barney takes advantage of the fact that the names in the phone book are sorted and opens the book to where he thinks the C's are located. If he goes too far into the book, he thumbs back a little. He continues thumbing back and forth until he locates the page containing "Collie, Colleen." You may recognize this second approach as a modified binary search and the first approach as a sequential search. We discuss these searches further in Section 1.2. The point here is that we have two distinct approaches to solving the problem, and the approaches have nothing to do with a programming language or style. A computer program is simply one way to implement these approaches.

Chapters 2 through 6 discuss various problem-solving techniques and apply those techniques to a variety of problems. Applying a technique to a problem results in a step-by-step procedure for solving the problem. This step-by-step procedure is called an algorithm for the problem. The purpose of studying these techniques and their applications is so that, when confronted with a new problem, you have a repertoire of techniques to consider as possible ways to solve the problem. We will often see that a given problem can be solved using several techniques but that one technique results in a much faster algorithm than the others. Certainly a modified binary search is faster than a sequential search when it comes to finding a name in a phone book. Therefore, we will be concerned not only with determining whether a problem can be solved using a given technique but also with analyzing how efficient the resulting algorithm is in terms of time and storage. When the algorithm is implemented on a computer, *time* means CPU cycles and *storage* means memory. You may wonder why efficiency should be a concern, because computers keep getting faster and memory keeps getting cheaper. In this chapter we discuss some fundamental concepts necessary to the material in the rest of the text. Along the way, we show why efficiency always remains a consideration, regardless of how fast computers get and how cheap memory becomes.

1.1 ALGORITHMS

So far we have mentioned the words "problem," "solution," and "algorithm." Most of us have a fairly good idea of what these words mean. However, to lay a sound foundation, let's define these terms concretely.

A computer program is composed of individual modules, understandable by a computer, that solve specific tasks (such as sorting). Our concern in this text is not the design of entire programs, but rather the design of the individual modules that accomplish the specific tasks. These specific tasks are called problems. Explicitly, we say that a **problem** is a question to which we seek an answer. Examples of problems follow.

Example 1.1   The following is an example of a problem:

Sort the list S of n numbers in nondecreasing order. The answer is the numbers in sorted sequence.

By a **list** we mean a collection of items arranged in a particular sequence. For example,

$$S = [10, 7, 11, 5, 13, 8]$$

is a list of six numbers in which the first number is 10, the second is 7, and so on. We say "nondecreasing order" in Example 1.1 instead of increasing order to allow for the possibility that the same number may appear more than once in the list.

Example 1.2   The following is an example of a problem:

Determine whether the number x is in the list S of n numbers. The answer is yes if x is in S and no if it is not.

A problem may contain variables that are not assigned specific values in the statement of the problem. These variables are called **parameters** to the problem. In Example 1.1 there are two parameters: S (the list) and n (the number of items in S). In Example 1.2 there are three parameters: S, n, and the number x. It is not necessary in these two examples to make n one of the parameters because its value is uniquely determined by S. However, making n a parameter facilitates our descriptions of problems.

Because a problem contains parameters, it represents a class of problems, one for each assignment of values to the parameters. Each specific assignment of values to the parameters is called an **instance** of the problem. A **solution** to an instance of a problem is the answer to the question asked by the problem in that instance.

Example 1.3   An instance of the problem in Example 1.1 is

$$S = [10, 7, 11, 5, 13, 8] \quad \text{and} \quad n = 6.$$

The solution to this instance is [5, 7, 8, 10, 11, 13].

Example 1.4   An instance of the problem in Example 1.2 is

$$S = [10, 7, 11, 5, 13, 8], \quad n = 6, \quad \text{and} \quad x = 5.$$

The solution to this instance is, "yes, x is in S."

We can find the solution to the instance in Example 1.3 by inspecting S and allowing the mind to produce the sorted sequence by cognitive steps that cannot be specifically described. This can be done because S is so small that at a conscious level, the mind seems to scan S rapidly and produce the solution almost immediately (and therefore one cannot describe the steps the mind follows to obtain the solution). However, if the instance had a value of 1000 for n, the mind would not be able to use this method, and it certainly would not be possible to convert such a method of sorting numbers to a computer program. To produce eventually a computer program that can solve all instances of a problem, we must specify a general step-by-step procedure for producing the solution to each instance. This step-by-step procedure is called an **algorithm**. We say that the algorithm *solves* the problem.

Example 1.5   An algorithm for the problem in Example 1.2 is as follows. Starting with the first item in S, compare x with each item in S in sequence until x is found or until S is exhausted. If x is found, answer yes; if x is not found, answer no.

We can communicate any algorithm in the English language as we did in Example 1.5. However, there are two drawbacks to writing algorithms in this manner. First, it is difficult to write a complex algorithm this way, and even if we did, a person would have a difficult time understanding the algorithm. Second, it is not clear how to create a computer language description of an algorithm from an English language description of it.

Because C++ is the language with which students are currently most familiar, we use a C++ like pseudocode to communicate algorithms. Anyone with programming experience in an Algol-like imperative language such as C, Pascal, or Java should have no difficulty with the pseudocode. We illustrate the pseudocode with an algorithm that solves a generalization of the problem in Example 1.2. For simplicity, Examples 1.1 and 1.2 were stated for numbers. However, in general we want to search and sort items that come from any ordered set. Often each item uniquely identifies a record, and therefore we commonly call the items *keys*. For example, a record may consist of personal information about an individual and have the person's social security number as its key. We write searching and sorting algorithms using the defined data type **keytype** for the items. It means the items are from any ordered set.

The following algorithm represents the list S by an array and, instead of merely returning yes or no, returns x's location in the array if x is in S and returns 0 otherwise. This particular searching algorithm does not require that the items come from an ordered set, but we still use our standard data type.

Algorithm 1.1   Sequential Search

Problem: Is the key x in the array S of n keys?

Inputs (parameters): positive integer n, array of keys S indexed from 1 to n, and a key x.

Outputs: *location*, the location of x in S (0 if x is not in S).

```
void seqsearch (int n,
                const keytype S[ ],
                keytype x,
                index& location)
```

```
{
    location = 1;
    while (location<=n && S[location] != x)
        location++;
    if (location> n)
        location = 0;
}
```

The pseudocode is similar, but not identical, to C++. A notable exception is our use of arrays. C++ only allows arrays to be indexed by integers starting at 0. Often we can explain algorithms more clearly using arrays indexed by other integer ranges, and sometimes we can explain them best using indices which are not integers at all. So we allow arbitrary sets to index our arrays. We always specify the ranges of indices in the **Inputs** and **Outputs** specifications for the algorithm. For example, in Algorithm 1.1 we specified that S is indexed from 1 to n. Since we are used to counting the items in a list starting with one, this is a good index range to use for a list. Of course, this particular algorithm can be implemented directly in C++ by declaring

keytype $S[n + 1]$;

and simply not using the $S[0]$ slot. Hereafter we will not discuss the implementation of algorithms in any particular programming language. Our purpose is only to present algorithms clearly so they can be readily understood and analyzed.

There are two other significant deviations from C++ regarding arrays. First, we allow variable length two-dimensional arrays as parameters to routines. See for example Algorithm 1.4 on page 9. Second, we declare local variable-length arrays. For example, if n is a parameter to procedure *example*, and we need a local array indexed from 2 to n, we declare

```
void example (int n)
{
    keytype S[2..n];
    .
    .
    .
}
```

The notation $S[2..n]$, which means an array S indexed from 2 to n, is strictly pseudocode; that is, it is not part of the C++ language.

Whenever we can demonstrate steps more succinctly and clearly using mathematical expressions or English-like descriptions than we could using actual C++ instructions, we do so. For example, suppose some instructions are to be executed only if a variable x is between the values *low* and *high*. We write

if *(low* ≤ *x* ≤ *high)* {   **if** *(low* <= *x* && *x* <= *high)*{
.   rather than   .
.   .
}   }

Suppose we wanted the variable *x* to take the value of variable *y* and *y* to take the value of *x*. We write

                                        temp = *x*;
exchange *x* and *y*;   rather than   *x* = *y*;
                                        y = *temp*;

Besides the data type **keytype**, we often use the following, which also are not predefined C++ data types:

Data Type	Meaning
index	An integer variable used as an index.
number	A variable that could be defined as integral (**int**) or real (**float**).
bool	A variable that can take the values "true" or "false".

We use the data type **number** when it is not important to the algorithm whether the numbers can take any real values or are restricted to the integers.

Sometimes we use the following nonstandard control structure:

repeat (*n* **times**) {
.
.
.
}

This means repeat the code *n* times. In C++ it would be necessary to introduce an extraneous control variable and write a **for** loop. We only use a **for** loop when we actually need to refer to the control variable within the loop.

When the name of an algorithm seems appropriate for a value it returns, we write the algorithm as a function. Otherwise, we write the algorithm as a procedure (void function in C++) and use reference parameters (that is, parameters that are passed by address) to return values. If the parameter is not an array, it is declared with an ampersand (&) at the end of the data type name. For our purposes this means that the parameter contains a value returned by the algorithm. Because arrays are automatically passed by reference in C++ and the ampersand is not used in C++ when passing arrays, we do not use the ampersand to indicate that an array contains values returned by the algorithm. Instead, since the reversed word **const** is used in C++ to prevent modification of a passed array, we use **const** to indicate that the array does not contain values returned by the algorithm.

In general, we avoid features peculiar to C++ so that the pseudocode is accessible to someone who knows only another high-level language. However, we do write instructions like $i++$ which means increment i by 1.

If you do not know C++, you may find the notation used for logical operators and certain relational operators unfamiliar. This notation is as follows:

Operator	C++ symbol
and	**&&**
or	‖
not	**!**

Comparison	C++ code
$x = y$	$(x == y)$
$x \neq y$	$(x \,!= y)$
$(x \leq y)$	$(x <= y)$
$x \geq y$	$(x >= y)$

More example algorithms follow. The first shows the use of a function. While procedures have the keyword **void** before the routine's name, functions have the data type returned by the function before the routine's name. The value is returned in the function via the **return** statement.

Algorithm 1.2　　Add Array Members

Problem: Add all the numbers in the array S of n numbers.

Inputs: positive integer n, array of numbers S indexed from 1 to n.

Outputs: *sum,* the sum of the numbers in S.

```
number sum (int n, const number S[ ])
{
    index i;
    number result;

    result = 0;
    for (i = 1; i <= n; i++)
        result = result + S[i];
    return result;
}
```

We discuss many sorting algorithms in this text. A simple one follows.

Algorithm 1.3　　Exchange Sort

Problem: Sort n keys in nondecreasing order.

Inputs: positive integer n, array of keys S indexed from 1 to n.

Outputs: the array S containing the keys in nondecreasing order.

```
void exchangesort (int n, keytype S[ ])
{
    index i, j;
    for (i = 1; i <= n − 1; i++)
        for (j = i + 1; j <= n; j++)
            if (S[j] < S[i])
                exchange S[i] and S[j];

}
```

The instruction

exchange $S[i]$ and $S[j]$

means that $S[i]$ is to take the value of $S[j]$ and $S[j]$ is to take the value of $S[i]$. This command looks nothing like a C++ instruction; whenever we can state something more simply by not using the details of C++ instructions we do so. Exchange Sort works by comparing the number in the ith slot with the numbers in the $(i + 1)$st through nth slots. Whenever a number in a given slot is found to be smaller than the one in the ith slot, the two numbers are exchanged. In this way, the smallest number ends up in the first slot after the first pass through for i loop, the second-smallest number ends up in the second slot after the second pass, and so on.

The next algorithm does matrix multiplication. Recall that if we have two 2×2 matrices,

$$A = \begin{bmatrix} a_{11} & a_{12} \\ a_{21} & a_{22} \end{bmatrix} \quad \text{and} \quad B = \begin{bmatrix} b_{11} & b_{12} \\ b_{21} & b_{22} \end{bmatrix},$$

their product $C = A \times B$ is given by

$$c_{ij} = a_{i1}b_{1j} + a_{i2}b_{2j}.$$

For example,

$$\begin{bmatrix} 2 & 3 \\ 4 & 1 \end{bmatrix} \times \begin{bmatrix} 5 & 7 \\ 6 & 8 \end{bmatrix} = \begin{bmatrix} 2 \times 5 + 3 \times 6 & 2 \times 7 + 3 \times 8 \\ 4 \times 5 + 1 \times 6 & 4 \times 7 + 1 \times 8 \end{bmatrix} = \begin{bmatrix} 28 & 38 \\ 26 & 36 \end{bmatrix}.$$

In general, if we have two $n \times n$ matrices A and B, their product C is given by

$$c_{ij} = \sum_{k=1}^{n} a_{ik}b_{kj} \qquad \text{for } 1 \le i, j \le n.$$

Directly from this definition, we obtain the following algorithm for matrix multiplication.

Algorithm 1.4   Matrix Multiplication

Problem: Determine the product of two $n \times n$ matrices.

Inputs: a positive integer n, two-dimensional arrays of numbers A and B, each of which has both its rows and columns indexed from 1 to n.

Outputs: a two-dimensional array of numbers C, which has both its rows and columns indexed from 1 to n, containing the product of A and B.

```
void matrixmult (int n,
                const number A[ ][ ],
                const number B[ ][ ],
                      number C[ ][ ])
{
   index i, j, k;

   for (i = 1; i <= n; i++)
     for (j = 1; j < = n; j++) {
       C[i][j] = 0;
       for (k = 1; k <= n; k++)
         C[i][j] = C[i][j] + A[i][k] * B[k][j];
     }
}
```

THE IMPORTANCE OF DEVELOPING
1.2 EFFICIENT ALGORITHMS

Previously we mentioned that, regardless of how fast computers become or how cheap memory gets, efficiency will always remain an important consideration. Next we show why this is so by comparing two algorithms for the same problem.

1.2.1 Sequential Search Versus Binary Search

Earlier we mentioned that the approach used to find a name in the phone book is a modified binary search, and is usually much faster than a sequential search. Next we compare algorithms for the two approaches to show how much faster the binary search is.

We have already written an algorithm that does a sequential search—namely, Algorithm 1.1. An algorithm for doing a binary search of an array that is sorted in nondecreasing order is similar to thumbing back and forth in a phone book. That is, given that we are searching for x, the algorithm first compares x with the middle item of the array. If they are equal, the algorithm is done. If x is smaller than the middle item, then x must be in the first half of the array (if it is present at all), and the algorithm repeats the searching procedure on the first half of the array. (That is, x is compared with the middle item of the first half of the array. If they are equal, the algorithm is done, etc.) If x is larger than the middle item of the array, the search is repeated on the second half of the array. This procedure is repeated until x is found or it is determined that x is not in the array. An algorithm for this method follows.

Algorithm 1.5   Binary Search

Problem: Determine whether x is in the sorted array S of n keys.

Inputs: positive integer n, sorted (nondecreasing order) array of keys S indexed from 1 to n, a key x.

Outputs: *location*, the location of x in S (0 if x is not in S).

```
void binsearch (int n,
                const keytype S[ ],
                keytype x,
                index& location)
{
    index low, high, mid;

    low = 1; high = n;
    location = 0;
    while (low <= high && location == 0) {
        mid = ⌊(low + high)/2⌋;
        if (x == S[mid])
            location = mid;
        else if (x < S[mid])
            high = mid − 1;
        else
            low = mid + 1;
    }
}
```

Let's compare the work done by Sequential Search and Binary Search. For focus we will determine the number of comparisons done by each algorithm. If the array S contains 32 items and x is not in the array, Algorithm 1.1 (Sequential Search) compares x with all 32 items before determining that x is not in the array.

In general, Sequential Search does n comparisons to determine that x is not in an array of size n. It should be clear that this is the most comparisons Sequential Search ever makes when searching an array of size n. That is, if x is in the array, the number of comparisons is no greater than n.

Next consider Algorithm 1.5 (Binary Search). There are two comparisons of x with $S[mid]$ in each pass through the **while** loop (except when x is found). In an efficient assembler language implementation of the algorithm, x would be compared with $S[mid]$ only once in each pass, the result of that comparison would set the condition code, and the appropriate branch would take place based on the value of the condition code. This means that there would be only one comparison of x with $S[mid]$ in each pass through the **while** loop. We will assume the algorithm is implemented in this manner. With this assumption, Figure 1.1 shows that the algorithm does six comparisons when x is larger than all the items in an array of size 32. Notice that $6 = \lg 32 + 1$. By "lg" we mean $\log_2$. The $\log_2$ is encountered so often in analysis of algorithms that we reserve the special symbol lg for it. You should convince yourself that this is the most comparisons Binary Search ever does. That is, if x is in the array, or if x is smaller than all the array items, or if x is between two array items, the number of comparisons is no greater than when x is larger than all the array items.

Suppose we double the size of the array so that it contains 64 items. Binary Search does only one comparison more because the first comparison cuts the array in half, resulting in a subarray of size 32 that is searched. Therefore, when x is larger than all the items in an array of size 64, Binary Search does seven comparisons. Notice that $7 = \lg 64 + 1$. In general, each time we double the size of the array we add only one comparison. Therefore, if n is a power of 2 and x is larger than all the items in an array of size n, the number of comparisons done by Binary Search is $\lg n + 1$.

Table 1.1 compares the number of comparisons done by Sequential Search and Binary Search for various values of n, when x is larger than all the items in the array. When the array contains around 4 billion items (about the number of people in the world), Binary Search does only 33 comparisons whereas Sequential Search compares x with all 4 billion items. Even if the computer was capable of completing one pass through the **while** loop in a nanosecond (one billionth of a second), Sequential Search would take 4 seconds to determine that x is not in the

Figure 1.1 The array items that Binary Search compares with x when x is larger than all the items in an array of size 32. The items are numbered according to the order in which they are compared.

Table 1.1 The number of comparisons done by Sequential Search and Binary Search when x is larger than all the array items

Array Size	Number of Comparisons by Sequential Search	Number of Comparisons by Binary Search
128	128	8
1,024	1,024	11
1,048,576	1,048,576	21
4,294,967,296	4,294,967,296	33

array, whereas Binary Search would make that determination almost instantaneously. This difference would be significant in an on-line application or if we needed to search for many items.

For convenience, we considered only arrays whose sizes were powers of 2 in the previous discussion of Binary Search. In Chapter 2 we will return to Binary Search, because it is an example of the divide-and-conquer approach, which is the focus of that chapter. At that time we will consider arrays whose sizes can be any positive integer.

As impressive as the searching example is, it is not absolutely compelling because Sequential Search still gets the job done in an amount of time tolerable to a human life span. Next we will look at an inferior algorithm that does not get the job done in a tolerable amount of time.

1.2.2 The Fibonacci Sequence

The algorithms discussed here compute the nth term of the Fibonacci Sequence, which is defined recursively as follows:

$$f_0 = 0$$
$$f_1 = 1$$
$$f_n = f_{n-1} + f_{n-2} \qquad \text{for } n \geq 2$$

Computing the first few terms, we have

$$f_2 = f_1 + f_0 = 1 + 0 = 1$$
$$f_3 = f_2 + f_1 = 1 + 1 = 2$$
$$f_4 = f_3 + f_2 = 2 + 1 = 3$$
$$f_5 = f_4 + f_3 = 3 + 2 = 5, \text{ etc.}$$

There are various applications of the Fibonacci Sequence in computer science and mathematics. Because the Fibonacci Sequence is defined recursively, we obtain the following recursive algorithm from the definition.

Algorithm 1.6 nth Fibonacci Term (Recursive)

Problem: Determine the nth term in the Fibonacci Sequence.

Inputs: a nonnegative integer n.

Outputs: *fib,* the nth term of the Fibonacci Sequence.

```
int fib (int n)
{
   if (n <= 1)
      return n;
   else
      return fib(n - 1) + fib(n - 2);
}
```

By ''nonnegative integer'' we mean an integer that is greater than or equal to 0, whereas by ''positive integer'' we mean an integer that is strictly greater than 0. We specify the input to the algorithm in this manner to make it clear what values the input can take. However, for the sake of avoiding clutter, we declare n simply as an integer in the expression of the algorithm. We will follow this convention throughout the text.

Although the algorithm was easy to create and is understandable, it is extremely inefficient. Figure 1.2 shows the recursion tree corresponding to the algorithm when computing *fib*(5). The children of a node in the tree contain the recursive calls made by the call at the node. For example, to obtain *fib*(5) at the top level we need *fib*(4) and *fib*(3), then to obtain *fib*(3) we need *fib*(2) and *fib*(1), etc. As the tree shows, the function is inefficient because values are computed over and over again. For example, *fib*(2) is computed three times.

How inefficient is this algorithm? The tree in Figure 1.2 shows that the algorithm computes the following numbers of terms to determine *fib*(n) for $0 \leq n \leq 6$:

n	*Number of Terms Computed*
0	1
1	1
2	3
3	5
4	9
5	15
6	25

The first six values can be obtained by counting the nodes in the subtree rooted at *fib*(n) for $1 \leq n \leq 5$, whereas the number of terms for *fib*(6) is the sum of the

Figure 1.2 The recursion tree corresponding to Algorithm 1.6 when computing the fifth Fibonacci term.

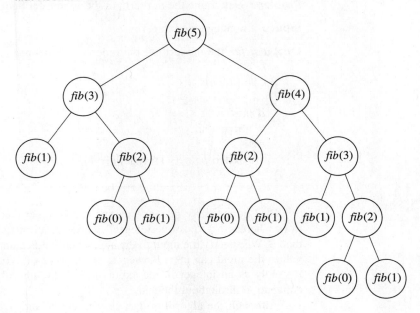

nodes in the trees rooted at *fib*(5) and *fib*(4) plus the one node at the root. These numbers do not suggest a simple expression like the one obtained for Binary Search. Notice, however, that in the case of the first seven values, the number of terms in the tree more than doubles every time n increases by 2. For example, there are nine terms in the tree when $n = 4$ and 25 terms when $n = 6$. Let's call $T(n)$ the number of terms in the recursion tree for n. If the number of terms more than doubled every time n increased by 2, we would have the following for n a positive power of 2:

$$
\begin{aligned}
T(n) &> 2 \times T(n - 2) \\
&> 2 \times 2 \times T(n - 4) \\
&> 2 \times 2 \times 2 \times T(n - 6) \\
&\qquad \vdots \\
&> \underbrace{2 \times 2 \times 2 \times \cdots \times 2}_{n/2 \text{ terms}} \times T(0)
\end{aligned}
$$

Because $T(0) = 1$, this would mean $T(n) > 2^{n/2}$. We use induction to show that this is true for $n \geq 2$ even if n is not a power of 2. The inequality does not hold for $n = 1$ because $T(1) = 1$, which is less than $2^{1/2}$. Induction is reviewed in Section A.3 in Appendix A.

Theorem 1.1 If $T(n)$ is the number of terms in the recursion tree corresponding to Algorithm 1.6, then, for $n \geq 2$,

$$T(n) > 2^{n/2}.$$

Proof: The proof is by induction on n.

Induction base: We need two base cases because the induction step assumes the results of two previous cases. For $n = 2$ and $n = 3$, the recursion in Figure 1.2 shows that

$$T(2) = 3 > 2 = 2^{2/2}$$
$$T(3) = 5 > 2.83 \approx 2^{3/2}$$

Induction hypothesis: One way to make the induction hypothesis is to assume that the statement is true for all $m < n$. Then, in the induction step, show that this implies that the statement must be true for n. This technique is used in this proof. Suppose for all m such that $2 \leq m < n$

$$T(m) > 2^{m/2}.$$

Induction step: We must show that $T(n) > 2^{n/2}$. The value of $T(n)$ is the sum of $T(n - 1)$ and $T(n - 2)$ plus the one node at the root. Therefore,

$$
\begin{aligned}
T(n) &= T(n - 1) + T(n - 2) + 1 \\
&> 2^{(n-1)/2} + 2^{(n-2)/2} + 1 \qquad\qquad \{\text{by induction hypothesis}\} \\
&> 2^{(n-2)/2} + 2^{(n-2)/2} = 2 \times 2^{(n/2)-1} = 2^{n/2}.
\end{aligned}
$$

We established that the number of terms computed by Algorithm 1.6 to determine the nth Fibonacci term is greater than $2^{n/2}$. We will return to this result to show how inefficient the algorithm is. But first let's develop an efficient algorithm for computing the nth Fibonacci term. Recall that the problem with the recursive algorithm is that the same value is computed over and over. As Figure 1.2 shows, *fib*(2) is computed three times in determining *fib*(5). If when computing a value, we save it in an array, then whenever we need it later we do not need to recompute it. The following iterative algorithm uses this strategy.

Algorithm 1.7

*n*th Fibonacci Term (Iterative)

Problem: Determine the *n*th term in the Fibonacci Sequence.

Inputs: a nonnegative integer *n*.

Outputs: *fib2,* the *n*th term in the Fibonacci Sequence.

```
int fib2 (int n)
{
    index i;
    int f[0..n];
```

```
f[0] = 0;
if (n > 0) {
    f[1] = 1;
    for (i = 2; i <= n; i++)
        f[i] = f[i - 1] + f[i - 2];
}
return f[n];
}
```

Algorithm 1.7 can be written without using the array f because only the two most recent terms are needed in each iteration of the loop. However, it is more clearly illustrated using the array.

To determine $fib2(n)$, the previous algorithm computes every one of the first $n + 1$ terms just once. So it computes $n + 1$ terms to determine the nth Fibonacci term. Recall that Algorithm 1.6 computes more than $2^{n/2}$ terms to determine the nth Fibonacci term. Table 1.2 compares these expressions for various values of n. The execution times are based on the simplifying assumption that one term can be computed in 10^{-9} second. The table shows the time it would take Algorithm 1.7 to compute the nth term on a hypothetical computer that could compute each term in a nanosecond, and it shows a lower bound on the time it would take to execute Algorithm 1.7. By the time n is 80, Algorithm 1.6 takes at least 18 minutes. When n is 120, it takes more than 36 years, an amount of time intolerable to a human life span. Even if we could build a computer one billion times as fast, Algorithm 1.6 would take over 40,000 years to compute the 200th term. This result can be obtained by dividing the time for the 200th term by one billion. We see that regardless of how fast computers become, Algorithm 1.6 will still take

Table 1.2 A comparison of Algorithms 1.6 and 1.7

n	$n + 1$	$2^{n/2}$	Execution Time Using Algorithm 1.7	Lower Bound on Execution Time Using Algorithm 1.6
40	41	1,048,576	41 ns*	1048 μs†
60	61	1.1×10^9	61 ns	1 s
80	81	1.1×10^{12}	81 ns	18 min
100	101	1.1×10^{15}	101 ns	13 days
120	121	1.2×10^{18}	121 ns	36 years
160	161	1.2×10^{24}	161 ns	3.8×10^7 years
200	201	1.3×10^{30}	201 ns	4×10^{13} years

*1 ns = 10^{-9} second.
†1 μs = 10^{-6} second.

an intolerable amount of time unless n is small. On the other hand, Algorithm 1.7 computes the nth Fibonacci term almost instantaneously. This comparison shows why the efficiency of an algorithm remains an important consideration regardless of how fast computers become.

Algorithm 1.6 is a divide-and-conquer algorithm. Recall that the divide-and-conquer approach produced a very efficient algorithm (Algorithm 1.5: Binary Search) for the problem of searching a sorted array. As shown in Chapter 2, the divide-and-conquer approach leads to very efficient algorithms for some problems, but very inefficient algorithms for other problems. Our efficient algorithm for computing the nth Fibonacci term (Algorithm 1.7) is an example of the dynamic programming approach, which is the focus of Chapter 3. We see that choosing the best approach can be essential.

We showed that Algorithm 1.6 computes at least an exponentially large number of terms, but could it be even worse? The answer is no. Using the techniques in Appendix B, it is possible to obtain an exact formula for the number of terms, and the formula is exponential in n. See Examples B.5 and B.9 in Appendix B for further discussion of the Fibonacci Sequence.

1.3 ANALYSIS OF ALGORITHMS

To determine how efficiently an algorithm solves a problem, we need to analyze the algorithm. We introduced efficiency analysis of algorithms when we compared the algorithms in the preceding section. However, we did those analyses rather informally. We will now discuss terminology used in analyzing algorithms and the standard methods for doing analyses. We will adhere to these standards in the remainder of the text.

1.3.1 Time Complexity Analysis

When analyzing the efficiency of an algorithm in terms of time, we do not determine the actual number of CPU cycles, because this depends on the particular computer on which the algorithm is run. Furthermore, we do not even want to count every instruction executed, because the number of instructions depends on the programming language used to implement the algorithm and the way the programmer writes the program. Rather, we want a measure that is independent of the computer, the programming language, the programmer, and all the complex details of the algorithm such as incrementing of loop indices, setting of pointers, etc. We learned that Algorithm 1.5 is much more efficient than Algorithm 1.1 by comparing the numbers of comparisons done by the two algorithms for various values of n, where n is the number of items in the array. This is a standard technique for analyzing algorithms. In general, the running time of an algorithm increases with the size of the input, and the total running time is roughly proportional to how many times some basic operation (such as a comparison instruction) is done. We therefore analyze the algorithm's efficiency by determining the number of times some basic operation is done as a function of the size of the input.

For many algorithms it is easy to find a reasonable measure of the size of the input, which we call the *input size*. For example, consider Algorithms 1.1 (Sequential Search), 1.2 (Add Array Members), 1.3 (Exchange Sort), and 1.5 (Binary Search). In all these algorithms, n, the number of items in the array, is a simple measure of the size of the input. Therefore, we can call n the input size. In Algorithm 1.4 (Matrix Multiplication), n, the number of rows and columns, is a simple measure of the size of the input. Therefore, we can again call n the input size. In some algorithms, it is more appropriate to measure the size of the input using two numbers. For example, when the input to an algorithm is a graph, we often measure the size of the input in terms of both the number of vertices and the number of edges. Therefore, we say that the input size consists of both parameters.

Sometimes we must be cautious about calling a parameter the input size. For example, in Algorithms 1.6 (nth Fibonacci Term, Recursive) and 1.7 (nth Fibonacci Term, Iterative), you may think that n should be called the input size. However, n is the input; it is not the *size* of the input. For this algorithm, a reasonable measure of the size of the input is the number of symbols used to encode n. If we use binary representation, the input size will be the number of bits it takes to encode n, which is $\lfloor \lg n \rfloor + 1$. For example,

$$n = 13 = \underbrace{1101_2}_{4 \text{ bits}}$$

Therefore, the size of the input $n = 13$ is 4. We gained insight into the relative efficiency of the two algorithms by determining the number of terms each computes as a function of n, but still n does not measure the size of the input. These considerations will be important in Chapter 9, where we will discuss the input size in more detail. Until then it will usually suffice to use a simple measure, such as the number of items in an array, as the input size.

After determining the input size, we pick some instruction or group of instructions such that the total work done by the algorithm is roughly proportional to the number of times this instruction or group of instructions is done. We call this instruction or group of instructions the *basic operation* in the algorithm. For example, x is compared with an item S in each pass through the loops in Algorithms 1.1 and 1.5. Therefore, the compare instruction is a good candidate for the basic operation in each of these algorithms. By determining how many times Algorithms 1.1 and 1.5 do this basic operation for each value of n, we gained insight into the relative efficiencies of the two algorithms.

In general, a *time complexity analysis* of an algorithm is the determination of how many times the basic operation is done for each value of the input size. Although we do not want to consider the details of how an algorithm is implemented, we will ordinarily assume that the basic operation is implemented as efficiently as possible. For example, we assume that Algorithm 1.5 is implemented such that the comparison is done just once. In this way, we analyze the most efficient implementation of the basic operation.

There is no hard-and-fast rule for choosing the basic operation. It is largely a matter of judgment and experience. As already mentioned, we ordinarily do not include the instructions that compose the control structure. For example, in Algorithm 1.1 we do not include the instructions that increment and compare the index in order to control the passes through the **while** loop. Sometimes it suffices simply to consider one pass through a loop as one execution of the basic operation. At the other extreme, for a very detailed analysis, one could consider the execution of each machine instruction as doing the basic operation once. As mentioned earlier, because we want our analyses to remain independent of the computer, we will never do that in this text.

At times we may want to consider two different basic operations. For example, in an algorithm that sorts by comparing keys, we often want to consider the comparison instruction and the assignment instruction each individually as the basic operation. By this we do not mean that these two instructions together compose the basic operation, but rather that we have two distinct basic operations, one being the comparison instruction and the other being the assignment instruction. We do this because ordinarily a sorting algorithm does not do the same number of comparisons as it does assignments. Therefore, we can gain more insight into the efficiency of the algorithm by determining how many times each is done.

Recall that a time complexity analysis of an algorithm determines how many times the basic operation is done for each value of the input size. In some cases the number of times it is done depends not only on the input size, but also on the input's values. This is the case in Algorithm 1.1 (Sequential Search). For example, if x is the first item in the array, the basic operation is done once, whereas if x is not in the array, it is done n times. In other cases, such as Algorithm 1.2 (Add Array Members), the basic operation is always done the same number of times for every instance of size n. When this is the case, $T(n)$ is defined as the number of times the algorithm does the basic operation for an instance of size n. $T(n)$ is called the every-case time complexity of the algorithm, and the determination of $T(n)$ is called an ***every-case time complexity analysis.*** Examples of every-case time complexity analyses follow.

Every-Case Time Complexity Analysis of Algorithm 1.2 (Add Array Members)

Other than control instructions, the only instruction in the loop is the one that adds an item in the array to *sum*. Therefore, we will call that instruction the basic operation.

Basic operation: the addition of an item in the array to *sum*.

Input size: n, the number of items in the array.

Regardless of the values of the numbers in the array, there are n passes through the **for** loop. Therefore, the basic operation is always done n times and

$$T(n) = n.$$

Every-Case Time Complexity Analysis of Algorithm 1.3 (Exchange Sort)

As mentioned previously, in the case of an algorithm that sorts by comparing keys, we can consider the comparison instruction or the assignment instruction as the basic operation. We will analyze the number of comparisons here.

Basic operation: the comparison of $S[j]$ with $S[i]$.

Input size: n, the number of items to be sorted.

We must determine how many passes there are through the **for** j loop. For a given n there are always $n - 1$ passes through the **for** i loop. In the first pass through the **for** i loop, there are $n - 1$ passes through the **for** j loop, in the second pass there are $n - 2$ passes through the **for** j loop, in the third pass there are $n - 3$ passes through the **for** j loop, . . . , and in the last pass there is one pass through the **for** j loop. Therefore, the total number of passes through the **for** j loop is given by

$$T(n) = (n - 1) + (n - 2) + (n - 3) + \cdots + 1 = \frac{(n - 1)n}{2}.$$

The last equality is derived in Example A.1 in Appendix A.

Every-Case Time Complexity Analysis of Algorithm 1.4 (Matrix Multiplication)

The only instruction in the innermost **for** loop is the one that does a multiplication and an addition. It is not hard to see that the algorithm can be implemented in such a way that fewer additions are done than multiplications. Therefore, we will consider only the multiplication instruction to be the basic operation.

Basic operation: multiplication instruction in the innermost **for** loop.

Input size: n, the number of rows and columns.

There are always n passes through the **for** i loop, in each pass there are always n passes through the **for** j loop, and in each pass through the **for** j loop there are always n passes through the **for** k loop. Because the basic operation is inside the **for** k loop,

$$T(n) = n \times n \times n = n^3.$$

As discussed previously, the basic operation in Algorithm 1.1 is not done the same number of times for all instances of size n. So this algorithm does not have an every-case time complexity. This is true for many algorithms. However, this does not mean that we cannot analyze such algorithms, because there are three other analysis techniques that can be tried. The first is to consider the maximum number of times the basic operation is done. For a given algorithm, $W(n)$ is defined as the maximum number of times the algorithm will ever do its basic operation for an input size of n. So $W(n)$ is called the worse-case time complexity of the algorithm, and the determination of $W(n)$ is called a ***worst-case time complexity analysis.*** If $T(n)$ exists, then clearly $W(n) = T(n)$. The following is an analysis of $W(n)$ in a case where $T(n)$ does not exist.

Worst-Case Time Complexity Analysis of Algorithm 1.1 (Sequential Search)

Basic operation: the comparison of an item in the array with x.

Input size: n, the number of items in the array.

The basic operation is done at most n times, which is the case if x is the last item in the array or if x is not in the array. Therefore,

$$W(n) = n.$$

Although the worst-case analysis informs us of the absolute maximum amount of time consumed, in some cases we may be more interested in knowing how the algorithm performs on the average. For a given algorithm, $A(n)$ is defined as the average (expected value) of the number of times the algorithm does the basic operation for an input size of n. (See Section A.8.2 in Appendix A for a discussion of average.) $A(n)$ is called the average-case time complexity of the algorithm, and the determination of $A(n)$ is called an ***average-case time complexity analysis.*** As is the case for $W(n)$, if $T(n)$ exists, then $A(n) = T(n)$.

To compute $A(n)$, we need to assign probabilities to all possible inputs of size n. It is important to assign probabilities based on all available information. For example, our next analysis will be an average-case analysis of Algorithm 1.1. We will assume that if x is in the array, it is equally likely to be in any of the array slots. If we know only that x may be somewhere in the array, our information gives us no reason to prefer one array slot over another. Therefore, it is reasonable to assign equal probabilities to all array slots. This means that we are determining the average search time when we search for all items the same number of times. If we have information indicating that the inputs will not arrive according to this distribution, we should not use this distribution in our analysis. For example, if the array contains first names and we are searching for names that have been chosen at random from all people in the United States, an array slot containing the common name "John" will probably be searched more often than one containing the uncommon name "Felix" (see Section A.8.1 in Appendix A for a discussion of randomness). We should not ignore this information and assume that all slots are equally likely.

As the following analysis illustrates, it is usually harder to analyze the average case than it is to analyze the worst case.

■■■■   **Average-Case Time Complexity Analysis of Algorithm 1.1 (Sequential Search)**

Basic operation: the comparison of an item in the array with x.

Input size: n, the number of items in the array.

We first analyze the case where it is known that x is in S, where the items in S are all distinct, and where we have no reason to believe that x is more likely to be in one array slot than it is to be in another. Based on this information, for $1 \le k \le n$, the probability that x is in the kth array slot is $1/n$. If x is in the kth array slot, the number of times the basic operation is done to locate x (and, therefore, to exit the loop) is k. This means that the average time complexity is given by

$$A(n) = \sum_{k=1}^{n} \left(k \times \frac{1}{n} \right) = \frac{1}{n} \times \sum_{k=1}^{n} k = \frac{1}{n} \times \frac{n(n+1)}{2} = \frac{n+1}{2}.$$

The third step in this quadruple equality is derived in Example A.1 of Appendix A. As we would expect, on the average, about half the array is searched.

Next we analyze the case where x may not be in the array. To analyze this case we must assign some probability p to the event that x is in the array. If x is in the array, we will again assume that it is equally likely to be in any of the slots from 1 to n. The probability that x is in the kth slot is then p/n, and the probability that it is not in the array is $1 - p$. Recall that there are k passes through the loop if x is found in the kth slot, and n passes through the loop if x is not in the array. The average time complexity is therefore given by

$$A(n) = \sum_{k=1}^{n} \left(k \times \frac{p}{n} \right) + n(1 - p)$$
$$= \frac{p}{n} \times \frac{n(n+1)}{2} + n(1 - p) = n\left(1 - \frac{p}{2}\right) + \frac{p}{2}.$$

The last step in this triple equality is derived with algebraic manipulations. If $p = 1$, $A(n) = (n+1)/2$, as before, whereas if $p = 1/2$, $A(n) = 3n/4 + 1/4$. This means that about 3/4 of the array is searched on the average.

Before proceeding, we offer a word of caution about the average. Although an average is often referred to as a typical occurrence, one must be careful in interpreting the average in this manner. For example, a meteorologist may say that a typical January 25 in Chicago has a high of 22 °F because 22 °F has been the average high for that date over the past 80 years. The paper may run an article saying that the typical family in Evanston, Illinois, earns $50,000 annually because that is the average income. An average can be called "typical" only if the actual cases do not deviate much from the average (that is, only if the standard deviation is small). This may be the case for the high temperature on January 25. However, Evanston is a community with wealthy areas and fairly poor areas. It is more typical for a family to make either $20,000 annually or $100,000 annually than to make $50,000. Recall in the previous analysis that $A(n)$ is $(n + 1)/2$ when it is known that x is in the array. This is not the typical search time, because all search times between 1 and n are equally typical. Such considerations are important in algorithms that deal with response time. For example, consider a system that monitors a nuclear power plant. If even a single instance has a bad response time, the results could be catastrophic. It is therefore important to know whether the average response time is 3 seconds because all response times are around 3 seconds or because most are 1 second and some are 60 seconds.

A final type of time complexity analysis is the determination of the smallest number of times the basic operation is done. For a given algorithm, $B(n)$ is defined as the minimum number of times the algorithm will ever do its basic operation for an input size of n. So $B(n)$ is called the best-case time complexity of the algorithm, and the determination of $B(n)$ is called a ***best-case time complexity analysis.*** As is the case for $W(n)$ and $A(n)$, if $T(n)$ exists, then $B(n) = T(n)$. Let's determine $B(n)$ for Algorithm 1.1.

Best-Case Time Complexity Analysis of Algorithm 1.1 (Sequential Search)

Basic operation: the comparison of an item in the array with x.

Input size: n, the number of items in the array.

Because $n \geq 1$, there must be at least one pass through the loop. If $x = S[1]$, there will be one pass through the loop regardless of the size of n. Therefore,

$$B(n) = 1.$$

For algorithms that do not have every-case time complexities, we do worst-case and average-case analyses much more often than best-case analyses. An average-case analysis is valuable because it tells us how much time the algorithm would take when used many times on many different inputs. This would be useful, for example, in the case of a sorting algorithm that was used repeatedly to sort all possible inputs. Often, a relatively slow sort can occasionally be tolerated if, on the average, the sorting time is good. In Section 2.4 we will see an algorithm, named Quicksort, that does exactly this. It is one of the most popular sorting algorithms. As noted previously, an average-case analysis would not suffice in a system that monitored a nuclear power plant. In this case, a worst-case analysis would be more useful because it would give us an upper bound on the time taken by the algorithm. For both the applications just discussed, a best-case analysis would be of little value.

We have only discussed analysis of the time complexity of an algorithm. All these same considerations also pertain to analysis of memory complexity, which is an analysis of how efficient the algorithm is in terms of memory. Although most of the analyses in this text are time complexity analyses, we will occasionally find it useful to do a memory complexity analysis.

In general, a ***complexity function*** can be any function from the nonnegative integers to the nonnegative reals. When not referring to the time complexity or memory complexity for some particular algorithm, we will usually use standard function notation, such as $f(n)$ and $g(n)$, to represent complexity functions.

Example 1.6   The functions

$$f(n) = n$$
$$f(n) = n^2$$
$$f(n) = \lg n$$
$$f(n) = 3n^2 + 4n$$

are all examples of complexity functions because they all map the nonnegative integers to the nonnegative reals.

1.3.2 Applying the Theory

When applying the theory of algorithm analysis, one must sometimes be aware of the time it takes to execute the basic operation, the overhead instructions, and the control instructions on the actual computer on which the algorithm is implemented. By "overhead instructions" we mean instructions such as initialization instructions before a loop. The number of times these instructions execute does not increase with input size. By "control instructions" we mean instructions such as incrementing an index to control a loop. The number of times these instructions execute increases with input size. The basic operation, overhead instructions, and control instructions are all properties of an algorithm and the implementation of the algorithm. They are not properties of a problem. This means that they are usually different for two different algorithms for the same problem.

Suppose we have two algorithms for the same problem with the following every-case time complexities: n for the first algorithm and n^2 for the second algorithm. The first algorithm appears more efficient. Suppose, however, a given computer takes 1000 times as long to process the basic operation once in the first algorithm as it takes to process the basic operation once in the second algorithm. By "process" we mean that we are including the time it takes to execute the control instructions. Therefore, if t is the time required to process the basic operation once in the second algorithm, $1000t$ is the time required to process the basic operation once in the first algorithm. For simplicity, let's assume that the time it takes to execute the overhead instructions is negligible in both algorithms. This means the times it takes the computer to process an instance of size n are $n \times 1000t$ for the first algorithm and $n^2 \times t$ for the second algorithm. We must solve the following inequality to determine when the first algorithm is more efficient:

$$n^2 \times t > n \times 1000t.$$

Dividing both sides by nt yields

$$n > 1000.$$

If the application never had an input size larger than 1000, the second algorithm should be implemented. Before proceeding, we should point out that it is not always so easy to determine precisely when one algorithm is faster than another. Sometimes we must use approximation techniques to analyze the inequalities obtained by comparing two algorithms.

Recall that we are assuming that the time it takes to process the overhead instructions is negligible. If this were not the case, these instructions would also have to be considered to determine when the first algorithm would be more efficient.

1.3.3 Analysis of Correctness

In this text, "analysis of an algorithm" means an efficiency analysis in terms of either time or memory. There are other types of analyses. For example, we can analyze the correctness of an algorithm by developing a proof that the algorithm actually does what it is supposed to do. Although we will often informally show that our algorithms are correct and will sometimes prove that they are, you should see Dijkstra (1976), Gries (1981), or Kingston (1990) for a comprehensive treatment of correctness.

1.4 ORDER

We just illustrated that an algorithm with a time complexity of n is more efficient than one with a time complexity of n^2 for sufficiently large values of n, regardless of how long it takes to process the basic operations in the two algorithms. Suppose now that we have two algorithms for the same problem, and that their every-case time complexities are $100n$ for the first algorithm and $0.01n^2$ for the second algorithm. Using an argument such as the one just given, we can show that the first algorithm will eventually be more efficient than the second one. For example, if it takes the same amount of time to process the basic operations in both algorithms and the overhead is about the same, the first algorithm will be more efficient if

$$0.01n^2 > 100n.$$

Dividing both sides by $0.01n$ yields

$$n > 10,000.$$

If it takes longer to process the basic operation in the first algorithm than in the second, then there is simply some larger value of n at which the first algorithm becomes more efficient.

Algorithms with time complexities such as n and $100n$ are called ***linear-time algorithms*** because their time complexities are linear in the input size n, whereas algorithms with time complexities such as n^2 and $0.01n^2$ are called ***quadratic-time algorithms*** because their time complexities are quadratic in the input size n. There is a fundamental principle here. That is, any linear-time algorithm is eventually more efficient than any quadratic-time algorithm. In the theoretical analysis of an algorithm, we are interested in eventual behavior. Next we will show how algorithms can be grouped according to their eventual behavior. In this way we can readily determine whether one algorithm's eventual behavior is better than another's.

1.4.1 An Intuitive Introduction to Order

Functions such as $5n^2$ and $5n^2 + 100$ are called ***pure quadratic*** functions because they contain no linear term, whereas a function such as $0.1n^2 + n + 100$ is called a ***complete quadratic*** function because it contains a linear term. Table 1.3 shows that eventually the quadratic term dominates this function. That is, the values of the other terms eventually become insignificant compared with the value of the quadratic term. Therefore, although the function is not a pure quadratic function, we can classify it with pure quadratic functions. This means that if some algorithm has this time complexity, we can call the algorithm a quadratic-time algorithm. Intuitively, it seems that we should always be able to throw away low-order terms when classifying complexity functions. For example, it seems that we should be able to classify $0.1n^3 + 10n^2 + 5n + 25$ with pure cubic functions. We will soon establish rigorously that we can do this. First let's impart an intuitive feel for how complexity functions are classified.

The set of all complexity functions that can be classified with pure quadratic functions is called $\Theta(n^2)$, where Θ is the Greek capital letter "theta." If a function is a member of the set $\Theta(n^2)$, we say that the function is order of n^2. For example, because we can throw away low-order terms,

$$g(n) = 5n^2 + 100n + 20 \in \Theta(n^2),$$

which means that $g(n)$ is order of n^2. As a more concrete example, recall from Section 1.3.1 that the time complexity for Algorithm 1.3 (Exchange Sort) is given by $T(n) = n(n-1)/2$. Because

$$\frac{n(n-1)}{2} = \frac{n^2}{2} - \frac{n}{2},$$

throwing away the lower-order term $n/2$ shows that $T(n) \in \Theta(n^2)$.

When an algorithm's time complexity is in $\Theta(n^2)$, the algorithm is called a quadratic-time algorithm or a ***$\Theta(n^2)$ algorithm***. We also say that the algorithm is ***$\Theta(n^2)$***. Exchange Sort is a quadratic-time algorithm.

Table 1.3 The quadratic term eventually dominates		
n	$0.1n^2$	$0.1n^2 + n + 100$
10	10	120
20	40	160
50	250	400
100	1,000	1,200
1000	100,000	101,100

Similarly, the set of complexity functions that can be classified with pure cubic functions is called $\Theta(n^3)$, and functions in that set are said to be order of n^3, and so on. We will call these sets **complexity categories.** The following are some of the most common complexity categories.

$$\Theta(\lg n) \qquad \Theta(n) \qquad \Theta(n \lg n) \qquad \Theta(n^2) \qquad \Theta(n^3) \qquad \Theta(2^n)$$

In this ordering, if $f(n)$ is in a category to the left of the category containing $g(n)$, then $f(n)$ eventually lies beneath $g(n)$ on a graph. Figure 1.3 plots the simplest members of these categories: n, $\lg n$, $n \lg n$, etc. Table 1.4 shows the execution times of algorithms whose time complexities are given by these functions. The simplifying assumption is that it takes 1 nanosecond (10^{-9} second) to process the basic operation for each algorithm. The table shows a possibly surprising result. One might expect that as long as an algorithm is not an exponential-time algorithm, it will be adequate. However, even the quadratic-time algorithm takes 31.7 years to process an instance with an input size of 1 billion. On the other hand, the $\Theta(n \lg n)$ algorithm takes only 29.9 seconds to process such an instance. Ordinarily an algorithm has to be $\Theta(n \lg n)$ or better for us to assume that it can process extremely large instances in tolerable amounts of time. This is not to say that algorithms whose time complexities are in the higher-order categories are not useful. Algorithms with quadratic, cubic, and even higher-order time complexities can often handle the actual instances that arise in many applications.

Before ending this discussion, we stress that there is more information in knowing a time complexity exactly than in simply knowing its order. For example, recall the hypothetical algorithms, discussed earlier, that have time complexities of $100n$ and $0.01n^2$. If it takes the same amount of time to process the basic operations and execute the overhead instructions in both algorithms, then the quadratic-time algorithm is more efficient for instances smaller than 10,000. If the application never requires instances larger than this, the quadratic-time algorithm should be implemented. If we knew only that the time complexities were in $\Theta(n)$ and $\Theta(n^2)$, respectively, we would not know this. The coefficients in this example are extreme, and in practice they are often less extreme. Furthermore, there are times when it is quite difficult to determine the time complexities exactly. Therefore, we are sometimes content to determine only the order.

Figure 1.3 Growth rates of some common complexity functions.

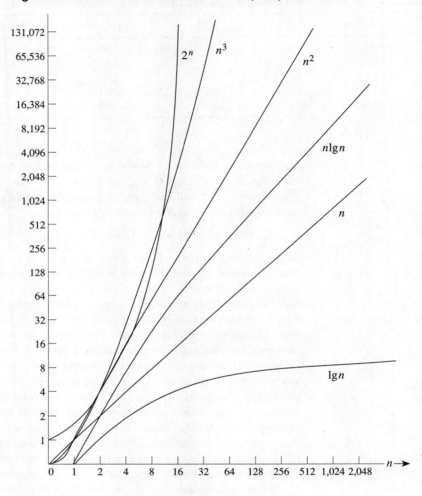

1.4.2 A Rigorous Introduction to Order

The previous discussion imparted an intuitive feel for order (Θ). Here we develop theory that enables us to define order rigorously. We accomplish this by presenting two other fundamental concepts. The first is "big O."

Definition   For a given complexity function $f(n)$, $O(f(n))$ is the set of complexity functions $g(n)$ for which there exists some positive real constant c and some nonnegative integer N such that for all $n \geq N$

$$g(n) \leq c \times f(n).$$

Table 1.4 Execution times for algorithms with the given time complexities

n	$f(n) = \lg n$	$f(n) = n$	$f(n) = n \lg n$	$f(n) = n^2$	$f(n) = n^3$	$f(n) = 2^n$
10	0.003 μs*	0.01 μs	0.033 μs	0.1 μs	1 μs	1 μs
20	0.004 μs	0.02 μs	0.086 μs	0.4 μs	8 μs	1 ms†
30	0.005 μs	0.03 μs	0.147 μs	0.9 μs	27 μs	1 s
40	0.005 μs	0.04 μs	0.213 μs	1.6 μs	64 μs	18.3 min
50	0.006 μs	0.05 μs	0.282 μs	2.5 μs	125 μs	13 days
10^2	0.007 μs	0.10 μs	0.664 μs	10 μs	1 ms	4×10^{13} years
10^3	0.010 μs	1.00 μs	9.966 μs	1 ms	1 s	
10^4	0.013 μs	10 μs	130 μs	100 ms	16.7 min	
10^5	0.017 μs	0.10 ms	1.67 ms	10 s	11.6 days	
10^6	0.020 μs	1 ms	19.93 ms	16.7 min	31.7 years	
10^7	0.023 μs	0.01 s	0.23 s	1.16 days	31,709 years	
10^8	0.027 μs	0.10 s	2.66 s	115.7 days	3.17×10^7 years	
10^9	0.030 μs	1 s	29.90 s	31.7 years		

*1 μs $= 10^{-6}$ second.
†1 ms $= 10^{-3}$ second.

If $g(n) \in O(f(n))$, we say that $g(n)$ is **big O** of $f(n)$. Figure 1.4(a) illustrates "big O." Although $g(n)$ starts out above $cf(n)$ in that figure, eventually it falls beneath $cf(n)$ and stays there. Figure 1.5 shows a concrete example. Although $n^2 + 10n$ is initially above $2n^2$ in that figure, for $n \geq 10$

$$n^2 + 10n \leq 2n^2.$$

We can therefore take $c = 2$ and $N = 10$ in the definition of "big O" to conclude that

$$n^2 + 10n \in O(n^2).$$

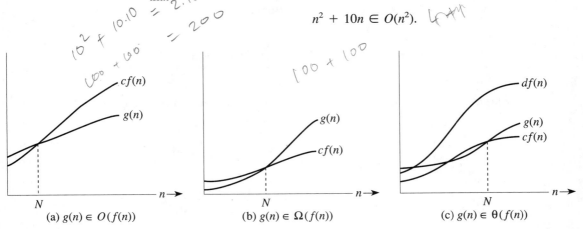

(a) $g(n) \in O(f(n))$ (b) $g(n) \in \Omega(f(n))$ (c) $g(n) \in \theta(f(n))$

Figure 1.4 Illustrating "big O," Ω, and Θ.

Figure 1.5 The function $n^2 + 10n$ eventually stays beneath the function $2n^2$.

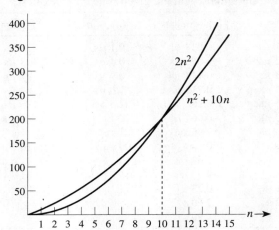

If, for example, $g(n)$ is in $O(n^2)$, then eventually $g(n)$ lies beneath some pure quadratic function cn^2 on a graph. This means that if $g(n)$ is the time complexity for some algorithm, eventually the running time of the algorithm will be at least as fast as quadratic. For the purposes of analysis, we can say that eventually $g(n)$ is at least as *good* as a pure quadratic function. "Big O" (and other concepts that will be introduced soon) are said to describe the *asymptotic* behavior of a function because they are concerned only with eventual behavior. We say that "big O" puts an *asymptotic upper bound* on a function.

The following examples illustrate how to show "big O."

Example 1.7   We show that $5n^2 \in O(n^2)$. Because, for $n \geq 0$,

$$5n^2 \leq 5n^2,$$

we can take $c = 5$ and $N = 0$ to obtain our desired result.

Example 1.8   Recall that the time complexity of Algorithm 1.3 (Exchange Sort) is given by

$$T(n) = \frac{n(n-1)}{2}.$$

Because, for $n \geq 0$,

$$\frac{n(n-1)}{2} \leq \frac{n(n)}{2} = \frac{1}{2}\,n^2,$$

we can take $c = 1/2$ and $N = 0$ to conclude that $T(n) \in O(n^2)$.

A difficulty students often have with "big O" is that they erroneously think there is some unique c and unique N that must be found to show that one function is "big O" of another. This is not the case at all. Recall that Figure 1.5 illustrates that $n^2 + 10n \in O(n^2)$ using $c = 2$ and $N = 10$. Alternatively, we could show it as follows.

Example 1.9   We show that $n^2 + 10n \in O(n^2)$. Because, for $n \geq 1$,
$$n^2 + 10n \leq n^2 + 10n^2 = 11n^2,$$
we can take $c = 11$ and $N = 1$ to obtain our result.

In general, one can show "big O" using whatever manipulations seem most straightforward.

Example 1.10   We show that $n^2 \in O(n^2 + 10n)$. Because, for $n \geq 0$,
$$n^2 \leq 1 \times (n^2 + 10n),$$
we can take $c = 1$ and $N = 0$ to obtain our result.

The purpose of this last example is to show that the function inside "big O" does not have to be one of the simple functions plotted in Figure 1.3. It can be any complexity function. Ordinarily, however, we take it to be a simple function like those plotted in Figure 1.3.

Example 1.11   We show that $n \in O(n^2)$. Because, for $n \geq 1$,
$$n \leq 1 \times n^2,$$
we can take $c = 1$ and $N = 1$ to obtain our result.

This last example makes a crucial point about "big O." A complexity function need not have a quadratic term to be in $O(n^2)$. It need only eventually lie beneath some pure quadratic function on a graph. Therefore, any logarithmic or linear complexity function is in $O(n^2)$. Similarly, any logarithmic, linear, or quadratic complexity function is in $O(n^3)$, and so on. Figure 1.6(a) shows some exemplary members of $O(n^2)$.

Just as "big O" puts an asymptotic upper bound on a complexity function, the following concept puts an *asymptotic lower bound* on a complexity function.

Figure 1.6 The sets $O(n^2)$, $\Omega(n^2)$, and $\Theta(n^2)$. Some exemplary members are shown.

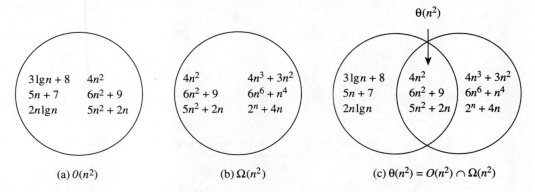

(a) $O(n^2)$ (b) $\Omega(n^2)$ (c) $\Theta(n^2) = O(n^2) \cap \Omega(n^2)$

Definition   For a given complexity function $f(n)$, $\Omega(f(n))$ is the set of complexity functions $g(n)$ for which there exists some positive real constant c and some nonnegative integer N such that, for all $n \geq N$,

$$g(n) \geq c \times f(n).$$

The symbol Ω is the Greek capital letter "omega." If $g(n) \in \Omega(f(n))$, we say that $g(n)$ is *omega* of $f(n)$. Figure 1.4(b) illustrates Ω. Some examples follow.

Example 1.12   We show that $5n^2 \in \Omega(n^2)$. Because, for $n \geq 0$,

$$5n^2 \geq 1 \times n^2,$$

we can take $c = 1$ and $N = 0$ to obtain our result.

Example 1.13   We show that $n^2 + 10n \in \Omega(n^2)$. Because, for $n \geq 0$,

$$n^2 + 10n \geq n^2,$$

we can take $c = 1$ and $N = 0$ to obtain our result.

Example 1.14   Consider again the time complexity of Algorithm 1.3 (Exchange Sort). We show that

$$T(n) = \frac{n(n-1)}{2} \in \Omega(n^2).$$

For $n \geq 2$,

$$n - 1 \geq \frac{n}{2}.$$

Therefore, for $n \geq 2$,

$$\frac{n(n-1)}{2} \geq \frac{n}{2} \times \frac{n}{2} = \frac{1}{4} n^2,$$

which means we can take $c = 1/4$ and $N = 2$ to obtain our result.

As is the case for "big O," there are no unique constants c and N for which the conditions in the definition of Ω hold. We can choose whichever ones make our manipulations easiest.

If a function is in $\Omega(n^2)$, then eventually the function lies above some pure quadratic function on a graph. For the purposes of analysis, this means that eventually it is at least as *bad* as a pure quadratic function. However, as the following example illustrates, the function need not be a quadratic function.

Example 1.15   We show that $n^3 \in \Omega(n^2)$. Because, if $n \geq 1$,

$$n^3 \geq 1 \times n^2,$$

we can take $c = 1$ and $N = 1$ to obtain our result.

Figure 1.6(b) shows some exemplary members of $\Omega(n^2)$.

If a function is in both $O(n^2)$ and $\Omega(n^2)$, we can conclude that eventually the function lies beneath some pure quadratic function on a graph and eventually it lies above some pure quadratic function on a graph. That is, eventually it is at least as *good* as some pure quadratic function and eventually it is at least as *bad* as some pure quadratic function. We can therefore conclude that its growth is similar to that of a pure quadratic function. This is precisely the result we want for our rigorous notion of order. We have the following definition.

Definition   For a given complexity function $f(n)$,

$$\Theta(f(n)) = O(f(n)) \cap \Omega(f(n)).$$

This means that $\Theta(f(n))$ is the set of complexity functions $g(n)$ for which there exists some positive real constants c and d and some nonnegative integer N such that, for all $n \geq N$,

$$c \times f(n) \leq g(n) \leq d \times f(n).$$

If $g(n) \in \Theta(f(n))$, we say that $g(n)$ is **order** of $f(n)$.

Example 1.16   Consider once more the time complexity of Algorithm 1.3. Examples 1.8 and 1.14 together establish that

$$T(n) = \frac{n(n-1)}{2} \quad \text{is in both} \quad O(n^2) \quad \text{and} \quad \Omega(n^2).$$

This means that

$$T(n) \in O(n^2) \cap \Omega(n^2) = \Theta(n^2).$$

Figure 1.6(c) depicts that $\Theta(n^2)$ is the intersection of $O(n^2)$ and $\Omega(n^2)$, whereas Figure 1.4(c) illustrates Θ. Notice in Figure 1.6(c) that the function $5n + 7$ is not in $\Omega(n^2)$, and the function $4n^3 + 3n^2$ is not in $O(n^2)$. Therefore, neither of these functions is in $\Theta(n^2)$. Although intuitively this seems correct, we have not yet proven it. The following example shows how such a proof proceeds.

Example 1.17   We show that n is not in $\Omega(n^2)$ using ***proof by contradiction.*** In this type of proof we assume something is true—in this case, that $n \in \Omega(n^2)$—and then we do manipulations that lead to a result that is not true. That is, the result *contradicts* something known to be true. We then conclude that what we assumed in the first place cannot be true.

Assuming that $n \in \Omega(n^2)$ means we are assuming that there exists some positive constant c and some nonnegative integer N such that, for $n \geq N$,

$$n \geq cn^2.$$

If we divide both sides of this inequality by cn, we have, for $n \geq N$,

$$\frac{1}{c} \geq n.$$

However, for any $n > 1/c$, this inequality cannot hold, which means that it cannot hold for all $n \geq N$. This contradiction proves that n is not in $\Omega(n^2)$.

We have one more definition concerning order that expresses relationships such as the one between the function n and the function n^2.

Definition   For a given complexity function $f(n)$, $o(f(n))$ is the set of all complexity functions $g(n)$ satisfying the following: For every positive real constant c there exists a nonnegative integer N such that, for all $n \geq N$,

$$g(n) \leq c \times f(n).$$

If $g(n) \in o(f(n))$, we say that $g(n)$ is ***small o*** of $f(n)$. Recall that "big O" means there must be *some* real positive constant c for which the bound holds. This definition says that the bound must hold for *every* real positive constant c. Because the bound holds for every positive c, it holds for arbitrarily small c. For example, if $g(n) \in o(f(n))$, there is an N such that, for $n > N$,

$$g(n) \leq 0.00001 \times f(n).$$

We see that $g(n)$ becomes insignificant relative to $f(n)$ as n becomes large. For the purposes of analysis, if $g(n)$ is in $o(f(n))$, then $g(n)$ is eventually much *better* than functions such as $f(n)$. The following examples illustrate this.

Example 1.18   We show that

$$n \in o(n^2).$$

Let $c > 0$ be given. We need to find an N such that, for $n \geq N$,

$$n \leq cn^2.$$

If we divide both sides of this inequality by cn, we get

$$\frac{1}{c} \leq n.$$

Therefore, it suffices to choose any $N \geq 1/c$.

   Notice that the value of N depends on the constant c. For example, if $c = 0.00001$, we must take N equal to at least 100,000. That is, for $n \geq 100,000$,

$$n \leq 0.00001n^2.$$

Example 1.19   We show that n is not in $o(5n)$. We will use proof by contradiction to show this. Let $c = \frac{1}{6}$. If $n \in o(5n)$, then there must exist some N such that, for $n \geq N$,

$$n \leq \frac{1}{6} 5n = \frac{5}{6} n.$$

This contradiction proves that n is not in $o(5n)$.

   The following theorem relates "small o" to our other asymptotic notation.

Theorem 1.2 If $g(n) \in o(f(n))$, then

$$g(n) \in O(f(n)) - \Omega(f(n)).$$

That is, $g(n)$ is in $O(f(n))$ but is not in $\Omega(f(n))$.

Proof: Because $g(n) \in o(f(n))$, for every positive real constant c there exists an N such that, for all $n \geq N$,

$$g(n) \leq c \times f(n),$$

which means that the bound certainly holds for some c. Therefore,

$$g(n) \in O(f(n)).$$

We will show that $g(n)$ is not in $\Omega(f(n))$ using proof by contradiction. If $g(n) \in \Omega(f(n))$, then there exists some real constant $c > 0$ and some N_1 such that, for all $n \geq N_1$,

$$g(n) \geq c \times f(n).$$

But, because $g(n) \in o(f(n))$, there exists some N_2 such that, for all $n \geq N_2$,

$$g(n) \leq \frac{c}{2} \times f(n).$$

Both inequalities would have to hold for all n greater than both N_1 and N_2. This contradiction proves that $g(n)$ cannot be in $\Omega(f(n))$.

You may think that $o(f(n))$ and $O(f(n)) - \Omega(f(n))$ must be the same set. This is not true. There are unusual functions that are in $O(f(n)) - \Omega(f(n))$ but that are not in $o(f(n))$. The following example illustrates this.

Example 1.20   Consider the function

$$g(n) = \begin{cases} n & \text{if } n \text{ is even} \\ 1 & \text{if } n \text{ is odd} \end{cases}$$

It is left as an exercise to show that

$$g(n) \in O(n) - \Omega(n) \qquad \text{but that} \qquad g(n) \text{ is not in } o(n).$$

Example 1.20 of course is quite contrived. When complexity functions represent the time complexities of actual algorithms, ordinarily the functions in $O(f(n)) - \Omega(f(n))$ are the same ones that are in $o(f(n))$.

Let's discuss Θ further. In the exercises we establish that

$$g(n) \in \Theta(f(n)) \qquad \text{if and only if} \qquad f(n) \in \Theta(g(n)).$$

For example,

$$n^2 + 10n \in \Theta(n^2) \qquad \text{and} \qquad n^2 \in \Theta(n^2 + 10n).$$

This means that Θ separates complexity functions into disjoint sets. We will call these sets *complexity categories.* Any function from a given category can represent the category. For convenience, we ordinarily represent a category by its simplest member. The previous complexity category is represented by $\Theta(n^2)$.

The time complexities of some algorithms do not increase with n. For example, recall that the best-case time complexity $B(n)$ for Algorithm 1.1 is 1 for every value of n. The complexity category containing such functions can be represented by any constant, and for simplicity we represent it by $\Theta(1)$.

The following are some important properties of order that make it easy to determine the orders of many complexity functions. They are stated without proof. The proofs of some will be derived in the exercises, whereas the proofs of others follow from results obtained in the next subsection. The second result we have already discussed. It is included here for completeness.

Properties of Order:

1. $g(n) \in O(f(n))$ if and only if $f(n) \in \Omega(g(n))$.
2. $g(n) \in \Theta(f(n))$ if and only if $f(n) \in \Theta(g(n))$.
3. If $b > 1$ and $a > 1$, then

$$\log_a n \in \Theta(\log_b n).$$

This implies that all logarithmic complexity functions are in the same complexity category. We will represent this category by $\Theta(\lg n)$.

4. If $b > a > 0$, then

$$a^n \in o(b^n).$$

This implies that all exponential complexity functions are not in the same complexity category.

5. For all $a > 0$

$$a^n \in o(n!).$$

This implies that $n!$ is *worse* than any exponential complexity function.

6. Consider the following ordering of complexity categories:

$$\Theta(\lg n) \quad \Theta(n) \quad \Theta(n \lg n) \quad \Theta(n^2) \quad \Theta(n^j) \quad \Theta(n^k) \quad \Theta(a^n) \quad \Theta(b^n) \quad \Theta(n!),$$

where $k > j > 2$ and $b > a > 1$. If a complexity function $g(n)$ is in a category that is to the left of the category containing $f(n)$, then

$$g(n) \in o(f(n)).$$

7. If $c \geq 0$, $d > 0$, $g(n) \in O(f(n))$, and $h(n) \in \Theta(f(n))$, then

$$c \times g(n) + d \times h(n) \in \Theta(f(n)).$$

Example 1.21 Property 3 states that all logarithmic complexity functions are in the same complexity category. For example,

$$\Theta(\log_4 n) = \Theta(\lg n).$$

This means that the relationship between $\log_4 n$ and $\lg n$ is the same as the one between $7n^2 + 5n$ and n^2.

Example 1.22 Property 6 states that any logarithmic function is eventually better than any polynomial, any polynomial is eventually better than any exponential function, and any exponential function is eventually better than the factorial function. For example,

$$\lg n \in o(n), \qquad n^{10} \in o(2^n), \qquad \text{and} \qquad 2^n \in o(n!).$$

Example 1.23   Properties 6 and 7 can be used repeatedly. For example, we can show that $5n + 3 \lg n + 10\, n \lg n + 7n^2 \in \Theta(n^2)$, as follows. Repeatedly applying Properties 6 and 7, we have

$$7n^2 \in \Theta(n^2),$$

which means

$$10\, n \lg n + 7n^2 \in \Theta(n^2),$$

which means

$$3 \lg n + 10\, n \lg n + 7n^2 \in \Theta(n^2),$$

which means

$$5n + 3 \lg n + 10\, n \lg n + 7n^2 \in \Theta(n^2).$$

In practice, we do not repeatedly appeal to the properties, but rather we simply realize that we can throw out low-order terms.

If we can obtain the exact time complexity of an algorithm, we can determine its order simply by throwing out low-order terms. When this is not possible, we can appeal back to the definitions of "big O" and Ω to determine order. For example, suppose for some algorithm we are unable to determine $T(n)$ [or $W(n)$, $A(n)$, or $B(n)$] exactly. If we can show that

$$T(n) \in O(f(n)) \qquad \text{and} \qquad T(n) \in \Omega(f(n))$$

by appealing directly to the definitions, we can conclude that $T(n) \in \Theta(f(n))$.

Sometimes it is fairly easy to show that $T(n) \in O(f(n))$ but difficult to determine whether $T(n)$ is in $\Omega(f(n))$. In such cases we may be content to show only that $T(n) \in O(f(n))$, because this implies that $T(n)$ is at least as *good* as functions such as $f(n)$. Similarly, we may be content to learn only that $T(n) \in \Omega(f(n))$, because this implies that $T(n)$ is at least as *bad* as functions such as $f(n)$.

Before closing, we mention that many authors say

$$f(n) = \Theta(n^2) \qquad \text{instead of} \qquad f(n) \in \Theta(n^2).$$

Both mean the same thing—namely, that $f(n)$ is a member of the set $\Theta(n^2)$. Similarly, it is common to write

$$f(n) = O(n^2) \qquad \text{instead of} \qquad f(n) \in O(n^2).$$

You are referred to Knuth (1976) for an account of the history of "order" and to Brassard (1985) for a discussion of the definitions of order given here. Our definitions of "big O," Ω, and Θ are for the most part standard. There are, however, other definitions of "small o. It is not standard to call the sets $\Theta(n)$,

$\Theta(n^2)$, etc., "complexity categories." Some authors call them "complexity classes," although this term is used more often to refer to the sets of problems discussed in Chapter 9. Other authors do not give them any particular name at all.

⊕ *1.4.3 Using a Limit to Determine Order*

We now show how order can sometimes be determined using a limit. This material is included for those familiar with limits and derivatives. Knowledge of this material is not required elsewhere in the text.

> **Theorem 1.3** We have the following:
>
> $$\lim_{n \to \infty} \frac{g(n)}{f(n)} = \begin{cases} c & \text{implies } g(n) \in \Theta(f(n)) \text{ if } c > 0 \\ 0 & \text{implies } g(n) \in o(f(n)) \\ \infty & \text{implies } f(n) \in o(g(n)) \end{cases}$$
>
> **Proof:** The proof is left as an exercise.

Example 1.24 Theorem 1.3 implies that

$$\frac{n^2}{2} \in o(n^3)$$

because

$$\lim_{n \to \infty} \frac{n^2/2}{n^3} = \lim_{n \to \infty} \frac{1}{2n} = 0.$$

Using Theorem 1.3 in Example 1.24 is not very exciting because the result could have easily been established directly. The following examples are more interesting.

Example 1.25 Theorem 1.3 implies that, for $b > a > 0$,

$$a^n \in o(b^n)$$

because

$$\lim_{n \to \infty} \frac{a^n}{b^n} = \lim_{n \to \infty} \left(\frac{a}{b}\right)^n = 0.$$

The limit is 0 because $0 < a/b < 1$.

This is Property 4 in the Properties of Order (near the end of Section 1.4.2).

Example 1.26

Theorem 1.3 implies that, for $a > 0$,

$$a^n \in o(n!).$$

If $a \leq 1$, the result is trivial. Suppose that $a > 1$. If n is so large that

$$\left\lceil \frac{n}{2} \right\rceil > a^4,$$

then

$$\frac{a^n}{n!} < \underbrace{\frac{a^n}{a^4 a^4 \cdots a^4}}_{\lceil n/2 \rceil \text{ times}} \leq \frac{a^n}{(a^4)^{n/2}} = \frac{a^n}{a^{2n}} = \left(\frac{1}{a}\right)^n.$$

Because $a > 1$, this implies that

$$\lim_{n \to \infty} \frac{a^n}{n!} = 0.$$

This is Property 5 in the Properties of Order.

The following theorem, whose proof can be found in most calculus texts, enhances the usefulness of Theorem 1.3.

Theorem 1.4 L'Hôpital's Rule   If $f(x)$ and $g(x)$ are both differentiable with derivatives $f'(x)$ and $g'(x)$, respectively, and if

$$\lim_{x \to \infty} f(x) = \lim_{x \to \infty} g(x) = \infty,$$

then

$$\lim_{x \to \infty} \frac{f(x)}{g(x)} = \lim_{x \to \infty} \frac{f'(x)}{g'(x)}$$

whenever the limit on the right exists.

Theorem 1.4 holds for functions of real valuables, whereas our complexity functions are functions of integer variables. However, most of our complexity functions (for example, $\lg n$, n, etc.) are also functions of real variables. Furthermore, if a function $f(x)$ is a function of a real variable x, then

$$\lim_{n \to \infty} f(n) = \lim_{x \to \infty} f(x),$$

where n is an integer, whenever the limit on the right exists. Therefore, we can apply Theorem 1.4 to complexity analysis, as the following examples illustrate.

Example 1.27
Theorems 1.3 and 1.4 imply that

$$\lg n \in o(n)$$

because

$$\lim_{x \to \infty} \frac{\lg x}{x} = \lim_{x \to \infty} \frac{d(\lg x)/dx}{dx/dx} = \lim_{x \to \infty} \frac{1/(x \ln 2)}{1} = 0.$$

Example 1.28
Theorems 1.3 and 1.4 imply that, for $b > 1$ and $a > 1$,

$$\log_a n \in \Theta(\log_b n)$$

because

$$\lim_{x \to \infty} \frac{\log_a x}{\log_b x} = \lim_{x \to \infty} \frac{d(\log_a x)/dx}{d(\log_b x)/dx} = \frac{1/(x \ln a)}{1/(x \ln b)} = \frac{\ln b}{\ln a} > 0.$$

This is Property 3 in the Properties of Order.

1.5 OUTLINE OF THIS BOOK

We are now ready to develop and analyze sophisticated algorithms. For the most part, our organization is by technique rather than by application area. As noted earlier, the purpose of this organization is to establish a repertoire of techniques that can be investigated as possible ways to approach a new problem. Chapter 2 discusses a technique called "divide-and-conquer." Chapter 3 covers dynamic programming. Chapter 4 addresses "the greedy approach." In Chapter 5, the backtracking technique is presented. Chapter 6 discusses a technique related to backtracking called "branch-and-bound." In Chapters 7 and 8, we switch from developing and analyzing algorithms to analyzing problems themselves. Such an analysis, which is called a computational complexity analysis, involves determining a lower bound for the time complexities of all algorithms for a given problem. Chapter 7 analyzes the Sorting Problem, and Chapter 8 analyzes the Searching Problem. Chapter 9 is devoted to a special class of problems. That class contains problems for which no one has ever developed an algorithm whose time complexity is better than exponential in the worst case. Yet no one has ever proven that such an algorithm is not possible. It turns out that there are thousands of such problems and that they are all closely related. The study of these problems has become a relatively new and exciting area of computer science. All of the algorithms discussed in the first nine chapters are developed for a computer containing a single processor that executes a single sequence of instructions. Owing to the drastic reduction in the price of computer hardware, there has been a recent increase in the development of parallel computers. Such computers have more than one processor, and all the processors can execute instructions simultaneously (in parallel). Algorithms written for such computers are called "parallel algorithms." Chapter 10 is an introduction to such algorithms.

Exercises

Section 1.1

1. Write an algorithm that finds the largest number in a list (an array) of n numbers.
2. Write an algorithm that finds the m smallest numbers in a list of n numbers.
3. Write an algorithm that prints out all the subsets of three elements of a set of n elements. The elements of this set are stored in a list that is the input to the algorithm.
4. Write an Insertion Sort algorithm that uses Binary Search to find the position where the next insertion should take place.
5. Write an algorithm that finds the greatest common divisor of two integers.
6. Write an algorithm that finds both the smallest and largest numbers in a list of n numbers. Try to find a method that does at most about $1.5n$ comparisons of array items.
7. Write an algorithm that determines whether or not an almost complete binary tree is a heap.

Section 1.2

8. Under what circumstances, when a searching operation is needed, would Sequential Search (Algorithm 1.1) not be appropriate?
9. Give a practical example in which you would not use Exchange Sort (Algorithm 1.3) to do a sorting task.

Section 1.3

10. Define basic operations for your algorithms in Exercises 1–7, and study the performance of these algorithms. If a given algorithm has an every-case time complexity, determine it. Otherwise, determine the worst-case time complexity.
11. Determine the worst-case, average-case, and best-case time complexities for the basic Insertion Sort and for the version given in Exercise 4, which uses Binary Search.
12. Write a linear-time algorithm that sorts n distinct integers ranging from 1 to 500, inclusive. (*Hint:* Use a 500-element array.)
13. Algorithm A performs $10n^2$ basic operations, and algorithm B performs $300 \ln n$ basic operations. For what value of n does algorithm B start to show its better performance?

14. There are two algorithms called Alg1 and Alg2 for a problem of size n. Alg1 runs in n^2 microseconds and Alg2 runs in $100n \log n$ microseconds. Alg1 can be implemented using 4 hours of programmer time and needs 2 minutes of CPU time. On the other hand, Alg2 requires 15 hours of programmer time and 6 minutes of CPU time. If programmers are paid 20 dollars per hour and CPU time costs 50 dollars per minute, how many times must a problem instance of size 500 be solved using Alg2 in order to justify its development cost?

Section 1.4

15. Show directly that $f(n) = n^2 + 3n^3 \in \Theta(n^3)$. That is, use the definitions of O and Ω to show that $f(n)$ is in both $O(n^3)$ and $\Omega(n^3)$.

16. Using the definitions of O and Ω, show that

$$6n^2 + 20n \in O(n^3) \quad \text{but} \quad 6n^2 + 20n \notin \Omega(n^3).$$

17. Using the Properties of Order in Section 1.4.2, show that

$$5n^5 + 4n^4 + 6n^3 + 2n^2 + n + 7 \in \Theta(n^5).$$

18. Let $p(n) = a_k n^k + a_{k-1} n^{k-1} + \cdots a_1 n + a_0$, where $a_k > 0$. Using the Properties of Order in Section 1.4.2, show that $p(n) \in \Theta(n^k)$.

19. Group the following functions by complexity category.

$$n \ln n \qquad (\lg n)^2 \qquad 5n^2 + 7n \qquad n^{5/2}$$
$$n! \qquad 2^{n!} \qquad 4^n \qquad n^n \qquad n^n + \ln n$$
$$5^{\lg n} \qquad \lg(n!) \qquad (\lg n)! \qquad \sqrt{n} \qquad e^n \qquad 8n + 12 \qquad 10^n + n^{20}$$

20. Establish properties 1, 2, 6, and 7 of the Properties of Order in Section 1.4.2.

21. Discuss the reflexive, symmetric, and transitive properties for asymptotic comparisons (O, Ω, Θ, o).

22. Suppose you have a computer that requires 1 minute to solve problem instances of size $n = 1000$. What instance sizes can be run in 1 minute if you buy a new computer that runs 1000 times faster than the old one, assuming the following time complexities $T(n)$ for our algorithm?
    (a) $T(n) \in \Theta(n)$
    (b) $T(n) \in \Theta(n^3)$
    (c) $T(n) \in \Theta(10^n)$

23. Derive the proof of Theorem 1.3.

24. Show the correctness of the following statements.
    (a) $\lg n \in O(n)$
    (b) $n \in O(n \lg n)$
    (c) $n \lg n \in O(n^2)$
    (d) $2^n \in \Omega(5^{\ln n})$
    (e) $\lg^3 n \in o(n^{0.5})$

Additional Exercises

25. Presently we can solve problem instances of size 100 in 1 minute using algorithm A, which is a $\Theta(2^n)$ algorithm. On the other hand, we will soon have to solve problem instances twice this large in 1 minute. Do you think it would help to buy a faster (and more expensive) computer?

26. What is the time complexity $T(n)$ of the nested loops below? For simplicity, you may assume that n is a power of 2. That is, $n = 2^k$ for some positive integer k.

```
        ⋮
for (i = 1; i <= n; i++) {
  j = n;
  while (j >= 1) {
    < body of the while loop>      // Needs Θ(1).
    j = ⌊j/2⌋;
  }
}
        ⋮
```

27. Give an algorithm for the following problem, and determine its time complexity. Given a list of n distinct positive integers, partition the list into two sublists, each of size $n/2$, such that the difference between the sums of the integers in the two sublists is maximized. You may assume that n is a multiple of 2.

28. What is the time complexity $T(n)$ of the nested loops below? For simplicity, you may assume that n is a power of 2. That is, $n = 2^k$ for some positive integer k.

```
        ⋮
i = n;
while (i >= 1) {
  j = i;
  while (j <= n) {
    < body of the inner while loop>      // Needs Θ(1).
    j = 2 * j;
  }
  i = ⌊i/2⌋;
}
        ⋮
```

29. Give a $\Theta(n \lg n)$ algorithm that computes the remainder when x^n is divided by p. For simplicity, you may assume that n is a power of 2. That is, $n = 2^k$ for some positive integer k.

30. Explain in English what functions are in the following sets.
    (a) $n^{O(1)}$ (b) $O(n^{O(1)})$ (c) $O(O(n^{O(1)}))$

31. Show that the function $f(n) = |\, n^2 \sin n\, |$ is in neither $O(n)$ nor $\Omega(n)$.

32. Justify the correctness of the following statements assuming that $f(n)$ and $g(n)$ are asymptotically positive functions.
    (a) $f(n) + g(n) \in O(\max(f(n), g(n)))$
    (b) $f^2(n) \in \Omega(f(n))$
    (c) $f(n) + o(f(n)) \in \Theta(f(n))$, where $o(f(n))$ means any function $g(n) \in o(f(n))$

33. Give an algorithm for the following problem. Given a list of n distinct positive integers, partition the list into two sublists, each of size $n/2$, such that the difference between the sums of the integers in the two sublists is minimized. Determine the time complexity of your algorithm. You may assume that n is a multiple of 2.

34. Algorithm 1.7 (*n*th Fibonacci Term, Iterative) is clearly linear in n, but is it a linear-time algorithm? In Section 1.3.1 we defined the input size as the size of the input. In the case of the *n*th Fibonacci term, n is the input, and the number of bits it takes to encode n could be used as the input size. Using this measure the size of 64 is $\lg 64 = 6$, and the size of 1024 is $\lg 1024 = 10$. Show that Algorithm 1.7 is exponential-time in terms of its input size. Show further that any algorithm for computing the *n*th Fibonacci term must be an exponential-time algorithm because the size of the output is exponential in the input size. See Section 9.2 for a related discussion of the input size.

35. Determine the time complexity of Algorithm 1.6 (*n*th Fibonacci Term, Recursive) in terms of its input size (See Exercise 34).

36. Can you verify the correctness of your algorithms for Exercises 1 to 7?

CHAPTER 2

Divide-and-Conquer

*O*ur first approach to designing algorithms, divide-and-conquer, is patterned after the brilliant strategy employed by the French emperor Napoleon in the Battle of Austerlitz on December 2, 1805. A combined army of Austrians and Russians outnumbered Napoleon's army by about 15,000 soldiers. The Austro-Russian army launched a massive attack against the French right flank. Anticipating their attack, Napoleon drove against their center and split their forces in two. Because the two smaller armies were individually no match for Napoleon, they each suffered heavy losses and were compelled to retreat. By *dividing* the large army into two smaller armies and individually conquering these two smaller armies, Napoleon was able to *conquer* the large army.

The divide-and-conquer approach employs this same strategy on an instance of a problem. That is, it divides an instance of a problem into two or more smaller instances. The smaller instances are usually instances of the original problem. If solutions to the smaller instances can be obtained readily, the solution to the original instance can be obtained by combining these solutions. If the smaller instances are still too large to be solved readily, they can be divided into still smaller instances. This process of dividing the instances continues until they are so small that a solution is readily obtainable.

The divide-and-conquer approach is a **top-down** approach. That is, the solution to a *top-level* instance of a problem is obtained by going *down* and obtaining solutions to smaller instances. The reader may recognize this as the method used by recursive routines. Recall that when writing recursion one thinks at the problem-solving level, and lets the system handle the details of obtaining the solution (by means of stack manipulations). When developing a divide-and-conquer algorithm, we usually think at this level and write it as a recursive routine. After this, we can sometimes create a more efficient iterative version of the algorithm.

We now introduce the divide-and-conquer approach with examples, starting with Binary Search.

2.1 BINARY SEARCH

We showed an iterative version of Binary Search (Algorithm 1.5) in Section 1.2. Here we present a recursive version because recursion illustrates the top-down approach used by divide-and-conquer. Stated in divide-and-conquer terminology, Binary Search locates a key x in a sorted (nondecreasing order) array by first comparing x with the middle item of the array. If they are equal, the algorithm is done. If not, the array is divided into two subarrays, one containing all the items to the left of the middle item and the other containing all the items to the right. If x is smaller than the middle item, this procedure is then applied to the left subarray. Otherwise, it is applied to the right subarray. That is, x is compared with the middle item of the appropriate subarray. If they are equal, the algorithm is done. If not, the subarray is divided in two. This procedure is repeated until x is found or it is determined that x is not in the array.

The steps of Binary Search can be summarized as follows.

If x equals the middle item, quit. Otherwise,

1. *Divide* the array into two subarrays about half as large. If x is smaller than the middle item, choose the left subarray. If x is larger than the middle item, choose the right subarray.
2. *Conquer* (solve) the subarray by determining whether x is in that subarray. Unless the subarray is sufficiently small, use recursion to do this.
3. *Obtain* the solution to the array from the solution to the subarray.

Binary Search is the simplest kind of divide-and-conquer algorithm because the instance is broken down into only one smaller instance and so there is no combination of outputs. The solution to the original instance is simply the solution to the smaller instance. The following example illustrates Binary Search.

Example 2.1 Suppose $x = 18$ and we have the following array:

10   12   13   14   18   20   25   27   30   35   40   45   47.

↑

Middle item

1. Divide the array: Because $x < 25$, we need to search

    10   12   13   14   18   20.

2. Conquer the subarray by determining whether x is in the subarray. (This is accomplished by recursively dividing the subarray):

    Yes, x is in the subarray.

3. Obtain the solution to the array from the solution to the subarray:

    Yes, x is in the array.

In Step 2 we simply assumed that the solution to the subarray was available. We did not discuss all the details involved in obtaining the solution because we wanted to show the solution at a problem-solving level. When developing a recursive algorithm for a problem, we need to

• Develop a way to obtain the solution to an instance from the solution to one or more smaller instances.

• Determine the terminal condition(s) that the smaller instance(s) is (are) approaching.

• Determine the solution in the case of the terminal condition(s).

We need not be concerned with the details of how the solution is obtained (in the case of a computer, by means of stack manipulations). Indeed, worrying about these details can sometimes hinder one's development of a complex recursive algorithm. For the sake of concreteness, Figure 2.1 shows the steps done by a human when searching with Binary Search.

A recursive version of Binary Search now follows.

Algorithm 2.1 Binary Search (Recursive)

Problem: Determine whether x is in the sorted array S of size n.

Inputs: positive integer n, sorted (nondecreasing order) array of keys S indexed from 1 to n, a key x.

Outputs: *location*, the location of x in S (0 if x is not in S).

```
index location (index low, index high)
{
    index mid;
```

```
if (low > high)
    return 0;
else {
    mid = ⌊(low + high)/2⌋;
    if (x == S[mid])
        return mid;
    else if (x < S[mid])
        return location(low, mid − 1);
    else
        return location(mid + 1, high);
}
}
```

Notice that *n, S,* and *x* are not parameters to function *location*. Because they remain unchanged in each recursive call, there is no need to make them parameters. In this text only the variables, whose values can change in the recursive

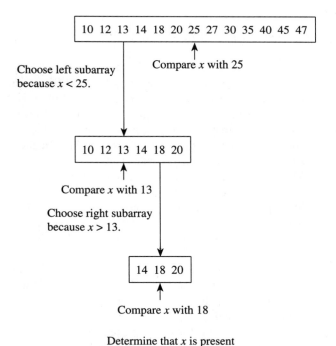

Figure 2.1 The steps done by a human when searching with Binary Search. (*Note:* $x = 18$.)

calls, are made parameters to recursive routines. There are two reasons for doing this. First, it makes the expression of recursive routines less cluttered. Second, in an actual implementation of a recursive routine, a new copy of any variable passed to the routine is made in each recursive call. If a variable's value does not change, the copy is unnecessary. This waste could be costly if the variable is an array. One way to circumvent this would be to pass the variable by address. Indeed, if the implementation language is C++, an array is automatically passed by address, and using the reserved word **const** guarantees the array cannot be modified. However, including all of this in our pseudocode expression of recursive algorithms again serves to clutter them and possibly diminish their clarity.

Each of the recursive algorithms could be implemented in a number of ways, depending on the language used for the implementation. For example, one possible way to implement them in C++ would be pass all the parameters to the recursive routine; another would be to use classes; and yet another would be to globally define the parameters that do not change in the recursive calls. We will illustrate how to implement the last one since this is the alternative consistent with our expression of the algorithms. If we did define S and x globally and n was the number of items in S, our top-level call to function *location* in Algorithm 2.1 would be as follows:

locationout = location(1, *n*);

Because the recursive version of Binary Search employs tail-recursion (that is, no operations are done after the recursive call), it is straightforward to produce an iterative version, as was done in Section 1.2. As previously discussed, we have written a recursive version because recursion clearly illustrates the divide-and-conquer process of dividing an instance into smaller instances. However, it is advantageous in languages such as C++ to replace tail-recursion by iteration. Most importantly, a substantial amount of memory can be saved by eliminating the stack developed in the recursive calls. Recall that when a routine calls another routine it is necessary to save the first routine's pending results by pushing them onto the stack of activation records. If the second routine calls another routine, the second routine's pending results must also be pushed onto the stack, and so on. When control is returned to a calling routine, its activation record is popped from the stack and the computation of the pending results is completed. In the case of a recursive routine, the number of activation records pushed onto the stack is determined by the depth reached in the recursive calls. For Binary Search, the stack reaches a depth that in the worst case is about $\lg n + 1$.

Another reason for replacing tail-recursion by iteration is that the iterative algorithm will execute faster (but only by a constant multiplicative factor) than the recursive version because no stack needs to be maintained. Because most modern LISP dialects compile tail-recursion to iterative code, there is no reason to replace tail-recursion by iteration in these dialects.

Binary Search does not have an every-case time complexity. We will do a worst-case analysis. We already did this informally in Section 1.2. Here we do the analysis more rigorously. Although the analysis refers to Algorithm 2.1, it pertains to Algorithm 1.5 as well. If you are not familiar with techniques for solving recurrence equations, you should study Appendix B before proceeding.

Worst-Case Time Complexity Analysis of Algorithm 2.1 (Binary Search, Recursive)

In an algorithm that searches an array, the most costly operation is usually the comparison of the search item with an array item. Thus, we have the following:

Basic operation: the comparison of x with $S[mid]$.

Input size: n, the number of items in the array.

We first analyze the case where n is a power of 2. There are two comparisons of x with $S[mid]$ in any call to function *location* in which x does not equal $S[mid]$. However, as discussed in our informal analysis of Binary Search in Section 1.2, we can assume that there is only one comparison, because this would be the case in an efficient assembler language implementation. Recall from Section 1.3 that we ordinarily assume that the basic operation is implemented as efficiently as possible.

As discussed in Section 1.2, one way the worst case can occur is when x is larger than all array items. If n is a power of 2 and x is larger than all the array items, each recursive call reduces the instance to one exactly half as big. For example, if $n = 16$, then $mid = \lfloor (1 + 16)/2 \rfloor = 8$. Because x is larger than all the array items, the top eight items are the input to the first recursive call. Similarly, the top four items are the input to the second recursive call, and so on. We have the following recurrence:

$$W(n) = \underbrace{W\left(\frac{n}{2}\right)}_{\substack{\text{Comparisons in} \\ \text{recursive call}}} + \underbrace{1}_{\substack{\text{Comparison at} \\ \text{top level}}}$$

If $n = 1$ and x is larger than the single array item, there is a comparison of x with that item followed by a recursive call with $low > high$. At this point the terminal condition is true, which means that there are no more comparisons. Therefore, $W(1)$ is 1. We have established the recurrence

$$
\boxed{
\begin{aligned}
&W(n) = W\left(\frac{n}{2}\right) + 1 \qquad \text{for } n > 1,\ n \text{ a power of 2} \\
&W(1) = 1
\end{aligned}
}
$$

This recurrence is solved in Example B.1 in Appendix B. The solution is

$$W(n) = \lg n + 1.$$

If n is not restricted to be a power of 2, then

$$W(n) = \lfloor \lg n \rfloor + 1 \in \Theta(\lg n),$$

where $\lfloor y \rfloor$ means the greatest integer less than or equal to y. We show how to establish this result in the exercises.

2.2 MERGESORT

A process related to sorting is merging. By ***two-way merging*** we mean combining two sorted arrays into one sorted array. By repeatedly applying the merging procedure, we can sort an array. For example, to sort an array of 16 items, we can divide it into two subarrays, each of size 8, sort the two subarrays, and then merge them to produce the sorted array. In the same way, each subarray of size 8 can be divided into two subarrays of size 4, and these subarrays can be sorted and merged. Eventually the size of the subarrays will become 1, and an array of size 1 is trivially sorted. This procedure is called "Mergesort." Given an array with n items (for simplicity, let n be a power of 2), Mergesort involves the following steps:

1. *Divide* the array into two subarrays each with $n/2$ items.
2. *Conquer* (solve) each subarray by sorting it. Unless the array is sufficiently small, use recursion to do this.
3. *Combine* the solutions to the subarrays by merging them into a single sorted array.

The following example illustrates these steps.

Example 2.2   Suppose the array contains these numbers in sequence:

$$27 \quad 10 \quad 12 \quad 20 \quad 25 \quad 13 \quad 15 \quad 22.$$

1. Divide the array:

    $$27 \quad 10 \quad 12 \quad 20 \qquad \text{and} \qquad 25 \quad 13 \quad 15 \quad 22.$$

2. Sort each subarray:

    $$10 \quad 12 \quad 20 \quad 27 \qquad \text{and} \qquad 13 \quad 15 \quad 22 \quad 25.$$

3. Merge the subarrays:

    $$10 \quad 12 \quad 13 \quad 15 \quad 20 \quad 22 \quad 25 \quad 27.$$

Figure 2.2 The steps done by a human when sorting with Mergesort.

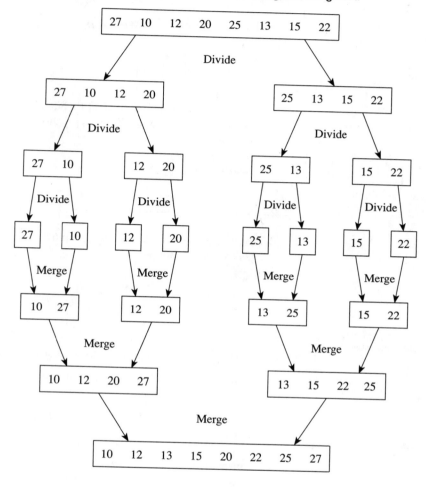

In Step 2 we think at the problem-solving level and assume that the solutions to the subarrays are available. To make matters more concrete, Figure 2.2 illustrates the steps done by a human when sorting with Mergesort. The terminal condition is when an array of size 1 is reached; at that time, the merging begins.

To implement Mergesort, we need an algorithm that merges two sorted arrays. First we give the algorithm for Mergesort.

Algorithm 2.2   Mergesort

Problem: Sort n keys in nondecreasing sequence.

Inputs: positive integer n, array of keys S indexed from 1 to n.

Outputs: the array S containing the keys in nondecreasing order.

```
void mergesort (int n, keytype S[ ])
{
    const int h = ⌊n/2⌋, m = n − h;
    keytype U[1..h], V[1..m];

    if (n > 1) {
        copy S[1] through S[h] to U[1] through U[h];
        copy S[h + 1] through S[n] to V[1] through V[m];
        mergesort(h, U);
        mergesort(m, V);
        merge(h, m, U, V, S);
    }
}
```

Before we can analyze Mergesort, we must write and analyze an algorithm that merges two sorted arrays.

Algorithm 2.3   Merge

Problem: Merge two sorted arrays into one sorted array.

Inputs: positive integers h and m, array of sorted keys U indexed from 1 to h, array of sorted keys V indexed from 1 to m.

Outputs: an array S indexed from 1 to $h + m$ containing the keys in U and V in a single sorted array.

```
void merge (int h, int m, const keytype U[ ],
                          const keytype V[ ],
                          keytype S[ ])
{
    index i, j, k;

    i = 1; j = 1; k = 1;
    while (i <= h && j <= m) {
        if (U[i] < V[j]) {
            S[k] = U[i];
            i++;
        }
        else {
            S[k] = V[j];
            j++;
        }
```

```
        k++;
    }
    if (i > h)
        copy V[j] through V[m] to S[k] through S[h + m];
    else
        copy U[i] through U[h] to S[k] through S[h + m];
    }
```

Table 2.1 illustrates how procedure *merge* works when merging two arrays of size 4.

Worst-Case Time Complexity Analysis of Algorithm 2.3 (Merge)

As mentioned in Section 1.3, in the case of algorithms that sort by comparing keys, the comparison instruction and the assignment instruction can each be considered the basic operation. Here we will consider the comparison instruction. When we discuss Mergesort further in Chapter 7, we will consider the number of assignments. In this algorithm, the number of comparisons depends on both h and m. We therefore have the following:

Basic operation: the comparison of $U[i]$ with $V[j]$.

Input size: h and m, the number of items in each of the two input arrays.

The worst case occurs when the loop is exited, because one of the indices—say, i—has reached its exit point h whereas the other index j has reached $m - 1$, 1 less than its exit point. For example, this can occur when the first $m - 1$ items in V are placed first in S, followed by all h items in U, at which time the loop is exited because i equals h. Therefore,

$$W(h, m) = h + m - 1.$$

Table 2.1 An example of merging two arrays U and V into one array S*

k	U				V				S (Result)							
1	**10**	12	20	27	**13**	15	22	25	10							
2	10	**12**	20	27	**13**	15	22	25	10	12						
3	10	12	**20**	27	**13**	15	22	25	10	12	13					
4	10	12	**20**	27	13	**15**	22	25	10	12	13	15				
5	10	12	**20**	27	13	15	**22**	25	10	12	13	15	20			
6	10	12	20	**27**	13	15	**22**	25	10	12	13	15	20	22		
7	10	12	20	**27**	13	15	22	**25**	10	12	13	15	20	22	25	
—	10	12	20	27	13	15	22	25	10	12	13	15	20	22	25	27 ← Final values

*The items compared are in boldface.

We can now analyze Mergesort.

Worst-Case Time Complexity Complexity Analysis of Algorithm 2.2 (Mergesort)

The basic operation is the comparison that takes place in *merge*. Because the number of comparisons increases with h and m, and h and m increase with n, we have the following:

Basic operation: the comparison that takes place in *merge*.

Input size: n, the number of items in the array S.

The total number of comparisons is the sum of the number of comparisons in the recursive call to *mergesort* with U as the input, the number of comparisons in the recursive call to *mergesort* with V as the input, and the number of comparisons in the top-level call to *merge*. Therefore,

$$W(n) = \underbrace{W(h)}_{\text{Time to sort } U} + \underbrace{W(m)}_{\text{Time to sort } V} + \underbrace{h + m - 1}_{\text{Time to merge}}.$$

We first analyze the case where n is a power of 2. In this case,

$$h = \lfloor n/2 \rfloor = \frac{n}{2}$$

$$m = n - h = n - \frac{n}{2} = \frac{n}{2}$$

$$h + m = \frac{n}{2} + \frac{n}{2} = n.$$

Our expression for $W(n)$ becomes

$$W(n) = W\left(\frac{n}{2}\right) + W\left(\frac{n}{2}\right) + n - 1$$

$$= 2W\left(\frac{n}{2}\right) + n - 1.$$

When the input size is 1, the terminal condition is met and no merging is done. Therefore, $W(1)$ is 0. We have established the recurrence

$$W(n) = 2W\left(\frac{n}{2}\right) + n - 1 \quad \text{for } n > 1, n \text{ a power of 2}$$

$$W(1) = 0$$

This recurrence is solved in Example B.19 in Appendix B. The solution is

$$W(n) = n \lg n - (n - 1) \in \Theta(n \lg n).$$

For n not a power of 2, we will establish in the exercises that

$$W(n) = W\left(\left\lfloor \frac{n}{2} \right\rfloor\right) + W\left(\left\lceil \frac{n}{2} \right\rceil\right) + n - 1,$$

where $\lceil y \rceil$ and $\lfloor y \rfloor$ are the smallest integer $\geq y$ and the largest integer $\leq y$, respectively. It is hard to analyze this case exactly because of floors and ceilings. However, using an induction argument like the one in Example B.25 in Appendix B, it can be shown that $W(n)$ is nondecreasing. Therefore, Theorem B.4 in that appendix implies that

$$W(n) \in \Theta(n \lg n).$$

An ***in-place sort*** is a sorting algorithm that does not use any extra space beyond that needed to store the input. Algorithm 2.2 is not an in-place sort because it uses the arrays U and V besides the input array S. If U and V are variable parameters (pass by address) in *merge,* a second copy of these arrays will not be created when *merge* is called. However, new arrays U and V will still be created each time *mergesort* is called. At the top level, the sum of the numbers of items in these two arrays is n. In the top-level recursive call, the sum of the numbers of items in the two arrays is about $n/2$, in the recursive call at the next level the sum of the numbers of items in the two arrays is about $n/4$, and in general the sum of the numbers of items in the two arrays at each recursion level is about one-half of the sum at the previous level. Therefore, the total number of extra array items created is about $n(1 + 1/2 + 1/4 + \cdots) = 2n$.

Algorithm 2.2 clearly illustrates the process of dividing an instance of a problem into smaller instances because two new arrays (smaller instances) are actually created from the input array (original instance). Therefore, this was a good way to introduce Mergesort and illustrate the divide-and-conquer approach. However, it is possible to reduce the amount of extra space to only one array containing n items. This is accomplished by doing much of the manipulation on the input array S. The following method for doing this is similar to the method used in Algorithm 2.1 (Binary Search, Recursive).

Algorithm 2.4 Mergesort 2

Problem: Sort n keys in nondecreasing sequence.

Inputs: positive integer n, array of keys S indexed from 1 to n.

Outputs: the array S containing the keys in nondecreasing order.

```
void mergesort2 (index low, index high)
{
    index mid;
```

```
    if (low < high) {
        mid = ⌊(low + high)/2⌋;
        mergesort2(low, mid);
        mergesort2(mid + 1, high);
        merge2(low, mid, high);
    }
}
```

Following our convention of making only variables, whose values can change in recursive calls, parameters to recursive routines, *n* and *S* are not parameters to procedure *mergesort2*. If the algorithm were implemented by defining *S* globally and *n* was the number of items in *S*, the top-level call to *mergesort2* would be as follows:

    mergesort2(1,n);

The merging procedure that works with *mergesort2* follows.

Algorithm 2.5

Merge 2

Problem: Merge the two sorted subarrays of *S* created in Mergesort 2.

Inputs: Indices *low, mid,* and *high,* and the subarray of *S* indexed from *low* to *high*. The keys in array slots from *low* to *mid* are already sorted in nondecreasing order, as are the keys in array slots from *mid* + 1 to *high*.

Outputs: the subarray of *S* indexed from *low* to *high* containing the keys in nondecreasing order.

```
void merge2 (index low, index mid, index high)
{
    index i, j, k;
    keytype U[low..high];      // A local array needed for the merging

    i = low; j = mid + 1; k = low;
    while (i ≤ mid && j ≤ high) {
        if (S[i] < S[j]) {
            U[k] = S[i];
            i++;
        }
        else {
            U[k] = S[j];
            j++;
        }
```

```
        k++;
    }
    if (i > mid)
        move S[j] through S[high] to U[k] through U[high];
    else
        move S[i] through S[mid] to U[k] through U[high];
        move U[low] through U[high] to S[low] through S[high];
}
```

2.3 THE DIVIDE-AND-CONQUER APPROACH

Having studied two divide-and-conquer algorithms in detail, you should now better understand the following general description of this approach.

The ***divide-and-conquer*** design strategy involves the following steps:

1. *Divide* an instance of a problem into one or more smaller instances.

2. *Conquer* (solve) each of the smaller instances. Unless a smaller instance is sufficiently small, use recursion to do this.

3. If necessary, *combine* the solutions to the smaller instances to obtain the solution to the original instance.

The reason we say "if necessary" in Step 3 is that in algorithms such as Binary Search (Algorithm 2.1) the instance is reduced to just one smaller instance. So there is no need to combine solutions.

More examples of the divide-and-conquer approach follow. In these examples we will not explicitly mention the steps previously outlined. It should be clear that we are following them.

2.4 QUICKSORT (PARTITION EXCHANGE SORT)

Next we look at a sorting algorithm, called "Quicksort," that was developed by Hoare (1962). Quicksort is similar to Mergesort in that the sort is accomplished by dividing the array into two partitions and then sorting each partition recursively. In Quicksort, however, the array is partitioned by placing all items smaller than some pivot item before that item and all items larger than or equal to the pivot item after it. The pivot item can be any item, and for convenience we will simply make it the first one. The following example illustrates how Quicksort works.

Example 2.3   Suppose the array contains these numbers in sequence:

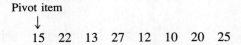

1. Partition the array so that all items smaller than the pivot item are to the left of it and all items larger are to the right:

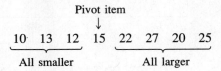

2. Sort the subarrays:

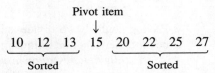

After the partitioning, the order of the items in the subarrays is unspecified and is a result of how the partitioning is implemented. We have ordered them according to how the partitioning routine, that will be presented shortly, would place them. The important thing is that all items smaller than the pivot item are to the left of it, and all items larger are to the right of it. Quicksort is then called

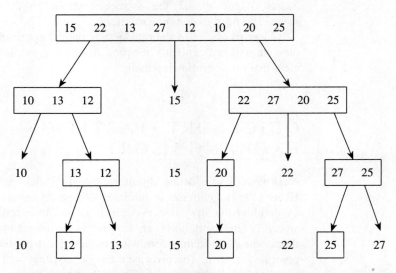

Figure 2.3 The steps done by a human when sorting with Quicksort. The subarrays are enclosed in rectangles whereas the pivot points are free.

recursively to sort each of the two subarrays. They are partitioned, and this procedure is continued until an array with one item is reached. Such an array is trivially sorted. Example 2.3 shows the solution at the problem-solving level. Figure 2.3 illustrates the steps done by a human when sorting with Quicksort. The algorithm follows.

Algorithm 2.6

Quicksort

Problem: Sort n keys in nondecreasing order.

Inputs: positive integer n, array of keys S indexed from 1 to n.

Outputs: the array S containing the keys in nondecreasing order.

```
void quicksort (index low, index high)
{
    index pivotpoint;

    if (high > low) {
        partition(low, high, pivotpoint);
        quicksort(low, pivotpoint − 1);
        quicksort(pivotpoint + 1, high);
    }
}
```

Following our usual convention, n and S are not parameters to procedure *quicksort*. If the algorithm were implemented by defining S globally and n was the number of items in S, the top-level call to *quicksort* would be as follows:

```
quicksort(1,n);
```

The partitioning of the array is done by procedure *partition*. Next we show an algorithm for this procedure.

Algorithm 2.7

Partition

Problem: Partition the array S for Quicksort.

Inputs: two indices, *low* and *high*, and the subarray of S indexed from *low* to *high*.

Outputs: *pivotpoint*, the pivot point for the subarray indexed from *low* to *high*.

```
void partition (index low, index high,
                index& pivotpoint)
```

```
{
    index i, j;
    keytype pivotitem;

    pivotitem = S[low];                              // Choose first item for pivotitem.
    j = low;
    for (i = low + 1; i <= high; i++)
        if (S[i] < pivotitem) {
            j++;
            exchange S[i] and S[j];
        }
    pivotpoint = j;
    exchange S[low] and S[pivotpoint];               // Put pivotitem at pivotpoint.
}
```

Procedure *partition* works by checking each item in the array in sequence. Whenever an item is found to be less than the pivot item, it is moved to the left side of the array. Table 2.2 shows how *partition* would proceed on the array in Example 2.3.

Table 2.2 An example of procedure *partition**

i	j	S[1]	S[2]	S[3]	S[4]	S[5]	S[6]	S[7]	S[8]	
—	—	15	22	13	27	12	10	20	25	←Initial values
2	1	**15**	**22**	13	27	12	10	20	25	
3	2	**15**	22	**13**	27	12	10	20	25	
4	2	**15**	⬚13	⬚22	**27**	12	10	20	25	
5	3	**15**	13	22	27	**12**	10	20	25	
6	4	**15**	13	⬚12	27	⬚22	**10**	20	25	
7	4	**15**	13	12	⬚10	22	⬚27	**20**	25	
8	4	**15**	13	12	10	22	27	20	**25**	
—	4	⬚10	13	12	⬚15	22	27	20	25	←Final values

*Items compared are in boldface. Items just exchanged appear in squares.

Next we analyze Partition and Quicksort.

Every-Case Time Complexity Analysis of Algorithm 2.7 (Partition)

Basic operation: the comparison of S[i] with *pivotitem*.

Input size: $n = high - low + 1$, the number of items in the subarray.

Because every item except the first is compared,

$$T(n) = n - 1.$$

> We are using n here to represent the size of the subarray, not the size of the array S. It represents the size of S only when *partition* is called at the top level.

Quicksort does not have an every-case complexity. We will do worst-case and average-case analyses.

Worst-Case Time Complexity Analysis of Algorithm 2.6 (Quicksort)

Basic operation: the comparison of $S[i]$ with *pivotitem* in *partition*.

Input size: n, the number of items in the array S.

Oddly enough, it turns out that the worse case occurs if the array is already sorted in nondecreasing order. The reason for this should become clear. If the array is already sorted in nondecreasing order, no items are less than the first item in the array, which is the pivot item. Therefore, when *partition* is called at the top level, no items are placed to the left of the pivot item, and the value of *pivotpoint* assigned by *partition* is 1. Similarly, in each recursive call *pivotpoint* receives the value of *low*. Therefore, the array is repeatedly partitioned into an empty subarray on the left and a subarray with one less item on the right. For the class of instances that are already sorted in nondecreasing order, we have

$$T(n) \;\;=\;\; \underbrace{T(0)}_{\substack{\text{Time to sort}\\\text{left subarray}}} \;+\; \underbrace{T(n-1)}_{\substack{\text{Time to sort}\\\text{right subarray}}} \;+\; \underbrace{n-1}_{\substack{\text{Time to}\\\text{partition}}}$$

We are using the notation $T(n)$ because we are presently determining the every-case complexity for the class of instances that are already sorted in nondecreasing order. Because $T(0) = 0$, we have the recurrence

$$
\begin{aligned}
&T(n) = T(n-1) + n - 1 \qquad \text{for } n > 0\\
&T(0) = 0
\end{aligned}
$$

This recurrence is solved in Example B.16 in Appendix B. The solution is

$$T(n) = \frac{n(n-1)}{2}.$$

We have established that the worst case is at least $n(n-1)/2$. Although intuitively it may now seem that this is as bad as things can get, we still need to show this. We will accomplish this by using induction to show that, for all n,

$$W(n) \le \frac{n(n-1)}{2}.$$

Induction base: For $n = 0$

$$W(0) = 0 \leq \frac{0(0-1)}{2}.$$

Induction hypothesis: Assume that, for $0 \leq k < n$,

$$W(k) \leq \frac{k(k-1)}{2}.$$

Induction step: We need to show that

$$W(n) \leq \frac{n(n-1)}{2}.$$

For a given n there is some instance with size n for which the processing time is $W(n)$. Let p be the value of *pivotpoint* returned by *partition* at the top level when this instance is processed. Because the time to process the instances of size $p - 1$ and $n - p$ can be no more than $W(p - 1)$ and $W(n - p)$, respectively, we have

$$W(n) \leq W(p-1) + W(n-p) + n - 1$$
$$\leq \frac{(p-1)(p-2)}{2} + \frac{(n-p)(n-p-1)}{2} + n - 1.$$

The last inequality is by the induction hypothesis. Algebraic manipulations can show that for $1 \leq p \leq n$ this last expression is

$$\leq \frac{n(n-1)}{2}.$$

This completes the induction proof.

We have shown that the worst-case time complexity is given by

$$W(n) = \frac{n(n-1)}{2} \in \Theta(n^2).$$

The worst case occurs when the array is already sorted because we always choose the first item for the pivot item. Therefore, if we have reason to believe that the array is close to being sorted, this is not a good choice for the pivot item. When we discuss Quicksort further in Chapter 7, we will investigate other methods for choosing the pivot item. If we use these methods, the worst case does not occur when the array is already sorted. But the worst-case time complexity is still $n(n-1)/2$.

In the worst case, Algorithm 2.6 is no faster than Exchange Sort (Algorithm 1.3). Why then is this sort called Quicksort? As we shall see, it is in its average-case behavior that Quicksort earns its name.

Average-Case Time Complexity Analysis of Algorithm 2.6 (Quicksort)

Basic operation: the comparison of $S[i]$ with *pivotitem* in *partition*.

Input size: n, the number of items in the array S.

We will assume that we have no reason to believe that the numbers in the array are in any particular order, and therefore that the value of *pivotpoint* returned by *partition* is equally likely to be any of the numbers from 1 through n. If there was reason to believe a different distribution, this analysis would not be applicable. The average obtained is, therefore, the average sorting time when every possible ordering is sorted the same number of times. In this case, the average-case time complexity is given by the following recurrence:

$$
A(n) = \overset{\underset{\displaystyle \text{Probability}}{\underset{\displaystyle \text{pivotpoint is } p}{\downarrow}}}{\sum_{p=1}^{n}} \;\underbrace{\frac{1}{n}\,[A(p-1) + A(n-p)]}_{\substack{\text{Average time to}\\\text{sort subarrays when}\\\text{pivotpoint is } p}} + \underbrace{n-1}_{\substack{\text{Time to}\\\text{partition}}} \tag{2.1}
$$

In the exercises we show that

$$
\sum_{p=1}^{n} [A(p-1) + A(n-p)] = 2 \sum_{p=1}^{n} A(p-1).
$$

Plugging this equality into Equality 2.1 yields

$$
A(n) = \frac{2}{n} \sum_{p=1}^{n} A(p-1) + n - 1.
$$

Multiplying by n we have

$$
nA(n) = 2 \sum_{p=1}^{n} A(p-1) + n(n-1). \tag{2.2}
$$

Applying Equality 2.2 to $n - 1$ gives

$$
(n-1)A(n-1) = 2 \sum_{p=1}^{n-1} A(p-1) + (n-1)(n-2). \tag{2.3}
$$

Subtracting Equality 2.3 from Equality 2.2 yields

$$
nA(n) - (n-1)A(n-1) = 2A(n-1) + 2(n-1),
$$

which simplifies to

$$
\frac{A(n)}{n+1} = \frac{A(n-1)}{n} + \frac{2(n-1)}{n(n+1)}.
$$

If we let

$$a_n = \frac{A(n)}{n + 1},$$

we have the recurrence

$$a_n = a_{n-1} + \frac{2(n - 1)}{n(n + 1)} \quad \text{for } n > 0$$
$$a_0 = 0.$$

Like the recurrence in Example B.22 in Appendix B, the approximate solution to this recurrence is given by

$$a_n \approx 2 \ln n,$$

which implies that

$$A(n) \approx (n + 1)2 \ln n = (n + 1)2(\ln 2)(\lg n)$$
$$\approx 1.38(n + 1) \lg n \in \Theta(n \lg n).$$

Quicksort's average-case time complexity is of the same order as Mergesort's time complexity. Mergesort and Quicksort are compared further in Chapter 7 and in Knuth (1973).

2.5 STRASSEN'S MATRIX MULTIPLICATION ALGORITHM

Recall that Algorithm 1.4 (Matrix Multiplication) multiplied two matrices strictly according to the definition of matrix multiplication. We showed that the time complexity of its number of multiplications is given by $T(n) = n^3$, where n is the number of rows and columns in the matrices. We can also analyze the number of additions. As you will show in the exercises, after the algorithm is modified slightly, the time complexity of the number of additions is given by $T(n) = n^3 - n^2$. Because both these time complexities are in $\Theta(n^3)$, the algorithm can become impractical fairly quickly. In 1969, Strassen published an algorithm whose time complexity is better than cubic in terms of both multiplications and additions/subtractions. The following example illustrates his method.

Example 2.4 Suppose we want the product C of two 2×2 matrices, A and B. That is,

$$\begin{bmatrix} c_{11} & c_{12} \\ c_{21} & c_{22} \end{bmatrix} = \begin{bmatrix} a_{11} & a_{12} \\ a_{21} & a_{22} \end{bmatrix} \times \begin{bmatrix} b_{11} & b_{12} \\ b_{21} & b_{22} \end{bmatrix}.$$

Strassen determined that, if we let

$$m_1 = (a_{11} + a_{22})(b_{11} + b_{22})$$
$$m_2 = (a_{21} + a_{22})b_{11}$$
$$m_3 = a_{11}(b_{12} - b_{22})$$
$$m_4 = a_{22}(b_{21} - b_{11})$$
$$m_5 = (a_{11} + a_{12})b_{22}$$
$$m_6 = (a_{21} - a_{11})(b_{11} + b_{12})$$
$$m_7 = (a_{12} - a_{22})(b_{21} + b_{22}),$$

the product C is given by

$$C = \begin{bmatrix} m_1 + m_4 - m_5 + m_7 & m_3 + m_5 \\ m_2 + m_4 & m_1 + m_3 - m_2 + m_6 \end{bmatrix}.$$

In the exercises, you will show that this is correct.

To multiply two 2×2 matrices, Strassen's Method requires seven multiplications and 18 additions/subtractions, whereas the straightforward method requires eight multiplications and four additions/subtractions. We have saved ourselves one multiplication at the expense of doing 14 additional additions or subtractions. This is not very impressive, and indeed it is not in the case of 2×2 matrices that Strassen's Method is of value. Because the commutativity of multiplication is not used in Strassen's formulas, those formulas pertain to larger matrices that are each divided into four submatrices. First we divide the matrices A and B, as illustrated in Figure 2.4. Assuming that n is a power of 2, the matrix A_{11}, for example, is meant to represent the following submatrix of A:

$$A_{11} = \begin{bmatrix} a_{11} & a_{12} \cdots a_{1,n/2} \\ a_{21} & a_{22} \cdots a_{2,n/2} \\ & \vdots \\ a_{n/2,1} & \cdots \quad a_{n/2,n/2} \end{bmatrix}$$

Using Strassen's Method, first we compute

$$M_1 = (A_{11} + A_{22})(B_{11} + B_{22}),$$

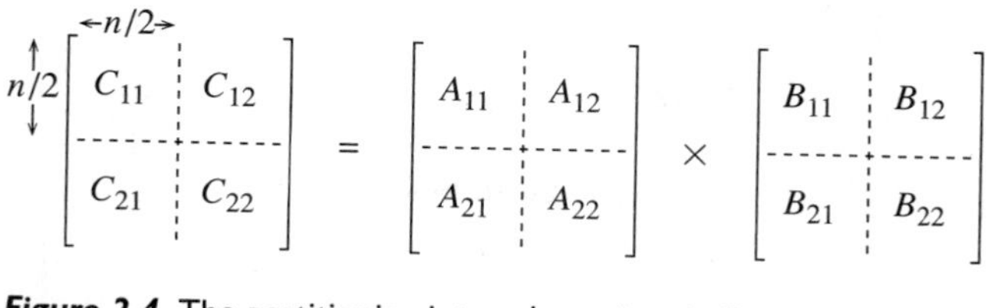

Figure 2.4 The partitioning into submatrices in Strassen's Algorithm.

where our operations are now matrix addition and multiplication. In the same way, we compute M_2 through M_7. Next we compute

$$C_{11} = M_1 + M_4 - M_5 + M_7$$

and C_{12}, C_{21}, and C_{22}. Finally, the product C of A and B is obtained by combining the four submatrices C_{ij}. The following example illustrates these steps.

Example 2.5 Suppose that

$$A = \begin{bmatrix} 1 & 2 & 3 & 4 \\ 5 & 6 & 7 & 8 \\ 9 & 1 & 2 & 3 \\ 4 & 5 & 6 & 7 \end{bmatrix} \qquad B = \begin{bmatrix} 8 & 9 & 1 & 2 \\ 3 & 4 & 5 & 6 \\ 7 & 8 & 9 & 1 \\ 2 & 3 & 4 & 5 \end{bmatrix}.$$

Figure 2.5 illustrates the partitioning in Strassen's Method. The computations proceed as follows:

$$\begin{aligned} M_1 &= (A_{11} + A_{22}) \times (B_{11} + B_{22}) \\ &= \left(\begin{bmatrix} 1 & 2 \\ 5 & 6 \end{bmatrix} + \begin{bmatrix} 2 & 3 \\ 6 & 7 \end{bmatrix} \right) \times \left(\begin{bmatrix} 8 & 9 \\ 3 & 4 \end{bmatrix} + \begin{bmatrix} 9 & 1 \\ 4 & 5 \end{bmatrix} \right) \\ &= \begin{bmatrix} 3 & 5 \\ 11 & 13 \end{bmatrix} \times \begin{bmatrix} 17 & 10 \\ 7 & 9 \end{bmatrix} \end{aligned}$$

When the matrices are sufficiently small, we multiply in the standard way. In this example, we do this when $n = 2$. Therefore,

$$\begin{aligned} M_1 &= \begin{bmatrix} 3 & 5 \\ 11 & 13 \end{bmatrix} \times \begin{bmatrix} 17 & 10 \\ 7 & 9 \end{bmatrix} \\ &= \begin{bmatrix} 3 \times 17 + 5 \times 7 & 3 \times 10 + 5 \times 9 \\ 11 \times 17 + 13 \times 7 & 11 \times 10 + 13 \times 9 \end{bmatrix} = \begin{bmatrix} 86 & 75 \\ 278 & 227 \end{bmatrix} \end{aligned}$$

After this, M_2 through M_7 are computed in the same way, and then the values of C_{11}, C_{12}, C_{21}, and C_{22} are computed. They are combined to yield C.

$$\overset{\leftarrow 2 \rightarrow}{} \; 2 \updownarrow \left[\begin{array}{c|c} C_{11} & C_{12} \\ \hline C_{21} & C_{22} \end{array}\right] = \left[\begin{array}{cc|cc} 1 & 2 & 3 & 4 \\ 5 & 6 & 7 & 8 \\ \hline 9 & 1 & 2 & 3 \\ 4 & 5 & 6 & 7 \end{array}\right] \times \left[\begin{array}{cc|cc} 8 & 9 & 1 & 2 \\ 3 & 4 & 5 & 6 \\ \hline 7 & 8 & 9 & 1 \\ 2 & 3 & 4 & 5 \end{array}\right]$$

Figure 2.5 The partitioning in Strassen's Algorithm with $n = 4$ and values given to the matrices.

Next we present an algorithm for Strassen's Method when n is a power of 2.

Algorithm 2.8

Strassen

Problem: Determine the product of two $n \times n$ matrices where n is a power of 2.

Inputs: an integer n that is a power of 2, and two $n \times n$ matrices A and B.

Outputs: the product C of A and B.

```
void strassen (int n
                n × n_matrix A,
                n × n_matrix B,
                n × n_matrix& C)
{
   if (n <= threshold)
      compute C = A × B using the standard algorithm;
   else {
      partition A into four submatrices A₁₁, A₁₂, A₂₁, A₂₂;
      partition B into four submatrices B₁₁, B₁₂, B₂₁, B₂₂;
      compute C = A × B using Strassen's Method;
         // example recursive call; strassen(n/2, A₁₁ + A₂₂, B₁₁ + B₂₂, M₁)
   }
}
```

The value of *threshold* is the point where we feel it is more efficient to use the standard algorithm than it would be to call procedure *strassen* recursively. In Section 2.7 we discuss a method for determining thresholds.

Every-Case Time Complexity Analysis of Number of Multiplications in Algorithm 2.8 (Strassen)

Basic operation: one elementary multiplication.

Input size: n, the number of rows and columns in the matrices.

For simplicity, we analyze the case where we keep dividing until we have two 1×1 matrices, at which point we simply multiply the numbers in each matrix. The actual threshold value used does not affect the order. When $n = 1$, exactly one multiplication is done. When we have two $n \times n$ matrices with $n > 1$, the algorithm is called exactly seven times with an $(n/2) \times (n/2)$ matrix passed each time, and no multiplications are done at the top level. We have established the recurrence

$$T(n) = 7T\left(\frac{n}{2}\right) \qquad \text{for } n > 1, n \text{ a power of 2}$$
$$T(1) = 1$$

This recurrence is solved in Example B.2 in Appendix B. The solution is

$$T(n) = n^{\lg 7} \approx n^{2.81} \in \Theta(n^{2.81}).$$

Every-Case Time Complexity Analysis of Number of Additions/Subtractions in Algorithm 2.8 (Strassen)

Basic operation: one elementary addition or subtraction.

Input size: n, the number of rows and columns in the matrices.

Again we assume that we keep dividing until we have two 1×1 matrices. When $n = 1$, no additions/subtractions are done. When we have two $n \times n$ matrices with $n > 1$, the algorithm is called exactly seven times with an $(n/2) \times (n/2)$ matrix passed in each time, and 18 matrix additions/subtractions are done on $(n/2) \times (n/2)$ matrices. When two $(n/2) \times (n/2)$ matrices are added or subtracted, $(n/2)^2$ additions or subtractions are done on the items in the matrices. We have established the recurrence

$$T(n) = 7T\left(\frac{n}{2}\right) + 18\left(\frac{n}{2}\right)^2 \quad \text{for } n > 1, n \text{ a power of 2}$$

$$T(1) = 0$$

This recurrence is solved in Example B.20 in Appendix B. The solution is

$$T(n) = 6n^{\lg 7} - 6n^2 \approx 6n^{2.81} - 6n^2 \in \Theta(n^{2.81}).$$

When n is not a power of 2, we must modify the previous algorithm. One simple modification is to add sufficient numbers of columns and rows of 0's to the original matrices to make the dimension a power of 2. Alternatively, in the recursive calls we could add just one extra row and one extra column of 0's whenever the number of rows and columns is odd. Strassen (1969) suggested the following, more complex modification. We embed the matrices in larger ones with $2^k m$ rows and columns, where $k = \lfloor \lg n - 4 \rfloor$ and $m = \lfloor n/2^k \rfloor + 1$. We use Strassen's Method up to a *threshold* value of m, and use the standard algorithm after reaching the *threshold*. It can be shown that the total number of arithmetic operations (multiplications, additions, and subtractions) is less than $4.7n^{2.81}$.

Table 2.3 compares the time complexities of the standard algorithm and Strassen's Algorithm for n a power of 2. Ignoring for the moment the overhead involved in the recursive calls, Strassen's Algorithm is always more efficient in terms of multiplications, and for large values of n, Strassen's Algorithm is more efficient in terms of additions/subtractions. In Section 2.7 we will discuss an analysis technique that accounts for the time taken by the recursive calls.

Shmuel Winograd developed a variant of Strassen's Algorithm that requires

Table 2.3 A comparison of two algorithms that multiply $n \times n$ matrices

	Standard Algorithm	Strassen's Algorithm
Multiplications	n^3	$n^{2.81}$
Additions/Subtractions	$n^3 - n^2$	$6n^{2.81} - 6n^2$

only 15 additions/subtractions. It appears in Brassard and Bratley (1988). For this algorithm, the time complexity of the additions/subtractions is given by

$$T(n) \approx 5n^{2.81} - 5n^2.$$

Coppersmith and Winograd (1987) developed a matrix multiplication algorithm whose time complexity for the number of multiplications is in $O(n^{2.38})$. However, the constant is so large that Strassen's Algorithm is usually more efficient.

It is possible to prove that matrix multiplication requires an algorithm whose time complexity is at least quadratic. Whether matrix multiplications can be done in quadratic time remains an open question, because no one has ever created a quadratic-time algorithm for matrix multiplication, and no one has proven that it is not possible to create such an algorithm.

One last point is that other matrix operations such as inverting a matrix and finding the determinant of a matrix are directly related to matrix multiplication. Therefore, we can readily create algorithms for these operations that are as efficient as Strassen's Algorithm for matrix multiplication.

2.6 ARITHMETIC WITH LARGE INTEGERS

Suppose that we need to do arithmetic operations on integers whose size exceeds the computer's hardware capability of representing integers. If we need to maintain all the significant digits in our results, switching to a floating point representation would be of no value. In such cases our only alternative is to use software to represent and manipulate the integers. We can accomplish this with the help of the divide-and-conquer approach. Our discussion focuses on integers represented in base 10. However, the methods developed can readily be modified for use in other bases.

2.6.1 Representation of Large Integers: Addition and Other Linear-Time Operations

A straightforward way to represent a large integer is to use an array of integers, where each array slot stores one digit. For example, the integer 543,127 can be represented in the array S as follows:

$$\underbrace{5}_{S\lfloor6\rfloor} \quad \underbrace{4}_{S\lfloor5\rfloor} \quad \underbrace{3}_{S\lfloor4\rfloor} \quad \underbrace{1}_{S\lfloor3\rfloor} \quad \underbrace{2}_{S\lfloor2\rfloor} \quad \underbrace{7}_{S\lfloor1\rfloor}.$$

To represent both positive and negative integers we need only reserve the high-order array slot for the sign. We could use 0 in that slot to represent a positive integer and 1 to represent a negative integer. We will assume this representation and use the defined data type large_integer to mean an array big enough to represent the integers in the application of interest.

It is not difficult to write linear-time algorithms for addition and subtraction, where n is the number of digits in the large integers. The basic operation consists of the manipulation of one decimal digit. In the exercises you are asked to write and analyze these algorithms. Furthermore, linear-time algorithms can readily be written that do the operation

$$u \times 10^m \qquad u \textbf{ divide } 10^m \qquad u \textbf{ rem } 10^m,$$

where u represents a large integer, m is a nonnegative integer, **divide** returns the quotient in integer division, and **rem** returns the remainder. This, too, is done in the exercises.

2.6.2 Multiplication of Large Integers

A simple quadratic-time algorithm for multiplying large integers is one that mimics the standard way learned in grammar school. We will develop one that is better than quadratic time. Our algorithm is based on using divide-and-conquer to split an n-digit integer into two integers of approximately $n/2$ digits. Following are two examples of such splits.

$$\underbrace{567,832}_{6 \text{ digits}} = \underbrace{567}_{3 \text{ digits}} \times 10^3 + \underbrace{832}_{3 \text{ digits}}$$

$$\underbrace{9,423,723}_{7 \text{ digits}} = \underbrace{9423}_{4 \text{ digits}} \times 10^3 + \underbrace{723}_{3 \text{ digits}}$$

In general, if n is the number of digits in the integer $u,$ we will split the integer into two integers, one with $\lceil n/2 \rceil$ and the other with $\lfloor n/2 \rfloor$, as follows:

$$\underbrace{u}_{n \text{ digits}} = \underbrace{x}_{\lceil n/2 \rceil \text{ digits}} \times 10^m + \underbrace{y}_{\lfloor n/2 \rfloor \text{ digits}}$$

With this representation, the exponent m of 10 is given by

$$m = \left\lfloor \frac{n}{2} \right\rfloor.$$

If we have two n-digit integers

$$u = x \times 10^m + y$$
$$v = w \times 10^m + z,$$

their product is given by

$$uv = (x \times 10^m + y)(w \times 10^m + z)$$
$$= xw \times 10^{2m} + (xz + wy) \times 10^m + yz.$$

We can multiply u and v by doing four multiplications on integers with about half as many digits and performing linear-time operations. The following example illustrates this method.

Example 2.6   Consider the following:

$$567{,}832 \times 9{,}423{,}723 = (567 \times 10^3 + 832)(9423 \times 10^3 + 723)$$
$$= 567 \times 9423 \times 10^6 + (567 \times 723 + 9423 \times 832)$$
$$\times 10^3 + 832 \times 723$$

Recursively, these smaller integers can then be multiplied by dividing them into yet smaller integers. This division process is continued until a threshold value is reached, at which time the multiplication can be done in the standard way.

Although we illustrate the method using integers with about the same number of digits, it is still applicable when this is not the case. We simply use $m = \lfloor n/2 \rfloor$ to split both of them, where n is the number of digits in the larger integer. The algorithm now follows. We keep dividing until one of the integers is 0 or we reach some threshold value for the larger integer, at which time the multiplication is done using the hardware of the computer (that is, in the usual way).

Algorithm 2.9   Large Integer Multiplication

Problem: Multiply two large integers, u and v.

Inputs: large integers u and v.

Outputs: *prod,* the product of u and v.

```
large_integer prod (large_integer u, large_integer v)
{
    large_integer x, y, w, z;
    int n, m;
```

```
n = maximum(number of digits in u, number of digits in v)
if (u == 0 || v == 0)
    return 0;
else if (n <= threshold)
    return u × v obtained in the usual way;
else {
    m = ⌊n/2⌋;
    x = u divide 10ᵐ; y = u rem 10ᵐ;
    w = v divide 10ᵐ; z = v rem 10ᵐ;
    return prod(x,w) × 10²ᵐ + (prod(x,z) + prod(w,y)) × 10ᵐ + prod(y,z);
    }
}
```

Notice that n is an implicit input to the algorithm because it is the number of digits in the larger of the two integers. Remember that **divide**, **rem**, and × represent linear-time functions that we need to write.

Worst-Case Time Complexity Analysis of Algorithm 2.9 (Large Integer Multiplication)

We analyze how long it takes to multiply two n-digit integers.

Basic operation: The manipulation of one decimal digit in a large integer when adding, subtracting, or doing **divide** 10^m, **rem** 10^m, or × 10^m. Each of these latter three calls results in the basic operation being done m times.

Input size: n, the number of digits in each of the two integers.

The worst case is when both integers have no digits equal to 0, because the recursion only ends when *threshold* is passed. We will analyze this case.

Suppose n is a power of 2. Then x, y, w, and z all have exactly $n/2$ digits, which means that the input size to each of the four recursive calls to *prod* is $n/2$. Because $m = n/2$, the linear-time operations of addition, subtraction, **divide** 10^m, **rem** 10^m, and × 10^m all have linear time complexities in terms of n. The maximum input size to these linear-time operations is not the same for all of them, and so the determination of the exact time complexity is not straightforward. It is much simpler to group all the linear-time operations in the one term cn, where c is a positive constant. Our recurrence is then

$$W(n) = 4W\left(\frac{n}{2}\right) + cn \qquad \text{for } n > s, \, n \text{ a power of 2}$$

$$W(s) = 0.$$

The actual value s at which we no longer divide the instance is less than or equal to *threshold* and is a power of 2, because all the inputs in this case are powers of 2.

For n not restricted to being a power of 2, it is possible to establish a recurrence like the previous one but involving floors and ceilings. Using an induction argument like the one in Example B.25 in Appendix B, we can show that $W(n)$ is eventually nondecreasing. Therefore, Theorem B.6 in Appendix B implies that

$$W(n) \in \Theta(n^{\lg 4}) = \Theta(n^2).$$

Our algorithm for multiplying large integers is still quadratic. The problem is that the algorithm does four multiplications on integers with half as many digits as the original integers. If we can reduce the numbers of these multiplications, we can obtain an algorithm that is better than quadratic. We do this in the following way. Recall that function *prod* must determine

$$xw, \qquad xz + yw, \qquad \text{and} \qquad yz, \tag{2.4}$$

and we accomplished this by calling function *prod* recursively four times to compute

$$xw, \qquad xz, \qquad yw, \qquad \text{and} \qquad yz.$$

If instead we set

$$r = (x + y)(w + z) = xw + (xz + yw) + yz,$$

then

$$xz + yw = r - xw - yz.$$

This means we can get the three values in Expression 2.4 by determining the following three values:

$$r = (x + y)(w + z), \qquad xw, \qquad \text{and} \qquad yz.$$

To get these three values we need to do only three multiplications, while doing some additional linear-time additions and subtractions. The algorithm that follows implements this method.

Algorithm 2.10

Large Integer Multiplication 2

Problem: Multiply two large integers, u and v.

Inputs: large integers u and v.

Outputs: *prod2*, the product of u and v.

```
large_integer prod2 (large_integer u, large_integer v)
{
    large_integer x, y, w, z, r, p, q;
    int n, m;
```

```
n = maximum(number of digits in u, number of digits in v);
if (u == 0 ‖ v == 0)
    return 0;
else if (n <= threshold)
    return u × v obtained in the usual way;
else {
    m = ⌊n/2⌋;
    x = u divide 10^m; y = u rem 10^m;
    w = v divide 10^m; z = v rem 10^m;
    r = prod2(x + y, w + z);
    p = prod2(x, w);
    q = prod2(y, z);
    return p × 10^{2m} + (r − p − q) × 10^m + q;
}
}
```

◆ ■■■■ **Worse-Case Time Complexity Analysis of Algorithm 2.10**
(Large Integer Multiplications 2)

We analyze how long it takes to multiply two n-digit integers.

Basic operation: The manipulation of one decimal digit in a large integer when adding, subtracting, or doing **divide** 10^m, **rem** 10^m, or **× 10^m**. Each of these latter three calls results in the basic operation being done m times.

Input size: n, the number of digits in each of the two integers.

The worst case happens when both integers have no digits equal to 0, because in this case the recursion ends only when the *threshold* is passed. We analyze this case.

If n is a power of 2, then x, y, w, and z all have $n/2$ digits. Therefore, as Table 2.4 illustrates,

$$\frac{n}{2} \le \text{digits in } x + y \le \frac{n}{2} + 1.$$

$$\frac{n}{2} \le \text{digits in } w + z \le \frac{n}{2} + 1.$$

This means we have the following input sizes for the given function calls:

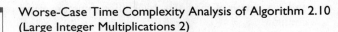

	Input Size
$prod2(x+y,w+z)$	$\frac{n}{2} \le \text{input size} \le \frac{n}{2} + 1$
$prod2(x,w)$	$\frac{n}{2}$
$prod2(y,z)$	$\frac{n}{2}$

				Number of Digits
n	x	y	$x + y$	in $x + y$
4	10	10	20	$2 = \dfrac{n}{2}$
4	99	99	198	$3 = \dfrac{n}{2} + 1$
8	1000	1000	2,000	$4 = \dfrac{n}{2}$
8	9999	9999	19,998	$5 = \dfrac{n}{2} + 1$

Table 2.4 Examples of the number of digits in $x + y$ in Algorithm 2.10

Because $m = n/2$, the linear-time operations of addition, subtraction, **divide** 10^m, **rem** 10^m, and $\times 10^m$ all have linear-time complexities in terms of n. Therefore, $W(n)$ satisfies

$$3W\left(\frac{n}{2}\right) + cn \le W(n) \le 3W\left(\frac{n}{2} + 1\right) + cn \qquad \text{for } n > s, \, n \text{ a power of 2}$$
$$W(s) = 0$$
,

where s is less than or equal to *threshold* and is a power of 2, because all the inputs in this case are powers of 2. For n not restricted to being a power of 2, it is possible to establish a recurrence like the previous one but involving floors and ceilings. Using an induction argument like the one in Example B.25 in Appendix B, we can show that $W(n)$ is eventually nondecreasing. Therefore, owing to the left inequality in this recurrence and Theorem B.6, we have

$$W(n) \in \Omega(n^{\log_2 3}).$$

Next we show that

$$W(n) \in O(n^{\log_2 3}).$$

To that end, let

$$W'(n) = W(n + 2).$$

Using the right inequality in the recurrence, we have

$$W'(n) = W(n + 2) \le 3W\left(\frac{n + 2}{2} + 1\right) + c[n + 2]$$

$$\le 3W\left(\frac{n}{2} + 2\right) + cn + 2c$$

$$\le 3W'\left(\frac{n}{2}\right) + cn + 2c.$$

Because $W(n)$ is nondecreasing, so is $W'(n)$. Therefore, owing to Theorem B.6 in Appendix B,

$$W'(n) \in O(n^{\log_2 3}),$$

and so

$$W(n) = W'(n-2) \in O(n^{\log_2 3}).$$

Combining our two results, we have

$$W(n) \in \Theta(n^{\log_2 3}) \approx \Theta(n^{1.58}).$$

Using Fast Fourier Transforms, Borodin and Munro (1975) developed a $\Theta(n(\lg n)^2)$ algorithm for multiplying large integers. The survey article (Brassard, Monet and Zuffelatto, 1986) concerns very large integer multiplication.

It is possible to write algorithms for other operations on large integers, such as division and square root, whose time complexities are of the same order as that of the algorithm for multiplication.

2.7 DETERMINING THRESHOLDS

As discussed in Section 2.1, recursion requires a fair amount of overhead in terms of computer time. If, for example, we are sorting only eight keys, is it really worth this overhead just so we can use a $\Theta(n \lg n)$ algorithm instead of a $\Theta(n^2)$ algorithm? Or perhaps, for such a small *n,* would Exchange Sort (Algorithm 1.3) be faster than our recursive Mergesort? We develop a method that determines for what values of *n* it is at least as fast to call an alternative algorithm as it is to divide the instance further. These values depend on the divide-and-conquer algorithm, the alternative algorithm, and the computer on which they are implemented. Ideally we would like to find an ***optimal threshold value*** of *n*. This would be an instance size such that for any smaller instance it would be at least as fast to call the other algorithm as it would be to divide the instance further, and for any larger instance size it would be faster to divide the instance again. However, as we shall see, an optimal threshold value does not always exist. Even if our analysis does not yield an optimal threshold value, we can use the results of the analysis to pick a threshold value. We then modify the divide-and-conquer algorithm so that the instance is no longer divided once *n* reaches that threshold value; instead, the alternative algorithm is called. We have already seen the use of thresholds in Algorithms 2.8, 2.9, and 2.10.

To determine a threshold, we must consider the computer on which the algorithm is implemented. This technique is illustrated using Mergesort and Exchange Sort. We use Mergesort's worst-case time complexity in this analysis. So we are actually trying to optimize the worse-case behavior. When analyzing

Mergesort, we determined that the worst case is given by the following recurrence:

$$W(n) = W\left(\left\lfloor \frac{n}{2} \right\rfloor\right) + W\left(\left\lceil \frac{n}{2} \right\rceil\right) + n - 1.$$

Let's assume that we are implementing Mergesort 2 (Algorithm 2.4). Suppose that on the computer of interest the time Mergesort 2 takes to divide and recombine an instance of size n is $32n$ μs, where μs stands for microseconds. The time to divide and recombine the instance includes the time to compute the value of *mid,* the time to do the stack operations for the two recursive calls, and the time to merge the two subarrays. Because there are several components to the division and recombination time, it is unlikely that the total time would simply be a constant times n. However, assume that this is the case to keep things as simple as possible. Because the term $n - 1$ in the recurrence for $W(n)$ is the recombination time, it is included in the time $32n$ μs. Therefore, for this computer, we have

$$W(n) = W\left(\left\lfloor \frac{n}{2} \right\rfloor\right) + W\left(\left\lceil \frac{n}{2} \right\rceil\right) + 32n \ \mu s$$

for Mergesort 2. Because only a terminal condition check is done when the input size is 1, we assume that $W(1)$ is essentially 0. For simplicity, we initially limit our discussion to n being a power of 2. In this case we have the following recurrence:

$$\boxed{\begin{aligned} &W(n) = 2W(n/2) + 32n \ \mu s \qquad \text{for } n > 1, \ n \text{ a power of 2} \\ &W(1) = 0 \ \mu s \end{aligned}}$$

The techniques in Appendix B can be used to solve this recurrence. The solution is

$$W(n) = 32 \ n\lg n \ \mu s.$$

Suppose on this same computer Exchange Sort takes exactly

$$\frac{n(n - 1)}{2} \ \mu s$$

to sort an instance of size n. Sometimes students erroneously believe that the optimal point where Mergesort 2 should call Exchange Sort can now be found by solving the inequality

$$\frac{n(n - 1)}{2} \ \mu s < 32n\lg n \ \mu s.$$

The solution is

$$n < 257.$$

Students sometimes believe that it is optimal to call Exchange Sort when $n < 257$ and Mergesort2 otherwise. This analysis is only approximate because we base it on n being a power of 2. But more importantly it is *incorrect,* because it only tells us that if we use Mergesort 2 and keep dividing until $n = 1$, then Exchange Sort is better for $n < 257$. We want to use Mergesort 2 and keep dividing until it is better to call Exchange Sort rather than divide the instance further. This is not the same as dividing until $n = 1$, and therefore the point where we call Exchange Sort should be less than 257. That this value should be less than 257 is a bit hard to grasp in the abstract. The following concrete example, which determines the point at which it is more efficient to call Exchange Sort rather than dividing the instance further, should make the matter clear. From now on, we no longer limit our considerations to n being a power of 2.

Example 2.7   We determine the optimal threshold for Algorithm 2.4 (Mergesort 2) when calling Algorithm 1.3 (Exchange Sort). Suppose we modify Mergesort 2 so that Exchange Sort is called when $n \le t$ for some threshold t. Assuming the hypothetical computer just discussed, for this version of Mergesort 2

$$W(n) = \begin{cases} \dfrac{n(n-1)}{2} \ \mu s & \text{for } n \le t \\[2ex] W\left(\left\lfloor \dfrac{n}{2} \right\rfloor\right) + W\left(\left\lceil \dfrac{n}{2} \right\rceil\right) + 32n \ \mu s & \text{for } n > t \end{cases} \tag{2.5}$$

We want to determine the optimal value of t. That value is the value for which the top and bottom expressions in Equality 2.5 are equal, because this is the point where calling Exchange Sort is as efficient as dividing the instance further. Therefore, to determine the optimal value of t, we must solve

$$W\left(\left\lfloor \frac{t}{2} \right\rfloor\right) + W\left(\left\lceil \frac{t}{2} \right\rceil\right) + 32t = \frac{t(t-1)}{2}. \tag{2.6}$$

Because $\lfloor t/2 \rfloor$ and $\lceil t/2 \rceil$ are both less than or equal to t, the execution time is given by the top expression in Equality 2.5 if the instance has either of these input sizes. Therefore,

$$W\left(\left\lfloor \frac{t}{2} \right\rfloor\right) = \frac{\lfloor t/2 \rfloor(\lfloor t/2 \rfloor - 1)}{2} \quad \text{and} \quad W\left(\left\lceil \frac{t}{2} \right\rceil\right) = \frac{\lceil t/2 \rceil(\lceil t/2 \rceil - 1)}{2}.$$

Substituting these equalities into Equation 2.6 yields

$$\frac{\lfloor t/2 \rfloor(\lfloor t/2 \rfloor - 1)}{2} + \frac{\lceil t/2 \rceil(\lceil t/2 \rceil - 1)}{2} + 32t = \frac{t(t-1)}{2}. \tag{2.7}$$

In general, in an equation with floors and ceilings, we can obtain a different solution when we insert an odd value for t than when we insert an even value for t. This is the reason there is not always an optimal threshold value. Such a case is investigated next. In this case, however, if we insert an even value for t, which is accomplished by setting $\lfloor t/2 \rfloor$ and $\lceil t/2 \rceil$ both equal to $t/2$, and solve Equation 2.7, we obtain

$$t = 128.$$

If we insert an odd value for t, which is accomplished by setting $\lfloor t/2 \rfloor$ equal to $(t-1)/2$ and $\lceil t/2 \rceil$ equal to $(t+1)/2$, and solve Equation 2.7, we obtain

$$t = 128.008.$$

Therefore, we have an optimal threshold value of 128.

Next we give an example where there is no optimal threshold value.

Example 2.8 Suppose for a given divide-and-conquer algorithm running on a particular computer we determine that

$$T(n) = 3T\left(\left\lceil \frac{n}{2} \right\rceil\right) + 16n \ \mu s,$$

where $16n \ \mu s$ is the time needed to divide and recombine an instance of size n. Suppose on the same computer a certain iterative algorithm takes $n^2 \ \mu s$ to process an instance of size n. To determine the value t at which we should call the iterative algorithm, we need to solve

$$3T\left(\left\lceil \frac{t}{2} \right\rceil\right) + 16t = t^2.$$

Because $\lceil t/2 \rceil \leq t$, the iterative algorithm is called when the input has this size, which means that

$$T\left(\left\lceil \frac{t}{2} \right\rceil\right) = \left\lceil \frac{t}{2} \right\rceil^2.$$

Therefore, we need to solve

$$3\left\lceil \frac{t}{2} \right\rceil^2 + 16t = t^2.$$

If we substitute an even value for t (by setting $\lceil t/2 \rceil = t/2$) and solve, we get

$$t = 64.$$

If we substitute an odd value for t (by setting $\lceil t/2 \rceil = (t+1)/2$) and solve, we get

$$t = 70.04.$$

Because the two values of t are not equal, there is no optimal threshold value. This means that if the size of an instance is an even integer between 64 and 70, it is more efficient to divide the instance one more time, whereas if the size is an

Table 2.5 Various instance sizes
illustrating that the threshold is 64
for n even and 70 for n odd in Example 2.8

n	n^2	$3\left\lceil\dfrac{n}{2}\right\rceil^2 + 16n$
62	3844	3875
63	3969	4080
64	4096	4096
65	4225	4307
68	4624	4556
69	4761	4779
70	4900	4795
71	5041	5024

odd integer between 64 and 70, it is more efficient to call the iterative algorithm. When the size is less than 64, it is always more efficient to call the iterative algorithm. When the size is greater than 70, it is always more efficient to divide the instance again. Table 2.5 illustrates that this is so.

2.8 WHEN NOT TO USE DIVIDE-AND-CONQUER

If possible, we should avoid divide-and-conquer in the following two cases:

1. An instance of size n is divided into two or more instances each almost of size n.

2. An instance of size n is divided into almost n instances of size n/c, where c is a constant.

The first partitioning leads to an exponential-time algorithm, where the second leads to a $\Theta(n^{\lg n})$ algorithm. Neither of these is acceptable for large values of n. Intuitively we can see why such partitionings lead to poor performance. For example, the first case would be like Napoleon dividing an opposing army of 30,000 soldiers into two armies of 29,999 soldiers (if this were somehow possible). Rather than dividing his enemy, he has almost doubled their number! If Napoleon did this, he would have met his Waterloo much sooner.

As you should now verify, Algorithm 1.6 (nth Fibonacci Term, Recursive) is a divide-and-conquer algorithm that divides the instance that computes the nth term into two instances that compute respectively the $(n-1)$st term and the $(n-2)$nd term. Although n is not the input size in that algorithm, the situation is the same as that just described concerning input size. That is, the number of terms computed by Algorithm 1.6 is exponential in *n,* whereas the number of terms computed by Algorithm 1.7 (*n*th Fibonacci Term, Iterative) is linear in *n.*

Sometimes, on the other hand, a problem requires exponentiality, and in such a case there is no reason to avoid the simple divide-and-conquer solution. Consider the Towers of Hanoi Problem, which is presented in Exercise 17. Briefly, the problem involves moving *n* disks from one peg to another given certain restrictions on how they may be moved. In the exercises you will show that the sequence of moves, obtained from the standard divide-and-conquer algorithm for the problem, is exponential in terms of *n* and that it is the most efficient sequence of moves given the problem's restrictions. Therefore, the problem requires an exponentially large number of moves in terms of *n.*

Exercises

Section 2.1

1. Use Binary Search (Algorithm 2.1) to search for the integer 120 in the following list (array) of integers. Show the actions step by step.

$$12 \quad 34 \quad 37 \quad 45 \quad 57 \quad 82 \quad 99 \quad 120 \quad 134$$

2. Suppose that, even unrealistically, we are to search a list of 700 million items using Binary Search (Algorithm 2.1). What is the maximum number of comparisons that this algorithm must perform before finding a given item or concluding that it is not in the list?

3. Let us assume that we always perform a successful search. That is, in Algorithm 2.1 the item *x* can always be found in the list *S*. Improve Algorithm 2.1 by removing all unnecessary operations.

4. Show that the worst-case time complexity for Binary Search (Algorithm 2.1) is given by

$$W(n) = \lfloor \lg n \rfloor + 1$$

when *n* is not restricted to being a power of 2. *Hint:* First show that the recurrence equation for $W(n)$ is given by

$$W(n) = 1 + W\left(\left\lfloor \frac{n}{2} \right\rfloor\right) \quad \text{for } n > 1$$
$$W(1) = 1$$

To do this, consider even and odd values of *n* separately. Then use induction to solve the recurrence equation.

5. Suppose that, in Algorithm 2.1 (line 4), the splitting function is changed to *mid = low;.* Explain the new search strategy. Analyze the performance of this strategy and show the results using order notation.

6. Write an algorithm that searches a sorted list of *n* items by dividing it into

three sublists of almost $n/3$ items. This algorithm finds the sublist that might contain the given item, and divides it into three smaller sublists of almost equal size. The algorithm repeats this process until it finds the item or concludes that the item is not in the list. Analyze your algorithm, and give the results using order notation.

7. Use the divide-and-conquer approach to write an algorithm that finds the largest item in a list of n items. Analyze your algorithm, and show the results in order notation.

Section 2.2

8. Use Mergesort (Algorithms 2.2 and 2.4) to sort the following list. Show the actions step by step.

123   34   189   56   150   12   9   240

9. Give the tree of recursive calls in Exercise 8.

10. Write for the following problem a recursive algorithm whose worst-case time complexity is not worse than $\Theta(n \lg n)$. Given a list of n distinct positive integers, partition the list into two sublists, each of size $n/2$, such that the difference between the sums of the integers in the two sublists is maximized. You may assume that n is a multiple of 2.

11. Write a nonrecursive algorithm for Mergesort (Algorithms 2.2 and 2.4).

12. Show that the recurrence equation for the worst-case time complexity for Mergesort (Algorithms 2.2 and 2.4) is given by

$$W(n) = W\left(\left\lfloor \frac{n}{2} \right\rfloor\right) + W\left(\left\lceil \frac{n}{2} \right\rceil\right) + n - 1$$

when n is not restricted to being a power of 2.

13. Write an algorithm that sorts a list of n items by dividing it into three sublists or almost $n/3$ items, sorting each sublist recursively and merging the three sorted sublists. Analyze your algorithm, and give the results using order notation.

Section 2.3

14. Given the recurrence relation

$$T(n) = 7T\left(\frac{n}{5}\right) + 10n \quad \text{for } n > 1$$
$$T(1) = 1$$

find $T(625)$.

15. Consider procedure *solve(P,I,O)* given below. This algorithm solves problem P by finding the output (solution) O corresponding to any input I.

```
procedure solve(P,I,O)
begin
  if size(I) = I then
    find solution O directly
  else
    partition I into 5 inputs I₁, I₂, I₃, I₄, I₅, where
    size(Iⱼ):= size(I)/3 for j = 1,...,5;
    for j:= I to 5 do
      solve(P,Iⱼ,Oⱼ)
    end;
    combine O₁, O₂, O₃, O₄, O₅ to get O for P with input I
  end
end;
```

Assume $g(n)$ basic operations for partitioning and combining and no basic operations for an instance of size 1.

(a) Write a recurrence equation $T(n)$ for the number of basic operations needed to solve P when the input size is n.

(b) What is the solution to this recurrence equation if $g(n) \in \Theta(n)$ (proof not required)?

(c) Assuming that $g(n) = n^2$, solve the recurrence equation exactly for $n = 27$.

(d) Find the general solution for n a power of 3.

16. Suppose that, in a divide-and-conquer algorithm, we always divide an instance of size n of a problem into 10 subinstances of size $n/3$, and the dividing and combining steps take a time in $\Theta(n^2)$. Write a recurrence equation for the running time $T(n)$, and solve the equation for $T(n)$.

17. Write a divide-and-conquer algorithm for the Towers of Hanoi Problem. The Towers of Hanoi Problem consists of three pegs and n disks of different sizes. The object is to move the disks that are stacked, in decreasing order of their size, on one of the three pegs to a new peg using the third one as a temporary peg. The problem should be solved according to the following rules: (1) when a disk is moved, it must be placed on one of the three pegs; (2) only one disk may be moved at a time, and it must be the top disk on one of the pegs; and (3) a larger disk may never be placed on top of a smaller disk.

(a) Show for your algorithm that $S(n) = 2^n - 1$. [Here $S(n)$ denotes the number of steps (moves), given an input of n disks.]

(b) Prove that any other algorithm takes at least as many moves as given in part (a).

18. When a divide-and-conquer algorithm divides an instance of size n of a problem into subinstances each of size n/c, the recurrence relation is typically given by

$$T(n) = aT\left(\frac{n}{c}\right) + g(n) \qquad \text{for } n > 1$$
$$T(1) = d$$

where $g(n)$ is the cost of the dividing and combining processes, and d is a constant. Let $n = c^k$.

(a) Show that

$$T(c^k) = d \times a^k + \sum_{j=1}^{k} [a^{k-j} \times g(c^j)]$$

(b) Solve the recurrence relation given that $g(n) \in \Theta(n)$.

Section 2.4

19. Use Quicksort (Algorithm 2.6) to sort the following list. Show the actions step by step.

$$123 \quad 34 \quad 189 \quad 56 \quad 150 \quad 12 \quad 9 \quad 240$$

20. Give the tree of recursive calls in Exercise 19.

21. Verify the following identity

$$\sum_{p=1}^{n} [A(p-1) + A(n-p)] = 2 \sum_{p=1}^{n} A(p-1).$$

This result is used in the discussion of the average-case time complexity analysis of Algorithm 2.6 (Quicksort).

22. Show that if

$$W(n) \leq \frac{(p-1)(p-2)}{2} + \frac{(n-p)(n-p-1)}{2},$$

then

$$W(n) \leq \frac{n(n-1)}{2} \qquad \text{for} \qquad 1 \leq p \leq n.$$

This result is used in the discussion of the worst-case time complexity analysis of Algorithm 2.6 (Quicksort).

23. Write a nonrecursive algorithm for Quicksort (Algorithm 2.6). Analyze your algorithm, and give the results using order notation.

24. Assuming that Quicksort uses the first item in the list as the pivot item:
    (a) Give a list of n items (for example, an array of 10 integers) representing the worst-case scenario.
    (b) Give a list of n items (for example, an array of 10 integers) representing the best-case scenario.

Section 2.5

25. Show that the number of additions performed by Algorithm 1.4 (Matrix Multiplication) can be reduced to $n^3 - n^2$ after a slight modification of this algorithm.

26. In Example 2.4, we gave Strassen's product of two 2×2 matrices. Verify the correctness of this product.

27. How many multiplications would be performed in finding the product of two 64×64 matrices using the standard algorithm?

28. How many multiplications would be performed in finding the product of two 64×64 matrices using Strassen's Method (Algorithm 2.8)?

29. Write a recurrence equation for the modified Strassen's Algorithm developed by Shmuel Winograd that uses 15 additions/subtractions instead of 18. Solve the recurrence equation, and verify your answer using the time complexity shown at the end of Section 2.5.

Section 2.6

30. Use Algorithm 2.10 (Large Integer Multiplication 2) to find the product of 1253 and 23,103.

31. How many multiplications are needed to find the product of the two integers in Exercise 30?

32. Write algorithms that perform the operations

    $u \times 10^m;$ u **divide** $10^m;$ u **rem** $10^m,$

    where u represents a large integer, m is a nonnegative integer, **divide** returns the quotient in integer division, and **rem** returns the remainder. Analyze your algorithms, and show that these operations can be done in linear time.

33. Modify Algorithm 2.9 (Large Integer Multiplication) so that it divides each n-digit integer into
    (a) three smaller integers of $n/3$ digits (you may assume that $n = 3^k$).
    (b) four smaller integers of $n/4$ digits (you may assume that $n = 4^k$).
    Analyze your algorithms, and show their time complexities in order notation.

Section 2.7

34. Implement both Exchange Sort and Quicksort algorithms on your computer to sort a list of n elements. Find the lower bound for n that justifies application of the Quicksort algorithm with its overhead.

35. Implement both the standard algorithm and Strassen's Algorithm on your computer to multiply two $n \times n$ matrices ($n = 2^k$). Find the lower bound for n that justifies application of Strassen's Algorithm with its overhead.

36. Suppose that on a particular computer it takes $12n^2$ μs to decompose and recombine an instance of size n in the case of Algorithm 2.8 (Strassen). Note that this time includes the time it takes to do all the additions and subtractions. If it takes n^3 μs to multiply two $n \times n$ matrices using the standard algorithm, determine thresholds at which we should call the standard algorithm instead of dividing the instance further. Is there a unique optimal threshold?

Section 2.8

37. Use the divide-and-conquer approach to write a recursive algorithm that computes $n!$. Define the input size (see Exercise 34 in Chapter 1), and answer the following questions. Does your function have an exponential time complexity? Does this violate the statement of case 1 given in Section 2.8?

38. Suppose that, in a divide-and-conquer algorithm, we always divide an instance of size n of a problem into n subinstances of size $n/3$, and the dividing and combining steps take linear time. Write a recurrence equation for the running time $T(n)$, and solve this recurrence equation for $T(n)$. Show your solution in order notation.

Additional Exercises

39. Write an efficient algorithm that searches for a value in an $n \times m$ table (two-dimensional array). This table is sorted along the rows and columns—that is,

$$Table[i][j] \leq Table[i][j + 1]$$
$$Table[i][j] \leq Table[i + 1][j]$$

40. Suppose that there are $n = 2^k$ teams in an elimination tournament, where there are $n/2$ games in the first round, with the $n/2 = 2^{k-1}$ winners playing in the second round, and so on.
    (a) Develop a recurrence equation for the number of rounds in the tournament.
    (b) How many rounds are there in the tournament when there are 64 teams?
    (c) Solve the recurrence equation of part (a).

41. Write a recursive $\Theta(n \lg n)$ algorithm whose parameters are three integers x, n, and p, and which computes the remainder when x^n is divided by p. For simplicity, you may assume that n is a power of 2—that is, that $n = 2^k$ for some positive integer k.

42. Use the divide-and-conquer approach to write a recursive algorithm that finds the maximum sum in any contiguous sublist of a given list of n real values. Analyze your algorithm, and show the results in order notation.

CHAPTER 3

Dynamic Programming

LEONARDO FIBONACCI CONSTRUCTING HIS SEQUENCE FROM THE BOTTOM UP.

*R*ecall that the number of terms computed by the divide-and-conquer algorithm for determining the *n*th Fibonacci term (Algorithm 1.6) is exponential in *n*. The reason is that the divide-and-conquer approach solves an instance of a problem by dividing it into smaller instances and then blindly solving these smaller instances. As discussed in Chapter 2, this is a top-down approach. It works in problems such as Mergesort, where the smaller instances are unrelated. They are unrelated because each consists of an array of keys that must be sorted independently. However, in problems such as the *n*th Fibonacci term, the smaller instances are related. For example, as shown in Section 1.2, to compute the fifth Fibonacci term we need to compute the fourth and third Fibonacci terms. However, the determinations of the fourth and third Fibonacci terms are related in that they both require the second Fibonacci term. Because the divide-and-conquer algorithm makes these two determinations independently, it ends up computing the second Fibonacci term more than once. In problems where the smaller instances are related, a divide-and-conquer algorithm often ends up repeatedly solving common instances, and the result is a very inefficient algorithm.

Dynamic programming, the technique discussed in this chapter, takes the opposite approach. Dynamic programming is similar to divide-and-conquer in that an instance of a problem is divided into smaller instances. However, in this approach we solve small instances first, store the results, and later, whenever we need a result, look it up instead of recomputing it. The term "dynamic programming" comes from control theory, and in this sense "programming" means the use of an array (table) in which a solution is constructed. As mentioned in Chapter 1, our efficient algorithm (Algorithm 1.7) for computing the nth Fibonacci term is an example of dynamic programming. Recall that this algorithm determines the nth Fibonacci term by constructing in sequence the first $n + 1$ terms in an array f indexed from 0 to n. In a dynamic programming algorithm, we construct a solution from the bottom up in an array (or sequence of arrays). Dynamic programming is therefore a ***bottom-up*** approach. Sometimes, as is the case for Algorithm 1.7, after developing the algorithm using an array (or sequence of arrays), we are able to revise the algorithm so that much of the originally allocated space is not needed.

The steps in the development of a dynamic programming algorithm are as follows:

1. *Establish* a recursive property that gives the solution to an instance of the problem.

2. Solve an instance of the problem in a *bottom-up* fashion by solving smaller instances first.

To illustrate these steps, we present another simple example of dynamic programming in Section 3.1. The remaining sections present more advanced applications of dynamic programming.

3.1 THE BINOMIAL COEFFICIENT

The ***binomial coefficient,*** which is discussed in Section A.7 in Appendix A, is given by

$$\binom{n}{k} = \frac{n!}{k!(n-k)!} \qquad \text{for } 0 \le k \le n.$$

For values of n and k that are not small, we cannot compute the binomial coefficient directly from this definition because $n!$ is very large even for moderate values of n. In the exercises we establish that

$$\binom{n}{k} = \begin{cases} \binom{n-1}{k-1} + \binom{n-1}{k} & 0 < k < n \\ 1 & k = 0 \quad \text{or} \quad k = n \end{cases} \qquad (3.1)$$

We can eliminate the need to compute $n!$ or $k!$ by using this recursive property. This suggests the following divide-and-conquer algorithm.

Algorithm 3.1

Binomial Coefficient Using Divide-and-Conquer

Problem: Compute the binomial coefficient.

Inputs: nonnegative integers n and k, where $k \leq n$.

Outputs: *bin*, the binomial coefficient $\binom{n}{k}$.

```
int bin (int n, int k)
{
    if (k == 0 || n == k)
        return 1;
    else
        return bin(n − 1, k − 1) + bin(n − 1, k);
}
```

Like Algorithm 1.6 (*n*th Fibonacci Term, Recursive), this algorithm is very inefficient. In the exercises you will establish that the algorithm computes

$$2\binom{n}{k} - 1$$

terms to determine $\binom{n}{k}$. The problem is that the same instances are solved in each recursive call. For example, $bin(n − 1, k − 1)$ and $bin(n − 1, k)$ both need the result of $bin(n − 2, k − 1)$, and this instance is solved separately in each recursive call. As mentioned in Section 2.8, the divide-and-conquer approach is always inefficient when an instance is divided into two smaller instances that are almost as large as the original instance.

A more efficient algorithm is developed next using dynamic programming. A recursive property has already been established in Equality 3.1. We will use that property to construct our solution in an array B, where $B[i][j]$ will contain $\binom{i}{j}$. The steps for constructing a dynamic programming algorithm for this problem are as follows:

1. *Establish* a recursive property. This has already been done in Equality 3.1. Written in terms of B, it is

$$B[i][j] = \begin{cases} B[i − 1][j − 1] + B[i − 1][j] & 0 < j < i \\ 1 & j = 0 \quad \text{or} \quad j = i \end{cases}$$

2. Solve an instance of the problem in a *bottom-up* fashion by computing the rows in B in sequence starting with the first row.

Step 2 is illustrated in Figure 3.1 (you may recognize the array in that figure as Pascal's Triangle). Each successive row is computed from the row preceding it using the recursive property established in Step 1. The final value computed, $B[n][k]$, is $\binom{n}{k}$. Example 3.1 illustrates these steps. Notice in the example that we compute only the first two columns. The reason is that $k = 2$ in the example, and in general we need to compute the values in each row only up to the kth column. Example 3.1 computes $B[0][0]$ because the binomial coefficient is defined for $n = k = 0$. Therefore, an algorithm would perform this step even though the value is not needed in the computation of other binomial coefficients.

Example 3.1   Compute $B[4][2] = \binom{4}{2}$.

Compute row 0:   {This is done only to mimic the algorithm exactly.}
                  {The value $B[0][0]$ is not needed in a later computation.}

$$B[0][0] = 1$$

Compute row 1:

$$B[1][0] = 1$$
$$B[1][1] = 1$$

Compute row 2:

$$B[2][0] = 1$$
$$B[2][1] = B[1][0] + B[1][1] = 1 + 1 = 2$$
$$B[2][2] = 1$$

Compute row 3:

$$B[3][0] = 1$$
$$B[3][1] = B[2][0] + B[2][1] = 1 + 2 = 3$$
$$B[3][2] = B[2][1] + B[2][2] = 2 + 1 = 3$$

Compute row 4:

$$B[4][0] = 1$$
$$B[4][1] = B[3][0] + B[3][1] = 1 + 3 = 4$$
$$B[4][2] = B[3][1] + B[3][2] = 3 + 3 = 6$$

Example 3.1 computes increasingly larger values of the binomial coefficient in sequence. At each iteration, the values needed for that iteration have already been computed and saved. This procedure is fundamental to the dynamic programming approach. The following algorithm implements this approach in computing the binomial coefficient.

Figure 3.1 The array B used to compute the binomial coefficient.

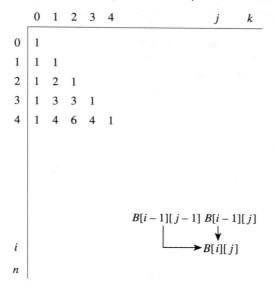

Algorithm 3.2

Binomial Coefficient Using Dynamic Programming

Problem: Compute the binomial coefficient.

Inputs: nonnegative integers n and k, where $k \leq n$.

Outputs: *bin2*, the binomial coefficient $\binom{n}{k}$.

```
int bin2 (int n, int k)
{
    index i, j;
    int B[0..n][0..k];

    for (i = 0; i <= n; i++)
        for (j = 0; j <= minimum(i, k); j++)
            if (j == 0 ‖ j == i)
                B[i][j] = 1;
            else
                B[i][j] = B[i − 1][j − 1] + B[i − 1][j];
    return B[n][k];
}
```

The parameters n and k are not the size of the input to this algorithm. Rather they are the input, and the input size is the number of symbols it takes to encode them. We discussed a similar situation in Section 1.3 regarding algorithms that compute the nth Fibonacci term. However, we can still gain insight into the efficiency of the algorithm by determining how much work it does as a function of n and k. For given n and k, let's compute the number of passes through the **for**-j loop. The following table shows the number of passes for each value of i:

i	0	1	2	3	$\cdots$	k	$k + 1$	$\cdots$	n
Number of passes	1	2	3	4	$\cdots$	$k + 1$	$k + 1$	$\cdots$	$k + 1$

The total number of passes is therefore given by

$$n - k + 1 \text{ times}$$
$$1 + 2 + 3 + 4 + \cdots + k + (k + 1) + (k + 1) \cdots + (k + 1).$$

Applying the result in Example A.1 in Appendix A, we find that this expression equals

$$\frac{k(k + 1)}{2} + (n - k + 1)(k + 1) = \frac{(2n - k + 2)(k + 1)}{2} \in \Theta(nk).$$

By using dynamic programming instead of divide-and-conquer, we have developed a much more efficient algorithm. As mentioned earlier, dynamic programming is similar to divide-and-conquer in that we find a recursive property that divides an instance into smaller instances. The difference is that in dynamic programming we use the recursive property to iteratively solve the instances in sequence, starting with the smallest instance, instead of blindly using recursion. In this way we solve each smaller instance just once. Dynamic programming is a good technique to try when divide-and-conquer leads to an inefficient algorithm.

The most straightforward way to present Algorithm 3.2 was to create the entire two-dimensional array B. However, once a row is computed, we no longer need the values in the row that precedes it. Therefore, the algorithm can be written using only a one-dimensional array indexed from 0 to k. This modification is investigated in the exercises. Another improvement to the algorithm would be to take advantage of the fact that $\binom{n}{k} = \binom{n}{n - k}$.

3.2 FLOYD'S ALGORITHM FOR SHORTEST PATHS

A common problem encountered by air travelers is the determination of the shortest way to fly from one city to another when a direct flight does not exist. Next we develop an algorithm that solves this and similar problems. First, let's informally review some graph theory. Figure 3.2 shows a weighted, directed graph. Recall that in a pictorial representation of a graph the circles represent ***vertices,*** and a line from one circle to another represents an ***edge*** (also called an *arc*). If each edge has a direction associated with it, the graph is called a *directed graph* or ***digraph.*** When drawing an edge in such a graph, we use an arrow to show the direction. In a digraph there can be two edges between two vertices, one going in each direction. For example, in Figure 3.2 there is an edge from v_1 to v_2 and an edge from v_2 to v_1. If the edges have values associated with them, the values are called ***weights*** and the graph is called a ***weighted graph.*** We assume here that these weights are nonnegative. Although the values are ordinarily called weights, in many applications they represent distances. Therefore, we talk of a path from one vertex to another. In a directed graph, a ***path*** is a sequence of vertices such that there is an edge from each vertex to its successor. For example, in Figure 3.2 the sequence $[v_1, v_4, v_3]$ is a path because there is an edge from v_1 to v_4 and an edge from v_4 to v_3. The sequence $[v_3, v_4, v_1]$ is not a path because there is no edge from v_4 to v_1. A path from a vertex to itself is called a ***cycle.*** The path $[v_1, v_4, v_5, v_1]$ in Figure 3.2 is a cycle. If a graph contains a cycle, it is ***cyclic;*** otherwise it is ***acyclic.*** A path is called ***simple*** if it never passes through the same vertex twice. The path $[v_1, v_2, v_3]$ in Figure 3.2 is simple, but the path $[v_1, v_4, v_5, v_1, v_2]$ is not simple. Notice that a simple path never contains a subpath that is a cycle. The ***length*** of a path in a weighted graph is the sum of the weights on the path; in an unweighted graph it is simply the number of edges in the path.

A problem that has many applications is finding the shortest paths from each vertex to all other vertices. Clearly, a shortest path must be a simple path. In Figure 3.2 there are three simple paths from v_1 to v_3—namely, $[v_1, v_2, v_3]$, $[v_1, v_4, v_3]$, and $[v_1, v_2, v_4, v_3]$. Because

$$length[v_1, v_2, v_3] = 1 + 3 = 4$$
$$length[v_1, v_4, v_3] = 1 + 2 = 3$$
$$length[v_1, v_2, v_4, v_3] = 1 + 2 + 2 = 5,$$

$[v_1, v_4, v_3]$ is the shortest path from v_1 to v_3. As mentioned previously, one common application of shortest paths is determining the shortest routes between cities.

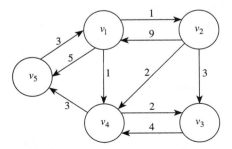

Figure 3.2 A weighted, directed graph.

The Shortest Paths Problem is an ***optimization problem.*** There can be more than one candidate solution to an instance of an optimization problem. Each candidate solution has a value associated with it, and a solution to the instance is any candidate solution that has an optimal value. Depending on the problem, the optimal value is either the minimum or the maximum. In the case of the Shortest Paths Problem, a candidate solution is a path from one vertex to another, the value is the length of the path, and the optimal value is the minimum of these lengths.

Because there can be more than one shortest path from one vertex to another, our problem is to find any one of the shortest paths. An obvious algorithm for this problem would be to determine, for each vertex, the lengths of all the paths from that vertex to each other vertex, and compute the minimum of these lengths. However, this algorithm is worse than exponential-time. For example, suppose there is an edge from every vertex to every other vertex. Then a subset of all the paths from one vertex to another vertex is the set of all those paths that start at the first vertex, end at the other vertex, and pass through all the other vertices. Because the second vertex on such a path can be any of $n - 2$ vertices, the third vertex on such a path can be any of $n - 3$ vertices, . . . , and the second-to-last vertex on such a path can be only one vertex, the total number of paths from one vertex to another vertex that pass through all the other vertices is

$$(n - 2)(n - 3) \cdots 1 = (n - 2)!,$$

which is worse than exponential. We encounter this same situation in many optimization problems. That is, the obvious algorithm that considers all possibilities is exponential-time or worse. Our goal is to find a more efficient algorithm.

Using dynamic programming, we create a cubic-time algorithm for the Shortest Paths Problem. First we develop an algorithm that determines only the lengths of the shortest paths. After that we modify it to produce shortest paths as well. We represent a weighted graph containing n vertices by an array W where

$$W[i][j] = \begin{cases} \text{weight on edge} & \text{if there is an edge from } v_i \text{ to } v_j \\ \infty & \text{if there is no edge from } v_i \text{ to } v_j \\ 0 & \text{if } i = j \end{cases}$$

Because vertex v_j is said to be ***adjacent*** to v_i if there is an edge from v_i to v_j, this array is called the ***adjacency matrix*** representation of the graph. The graph in Figure 3.2 is represented in this manner in Figure 3.3. The array D in Figure 3.3 contains the lengths of the shortest paths in the graph. For example, $D[3][5]$ is 7 because 7 is the length of a shortest path from v_3 to v_5. If we can develop a way to calculate the values in D from those in W, we will have an algorithm for the Shortest Paths Problem. We accomplish this by creating a sequence of $n + 1$ arrays $D^{(k)}$, where $0 \le k \le n$ and where

$D^{(k)}[i][j] = $ length of a shortest path from v_i to v_j using only
vertices in the set $\{v_1, v_2, \ldots, v_k\}$ as intermediate vertices

Figure 3.3 W represents the graph in Figure 3.2 and D contains the lengths of the shortest paths. Our algorithm for the Shortest Paths problem computes the values in D from those in W.

	1	2	3	4	5			1	2	3	4	5
1	0	1	∞	1	5		1	0	1	3	1	4
2	9	0	3	2	∞		2	8	0	3	2	5
3	∞	∞	0	4	∞		3	10	11	0	4	7
4	∞	∞	2	0	3		4	6	7	2	0	3
5	3	∞	∞	∞	0		5	3	4	6	4	0

W   D

Before showing why this enables us to compute D from W, let's illustrate the meaning of the items in these arrays.

Example 3.2 We will calculate some exemplary values of $D^{(k)}[i][j]$ for the graph in Figure 3.2.

$D^{(0)}[2][5] = length[v_2, v_5] = \infty.$

$D^{(1)}[2][5] = minimum(length[v_2, v_5], length[v_2, v_1, v_5])$

$\qquad\qquad = minimum(\infty, 14) = 14.$

$D^{(2)}[2][5] = D^{(1)}[2][5] = 14.$ {For any graph these are equal because a} {shortest path starting at v_2 cannot} {pass through v_2.}

$D^{(3)}[2][5] = D^{(2)}[2][5] = 14.$ {For this graph these are equal because} {including v_3 yields no new paths} {from v_2 to v_5.}

$D^{(4)}[2][5] = minimum(length[v_2, v_1, v_5], length[v_2, v_4, v_5],$
$\qquad\qquad\qquad\quad length[v_2, v_1, v_4, v_5], length[v_2, v_3, v_4, v_5])$

$\qquad\qquad = minimum(14, 5, 13, 10) = 5.$

$D^{(5)}[2][5] = D^{(4)}[2][5] = 5.$ {For any graph these are equal because a} {shortest path ending at v_5 cannot} {pass through v_5.}

The last value computed, $D^{(5)}[2][5]$, is the length of a shortest path from v_2 to v_5 that is allowed to pass through any of the other vertices. This means that it is the length of a shortest path.

Because $D^{(n)}[i][j]$ is the length of a shortest path from v_i to v_j that is allowed to pass through any of the other vertices, it is the length of a shortest path from v_i to v_j. Because $D^{(0)}[i][j]$ is the length of a shortest path that is not allowed to pass through any other vertices, it is the weight on the edge from v_i to v_j. We have established that

$$D^{(0)} = W \qquad \text{and} \qquad D^{(n)} = D.$$

Therefore, to determine D from W we need only find a way to obtain $D^{(n)}$ from $D^{(0)}$. The steps for using dynamic programming to accomplish this are as follows:

1. *Establish* a recursive property (process) with which we can compute $D^{(k)}$ from $D^{(k-1)}$.

2. Solve an instance of the problem in a *bottom-up* fashion by repeating the process (established in Step 1) for $k = 1$ to n. This creates the sequence

$$\underset{\underset{W}{\uparrow}}{D^{(0)}}, D^{(1)}, D^{(2)}, \ldots, \underset{\underset{D}{\uparrow}}{D^{(n)}}. \tag{3.2}$$

We accomplish Step 1 by considering two cases:

Case 1. At least one shortest path from v_i to v_j, using only vertices in $\{v_1, v_2, \ldots, v_k\}$ as intermediate vertices, does not use v_k. Then

$$D^{(k)}[i][j] = D^{(k-1)}[i][j]. \tag{3.3}$$

An example of this case in Figure 3.2 is that

$$D^{(5)}[1][3] = D^{(4)}[1][3] = 3,$$

because when we include vertex v_5, the shortest path from v_1 to v_3 is still $[v_1, v_4, v_3]$.

Case 2. All shortest paths from v_i to v_j, using only vertices in $\{v_1, v_2, \ldots, v_k\}$ as intermediate vertices, do use v_k. In this case any shortest path appears as in Figure 3.4. Because v_k cannot be an intermediate vertex on the subpath from v_i to v_k, that subpath uses only vertices in $\{v_1, v_2, \ldots, v_{k-1}\}$ as intermediates. This implies that the subpath's length must be equal to $D^{(k-1)}[i][k]$ for the following reasons: First, the subpath's length cannot be shorter because $D^{(k-1)}[i][k]$ is the length of a shortest path from v_1 to v_k using only vertices in $\{v_1, v_2, \ldots, v_{k-1}\}$

Figure 3.4 The shortest path uses v_k.

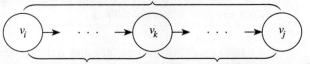

A shortest path from v_i to v_j using only vertices in $\{v_1, v_2, \ldots, v_k\}$

A shortest path from v_i to v_k using   A shortest path from v_k to v_j using
only vertices in $\{v_1, v_2, \ldots, v_{k-1}\}$ only vertices in $\{v_1, v_2, \ldots, v_{k-1}\}$

as intermediates. Second, the subpath's length cannot be longer because if it were, we could replace it in Figure 3.4 by a shortest path, which contradicts the fact that the entire path in Figure 3.4 is a shortest path. Similarly, the length of the subpath from v_k to v_j in Figure 3.4 must be equal to $D^{(k-1)}[k][j]$. Therefore, in the second case

$$D^{(k)}[i][j] = D^{(k-1)}[i][k] + D^{(k-1)}[k][j]. \qquad (3.4)$$

An example of the second case in Figure 3.2 is that

$$D^{(2)}[5][3] = 7 = 4 + 3 = D^{(1)}[5][2] + D^{(1)}[2][3].$$

Because we must have either Case 1 or Case 2, the value of $D^{(k)}[i][j]$ is the minimum of the values on the right in Equalities 3.3 and 3.4. This means that we can determine $D^{(k)}$ from $D^{(k-1)}$ as follows:

$$D^{(k)}[i][j] = minimum(\underbrace{D^{(k-1)}[i][j]}_{\text{Case 1}}, \underbrace{D^{(k-1)}[i][k] + D^{(k-1)}[k][j]}_{\text{Case 2}})$$

We have accomplished Step 1 in the development of a dynamic programming algorithm. To accomplish Step 2, we use the recursive property in Step 1 to create the sequence of arrays shown in Expression 3.2. Let's do an example showing how each of these arrays is computed from the previous one.

Example 3.3
Given the graph in Figure 3.2, which is represented by the adjacency matrix W in Figure 3.3, some sample computations are as follows (recall that $D^{(0)} = W$):

$$D^{(1)}[2][4] = minimum(D^{(0)}[2][4], D^{(0)}[2][1] + D^{(0)}[1][4])$$
$$= minimum(2, 9 + 1) = 2$$
$$D^{(1)}[5][2] = minimum(D^{(0)}[5][2], D^{(0)}[5][1] + D^{(0)}[1][2])$$
$$= minimum(\infty, 3 + 1) = 4$$
$$D^{(1)}[5][4] = minimum(D^{(0)}[5][4], D^{(0)}[5][1] + D^{(0)}[1][4])$$
$$= minimum(\infty, 3 + 1) = 4$$

Once the whole array $D^{(1)}$ is computed, the array $D^{(2)}$ is computed. A sample computation is

$$D^{(2)}[5][4] = minimum(D^{(1)}[5][4], D^{(1)}[5][2] + D^{(1)}[2][4])$$
$$= minimum(4, 4 + 2) = 4$$

After computing all of $D^{(2)}$, we continue in sequence until $D^{(5)}$ is computed. This final array is D, the lengths of shortest paths. It appears on the right in Figure 3.3.

Next we present the algorithm developed by Floyd (1962) and known as "Floyd's Algorithm." Following the algorithm, we explain why it uses only one array D besides the input array W.

Algorithm 3.3

Floyd's Algorithm for Shortest Paths

Problem: Compute the shortest paths from each vertex in a weighted graph to each of the other vertices. The weights are nonnegative numbers.

Inputs: A weighted, directed graph and n, the number of vertices in the graph. The graph is represented by a two-dimensional array W, which has both its rows and columns indexed from 1 to n, where $W[i][j]$ is the weight on the edge from the ith vertex to the jth vertex.

Outputs: A two-dimensional array D, which has both its rows and columns indexed from 1 to n, where $D[i][j]$ is the length of a shortest path from the ith vertex to the jth vertex.

```
void floyd (int n
            const number W[ ][ ],
            number D[ ][ ])
{
   index i, j, k;

   D = W;
   for (k = 1; k <= n; k++)
      for (i = 1; i <= n; i++)
         for (j = 1; j <= n; j++)
            D[i][j] = minimum(D[i][j], D[i][k] + D[k][j]);
}
```

We can perform our calculations using only one array D because the values in the kth row and the kth column are not changed during the kth iteration of the loop. That is, in the kth iteration the algorithm assigns

$$D[i][k] = minimum(D[i][k], D[i][k] + D[k][k]),$$

which clearly equals $D[i][k]$, and

$$D[k][j] = minimum(D[k][j], D[k][k] + D[k][j]),$$

which clearly equals $D[k][j]$.

During the kth iteration, $D[i][j]$ is computed from only its own value and values in the kth row and the kth column. Because these values have maintained their values from the $(k - 1)$st iteration, they are the values we want. As mentioned before, sometimes after developing a dynamic programming algorithm, it is possible to revise the algorithm to make it more efficient in terms of space. Next we analyze Floyd's Algorithm.

Every-Case Time Complexity Analysis of Algorithm 3.3
(Floyd's Algorithm for Shortest Paths)

Basic operation: The instructions in the **for**-*j* loop.

Input size: *n*, the number of vertices in the graph.

We have a loop within a loop within a loop, with *n* passes through each loop. So

$$T(n) = n \times n \times n = n^3 \in \Theta(n^3).$$

The following modification to Algorithm 3.3 produces shortest paths.

Algorithm 3.4

Floyd's Algorithm for Shortest Paths 2

Problem: Same as in Algorithm 3.3, except shortest paths are also created.

Additional outputs: an array *P*, which has both its rows and columns indexed from 1 to *n*, where

$$P[i][j] = \begin{cases} \text{highest index of an intermediate vertex on the shortest path} \\ \text{from } v_i \text{ to } v_j \text{ if at least one intermediate vertex exists.} \\ 0 \text{ if no intermediate vertex exists.} \end{cases}$$

```
void floyd2 (int n,
             const number W[ ][ ],
                   number D[ ][ ],
                   index    P[ ][ ])
{
   index i, j, k;

   for (i = 1; i <= n; i++)
     for (j = 1; j <= n; j++)
       P[i][j] = 0;
   D = W;
   for (k = 1; k <= n; k++)
     for (i = 1; i <= n; i++)
       for (j = 1; j <= n; j++)
         if (D[i][k] + D[k][j] < D[i][j]) {
             P[i][j] = k;
             D[i][j] = D[i][k] + D[k][j];
         }
}
```

Figure 3.5 shows the array P that is created when the algorithm is applied to the graph in Figure 3.2.

The following algorithm produces a shortest path from vertex v_q to v_r using the array P.

Algorithm 3.5   Print Shortest Path

Problem: Print the intermediate vertices on a shortest path from one vertex to another vertex in a weighted graph.

Inputs: the array P produced by Algorithm 3.4, and two indices, q and r, of vertices in the graph that is the input to Algorithm 3.4.

$$P[i][j] = \begin{cases} \text{highest index of an intermediate vertex on the shortest path} \\ \text{from } v_i \text{ to } v_j \text{ if at least one intermediate vertex exists.} \\ 0 \text{ if no intermediate vertex exists.} \end{cases}$$

Outputs: the intermediate vertices on a shortest path from v_q to v_r.

```
void path (index q, r)
{
   if (P[q][r] != 0) {
      path(q, P[q][r]);
      cout << " v" << P[q][r];
      path(P[q][r], r);
   }
}
```

	1	2	3	4	5
1	0	0	4	0	4
2	5	0	0	0	4
3	5	5	0	0	4
4	5	5	0	0	0
5	0	1	4	1	0

Figure 3.5 The array P produced when Algorithm 3.4 is applied to the graph in Figure 3.2.

Recall the convention established in Chapter 2 of making only variables, whose values can change in the recursive calls, inputs to recursive routines. Therefore, the array P is not an input to *path*. If the algorithm were implemented by defining P globally, and we wanted a shortest path from v_q to v_r, the top-level call to *path* would be as follows:

> *path(q,r);*

Given the value of P in Figure 3.5, if the values of q and r were 5 and 3 respectively, the output would be

$$v1 \quad v4.$$

These are the intermediate vertices on a shortest path from v_5 to v_3.

In the exercises we establish that $W(n) \in \Theta(n)$ for Algorithm 3.5.

3.3 DYNAMIC PROGRAMMING AND OPTIMIZATION PROBLEMS

Recall that Algorithm 3.4 not only determines the lengths of the shortest paths but also constructs shortest paths. The construction of the optimal solution is a third step in the development of a dynamic programming algorithm for an optimization problem. This means that the steps in the development of such an algorithm are as follows:

1. *Establish* a recursive property that gives the optimal solution to an instance of the problem.
2. Compute the value of an optimal solution in a *bottom-up* fashion.
3. Construct an optimal solution in a *bottom-up fashion.*

Steps 2 and 3 are ordinarily accomplished at about the same point in the algorithm. Because Algorithm 3.2 is not an optimization problem, there is no third step.

Although it may seem that any optimization problem can be solved using dynamic programming, this is not the case. The principle of optimality must apply in the problem. That principle can be stated as follows:

Definition The ***principle of optimality*** is said to apply in a problem if an optimal solution to an instance of a problem always contains optimal solutions to all subinstances.

The principle of optimality is difficult to state, and can be better understood by looking at an example. In the case of the Shortest Paths Problem we showed that if v_k is a vertex on an optimal path from v_i to v_j, then the subpaths from v_i to v_k and from v_k to v_j must also be optimal. Therefore, the optimal solution to the instance contains optimal solutions to all subinstances, and the principle of optimality applies.

If the principle of optimality applies in a given problem, we can develop a recursive property that gives an optimal solution to an instance in terms of optimal solutions to subinstances. The important but subtle reason we can then use dynamic programming to construct an optimal solution to an instance is that the optimal solutions to the subinstances can be any optimal solutions. For example, in the case of the Shortest Paths Problem, if the subpaths are any shortest paths, the combined path will be optimal. We can therefore use the recursive property to construct optimal solutions to increasingly large instances from the bottom up. Each solution along the way will always be optimal.

Although the principle of optimality may appear obvious, in practice it is necessary to show that the principle applies before assuming that an optimal solution can be obtained using dynamic programming. The following example shows that it does not apply in every optimization problem.

Example 3.4   Consider the Longest Paths Problem of finding the longest simple paths from each vertex to all other vertices. We restrict the Longest Paths Problem to simple paths because with a cycle we could always create an arbitrarily long path by repeatedly passing through the cycle. In Figure 3.6 the optimal (longest) simple path from v_1 to v_4 is $[v_1, v_3, v_2, v_4]$. However, the subpath $[v_1, v_3]$ is not an optimal (longest) path from v_1 to v_3 because

$$length[v_1, v_3] = 1 \quad \text{and} \quad length[v_1, v_2, v_3] = 4.$$

Therefore, the principle of optimality does not apply. The reason for this is that the optimal paths from v_1 to v_3 and from v_3 to v_4 cannot be strung together to give an optimal path from v_1 to v_4. Doing this would create a cycle rather than an optimal path.

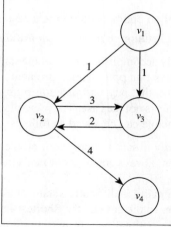

Figure 3.6 A weighted, directed graph with a cycle.

The remainder of this chapter is concerned with optimization problems. When developing the algorithms, we will not explicitly mention the steps outlined earlier. It should be clear that they are being followed.

3.4 CHAINED MATRIX MULTIPLICATION

Suppose we want to multiply a 2×3 matrix times a 3×4 matrix as follows:

$$\begin{bmatrix} 1 & 2 & 3 \\ 4 & 5 & 6 \end{bmatrix} \times \begin{bmatrix} 7 & 8 & 9 & 1 \\ 2 & 3 & 4 & 5 \\ 6 & 7 & 8 & 9 \end{bmatrix} = \begin{bmatrix} 29 & 35 & 41 & 38 \\ 74 & 89 & 104 & 83 \end{bmatrix}$$

The resultant matrix is a 2×4 matrix. If we use the standard method of multiplying matrices (that is, the one obtained from the definition of matrix multiplication), it takes three elementary multiplications to compute each item in the product. For example, the first item in the first column is given by

$$\underbrace{1 \times 7 + 2 \times 2 + 3 \times 6.}_{\text{3 multiplications}}$$

Because there are $2 \times 4 = 8$ entries in the product, the total number of elementary multiplications is

$$2 \times 4 \times 3 = 24.$$

In general, to multiply an $i \times j$ matrix times a $j \times k$ matrix, using the standard method, it is necessary to do

$$i \times j \times k \text{ elementary multiplications.}$$

Consider the multiplication of the following four matrices:

$$\begin{array}{ccccccc} A & \times & B & \times & C & \times & D \\ 20 \times 2 & & 2 \times 30 & & 30 \times 12 & & 12 \times 8 \end{array}$$

The dimension of each matrix appears under the matrix. Matrix multiplication is an associative operation meaning the order in which we multiply does not matter. For example, $A(B(CD))$ and $(AB)(CD)$ both give the same answer. There are five different orders in which we can multiply four matrices, each possibly resulting in a different number of elementary multiplications. In the case of the previous matrices, we have the following number of elementary multiplications for each order.

$A(B(CD))$	$30 \times 12 \times 8 +$	$2 \times 30 \times 8 +$	$20 \times 2 \times 8 =$	3,680
$(AB)(CD)$	$20 \times 2 \times 30 +$	$30 \times 12 \times 8 +$	$20 \times 30 \times 8 =$	8,880
$A((BC)D)$	$2 \times 30 \times 12 +$	$2 \times 12 \times 8 +$	$20 \times 2 \times 8 =$	1,232
$((AB)C)D$	$20 \times 2 \times 30 +$	$20 \times 30 \times 12 +$	$20 \times 12 \times 8 =$	10,320
$(A(BC))D$	$2 \times 30 \times 12 +$	$20 \times 2 \times 12 +$	$20 \times 12 \times 8 =$	3,120

The third order is the optimal order for multiplying the four matrices.

Our goal is to develop an algorithm that determines the optimal order for multiplying n matrices. The optimal order depends only on the dimensions of the matrices. Therefore, besides n, these dimensions would be the only input to the algorithm. The brute-force algorithm is to consider all possible orders and take the minimum as we just did. We will show that this algorithm is at least exponential-time. To this end, let t_n be the number of different orders in which we can multiply n matrices: $A_1, A_2, \ldots, A_n$. A subset of all the orders is the set of orders for which A_1 is the last matrix multiplied. As illustrated below, the number of different orders in this subset is t_{n-1}, because it is the number of different orders with which we can multiply A_2 through A_n.

$$A_1 \underbrace{(A_2 A_3 \cdots A_n)}_{t_{n-1} \text{ different orders}}$$

A second subset of all the orders is the set of orders for which A_n is the last matrix multiplied. Clearly, the number of different orders in this subset is also t_{n-1}. Therefore,

$$t_n \geq t_{n-1} + t_{n-1} = 2t_{n-1}.$$

Because there is only one way to multiply two matrices, $t_2 = 1$. Using the techniques in Appendix B, we can solve this recurrence to show that

$$t_n \geq 2^{n-2}.$$

It is not hard to see that the principle of optimality applies in this problem. That is, the optimal order for multiplying n matrices includes the optimal order for multiplying any subset of the n matrices. For example, if the optimal order for multiplying six particular matrices is

$$A_1((((A_2 A_3)A_4)A_5)A_6),$$

then

$$(A_2 A_3)A_4$$

must be the optimal order for multiplying matrices A_2 through A_4. This means we can use dynamic programming to construct a solution.

Because we are multiplying the $(k-1)$st matrix A_{k-1} times the kth matrix A_k, the number of columns in A_{k-1} must equal the number of rows in A_k. For example, in the product discussed earlier, the first matrix has three columns and the second has three rows. If we let d_0 be the number of rows in A_1 and d_k be the number of columns in A_k for $1 \leq k \leq n$, the dimension of A_k is $d_{k-1} \times d_k$. This is illustrated in Figure 3.7.

As in the previous section, we will use a sequence of arrays to construct our solution. For $1 \leq i \leq j \leq n$, let

$M[i][j] = $ minimum number of multiplications needed to multiply A_i through A_j if $i < j$

$M[i][i] = 0.$

Figure 3.7 The number of columns in A_{k-1} is the same as the number of rows in A_k.

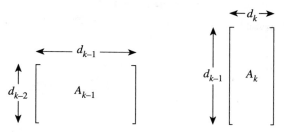

Before discussing how we will use these arrays, let's illustrate the meanings of the items in them.

Example 3.5 Suppose we have the following six matrices:

$$A_1 \quad \times \quad A_2 \quad \times \quad A_3 \quad \times \quad A_4 \quad \times \quad A_5 \quad \times \quad A_6$$

$$5 \times 2 \qquad 2 \times 3 \qquad 3 \times 4 \qquad 4 \times 6 \qquad 6 \times 7 \qquad 7 \times 8$$

$$d_0 \quad d_1 \qquad d_1 \quad d_2 \qquad d_2 \quad d_3 \qquad d_3 \quad d_4 \qquad d_4 \quad d_5 \qquad d_5 \quad d_6$$

To multiply A_4, A_5, and A_6, we have the following two orders and numbers of elementary multiplications:

$(A_4A_5)A_6$ Number of multiplications $= d_3 \times d_4 \times d_5 + d_3 \times d_5 \times d_6$

$$= 4 \times 6 \times 7 + 4 \times 7 \times 8 = 392$$

$A_4(A_5A_6)$ Number of multiplications $= d_4 \times d_5 \times d_6 + d_3 \times d_4 \times d_6$

$$= 6 \times 7 \times 8 + 4 \times 6 \times 8 = 528$$

Therefore,

$$M[4][6] = minimum(392, 528) = 392.$$

The optimal order for multiplying six matrices must have one of these factorizations:

1. $A_1(A_2A_3A_4A_5A_6)$
2. $(A_1A_2)(A_3A_4A_5A_6)$
3. $(A_1A_2A_3)(A_4A_5A_6)$
4. $(A_1A_2A_3A_4)(A_5A_6)$
5. $(A_1A_2A_3A_4A_5)A_6$

where inside each parentheses the products are obtained according to the optimal order for the matrices inside the parentheses. Of these factorizations, the one that yields the minimum number of multiplications must be the optimal one. The number of multiplications for the kth factorization is the minimum number needed

Figure 3.8 The array M developed in Example 3.6. $M[1][4]$, which is circled, is computed from the pairs of entries indicated.

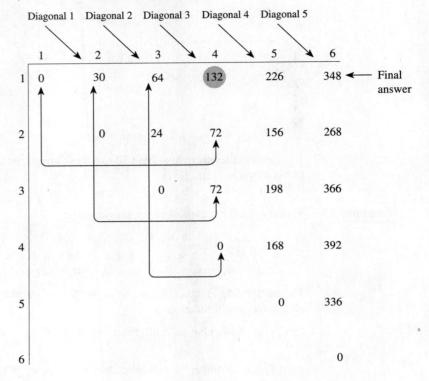

to obtain each factor plus the number needed to multiply the two factors. This means that it equals

$$M[1][k] + M[k + 1][6] + d_0 d_k d_6.$$

We have established that

$$M[1][6] = \underset{1 \le k \le 5}{minimum}(M[1][k] + M[k + 1][6] + d_0 d_k d_6).$$

There is nothing in the preceding argument that restricts the first matrix to being A_1 or the last matrix to being A_6. For example, we could have obtained a similar result for multiplying A_2 through A_6. Therefore, we can generalize this result to obtain the following recursive property when multiplying n matrices. For $1 \le i \le j \le n$

$$
\begin{aligned}
M[i][j] &= \underset{i \le k \le j-1}{minimum}(M[i][k] + M[k + 1][j] + d_{i-1} d_k d_j) \quad \text{if } i < j \\
M[i][i] &= 0.
\end{aligned}
$$

(3.5)

A divide-and-conquer algorithm based on this property is exponential-time. We develop a more efficient algorithm using dynamic programming to compute the values of $M[i][j]$ in steps. A grid similar to Pascal's triangle is used (see Section 3.1). The calculations, which are a little more complex than those in Section 3.1, are based on the following property of Equality 3.5: $M[i][j]$ is calculated from all entries on the same row as $M[i][j]$ but to the left of it along with all entries in the same column as $M[i][j]$ but beneath it. Using this property, we can compute the entries in M as follows: first we set all those entries in the main diagonal to 0; next we compute all those entries in the diagonal just above it, which we call diagonal 1; next we compute all those entries in diagonal 2; and so on. We continue in this manner until we compute the only entry in diagonal 5, which is our final answer, $M[1][6]$. This procedure is illustrated in Figure 3.8 for the matrices in Example 3.5. The following example shows the calculations.

Example 3.6

Suppose we have the six matrices in Example 3.5. The steps in the dynamic programming algorithm follow. The results appear in Figure 3.8.

Compute diagonal 0:

$$M[i][i] = 0 \qquad \text{for } 1 \leq i \leq 6.$$

Compute diagonal 1:

$$\begin{aligned}
M[1][2] &= \underset{1 \leq k \leq 1}{minimum}(M[1][k] + M[k+1][2] + d_0 d_k d_2) \\
&= M[1][1] + M[2][2] + d_0 d_1 d_2 \\
&= 0 + 0 + 5 \times 2 \times 3 = 30
\end{aligned}$$

The values of $M[2][3]$, $M[3][4]$, $M[4][5]$, and $M[5][6]$ are computed in the same way. They appear in Figure 3.8.

Compute diagonal 2:

$$\begin{aligned}
M[1][3] &= \underset{1 \leq k \leq 2}{minimum}(M[1][k] + M[k+1][3] + d_0 d_k d_3) \\
&= minimum(M[1][1] + M[2][3] + d_0 d_1 d_3, \\
&\qquad\qquad\quad M[1][2] + M[3][3] + d_0 d_2 d_3) \\
&= minimum(0 + 24 + 5 \times 2 \times 4, 30 + 0 + 5 \times 3 \times 4) = 64
\end{aligned}$$

The values of $M[2][4]$, $M[3][5]$, and $M[4][6]$ are computed in the same way and are shown in Figure 3.8.

Compute diagonal 3:

$$M[1][4] = \underset{1 \leq k \leq 3}{minimum}(M[1][k] + M[k+1][4] + d_0 d_k d_4)$$

$$= minimum(M[1][1] + M[2][4] + d_0 d_1 d_4,$$
$$M[1][2] + M[3][4] + d_0 d_2 d_4,$$
$$M[1][3] + M[4][4] + d_0 d_3 d_4)$$
$$= minimum(0 + 72 + 5 \times 2 \times 6, 30 + 72 + 5 \times 3 \times 6,$$
$$64 + 0 + 5 \times 4 \times 6) = 132$$

The values of $M[2][5]$ and $M[3][6]$ are computed in the same manner and are shown in Figure 3.8.

Compute diagonal 4:

The entries in diagonal 4 are computed in the same manner and are shown in Figure 3.8.

Compute diagonal 5:

Finally, the entry in diagonal 5 is computed in the same manner. This entry is the solution to our instance; it is the minimum number of elementary multiplications, and its value is given by

$$M[1][6] = 348.$$

The algorithm that follows implements this method. The dimensions of the n matrices—namely, the values of d_0 through d_n—are the only inputs to the algorithm. Matrices themselves are not inputs because the values in the matrices are irrelevant to the problem. The array P produced by the algorithm can be used to print the optimal order. We discuss this after analyzing Algorithm 3.6.

Algorithm 3.6   Minimum Multiplications

Problem: Determining the minimum number of elementary multiplications needed to multiply n matrices and an order that produces that minimum number.

Inputs: the number of matrices n, and an array of integers d, indexed from 0 to n, where $d[i - 1] \times d[i]$ is the dimension of the ith matrix.

Outputs: *minmult,* the minimum number of elementary multiplications needed to multiply the n matrices; a two-dimensional array P from which the optimal order can be obtained. P has its rows indexed from 1 to $n - 1$ and its columns indexed from 1 to n. $P[i][j]$ is the point where matrices i through j are split in an optimal order for multiplying the matrices.

```
int minmult (int n,
             const int d[ ],
             index P[ ][ ])
{
    index i, j, k, diagonal;
    int M[1..n][1..n];
```

```
    for (i = 1; i <= n; i++)
      M[i][i] = 0;
    for (diagonal = 1; diagonal <= n - 1; diagonal++)   // Diagonal-1 is just
      for (i = 1; i <= n - diagonal; i++) {             // above the main
        j = i + diagonal;                               // diagonal.
        M[i][j] = minimum (M[i][k] + M[k + 1][j] + d[i - 1]*d[k]*d[j]);
                  i≤k≤j-1
        P[i][j] = a value of k that gave the minimum;
      }
    return M[1][n];
}
```

Next we analyze Algorithm 3.6.

**Every-Case Time Complexity Analysis of Algorithm 3.6
(Minimum Multiplications)**

Basic operation: We can consider the instructions executed for each value of k to be the basic operation. Included is a comparison to test for the minimum.

Input size: n, the number of matrices to be multiplied.

We have a loop within a loop within a loop. Because $j = i + diagonal$, for given values of *diagonal* and i, the number of passes through the k loop is

$$j - 1 - i + 1 = i + diagonal - 1 - i + 1 = diagonal.$$

For a given value of *diagonal*, the number of passes through the **for**-i loop is $n - diagonal$. Because *diagonal* goes from 1 to $n - 1$, the total number of times the basic operation is done equals

$$\sum_{diagonal=1}^{n-1} [(n - diagonal) \times diagonal].$$

In the exercises we establish that this expression equals

$$\frac{n(n - 1)(n + 1)}{6} \in \Theta(n^3).$$

Next we show how an optimal order can be obtained from the array P. The values of that array, when the algorithm is applied to the dimensions in Example 3.5, are shown in Figure 3.9. The fact that, for example, $P[2][5] = 4$ means that the optimal order for multiplying matrices A_2 through A_5 has the factorization

$$(A_2 A_3 A_4)A_5,$$

Figure 3.9 The array P produced when Algorithm 3.6 is applied to the dimensions in Example 3.5.

	1	2	3	4	5	6
1		1	1	1	1	1
2			2	3	4	5
3				3	4	5
4					4	5
5						5

where inside the parentheses the matrices are multiplied according to the optimal order. That is, $P[2][5]$, which is 4, is the point where the matrices should be split to obtain the factors. We can produce an optimal order by visiting $P[1][n]$ first to determine the top-level factorization. Because $n = 6$ and $P[1, 6] = 1$, the top-level factorization in the optimal order is

$$A_1(A_2A_3A_4A_5A_6).$$

Next we determine the factorization in the optimal order for multiplying A_2 through A_6 by visiting $P[2][6]$. Because the value of $P[2][6]$ is 5, that factorization is

$$(A_2A_3A_4A_5)A_6.$$

We now know that the factorization in the optimal order is

$$A_1((A_2A_3A_4A_5)A_6),$$

where the factorization for multiplying A_2 through A_5 must still be determined. Next we look up $P[2][5]$ and continue in this manner until all the factorizations are determined. The answer is

$$A_1((((A_2A_3)A_4)A_5)A_6).$$

The following algorithm implements the method just described.

Algorithm 3.7

Print Optimal Order

Problem: Print the optimal order for multiplying n matrices.

Inputs: positive integer n, and the array P produced by Algorithm 3.6. $P[i][j]$ is the point where matrices i through j are split in an optimal order for multiplying those matrices.

Outputs: the optimal order for multiplying the matrices.

```
void order (index i, index j)
{
  if (i == j)
    cout << "A" << i;
  else {
    k = P[i][j];
    cout << "(";
    order(i, k);
    order(k + 1, j);
    cout << ")";
  }
}
```

Following our usual convention for recursive routines, P and n are not inputs to *order,* but are inputs to the algorithm. If the algorithm were implemented by defining P and n globally, the top-level call to *order* would be as follows:

order(1, n);

When the dimensions are those in Example 3.5, the algorithm prints the following:

$$(A1((((A2A3)A4)A5)A6)).$$

There are parentheses around the entire expression because the algorithm puts parentheses around every compound term. In the exercises we establish for Algorithm 3.7 that

$$T(n) \in \Theta(n).$$

Our $\Theta(n^3)$ algorithm for chained matrix multiplication is from Godbole (1973). Yao (1982) developed methods for speeding up certain dynamic programming solutions. Using those methods, it is possible to create a $\Theta(n^2)$ algorithm for chained matrix multiplication. Hu and Shing (1982, 1984) describe a $\Theta(n \lg n)$ algorithm for chained matrix multiplication.

3.5 OPTIMAL BINARY SEARCH TREES

Next we obtain an algorithm for determining the optimal way of organizing a set of items in a binary search tree. Before discussing what kind of organization is considered optimal, let's review such trees. For any node in a binary tree, the subtree whose root is the left child of the node is called the *left subtree* of the node. The left subtree of the root of the tree is called the left subtree of the tree. The *right subtree* is defined analogously.

Definition   A *binary search tree* is a binary tree of items (ordinarily called keys), that come from an ordered set, such that

1.   Each node contains one key.
2.   The keys in the left subtree of a given node are less than or equal to the key in that node.
3.   The keys in the right subtree of a given node are greater than or equal to the key in that node.

Figure 3.10 shows two binary search trees, each with the same keys. In the tree on the left, look at the right subtree of the node containing "Ralph." That subtree contains "Tom," "Ursula," and "Wally," and these names are all greater than "Ralph" according to an alphabetic ordering. Although in general a key can occur more than once in a binary search tree, for simplicity we assume that the keys are distinct.

The *depth* of a node in a tree is the number of edges in the unique path from the root to the node. This is also called the *level* of the node in the tree. Usually we say that a node *has* a depth and that the node is *at* a level. For example, in the tree on the left in Figure 3.10, the node containing "Ursula" has a depth of 2. Alternatively, we could say that the node is at level 2. The root has a depth of 0 and is at level 0. The *depth* of a tree is the maximum depth of all nodes in the tree. The tree on the left in Figure 3.10 has a depth of 3, whereas the tree on the right has a depth of 2. A binary tree is called *balanced* if the depth of the two subtrees of every node never differ by more than 1. The tree on the left in Figure 3.10 is not balanced because the left subtree of the root has a depth of 0, and the right subtree has a depth of 2. The tree on the right in Figure 3.10 is balanced.

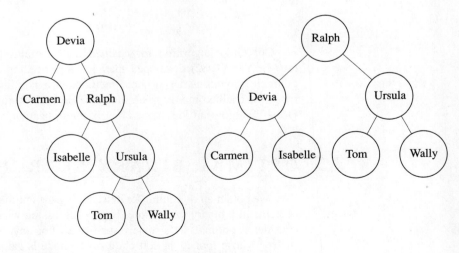

Figure 3.10 Two binary search trees.

Ordinarily, a binary search tree contains records that are retrieved according to the values of the keys. Our goal is to organize the keys in a binary search tree so that the average time it takes to locate a key is minimized (see Section A.8.2 for a discussion of the average). A tree that is organized in this fashion is called *optimal.* It is not hard to see that, if all keys have the same probability of being the search key, the tree on the right in Figure 3.10 is optimal. We are concerned with the case where the keys do not have the same probability. An example of this case would be a search of one of the trees in Figure 3.10 for a name picked at random from people in the United States. Because ''Tom'' is a more common name than ''Ursula,'' we would assign a greater probability to ''Tom.'' (See Section A.8.1 in Appendix A for a discussion of randomness.)

We will discuss the case where it is known that the search key is in the tree. A generalization to the case where it may not be in the tree is investigated in the exercises. To minimize the average search time, we need to know the time complexity of locating a key. Therefore, before proceeding, let's write and analyze an algorithm that searches for a key in a binary search tree. The algorithm uses the following data types:

```
struct nodetype
{
   keytype key;
   nodetype* left;
   nodetype* right;
};

typedef nodetype* node_pointer;
```

This declaration means that a node_pointer variable is a pointer to a nodetype record. That is, its value is the memory address of such a record.

Algorithm 3.8

Search Binary Tree

Problem: Determine the node containing a key in a binary search tree. It is assumed that the key is in the tree.

Inputs: a pointer *tree* to a binary search tree and a key *keyin*.

Outputs: a pointer *p* to the node containing the key.

```
void search (node_pointer tree,
             keytype keyin,
             node_pointer& p)
{
   bool found;
```

```
    p = tree;
    found = false;
    while (! found)
      if (p-> key == keyin)
        found = true;
      else if (keyin < p-> key);
        p = p-> left;                        // Advance to left child.
      else
        p = p-> right;                       // Advance to right child.
    }
```

The number of comparisons done by procedure *search* to locate a key is called the **search time.** Our goal is to determine a tree for which the average search time is minimal. As discussed in Section 1.2, we assume that comparisons are implemented efficiently. With this assumption, only one comparison is done in each iteration of the **while** loop in the previous algorithm. Therefore, the search time for a given key is

$$depth(key) + 1,$$

where *depth(key)* is the depth of the node containing the key. For example, because the depth of the node containing ''Ursula'' is 2 in the left tree in Figure 3.10, the search time for ''Ursula'' is

$$depth(\text{Ursula}) + 1 = 2 + 1 = 3.$$

Let $Key_1, Key_2, \ldots, Key_n$ be the n keys in order, and let p_i be the probability that Key_i is the search key. If c_i is the number of comparisons needed to find Key_i in a given tree, the average search time for that tree is

$$\sum_{i=1}^{n} c_i p_i.$$

This is the value we want to minimize.

Example 3.7   Figure 3.11 shows the five different trees when $n = 3$. The actual values of the keys are not important. The only requirement is that they be ordered. If

$$p_1 = 0.7 \qquad p_2 = 0.2, \qquad \text{and} \qquad p_3 = 0.1,$$

the average search times for the trees in Figure 3.11 are:

1. $3(0.7) + 2(0.2) + 1(0.1) = 2.6$
2. $2(0.7) + 3(0.2) + 1(0.1) = 2.1$
3. $2(0.7) + 1(0.2) + 2(0.1) = 1.8$

4. $1(0.7) + 3(0.2) + 2(0.1) = 1.5$

5. $1(0.7) + 2(0.2) + 3(0.1) = 1.4$

The fifth tree is optimal.

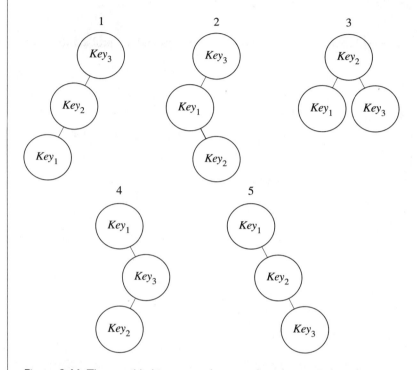

Figure 3.11 The possible binary search trees when there are three keys.

In general, we cannot find an optimal binary search tree by considering all binary search trees, because the number of such trees is at least exponential in n. We prove this by showing that if we just consider all binary search trees with a depth of $n - 1$, we have an exponential number of trees. In a binary search tree with a depth of $n - 1$, the single node at each of the $n - 1$ levels beyond the root can be either to the left or to the right of its parent, which means there are two possibilities at each of those levels. This means that the number of different binary search trees with a depth of $n - 1$ is 2^{n-1}.

Dynamic programming will be used to develop a more efficient algorithm. To that end, suppose that keys Key_i through Key_j are arranged in a tree that minimizes

$$\sum_{m=i}^{j} c_m p_m,$$

where c_m is the number of comparisons needed to locate Key_m in the tree. We will call such a tree ***optimal*** for those keys and denote the optimal value by $A[i][j]$. Because it takes one comparison to locate a key in a tree containing one key, $A[i][i] = p_i$.

Example 3.8   Suppose we have three keys and the probabilities in Example 3.7. That is,

$$p_1 = 0.7, \qquad p_2 = 0.2, \qquad \text{and} \qquad p_3 = 0.1.$$

To determine $A[2][3]$ we must consider the two trees in Figure 3.12. For those two trees we have the following:

1. $1(p_2) + 2(p_3) = 1(0.2) + 2(0.1) = 0.4$
2. $2(p_2) + 1(p_3) = 2(0.2) + 1(0.1) = 0.5$

The first tree is optimal, and

$$A[2][3] = 0.4.$$

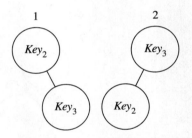

Figure 3.12 The binary search trees composed of Key_2 and Key_3.

Notice that the optimal tree obtained in Example 3.8 is the right subtree of the root of the optimal tree obtained in Example 3.7. Even if this tree was not the exact same one as that right subtree, the average time spent searching in it would have to be the same. Otherwise, we could substitute it for that subtree, resulting in a tree with a smaller average search time. In general, any subtree of an optimal tree must be optimal for the keys in that subtree. Therefore, the principle of optimality applies.

Next, let tree 1 be an optimal tree given the restriction that Key_1 is at the root, tree 2 be an optimal tree given the restriction that Key_2 is at the root, ..., tree n be an optimal tree given the restriction that Key_n is at the root. For $1 \leq k \leq n$, the subtrees of tree k must be optimal, and therefore the average search times in these subtrees are as depicted in Figure 3.13. This figure also shows that for each $m \neq k$ it takes exactly one more comparison (the one at the root) to locate Key_m in tree k than it does to locate that key in the subtree that contains

Figure 3.13 Optimal binary search tree given that Key_k is at the root.

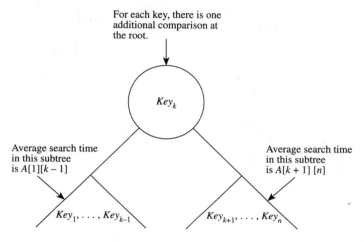

For each key, there is one additional comparison at the root.

Key_k

Average search time in this subtree is $A[1][k-1]$

$Key_1, \ldots, Key_{k-1}$

Average search time in this subtree is $A[k+1][n]$

$Key_{k+1}, \ldots, Key_n$

it. This one comparison adds $1 \times p_m$ to the average search time for Key_m in tree k. We've established that the average search time for tree k is given by

$$\underbrace{A[1][k-1]}_{\substack{\text{Average time} \\ \text{in left} \\ \text{subtree}}} + \underbrace{p_1 + \cdots + p_{k-1}}_{\substack{\text{Additional time} \\ \text{comparing at root}}} + \underbrace{p_k}_{\substack{\text{Average time} \\ \text{searching} \\ \text{for root}}} + \underbrace{A[k+1][n]}_{\substack{\text{Average time} \\ \text{in right} \\ \text{subtree}}} + \underbrace{p_{k+1} + \cdots + p_n}_{\substack{\text{Additional time} \\ \text{comparing at root}}},$$

which equals

$$A[1][k-1] + A[k+1][n] + \sum_{m=1}^{n} p_m.$$

Because one of the k trees must be optimal, the average search time for the optimal tree is given by

$$A[1][n] = \underset{1 \le k \le n}{minimum}(A[1][k-1] + A[k+1][n]) + \sum_{m=1}^{n} p_m,$$

where $A[1][0]$ and $A[n+1][n]$ are defined to be 0. Although the sum of the probabilities in this last expression is clearly 1, we have written it as a sum because we now wish to generalize the result. To that end, there is nothing in the previous discussion that requires that the keys be Key_1 through Key_n. That is, in general, the discussion pertains to Key_i through Key_j where $i < j$. We have therefore derived the following:

$$A[i][j] = \underset{i \le k \le j}{minimum}(A[i][k-1] + A[k+1][j]) + \sum_{m=i}^{j} p_m \qquad i < j$$

$$A[i][i] = p_i \hspace{4cm} (3.6)$$

$A[i][i-1]$ and $A[j+1][j]$ are defined to be 0.

Using Equality 3.6, we can write an algorithm that determines an optimal binary search tree. Because $A[i][j]$ is computed from entries in the ith row but to the left of $A[i][j]$ and from entries in the jth column but beneath $A[i][j]$, we proceed by computing in sequence the values on each diagonal (as was done in Algorithm 3.6). Because the steps in the algorithm are so similar to those in Algorithm 3.6, we do not include an example illustrating these steps. Rather, we simply give the algorithm, followed by a comprehensive example showing the results of applying the algorithm. The array R produced by the algorithm contains the indices of the keys chosen for the root at each step. For example, $R[1][2]$ is the index of the key in the root of an optimal tree containing the first two keys, and $R[2][4]$ is the index of the key in the root of an optimal tree containing the second, third, and fourth keys. After analyzing the algorithm, we will discuss how to build an optimal tree from R.

Algorithm 3.9

Optimal Binary Search Tree

Problem: Determine an optimal binary search tree for a set of keys, each with a given probability of being the search key.

Inputs: n, the number of keys, and an array of real numbers p indexed from 1 to n, where $p[i]$ is the probability of searching for the ith key.

Outputs: a variable *minavg*, whose value is the average search time for an optimal binary search tree; and a two-dimensional array R from which an optimal tree can be constructed. R has its rows indexed from 1 to $n + 1$ and its columns indexed from 0 to n. $R[i][j]$ is the index of the key in the root of an optimal tree containing the ith through the jth keys.

```
void optsearchtree (int n,
                    const float p[ ],
                    float& minavg,
                    index R[ ][ ])
{
    index i, j, k, diagonal;
    float A[1..n + 1][0..n];

    for (i = 1; i <= n; i++) {
        A[i][i − 1] = 0;
        A[i][i] = p[i];
        R[i][i] = i;
        R[i][i − 1] = 0;
    }
```

```
A[n + 1][n] = 0;
R[n + 1][n] = 0;
for (diagonal = 1; diagonal <= n - 1; diagonal++)    // Diagonal-1 is just
    for (i = 1; i <= n - diagonal; i++) {            // above the main
                                                      // diagonal.
        j = i + diagonal;
```
$$A[i][j] = \underset{i \leq k \leq j}{minimum}\ (A[i][k-1] + A[k+1][j]) + \sum_{m=i}^{j} p_m;$$
```
        R[i][j] = a value of k that gave the minimum;
    }
    minavg = A[1][n];
}
```

Every-Case Time Complexity Analysis of Algorithm 3.9
(Optimal Binary Search Tree)

Basic operation: The instructions executed for each value of k. They include a comparison to test for the minimum. The value of $\sum_{m=i}^{j} p_m$ does not need to be computed from scratch each time. In the exercises you will find an efficient way to compute these sums.

Input size: n, the number of keys.

The control of this algorithm is almost identical to that in Algorithm 3.6. The only difference is that for given values of *diagonal* and i the basic operation is done $diagonal + 1$ times. An analysis like the one of Algorithm 3.6 establishes that

$$T(n) = \frac{n(n-1)(n+4)}{6} \in \Theta(n^3).$$

The following algorithm constructs a binary tree from the array R. Recall that R contains the indices of the keys chosen for the root at each step.

Algorithm 3.10

Build Optimal Binary Search Tree

Problem: Build an optimal binary search tree.

Inputs: n, the number of keys, an array *Key* containing the n keys in order, and the array R produced by Algorithm 3.9. $R[i][j]$ is the index of the key in the root of an optimal tree containing the ith through the jth keys.

Outputs: a pointer *tree* to an optimal binary search tree containing the *n* keys.

```
node_pointer tree (index i, j)
{
    index k;
    node_pointer p;

    k = R[i][j];
    if (k == 0)
        return NULL;
    else {
        p = new nodetype;
        p-> key = Key[k];
        p-> left = tree(i, k − 1);
        p-> right = tree(k + 1, j);
        return p;
    }
}
```

The instruction *p* = **new nodetype** gets a new node and puts its address in *p*. Following our convention for recursive algorithms, the parameters *n*, *Key*, and *R* are not inputs to function *tree*. If the algorithm were implemented by defining *n*, *Key*, and *R* globally, a pointer *root* to the root of an optimal binary search tree is obtained by calling *tree* as follows:

root = *tree*(1, *n*);

We did not illustrate the steps in Algorithm 3.9 because it is similar to Algorithm 3.6 (Minimum Multiplications). Likewise, we will not illustrate the steps in Algorithm 3.10 because this algorithm is similar to Algorithm 3.7 (Print Optimal Order). Rather, we provide one comprehensive example showing the results of applying both Algorithms 3.9 and 3.10.

Example 3.9 Suppose we have the following values of the array *Key:*

Don	Isabelle	Ralph	Wally
Key[1]	*Key*[2]	*Key*[3]	*Key*[4]

and

$$p_1 = \frac{3}{8} \qquad p_2 = \frac{3}{8} \qquad p_3 = \frac{1}{8} \qquad p_4 = \frac{1}{8}.$$

The arrays *A* and *R* produced by Algorithm 3.9 are shown in Figure 3.14, and the tree created by Algorithm 3.10 is shown in Figure 3.15. The minimal average search time is 7/4.

	0	1	2	3	4
1	0	$\frac{3}{8}$	$\frac{9}{8}$	$\frac{11}{8}$	$\frac{7}{4}$
2		0	$\frac{3}{8}$	$\frac{5}{8}$	1
3			0	$\frac{1}{8}$	$\frac{3}{8}$
4				0	$\frac{1}{8}$
5					0

A

	0	1	2	3	4
1	0	1	1	2	2
2		0	2	2	2
3			0	3	3
4				0	4
5					0

R

Figure 3.14 The arrays A and R, produced when Algorithm 3.9 is applied to the instance in Example 3.9.

Notice that $R[1][2]$ could be 1 or 2. The reason is that either of these indices could be the index of the root in an optimal tree containing only the first two keys. Therefore, both these indices give the minimum value of $A[1][2]$ in Algorithm 3.9, which means that either could be chosen for $R[1][2]$.

Figure 3.15 The tree produced when Algorithms 3.9 and 3.10 are applied to the instance in Example 3.9.

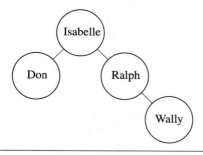

The previous algorithm for determining an optimal binary search tree is from Gilbert and Moore (1959). A $\Theta(n^2)$ algorithm can be obtained using the dynamic programming speed-up method in Yao (1982).

3.6 THE TRAVELING SALESPERSON PROBLEM

Suppose a salesperson is planning a sales trip that includes 20 cities. Each city is connected to some of the other cities by a road. To minimize travel time, we want to determine a shortest route that starts at the salesperson's home city, visits each

Figure 3.16 The optimal
tour is [v_1, v_3, v_4, v_2, v_1].

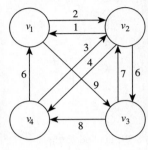

to determine a shortest route that starts at the salesperson's home city, visits each of the cities once, and ends up at the home city. This problem of determining a shortest route is called the Traveling Salesperson Problem.

An instance of this problem can be represented by a weighted graph, where each vertex represents a city. As in Section 3.2, we generalize the problem to include the case where the weight (distance) going in one direction can be different than the weight going in another direction. Again we assume that the weights are nonnegative numbers. Figures 3.2 and 3.16 show such weighted graphs. A *tour* (also called a Hamiltonian Circuit) in a directed graph is a path from a vertex to itself that passes through each of the other vertices exactly once. An *optimal tour* in a weighted, directed graph is such a path of minimum length. The Traveling Salesperson Problem is to find an optimal tour in a weighted, directed graph when at least one tour exists. Because the starting vertex is irrelevant to the length of an optimal tour, we will consider v_1 to be the starting vertex. The following are the three tours and lengths for the graph in Figure 3.16:

$$length[v_1, v_2, v_3, v_4, v_1] = 22$$
$$length[v_1, v_3, v_2, v_4, v_1] = 26$$
$$length[v_1, v_3, v_4, v_2, v_1] = 21$$

The last tour is optimal. We solved this instance by simply considering all possible tours. In general, there can be an edge from every vertex to every other vertex. If we consider all possible tours, the second vertex on the tour can be any of $n - 1$ vertices, the third vertex on the tour can be any of $n - 2$ vertices, . . . , the nth vertex on the tour can be only one vertex. Therefore, the total number of tours is

$$(n - 1)(n - 2) \cdots 1 = (n - 1)!,$$

which is worse than exponential.

Can dynamic programming be applied to this problem? Notice that if v_k is the first vertex after v_1 on an optimal tour, the subpath of that tour from v_k to v_1 must be a shortest path from v_k to v_1 that passes through each of the other vertices exactly once. This means that the principle of optimality applies, and we can use dynamic programming. To that end, we represent the graph by an adjacency matrix W, as was done in Section 3.2. Figure 3.17 shows the adjacency matrix representation of the graph in Figure 3.16. Let

Figure 3.17 The adjacency matrix representation W of the graph in Figure 3.16.

	1	2	3	4
1	0	2	9	∞
2	1	0	6	4
3	∞	7	0	8
4	6	3	∞	0

$$V = \text{set of all the vertices}$$
$$A = \text{a subset of } V$$
$$D[v_i][A] = \text{length of a shortest path from } v_i \text{ to } v_1 \text{ passing}$$
$$\text{through each vertex in } A \text{ exactly once.}$$

Example 3.10   For the graph in Figure 3.16,

$$V = \{v_1, v_2, v_3, v_4\}.$$

Notice that $\{v_1, v_2, v_3, v_4\}$ uses curly braces to represent a set, whereas $[v_1, v_2, v_3, v_4]$ uses square brackets to represent a path. If $A = \{v_3\}$, then

$$D[v_2][A] = length[v_2, v_3, v_1]$$
$$= \infty.$$

If $A = \{v_3, v_4\}$, then

$$D[v_2][A] = minimum(length[v_2, v_3, v_4, v_1], length[v_2, v_4, v_3, v_1])$$
$$= minimum(20, \infty) = 20.$$

Because $V - \{v_1, v_j\}$ contains all the vertices except v_1 and v_j and the principle of optimality applies, we have

$$\text{Length of an optimal tour} = \underset{2 \leq j \leq n}{minimum}(W[1][j] + D[v_j][V - \{v_1, v_j\}]),$$

and, in general for $i \neq 1$ and i not in A,

$$D[v_i][A] = \underset{v_j \in A}{minimum}(W[i][j] + D[v_j][A - \{v_j\}]) \quad \text{if } A \neq \emptyset$$

$$D[v_i][\emptyset] = W[i][1].$$

(3.7)

We can create a dynamic programming algorithm for the Traveling Salesperson Problem using Equality 3.7. But first, let's illustrate how the algorithm would proceed.

Example 3.11   Determine an optimal tour for the graph represented in Figure 3.17.

First consider the empty set:

$$D[v_2][\emptyset] = 1$$
$$D[v_3][\emptyset] = \infty$$
$$D[v_4][\emptyset] = 6$$

Next consider all sets containing one element:

$$D[v_3][\{v_2\}] = \underset{v_j \in \{v_2\}}{minimum}(W[3][j] + D[v_j][\{v_2\} - \{v_j\}])$$
$$= W[3][2] + D[v_2][\varnothing] = 7 + 1 = 8$$

Similarly,

$$D[v_4][\{v_2\}] = 3 + 1 = 4$$
$$D[v_2][\{v_3\}] = 6 + \infty = \infty$$
$$D[v_4][\{v_3\}] = \infty + \infty = \infty$$
$$D[v_2][\{v_4\}] = 4 + 6 = 10$$
$$D[v_3][\{v_4\}] = 8 + 6 = 14$$

Next consider all sets containing two elements:

$$D[v_4][\{v_2, v_3\}] = \underset{v_j \in \{v_2, v_3\}}{minimum}(W[4][j] + D[v_j][\{v_2, v_3\} - \{v_j\}])$$
$$= minimum(W[4][2] + D[v_2][\{v_3\}], W[4][3] + D[v_3][\{v_2\}])$$
$$= minimum(3 + \infty, \infty + 8) = \infty$$

Similarly,

$$D[v_3][\{v_2, v_4\}] = minimum(7 + 10, 8 + 4) = 12$$
$$D[v_2][\{v_3, v_4\}] = minimum(6 + 14, 4 + \infty) = 20$$

Finally, compute the length of an optimal tour:

$$D[v_1][\{v_2, v_3, v_4\}] = \underset{v_j \in \{v_2, v_3, v_4\}}{minimum}(W[1][j] + D[v_j][\{v_2, v_3, v_4\} - \{v_j\}])$$
$$= minimum(W[1][2] + D[v_2][\{v_3, v_4\}],$$
$$W[1][3] + D[v_3][\{v_2, v_4\}],$$
$$W[1][4] + D[v_4][\{v_2, v_3\}])$$
$$= minimum(2 + 20, 9 + 12, \infty + \infty) = 21.$$

The dynamic programming algorithm for the Traveling Salesperson Problem follows.

Algorithm 3.11

The Dynamic Programming Algorithm
for the Traveling Salesperson Problem

Problem: Determine an optimal tour in a weighted, directed graph. The weights are nonnegative numbers.

Inputs: a weighted, directed graph, and n, the number of vertices in the graph. The graph is represented by a two-dimensional array W, which has both its rows and columns indexed from 1 to n, where $W[i][j]$ is the weight on the edge from ith vertex to the jth vertex.

Outputs: a variable *minlength,* whose value is the length of an optimal tour, and a two-dimensional array P from which an optimal tour can be constructed. P has its rows indexed from 1 to n and its columns indexed by all subsets of $V - \{v_1\}$. $P[i][A]$ is the index of the first vertex after v_i on a shortest path from v_i to v_1 that passes through all the vertices in A exactly once.

```
void travel (int n,
             const number W[ ][ ],
             index P[ ][ ],
             number& minlength)
{
   index i, j, k;
   number D[1..n][subset of V − {v₁}];

   for (i = 2; i <= n; i++)
      D[i][∅] = W[i][1];
   for (k = 1; k <= n − 2; k++)
      for (all subsets A ⊆ V − {v₁} containing k vertices)
         for (i such that i ≠ 1 and vᵢ is not in A) {
            D[i][A] = minimum (W[i][j] + D[vⱼ][A − {vⱼ}]);
                      vj∈A
            P[i][A] = value of j that gave the minimum;
         }
   D[1][V − {v₁}] = minimum (W[1][j] + D[vⱼ][V − {v₁}]);
                    2≤j≤n
   P[1][V − {v₁}] = value of j that gave the minimum;
   minlength = D[1][V − {v₁}];
}
```

The sets A and V and their members v_i are not defined as variables in the algorithm because they would not be defined in an implementation of the algorithm. However, expressing the algorithm without referring to them gets us too involved in the implementation and hinders the clarity of the algorithm. Before showing how an optimal tour can be obtained from the array P, we analyze the algorithm. First we need a theorem:

Theorem 3.1 For all $n \geq 1$

$$\sum_{k=1}^{n} k\binom{n}{k} = n2^{n-1}.$$

Proof: It is left as an exercise to show that

$$k\binom{n}{k} = n\binom{n-1}{k-1}.$$

Therefore,

$$\sum_{k=1}^{n} k\binom{n}{k} = \sum_{k=1}^{n} n\binom{n-1}{k-1}$$

$$= n\sum_{k=0}^{n-1}\binom{n-1}{k}$$

$$= n2^{n-1}.$$

The last equality is obtained by applying the result found in Example A.10 in Appendix A.

The analysis of Algorithm 3.11 follows.

Every-Case Time and Space Complexity Analysis of Algorithm 3.11 (The Dynamic Programming Algorithm for the Traveling Salesperson Problem)

Basic operation: The time in both the first and last loops is insignificant compared to the time in the middle loop, because the middle loop contains various levels of nesting. Therefore, we will consider the instructions executed for each value of v_j to be the basic operation. They include an addition instruction.

Input size: n, the number of vertices in the graph.

For each set A containing k vertices, we must consider $n - 1 - k$ vertices, and for each of these vertices the basic operation is done k times. Because the number of subsets A of $V - \{v_1\}$ containing k vertices is equal to $\binom{n-1}{k}$, the total number of times the basic operation is done is given by

$$T(n) = \sum_{k=1}^{n-2} (n-1-k)k\binom{n-1}{k}. \tag{3.8}$$

It is not hard to show that

$$(n-1-k)\binom{n-1}{k} = (n-1)\binom{n-2}{k}.$$

Substituting this equality into Equality 3.8, we have

$$T(n) = (n-1)\sum_{k=1}^{n-2} k\binom{n-2}{k}.$$

Finally, applying Theorem 3.1, we have

$$T(n) = (n-1)(n-2)2^{n-3} \in \Theta(n^2 2^n).$$

Because the memory used in this algorithm is also large, we will analyze the memory complexity, which we call $M(n)$. The memory used to store the arrays $D[v_i][A]$ and $P[v_i][A]$ is clearly the dominant amount of memory. So we will determine how large these arrays must be. Because $V - \{v_1\}$ contains $n - 1$ vertices, we can apply the result in Example A.10 in Appendix A to conclude that it has 2^{n-1} subsets A. The first index of the arrays D and P ranges in value between 1 and n. Therefore,

$$M(n) = 2 \times n2^{n-1} = n2^n \in \Theta(n2^n).$$

At this point you may be wondering what we have gained, because our new algorithm is still $\Theta(n^2 2^n)$. The following example shows that even an algorithm with this time complexity can sometimes be useful.

Example 3.12

Ralph and Nancy are both competing for the same sales position. The boss tells them on Friday that, starting on Monday, whoever can cover the entire 20-city territory faster will get the position. The territory includes the home office, and they must return to the home office when they are done. There is a road from every city to every other city. Ralph figures he has the whole weekend to determine his route; so he simply runs the brute-force algorithm that considers all $(20 - 1)!$ tours on his computer. Nancy recalls the dynamic programming algorithm from her algorithms course. Figuring she should take every advantage she can, she runs that algorithm on her computer. Assuming that the time to process the basic instruction in Nancy's algorithm is 1 microsecond, and that it takes 1 microsecond for Ralph's algorithm to compute the length of each tour, the time taken by each algorithm is given about by the following:

Brute-force algorithm: $\quad\quad\quad\quad\quad\quad\quad\quad$ 19! μs = 3857 years

Dynamic programming algorithm: $\quad (20 - 1)(20 - 2)2^{20-3}$ μs = 45 seconds.

We see that even a $\Theta(n^2 2^n)$ algorithm can be useful when the alternative is a factorial-time algorithm. The memory used by the dynamic programming algorithm in this example is

$$20 \times 2^{20} = 20,971,520 \text{ array slots.}$$

Although this is quite large, it is feasible by today's standards.

Using the $\Theta(n^2 2^n)$ algorithm to find the optimal tour is practical only because n is small. If, for example, there were 60 cities, that algorithm, too, would take many years.

Let's discuss how to retrieve an optimal tour from the array P. We don't give the algorithm; rather, we simply illustrate how it would proceed. The members of the array P needed to determine an optimal tour for the graph represented in Figure 3.16 are:

3	4	2
$P[1, \{v_2, v_3, v_4\}]$	$P[3, \{v_2, v_4\}]$	$P[4, \{v_2\}]$

We obtain an optimal tour as follows:

$$\text{Index of first node} = P\,[1][\{v_2,\, v_3,\, v_4\}] = 3$$
$$\text{Index of second node} = P\,[3][\{v_2,\, v_4\}] \quad = 4$$
$$\text{Index of third node} = P\,[4][\{v_2\}] \qquad = 2$$

The optimal tour is, therefore,

$$[v_1,\, v_3,\, v_4,\, v_2,\, v_1].$$

No one has ever found an algorithm for the Traveling Salesperson Problem whose worst-case time complexity is better than exponential. Yet no one has ever proved that such an algorithm is not possible. This problem is one of a large class of closely related problems that share this property and are the focus of Chapter 9.

Exercises

Section 3.1

1. Establish Equality 3.1 given in this section.

2. Use induction on n to show that the divide-and-conquer algorithm for the Binomial Coefficient Problem (Algorithm 3.1), based on Equality 3.1, computes $2\dbinom{n}{k} - 1$ terms to determine $\dbinom{n}{k}$.

3. Implement both Algorithms for the Binomial Coefficient Problem (Algorithms 3.1 and 3.2) on your system, and study their performances using different problem instances.

4. Modify Algorithm 3.2 (Binomial Coefficient Using Dynamic Programming) so that it uses only a one-dimensional array indexed from 0 to k.

Section 3.2

5. Use Floyd's Algorithm for the Shortest Paths Problem 2 (Algorithm 3.4) to construct the matrix D, which contains the lengths of the shortest paths, and the matrix P, which contains the highest indices of the intermediate vertices on the shortest paths, for the following graph. Show the actions step by step.

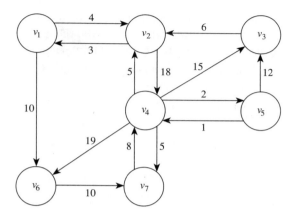

6. Use the Print Shortest Path algorithm (Algorithm 3.5) to find the shortest path from vertex v_7 to vertex v_3, in the graph of Exercise 5, using the matrix P found in that exercise. Show the actions step by step.

7. Analyze the Print Shortest Path algorithm (Algorithm 3.5), and show that it has a linear time complexity.

8. Implement Floyd's Algorithm for the Shortest Paths Problem 2 (Algorithm 3.4) on your system, and study its performance using different graphs.

9. Can Floyd's Algorithm for the Shortest Paths Problem 2 (Algorithm 3.4) be modified to give just the shortest path from a given vertex to another specified vertex in a graph? Justify your answer.

10. Can Floyd's Algorithm for the Shortest Paths Problem 2 (Algorithm 3.4) be used to find the shortest paths in a graph with some negative weights? Justify your answer.

Section 3.3

11. Find an optimization problem in which the principle of optimality does not apply, and therefore the optimal solution cannot be obtained using dynamic programming. Justify your answer.

Section 3.4

12. Find the optimal order, and its cost, for evaluating the product $A_1 \times A_2 \times A_3 \times A_4 \times A_5$, where

A_1 is (10×4)
A_2 is (4×5)
A_3 is (5×20)
A_4 is (20×2)
A_5 is (2×50).

13. Implement the Minimum Multiplications algorithm (Algorithm 3.6) and the Print Optimal Order algorithm (Algorithm 3.7) on your system, and study their performances using different problem instances.

14. Show that a divide-and-conquer algorithm based on Equality 3.5 has an exponential time complexity.

15. Establish the equality

$$\sum_{diagonal=1}^{n-1} [(n - diagonal) \times diagonal] = \frac{n(n - 1)(n + 1)}{6}.$$

This is used in the every-case time complexity analysis of Algorithm 3.6.

16. Show that to fully parenthesize an expression having n matrices we need $n - 1$ pairs of parentheses.

17. Analyze Algorithm 3.7, and show that it has a linear time complexity.

18. Write an efficient algorithm that will find an optimal order for multiplying n matrices $A_1 \times A_2 \times \cdots \times A_n$ where the dimension of each matrix is 1×1, $1 \times d, d \times 1$, or $d \times d$ for some positive integer d. Analyze your algorithm, and show the results using order notation.

Section 3.5

19. How many different binary search trees can be constructed using six distinct keys?

20. Create the optimal binary search tree for the following items, where the probability occurrence of each word is given in parentheses: CASE (.05), ELSE (.15), END (.05), IF (.35), OF (.05), THEN (.35).

21. Find an efficient way to compute $\sum_{m=i}^{j} p_m$, which is used in the Optimal Binary Search Tree algorithm (Algorithm 3.9).

22. Implement the Optimal Binary Search Tree algorithm (Algorithm 3.9) and the Build Optimal Binary Search Tree algorithm (Algorithm 3.10) on your system, and study their performances using different problem instances.

23. Analyze Algorithm 3.10, and show its time complexity using order notation.

24. Generalize the Optimal Binary Search Tree algorithm (Algorithm 3.9) to the case where the search key may not be in the tree. That is, you should let q_i, where $i = 0, 1, 2, \ldots, n$, be the probability that a missing search key can be situated between Key_i and Key_{i+1}. Analyze your generalized algorithm, and show the results using order notation.

25. Show that a divide-and-conquer algorithm based on Equality 3.6 has an exponential time complexity.

Section 3.6

26. Find an optimal circuit for the weighted, direct graph represented by the following matrix W. Show the actions step by step.

$$W = \begin{bmatrix} 0 & 8 & 13 & 18 & 20 \\ 3 & 0 & 7 & 8 & 10 \\ 4 & 11 & 0 & 10 & 7 \\ 6 & 6 & 7 & 0 & 11 \\ 10 & 6 & 2 & 1 & 0 \end{bmatrix}$$

27. Write a more detailed version of the dynamic programming algorithm for the Traveling Salesperson Problem (Algorithm 3.11).

28. Implement your detailed version of Algorithm 3.11 from Exercise 27 on your system, and study its performance using several problem instances.

Additional Exercises

29. Like algorithms for computing the nth Fibonacci term (see Exercise 34 in Chapter 1) the input size in Algorithm 3.2 (Binomial Coefficient Using Dynamic Programming) is the number of symbols it takes to encode the numbers n and k. Analyze the algorithm in terms of its input size.

30. Determine the number of possible orders for multiplying n matrices A_1, $A_2, \ldots, A_n$.

31. Show that the number of binary search trees with n keys is given by the formula

$$\frac{1}{(n + 1)} \binom{2n}{n}$$

32. Can you develop a quadratic-time algorithm for the Optimal Binary Search Tree Problem (Algorithm 3.9)?

33. Use the dynamic programming approach to write an algorithm to find the maximum sum in any contiguous sublist of a given list of n real values. Analyze your algorithm, and show the results using order notation.

34. Let us consider two sequences of characters S_1 and S_2. For example, we could have $S_1 = $ A\$CMA*MN and $S_2 = $ AXMC4ANB. Assuming that a subsequence of a sequence can be constructed by deleting any number of characters from any positions, use the dynamic programming approach to create an algorithm that finds the longest common subsequence of S_1 and S_2. This algorithm returns the maximum-length common subsequence of each sequence.

CHAPTER 4

The Greedy Approach

C harles Dickens' classic character Ebenezer Scrooge may well be the most greedy person ever, fictional or real. Recall that Scrooge never considered the past or future. Each day his only drive was to greedily grab as much gold as he could. After the Ghost of Christmas Past reminded him of the past and the Ghost of Christmas Future warned him of the future, he changed his greedy ways.

A greedy algorithm proceeds in the same way as Scrooge did. That is, it grabs data items in sequence, each time taking the one that is deemed ''best'' according to some criterion, without regard for the choices it has made before or will make in the future. One should not get the impression that there is something wrong with greedy algorithms because of the negative connotations of Scrooge and the word ''greedy.'' They often lead to very efficient and simple solutions.

Like dynamic programming, greedy algorithms are often used to solve optimization problems. However, the greedy approach is more straightforward. In dynamic programming, a recursive property is used to divide an instance into smaller instances. In the greedy approach, there is no division into smaller instances. A ***greedy algorithm*** arrives at a solution by making a sequence of choices, each of which simply looks the best at the moment. That is, each choice is locally optimal. The hope is that a globally optimal solution will be obtained, but this is not always the case. For a given algorithm, we must determine whether the solution is always optimal.

A simple example illustrates the greedy approach. Joe the sales clerk often encounters the problem of giving change for a purchase. Customers usually don't want to receive a lot of coins. For example, most customers would be aggravated if he gave them 87 pennies when the change was $0.87. Therefore, his goal is not only to give the correct change, but to do so with as few coins as possible. A solution to an instance of Joe's change problem is a set of coins that adds up to the amount he owes the customer, and an optimal solution is such a set of minimum size. A greedy approach to the problem could proceed as follows. Initially there are no coins in the change. Joe starts by looking for the largest coin (in value) he can find. That is, his criterion for deciding which coin is best (locally optimal) is the value of the coin. This is called the *selection procedure* in a greedy algorithm. Next he sees if adding this coin to the change would make the total value of the change exceed the amount owed. This is called the *feasibility check* in a greedy algorithm. If adding the coin would not make the change exceed the amount owed, he adds the coin to the change. Next he checks to see if the value of the change is now equal to the amount owed. This is the *solution check* in a greedy algorithm. If they are not equal, he gets another coin using his selection procedure, and repeats the process. He does this until the value of the change equals the amount owed or he runs out of coins. In the latter case, he is not able to return the exact amount owed. The following is a high-level algorithm for this procedure.

```
While (there are more coins and the instance is not solved) {

    Grab the largest remaining coin;                    // selection procedure

    If (adding the coin makes the change exceed the     // feasibility check
                            amount owed)

        reject the coin;
    else
        add the coin to the change;

    If (the total value of the change equals the        // solution check
                        the amount owed)
        the instance is solved;
}
```

Figure 4.1 A greedy algorithm for giving change.

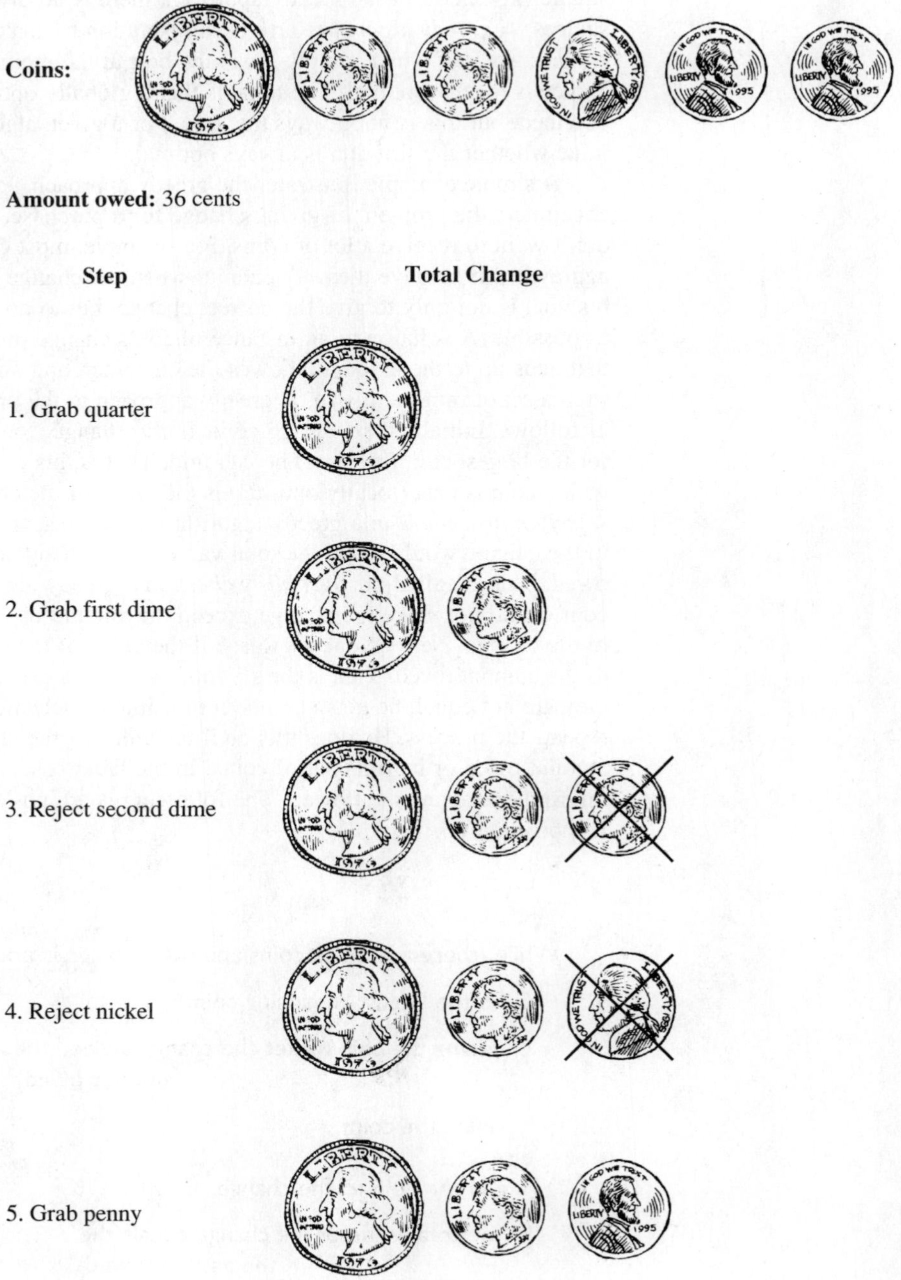

Coins:

Amount owed: 36 cents

Step	Total Change

1. Grab quarter

2. Grab first dime

3. Reject second dime

4. Reject nickel

5. Grab penny

In the feasibility check, when we determine that adding a coin would make the change exceed the amount owed, we learn that the set obtained by adding that coin cannot be completed to give a solution to the instance. Therefore, that set is unfeasible and is rejected. An example application of this algorithm appears in Figure 4.1. Again, the algorithm is called ''greedy'' because the selection procedure simply consists of greedily grabbing the next-largest coin without considering the potential drawbacks of making such a choice. There is no opportunity to reconsider a choice. Once a coin is accepted, it is permanently included in the solution; once a coin is rejected, it is permanently excluded from the solution. This procedure is very simple, but does it result in an optimal solution? That is, in the change problem, when a solution is possible, does the solution provided by the algorithm contain the minimum number of coins necessary to give the correct change? If the coins consist of U.S. coins (penny, nickel, dime, quarter, half dollar) and if there is at least one type of each coin available, the greedy algorithm always returns an optimal solution when a solution exists. This is proven in the exercises. There are cases other than those involving standard U.S. coins for which the greedy algorithm produces optimal solutions. Some of these also are investigated in the exercises. Notice here that if we include a 12-cent coin with the U.S. coins, the greedy algorithm does not always give an optimal solution. Figure 4.2 illustrates this. In that figure, the greedy solution contains five coins, whereas the optimal solution, which consists of the dime, nickel, and penny, contains only three coins.

As the Change Problem shows, a greedy algorithm does not guarantee an optimal solution. We must always determine whether this is the case for a particular greedy algorithm. Sections 4.1, 4.2, and 4.3 discuss problems for which the greedy approach always yields an optimal solution. Section 4.4 investigates a problem in which it does not. In that section, we compare the greedy approach with dynamic programming to illuminate when each approach might be applicable.

We close here with a general outline of the greedy approach. A greedy algorithm starts with an empty set and adds items to the set in sequence until the set represents a solution to an instance of a problem. Each iteration consists of the following components:

- A **selection procedure** chooses the next item to add to the set. The selection is performed according to a greedy criterion that satisfies some locally optimal consideration at the time.

- A **feasibility check** determines if the new set is feasible by checking whether it is possible to complete this set in such a way as to give a solution to the instance.

- A **solution check** determines whether the new set constitutes a solution to the instance.

Figure 4.2 The greedy algorithm is not optimal if a 12-cent coin is included.

Coins:

Amount owed: 16 cents

| | |
| **Step** | **Total Change** |

1. Grab 12-cent coin

2. Reject dime

3. Reject nickel

4. Grab four pennies

4.1 MINIMUM SPANNING TREES

Suppose an urban planner wants to connect certain cities with roads so that it is possible for someone to drive from any city to any other city. If there are budgetary restrictions, the planner may want to do this with the minimum amount of road. We will develop an algorithm that solves this and similar problems. First, let's informally review more graph theory. Figure 4.3(a) shows a connected, weighted, undirected graph *G*. We assume here that the weights are nonnegative numbers. The graph is ***undirected*** because the edges do not have direction. This is represented pictorially by an absence of arrows on the edges. Because the edges

Figure 4.3 A weighted graph and three subgraphs.

(a) A connected, weighted,
undirected graph G.

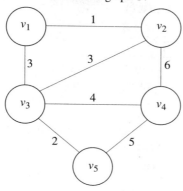

(b) If (v_4, v_5) were removed from this subgraph,
the graph would remain connected.

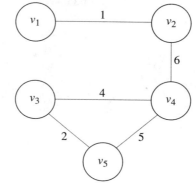

(c) A spanning tree for G.

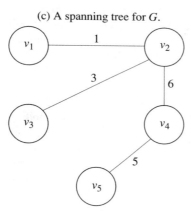

(d) A minimum spanning tree for G.

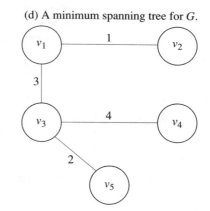

do not have direction, we say an edge is between two vertices. A *path* in an undirected graph is a sequence of vertices such that there is an edge between each vertex and its successor. Because the edges have no direction, there is a path from vertex u to vertex v if and only if there is a path from v to u. Therefore, for undirected graphs we simply say that there is a path between two vertices. An undirected graph is called *connected* if there is a path between every pair of vertices. All the graphs in Figure 4.3 are connected. If we removed the edge between v_2 and v_4 from the graph in Figure 4.3(b), it would no longer be connected.

In an undirected graph, as in a directed graph, a path from a vertex to itself is called a **cycle,** and a graph with no cycles is called *acyclic.* The graphs in

Figure 4.3(c) and (d) are acyclic, whereas the ones in Figure 4.3(a) and (b) are not. A **tree,** as it is defined here, is an acyclic, connected, undirected graph. Equivalently, a tree can be defined as an undirected graph in which there is exactly one path between every pair of vertices. The graphs in Figure 4.3(c) and (d) are trees. With this definition, no vertex is singled out as the root, and a ***rooted tree*** is defined as a tree with one vertex designated as the root. Therefore, a rooted tree is what is often called a tree (as was done in Section 3.5).

Consider the problem of removing edges from a connected, weighted, undirected graph G to form a subgraph such that all the vertices remain connected and the sum of the weights on the remaining edges is as small as possible. Such a problem has numerous applications. As mentioned earlier, in road construction we may want to connect a set of cities with a minimum amount of road. Similarly, in telecommunications we may want to use a minimal length of cable, and in plumbing we may want to use a minimal amount of pipe. A subgraph with minimum weight must be a tree, because if a subgraph were not a tree, it would contain a cycle, and we could remove any edge on the cycle, resulting in a connected graph with a smaller weight. To illustrate this, look at Figure 4.3. The subgraph in Figure 4.3(b) of the graph in Figure 4.3(a) cannot have minimum weight because if we remove any edge on the cycle $[v_3, v_4, v_5, v_3]$, the subgraph remains connected. For example, we could remove the edge connecting v_4 and v_5, resulting in a connected graph with a smaller weight.

A *spanning tree* for G is a connected subgraph that contains all the vertices in G and is a tree. The trees in Figure 4.3(c) and (d) are spanning trees for G. A connected subgraph of minimum weight must be a spanning tree, but not every spanning tree has minimum weight. For example, the spanning tree in Figure 4.3(c) does not have minimum weight, because the spanning tree in Figure 4.3(d) has a lesser weight. An algorithm for our problem must obtain a spanning tree of minimum weight. Such a tree is called a ***minimum spanning tree.*** The tree in Figure 4.3(d) is a minimum spanning tree for G. A graph can have more than one minimum spanning tree. There is another one for G, which you may wish to find.

To find a minimum spanning tree by the brute-force method of considering all spanning trees is worse than exponential in the worst case. We will solve the problem more efficiently using the greedy approach. First we need the formal definition of an undirected graph.

Definition

An ***undirected graph*** G consists of a finite set V whose members are called the vertices of G, together with a set E of pairs of vertices in V. These pairs are called the edges of G. We denote G by

$$G = (V, E).$$

We will denote members of V by v_i and the edge between v_i and v_j by

$$(v_i, v_j).$$

Example 4.1   For the graph in Figure 4.3(a),

$$V = \{v_1, v_2, v_3, v_4, v_5\}$$
$$E = \{(v_1, v_2), (v_1, v_3), (v_2, v_3), (v_2, v_4), (v_3, v_4),$$
$$(v_3, v_5), (v_4, v_5)\}$$

The order in which we list the vertices to denote an edge is irrelevant in an undirected graph. For example, (v_1, v_2) denotes the same edge as (v_2, v_1). We have listed the vertex with the lower index first.

A spanning tree T for G has the same vertices V as G, but the set of edges of T is a subset F of E. We will denote a spanning tree by $T = (V, F)$. Our problem is to find a subset F of E such that $T = (V, F)$ is a minimum spanning tree for G. A high-level greedy algorithm for the problem could proceed as follows:

```
F = ∅;                                         // Initialize set of
                                               // edges to empty.
while (the instance is not solved) {

    select an edge according to some locally   // selection procedure
    optimal consideration;

    if (adding the edge to F does not create a cycle)  // feasibility check
        add it;

    if (T = (V,F) is a spanning tree)          // solution check
        the instance is solved;
}
```

This algorithm simply says ''select an edge according to some locally optimal consideration.'' There is no unique locally optimal property for a given problem. We will investigate two different greedy algorithms for this problem, Prim's Algorithm and Kruskal's Algorithm. Each uses a different locally optimal property. Recall that there is no guarantee that a given greedy algorithm always yields an optimal solution. It is necessary to prove whether or not this is the case. We will prove that both Prim's and Kruskal's Algorithms always produce minimum spanning trees.

4.1.1 Prim's Algorithm

Prim's Algorithm starts with an empty subset of edges F and a subset of vertices Y initialized to contain an arbitrary vertex. We will initialize Y to $\{v_1\}$. A vertex

Figure 4.4 A weighted graph (in upper left corner) and the steps in Prim's Algorithm for that graph. The vertices in *Y* and the edges in *F* are shaded at each step.

Determine a minimum spanning tree.

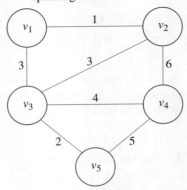

1. Vertex v_1 is selected first.

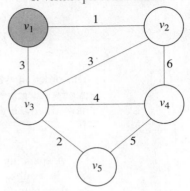

2. Vertex v_2 is selected because it is nearest to $\{v_1\}$.

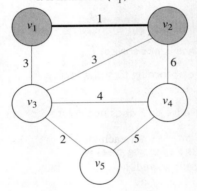

3. Vertex v_3 is selected because it is nearest to $\{v_1, v_2\}$.

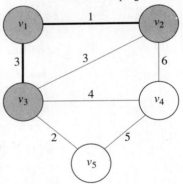

4. Vertex v_5 is selected because it is nearest to $\{v_1, v_2, v_3\}$.

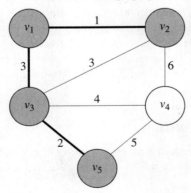

5. Vertex v_4 is selected.

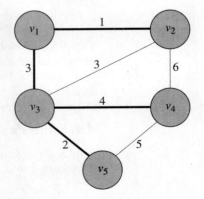

nearest to Y is a vertex in $V - Y$ that is connected to a vertex in Y by an edge of minimum weight. (Recall from Chapter 3 that weight and distance terminology are used interchangeably for weighted graphs.) In Figure 4.3(a), v_2 is nearest to Y when $Y = \{v_1\}$. The vertex that is nearest to Y is added to Y and the edge is added to F. Ties are broken arbitrarily. In this case, v_2 is added to Y, and (v_1, v_2) is added to F. This process of adding nearest vertices is repeated until $Y = V$. The following is a high-level algorithm for this procedure:

```
F = ∅;                          // Initialize set of edges to empty.

Y = {v₁};                       // Initialize set of vertices to
                                // contain only the first one.

while (the instance is not solved) {

    select a vertex in V − Y that is    // selection procedure and
    nearest to Y;                       // feasibility check

    add the vertex to Y;
    add the edge to F;

    if (Y ==V)                  // solution check
        the instance is solved;
}
```

The selection procedure and feasibility check are done together because taking the new vertex from $V - Y$ guarantees that a cycle is not created. Figure 4.4 illustrates Prim's Algorithm. At each step in that figure, Y contains the shaded vertices and F contains the shaded edges.

The high-level algorithm works fine for a human creating a minimum spanning tree for a small graph from a picture of the graph. The human merely finds the vertex nearest to Y by inspection. However, for the purposes of writing an algorithm that can be implemented in a computer language, we need to describe a step-by-step procedure. To this end, we represent a weighted graph by its adjacency matrix. That is, we represent it by an $n \times n$ array W of numbers where

$$W[i][j] = \begin{cases} \text{weight on edge} & \text{if there is an edge between } v_i \text{ and } v_j \\ \infty & \text{if there is no edge between } v_i \text{ and } v_j \\ 0 & \text{if } i = j \end{cases}$$

The graph in Figure 4.3(a) is represented in this manner in Figure 4.5. We maintain two arrays, *nearest* and *distance*, where, for $i = 2, \ldots, n$,

$$nearest[i] = \text{index of the vertex in } Y \text{ nearest to } v_i$$
$$distance[i] = \text{weight on edge between } v_i \text{ and the vertex indexed by } nearest[i]$$

Figure 4.5 The array representation W of the graph in Figure 4.3(a).

	1	2	3	4	5
1	0	1	3	∞	∞
2	1	0	3	6	∞
3	3	3	0	4	2
4	∞	6	4	0	5
5	∞	∞	2	5	0

Because at the start $Y = \{v_1\}$, *nearest*[i] is initialized to 1 and *distance*[i] is initialized to the weight on the edge between v_1 and v_i. As vertices are added to *Y*, these two arrays are updated to reference the new vertex in *Y* nearest to each vertex outside of *Y*. To determine which vertex to add to *Y*, in each iteration we compute the index for which *distance*[i] is the smallest. We call this index *vnear*. The vertex indexed by *vnear* is added to *Y* by setting *distance*[vnear] to -1. The following algorithm implements this procedure.

Algorithm 4.1

Prim's Algorithm

Problem: Determine a minimum spanning tree.

Inputs: integer $n \geq 2$, and a connected, weighted, undirected graph containing *n* vertices. The graph is represented by a two-dimensional array *W*, which has both its rows and columns indexed from 1 to *n*, where *W*[i][j] is the weight on the edge between the *i*th vertex and the *j*th vertex.

Outputs: set of edges *F* in a minimum spanning tree for the graph.

```
void prim (int n,
           const number W[ ][ ],
           set_of_edges& F)
{
   index i, vnear;
   number min;
   edge e;
   index nearest[2..n];
   number distance[2..n];

   F = ∅;
   for (i = 2; i <= n; i++) {          // For all vertices, initialize vₗ
      nearest[i] = 1;                  // to be the nearest vertex in
      distance[i] = W[1][i];           // Y and initialize the distance
   }                                   // from Y to be the weight
                                       // on the edge to vₗ.
```

```
repeat (n - 1 times) {                          // Add all n - 1 vertices to Y.
    min = ∞;
    for (i = 2; i <= n; i++)                     // Check each vertex for
        if (0 ≤ distance[i] < min) {             // being nearest to Y.
            min = distance[i];
            vnear = i;
        }
    e = edge connecting vertices indexed
            by vnear and nearest[vnear];
    add e to F;
    distance[vnear] = -1;                        // Add vertex indexed by
    for (i = 2; i <= n; i++)                      // vnear to Y.
        if (W[i][vnear] < distance[i]) {         // For each vertex not in Y,
            distance[i] = W[i][vnear];           // update its distance from Y.
            nearest[i] = vnear;
        }
    }
}
```

Every-Case Time Complexity Analysis of Algorithm 4.1 (Prim's Algorithm)

Basic operation: There are two loops, each with $n - 1$ iterations, inside the **repeat** loop. Executing the instructions inside each of them can be considered to be doing the basic operation once.

Input size: n, the number of vertices.

Because the **repeat** loop has $n - 1$ iterations, the time complexity is given by

$$T(n) = 2(n - 1)(n - 1) \in \Theta(n^2)$$

Clearly, Prim's Algorithm produces a spanning tree. However, is it necessarily minimal? Because at each step we select the vertex nearest to Y, intuitively it seems that the tree should be minimal. However, we need to prove whether or not this is the case. Although greedy algorithms are often easier to develop than dynamic programming algorithms, usually it is more difficult to determine whether or not a greedy algorithm always produces an optimal solution. Recall that for a dynamic programming algorithm we need only show that the principle of optimality applies. For a greedy algorithm we usually need a formal proof. Next we give such a proof for Prim's Algorithm.

Let an undirected graph $G = (V, E)$ be given. A subset F of E is called **promising** if edges can be added to it so as to form a minimum spanning tree. The subset $\{(v_1, v_2), (v_1, v_3)\}$ in Figure 4.3(a) is promising, and the subset $\{(v_2, v_4)\}$ is not promising.

Lemma 4.1 Let $G = (V, E)$ be a connected, weighted, undirected graph, let F be a promising subset of E, and let Y be the set of vertices connected by the edges in F. If e is an edge of minimum weight that connects a vertex in Y to a vertex in $V - Y$, then $F \cup \{e\}$ is promising.

Proof: Because F is promising, there must be some set of edges F' such that

$$F \subseteq F'$$

and (V, F') is a minimum spanning tree. If $e \in F'$, then

$$F \cup \{e\} \subseteq F',$$

which means $F \cup \{e\}$ is promising and we're done. Otherwise, because (V, F') is a spanning tree, $F' \cup \{e\}$ must contain exactly one cycle and e must be in the cycle. Figure 4.6 illustrates this. The cycle is $[v_1, v_2, v_4, v_3]$. As can be seen in Figure 4.6, there must be another edge $e' \in F'$ in the cycle that also connects a vertex in Y to one in $V - Y$. If we remove e' from $F' \cup \{e\}$, the cycle disappears, which means that we have a spanning tree. Because e is an edge of minimum weight that connects a vertex in Y to one in $V - Y$, the weight of e must be less than or equal to the weight of e' (in fact, they must be equal). So

$$F' \cup \{e\} - \{e'\}$$

is a minimum spanning tree. Now

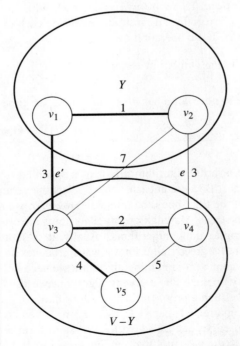

Figure 4.6 A graph illustrating the proof in Lemma 4.1. The edges in F' are shaded.

$$F \cup \{e\} \subseteq F' \cup \{e\} - \{e'\},$$

because e' cannot be in F (recall that edges in F connect only vertices in Y). Therefore, $F \cup \{e\}$ is promising, which completes the proof.

Theorem 4.1 Prim's Algorithm always produces a minimum spanning tree.

Proof: We use induction to show that the set F is promising after each iteration of the **repeat** loop.

Induction base: Clearly the empty set $\emptyset$ is promising.

Induction hypothesis: Assume that, after a given iteration of the **repeat** loop, the set of edges so far selected—namely, F—is promising.

Induction step: We need to show that the set $F \cup \{e\}$ is promising, where e is the edge selected in the next iteration. Because the edge e selected in the next iteration is an edge of minimum weight that connects a vertex in Y to one in $V - Y$, $F \cup \{e\}$ is promising, by Lemma 4.1. This completes the induction proof.

By the induction proof, the final set of edges is promising. Because this set consists of the edges in a spanning tree, that tree must be a minimum spanning tree.

4.1.2 Kruskal's Algorithm

Kruskal's Algorithm for the Minimum Spanning Tree Problem starts by creating disjoint subsets of V, one for each vertex and containing only that vertex. It then inspects the edges according to nondecreasing weight (ties are broken arbitrarily). If an edge connects two vertices in disjoint subsets, the edge is added and the subsets are merged into one set. This process is repeated until all the subsets are merged into one set. The following is a high-level algorithm for this procedure.

```
F = ∅;                                        // Initialize set of
                                              // edges to empty.

create disjoint subsets of V, one for each
vertex and containing only that vertex;

sort the edges in E in nondecreasing order;

while (the instance is not solved) {

   select next edge;                          // selection procedure

   if (the edge connects two vertices in      // feasiblity check
                  disjoint subsets) {
      merge the subsets;
      add the edge to F;
   }

   if (all the subsets are merged)            // solution check
      the instance is solved;

}
```

Figure 4.7 A weighted graph (in upper left corner) and the steps in Kruskal's Algorithm for that graph.

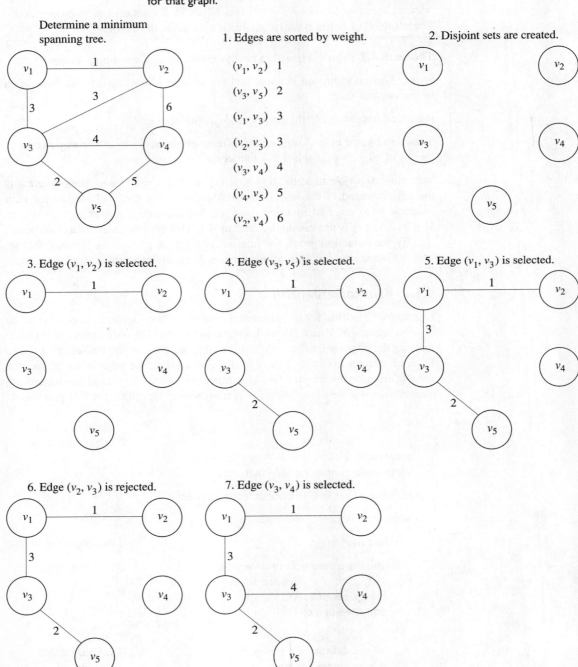

Determine a minimum spanning tree.

1. Edges are sorted by weight.

(v_1, v_2) 1

(v_3, v_5) 2

(v_1, v_3) 3

(v_2, v_3) 3

(v_3, v_4) 4

(v_4, v_5) 5

(v_2, v_4) 6

2. Disjoint sets are created.

3. Edge (v_1, v_2) is selected.

4. Edge (v_3, v_5) is selected.

5. Edge (v_1, v_3) is selected.

6. Edge (v_2, v_3) is rejected.

7. Edge (v_3, v_4) is selected.

Figure 4.7 illustrates Kruskal's Algorithm.

To write a formal version of Kruskal's Algorithm, we need a disjoint set abstract data type. Such a data type is implemented in Appendix C. Because that implementation is for disjoint subsets of indices, we need only refer to the vertices by index to use the implementation. The disjoint set abstract data type consists of data types **index** and **set_pointer**, and routines *initial, find, merge,* and *equal,* such that if we declare

> **index** *i*;
> **set_pointer** *p, q*;

then

- *initial(n)* initializes *n* disjoint subsets, each of which contains exactly one of the indices between 1 and *n*.
- *p = find(i)* makes *p* point to the set containing index *i;*
- *merge(p,q)* merges the two sets, to which *p* and *q* point, into the set.
- *equal(p,q)* returns true if *p* and *q* both point to the same set.

The algorithm follows.

Algorithm 4.2 Kruskal's Algorithm

Problem Determine a minimum spanning tree.

Inputs: integer $n \geq 2$, positive integer *m,* and a connected, weighted, undirected graph containing *n* vertices and *m* edges. The graph is represented by a set *E* that contains the edges in the graph along with their weights.

Outputs: *F,* a set of edges in a minimum spanning tree.

```
void kruskal (int n, int m,
              set_of_edges E,
              set_of_edges& F)
{
   index i, j;
   set_pointer p, q;
   edge e;
```

```
Sort the m edges in E by weight in nondecreasing order;
F = ∅;
initial(n);                                    // Initialize n disjoint subsets.
while (number of edges in F is less than n − 1) {
    e = edge with least weight not yet considered;
    i, j = indices of vertices connected by e;
    p = find(i);
    q = find(j);
    if (! equal(p, q)) {
        merge(p, q);
        add e to F;
    }
}
}
```

The **while** loop is exited when there are $n - 1$ edges in F, because there are $n - 1$ edges in a spanning tree.

Worst-Case Time-Complexity Analysis of Algorithm 4.2 (Kruskal's Algorithm)

Basic operation: a comparison instruction.

Input size: n, the number of vertices, and m, the number of edges.

There are three considerations in this algorithm:

1. The time to sort the edges. We obtained a sorting algorithm in Chapter 2 (Mergesort) that is worst-case $\Theta(m \lg m)$. In Chapter 7 we will show, for algorithms that sort by comparison of keys, that it is not possible to improve on this performance. Therefore, the time complexity for sorting the edges is given by

$$W(m) \in \Theta(m \lg m).$$

2. The time in the **while** loop. The time it takes to manipulate the disjoint sets is dominant in this loop (because everything else is constant). In the worst case, every edge is considered before the **while** loop is exited, which means there are m passes through the loop. Using the implementation called Disjoint Set Data Structure II in Appendix C, the time complexity for m passes through a loop that contains a constant number of calls to routines *find*, *equal*, and *merge* is given by

$$W(m) \in \Theta(m \lg m),$$

where the basic operation is a comparison instruction.

3. The time to initialize n disjoint sets. Using the disjoint set data structure implementation mentioned previously, the time complexity for the initialization is given by

$$T(n) \in \Theta(n).$$

Because $m \geq n - 1$, the sorting and the manipulations of the disjoint sets dominate the initialization time, which means that

$$W(m, n) \in \Theta(m \lg m).$$

It may appear that the worst case has no dependence on n. However, in the worst case every vertex can be connected to every other vertex, which would mean that

$$m = \frac{n(n - 1)}{2} \in \Theta(n^2).$$

Therefore, we can also write the worst case as follows:

$$W(m, n) \in \Theta(n^2 \lg n^2) = \Theta(n^2 2 \lg n) = \Theta(n^2 \lg n).$$

It is useful to use both expressions for the worst case when comparing Kruskal's Algorithm with Prim's Algorithm.

We need the following lemma to prove that Kruskal's Algorithm always produces an optimal solution.

Lemma 4.2 Let $G = (V, E)$ be a connected, weighted, undirected graph, let F be a promising subset of E, and let e be an edge of minimum weight in $E - F$ such that $F \cup \{e\}$ has no cycles. Then $F \cup \{e\}$ is promising.

Proof: The proof is similar to the proof of Lemma 4.1. Because F is promising, there must be some set of edges F' such that

$$F \subseteq F'$$

and (V, F') is a minimum spanning tree. If $e \in F'$, then

$$F \cup \{e\} \subseteq F',$$

which means that $F \cup \{e\}$ is promising and we're done. Otherwise, because (V, F') is a spanning tree, $F' \cup \{e\}$ must contain exactly one cycle and e must be in the cycle. Because $F \cup \{e\}$ contains no cycles, there must be some edge $e' \in F'$ that is in the cycle and that is not in F. That is, $e' \in E - F$. The set $F \cup \{e'\}$ has no cycles because it is a subset of F'. Therefore, the weight of e is no greater than the weight of e'. (Recall that we assumed e is an edge of minimum weight in $E - F$ such that $F \cup \{e\}$ has no cycles.) If we remove e' from $F' \cup \{e\}$, the cycle in this set disappears, which means we have a spanning tree. Indeed

$$F' \cup \{e\} - \{e'\}$$

is a minimum spanning tree because, as we have shown, the weight of e is no greater than the weight of e'. Because e' is not in F,

$$F \cup \{e\} \subseteq F' \cup \{e\} - \{e'\}.$$

Therefore, $F \cup \{e\}$ is promising, which completes the proof.

Theorem 4.2 Kruskal's Algorithm always produces a minimum spanning tree.

Proof: The proof is by induction, starting with the empty set of edges. You are asked to apply Lemma 4.2 to complete the proof in the exercises.

4.1.3 Comparing Prim's Algorithm with Kruskal's Algorithm

We obtained the following time complexities:

Prim's Algorithm: $T(n) \in \Theta(n^2)$

Kruskal's Algorithm: $W(m, n) \in \Theta(m \lg m)$ and $W(m, n) \in \Theta(n^2 \lg n)$

We also showed that in a connected graph

$$n - 1 \leq m \leq \frac{n(n - 1)}{2}.$$

For a graph whose number of edges m is near the low end of these limits (the graph is very sparse), Kruskal's Algorithm is $\Theta(n \lg n)$, which means that Kruskal's Algorithm should be faster. However, for a graph whose number of edges is near the high end (the graph is highly connected), Kruskal's Algorithm is $\Theta(n^2 \lg n)$, which means that Prim's Algorithm should be faster.

4.1.4 Final Discussion

As mentioned before, the time complexity of an algorithm sometimes depends on the data structure used to implement it. Using heaps, Johnson (1977) created a $\Theta(m \lg n)$ implementation of Prim's Algorithm. For a sparse graph, this is $\Theta(n \lg n)$, which is an improvement over our implementation. But for a dense graph it is $\Theta(n^2 \lg n)$, which is slower than our implementation. Using the Fibonacci Heap, Fredman and Tarjan (1987) developed the fastest implementation of Prim's Algorithm. Their implementation is $\Theta(m + n \lg n)$. For a sparse graph, this is $\Theta(n \lg n)$, and for a dense graph it is $\Theta(n^2)$.

Prim's Algorithm originally appeared in Jarník (1930) and was published by its namesake in Prim (1957). Kruskal's Algorithm is from Kruskal (1956). The history of the Minimum Spanning Tree Problem is discussed in Graham and Hell (1985). Other algorithms for the problem can be found in Yao (1975) and Tarjan (1983).

4.2 DIJKSTRA'S ALGORITHM FOR SINGLE-SOURCE SHORTEST PATHS

In Section 3.2, we developed a $\Theta(n^3)$ algorithm for determining the shortest paths from each vertex to all other vertices in a weighted, directed graph. If we wanted to know only the shortest paths from one particular vertex to all the others, that algorithm would be overkill. Next we will use the greedy approach to develop a $\Theta(n^2)$ algorithm for this problem (called the Single-Source Shortest Paths Problem). This algorithm is due to Dijkstra (1959). We present the algorithm, assuming that there is a path from the vertex of interest to each of the other vertices. It is a simple modification to handle the case where this is not so.

This algorithm is similar to Prim's Algorithm for the Minimum Spanning Tree Problem. We initialize a set Y to contain only the vertex whose shortest paths are to be determined. For focus, we say that the vertex is v_1. We initialize a set F of edges to being empty. First we choose a vertex v that is nearest to v_1, add it to Y, and add the edge $<v_1, v>$ to F. (By $<v_1, v>$ we mean the directed edge from v_1 to v.) That edge is clearly a shortest path from v_1 to v. Next we check the paths from v_1 to the vertices in $V - Y$ that allow only vertices in Y as intermediate vertices. A shortest of these paths is a shortest path (this needs to be proven). The vertex at the end of such a path is added to Y, and the edge (on the path) that touches that vertex is added to F. This procedure is continued until Y equals V, the set of all vertices. At this point, F contains the edges in shortest paths. The following is a high-level algorithm for this approach.

```
Y = {v₁};

F = ∅;

while (the instance is not solved) {

    select a vertex v from V − Y, that has a      // selection procedure
    shortest path from v₁, using only vertices    // and feasibility check
    in Y as intermediates;

    add the new vertex v to Y;
    add the edge (on the shortest path) that touches v to F;

    if (Y == V)
        the instance is solved;                   // solution check
}
```

Figure 4.8 illustrates Dijkstra's Algorithm. As was the case for Prim's Algorithm, the high-level algorithm works only for a human solving an instance by inspection on a small graph. Next we give a detailed algorithm. For this algorithm, the weighted graph is represented by a two-dimensional array exactly as was done in Section 3.2. This algorithm is very similar to Algorithm 4.1 (Prim). The dif-

Figure 4.8 A weighted, directed graph (in upper left corner) and the steps in Dijkstra's Algorithm for that graph. The vertices in Y and the edges in F are shaded at each step.

Compute shortest paths from v_1.

1. Vertex v_5 is selected because it is nearest to v_1.

2. Vertex v_4 is selected because it has the shortest path from v_1 using only vertices in $\{v_5\}$ as intermediates.

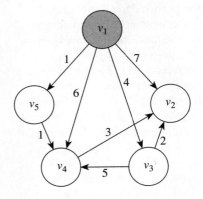 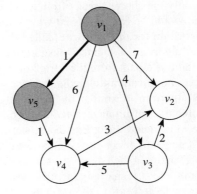 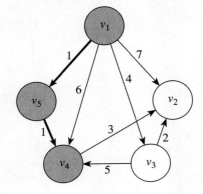

3. Vertex v_3 is selected because it has the shortest path from v_1 using only vertices in $\{v_4, v_5\}$ as intermediates.

4. The shortest path from v_1 to v_2 is $[v_1, v_5, v_4, v_2]$.

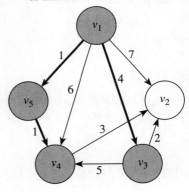 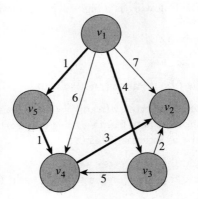

ference is that instead of the arrays *nearest* and *distance,* we have arrays *touch* and *length,* where for i = 2, . . . , n,

touch[i] = index of vertex v in Y such that the edge $<v, v_i>$ is the last edge on the current shortest path from v_1 to v_i using only vertices in Y as intermediates.

length[i] = length of the current shortest path from v_1 to v_i using only vertices in Y as intermediates.

The algorithm follows.

Algorithm 4.3

Dijkstra's Algorithm

Problem: Determine the shortest paths from v_1 to all other vertices in a weighted, directed graph.

Inputs: integer $n \geq 2$, and a connected, weighted, directed graph containing n vertices. The graph is represented by a two-dimensional array W, which has both its rows and columns indexed from 1 to n, where $W[i][j]$ is the weight on the edge from the ith vertex to the jth vertex.

Outputs: set of edges F containing edges in shortest paths.

```
void dijkstra (int n,
               const number W[ ][ ],
               set_of_edges& F)
{
   index i, vnear;
   edge e;
   index touch[2..n];
   number length[2..n];

   F = ∅;
   for (i = 2; i <= n; i++) {          // For all vertices, initialize v₁
      touch[i] = 1;                    // to be the last vertex on the
      length[i] = W[1][i];             // current shortest path from
   }                                   // v₁, and initialize length of
                                       // that path to be the weight
                                       // on the edge from v₁.

   repeat (n − 1 times) {              // Add all n − 1 vertices to Y.
      min = ∞;
      for (i = 2; i <= n; i++)         // Check each vertex for
         if (0 ≤ length[i] < min) {    // having shortest path.
            min = length[i];
            vnear = i;
         }
      e = edge from vertex indexed by touch[vnear]
          to vertex indexed by vnear;
      add e to F;
      for (i = 2; i <= n; i++)
         if (length[vnear] + W[vnear][i] < length[i]) {
            length[i] = length[vnear] + W[vnear][i];
            touch[i] = vnear;          // For each vertex not in Y,
         }                             // update its shortest path.
      length[vnear] = −1;              // Add vertex indexed by vnear
   }                                   // to Y.
}
```

Because we are assuming that there is a path from v_1 to every other vertex, the variable *vnear* has a new value in each iteration of the **repeat** loop. If this were not the case, the algorithm, as written, would end up adding the last edge over and over until $n - 1$ iterations of the **repeat** loop were completed.

Algorithm 4.3 determines only the edges in the shortest paths. It does not produce the lengths of those paths. These lengths could be obtained from the edges. Alternatively, a simple modification of the algorithm would enable it to compute the lengths and store them in an array as well.

The control in Algorithm 4.3 is identical to that in Algorithm 4.1. Therefore, from the analysis of that Algorithm 4.1, we know for Algorithm 4.3 that

$$T(n) = 2(n - 1)^2 \in \Theta(n^2).$$

Although we do not do it here, it is possible to prove that Algorithm 4.3 always produces shortest paths. The proof uses an induction argument similar to the one used to prove that Prim's Algorithm (Algorithm 4.1) always produces a minimum spanning tree.

As is the case for Prim's Algorithm, Dijkstra's Algorithm can be implemented using a heap or a Fibonacci Heap. The heap implementation is $\Theta(m \lg n)$, and the Fibonacci Heap implementation is $\Theta(m + n \lg n)$, where m is the number of edges. See Fredman and Tarjan (1987) for this latter implementation.

4.3   SCHEDULING

Suppose a hair stylist has several customers waiting for different treatments (e.g., simple cut, cut with shampoo, permanent, hair coloring). The treatments don't all take the same amount of time, but the stylist knows how long each takes. A reasonable goal would be to schedule the customers in such a way as to minimize the total time they spend both waiting and being served (getting treated). Such a schedule is considered optimal. The time spent both waiting and being served is called the *time in the system.* The problem of minimizing the total time in the system has many applications. For example, we may want to schedule users' access to a disk drive to minimize the total time they spend waiting and being served.

Another scheduling problem is when each job (customer) takes the same amount of time to complete, but has a deadline by which it must start to yield a profit associated with the job. The goal is to schedule the jobs to maximize the total profit. We will consider *scheduling with deadlines* after discussing the simpler scheduling problem of minimizing the total time in the system.

4.3.1 Minimizing Total Time in the System

A simple solution to minimizing the total time in the system is to consider all possible schedules and take the minimum. This is illustrated in the following example.

Example 4.2   Suppose there are three jobs and the service times for these jobs are

$$t_1 = 5, \qquad t_2 = 10, \qquad \text{and} \qquad t_3 = 4.$$

The actual time units are not relevant to the problem. If we schedule them in the order 1, 2, 3, the times spent in the system for the three jobs are as follows:

Job	Time in the System
1	5 (service time)
2	5 (wait for job 1) + 10 (service time)
3	5 (wait for job 1) + 10 (wait for job 2) + 4 (service time)

The total time in the system for this schedule is

$$\underbrace{5}_{\substack{\text{Time for}\\\text{job 1}}} + \underbrace{(5 + 10)}_{\substack{\text{Time for}\\\text{job 2}}} + \underbrace{(5 + 10 + 4)}_{\substack{\text{Time for}\\\text{job 3}}} = 39.$$

This same method of computation yields the following list of all possible schedules and total times in the system:

Schedule	Total Time in the System
[1, 2, 3]	5 + (5 + 10) + (5 + 10 + 4) = 39
[1, 3, 2]	5 + (5 + 4) + (5 + 4 + 10) = 33
[2, 1, 3]	10 + (10 + 5) + (10 + 5 + 4) = 44
[2, 3, 1]	10 + (10 + 4) + (10 + 4 + 5) = 43
[3, 1, 2]	4 + (4 + 5) + (4 + 5 + 10) = 32
[3, 2, 1]	4 + (4 + 10) + (4 + 10 + 5) = 37

Schedule [3, 1, 2] is optimal with a total time of 32.

Clearly, an algorithm that considers all possible schedules is factorial-time. Notice in the previous example that an optimal schedule occurs when the job with the smallest service time (job 3, with a service time of 4) is scheduled first, followed by the job with the second-smallest service time (job 1, with a service time of 5), followed finally by the job with the largest service time (job 2, with a service time of 10). Intuitively, it seems that such a schedule would be optimal because it gets the shortest jobs out of the way first. A high-level greedy algorithm for this approach is as follows:

```
sort the jobs by service time in nondecreasing order;

while (the instance is not solved) {

    schedule the next job;                    // selection procedure and
                                              // feasibility check

    if (there are no more jobs)               // solution check
        the instance is solved;
}
```

We wrote this algorithm in the general form of the greedy approach to show that it is indeed a greedy algorithm. However, clearly all the algorithm does is sort the jobs according to service time. Its time complexity is therefore given by

$$W(n) \in \Theta(n \lg n).$$

Although intuitively it seems that the schedule created by this algorithm is optimal, this needs to be proved. The following theorem proves the stronger result that this schedule is the only optimal one.

Theorem 4.3 The only schedule that minimizes the total time in the system is one that schedules jobs in nondecreasing order by service time.

Proof: For $1 \leq i \leq n - 1$, let t_i be the service time for the ith job scheduled in some particular optimal schedule (one that minimizes the total time in the system). We need to show that the schedule has the jobs scheduled in nondecreasing order by service time. We show this using proof by contradiction. If they are not scheduled in nondecreasing order, then for at least one i where $1 \leq i \leq n - 1$,

$$t_i > t_{i+1}.$$

We can rearrange our original schedule by interchanging the ith and $(i + 1)$st jobs. By doing this, we have taken t_i units off the time the $(i + 1)$st job (in the original schedule) spends in the system. The reason is that it no longer waits while the ith job (in the original schedule) is being served. Similarly, we have added t_{i+1} units to the time the ith job (in the original schedule) spends in the system. Clearly, we have not changed the time that any other job spends in the system. Therefore, if T is the total time in the system in our original schedule and T' is the total time in the rearranged schedule,

$$T' = T + t_{i+1} - t_i.$$

Because $t_i > t_{i+1}$,

$$T' < T,$$

which contradicts the optimality of our original schedule.

It is straightforward to generalize our algorithm to handle the Multiple-Server Scheduling Problem. Suppose there are m servers. Order those servers in an arbitrary manner. Order the jobs again by service time in nondecreasing order. Let the first server serve the first job, the second server the second job, . . . , and the mth server the mth job. The first server will finish first because that server serves the job with the shortest service time. Therefore, the first server serves the $(m + 1)$st job. Similarly, the second server serves the $(m + 2)$nd job, and so on. The scheme is as follows:

Server 1 serves jobs 1, $(1 + m)$, $(1 + 2m)$, $(1 + 3m)$, . . .
Server 2 serves jobs 2, $(2 + m)$, $(2 + 2m)$, $(2 + 3m)$, . . .
$$\vdots$$
Server i serves jobs i, $(i + m)$, $(i + 2m)$, $(i + 3m)$, . . .
$$\vdots$$
Server m serves jobs m, $(m + m)$, $(m + 2m)$, $(m + 3m)$, ...

Clearly, the jobs end up being processed in the following order:

$$1, 2, \ldots, m, 1 + m, 2 + m, \ldots, m + m, 1 + 2m, \ldots.$$

That is, the jobs are processed in nondecreasing order by service time.

4.3.2 Scheduling with Deadlines

In this scheduling problem, each job takes one unit of time to finish and has a deadline and a profit. If the job starts before or at its deadline, the profit is obtained. The goal is to schedule the jobs so as to maximize the total profit. Not all jobs have to be scheduled. We need not consider any schedule that has a job scheduled after its deadline because that schedule has the same profit as one that doesn't schedule the job at all. We call such a schedule impossible. The following example illustrates this problem.

Example 4.3 Suppose we have the following jobs, deadlines, and profits:

Job	Deadline	Profit
1	2	30
2	1	35
3	2	25
4	1	40

When we say that job 1 has a deadline of 2, we mean that job 1 can start at time 1 or time 2. There is no time 0. Because job 2 has a deadline of 1, that job can start only at time 1. The possible schedules and total profits are as follows:

Schedule	Total profit
[1, 3]	30 + 25 = 55
[2, 1]	35 + 30 = 65
[2, 3]	35 + 25 = 60
[3, 1]	25 + 30 = 55
[4, 1]	40 + 30 = 70
[4, 3]	40 + 25 = 65

Impossible schedules have not been listed. For example, schedule [1, 2] is not possible, and is therefore not listed, because job 1 would start first at time 1, take one unit of time to finish, causing job 2 to start at time 2. However, the deadline for job 2 is time 1. Schedule [1, 3], for example, is possible because job 1 is started before its deadline, and job 3 is started at its deadline. We see that schedule [4, 1] is optimal with a total profit of 70.

To consider all schedules, as is done in Example 4.3, takes factorial time. Notice in the example that the job with the greatest profit (job 4) is included in the optimal schedule, but the job with the second-greatest profit (job 2) is not. Because both jobs have deadlines equal to 1, both cannot be scheduled. Of course, the one with the greatest profit is the one scheduled. The other job scheduled is job 1, because its profit is bigger than that of job 3. This suggests that a reasonable greedy approach to solving the problem would be to first sort the jobs in nonincreasing order by profit. Next inspect each job in sequence and add it to the schedule if it is possible. Before we can create even a high-level algorithm for this approach, we need some definitions. A sequence is called a *feasible sequence* if all the jobs in the sequence start by their deadlines. For example, [4, 1] is a feasible sequence in Example 4.3, but [1, 4] is not a feasible sequence. A set of jobs is called a *feasible set* if there exists at least one feasible sequence for the jobs in the set. In Example 4.3, {1, 4} is a feasible set because the scheduling sequence [4, 1] is feasible, whereas {2, 4} is not a feasible set because no scheduling sequence allows both jobs to start by their deadlines. Our goal is to find a feasible sequence with maximum total profit. We call such a sequence an *optimal sequence* and the set of jobs in the sequence an *optimal set of jobs.* We can now present a high-level greedy algorithm for the Scheduling with Deadlines Problem.

```
sort the jobs in nonincreasing order by profit;

S = ∅;

while (the instance is not solved) {
    select next job;                              //selection procedure
    if (S is feasible with this job added)        //feasbility check
        add this job to S;
```

```
        if (there are no more jobs)                    // solution check
            the instance is solved;
    }
```

The following example illustrates this algorithm.

Example 4.4   Suppose we have the following jobs, deadlines, and profits:

Job	Deadline	Profit
1	3	40
2	1	35
3	1	30
4	3	25
5	1	20
6	3	15
7	2	10

We have already sorted the jobs before labeling them. The previous greedy algorithm does the following:

1. S is set to $\varnothing$.
2. S is set to $\{1\}$ because the sequence $[1]$ is feasible.
3. S is set to $\{1, 2\}$ because the sequence $[2, 1]$ is feasible.
4. $\{1, 2, 3\}$ is rejected because there is no feasible sequence for this set.
5. S is set to $\{1, 2, 4\}$ because the sequence $[2, 1, 4]$ is feasible.
6. $\{1, 2, 4, 5\}$ is rejected because there is no feasible sequence for this set.
7. $\{1, 2, 4, 6\}$ is rejected because there is no feasible sequence for this set.
8. $\{1, 2, 4, 7\}$ is rejected because there is no feasible sequence for this set.

The final value of S is $\{1, 2, 4\}$, and a feasible sequence for this set is $[2, 1, 4]$. Because jobs 1 and 4 both have deadlines of 3, we could use the feasible sequence $[2, 4, 1]$ instead.

Before proving that this algorithm always produces an optimal sequence, let's write a formal version of it. To do this, we need an efficient way to determine whether a set is feasible. To consider all possible sequences is not acceptable because it would take factorial time to do this. The following lemma enables us to check efficiently whether or not a set is feasible.

Lemma 4.3 Let S be a set of jobs. Then S is feasible if and only if the sequence obtained by ordering the jobs in S according to nondecreasing deadlines is feasible.

Proof: Suppose S is feasible. Then there exists at least one feasible sequence for the jobs in S. In this sequence, suppose that job x is scheduled before job y, and job y has a smaller (earlier) deadline than job x. If we interchange these two jobs in the sequence, job y will still start by its deadline because it will have started even earlier, and because the deadline for job x is larger than the deadline for job y and the new time slot given to job x was adequate for job y, job x will also start by its deadline. Therefore, the new sequence will still be feasible. We can prove that the ordered sequence is feasible by repeatedly using this fact while we do an Exchange Sort (Algorithm 1.3) on the original feasible sequence. In the other direction, of course, S is feasible if the ordered sequence is feasible.

Example 4.5

Suppose we have the jobs in Example 4.4. To determine whether $\{1, 2, 4, 7\}$ is feasible, Lemma 4.3 says we need only check the feasibility of the sequence

$$[\, 2, \quad 7, \quad 1, \quad 4 \,].$$
$$\uparrow \quad \uparrow \quad \uparrow \quad \uparrow$$
$$1 \quad 2 \quad 3 \quad 3$$

The deadline of each job has been listed under the job. Because job 4 is not scheduled by its deadline, the sequence is not feasible. By Lemma 4.3, the set is not feasible.

The algorithm follows. It is assumed that the jobs have already been sorted by profit in nonincreasing order, before being passed to the algorithm. Because the profits are needed only to sort the jobs, they are not listed as parameters of the algorithm.

Algorithm 4.4

Scheduling with Deadlines

Problem: Determine the schedule with maximum total profit given that each job has a profit that will be obtained only if the job is scheduled by its deadline.

Inputs: n, the number of jobs, and array of integers *deadline*, indexed from 1 to n, where *deadline*$[i]$ is the deadline for the ith job. The array has been sorted in nonincreasing order according to the profits associated with the jobs.

Outputs: an optimal sequence J for the jobs.

```
void schedule (int n,
               const int deadline[ ],
               sequence_of_integer& j)
{
   index i;
   sequence_of_integer K;
```

```
J = [1];
for (i = 2; i <= n; i++) {
    K = J with i added according to nondecreasing values of deadline[i];
    if (K is feasible)
        J = K;
}
}
```

Before analyzing this algorithm, let's apply it.

Example 4.6

Suppose we have the jobs in Example 4.4. Recall that they had the following deadlines:

Job	Deadline
1	3
2	1
3	1
4	3
5	1
6	3
7	2

Algorithm 4.4 does the following:

1. J is set to [1].
2. K is set to [2, 1] and is determined to be feasible.
   J is set to [2, 1] because K is feasible.
3. K is set to [2, 3, 1] and is rejected because it is not feasible.
4. K is set to [2, 1, 4] and is determined to be feasible.
   J is set to [2, 1, 4] because K is feasible.
5. K is set to [2, 5, 1, 4] and is rejected because it is not feasible.
6. K is set to [2, 1, 6, 4] and is rejected because it is not feasible.
7. K is set to [2, 7, 1, 4] and is rejected because it is not feasible.

The final value of J is [2, 1, 4].

Worst-Case Time Complexity Analysis of Algorithm 4.4 (Scheduling With Deadlines)

Basic operation: We need to do comparisons to sort the jobs, we need to do more comparisons when we set K equal to J with job i added, and we need to do more comparisons to check if K is feasible. Therefore, a comparison instruction is the basic operation.

Input size: n, the number of jobs.

It takes a time of $\Theta(n \lg n)$ to sort the jobs before passing them to the procedure. In each iteration of the **for**-i loop, we need to do at most $i - 1$ comparisons to add the ith job to K, and at most i comparisons to check if K is feasible. Therefore, the worst case is

$$\sum_{i=2}^{n} [(i - 1) + i] = n^2 - 1 \in \Theta(n^2).$$

The first equality is obtained in Example A.1 in Appendix A. Because this time dominates the sorting time,

$$W(n) \in \Theta(n^2).$$

Finally, we prove that the algorithm always gives an optimal solution.

Theorem 4.4 Algorithm 4.4 always produces an optimal set of jobs.

Proof: The proof is by induction on the number of jobs n.

Induction base: Clearly, the theorem holds if there is one job.

Induction hypothesis: Suppose the set of jobs our algorithm obtains from the first n jobs is optimal for the first n jobs.

Induction step: We need to show that the set of jobs our algorithm obtains from the first $n + 1$ jobs is optimal for the first $n + 1$ jobs. To that end, let A be the set of jobs our algorithm obtains from the first $n + 1$ jobs and let B be an optimal set of jobs obtained from the first $n + 1$ jobs.

There are two cases:

Case 1 B does not include job $(n + 1)$.

In this case B is a set of jobs obtained from the first n jobs. However, by the induction hypothesis, A includes an optimal set of jobs obtained from the first n jobs. Therefore, the total profit of the jobs in B can be no greater than the total profit of the jobs in A, and A must be optimal.

Case 2 B includes job $(n + 1)$.

Suppose A includes job $(n + 1)$. Then

$$B = B' \cup \{\text{job } (n + 1)\} \qquad \text{and} \qquad A = A' \cup \{\text{job } (n + 1)\},$$

where B' is a set obtained from the first n jobs and A' is the set our algorithm obtains from the first n jobs. By the induction hypothesis, A' is optimal for the first n jobs. Therefore,

$$profit\ (B) = profit\ (B') + profit\ (n + 1)$$
$$\leq profit\ (A') + profit\ (n + 1) = profit\ (A),$$

where *profit* $(n + 1)$ is the profit of job $(n + 1)$ and *profit* (A) is the total profit of the jobs in A. Since B is optimal for the first $n + 1$ jobs, we can conclude that A is also.

Suppose A does not include job $(n + 1)$. Consider the time slot occupied by job $(n + 1)$ in B. If that slot was available when our algorithm considered job $(n + 1)$, it would schedule that job. Therefore, that time slot must be given to some job in A, which we will call job i. Because the jobs are sorted by profit in nonincreasing order, job i's profit is at least as great as job $(n + 1)$'s profit.

If job i is not in B, we can replace job $(n + 1)$ with job i in B. The result is a set of jobs that has a total profit at least as great as the total profit of the jobs in B. However, this set is obtained from the first n jobs. Therefore, by the induction hypothesis, its total profit can be no greater than the total profit of the jobs in A, which means that A is optimal.

If job i is in B, then whatever time slot it occupies in B must be occupied by some job in A, which we will call job j. [Otherwise, our algorithm could have put job i in that slot and scheduled job $(n + 1)$.] As Figure 4.9 illustrates, in B we can replace job $(n + 1)$ by job i and job i by job j. Because job j's profit is at least as great as job $(n + 1)$'s profit, the result is again a set of jobs that has a total profit at least as great as the total profit of the jobs in B. We then proceed as before to conclude that A is optimal.

Figure 4.9 If in B we replace job $(n + 1)$ by job i and job i by job j, the total profit will be at least as great as it was before.

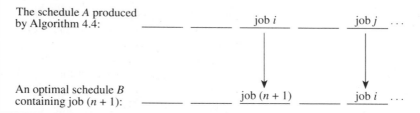

Using Disjoint Set Data Structure III, which is presented in Appendix C, it is possible to create a $\Theta(n \lg m)$ version of procedure *schedule* (in Algorithm 4.4), where m is the minimum of n and the largest of the deadlines for the n jobs. Because the time to sort is still in $\Theta(n \lg n)$, the entire algorithm is $\Theta(n \lg n)$. This modification will be discussed in the exercises.

4.4 THE GREEDY APPROACH VERSUS DYNAMIC PROGRAMMING: THE KNAPSACK PROBLEM

The greedy approach and dynamic programming are two ways to solve optimization problems. Often a problem can be solved using either approach. For example, the Single-Source Shortest Paths Problem is solved using dynamic programming in Algorithm 3.3 and is solved using the greedy approach in Algorithm 4.3. However, the dynamic programming algorithm is overkill in that it produces the shortest paths from all sources. There is no way to modify the algorithm to produce more efficiently only shortest paths from a single source because the entire array D is needed regardless. Therefore, the dynamic programming approach yields a $\Theta(n^3)$ algorithm for the problem, whereas the greedy approach yields a $\Theta(n^2)$ algorithm. Often when the greedy approach solves a problem, the result is a simpler, more efficient algorithm.

On the other hand, it is usually more difficult to determine whether a greedy algorithm always produces an optimal solution. As the Change Problem shows, not all greedy algorithms do. A proof is needed to show that a particular greedy algorithm always produces an optimal solution, whereas a counterexample is needed to show that it does not. Recall that in the case of dynamic programming we need only determine whether the principle of optimality applies.

To illuminate further the differences between the two approaches, we will present two very similar problems, the 0-1 Knapsack Problem and the Fractional Knapsack Problem. We will develop a greedy algorithm that successfully solves the Fractional Knapsack Problem but fails in the case of the 0-1 Knapsack Problem. Then we will successfully solve the 0-1 Knapsack Problem using dynamic programming.

4.4.1 A Greedy Approach to the 0-1 Knapsack Problem

An example of this problem concerns a thief breaking into a jewelry store carrying a knapsack. The knapsack will break if the total weight of the items stolen exceeds some maximum weight W. Each item has a value and a weight. The thief's dilemma is to maximize the total value of the items while not making the total weight exceed W. This problem is called the 0-1 Knapsack Problem. It can be formalized as follows.

Suppose there are n items. Let

$$S = \{item_1, item_2, \ldots, item_n\}$$
$$w_i = \text{weight of } item_i$$
$$p_i = \text{profit of } item_i$$
$$W = \text{maximum weight the knapsack can hold,}$$

where w_i, p_i, and W are positive integers. Determine a subset A of S such that

$$\sum_{item_i \in A} p_i \quad \text{is maximized subject to} \quad \sum_{item_i \in A} w_i \leq W.$$

The brute-force solution is to consider all subsets of the n items; discard those subsets whose total weight exceeds W; and, of those remaining, take one with maximum total profit. Example A.10 in Appendix A shows that there are 2^n subsets of a set containing n items. Therefore, the brute-force algorithm is exponential-time.

An obvious greedy strategy is to steal the items with the largest profit first.

That is, steal them in nonincreasing order according to profit. This strategy, how-ever, would not work very well if the most profitable item had a large weight in comparison with its profit. For example, suppose we had three items, the first weighing 25 pounds and having a profit of $10, and the second and third each weighing 10 pounds and having a profit of $9. If the capacity W of the knapsack was 30 pounds, this greedy strategy would yield only a profit of $10, whereas the optimal solution is $18.

Another obvious greedy strategy is to steal the lightest items first. This strat-egy fails badly when the light items have small profits compared with their weights.

To avoid the pitfalls of the previous two greedy algorithms, a more sophis-ticated greedy strategy is to steal the items with the largest profit per unit weight first. That is, we order the items in nonincreasing order according to profit per unit weight, and select them in sequence. An item is put in the knapsack if its weight does not bring the total weight above W. This approach is illustrated in Figure 4.10. In that figure, the weight and profit for each item are listed by the item, and the value of W, which is 30, is listed in the knapsack. We have the following profits per unit weight:

$$item_1: \frac{\$50}{5} = \$10 \qquad item_2: \frac{\$60}{10} = \$6 \qquad item_3: \frac{\$140}{20} = \$7$$

Ordering them by profit per unit weight yields

$$item_1, \ item_3, \ item_2.$$

As can be seen in the figure, this greedy approach chooses $item_1$ and $item_3$, resulting in a total profit of $190, whereas the optimal solution is to choose $item_2$ and $item_3$, resulting in a total profit of $200. The problem is that after $item_1$ and

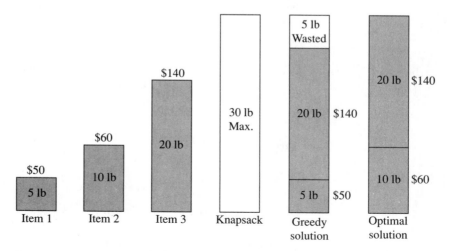

Figure 4.10 A greedy solution and an optimal solution to the 0-1 Knapsack Problem.

$item_3$ are chosen, there are 5 pounds of capacity left, but it is wasted because $item_2$ weighs 10 pounds. Even this more sophisticated greedy algorithm does not solve the 0-1 Knapsack Problem.

4.4.2 A Greedy Approach to the Fractional Knapsack Problem

In the Fractional Knapsack Problem, the thief does not have to steal all of an item, but rather can take any fraction of the item. We can think of the items in the 0-1 Knapsack Problem as being gold or silver ingots and the items in the Fractional Knapsack Problem as being bags of gold or silver dust. Suppose we have the items in Figure 4.10. If our greedy strategy is again to choose the items with the largest profit per unit weight first, all of $item_1$ and $item_3$ will be taken as before. However, we can use the 5 pounds of remaining capacity to take 5/10 of $item_2$. Our total profit is

$$\$50 + \$140 + \frac{5}{10}(\$60) = \$220.$$

Our greedy algorithm never wastes any capacity in the Fractional Knapsack Problem as it does in the 0-1 Knapsack Problem. As a result, it always yields an optimal solution. You are asked to prove this in the exercises.

4.4.3 A Dynamic Programming Approach to the 0-1 Knapsack Problem

If we can show that the principle of optimality applies, we can solve the 0-1 Knapsack Problem using dynamic programming. To that end, let A be an optimal subset of the n items. There are two cases: either A contains $item_n$ or it does not. If A does not contain $item_n$, A is equal to an optimal subset of the first $n - 1$ items. If A does contain $item_n$, the total profit of the items in A is equal to p_n plus the optimal profit obtained when the items can be chosen from the first $n - 1$ items under the restriction that the total weight cannot exceed $W - w_n$. Therefore, the principle of optimality applies.

The result just obtained can be generalized as follows. If for $i > 0$ and $w > 0$ we let $P[i][w]$ be the optimal profit obtained when choosing items only from the first i items under the restriction that the total weight cannot exceed w,

$$P[i][w] = \begin{cases} maximum(P[i - 1][w], p_i + P[i - 1][w - w_i]) & \text{if } w_i \leq w \\ P[i - 1][w] & \text{if } w_i > w \end{cases}$$

The maximum profit is equal to $P[n][W]$. We can determine this value using a two-dimensional array P, whose rows are indexed from 0 to n and whose columns are indexed from 0 to W. We compute the values in the rows of the array in sequence using the previous expression for $P[i][w]$. The values of $P[0][w]$ and

$P[i][0]$ are set to 0. You are asked to actually write the algorithm in the exercises. It is straightforward that the number of array entries computed is

$$nW \in \Theta(nW).$$

4.4.4 A Refinement of the Dynamic Programming Algorithm for the 0-1 Knapsack Problem

The fact that the previous expression for the number of array entries computed is linear in n can mislead one into thinking that the algorithm is efficient for all instances containing n items. This is not the case. The other term in that expression is W, and there is no relationship between n and W. Therefore, for a given n, we can create instances with arbitrarily large running times by taking arbitrarily large values of W. For example, the number of entries computed is in $\Theta(n \times n!)$ if W equals $n!$. If $n = 20$ and $W = 20!$, the algorithm will take thousands of years to run on a modern-day computer. When W is extremely large in comparison with n, this algorithm is worse than the brute-force algorithm that simply considers all subsets.

The algorithm can be improved so that the worst-case number of entries computed is in $\Theta(2^n)$. With this improvement, it never performs worse than the brute-force algorithm and often performs much better. The improvement is based on the fact that it is not necessary to determine the entries in the ith row for every w between 1 and W. Rather, in the nth row we need only determine $P[n][W]$. Therefore, the only entries needed in the $(n - 1)$st row are the ones needed to compute $P[n][W]$. Because

$$P[n][W] = \begin{cases} maximum(P[n - 1][W], p_n + P[n - 1][W - w_n]) & \text{if } w_n \leq W \\ P[n - 1][W] & \text{if } w_n > W, \end{cases}$$

the only entries needed in the $(n - 1)$st row are

$$P[n - 1][W] \qquad \text{and} \qquad P[n - 1][W - w_n].$$

We continue to work backward from n to determine which entries are needed. That is, after we determine which entries are needed in the ith row, we determine which entries are needed in the $(i - 1)$st row using the fact that

$$P[i][w] \qquad \text{is computed from} \qquad P[i - 1][w] \quad \text{and} \quad P[i - 1][w - w_i].$$

We stop when $n = 1$ or $w \leq 0$. After determining the entries needed, we do the computations starting with the first row. The following example illustrates this method.

Example 4.7 Suppose we have the items in Figure 4.10 and $W = 30$. First we determine which entries are needed in each row.

Determine entries needed in row 3:
    We need

$$P[3][W] = P[3][30].$$

Determine entries needed in row 2:
  To compute $P[3][30]$, we need

$$P[3-1][30] = P[2][30] \quad \text{and} \quad P[3-1][30-w_3] = P[2][10].$$

Determine entries needed in row 1:
  To compute $P[2][30]$, we need

$$P[2-1][30] = P[1][30] \quad \text{and} \quad P[2-1][30-w_2] = P[1][20].$$

To compute $P[2][10]$, we need

$$P[2-1][10] = P[1][10] \quad \text{and} \quad P[2-1][10-w_2] = P[1][0].$$

Next we do the computations.

Compute row 1:

$$P[1][w] = \begin{cases} maximum(P[0][w], \$50 + P[0][w-5]) & \text{if } w_1 = 5 \le w \\ P[0][w] & \text{if } w_1 = 5 > w \end{cases}$$

$$= \begin{cases} \$50 & \text{if } w_1 = 5 \le w \\ \$0 & \text{if } w_1 = 5 > w. \end{cases}$$

Therefore,

$$P[1][0] = \$0$$
$$P[1][10] = \$50$$
$$P[1][20] = \$50$$
$$P[1][30] = \$50$$

Compute row 2:

$$P[2][10] = \begin{cases} maximum(P[1][10], \$60 + P[1][0]) & \text{if } w_2 = 10 \le 10 \\ P[1][10] & \text{if } w_2 = 10 > 10 \end{cases}$$

$$= \$60$$

$$P[2][30] = \begin{cases} maximum(P[1][30], \$60 + P[1][20]) & \text{if } w_2 = 10 \le 30 \\ P[1][30] & \text{if } w_2 = 10 > 30 \end{cases}$$

$$= \$60 + \$50 = \$110$$

Compute row 3:

$$P[3][30] = \begin{cases} maximum(P[2][30], \$140 + P[2][10]) & \text{if } w_3 = 20 \le 30 \\ P[2][30] & \text{if } w_3 = 20 > 30 \end{cases}$$

$$= \$140 + \$60 = \$200$$

This version of the algorithm computes only seven entries, whereas the original version would have computed $(3)(30) = 90$ entries.

Let's determine how efficient this version is in the worst case. Notice that we compute at most 2^i entries in the $(n - i)$th row. Therefore, at most the total number of entries computed is

$$1 + 2 + 2^2 + \cdots + 2^{n-1} = 2^n - 1.$$

This equality is obtained in Example A.3 in Appendix A. It is left as an exercise to show that the following is an instance for which about 2^n entries are computed (the profits can have any values):

$$w_i = 2^{i-1} \quad \text{for} \quad 1 \leq i \leq n \quad \text{and} \quad W = 2^n - 2.$$

Combining these two results, we can conclude that the worst-case number of entries computed is in

$$\Theta(2^n).$$

The previous bound is in terms of only n. Let's also obtain a bound in terms of n and W combined. We know that the number of entries computed is in $O(nW)$, but perhaps this version avoids ever reaching this bound. This is not the case. In the exercises you will show that if $n = W + 1$ and $w_i = 1$ for all i, then the total number of entries computed is about

$$1 + 2 + 3 + \cdots + n = \frac{n(n + 1)}{2} = \frac{(W + 1)(n + 1)}{2}.$$

The first equality is obtained in Example A.1 in Appendix A, and the second derives from the fact that $n = W + 1$ in this instance. Therefore, this bound is reached for arbitrarily large values of n and W

$$\Theta(nW).$$

Combining our two results, the worst-case number of entries computed is in

$$O(minimum(2^n, nW)).$$

We do not need to create the entire array to implement the algorithm. Instead, we can store just the entries that are needed. The entire array exists only implicitly. If the algorithm is implemented in this manner, the worst-case memory usage has these same bounds.

We could write a divide-and-conquer algorithm using the expression for $P[i][w]$ that was used to develop the dynamic programming algorithm. For this algorithm the worst-case number of entries computed is also in $\Theta(2^n)$. The main advantage of the dynamic programming algorithm is the additional bound in terms of nW. The divide-and-conquer algorithm does not have this bound. Indeed, this bound is obtained because of the fundamental difference between dynamic programming and divide-and-conquer. That is, dynamic programming does not process the same instance more than once. The bound in terms of nW is very significant when W is not large in comparison with n.

As is the case for the Traveling Salesperson Problem, no one has ever found an algorithm for the 0-1 Knapsack Problem whose worst-case time complexity is better than exponential, yet no one has proven that such an algorithm is not possible. Such problems are the focus of Chapter 9.

Exercises

Section 4.1

1. Show that the greedy approach always finds an optimal solution for the Change Problem when the coins are in the denominations $D^0, D^1, D^2, \ldots,$ D^i for some integers $i > 0$ and $D > 0$.

2. Use Prim's Algorithm (Algorithm 4.1) to find a minimum spanning tree for the following graph. Show the actions step by step.

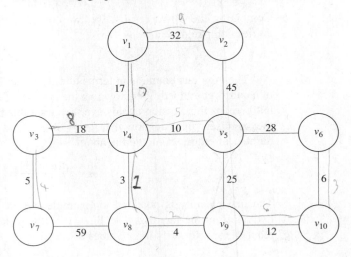

3. Draw a graph that has more than one minimum spanning tree.

4. Implement Prim's Algorithm (Algorithm 4.1) on your system, and study its performance using different graphs.

5. Modify Prim's Algorithm (Algorithm 4.1) to check if an undirected, weighted graph is connected. Analyze your algorithm, and show the results using order notation.

6. Use Kruskal's Algorithm (Algorithm 4.2) to find a minimum spanning tree for the graph in Exercise 2. Show the actions step by step.

7. Implement Kruskal's Algorithm (Algorithm 4.2) on your system, and study its performance using different graphs.

8. Do you think it is possible for a minimum spanning tree to have a cycle? Justify your answer.

9. Assume that in a network of computers any two computers can be linked. Given a cost estimate for each possible link, should Algorithm 4.1 (Prim's Algorithm) or Algorithm 4.2 (Kruskal's Algorithm) be used? Justify your answer.

10. Apply Lemma 4.2 to complete the proof of Theorem 4.2.

Section 4.2

11. Use Dijkstra's Algorithm (Algorithm 4.3) to find the shortest paths from the vertex v_4 to all the other vertices of the graph in Exercise 2. Show the actions step by step. Assume that each undirected edge represents two directed edges with the same weight.

12. Implement Dijkstra's Algorithm (Algorithm 4.3) on your system, and study its performance using different graphs.

13. Modify Dijkstra's Algorithm (Algorithm 4.3) so that it computes the lengths of the shortest paths. Analyze the modified algorithm, and show the results using order notation.

14. Modify Dijkstra's Algorithm (Algorithm 4.3) so that it checks if a directed graph has a cycle. Analyze your algorithm, and show the results using order notation.

15. Can Dijkstra's Algorithm (Algorithm 4.3) be used to find the shortest paths in a graph with some negative weights? Justify your answer.

16. Use induction to prove the correctness of Dijkstra's Algorithm (Algorithm 4.3).

Section 4.3

17. Consider the following jobs and service times. Use the algorithm in Section 4.3.1 to minimize the total amount of time spent in the system.

Job	Service Time
1	7
2	3
3	10
4	5

18. Implement the algorithm in Section 4.3.1 on your system, and run it on the instance in Exercise 17.

19. Write an algorithm for the generalization of the Single-Server Scheduling Problem to the Multiple-Server Scheduling Problem in Section 4.3.1. Analyze your algorithm, and show the results using order notation.

20. Consider the following jobs, deadlines, and profits. Use the Scheduling with Deadlines Algorithm (Algorithm 4.4) to maximize the total profit.

Job	Deadline	Profit
1	2	40
2	4	15
3	3	60
4	2	20
5	3	10
6	1	45
7	1	55

21. Consider procedure *schedule* in the Scheduling with Deadlines Algorithm (Algorithm 4.4). Let d be the maximum of the deadlines for n jobs. Modify the procedure so that it adds a job as late as possible to the schedule being built, but no later than its deadline. Do this by initializing $d + 1$ disjoint sets, containing the integers $0, 1, \ldots, d$. Let *small(S)* be the smallest member of set S. When a job is scheduled, find the set S containing the minimum of its deadline and n. If *small(S)* $= 0$, reject the job. Otherwise, schedule it at time *small(S)*, and merge S with the set containing *small(S)* $- 1$. Assuming we use Disjoint Set Data Structure III in Appendix C, show that this version is $\theta(n \lg m)$, where m is the minimum of d and n.

22. Implement the algorithm developed in Exercise 21.

23. Suppose we minimize the average time to store n files of lengths $l_1, l_2, \ldots,$ l_n on a tape. If the probability of requesting file k is given by p_k, the expected access time to load these n files in the order $k_1, k_2, \ldots, k_n$ is given by the formula

$$T_{average} = C \sum_{f=1}^{n} (p_{k_f} \sum_{i=1}^{f} l_{k_i}).$$

The constant C represents parameters such as the speed of the drive and the recording density.
(a) In what order should a greedy approach store these files to guarantee minimum average access time?
(b) Write the algorithm that stores the files, analyze your algorithm, and show the results using order notation.

Section 4.4

24. Write the dynamic programming algorithm for the 0-1 Knapsack Problem.

25. Use a greedy approach to construct an optimal binary search tree by considering the most probable key, Key_k, for the root, and constructing the left and right subtrees for $Key_1, Key_2, \ldots, Key_{k-1}$ and $Key_{k+1}, Key_{k+2}, \ldots, Key_n$ recursively in the same way.
(a) Assuming the keys are already sorted, what is the worst-case time complexity of this approach? Justify your answer.
(b) Use an example to show that this greedy approach does not always find an optimal binary search tree.

26. Suppose we assign n persons to n jobs. Let C_{ij} be the cost of assigning the ith person to the jth job. Use a greedy approach to write an algorithm that finds an assignment that minimizes the total cost of assigning all n persons to all n jobs. Analyze your algorithm, and show the results using order notation.

27. Use the dynamic programming approach to write an algorithm for the problem of Exercise 26. Analyze your algorithm, and show the results using order notation.

28. Use a greedy approach to write an algorithm that minimizes the number of record moves in the problem of merging n files. Use a two-way merge pattern (two files are merged during each merge step.) Analyze your algorithm, and show the results using order notation.

29. Use the dynamic programming approach to write an algorithm for Exercise 28. Analyze your algorithm, and show the results using order notation.

30. Prove that the greedy approach to the Fractional Knapsack Problem yields an optimal solution.

31. Show that the worst-case number of entries computed by the refined dynamic programming algorithm for the 0-1 Knapsack Problem is in $\Omega(2^n)$. Do this by considering the instance where $W = 2^n - 2$ and $w_i = 2^{i-1}$ for $1 \leq i \leq n$.

32. Show that in the refined dynamic programming algorithm for the 0-1 Knapsack Problem, the total number of entries computed is about $(W + 1) \times (n + 1)/2$, when $n = W + 1$ and $w_i = 1$ for all i.

Additional Exercises

33. Show with a counterexample that the greedy approach does not always yield an optimal solution for the Change Problem when the coins are U.S. coins and we do not have at least one of each type of coin.

34. Prove that a complete graph (a graph in which there is an edge between every pair of vertices) has n^{n-2} spanning trees. Here n is the number of vertices in the graph.

35. Use a greedy approach to write an algorithm for the Traveling Salesperson Problem. Show that your algorithm does not always find a minimum-length tour.

36. Prove that the algorithm for the Multiple-Server Scheduling Problem of Exercise 19 always finds an optimal schedule.

CHAPTER 5

Backtracking

*I*f you were trying to find your way through the well-known maze of hedges by Hampton Court Palace in England, you would have no choice but to follow a hopeless path until you reached a dead end. When that happened, you'd go back to a fork and pursue another path. Anyone who has ever tried solving a maze puzzle has experienced the frustration of hitting dead ends. Think how much easier it would be if there were a sign, positioned a short way down a path, that told you that the path led to nothing but dead ends. If the sign were positioned near the beginning of the path, the time savings could be enormous, because all forks after that sign would be eliminated from consideration. This means that not one but many dead ends would be avoided. There are no such signs in the famous maze of hedges or in most maze puzzles. However, as we shall see, they do exist in backtracking algorithms.

Backtracking is very useful for problems such a the 0-1 Knapsack Problem. Although in Section 4.4.3 we found a dynamic programming algorithm for this problem that is efficient if the capacity W of the knapsack is not large, the algorithm is still exponential-time in the worst case. The 0-1 Knapsack Problem is in the class of problems discussed in Chapter 9. No one has ever found algorithms for any of those problems whose worst-case time complexities are better than exponential, but no one has ever proved that such algorithms are not possible. One way to try to handle the 0-1 Knapsack Problem would be to actually generate all the subsets, but this would be like following every path in a maze until a dead end is reached. Recall from Section 4.4.1 that there are 2^n subsets, which means that this brute-force method is feasible only for small values of n. However, if while generating the subsets we can find signs that tell us that many of them need not be generated, we can often avoid much unnecessary labor. This is exactly what a backtracking algorithm does. Backtracking algorithms for problems such as the 0-1 Knapsack Problem are still exponential-time (or even worse) in the worst case. They are useful because they are efficient for many large instances, not because they are efficient for all large instances. We return to the 0-1 Knapsack Problem in Section 5.7. Before that, we introduce backtracking with a simple example in Section 5.1, and solve several other problems in the other sections.

5.1 THE BACKTRACKING TECHNIQUE

Backtracking is used to solve problems in which a *sequence* of objects is chosen from a specified *set* so that the sequence satisfies some *criterion.* The classic example of backtracking is the n-Queens Problem. The goal in this problem is to position n queens on an $n \times n$ chessboard so that no two queens threaten each other. That is, no two queens may be in the same row, column, or diagonal. The *sequence* in this problem is the n positions where the queens are placed, the *set* for each choice is the n^2 possible positions on the chessboard, and the *criterion* is that no two queens can threaten each other. The n-Queens Problem is a generalization of its instance when $n = 8$, which is the instance using a standard chessboard. For the sake of brevity, we will illustrate backtracking using the instance when $n = 4$.

Backtracking is a modified depth-first search of a tree (here "tree" means a rooted tree). So let's review the depth-first search before proceeding. Although the depth-first search is defined for graphs in general, we will discuss only searching of trees, because backtracking involves only a tree search. A *preorder* tree traversal is a *depth-first search* of the tree. This means that the root is visited first, and a visit to a node is followed immediately by visits to all descendants of the node. Although a depth-first search does not require that the children be visited in any particular order, we will visit the children of a node from left to right in the applications in this chapter. Figure 5.1 shows a depth-first search of a tree performed in this manner. The nodes are numbered in the order in which they are visited. Notice that in a depth-first search a path is followed as deep as possible until a dead end is reached. At a dead end we back up until we reach a node with an unvisited child, and then we again proceed to go as deep as possible.

Figure 5.1 A tree with nodes numbered according to a depth-first search.

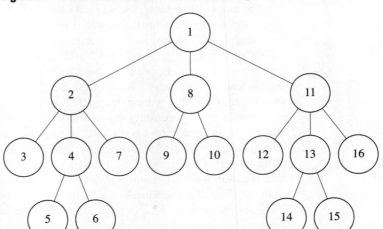

There is a simple recursive algorithm for doing a depth-first search. Because we are presently interested only in preorder traversals of trees, we give a version that specifically accomplishes this. The procedure is called by passing the root at the top level.

```
void depth_first_tree_search (node v)
{
    node u;

    visit v;
    for (each child u of v)
        depth_first_tree_search(u);
}
```

This general-purpose algorithm does not state that the children must be visited in any particular order. However, as mentioned previously, we visit them from left to right.

Now let's illustrate the backtracking technique with the instance of the *n*-Queens Problem when $n = 4$. Our task is to position four queens on a 4×4 chessboard so that no two queens threaten each other. We can immediately simplify matters by realizing that no two queens can be in the same row. The instance can then be solved by assigning each queen a different row and checking which column combinations yield solutions. Because each queen can be placed in one of four columns, there are $4 \times 4 \times 4 \times 4 = 256$ candidate solutions.

We can create the candidate solutions by constructing a tree in which the column choices for the first queen (the queen in row 1) are stored in level-1 nodes

Figure 5.2 A portion of the state space tree for the instance of the *n*-Queens Problem in which *n* = 4. The ordered pair <*i, j*> at each node means that the queen in the *i*th row is placed in the *j*th column. Each path from the root to a leaf is a candidate solution.

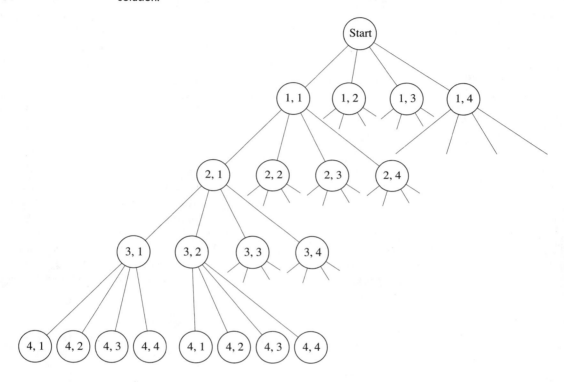

in the tree (recall that the root is at level 0), the column choices for the second queen (the queen in row 2) are stored in level-2 nodes, and so on. A path from the root to a leaf is a candidate solution (recall that a *leaf* in a tree is a node with no children). This tree is called a *state space tree*. A small portion of it appears in Figure 5.2. The entire tree has 256 leaves, one for each candidate solution. Notice that an ordered pair <*i, j*> is stored at each node. This ordered pair means that the queen in the *i*th row is placed in the *j*th column.

To determine the solutions, we check each candidate solution (each path from the root to a leaf) in sequence, starting with the leftmost path. The first few paths checked are as follows:

$$[<1, 1>, <2, 1>, <3, 1>, <4, 1>]$$
$$[<1, 1>, <2, 1>, <3, 1>, <4, 2>]$$
$$[<1, 1>, <2, 1>, <3, 1>, <4, 3>]$$
$$[<1, 1>, <2, 1>, <3, 1>, <4, 4>]$$
$$[<1, 1>, <2, 1>, <3, 2>, <4, 1>]$$

Notice that the nodes are visited according to a depth-first search in which the children of a node are visited from left to right. A simple depth-first search of a state space tree is like following every path in a maze until you reach a dead end. It does not take advantage of any signs along the way. We can make the search more efficient by looking for such signs. For example, as illustrated in Figure 5.3(a), no two queens can be in the same column. Therefore, there is no point in constructing and checking any paths in the entire branch emanating from the node containing $<2, 1>$ in Figure 5.2 (because we have already placed queen 1 in column 1, we cannot place queen 2 there). This sign tells us that this node can lead to nothing but dead ends. Similarly, as illustrated in Figure 5.3(b), no two queens can be on the same diagonal. Therefore, there is no point in constructing and checking the entire branch emanating from the node containing $<2, 2>$ in Figure 5.2.

Backtracking is the procedure whereby, after determining that a node can lead to nothing but dead ends, we go back ("backtrack") to the node's parent and proceed with the search on the next child. We call a node *nonpromising* if when visiting the node we determine that it cannot possibly lead to a solution. Otherwise, we call it *promising.* To summarize, backtracking consists of doing a depth-first search of a state space tree, checking whether each node is promising, and, if it is nonpromising, backtracking to the node's parent. This is called *pruning* the state space tree, and the subtree consisting of the visited nodes is called the *pruned state space tree.* A general algorithm for the backtracking approach is as follows:

```
void checknode (node v)
{
   node u;

   if (promising(v))
      if (there is a solution at v)
         write the solution;
      else
         for (each child u of v)
            checknode(u);
}
```

The root of the state space tree is passed to *checknode* at the top level. A visit to a node consists of first checking whether it is promising. If it is promising and there is a solution at the node, the solution is printed. If there is not a solution at a promising node, the children of the node are visited. The function *promising* is different in each application of backtracking. We call it the *promising function* for the algorithm. A backtracking algorithm is identical to a depth-first search,

Figure 5.3 Diagram showing that if the first queen is placed in column 1, the second queen cannot be placed in column 1 (a) or column 2 (b).

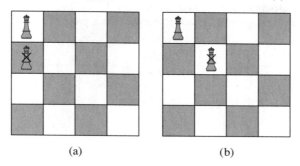

(a)   (b)

except that the children of a node are visited only when the node is promising and there is not a solution at the node. (Unlike the algorithm for the *n*-Queens Problem, in some backtracking algorithms a solution can be found before reaching a leaf in the state space tree.) We have called the backtracking procedure *checknode* rather than *backtrack* because backtracking does not occur when the procedure is called. Rather, it occurs when we find that a node is nonpromising and proceed to the next child of the parent. A computer implementation of the recursive algorithm accomplishes backtracking by popping the activation record for a nonpromising node from the stack of activation records.

Next we use backtracking to solve the instance of the *n*-Queens Problem when $n = 4$.

Example 5.1

Recall that the function *promising* is different for each application of backtracking. For the *n*-Queens Problem, it must return false if a node and any of the node's ancestors place queens in the same column or diagonal. Figure 5.4 shows a portion of the pruned state space tree produced when backtracking is used to solve the instance in which $n = 4$. Only the nodes checked to find the first solution are shown. Figure 5.5 shows the actual chessboards. A node is marked with a cross in Figure 5.4 if it is nonpromising. Similarly, there is a cross in a nonpromising position in Figure 5.5. The shaded node in Figure 5.4 is the node where the first solution is found. A walk-through of the traversal done by backtracking follows. We refer to a node by the ordered pair stored at that node. Some of the nodes contain the same ordered pair, but you can tell which node we mean by traversing the tree in Figure 5.4 while we do the walk-through.

(a) $<1, 1>$ is promising   {because queen 1 is the first queen positioned}

(b) $<2, 1>$ is nonpromising.   {because queen 1 is in column 1}
    $<2, 2>$ is nonpromising.   {because queen 1 is on left diagonal}
    $<2, 3>$ is promising.

Figure 5.4 A portion of the pruned state space tree produced when backtracking is used to solve the instance of the *n*-Queens Problem in which $n = 4$. Only the nodes checked to find the first solution are shown. That solution is found at the shaded node. Each nonpromising node is marked with a cross.

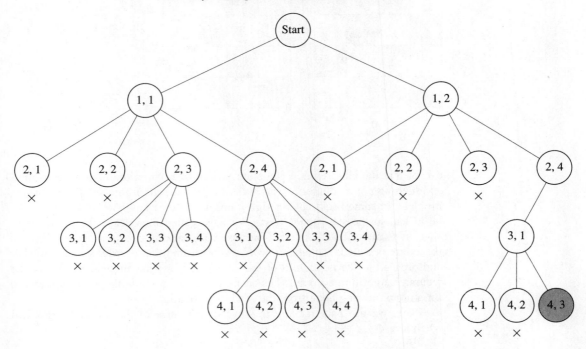

(c) <3, 1> is nonpromising.   {because queen 1 is in column 1}
      <3, 2> is nonpromising.   {because queen 2 is on right diagonal}
      <3, 3> is nonpromising.   {because queen 2 is in column 3}
      <3, 4> is nonpromising.   {because queen 2 is on left diagonal}

(d) Backtrack to <1, 1>.
      <2, 4> is promising.

(e) <3, 1> is nonpromising.   {because queen 1 is in column 1}
      <3, 2> is promising.   {This is the second time we've tried <3, 2>.}

(f) <4, 1> is nonpromising.   {because queen 1 is in column 1}
      <4, 2> is nonpromising.   {because queen 3 is in column 2}
      <4, 3> is nonpromising.   {because queen 3 is on left diagonal}
      <4, 4> is nonpromising.   {because queen 2 is in column 4}

(g) Backtrack to <2, 4>.
      <3, 3> is nonpromising.   {because queen 2 is on right diagonal}
      <3, 4> is nonpromising.   {because queen 2 is in column 4}

Figure 5.5 The actual chessboard positions that are tried when backtracking is used to solve the instance of the *n*-Queens Problem in which *n* = 4. Each nonpromising position is marked with a cross.

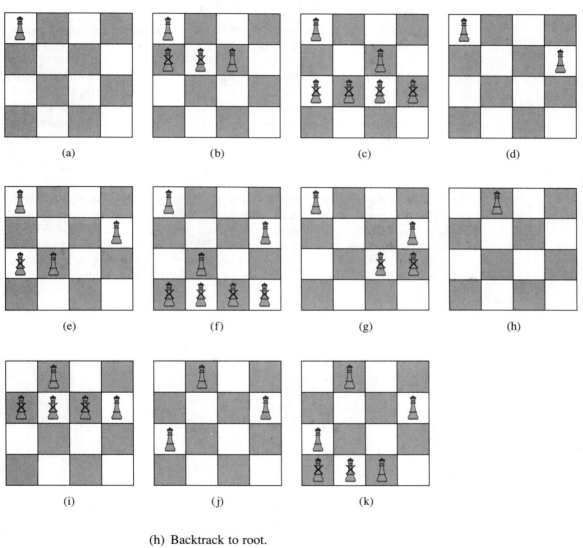

 (a)   (b)   (c)   (d)

 (e)   (f)   (g)   (h)

 (i)   (j)   (k)

(h) Backtrack to root.
  <1, 2> is promising.

(i) <2, 1> is nonpromising. {because queen 1 is on right diagonal}
  <2, 2> is nonpromising. {because queen 1 is in column 2}
  <2, 3> is nonpromising. {because queen 1 is on left diagonal}
  <2, 4> is promising.

(j) <3, 1> is promising.   {This is the third time we've tried <3, 1>.}

(k) <4, 1> is nonpromising.   {because queen 3 is in column 1}
    <4, 2> is nonpromising.   {because queen 1 is in column 2}
    <4, 3> is promising.

At this point the first solution has been found. It appears in Figure 5.5(k), and the node at which it is found is shaded in Figure 5.4.

Notice that a backtracking algorithm need not actually create a tree. Rather, it only needs to keep track of the values in the current branch being investigated. This is the way we implement backtracking algorithms. We say that the state space tree exists *implicitly* in the algorithm because it is not actually constructed.

A node count in Figure 5.4 shows that the backtracking algorithm checks 27 nodes before finding a solution. In the exercises you will show that, without backtracking, a depth-first search of the state space tree checks 155 nodes before finding that same solution.

You may have observed that there is some inefficiency in our general algorithm for backtracking (procedure *checknode*). That is, we check whether a node is promising after passing it to the procedure. This means that activation records for nonpromising nodes are unnecessarily placed on the stack of activation records. We could avoid this by checking whether a node is promising before passing it. A general algorithm for backtracking that does this is as follows:

```
void expand(node v)
{
   node u;

   for (each child u of v)
     if (promising(u))
        if (there is a solution at u)
           write the solution;
     else
        expand(u);
}
```

The node passed at the top level to the procedure is again the root of the tree. We call this procedure *expand* because it is called when we expand a promising node. A computer implementation of this algorithm accomplishes backtracking from a nonpromising node by not pushing an activation record for the node onto the stack of activation records.

In explaining algorithms in this chapter we use the first version of the algorithm (procedure *checknode*) because we have found that this version typically produces algorithms that are easier to understand. The reason is that one execution of *checknode* consists of the steps done when visiting a single node. That is, it consists of the following steps. Determine if the node is promising. If it is promising, then if there is a solution at the node, print the solution; otherwise, visit its children. On the other hand, one execution of *expand* involves doing the same steps for all children of a node. After seeing the first version of an algorithm, it is not hard to write the second version.

Next we will develop backtracking algorithms for several problems, starting with the *n*-Queens Problem. In all these problems, the state space tree contains an exponentially large or larger number of nodes. Backtracking is used to avoid unnecessary checking of nodes. Given two instances with the same value of *n*, a backtracking algorithm may check very few nodes for one of them but the entire state space tree for the other. This means that we will not obtain efficient time complexities for our backtracking algorithms as we did for the algorithms in the preceding chapters. Therefore, instead of the types of analyses done in those chapters, we will analyze our backtracking algorithms using the Monte Carlo Technique. This technique enables us to determine whether we can expect a given backtracking algorithm to be efficient for a particular instance. The Monte Carlo Technique is discussed in Section 5.3.

5.2 THE *n*-QUEENS PROBLEM

We have already discussed the goal in the *n*-Queens Problem. The promising function must check whether two queens are in the same column or diagonal. If we let **col(i)** be the column where the queen in the *i*th row is located, then, to check whether the queen in the *k*th row is in the same column, we need to check whether

$$col(i) = col(k).$$

Next let's see how to check the diagonals. Figure 5.6 illustrates the instance in which $n = 8$. In that figure, the queen in row 6 is being threatened in its left diagonal by the queen in row 3, and in its right diagonal by the queen in row 2. Notice that

$$col(6) - col(3) = 4 - 1 = 3 = 6 - 3.$$

That is, for the queen threatening from the left, the difference in the columns is the same as the difference in the rows. Furthermore,

$$col(6) - col(2) = 4 - 8 = -4 = 2 - 6.$$

That is, for the queen threatening from the right, the difference in the columns is the negative of the difference in the rows. These are examples of the general result that if the queen in the *k*th row threatens the queen in the *i*th row along one of its diagonals, then

$$col(i) - col(k) = i - k \quad \text{or} \quad col(i) - col(k) = k - i.$$

Next we present the algorithm.

5 Backtracking

Figure 5.6 The queen in row 6 is being threatened in its left diagonal by the queen in row 3 and in its right diagonal by the queen in row 2.

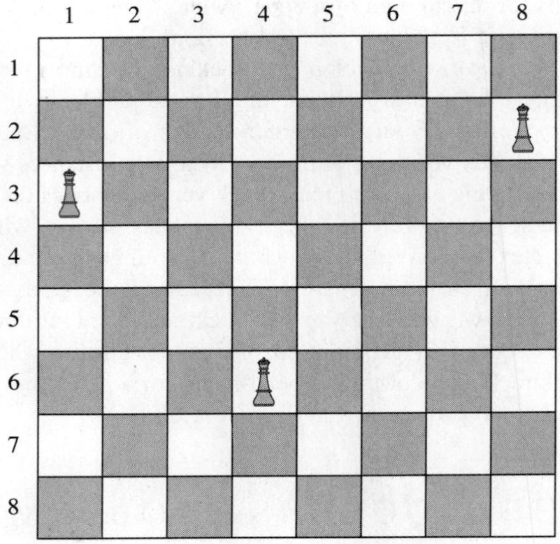

Algorithm 5.1

The Backtracking Algorithm for the *n*-Queens Problem

Problem: Position *n* queens on a chessboard so that no two are in the same row, column, or diagonal.

Inputs: positive integer *n*.

Outputs: all possible ways *n* queens can be placed on an $n \times n$ chessboard so that no two queens threaten each other. Each output consists of an array of integers *col* indexed from 1 to *n*, where *col*[*i*] is the column where the queen in the *i*th row is placed.

```
void queens (index i)
{
   index j;
   if (promising(i))
     if (i == n)
        cout << col[1] through col[n];
     else
        for (j = 1; j <= n; j++) {        // See if queen in (i + 1)st row
          col[i + 1] = j;                 // can be positioned in each of
          queens(i + 1);                  // the n columns.
        }
}
```

```
bool promising (index i)
{
   index k;
   bool switch;

   k = 1;
   switch = true;                        // Check if any queen threatens
   while (k < i && switch) {             // queen in the ith row.
      if (col[i] == col[k] || abs(col[i] − col[k]) == i − k)
         switch = false;
      k++;
   }
   return switch;
}
```

When an algorithm consists of more than one routine, we do not order the routines according to the rules of any particular programming language. Rather we just present the main routine first. In algorithm 5.1, that routine is *queens*. Following the convention discussed in Section 2.1, *n* and *col* are not inputs to the recursive routine *queens*. If the algorithm were implemented by defining *n* and *col* globally, the top-level call to *queens* would be

queens(0);

Algorithm 5.1 produces all solutions to the *n*-Queens Problem because that is how we stated the problem. We stated the problem this way to eliminate the need to exit when a solution is found. This makes the algorithm less cluttered. In general, the problems in this chapter can be stated to require one, several, or all solutions. In practice, which is done depends on the needs of the application. Most of our algorithms are written to produce all solutions. It is a simple modification to make the algorithms stop after finding one solution.

It is difficult to analyze Algorithm 5.1 theoretically. To do this, we have to determine the number of nodes checked as a function of *n*, the number of queens. We can get an upper bound on the number of nodes in the pruned state space tree by counting the number of nodes in the entire state space tree. This latter tree contains 1 node at level 0, *n* nodes at level 1, n^2 nodes at level 2, . . . , and n^n nodes at level *n*. The total number of nodes is

$$1 + n + n^2 + n^3 + \cdots + n^n = \frac{n^{n+1} - 1}{n - 1}.$$

This equality is obtained in Example A.4 in Appendix A. For the instance in which $n = 8$, the state space tree contains

$$\frac{8^{8+1} - 1}{8 - 1} = 19{,}173{,}961 \text{ nodes.}$$

This analysis is of limited value because the whole purpose of backtracking is to avoid checking many of these nodes.

Another analysis we could try is to obtain an upper bound on the number of promising nodes. To compute such a bound, we can use the fact that no two queens can ever be placed in the same column. For example, consider the instance in which $n = 8$. The first queen can be positioned in any of the eight columns. Once the first queen is positioned, the second can be positioned in at most seven columns; once the second is positioned, the third can be positioned in at most six columns; and so on. Therefore, there are at most

$$1 + 8 + 8 \times 7 + 8 \times 7 \times 6 + 8 \times 7 \times 6 \times 5 + \cdots + 8!$$

$$= 109{,}601 \text{ promising nodes.}$$

Generalizing this result to an arbitrary n, there are at most

$$1 + n + n(n - 1) + n(n - 1)(n - 2) + \cdots + n! \text{ promising nodes.}$$

This analysis does not give us a very good idea as to the efficiency of the algorithm for the following reasons: First, it does not take into account the diagonal check in function *promising*. Therefore, there could be far less promising nodes than this upper bound. Second, the total number of nodes checked includes both promising and nonpromising nodes. As we shall see, the number of nonpromising nodes can be substantially greater than the number of promising nodes.

A straightforward way to determine the efficiency of the algorithm is to actually run the algorithm on a computer and count how many nodes are checked. Table 5.1 shows the results for several values of n. The backtracking algorithm is compared with two other algorithms for the n-Queens Problem. Algorithm 1 is a depth-first search of the state space tree without backtracking. The number of nodes it checks is the number in the state space tree. Algorithm 2 uses only the fact that no two queens can be in the same row or in the same column. Algorithm 2 generates $n!$ candidate solutions by trying the row-1 queen in each

Table 5.1 An illustration of how much checking is saved by backtracking in the n-Queens Problem*

n	Number of Nodes Checked by Algorithm 1[†]	Number of Candidate Solutions Checked by Algorithm 2[‡]	Number of Nodes Checked by Backtracking	Number of Nodes Found Promising by Backtracking
4	341	24	61	17
8	19,173,961	40,320	15,721	2057
12	9.73×10^{12}	4.79×10^{8}	1.01×10^{7}	8.56×10^{5}
14	1.20×10^{16}	8.72×10^{10}	3.78×10^{8}	2.74×10^{7}

*Entries indicate numbers of checks required to find all solutions.
[†]Algorithm 1 does a depth-first search of the state space tree without backtracking.
[‡]Algorithm 2 generates the $n!$ candidate solutions that place each queen in a different row and column.

of the n columns, the row-2 queen in each of the $n - 1$ columns not occupied by the first queen, the row-3 queen in each of the $n - 2$ columns not occupied by either of the first two queens, and so on. After generating a candidate solution, it checks whether two queens threaten each other in a diagonal. Notice that the advantage of the backtracking algorithm increases dramatically with n. When $n = 4$, Algorithm 1 checks less than six times as many nodes as the backtracking algorithm, and the backtracking algorithm seems slightly inferior to Algorithm 2. But when $n = 14$, Algorithm 1 checks almost 32,000,000 times as many nodes as does the backtracking algorithm, and the number of candidate solutions generated by Algorithm 2 is about 230 times the number of nodes checked by backtracking. We have listed the number of promising nodes in Table 5.1 to show that many of the nodes checked can be nonpromising. This means that our second way of implementing backtracking (procedure *expand,* which is discussed in Section 5.1) can save a significant amount of time.

Actually running an algorithm to determine its efficiency (as was done to create Table 5.1) is not really an analysis. We did this to illustrate how much time backtracking can save. The purpose of an analysis is to determine ahead of time whether an algorithm is efficient. In the next section we show how the Monte Carlo Technique can be used to estimate the efficiency of a backtracking algorithm.

Recall that in our state space tree for the n-Queens Problem we use the fact that no two queens can be in the same row. Alternatively, we could create a state space tree that tries every queen in each of the n^2 board positions. We would backtrack in this tree whenever a queen was placed in the same row, column, or diagonal as a queen already positioned. Every node in this state space tree would have n^2 children, one for each board position. There would be $(n^2)^n$ leaves, each representing a different candidate solution. An algorithm that backtracked in this state space tree would find no more promising nodes than our algorithm finds, but it would still be slower than ours because of the extra time needed to do a row check in function *promising* and because of the extra nonpromising nodes that would be investigated (that is, any node that attempted to place a queen in a row that was already occupied). In general, it is most efficient to build as much information as possible into the state space tree.

The time spent in the promising function is a consideration in any backtracking algorithm. That is, our goal is not strictly to cut down on the number of nodes checked; rather, it is to improve overall efficiency. A very time-consuming promising function could offset the advantage of checking fewer nodes. In the case of Algorithm 5.1, the promising function can be improved by keeping track of the sets of columns, of left diagonals, and of right diagonals controlled by the queens already placed. In this way, it is not necessary to check whether the queens already positioned threaten the current queen. We need only check if the current queen is being placed in a controlled column or diagonal. This improvement is investigated in the exercises.

5.3 USING A MONTE CARLO ALGORITHM TO ESTIMATE THE EFFICIENCY OF A BACKTRACKING ALGORITHM

As mentioned previously, the state space tree for each of the algorithms presented in the following sections contains an exponentially large or larger number of nodes. Given two instances with the same value of n, one of them may require that very few nodes be checked whereas the other requires that the entire state space tree be checked. If we had an estimate of how efficiently a given backtracking algorithm would process a particular instance, we could decide whether using the algorithm on that instance was reasonable. We can obtain such an estimate using a Monte Carlo algorithm.

Monte Carlo algorithms are probabilistic algorithms. By a ***probabilistic algorithm,*** we mean one in which the next instruction executed is sometimes determined at random. By a ***deterministic algorithm,*** we mean one in which this cannot happen. All the algorithms discussed so far are deterministic algorithms. A ***Monte Carlo algorithm*** estimates the expected value of a random variable, defined on a sample space, from its average value on a random sample of the sample space. (See Section A.8.1 in Appendix A for a discussion of sample spaces, random samples, random variables, and expected values.) There is no guarantee that the estimate is close to the true expected value, but the probability that it is close increases as the time available to the algorithm increases.

We can use a Monte Carlo algorithm to estimate the efficiency of a backtracking algorithm for a particular instance as follows. We generate a "typical path" in the tree consisting of the nodes that would be checked given that instance, and then estimate the number of nodes in this tree from the path. The estimate is an estimate of the total number of nodes that would be checked to find all solutions. That is, it is an estimate of the number of nodes in the pruned state space tree. The following conditions must be satisfied by the algorithm in order for the technique to apply:

1. The same promising function must be used on all nodes at the same level in the state space tree.
2. Nodes at the same level in the state space tree must have the same number of children.

Notice that Algorithm 5.1 (The Backtracking Algorithm for the n-Queens Problem) satisfies these conditions.

The Monte Carlo Technique requires that we randomly generate a promising child of a node. By this we mean that a random process is used to generate the promising child. (See Section A.8.1 in Appendix A for a discussion of random processes.) When implementing the technique on a computer, we can generate only a pseudorandom promising child. The technique is as follows:

1. Let m_0 be the number of promising children of the root.
2. Randomly generate a promising node at level 1. Let m_1 be the number of promising children of this node.
3. Randomly generate a promising child of the node obtained in the previous step. Let m_2 be the number of promising children of this node.

$$\vdots$$

4. Randomly generate a promising child of the node obtained in the previous step. Let m_i be the number of promising children of this node.

$$\vdots$$

This process continues until no promising children are found. Because we assume that nodes at the same level in the state space tree all have the same number of children, m_i is an estimate of the average number of promising children of nodes at level i. Let

$$t_i = \text{total number of children of a node at level } i.$$

Because all t_i children of a node are checked and only the m_i promising children have children that are checked, an estimate of the total number of nodes checked by the backtracking algorithm to find all solutions is given by

$$1 + t_0 + m_0 t_1 + m_0 m_1 t_2 + \cdots + m_0 m_1 \cdots m_{i-1} t_i + \cdots.$$

A general algorithm for computing this estimate follows. In this algorithm, a variable *mprod* is used to represent the produce $m_0 m_1 \cdots m_{i-1}$ at each level.

Algorithm 5.2 Monte Carlo Estimate

Problem: Estimate the efficiency of a backtracking algorithm using a Monte Carlo algorithm.

Inputs: an instance of the problem that the backtracking algorithm solves.

Outputs: an estimate of the number of nodes in the pruned state space tree produced by the algorithm, which is the number of the nodes the algorithm will check to find all solutions to the instance.

```
int estimate ( )
{
    node v;
    int m, mprod, t, numnodes;
```

```
v = root of state space tree;
numnodes = 1;
m = 1;
mprod = 1;
while (m != 0) {
   t = number of children of v;
   mprod = mprod * m;
   numnodes = numnodes + mprod * t;
   m = number of promising children of v;
   if (m != 0)
      v = randomly selected promising child of v;
}
return numnodes;
}
```

A specific version of Algorithm 5.2 for Algorithm 5.1 (The Backtracking Algorithm for the *n*-Queens Problem) follows. We pass *n* to this algorithm because *n* is the parameter to Algorithm 5.1.

Algorithm 5.3

Monte Carlo Estimate for Algorithm 5.1
(The Backtracking Algorithm for the *n*-Queens Problem)

Problem: Estimate the efficiency of Algorithm 5.1.

Inputs: positive integer *n*.

Outputs: an estimate of the number of nodes in the pruned state space tree produced by Algorithm 5.1, which is the number of the nodes the algorithm will check before finding all ways to position *n* queens on an $n \times n$ chessboard so that no two queens threaten each other.

```
int estimate_n_queens (int n)
{
   index i, j, col[1..n];
   int m, mprod, numnodes;
   set_of_index prom_children;
```

```
i = 0;
numnodes = 1;
m = 1;
mprod = 1;
while (m != 0 && i != n) {
   mprod = mprod * m;
   numnodes = numnodes + mprod * n;     // number of children t is n.
   i++;
   m = 0;
   prom_children = ∅;                   // Initialize set of promising
   for (j = 1; j <= n; j++) {           // children to empty.
      col[i] = j;
      if (promising(i)) {               // Determine promising
         m++;                           // children. Function
         prom_children = prom_children ∪ {j};  // promising is the one in
      }                                 // Algorithm 5.1.
   }
   if (m != 0) {
      j = random selection from prom_children;
      col[i] = j;
   }
}
return numnodes;
}
```

When a Monte Carlo algorithm is used, the estimate should be run more than once, and the average of the results should be used as the actual estimate. Using standard methods from statistics, one can determine a confidence interval for the actual number of nodes checked from the results of the trials. As a rule of thumb, around 20 trials are ordinarily sufficient. We caution that although the probability of obtaining a good estimate is high when the Monte Carlo algorithm is run many times, there is never a guarantee that it is a good estimate.

The n-Queens Problem has only one instance for each value of n. This is not so for most problems solved with backtracking algorithms. The estimate produced by any one application of the Monte Carlo Technique is for one particular instance. As discussed before, given two instances with the same value of n, one may require that very few nodes be checked whereas the other requires that the entire state space tree be checked.

The estimate obtained using a Monte Carlo estimate is not necessarily a good indication of how many nodes will be checked before the first solution is found. To obtain only one solution, the algorithm may check a small fraction of the nodes it would check to find all solutions. For example, Figure 5.4 shows that the two branches that place the first queen in the third and fourth columns, respectively, need not be traversed to find only one solution.

5.4 THE SUM-OF-SUBSETS PROBLEM

Recall our thief and the 0-1 Knapsack Problem from Section 4.4.1. In this problem, there is a set of items the thief can steal, and each item has its own weight and profit. The thief's knapsack will break if the total weight of the items in it exceeds W. Therefore, the goal is to maximize the total value of the stolen items while not making the total weight exceed W. Suppose here that the items all have the same profit per unit weight. Then an optimal solution for the thief would simply be a set of items that maximized the total weight, subject to the constraint that its total weight did not exceed W. The thief might first try to determine whether there was a set whose total weight equaled W, because this would be best. The problem of determining such sets is called the Sum-of-Subsets Problem.

Specifically, in the Sum-of-Subsets Problem, there are n positive integers (weights) w_i and a positive integer W. The goal is to find all subsets of the integers that sum to W. As mentioned earlier, we usually state our problems so as to find all solutions. For the purposes of the thief's application, however, only one solution need be found.

Example 5.2 Suppose that $n = 5$, $W = 21$, and

$$w_1 = 5 \qquad w_2 = 6 \qquad w_3 = 10 \qquad w_4 = 11 \qquad w_5 = 16.$$

Because

$$w_1 + w_2 + w_3 = 5 + 6 + 10 = 21$$
$$w_1 + w_5 = 5 + 16 = 21$$
$$w_3 + w_4 = 10 + 11 = 21,$$

the solutions are $\{w_1, w_2, w_3\}$, $\{w_1, w_5\}$, and $\{w_3, w_4\}$.

This instance can be solved by inspection. For larger values of n, a systematic approach is necessary. One approach is to create a state space tree. A possible way to structure the tree appears in Figure 5.7. For the sake of simplicity, the tree in this figure is for only three weights. We go to the left from the root to include w_1, and we go to the right to exclude w_1. Similarly, we go to the left from a node at level 1 to include w_2, and we go to the right to exclude w_2, etc. Each subset is represented by a path from the root to a leaf. When we include w_i, we write w_i on the edge where we include it. When we do not include w_i, we write 0.

Figure 5.7 A state space tree for instances of the Sum-of-Subsets Problem in which $n = 3$.

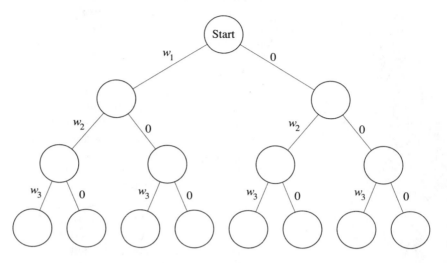

Example 5.3 Figure 5.8 shows the state space tree for $n = 3$, $W = 6$, and

$$w_1 = 2 \qquad w_2 = 4 \qquad w_3 = 5.$$

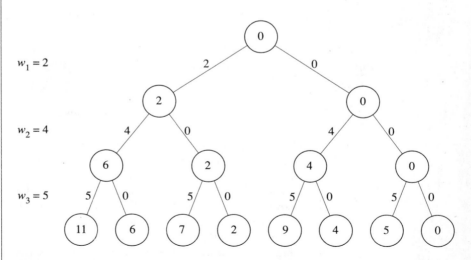

Figure 5.8 A state space tree for the Sum-of-Subsets Problem for the instance in Example 5.3. Stored at each node is the total weight included up to that node.

At each node, we have written the sum of the weights that have been included up to that point. Therefore, each leaf contains the sum of the weights in the subset leading to that leaf. The second leaf from the left is the only one containing a 6. Because the path to this leaf represents the subset $\{w_1, w_2\}$, this subset is the only solution.

If we sort the weights in nondecreasing order before doing the search, there is an obvious sign telling us that a node is nonpromising. If the weights are sorted in this manner, then w_{i+1} is the lightest weight remaining when we are at the ith level. Let *weight* be the sum of the weights that have been included up to a node at level i. If w_{i+1} would bring the value of *weight* above W, then so would any other weight following it. Therefore, unless *weight* equals W (which means that there is a solution at the node), a node at the ith level is nonpromising if

$$weight + w_{i+1} > W.$$

There is another, less obvious sign telling us that a node is nonpromising. If, at a given node, adding all the weights of the remaining items to *weight* does not make *weight* at least equal to W, then *weight* could never become equal to W by expanding beyond the node. This means that if **total** is the total weight of the remaining weights, a node is nonpromising if

$$weight + total < W.$$

The following example illustrates these backtracking strategies.

Example 5.4   Figure 5.9 shows the pruned state space tree when backtracking is used with $n = 4$, $W = 13$, and

$$w_1 = 3 \qquad w_2 = 4 \qquad w_3 = 5 \qquad w_4 = 6.$$

The only solution is found at the shaded node. The solution is $\{w_1, w_2, w_4\}$. The nonpromising nodes are marked with crosses. The nodes containing 12, 8, and 9 are nonpromising because adding the next weight (6) would make the value of *weight* exceed W. The nodes containing 7, 3, 4, and 0 are nonpromising because there is not enough total weight remaining to bring the value of *weight* up to W. Notice that a leaf in the state space tree that does not contain a solution is automatically nonpromising because there are no weights remaining that could bring *weight* up to W. The leaf containing 7 illustrates this. There are only 15 nodes in the pruned state space tree, whereas the entire state space tree contains 31 nodes.

Figure 5.9 The pruned state space tree produced using backtracking in Example 5.4. Stored at each node is the total weight included up to that node. The only solution is found at the shaded node. Each nonpromising node is marked with a cross.

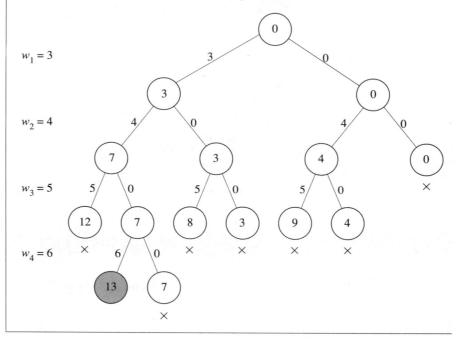

When the sum of the weights included up to a node equals W, there is a solution at that node. Therefore, we cannot get another solution by including more items. This means that if

$$W = weight,$$

we should print the solution and backtrack. This backtracking is provided automatically by our general procedure *checknode* because it never expands beyond a promising node where a solution is found. Recall that when we discussed *checknode* we mentioned that some backtracking algorithms sometimes find a solution before reaching a leaf in the state space tree. This is one such algorithm.

Next we present the algorithm that employs these strategies. The algorithm uses an array *include*. It sets *include*[i] to "yes" if $w[i]$ is to be included and to "no" if it is not.

Algorithm 5.4

The Backtracking Algorithm for the Sum-of-Subsets Problem

Problem: Given n positive integers (weights) and a positive integer W, determine all combinations of the integers that sum to W.

Inputs: positive integer *n*, sorted (nondecreasing order) array of positive integers *w* indexed from 1 to *n*, and a positive integer *W*.

Outputs: all combinations of the integers that sum to *W*.

```
void sum_of_subsets (index i,
                        int weight, int total)
{
  if (promising(i))
    if (weight == W)
      cout << include[1] through include[i];
    else {
      include[i + 1] = "yes";                    // Include w[i + 1].
      sum_of_subsets(i + 1, weight + w[i + 1], total - w[i + 1]);
      include[i + 1] = "no";                     // Do not include w[i + 1].
      sum_of_subsets(i + 1, weight, total - w[i + 1]);
    }
}

bool promising (index i);
{
return (weight + total >= W) && (weight == W || weight + w[i + 1] <= W);
}
```

Following our usual convention, *n, w, W,* and *include* are not inputs to our routines. If these variables were defined globally, the top-level call to *sum_of_subsets* would be as follows:

sum_of_subsets(0, 0, *total*);

where initially

$$total = \sum_{j=1}^{n} w[j].$$

Recall that a leaf in the state space tree that does not contain a solution is nonpromising because there are no weights left that could bring the value of *weight* up to *W*. This means that the algorithm should not need to check for the terminal condition $i = n$. Let's verify that the algorithm implements this correctly. When $i = n$, the value of *total* is 0 (because there are no weights remaining). Therefore, at this point

$$weight + total = weight + 0 = weight,$$

which means that

$$weight \, + \, total \geq W$$

is true only if $weight \geq W$. Because we always keep $weight \leq W$, we must have $weight = W$. Therefore, when $i = n$, function *promising* returns true only if $weight = W$. But in this case there is no recursive call because we found a solution. Therefore, we do not need to check for the terminal condition $i = n$. Notice that there is never a reference to the nonexistent array item $w[n + 1]$ in function *promising* because of our assumption that the second condition in an **or** expression is not evaluated when the first condition is true.

The number of nodes in the state space tree searched by Algorithm 5.4 is equal to

$$1 + 2 + 2^2 + \cdots + 2^n = 2^{n+1} - 1.$$

This equality is obtained in Example A.3 in Appendix A. Given only this result, the possibility exists that the worst case could be much better than this. That is, it could be that for every instance only a small portion of the state space tree is searched. This is not the case. For each n, it is possible to construct an instance for which the algorithm visits an exponentially large number of nodes. This is true even if we want only one solution. To this end, if we take

$$\sum_{i=1}^{n-1} w_i < W \qquad w_n = W,$$

there is only one solution $\{w_n\}$, and it will not be found until an exponentially large number of nodes are visited. As stressed before, even though the worst case is exponential, the algorithm can be efficient for many large instances. In the exercises you are asked to write programs using the Monte Carlo Technique to estimate the efficiency of Algorithm 5.4 on various instances.

Even if we state the problem so as to require only one solution, the Sum-of-Subsets Problem, like the 0-1 Knapsack Problem, is in the class of problems discussed in Chapter 9.

5.5 GRAPH COLORING

The m-Coloring Problem concerns finding all ways to color an undirected graph using at most m different colors, so that no two adjacent vertices are the same color. We usually call the m-Coloring Problem a unique problem for each value of m.

Example 5.5 Consider the graph in Figure 5.10. There is no solution to the 2-Coloring Problem for this graph because, if we can use at most two different colors, there is no way to color the vertices so that no adjacent vertices are the same color. One solution to the 3-Coloring Problem for this graph is as follows:

Vertex	Color
v_1	color 1
v_2	color 2
v_3	color 3
v_4	color 2

There are a total of six solutions to the 3-Coloring Problem for this graph. However, the six solutions are only different in the way the colors are permuted. For example, another solution is to color v_1 color 2, v_2 and v_4 color 1, and v_3 color 3.

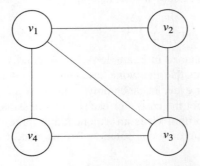

Figure 5.10 Graph for which there is no solution to the 2-Coloring Problem. A solution to the 3-Coloring Problem for this graph is shown in Example 5.5.

An important application of graph coloring is the coloring of maps. A graph is called **planar** if it can be drawn in a plane in such a way that no two edges cross each other. The graph at the bottom of Figure 5.11 is planar. However, if we were to add the edges (v_1, v_5) and (v_2, v_4) it would no longer be planar. To every map there corresponds a planar graph. Each region in the map is represented by a vertex. If one region is adjacent to another region, we join their corresponding vertices by an edge. Figure 5.11 shows a map at the top and its planar graph representation at the bottom. The m-Coloring Problem for planar graphs is to determine how many ways the map can be colored, using at most m colors, so that no two adjacent regions are the same color.

A straightforward state space tree for the m-Coloring Problem is one in which each possible color is tried for vertex v_1 at level 1, each possible color is tried for vertex v_2 at level 2, and so on until each possible color has been tried for vertex v_n at level n. Each path from the root to a leaf is a candidate solution. We check whether a candidate solution is a solution by determining whether any two adjacent vertices are the same color. To avoid confusion, remember in the following discussion that "node" refers to a node in the state space tree and "vertex" refers to a vertex in the graph being colored.

We can backtrack in this problem because a node is nonpromising if a vertex

Figure 5.11 Map (top) and its planar graph representation (bottom).

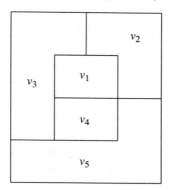

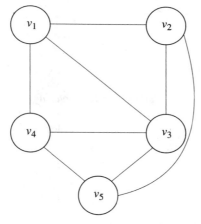

that is adjacent to the vertex being colored at the node has already been colored the color that is being used at the node. Figure 5.12 shows a portion of the pruned state space tree that results when this backtracking strategy is applied to a 3-coloring of the graph in Figure 5.10. The number in a node is the number of the color used on the vertex being colored at the node. The first solution is found at the shaded node. Nonpromising nodes are labeled with crosses. After v_1 is colored color 1, choosing color 1 for v_2 is nonpromising because v_1 is adjacent to v_2. Similarly, after v_1, v_2, and v_3 have been colored colors 1, 2, and 3, respectively, choosing color 1 for v_4 is nonpromising because v_1 is adjacent to v_4.

Next we present an algorithm that solves the m-Coloring Problem for all values of m. In this algorithm the graph is represented by an adjacency matrix, as was done in Section 4.1. However, because the graph is unweighted, each entry in the matrix is simply true or false depending on whether or not there is an edge between the two vertices.

Algorithm 5.5   The Backtracking Algorithm for the *m*-Coloring Problem

Problem: Determine all ways in which the vertices in an undirected graph can be colored, using only *m* colors, so that adjacent vertices are not the same color.

Inputs: positive integers *n* and *m*, and an undirected graph containing *n* vertices. The graph is represented by a two-dimensional array *W*, which has both its rows and columns indexed from 1 to *n*, where $W[i][j]$ is true if there is an edge between *i*th vertex and the *j*th vertex and false otherwise.

Outputs: all possible colorings of the graph, using at most *m* colors, so that no two adjacent vertices are the same color. The output for each coloring is an array *vcolor* indexed from 1 to *n*, where *vcolor*[*i*] is the color (an integer between 1 and *m*) assigned to the *i*th vertex.

```
void m_coloring (index i)
{
   int color;

   if (promising(i))
      if (i == n)
         cout << vcolor[1] through vcolor[n];
      else
         for (color = 1; color <= m; color++) {   // Try every color for
            vcolor[i + 1] = color;                 // next vertex.
            m_coloring(i + 1);
         }
}

bool promising (index i)
{
   index j;
   bool switch;

   switch = true;
   j = 1;
   while (j < i && switch) {                       // Check if an adjacent
      if (W[i][j] && vcolor[i] == vcolor[j])       // vertex is already this
         switch = false;                           // color.
      j++;
   }
   return switch;
}
```

Following our usual convention, *n, m, W,* and *vcolor* are not inputs to either routine. In an implementation of the algorithm, the routines would be defined

Figure 5.12 A portion of the pruned state space tree produced using backtracking to do a 3-coloring of the graph in Figure 5.10. The first solution is found at the shaded node. Each nonpromising node is marked with a cross.

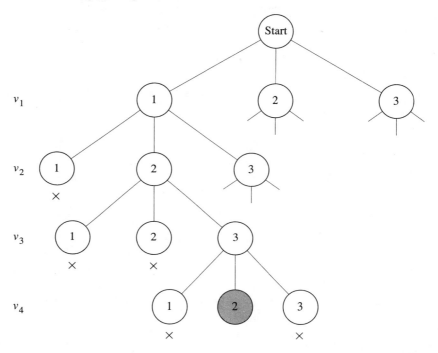

locally in a simple procedure that had n, m, and W as inputs, and *vcolor* defined locally. The top level call to *m_coloring* would be

   m_coloring(0).

The number of nodes in the state space tree for this algorithm is equal to

$$1 + m + m^2 + \cdots + m^n = \frac{m^{n+1} - 1}{m - 1}.$$

This equality is obtained in Example A.4 in Appendix A. For a given m and n, it is possible to create an instance that checks at least an exponentially large number of nodes (in terms of n). For example, if m is only 2, and we take a graph in which v_n has an edge to every other node, and the only other edge is one between v_{n-2} and v_{n-1}, no solution exists, but almost every node in the state space tree will be visited to determine this. As with any backtracking algorithm, the algorithm can be efficient for a particular large instance. The Monte Carlo Technique described in Section 5.3 is applicable to this algorithm, which means that it can be used to estimate the efficiency for a particular instance.

In the exercises, you are asked to solve the 2-Coloring Problem with an algorithm whose worst-case time complexity is not exponential in n. For $m \geq 3$, no one has ever developed an algorithm that is efficient in the worst case. Like the Sum-of-Subsets Problem and the 0-1 Knapsack Problem, the m-Coloring Problem for $m \geq 3$ is in the class of problems discussed in Chapter 9. This is the case even if we are looking for only one m-coloring of the graph.

5.6 THE HAMILTONIAN CIRCUITS PROBLEM

Recall Example 3.12, in which Nancy and Ralph were competing for the same sales position. The one who could cover all 20 cities in the sales territory the fastest was to win the job. Using the dynamic programming algorithm, with a time complexity given by

$$T(n) = (n - 1)(n - 2)2^{n-3},$$

Nancy found a shortest tour in 45 seconds. Ralph tried computing all 19! tours. Because his algorithm takes over 3,800 years, it is still running. Of course, Nancy won the job. Suppose she did such a good job that the boss doubled her territory, giving her a 40-city territory. In this territory, however, not every city is connected to every other city by a road. Recall that we assumed that Nancy's dynamic programming algorithm took 1 microsecond to process its basic operation. A quick calculation shows that it would take this algorithm

$$(40 - 1)(40 - 2)2^{40-3} \ \mu s = 6.46 \ \text{years}$$

to determine a shortest tour for the 40-city territory. Because this amount of time is intolerable, Nancy must look for another algorithm. She reasons that perhaps it is too hard to find an optimal tour, and so she becomes content with just finding any tour. If there were a road from every city to every other city, any permutation of cities would constitute a tour. However, recall that this is not the case in Nancy's new territory. Therefore, her problem now is to find any tour in a graph. This problem is called the Hamiltonian Circuits Problem, named after Sir William Hamilton, who suggested it. The problem can be stated for either a directed graph (the way we stated the Traveling Salesperson Problem) or an undirected graph. Because it is usually stated for an undirected graph, this is the way we will state it here. As applied to Nancy's dilemma, this means that there is a unique two-way road connecting two cities when they are connected at all.

Specifically, given a connected, undirected graph, a *Hamiltonian Circuit* (also called a tour) is a path that starts at a given vertex, visits each vertex in the graph exactly once, and ends at the starting vertex. The graph in Figure 5.13(a) contains the Hamiltonian Circuit $[v_1, v_2, v_8, v_7, v_6, v_5, v_4, v_3, v_1]$, but the one in Figure 5.13(b) does not contain a Hamiltonian Circuit. The Hamiltonian Circuits Problem determines the Hamiltonian Circuits in a connected, undirected graph.

A state space tree for this problem is as follows. Put the starting vertex at

Figure 5.13 The graph in (a) contains the Hamiltonian Circuit
$[v_1, v_2, v_8, v_7, v_6, v_5, v_4, v_3, v_1]$; the graph in (b) contains no Hamiltonian Circuit.

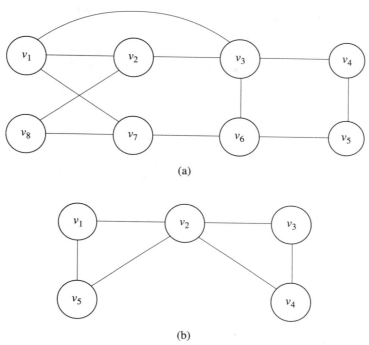

(a)

(b)

level 0 in the tree; call it the zeroth vertex on the path. At level 1, consider each
vertex other than the starting vertex as the first vertex after the starting one. At
level 2, consider each of these same vertices as the second vertex, and so on.
Finally, at level $n - 1$, consider each of these same vertices as the $(n - 1)$st
vertex.

The following considerations enable us to backtrack in this state space tree:

1. The ith vertex on the path must be adjacent to the $(i - 1)$st vertex on the
    path.
2. The $(n - 1)$st vertex must be adjacent to the 0th vertex (the starting one).
3. The ith vertex cannot be one of the first $i - 1$ vertices.

The algorithm that follows uses these considerations to backtrack. This algorithm is hard-coded to make v_1 the starting vertex.

Algorithm 5.6   The Backtracking Algorithm for the Hamiltonian Circuits Problem

Problem: Determine all Hamiltonian Circuits in a connected, undirected graph.

Inputs: positive integer n and an undirected graph containing n vertices. The
graph is represented by a two-dimensional array W, which has both its rows and

columns indexed from 1 to *n*, where $W[i][j]$ is true if there is an edge between the *i*th vertex and the *j*th vertex and false otherwise.

Outputs: all paths that start at a given vertex, visit each vertex in the graph exactly once, and end up at the starting vertex. The output for each path is an array of indices *vindex* indexed from 0 to $n - 1$, where $vindex[i]$ is the index of the *i*th vertex on the path. The index of the starting vertex is $vindex[0]$.

```
void hamiltonian (index i)
{
  index j;

  if (promising(i)
    if (i == n - 1)
      cout << vindex[0] through vindex[n - 1];
    else
      for (j = 2; j <= n; j++) {          // Try all vertices as
        vindex[i + 1] = j;                // next one.
        hamiltonian(i + 1);
      }
}


bool promising (index i)
{
  index j;
  bool switch;

  if (i == n - 1 && ! W[vindex[n - 1]] [vindex[0]])   // First vertex must
    switch = false;                                   // be adjacent to
  else if (i > 0 && ! W[vindex[i - 1]][vindex[i]])    // last. ith vertex
    switch = false;                                   // must be adjacent
  else {                                              // to (i - 1)st.
    switch = true;
    j = 1;
  while (j < i && switch) {                            // Check if vertex is
      if (vindex[i] == vindex[j])                      // already selected.
        switch = false;
      j++;
    }
  }
  return switch;
}
```

Following our convention, *n, W,* and *vindex* are not inputs to either routine. If these variables were defined globally, the top-level call to *hamiltonian* would be as follows:

vindex[0] = 1;   // Make v_1 the starting vertex.
hamiltonian(0);

The number of nodes in the state space tree for this algorithm is

$$1 + (n - 1) + (n - 1)^2 + \cdots + (n - 1)^{n-1} = \frac{(n - 1)^n - 1}{n - 2},$$

which is much worse that exponential. This equality is obtained in Example A.4 in Appendix A. Although the following instance does not check the entire state space tree, it does check a worse-than-exponential number of nodes. Let the only edge to v_1 be one from v_2, and let all the vertices other than v_1 have edges to each other. There is no Hamiltonian Circuit for the graph, and the algorithm will check a worse-than-exponential number of nodes to learn this.

Returning to Nancy's dilemma, the possibility exists that the backtracking algorithm (for the Hamiltonian Circuits Problem) will take even longer that the dynamic programming algorithm (for the Traveling Salesperson Problem) to solve her particular 40-city instance. Because the conditions for using the Monte Carlo Technique are satisfied in this problem, she can use that technique to estimate the efficiency for her instance. However, the Monte Carlo Technique estimates the time to find all circuits. Because Nancy needs only one circuit, she can have the algorithm stop when the first circuit is found (if there is a circuit). You are encouraged to develop an instance when $n = 40$, estimate how quickly the algorithm should find all circuits in the instance, and run the algorithm to find one circuit. In this way you can create your own ending to the story.

Even if we want only one tour, the Hamiltonial Circuits Problem is in the class of problems discussed in Chapter 9.

5.7 THE 0-1 KNAPSACK PROBLEM

We solved this problem using dynamic programming in Section 4.4. Here we solve it using backtracking. After that we compare the backtracking algorithm with the dynamic programming algorithm.

5.7.1 A Backtracking Algorithm for the 0-1 Knapsack Problem

Recall that in this problem we have a set of items, each of which has a weight and a profit. The weights and profits are positive integers. A thief plans to carry off stolen items in a knapsack, and the knapsack will break if the total weight of the items placed in it exceeds some positive integer *W*. The thief's objective is to determine a set of items that maximizes the total profit under the constraint that the total weight cannot exceed *W*.

We can solve this problem using a state space tree exactly like the one in the

Sum-of-Subsets Problem (see Section 5.4). That is, we go to the left from the root to include the first item, and we go to the right to exclude it. Similarly, we go to the left from a node at level 1 to include the second item, and we go to the right to exclude it, and so on. Each path from the root to a leaf is a candidate solution.

This problem is different from the others discussed in this chapter in that it is an optimization problem. This means that we do not know if a node contains a solution until the search is over. Therefore, we backtrack a little differently. If the items included up to a node have a greater total profit than the best solution so far, we change the value of the best solution so far. However, we may still find a better solution at one of the node's descendants (by stealing more items). Therefore, for optimization problems we always visit a promising node's children. The following is a general algorithm for backtracking in the case of optimization problems.

```
void checknode (node v)
{
   node u;

   if (value(v) is better than best)
      best = value(v);
   if (promising(v))
      for (each child u of v)
         checknode(u);
}
```

The variable *best* has the value of the best solution found so far, and *value(v)* is the value of the solution at the node. After *best* is initialized to a value that is worse than the value of any candidate solution, the root is passed at the top level. Notice that a node is promising only if we should expand to its children. Recall that our other algorithms also call a node promising if there is a solution at the node.

Next we apply this technique to the 0-1 Knapsack Problem. First let's look for signs telling us that a node is nonpromising. An obvious sign that a node is nonpromising is that there is no capacity left in the knapsack for more items. Therefore, if *weight* is the sum of the weights of the items that have been included up to some node, the node is nonpromising if

$$weight \geq W.$$

It is nonpromising even if *weight* equals W because, in the case of optimization problems, "promising" means that we should expand to the children.

We can use considerations from the greedy approach to find a less obvious sign. Recall that this approach failed to give an optimal solution to this problem in Section 4.4. Here we will only use greedy considerations to limit our search; we will not develop a greedy algorithm. To that end, we first order the items in nonincreasing order according to the values of p_i/w_i, where w_i and p_i are the weight and profit, respectively, of the ith item. Suppose we are trying to determine whether a particular node is promising. No matter how we choose the remaining items, we cannot obtain a higher profit than we would obtain if we were allowed to use the restrictions in the Fractional Knapsack Problem from this node on (recall that in this problem the thief can steal any fraction of an item taken). Therefore, we can obtain an upper bound on the profit that could be obtained by expanding beyond that node as follows. Let *profit* be the sum of the profits of the items included up to the node. Recall that *weight* is the sum of the weights of those items. We initialize variables *bound* and *totweight* to *profit* and *weight*, respectively. Next we greedily grab items, adding their profits to *bound* and their weights to *totweight*, until we get to an item that if grabbed would bring *totweight* above W. We grab the fraction of that item allowed by the remaining weight, and we add the value of that fraction to *bound*. If we are able to get only a fraction of this last weight, this node cannot lead to a profit equal to *bound*, but *bound* is still an upper bound on the profit we could achieve by expanding beyond the node. Suppose the node is at level i, and the node at level k is the one that would bring the sum of the weights above W. Then

$$totweight = weight + \sum_{j=i+1}^{k-1} w_j, \quad \text{and}$$

$$bound = \underbrace{\left(profit + \sum_{j=i+1}^{k-1} p_j\right)}_{\substack{\text{Profit from first} \\ k-1 \text{ items taken}}} + \underbrace{(W - totweight)}_{\substack{\text{Capacity available} \\ \text{for } k\text{th item}}} \times \underbrace{\frac{p_k}{w_k}}_{\substack{\text{Profit per unit} \\ \text{weight for } k\text{th item}}}.$$

If *maxprofit* is the value of the profit in the best solution found so far, then a node at level i is nonpromising if

$$bound \leq maxprofit.$$

We are using greedy considerations only to obtain a bound that tells us whether we should expand beyond a node. We are not using it to greedily grab items with no opportunity to reconsider later (as is done in the greedy approach).

Before presenting the algorithm, we show an example.

Example 5.6 Suppose that $n = 4$, $W = 16$, and we have the following:

i	p_i	w_i	$\frac{p_i}{w_i}$
1	$40	2	$20
2	$30	5	$6
3	$50	10	$5
4	$10	5	$2

We have already ordered the items according to p_i/w_i. For simplicity, we chose values of p_i and w_i that make p_i/w_i an integer. In general, this need not be the case. Figure 5.14 shows the pruned state space tree produced by using the backtracking considerations just discussed. The total profit, total weight, and bound are specified from top to bottom at each node. These are the values of the variables *profit, weight,* and *bound* mentioned in the previous discussion. The maximum profit is found at the shaded node. Each node is labeled with its level and its position from the left in the tree. For example, the shaded node is labeled (3, 3) because it is at level 3 and it is the third node from the left at that level. Next we

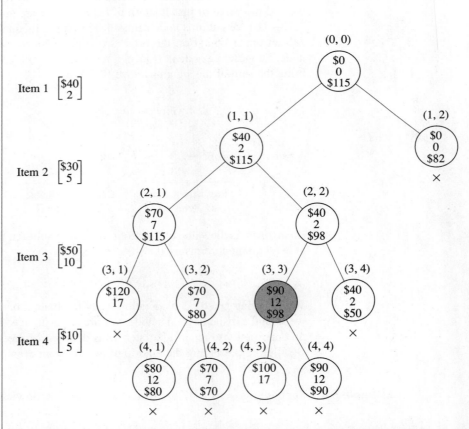

Figure 5.14 The pruned state space tree produced using backtracking in Example 5.6. Stored at each node from top to bottom are the total profit of the items stolen up to the node, their total weight, and the bound on the total profit that could be obtained by expanding beyond the node. The optimal solution is found at the shaded node. Each nonpromising node is marked with a cross.

present the steps that produced the pruned tree. In these steps we refer to a node
by its label.

1. Set *maxprofit* to $0.
2. Visit node (0, 0) (the root).
   (a) Compute its profit and weight.

$$profit = \$0$$
$$weight = 0$$

   (b) Compute its bound. Because $2 + 5 + 10 = 17$, and $17 > 16$, the value
       of W, the third item would bring the sum of the weights above W. There-
       fore, $k = 3$, and we have

$$totweight = weight + \sum_{j=0+1}^{3-1} w_j = 0 + 2 + 5 = 7$$

$$bound = profit + \sum_{j=0+1}^{3-1} p_j + (W - totweight) \times \frac{p_3}{w_3}$$

$$= \$0 + \$40 + \$30 + (16 - 7) \times \frac{\$50}{10} = \$115.$$

   (c) Determine that it is promising because its weight 0 is less than 16, the
       value of W, and its bound $115 is greater than $0, the value of *maxprofit*.
3. Visit node (1, 1).
   (a) Compute its profit and weight.

$$profit = \$0 + \$40 = \$40$$
$$weight = 0 + 2 = 2$$

   (b) Because its weight 2 is less than or equal to 16, the value of W, and its
       profit $40 is greater than $0, the value of *maxprofit*, set *maxprofit* to $40.
   (c) Compute its bound. Because $2 + 5 + 10 = 17$, and $17 > 16$, the value
       of W, the third item would bring the sum of the weights above W. There-
       fore, $k = 3$, and we have

$$totweight = weight + \sum_{j=1+1}^{3-1} w_j = 2 + 5 = 7$$

$$bound = profit + \sum_{j=1+1}^{3-1} p_j + (W - totweight) \times \frac{p_3}{w_3}$$

$$= \$40 + \$30 + (16 - 7) \times \frac{\$50}{10} = \$115.$$

   (d) Determine that it is promising because its weight 2 is less than 16, the
       value of W, and its bound $115 is greater than $0, the value of *maxprofit*.
4. Visit node (2, 1).
   (a) Compute its profit and weight.

$$profit = \$40 + \$30 = \$70$$
$$weight = 2 + 5 = 7$$

(b) Because its weight 7 is less than or equal to 16, the value of W, and its profit \$70 is greater than \$40, the value of *maxprofit,* set *maxprofit* to \$70.

(c) Compute its bound.

$$totweight = weight + \sum_{j=2+1}^{3-1} w_j = 7$$
$$bound = \$70 + (16 - 7) \times \frac{\$50}{10} = \$115$$

(d) Determine that it is promising because its weight 7 is less than 16, the value of W, and its bound \$115 is greater than \$70, the value of *maxprofit*.

5. Visit node (3, 1).

(a) Compute its profit and weight.

$$profit = \$70 + \$50 = \$120$$
$$weight = 7 + 10 = 17$$

(b) Because its weight 17 is greater than 16, the value of W, *maxprofit* does not change.

(c) Determine that it is nonpromising because its weight 17 is greater than or equal to 16, the value of W.

(d) The bound for this node is not computed, because its weight has determined it to be nonpromising.

6. Backtrack to node (2, 1).

7. Visit node (3, 2).

(a) Compute its profit and weight. Because we are not including item 3,

$$profit = \$70$$
$$weight = 7$$

(b) Because its profit \$70 is less than or equal to \$70, the value of *maxprofit,* *maxprofit* does not change.

(c) Compute its bound. The fourth weight would not bring the sum of the items above W, and there are only four items. Therefore, $k = 5$, and

$$bound = profit + \sum_{j=3+1}^{5-1} p_j = \$70 + \$10 = \$80.$$

(d) Determine that it is promising because its weight 7 is less than 16, the value of W, and its bound \$80 is greater than \$70, the value of *maxprofit*.

(From now on we leave the computations of profits, weights, and bounds as exercises. Furthermore, when *maxprofit* does not change, we will not mention it.)

8. Visit node (4, 1)
   (a) Compute its profit and weight to be $80 and 12.
   (b) Because its weight 12 is less than or equal to 16, the value of W, and its profit $80 is greater than $70, the value of *maxprofit*, set *maxprofit* to $80.
   (c) Compute its bound to be $80.
   (d) Determine that it is nonpromising because its bound $80 is less than or equal to $80, the value of *maxprofit*. Leaves in the state space tree are automatically nonpromising because their bounds are always less than or equal to *maxprofit*.

9. Backtrack to node (3, 2).

10. Visit node (4, 2).
    (a) Compute its profit and weight to be $70 and 7.
    (b) Compute its bound to be $70.
    (c) Determine that it is nonpromising because its bound $70 is less than or equal to $80, the value of *maxprofit*.

11. Backtrack to node (1, 1).

12. Visit node (2, 2).
    (a) Compute its profit and weight to be $40 and 2.
    (b) Compute its bound to be $98.
    (c) Determine that it is promising because its weight 2 is less than 16, the value of W, and its bound $98 is greater than $80, the value of *maxprofit*.

13. Visit node (3, 3).
    (a) Compute its profit and weight to be $90 and 12.
    (b) Because its weight 12 is less than or equal to 16, the value of W, and its profit $90 is greater than $80, the value of *maxprofit*, set *maxprofit* to $90.
    (c) Compute its bound to be $98.
    (d) Determine that it is promising because its weight 12 is less than 16, the value of W, and its bound $98 is greater than $90, the value of *maxprofit*.

14. Visit node (4, 3).
    (a) Compute its profit and weight to be $100 and 17.
    (b) Determine that it is nonpromising because its weight 17 is greater than or equal to 16, the value of W.
    (c) The bound for this node is not computed because its weight has determined it to be nonpromising.

15. Backtrack to node (3, 3).

16. Visit node (4, 4).
    (a) Compute its profit and weight to be $90 and 12.
    (b) Compute its bound to be $90.
    (c) Determine that it is nonpromising because its bound $90 is less than or equal to $90, the value of *maxprofit*.

17. Backtrack to node (2, 2).
18. Visit node (3, 4).
    (a) Compute its profit and weight to be $40 and 2.
    (b) Compute its bound to be $50.
    (c) Determine that it is nonpromising because its bound $50 is less than or equal to $90, the value of *maxprofit*.
19. Backtrack to root.
20. Visit node (1, 2).
    (a) Compute its profit and weight to be $0 and 0.
    (b) Compute its bound to be $82.
    (c) Determine that it is nonpromising because its bound $82 is less than or equal to $90, the value of *maxprofit*.
21. Backtrack to root.
    (a) Root has no more children. We are done.

There are only 13 nodes in the pruned state space tree, whereas the entire state space tree has 31 nodes.

Next we present the algorithm. Because this is an optimization problem, we have the added task of keeping track of the current best set of items and the total value of their profits. We do this in an array *bestset* and a variable *maxprofit*. Unlike the other problems in this chapter, we state this problem so as to find just one optimal solution.

Algorithm 5.7   The Backtracking Algorithm for the 0-1 Knapsack Problem

Problem: Let n items be given, where each item has a weight and a profit. The weights and profits are positive integers. Furthermore, let a positive integer W be given. Determine a set of items with maximum total profit, under the constraint that the sum of their weights cannot exceed W.

Inputs: Positive integers n and W; arrays w and p, each indexed from 1 to n, and each containing positive integers sorted in nonincreasing order according to the values of $p[i]/w[i]$.

Outputs: An *array bestset* indexed from 1 to n, where the values of *bestset*[i] is "yes" if the ith item is included in the optimal set and is "no" otherwise; an integer *maxprofit* that is the maximum profit.

void *knapsack* (**index** *i*,
                    int *profit*, **int** *weight*)

```
{
   if (weight <= W && profit > maxprofit) {        // This set is best so far.
      maxprofit = profit;
      numbest = i;                                 // Set numbest to number
      bestset = include;                           // of items considered. Set
   }                                               // bestset to this solution.
   if (promising(i)) {
      include[i + 1] = "yes";                      // Include w[i + 1].
      knapsack(i + 1, profit + p[i + 1], weight + w[i + 1]);
      include[i + 1] = "no";                       // Do not include w[i + 1].
      knapsack(i + 1, profit, weight);
   }
}

bool promising (index i)
{
   index j, k;
   int totweight;
   float bound;

   if (weight >= W)                                // Node is promising only
      return false;                                // if we should expand to
   else {                                          // its children. There must
      j = i + 1;                                   // be some capacity left for
      bound = profit;                              // the children.
      totweight = weight;
      while (j <= n && totweight + w[j] <= W) {    // Grab as many items as
         totweight = totweight + w[j];             // possible.
         bound = bound + p[j];
         j++;
      }
      k = j;                                       // Use k for consistency
      if (k <= n)                                  // with formula in text.
         bound = bound + (W - totweight) * p[k]/w[k];  // Grab fraction of kth
      return bound > maxprofit;                    // item.
   }
}
```

Following our usual convention, *n, w, p, W, maxprofit, include, bestset,* and *numbest* are not inputs to either routine. If these variables were defined globally, the following code would produce the maximum profit and a set that has that profit:

```
numbest = 0;
maxprofit = 0;
Knapsack(0, 0, 0);
cout ≪ maxprofit;                    // Write the maximum profit.
for (j = 1; j <= numbest; j++)       // Show an optimal set of items.
   cout ≪ bestset[i];
```

Recall that leaves in the state space tree are automatically nonpromising because their bounds cannot be greater than *maxprofit*. Therefore, we should not need a check for the terminal condition that $i = n$ in function *promising*. Let's confirm that our algorithm does not need to do this check. If $i = n$, *bound* does not change from its initial value *profit*. Because *profit* is less than or equal to *maxprofit*, the expression *bound>maxprofit* is false, which means that function *promising* returns false.

Our upper bound does not change value as we repeatedly proceed to the left in the state space tree until we reach the node at level k. (This can be seen by looking again at the first few steps in Example 5.6.) Therefore, each time a value of k is established, we can save its value and proceed to the left without calling function *promising* until we reach the node at the $(k - 1)$st level. We know that the left child of this node is nonpromising because including the kth item would bring the value of *weight* above W. Therefore, we proceed only to the right from this node. It is only after a move to the right that we need to call function *promising* and determine a new value of k. In the exercises you are asked to write this improvement.

The state space tree in the 0-1 Knapsack Problem is the same as that in the Sum-of-Subsets Problem. As shown in Section 5.4, the number of nodes in that tree is

$$2^{n+1} - 1.$$

Algorithm 5.7 checks all nodes in the state space tree for the following instances. For a given n, let $W = n$, and

$$p_i = 1 \qquad w_i = 1 \qquad \text{for } 1 \leq i \leq n - 1$$
$$p_n = n \qquad w_n = n$$

The optimal solution is to take only the nth item, and this solution will not be found until we go all the way to the right to a depth of $n - 1$ and then go left. Before the optimal solution is found, however, every nonleaf will be found to be promising, which means that all nodes in the state space tree will be checked. Because the Monte Carlo Technique applies in this problem, it can be used to estimate the efficiency of the algorithm for a particular instance.

5.7.2 Comparing the Dynamic Programming Algorithm and the Backtracking Algorithm for the 0-1 Knapsack Problem

Recall from Section 4.4 that the worst-case number of entries that is computed by the dynamic programming algorithm for the 0-1 Knapsack Problem is in $O(minimum(2^n, nW))$. In the worst case, the backtracking algorithm checks $\Theta(2^n)$ nodes. Owing to the additional bound of nW, it may appear that the dynamic programming algorithm is superior. However, in backtracking algorithms the worst case gives little insight into how much checking is usually saved by backtracking. With so many considerations, it is difficult to analyze theoretically the relative efficiencies of the two algorithms. In cases such as this, the algorithms can be compared by running them on many sample instances and seeing which algorithm usually performs better. Horowitz and Sahni (1978) did this and found that the backtracking algorithm is usually more efficient than the dynamic programming algorithm.

Horowitz and Sahni (1974) coupled the divide-and-conquer approach with the dynamic programming approach to develop an algorithm for the 0-1 Knapsack Problem that is $O(2^{n/2})$ in the worst case. They showed that this algorithm is usually more efficient than the backtracking algorithm.

Exercises

Sections 5.1 and 5.2

1. Apply the Backtracking Algorithm for the n-Queens Problem (Algorithm 5.1) to the problem instance in which $n = 8$, and show the actions step by step. Draw the pruned state space tree produced by this algorithm up to the point where the first solution is found.

2. Write a backtracking algorithm for the n-Queens Problem that uses a version of procedure *expand* instead of a version of procedure *checknode*.

3. Show that, without backtracking, 155 nodes must be checked before the first solution to the $n = 4$ instance of the n-Queens Problem is found (in contrast to the 27 nodes in Figure 5.4).

4. Implement the Backtracking Algorithm for the n-Queens Problem (Algorithm 5.1) on your system, and run it on problem instances in which $n = 4$, 8, 10, and 12.

5. Improve the Backtracking Algorithm for the n-Queens Problem (Algorithm 5.1) by having the promising function keep track of the set of columns, of left diagonals, and of right diagonals controlled by the queens already placed.

6. Modify the Backtracking Algorithm for the n-Queens Problem (Algorithm 5.1) so that, instead of generating all possible solutions, it finds only a single solution.

7. Suppose we have a solution to the n-Queens Problem instance in which $n = 4$. Can we extend this solution to find a solution to the problem instance in which $n = 5$, then use the solutions for $n = 4$ and $n = 5$ to construct a solution to the instance in which $n = 6$, and continue this dynamic programming approach to find a solution to any instance in which $n > 4$? Justify your answer.

8. Find at least two instances of the n-Queens Problem that have no solutions.

Section 5.3

9. Implement Algorithm 5.3 (Monte Carlo Estimate for the Backtracking Algorithm for the n-Queens Problem) on your system, run it 20 times on the problem instance in which $n = 8$, and find the average of the 20 estimates.

10. Modify the Backtracking Algorithm for the n-Queens Problem (Algorithm 5.1) so that it finds the number of nodes checked for an instance of a problem, run it on the problem instance in which $n = 8$, and compare the result against the average of Exercise 9.

Section 5.4

11. Use the Backtracking Algorithm for the Sum-of-Subsets Problem (Algorithm 5.4) to find all combinations of the following numbers that sum to $W = 52$.

$$w_1 = 2 \quad w_2 = 10 \quad w_3 = 13 \quad w_4 = 17 \quad w_5 = 22 \quad w_6 = 42$$

Show the actions step by step.

12. Implement the Backtracking Algorithm for the Sum-of-Subsets Problem (Algorithm 5.4) on your system, and run it on the problem instance of Exercise 11.

13. Write a backtracking algorithm for the Sum-of-Subsets Problem that does not sort the weights in advance. Compare the performance of this algorithm with that of Algorithm 5.4.

14. Modify the Backtracking Algorithm for the Sum-of-Subsets Problem (Algorithm 5.4) so that, instead of generating all possible solutions, it finds only a single solution. How does this algorithm perform with respect to Algorithm 5.4?

15. Use the Monte Carlo Technique to estimate the efficiency of the Backtracking Algorithm for the Sum-of-Subsets Problem (Algorithm 5.4).

Section 5.5

16. Use the Backtracking Algorithm for the *m*-Coloring Problem (Algorithm 5.5) to find all possible colorings of the graph below using the three colors red, green, and white. Show the actions step by step.

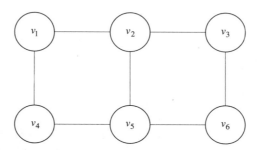

17. Suppose that to color a graph properly we choose a starting vertex and a color to color as many vertices as possible. Then we select a new color and a new uncolored vertex to color as many more vertices as possible. We repeat this process until all the vertices of the graph are colored or all the colors are exhausted. Write an algorithm for this greedy approach to color a graph of *n* vertices. Analyze this algorithm and show the results using order notation.

18. Use the algorithm of Exercise 17 to color the graph of Exercise 16.

19. Suppose we are interested in minimizing the number of colors used in coloring a graph. Does the greedy approach of Exercise 17 guarantee an optimal solution? Justify your answer.

20. Compare the performance of the Backtracking Algorithm for the *m*-Coloring Problem (Algorithm 5.5) and the greedy algorithm of Exercise 17. Considering the result(s) of the comparison, and your answer to Exercise 19, why might one be interested in using an algorithm based on the greedy approach?

21 Write an algorithm for the 2-coloring problem whose time complexity is not worst-case exponential in *n*.

22. List some of the practical applications that are representable in terms of the *m*-Coloring Problem.

Section 5.6

23. Use the Backtracking Algorithm for the Hamiltonian Circuits Problem (Algorithm 5.6) to find all possible Hamiltonian Circuits of the following graph.

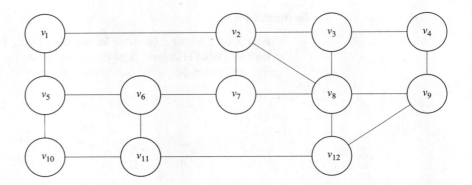

Show the actions step by step.

24. Implement the Backtracking Algorithm for the Hamiltonian Circuits Problem (Algorithm 5.6) on your system, and run it on the problem instance of Exercise 23.

25. Change the starting vertex in the Backtracking Algorithm for the Hamiltonian Circuits Problem (Algorithm 5.6) in Exercise 24 and compare its performance with that of Algorithm 5.6.

26. Modify the Backtracking Algorithm for the Hamiltonian Circuits Problem (Algorithm 5.6) so that, instead of generating all possible solutions, it finds only a single solution. How does this algorithm perform with respect to Algorithm 5.6?

27. Analyze the Backtracking Algorithm for the Hamiltonian Circuits Problem (Algorithm 5.6), and show the worst-case complexity using order notation.

28. Use the Monte Carlo Technique to estimate the efficiency of the Backtracking Algorithm for the Hamiltonian Circuits Problem (Algorithm 5.6).

Section 5.7

29. Compute the remaining values and bounds after visiting node (4, 1) in Example 5.6 (Section 5.7.1).

30. Use the Backtracking Algorithm for the 0-1 Knapsack Problem (Algorithm 5.7) to maximize the profit for the following problem instance. Show the actions step by step.

i	P_i	w_i	$\dfrac{p_i}{w_i}$	
1	$20	2	10	
2	$30	5	6	
3	$35	7	5	$W = 19$
4	$12	3	4	
5	$ 3	1	3	

31. Implement the Backtracking Algorithm for the 0-1 Knapsack Problem (Algorithm 5.7) on your system, and run it on the problem instance of Exercise 30.

32. Implement the dynamic programming algorithm for the 0-1 Knapsack Problem (see Section 4.4.3), and compare the performance of this algorithm with the Backtracking Algorithm for the 0-1 Knapsack Problem (Algorithm 5.7) using large instances of the problem.

33. Improve the Backtracking Algorithm for the 0-1 Knapsack Problem (Algorithm 5.7) by calling the promising function after only a move to the right.

34. Use the Monte Carlo Technique to estimate the efficiency of the Backtracking Algorithm for the 0-1 Knapsack Problem (Algorithm 5.7).

Additional Exercises

35. List three more applications of backtracking.

36. Modify the Backtracking Algorithm for the n-Queens Problem (Algorithm 5.1) so that it produces only the solutions that are invariant under reflections or rotations.

37. Given an $n \times n \times n$ cube containing n^3 cells, we are to place n queens in the cube so that no two queens challenge each other (so that no two queens are in the same row, column, or diagonal). Can the n-Queens Algorithm (Algorithm 5.1) be extended to solve this problem? If so, write the algorithm and implement it on your system to solve problem instances in which $n = 4$ and $n = 8$.

38. Modify the Backtracking Algorithm for the Sum-of-Subsets (Algorithm 5.4) to produce the solutions in a variable-length list.

39. Explain how we can use the Backtracking Algorithm for the m-Coloring Problem (Algorithm 5.5) to color the edges of the graph of Exercise 16 using the same three colors so that edges with a common end receive different colors.

40. Modify the Backtracking Algorithm for the Hamiltonian Circuits Problem (Algorithm 5.6) so that it finds a Hamiltonian Circuit with minimum cost for a weighted graph. How does your algorithm perform?

41. Modify the Backtracking Algorithm for the 0-1 Knapsack Problem (Algorithm 5.7) to produce a solution in a variable-length list.

CHAPTER 6

Branch-and-Bound

We've provided our thief with two algorithms for the 0-1 Knapsack Problem: the dynamic programming algorithm in Section 4.4 and the backtracking algorithm in Section 5.7. Because both these algorithms are exponential-time in the worst case, they could both take many years to solve our thief's particular instance. In this chapter, we provide our thief with yet another approach, called branch-and-bound. As we shall see, the branch-and-bound algorithm developed here is an improvement on the backtracking algorithm. Therefore, even if the other two algorithms fail to solve our thief's instance efficiently, the branch-and-bound algorithm might do so.

The branch-and-bound design strategy is very similar to backtracking in that a state space tree is used to solve a problem. The differences are that the branch-and-bound method (1) does not limit us to any particular way of traversing the tree and (2) is used only for optimization problems. A branch-and-bound algorithm computes a number (bound) at a node to determine whether the node is promising. The number is a bound on the value of the solution that could be obtained by expanding beyond the node. If that bound is no better than the value of the best solution found so far, the node is **nonpromising.** Otherwise, it is **promising.** Because the optimal value is a minimum in some problems and a maximum in others, by "better" we mean smaller or larger depending on the problem. As is the case for backtracking algorithms, branch-and-bound algorithms are ordinarily exponential-time (or worse) in the worst case. However, they can be very efficient for many large instances.

The backtracking algorithm for the 0-1 Knapsack Problem in Section 5.7 is actually a branch-and-bound algorithm. In that algorithm, the promising function returns false if the value of *bound* is not greater than the current value of *maxprofit*. A backtracking algorithm, however, does not exploit the real advantage of using branch-and-bound. Besides using the bound to determine whether a node is promising, we can compare the bounds of promising nodes and visit the children of the one with the best bound. In this way we often can arrive at an optimal solution faster than we would by methodically visiting the nodes in some predetermined order (such as a depth-first search). This approach is called **best-first search with branch-and-bound pruning.** The implementation of the approach is a simple modification of another methodical approach called **breadth-first search with branch-and-bound pruning.** Therefore, even though this latter technique has no advantage over depth-first search, in Section 6.1 we will first solve the 0-1 Knapsack Problem using a breadth-first search. This will enable us to more easily explain best-first search and use it to solve the 0-1 Knapsack Problem. Sections 6.2 and 6.3 apply the best-first search approach to two more problems.

Before proceeding, we review breadth-first search. In the case of a tree, a **breadth-first search** consists of visiting the root first, followed by all nodes at level 1, followed by all nodes at level 2, and so on. Figure 6.1 shows a breadth-

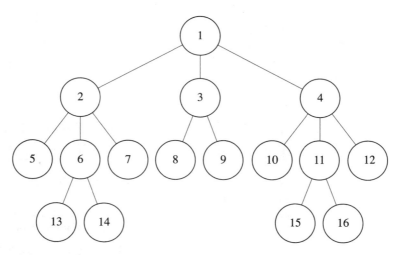

Figure 6.1 A breadth-first search of a tree. The nodes are numbered in the order in which they are visited. The children of a node are visited from left to right.

first search of a tree in which we proceed from left to right. The nodes are numbered according to the order in which they are visited.

Unlike depth-first search, there is no simple recursive algorithm for breadth-first search. However, we can implement it using a queue. The algorithm that follows does this. The algorithm is written specifically for trees because presently we are interested only in trees. We insert an item at the end of the queue with a procedure called *enqueue,* and we remove an item from the front with a procedure called *dequeue.*

```
void breadth_first_tree_search (tree T);
{
    queue_of_node Q;
    node u, v,

    initialize(Q);                                      // Initialize Q to be empty.
    v = root of T;
    visit v;
    enqueue(Q, v);
    while (! empty(Q)) {
        dequeue(Q, v);
        for (each child u of v) {
            visit u;
            enqueue(Q, u);
        }
    }
}
```

If you are not convinced that this procedure produces a breadth-first search, you should walk through an application of this algorithm to the tree in Figure 6.1. In that tree, as mentioned previously, a node's children are visited from left to right.

6.1 ILLUSTRATING BRANCH-AND-BOUND WITH THE 0-1 KNAPSACK PROBLEM

We show how to use the branch-and-bound design strategy by applying it to the 0-1 Knapsack Problem. First we discuss a simple version called breadth-first search with branch-and-bound pruning. After that, we show an improvement on the simple version called best-first search with branch-and-bound pruning.

6.1.1 Breadth-First Search with Branch-and-Bound Pruning

Let's demonstrate this approach with an example.

Example 6.1

Suppose we have the instance of the 0-1 Knapsack Problem presented in Exercise 5.6. That is, $n = 4$, $W = 16$, and we have the following:

i	p_i	w_i	$\dfrac{p_i}{w_i}$
1	$40	2	$20
2	$30	5	$6
3	$50	10	$5
4	$10	5	$2

As in Example 5.6, the items have already been ordered according to p_i/w_i. Using breadth-first search with branch-and-bound pruning, we proceed exactly as we did using backtracking in Example 5.6, except that we do a breadth-first search instead of a depth-first search. That is, we let *weight* and *profit* be the total weight and total profit of the items that have been included up to a node. To determine whether the node is promising, we initialize *totweight* and *bound* to *weight* and *profit*, respectively, and then greedily grab items, adding their weights and profits to *totweight* and *bound*, until we reach an item whose weight would bring *totweight* above W. We grab the fraction of that item allowed by the available weight, and add the profit of that fraction to *totweight*. In this way, *bound* becomes an upper bound on the amount of profit we could obtain by expanding beyond the node. If the node is at level i, and the node at level k is the one whose weight would bring the weight above W, then

$$totweight = weight + \sum_{j=i+1}^{k-1} w_j$$

and

$$bound = \left(profit + \sum_{j=i+1}^{k-1} p_j\right) + (W - totweight) \times \frac{p_k}{w_k}.$$

A node is nonpromising if this bound is less than or equal to *maxprofit*, which is the value of the best solution found up to that point. Recall that a node is also nonpromising if

$$weight \geq W.$$

The pruned state space tree produced using a breadth-first search on the instance in this example, with branches pruned using the bounds indicated above, is shown in Figure 6.2. The values of *profit, weight,* and *bound* are specified from top to

Figure 6.2 The pruned state space tree produced using breadth-first search with branch-and-bound pruning in Example 6.1. Stored at each node from top to bottom are the total profit of the items stolen up to that node, their total weight, and the bound on the total profit that could be obtained by expanding beyond the node. The shaded node is the one at which an optimal solution is found.

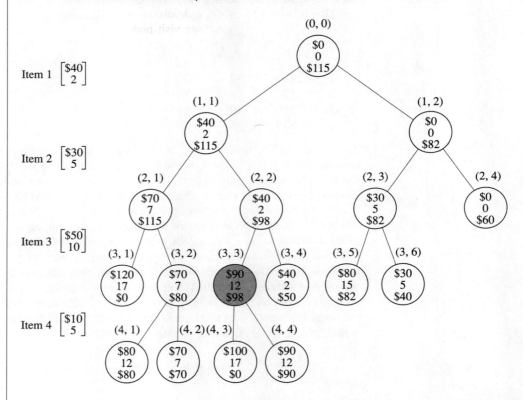

bottom at each node. The shaded node is where the maximum profit is found. The nodes are labeled according to their levels and positions from the left in the tree.

Because the steps are so similar to those in Example 5.6, we will not walk through them. We mention only a few important points. We refer to a node by its level and position from the left in the tree. First, notice that nodes (3, 1) and (4, 3) have bounds of $0. A branch-and-bound algorithm decides whether to expand beyond a node by checking whether its bound is better than the value of the best solution found so far. Therefore, when a node is nonpromising because its weight is not less than W, we set its bound to $0. In this way, we ensure that its bound cannot be better than the value of the best solution found so far. Second, recall that when backtracking (depth-first search) was used on this instance, node (1, 2) was found to be nonpromising and we did not expand beyond the node.

However, in the case of a breadth-first search this node is the third node visited. At the time it is visited, the value of *maxprofit* is only $40. Because its bound $82 exceeds *maxprofit* at this point, we expand beyond the node. Last of all, in a simple breadth-first search with branch-and-bound pruning, the decision of whether or not to visit a node's children is made at the time the node is visited. That is, if the branches to the children are pruned, they are pruned when the node is visited. Therefore, when we visit node (2, 3), we decide to visit its children because the value of *maxprofit* at that time is only $70, whereas the bound for the node is $82. Unlike a depth-first search, in a breadth-first search the value of *maxprofit* can change by the time we actually visit the children. In this case, *maxprofit* has a value of $90 by the time we visit the children of node (2, 3). We then waste our time checking these children. We avoid this in our best-first search, which is described in the next subsection.

Now that we have illustrated the technique, we present a general algorithm for breadth-first search with branch-and-bound pruning. Although we refer to the state space tree T as the input to this general-purpose algorithm, in actual applications the state space tree exists only implicitly. The parameters of the problem are the actual inputs to the algorithm and determine the state space tree T.

```
void breadth_first_branch_and_bound (state_space_tree T,
                                     number& best)
{
  queue_of_node Q;
  node u, v,

  initialize (Q);                            // Initialize Q to be empty.
  v = root of T;                             // Visit root.
  enqueue(Q, v);
  best = value(v);
  while (! empty(Q)) {
    dequeue (Q, v);
    for (each child u of v) {                // Visit each child.
      if (value(u) is better than best)
        best = value(u);
      if (bound(u) is better than best)
        enqueue (Q, u);
    }
  }
}
```

This algorithm is a modification of the breadth-first search algorithm presented at the beginning of this chapter. In this algorithm, however, we expand beyond a node (visit a node's children) only if its bound is better than the value of the current best solution. The value of the current best solution (the variable *best*) is initialized to the value of the solution at the root. In some applications there is no solution at the root because we must be at a leaf in the state space tree to have a solution. In such cases, we initialize *best* to a value that is worse than that of any solution. The functions *bound* and *value* are different in each application of *breadth_first_branch_and_bound*. As we shall see, we often do not actually write a function *value*. We simply compute the value directly.

Next we present a specific algorithm for the 0-1 Knapsack Problem. Because we do not have the benefit of recursion (which means we do not have new variables being created at each recursive call), we must store all the information pertinent to a node at that node. Therefore, the nodes in our algorithm will be of the following type:

```
struct node
{
    int level;                              // the node's level in the tree
    int profit;
    int weight;
};
```

Algorithm 6.1

The Breadth-First Search with Branch-and-Bound Pruning Algorithm for the 0-1 Knapsack Problem

Problem: Let *n* items be given, where each item has a weight and a profit. The weights and profits are positive integers. Furthermore, let a positive integer *W* be given. Determine a set of items with maximum total profit, under the constraint that the sum of their weights cannot exceed *W*.

Inputs: positive integers *n* and *W*, arrays of positive integers *w* and *p*, each indexed from 1 to *n*, and each of which is sorted in nonincreasing order according to the values of $p[i]/w[i]$.

Outputs: an integer *maxprofit* that is the sum of the profits in an optimal set.

```
void knapsack2 (int n,
                const int p[ ], const int w[ ],
                int W,
                int& maxprofit)
{
    queue_of_node Q;
    node u, v;
```

```
    initialize(Q);                              // Initialize Q to be empty.
    v.level = 0; v.profit = 0; v.weight = 0;     // Initialize v to be the root.
    maxprofit = 0;
    enqueue(Q, v);
    while (! empty(Q)) {
      dequeue(Q, v);
      u.level = v.level + 1;                     // Set u to a child of v.
      u.weight = v.weight + w[u.level];          // Set u to the child that
      u.profit = v.profit + p[u.level];          // includes the next item.
      if (u.weight <= W && u.profit > maxprofit)
        maxprofit = u.profit;
      if (bound(u) > maxprofit)
        enqueue(Q, u);
      u.weight = v.weight;                       // Set u to the child that
      u.profit = v.profit;                       // does not include the
      if (bound(u) > maxprofit)                  // next item.
        enqueue(Q, u);
    }
}

float bound (node u)
{
  index j, k;
  int totweight;
  float result;

  if (u.weight > = W)
    return 0;
  else {
    result = u.profit;
    j = u.level + 1;
    totweight = u.weight;
    while (j <= n && totweight + w[j] <= W){      // Grab as many items
      totweight = totweight + w[j];               // as possible.
      result = result + p[j];
      j++;
    }
    k = j;                                        // Use k for consistency
    if (k <= n)                                   // with formula in text.
      result = result + (W − totweight) * p[k]/w[k];  // Grab fracton of kth
    return result;                                // item.
  }
}
```

We do not need to check whether *u.profit* exceeds *maxprofit* when the current item is not included, because in this case *u.profit* is the profit associated with *u*'s parent, which means that it cannot exceed *maxprofit*. We do not need to store the bound at a node (as depicted in Figure 6.2) because we have no need to refer to the bound after we compare it with *maxprofit*.

Function *bound* is essentially the same as function *promising* in Algorithm 5.7. The difference is that we have written *bound* according to guidelines for creating branch-and-bound algorithms, and therefore *bound* returns an integer. Function *promising* returns a boolean value because it was written according to backtracking guidelines. In our branch-and-bound algorithm, the comparison with *maxprofit* is done in the calling procedure. There is no need to check for the condition $i = n$ in function *bound* because in this case the value returned by *bound* is less than or equal to *maxprofit*, which means that the node is not put in the queue.

Algorithm 6.1 does not produce an optimal set of items; it only determines the sum of the profits in an optimal set. The algorithm can be modified to produce an optimal set as follows. At each node we also store a variable *items*, which is the set of items that have been included up to the node, and we maintain a variable *bestitems*, which is the current best set of items. When *maxprofit* is set equal to *u.profit*, we also set *bestitems* equal to *u.items*.

6.1.2 Best-First Search with Branch-and-Bound Pruning

In general, the breadth-first search strategy has no advantage over a depth-first search (backtracking). However, we can improve our search by using our bound to do more than just determine whether a node is promising. After visiting all the children of a given node, we can look at all the promising, unexpanded nodes and expand beyond the one with the best bound. Recall that a node is promising if its bound is better than the value of the best solution found so far. In this way we often arrive at an optimal solution more quickly than if we simply proceeded blindly in a predetermined order. The example that follows illustrates this method.

Example 6.2   Suppose we have the instance of the 0-1 Knapsack Problem in Example 6.1. A best-first search produces the pruned state space tree in Figure 6.3. The values of *profit, weight,* and *bound* are again specified from top to bottom at each node in the tree. The shaded node is where the maximum profit is found. Next we show the steps that produced this tree. We again refer to a node by its level and its position from the left in the tree. Values and bounds are computed in the same way as in Examples 5.6 and 6.1. We do not show the computations while walking

Figure 6.3 The pruned state space tree produced using best-first search with branch-and-bound pruning in Example 6.2. Stored at each node from top to bottom are the total profit of the items stolen up to the node, their total weight, and the bound on the total profit that could be obtained by expanding beyond the node. The shaded node is the one at which an optimal solution is found.

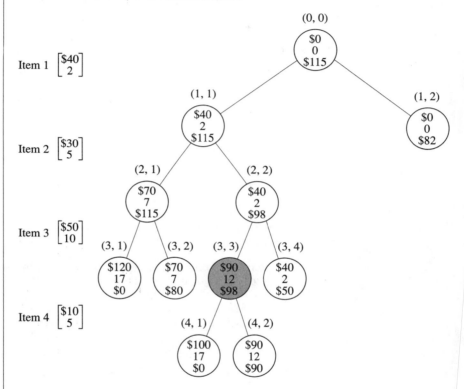

through the steps. Furthermore, we only mention when a node is found to be nonpromising; we do not mention when it is found to be promising.

The steps are as follows:

1. Visit node (0, 0) (the root).
   (a) Set its profit and weight to $0 and 0.
   (b) Compute its bound to be $115. (See Example 5.6 for the computation.)
   (c) Set *maxprofit* to 0.
2. Visit node (1, 1).
   (a) Compute its profit and weight to be $40 and 2.

(b) Because its weight 2 is less than or equal to 16, the value of W, and its profit \$40 is greater than \$0, the value of *maxprofit*, set *maxprofit* to \$40.

(c) Compute its bound to be \$115.

3. Visit node (1, 2).
   (a) Compute its profit and weight to be \$0 and 0.
   (b) Compute its bound to be \$82.

4. Determine promising, unexpanded node with the greatest bound.
   (a) Because node (1, 1) has a bound of \$115 and node (1, 2) has a bound of \$82, node (1, 1) is the promising, unexpanded node with the greatest bound. We visit its children next.

5. Visit node (2, 1).
   (a) Compute its profit and weight to be \$70 and 7.
   (b) Because its weight 7 is less than or equal to 16, the value of W, and its profit \$70 is greater than \$40, the value of *maxprofit*, set *maxprofit* to \$70.
   (c) Compute its bound to be \$115.

6. Visit node (2, 2).
   (a) Compute its profit and weight to be \$40 and 2.
   (b) Compute its bound to be \$98.

7. Determine promising, unexpanded node with the greatest bound.
   (a) That node is node (2, 1). We visit its children next.

8. Visit node (3, 1).
   (a) Compute its profit and weight to be \$120 and 17.
   (b) Determine that it is nonpromising because its weight 17 is greater than or equal to 16, the value of W. We make it nonpromising by setting its bound to \$0.

9. Visit node (3, 2).
   (a) Compute its profit and weight to be \$70 and 7.
   (b) Compute its bound to be \$80.

10. Determine promising, unexpanded node with the greatest bound.
    (a) That node is node (2, 2). We visit its children next.

11. Visit node (3, 3).
    (a) Compute its profit and weight to be \$90 and 12.
    (b) Because its weight 12 is less than or equal to 16, the value of W, and its profit \$90 is greater than \$70, the value of *maxprofit*, set *maxprofit* to \$90.
    (c) At this point, nodes (1, 2) and (3, 2) become nonpromising because their bounds, \$82 and \$80 respectively, are less than or equal to \$90, the new value of *maxprofit*.
    (d) Compute its bound to be \$98.

12. Visit node (3, 4).
    (a) Compute its profit and weight to be $40 and 2.
    (b) Compute its bound to be $50.
    (c) Determine that it is nonpromising because its bound $50 is less than or equal to $90, the value of *maxprofit*.

13. Determine promising, unexpanded node with the greatest bound.
    (a) The only unexpanded, promising node is node (3, 3). We visit its children next.

14. Visit node (4, 1).
    (a) Compute its profit and weight to be $100 and 17.
    (b) Determine that it is nonpromising because its weight 17 is greater than or equal to 16, the value of *W*. We set its bound to $0.

15. Visit node (4, 2).
    (a) Compute its profit and weight to be $90 and 12.
    (b) Compute its bound to be $90.
    (c) Determine that it is nonpromising because its bound $90 is less than or equal to $90, the value of *maxprofit*. Leaves in the state space tree are automatically nonpromising because their bounds cannot exceed *maxprofit*.

Because there are now no promising, unexpanded nodes, we are done.

Using best-first search, we have checked only 11 nodes, which is 6 less than the number checked using breadth-first search (Figure 6.2) and 2 less than the number checked using depth-first search (see Figure 5.14). A savings of 2 is not very impressive; however, in a large state space tree, the savings can be very significant when the best-first search quickly hones in on an optimal solution. It must be stressed, however, that there is no guarantee that the node that appears to be best will actually lead to an optimal solution. In Example 6.2, node (2, 1) appears to be better than node (2, 2), but node (2, 2) leads to the optimal solution. In general, best-first search can still end up creating most or all of the state space tree for some instances.

The implementation of best-first search consists of a simple modification to breadth-first search. Instead of using a queue, we use a priority queue. In a ***priority queue,*** the element with the highest priority is always removed next. In best-first search applications, the element with the highest priority is the node with the best bound. A priority queue can be implemented as a linked list, but more efficiently as a heap (see Section 7.6 for a discussion of heaps). The implementation of a priority queue is investigated in the exercises. A general algorithm for the best-first search method follows. Again, the tree *T* exists only implicitly. In the algorithm, *insert(PQ,v)* is a procedure that adds *v* to the priority queue *PQ*, whereas *remove(PQ,v)* is a procedure that removes the node with the best bound and assigns its value to *v*.

```
void best_first_branch_and_bound (state_space_tree T,
                                  number& best)
{
  priority_queue_of_node PQ;
  node u, v;

  initialize(PQ);                            // Initialize PQ to be empty.
  v = root of T;
  best = value(v);
  insert(PQ, v);
  while (! empty(PQ)) {                       // Remove node with best
    remove(PQ, v);                            // bound.
    if (bound(v) is better than best)         // Check if node is still
      for (each child u of v) {               // promising.
        if (value(u) is better than best)
          best = value(u);
        if (bound(u) is better than best)
          insert(PQ, u);
      }
  }
}
```

Besides using a priority queue instead of a queue, we have added a check following the removal of a node from the priority queue. The check determines if the bound for the node is still better than *best*. This is how we determine that a node has become nonpromising after visiting the node. For example, node $(1, 2)$ in Figure 6.3 is promising at the time we visit it. In our implementation, this is when we insert it in *PQ*. However, it becomes nonpromising when *maxprofit* takes the value $90. In our implementation, this is before we remove it from *PQ*. We learn this by comparing its bound with *maxprofit* after removing it from *PQ*. In this way, we avoid visiting children of a node that becomes nonpromising after it is visited.

The specific algorithm for the 0-1 Knapsack Problem follows. Because we need the bound for a node at insertion time, at removal time, and to order the nodes in the priority queue, we store the bound at the node. The type declaration is as follows:

```
struct node
{
  int level;                                 // the node's level in the tree
  int profit;
  int weight;
  float bound;
};
```

Algorithm 6.2

The Best-First Search with Branch-and-Bound Pruning Algorithm
for the 0-1 Knapsack Problem

Problem: Let n items be given, where each item has a weight and a profit. The weights and profits are positive integers. Furthermore, let a positive integer W be given. Determine a set of items with maximum total profit, under the constraint that the sum of their weights cannot exceed W.

Inputs: positive integers n and W, arrays of positive integers w and p, each indexed from 1 to n, and each of which is sorted in nonincreasing order according to the values of $p[i]/w[i]$.

Outputs: an integer *maxprofit* that is the sum of the profits of an optimal set.

```
void knapsack3 (int n,
                const int p[ ], const int w[ ],
                int W,
                int& maxprofit)
{
   priority_queue_of_node PQ;
   node u, v;

   initialize(PQ);                               // Initialize PQ to be empty.
   v.level = 0; v.profit = 0; v.weight = 0;      Initialize v to be the root.
   maxprofit = 0;
   v.bound = bound(v);
   insert(PQ, v);
   while (! empty(PQ)) {                         // Remove node with
      remove(PQ, v);                             // best bound.
      if (v.bound > maxprofit) {                 // Check if node is still
         u.level = v.level + 1;                  // promising.
         u.weight = v.weight + w[u.level];       // Set u to the child
         u.profit = v.profit + p[u.level];       // that includes the
         if (u.weight <= W && u.profit > maxprofit)  // next item.
            maxprofit = u.profit;
         u.bound = bound(u);
         if (u.bound > maxprofit)
            insert(PQ, u);
         u.weight = v.weight;                     // Set u to the child
         u.profit = v.profit;                     // that does not include
         u.bound = bound(u);                      // the next item.
         if (u.bound > maxprofit)
            insert(PQ, u);
      }
   }
}
```

Function *bound* is the one in Algorithm 6.1.

6.2 THE TRAVELING SALESPERSON PROBLEM

In Example 3.12, Nancy won the sales position over Ralph because she found an optimal tour for the 20-city sales territory in 45 seconds using a $\Theta(n^2 2^n)$ dynamic programming algorithm to solve the Traveling Salesperson Problem. Ralph used the brute-force algorithm that generates all 19! tours. Because the brute-force algorithm takes over 3,800 years, it is still running. We last saw Nancy in Section 5.6 when her sales territory was expanded to 40 cities. Because her dynamic programming algorithm would take more than six years to find an optimal tour for this territory, she became content with just finding any tour. She used the backtracking algorithm for the Hamiltonian Circuits Problem to do this. Even if this algorithm did find a tour efficiently, that tour could be far from optimal. For example, if there were a long, winding road of 100 miles between two cities that were 2 miles apart, the algorithm could produce a tour containing that road even if it were possible to connect the two cities by a city that is a mile from each of them. This means Nancy could be covering her territory very inefficiently using the tour produced by the backtracking algorithm. Given this, she might decide that she better go back to looking for an optimal tour. If the 40 cities were highly connected, having the backtracking algorithm produce all the tours would not work, because there would be a worst-than-exponential number of tours. Let's assume that Nancy's instructor did not get to the branch-and-bound technique in her algorithms course (this is why she settled for any tour in Section 5.6). After going back to her algorithms text and discovering that the branch-and-bound technique is specifically designed for optimization problems, Nancy decides to apply it to the Traveling Salesperson Problem. She might proceed as follows.

Recall that the goal in this problem is to find the shortest path in a directed graph that starts at a given vertex, visits each vertex in the graph exactly once, and ends up back at the starting vertex. Such a path is called an ***optimal tour.*** Because it does not matter where we start, the starting vertex can simply be the first vertex. Figure 6.4 shows the adjacency matrix representation of a graph containing five vertices, in which there is an edge from every vertex to every other vertex, and an optimal tour for that graph.

An obvious state space tree for this problem is one in which each vertex other than the starting one is tried as the first vertex (after the starting one) at level 1, each vertex other than the starting one and the one chosen at level 1 is tried as the second vertex at level 2, and so on. A portion of this state space tree, in which there are five vertices and in which there is an edge from every vertex to every other vertex, is shown in Figure 6.5. In what follows, the term "node" means a node in the state space tree, and the term "vertex" means a vertex in the graph. At each node in Figure 6.5, we have included the path chosen up to that node. For simplicity, we have denoted a vertex in the graph simply by its index. A node that is not a leaf represents all those tours that start with the path stored at that node. For example, the node containing [1, 2, 3] represents all those tours that start with the path [1, 2, 3]. That is, it represents the tours [1, 2, 3, 4,

Figure 6.4 Adjacency matrix representation of a graph that has an edge from every vertex to every other vertex (left), and the nodes in the graph and the edges in an optimal tour (right).

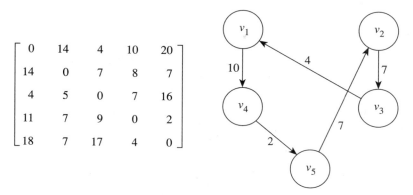

$$\begin{bmatrix} 0 & 14 & 4 & 10 & 20 \\ 14 & 0 & 7 & 8 & 7 \\ 4 & 5 & 0 & 7 & 16 \\ 11 & 7 & 9 & 0 & 2 \\ 18 & 7 & 17 & 4 & 0 \end{bmatrix}$$

5, 1] and [1, 2, 3, 5, 4, 1]. Each leaf represents a tour. We need to find a leaf that contains an optimal tour. We stop expanding the tree when there are four vertices in the path stored at a node because at that time the fifth one is uniquely determined. For example, the far left leaf represents the tour [1, 2, 3, 4, 5, 1], because once we have specified the path [1, 2, 3, 4], the next vertex must be the fifth one.

To use best-first search, we need to be able to determine a bound for each node. Because of the objective in the 0-1 Knapsack Problem (to maximize profit while keeping the total weight from exceeding W), we computed an upper bound on the amount of profit that could be obtained by expanding beyond a given node, and we called a node promising only if its bound was greater than the current maximum profit. In this problem, we need to determine a lower bound on the length of any tour that can be obtained by expanding beyond a given node, and we call the node promising only if its bound is less than the current minimum tour length. We can obtain a bound as follows. In any tour, the length of the edge taken when leaving a vertex must be at least as great as the length of the shortest edge emanating from that vertex. Therefore, a lower bound on the *cost* (length of the edge taken) of leaving vertex v_1 is given by the minimum of all the nonzero entries in row 1 of the adjacency matrix, a lower bound on the cost of leaving vertex v_2 is given by the minimum of all the nonzero entries in row 2, and so on. The lower bounds on the costs of leaving the five vertices in the graph represented in Figure 6.4 are as follows:

$$\begin{array}{lll} v_1 & minimum(14, 4, 10, 20) & = 4 \\ v_2 & minimum(14, 7, 8, 7) & = 7 \\ v_3 & minimum(4, 5, 7, 16) & = 4 \\ v_4 & minimum(11, 7, 9, 2) & = 2 \\ v_5 & minimum(18, 7, 17, 4) & = 4 \end{array}$$

Figure 6.5 A state space tree for an instance of the Traveling Salesperson Problem in which there are five vertices. The indices of the vertices in the partial tour are stored at each node.

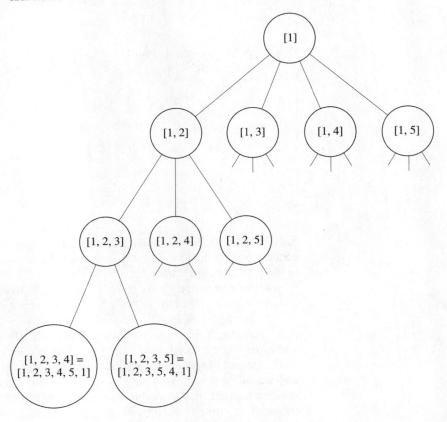

Because a tour must leave every vertex exactly once, a lower bound on the length of a tour is the sum of these minimums. Therefore, a lower bound on the length of a tour is

$$4 + 7 + 4 + 2 + 4 = 21.$$

This is not to say that there is a tour with this length. Rather, it says that there can be no tour with a shorter length.

Suppose we have visited the node containing [1, 2] in Figure 6.5. In that case we have already committed to making v_2 the second vertex on the tour, and the cost of getting to v_2 is the weight on the edge from v_1 to v_2, which is 14. Any tour obtained by expanding beyond this node, therefore, has the following lower bounds on the costs of leaving the vertices:

v_1			14
v_2	$minimum(7, 8, 7)$	$=$	7
v_3	$minimum(4, 7, 16)$	$=$	4
v_4	$minimum(11, 9, 2)$	$=$	2
v_5	$minimum(18, 17, 4)$	$=$	4

To obtain the minimum for v_2 we do not include the edge to v_1, because v_2 cannot return to v_1. To obtain the minimums for the other vertices we do not include the edge to v_2, because we have already been at v_2. A lower bound on the length of any tour, obtained by expanding beyond the node containing [1, 2], is the sum of these minimums, which is

$$14 + 7 + 4 + 2 + 4 = 31.$$

To further illustrate the technique for determining the bound, suppose we have visited the node containing [1, 2, 3] in Figure 6.5. We have committed to making v_2 the second vertex and v_3 the third vertex. Any tour obtained by expanding beyond this node has the following lower bounds on the costs of leaving the vertices:

v_1			14
v_2			7
v_3	$minimum(7, 16)$	$=$	7
v_4	$minimum(11, 2)$	$=$	2
v_5	$minimum(18, 4)$	$=$	4

To obtain the minimums for v_4 and v_5 we do not consider the edges to v_2 and v_3, because we have already been to these vertices. The lower bound on the length of any tour we could obtain by expanding beyond the node containing [1, 2, 3] is

$$14 + 7 + 7 + 2 + 4 = 34.$$

In the same way, we can obtain a lower bound on the length of a tour that can be obtained by expanding beyond any node in the state space tree, and use these lower bounds in our best-first search. The following example illustrates this technique. We will not actually do any calculations in the example. They would be done as just illustrated.

Example 6.3   Given the graph in Figure 6.4 and using the bounding considerations outlined previously, a best-first search with branch-and-bound pruning produces the tree in Figure 6.6. The bound is stored at a nonleaf, whereas the length of the tour is stored at a leaf. We show the steps that produced the tree. We initialize the value of the best solution to ∞ (infinity) because there is no candidate solution at the root (candidate solutions exist only at leaves in the state space tree). We do not compute bounds for leaves in the state space tree because the algorithm is written so as not to expand beyond leaves. When referring to a node, we refer to the partial tour stored at the node. This is different from the way we referred to a node when illustrating the 0-1 Knapsack Problem.

The steps are as follows:

1. Visit node containing [1] (the root).
   (a) Compute bound to be 21.   {This is a lower bound on the}
   (b) Set *minlength* to ∞.   {length of a tour.}

2. Visit node containing [1, 2].
   (a) Compute bound to be 31.

3. Visit node containing [1, 3].
   (a) Compute bound to be 22.

4. Visit node containing [1, 4].
   (a) Compute bound to be 30.

5. Visit node containing [1, 5].
   (a) Compute bound to be 42.

6. Determine promising, unexpanded node with the smallest bound.
   (a) That node is the node containing [1, 3]. We visit its children next.

7. Visit node containing [1, 3, 2].
   (a) Compute bound to be 22.

8. Visit node containing [1, 3, 4].
   (a) Compute bound to be 27.

9. Visit node containing [1, 3, 5].
   (a) Compute bound to be 39.

10. Determine promising, unexpanded node with the smallest bound.
    (a) That node is the node containing [1, 3, 2]. We visit its children next.

11. Visit node containing [1, 3, 2, 4].
    (a) Because this node is a leaf, compute tour length to be 37.
    (b) Because its length 37 is less than ∞, the value of *minlength*, set *minlength* to 37.
    (c) The nodes containing [1, 5] and [1, 3, 5] become nonpromising because their bounds 42 and 39 are greater than or equal to 37, the new value of *minlength*.

12. Visit node containing [1, 3, 2, 5].
    (a) Because this node is a leaf, compute tour length to be 31.

Figure 6.6 The pruned state space tree produced using best-first search with branch-and-bound pruning in Example 6.3. At each node that is not a leaf in the state space tree, the partial tour is at the top and the bound on the length of any tour that could be obtained by expanding beyond the node is at the bottom. At each leaf in the state space tree, the tour is at the top and its length is at the bottom. The shaded node is the one at which an optimal tour is found.

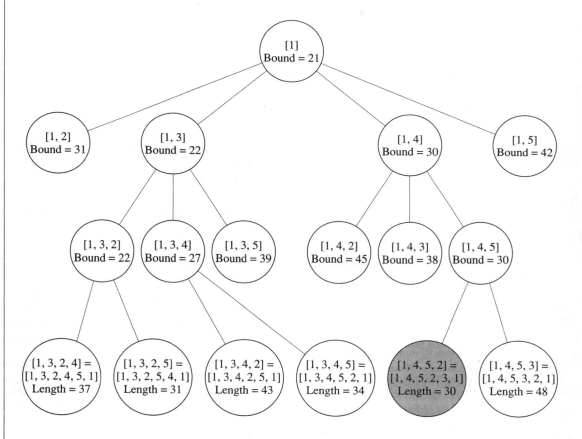

(b) Because its length 31 is less than 37, the value of *minlength*, set *minlength* to 31.

(c) The node containing [1, 2] becomes nonpromising because its bound 31 is greater than or equal to 31, the new value of *minlength*.

13. Determine promising, unexpanded node with the smallest bound.
    (a) That node is the node containing [1, 3, 4]. We visit its children next.
14. Visit node containing [1, 3, 4, 2].
    (a) Because this node is a leaf, compute tour length to be 43.
15. Visit node containing [1, 3, 4, 5].
    (a) Because this node is a leaf, compute tour length to be 34.

16. Determine promising, unexpanded node with the smallest bound.
    (a) The only promising, unexpanded node is the node containing [1, 4]. We visit its children next.
17. Visit node containing [1, 4, 2].
    (a) Compute bound to be 45.
    (b) Determine that the node is nonpromising because its bound 45 is greater than or equal to 31, the value of *minlength.*
18. Visit node containing [1, 4, 3].
    (a) Compute bound to be 38.
    (b) Determine that the node is nonpromising because its bound 38 is greater than or equal to 31, the value of *minlength.*
19. Visit node containing [1, 4, 5].
    (a) Compute bound to be 30.
20. Determine promising, unexpanded node with the smallest bound.
    (a) The only promising, unexpanded node is the node containing [1, 4, 5]. We visit its children next.
21. Visit node containing [1, 4, 5, 2].
    (a) Because this node is a leaf, compute tour length to be 30.
    (b) Because its length 30 is less than 31, the value of *minlength,* set *minlength* to 30.
22. Visit node containing [1, 4, 5, 3].
    (a) Because this node is a leaf, compute tour length to be 48.
23. Determine promising, unexpanded node with the smallest bound.
    (a) There are no more promising, unexpanded nodes. We are done.

We have determined that the node containing [1, 4, 5, 2], which represents the tour [1, 4, 5, 2, 3, 1], contains an optimal tour, and that the length of an optimal tour is 30.

There are 17 nodes in the tree in Figure 6.6, whereas the number of nodes in the entire state space tree is $1 + 4 + 4 \times 3 + 4 \times 3 \times 2 = 41$.

We will use the following data type in the algorithm that implements the strategy used in the previous example:

```
struct node
{
    int level;                          // the node's level in the tree
    ordered_set path;
    number bound;
};
```

The field *path* contains the partial tour stored at the node. For example, in Figure 6.6 the value of *path* for the far left child of the root is [1, 2]. The algorithm follows.

Algorithm 6.3

The Best-First Search with Branch-and-Bound Pruning Algorithm
for the Traveling Salesperson Problem

Problem: Determine an optimal tour in a weighted, directed graph. The weights
are nonnegative numbers.

Inputs: a weighted, directed graph, and n, the number of vertices in the graph.
The graph is represented by a two-dimensional array W, which has both its rows
and columns indexed from 1 to n, where $W[i][j]$ is the weight on the edge from
the ith vertex to the jth vertex.

Outputs: variable *minlength,* whose value is the length of an optimal tour, and
variable *opttour,* whose value is an optimal tour.

```
void travel2 (int n,
              const number W[ ] [ ],
              ordered-set& opttour,
              number& minlength)
{
   priority_queue_of_node PQ; node u, v;

   initialize(PQ);                        // InitializePQ to be empty.
   v.level = 0;
   v.path = [I];                          // Make first vertex the starting
   v.bound = bound(v);                    // one.
   minlength = ∞;
   insert(PQ, v);
   while (! empty(PQ)) {
      remove(PQ, v);                      // Remove node with best bound.
      if (v.bound < minlength) {
         u.level = v.level + I;           // Set u to a child of v.
         if (u.level == n − I) {          // Check if u completes a tour.
            u.path = v.path;
            put I at the end of u.path;    // Make first vertex the last one.
            if (length(u) < minlength) {   // Function length computes the
               minlength = length(u);      // length of the tour.
               opttour = u.path;
            }
         }
         else
            for (all i such that 2 ≤ i ≤ n && i is not in v.path) {
               u.path = v.path;
               put i at the end of u.path;
               u.bound = bound(u);
               if (u.bound < minlength)
                  insert(PQ, u);
            }
      }
   }
}
```

You are asked to write functions *length* and *bound* in the exercises. Function *length* returns the length of the tour *u.path,* and function *bound* returns the bound for a node using the considerations discussed.

A problem does not necessarily have a unique bounding function. In the Traveling Salesperson Problem, for example, we could observe that every vertex must be visited exactly once, and then use the minimums of the values in the columns in the adjacency matrix instead of the minimums of the values in the rows. Alternatively, we could take advantage of both the rows and the columns by noting that every vertex must be entered and exited exactly once. For a given edge, we could associate half of its weight with the vertex it leaves and the other half with the vertex it enters. The cost of visiting a vertex is then the sum of the weights associated with entering and exiting it. For example, suppose we are determining the initial bound on the length of a tour. The minimum cost of entering v_2 is obtained by taking $1/2$ of the minimum of the values in the second column. The minimum cost of exiting v_2 is obtained by taking $1/2$ of the minimum of the values in the second row. The minimum cost of visiting v_2 is then given by

$$\frac{minimum(14,\ 5,\ 7,\ 7)\ +\ minimum(14,\ 7,\ 8,\ 7)}{2} = 6.$$

Using this bounding function, a branch-and-bound algorithm checks only 15 vertices in the instance in Example 6.3.

When two or more bounding functions are available, one bounding function may produce a better bound at one node whereas another produces a better bound at another node. Indeed, as you are asked to verify in the exercises, this is the case for our bounding functions for the Traveling Salesperson Problem. When this is the case, the algorithm can compute bounds using all available bounding functions, and then use the best bound. However, as discussed in Chapter 5, our goal is not to visit as few nodes as possible, but rather to maximize the overall efficiency of the algorithm. The extra computations done when using more than one bounding function may not be offset by the savings realized by visiting fewer nodes.

Recall that a branch-and-bound algorithm might solve one large instance efficiently but check an exponential (or worse) number of nodes for another large instance. Returning to Nancy's dilemma, what is she to do if even the branch-and-bound algorithm cannot solve her 40-city instance efficiently? Another approach to handling problems such as the Traveling Salesperson Problem is to develop approximation algorithms. **Approximation algorithms** are not guaranteed to yield optimal solutions, but rather yield solutions that are reasonably close to optimal. They are discussed in Section 9.5. In that section we return to the Traveling Salesperson Problem.

ABDUCTIVE INFERENCE

⊙ **6.3** (DIAGNOSIS)

This section requires knowledge of discrete probability theory and Bayes' Theorem.

An important problem in artificial intelligence and expert systems is determining the most probable explanation for some findings. For example, in medicine we want to determine the most probable set of diseases given a set of symptoms. In the case of an electronic circuit, we want to find the most probable explanation for a failure at some point in the circuit. Another example is the determination of the most probable causes for the failure of an automobile to function properly. This process of determining the most probable explanation for a set of findings is called **abductive inference.**

For the sake of focus, we use medical terminology. Assume that there are n diseases, $d_1, d_2, \ldots, d_n$, each of which may be present in a patient. We know that the patient has a certain set of symptoms S. Our goal is to find the set of diseases that are most probably present. Technically, there could be two or more sets that are probably present. However, we often discuss the problem as if a unique set is most probably present.

The **belief network** has become a standard for representing probabilistic relationships such as those between diseases and symptoms. It is beyond our scope to discuss belief networks here. They are discussed in detail in Neapolitan (1990) and Pearl (1988). For many belief network applications, there exist efficient algorithms for determining the prior probability (before any symptoms are discovered) that a particular set of diseases contains the only diseases present in the patient. These algorithms are also discussed in Neapolitan (1990) and Pearl (1988). Here we will simply assume that the results of the algorithms are available to us. For example, these algorithms can determine the prior probability that d_1, d_3, and d_6 are the only diseases present in the patient. We will denote this probability by

$$p(d_1, d_3, d_6) \quad \text{and by} \quad p(D),$$

where

$$D = \{d_1, d_3, d_6\}.$$

These algorithms can also determine the probability that d_1, d_3, and d_6 are the only diseases present conditional on the information that the symptoms in S are present. We will denote this conditional probability by

$$p(d_1, d_3, d_6 \mid S) \quad \text{and by} \quad p(D \mid S).$$

Given that we can compute these probabilities (using the algorithms mentioned previously), we can solve the problem of determining the most probable set of diseases (conditional on the information that some symptoms are present) using a state space tree like the one in the 0-1 Knapsack Problem. We go to the left of the root to include d_1, and we go to the right to exclude it. Similarly, we go to the left of a node at level 1 to include d_2, and we go to the right to exclude it, and so on. Each leaf in the state space tree represents a possible solution (that is, the set of diseases that have been included up to that leaf). To solve the problem, we compute the conditional probability of the set of diseases at each leaf, and determine which one has the largest conditional probability.

To prune using best-first search, we need to find a bounding function. The following theorem accomplishes this for a large class of instances.

Theorem 6.1 If D and D' are two sets of diseases such that

$$p(D') \leq p(D),$$

then

$$p(D' \mid S) \leq \frac{p(D)}{p(S)}.$$

Proof: According to Bayes' Theorem,

$$p(D' \mid S) = \frac{p(S \mid D')p(D')}{p(S)}$$

$$\leq \frac{p(S \mid D')p(D)}{p(S)}$$

$$\leq \frac{p(D)}{p(S)}.$$

The first inequality is by the assumption in this theorem, and the second follows from the fact that any probability is less than or equal to 1. This proves the theorem.

For a given node, let D be the set of diseases that have been included up to that node, and for some descendent of that node, let D' be the set of diseases that have been included up to that descendent. Then $D \subseteq D'$. Often it is reasonable to assume that

$$p(D') \leq p(D) \qquad \text{when} \qquad D \subseteq D'.$$

The reason is that usually it is at least as probable that a patient has a set of diseases as it is that the patient has that set plus even more diseases (recall that these are prior probabilities before any symptoms are observed). If we make this assumption, by Theorem 6.1

$$p(D' \mid S) \leq \frac{p(D)}{p(S)}.$$

Therefore, $p(D)/p(S)$ is an upper bound on the conditional probability of the set of diseases in any descendant of the node. The following example illustrates how this bound is used to prune branches.

Example 6.4   Suppose there are four possible diseases d_1, d_2, d_3, and d_4 and a set of symptoms S. The input to this example would also include a belief network containing the probabilistic relationships among the diseases and the symptoms. The probabilities used in this example would be computed from this belief network using the methods discussed earlier. These probabilities are not computed elsewhere in this text. We assign arbitrary probabilities to illustrate the best-first search algorithm. When using the results from one algorithm (in this case, the one for doing inference in a belief network) in another algorithm (in this case, the best-first search algorithm), it is important to recognize where the first algorithm supplies results that can simply be assumed in the second algorithm.

Figure 6.7 is the pruned state space tree produced by a best-first search. Probabilities have been given arbitrary values in the tree. The conditional probability is at the top and the bound is at the bottom in each node. The shaded node is the node at which the best solution is found. As was done in Section 6.1, nodes are labeled according to their depth and position from the left in the tree. The steps that produce the tree follow. The variable *best* is the current best solution, whereas $p(best \mid S)$ is its conditional probability. Our goal is to determine a value of *best* that maximizes this conditional probability. It is also assumed arbitrarily that

$$p(S) = .01.$$

1. Visit node (0, 0) (the root).
   (a) Compute its conditional probability. {$\emptyset$ is the empty set. This means that no diseases are present.}

   $p(\emptyset \mid S) = .1$ {The computations would be done by another}
   {algorithm. We are assigning arbitrary values.}

   (b) Set

   $$best = \emptyset \quad \text{and} \quad p(best \mid S) = p(\emptyset \mid S) = .1.$$

   (c) Compute its prior probability and bound.

   $$(p(\emptyset) = .9$$
   $$bound = \frac{p(\emptyset)}{p(S)} = \frac{.9}{.01} = 90$$

Figure 6.7 The pruned state space tree produced using best-first search with branch-and-bound pruning in Example 6.4. At each node, the conditional probability of the diseases included up to that node is at the top, and the bound on the conditional probability that could be obtained by expanding beyond the node is at the bottom. The shaded node is the one at which an optimal set is found.

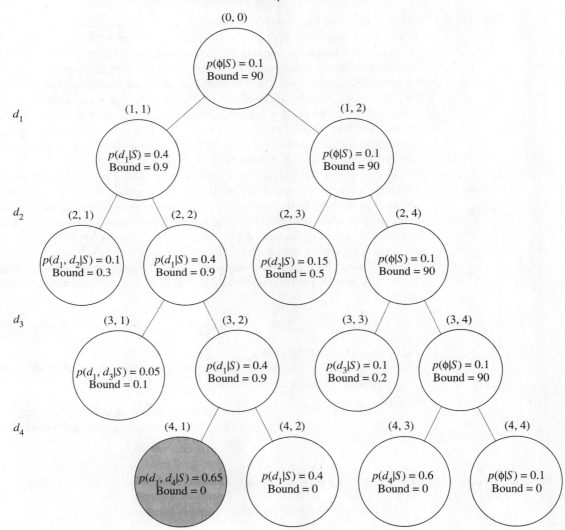

2. Visit node (1, 1).
   (a) Compute its conditional probability.

$$p(d_1 \mid S) = .4$$

   (b) Because $.4 > p(best \mid S)$, set

$$best = \{d_1\} \qquad \text{and} \qquad p(best \mid S) = .4.$$

   (c) Compute its prior probability and bound.

$$p(d_1) = .009$$

$$bound = \frac{p(d_1)}{p(S)} = \frac{.009}{.01} = .9$$

3. Visit node (1, 2).
   (a) Its conditional probability is simply that of its parent—namely, .1.
   (b) Its prior probability and bound are simply those of its parent—namely, .9 and 90.

4. Determine promising, unexpanded node with the largest bound.
   (a) That node is node (1, 2). We visit its children next.

5. Visit node (2, 3).
   (a) Compute its conditional probability.

$$p(d_2 \mid S) = .15$$

   (b) Compute its prior probability and bound.

$$p(d_2) = .005$$

$$bound = \frac{p(d_2)}{p(S)} = \frac{.005}{.01} = .5$$

6. Visit node (2, 4).
   (a) Its conditional probability is simply that of its parent—namely, .1.
   (b) Its prior probability and bound are simply those of its parent—namely, .9 and 90.

7. Determine promising, unexpanded node with the largest bound.
   (a) That node is node (2, 4). We visit its children next.

8. Visit node (3, 3).
   (a) Compute its conditional probability.

$$p(d_3 \mid S) = .1$$

   (b) Compute its prior probability and bound.

$$p(d_3) = .002$$

$$bound = \frac{p(d_3)}{p(S)} = \frac{.002}{.01} = .2$$

(c) Determine that it is nonpromising because its bound .2 is less than or equal to .4, the value of $p(best \mid S)$.

9. Visit node (3, 4).
   (a) Its conditional probability is simply that of its parent—namely, .1.
   (b) Its prior probability and bound are simply those of its parent—namely, .9 and 90.

10. Determine promising, unexpanded node with the largest bound.
    (a) That node is node (3, 4). We visit its children next.

11. Visit node (4, 3).
    (a) Compute its conditional probability.

    $$p(d_4 \mid S) = .6$$

    (b) Because $.6 > p(best \mid S)$, set

    $$best = \{d_4\} \quad \text{and} \quad p(best \mid S) = .6.$$

    (c) Set its bound to 0 because it is a leaf in the state space tree.
    (d) At this point, the node (2, 3) becomes nonpromising because its bound .5 is less than or equal to .6, the new value of $p(best \mid S)$.

12. Visit node (4, 4).
    (a) Its conditional probability is simply that of its parent—namely, .1.
    (b) Set its bound to 0 because it is a leaf in the state space tree.

13. Determine promising, unexpanded node with the largest bound.
    (a) That node is node (1, 1). We visit its children next.

14. Visit node (2, 1).
    (a) Compute its conditional probability.

    $$p(d_1, d_2 \mid S) = .1$$

    (b) Compute its prior probability and bound.

    $$p(d_1, d_2) = .003$$
    $$bound = \frac{p(d_1, d_2)}{p(S)} = \frac{.003}{.01} = .3$$

    (c) Determine that it is nonpromising because its bound .3 is less than or equal to .6, the value of $p(best \mid S)$.

15. Visit node (2, 2).
    (a) Its conditional probability is simply that of its parent—namely, .4.
    (b) Its prior probability and bound are simply those of its parent—namely, .009 and .9.

16. Determine promising, unexpanded node with the greatest bound.
    (a) The only promising, unexpanded node is node (2, 2). We visit its children next.

17. Visit node (3, 1).
    (a) Compute its conditional probability.

$$p(d_1, d_3 \mid S) = .05$$

    (b) Compute its prior probability and bound.

$$p(d_1, d_3) = .001$$

$$bound = \frac{p(d_1, d_3)}{p(S)} = \frac{.001}{.01} = .1$$

    (c) Determine that it is nonpromising because its bound .1 is less than or equal to .6, the value of $p(best \mid S)$.
18. Visit node (3, 2).
    (a) Its conditional probability is simply that of its parent—namely, .4.
    (b) Its prior probability and bound are simply those of its parent—namely, .009 and .9.
19. Determine promising, unexpanded node with the largest bound.
    (a) The only promising, unexpanded node is node (3, 2). We visit its children next.
20. Visit node (4, 1).
    (a) Compute its conditional probability.

$$p(d_1, d_4 \mid S) = .65.$$

    (b) Because $.65 > p(best \mid S)$, set

$$best = \{d_1, d_4\} \quad \text{and} \quad p(best \mid S) = .65.$$

    (c) Set its bound to 0 because it is a leaf in the state space tree.
21. Visit node (4, 2).
    (a) Its conditional probability is simply that of its parent—namely, .4.
    (b) Set its bound to 0 because it is a leaf in the state space tree.
22. Determine promising, unexpanded node with the largest bound.
    (a) There are no more promising, unexpanded nodes. We are done.

We have determined that the most probable set of diseases is $\{d_1, d_4\}$ and that $p(d_1, d_4 \mid S) = .65$.

A reasonable strategy in this problem would be to initially sort the diseases in nonincreasing order according to their conditional probabilities. There is no guarantee, however, that this strategy will minimize the search time. We have not done this in Example 6.4, and 15 nodes were checked. In the exercises, you establish that if the diseases were sorted, 23 nodes would be checked.

Next we present the algorithm. It uses the following declaration:

```
struct node
{
   int level;                                    // the node's level in the tree
   set_of_indices D;
   float bound;
};
```

The field D contains the indices of the diseases included up to the node. One of the inputs to this algorithm is a belief network *BN*. As mentioned previously, a belief network represents the probabilistic relationships among diseases and symptoms. The algorithms referenced at the beginning of this section can compute the necessary probabilities from such a network.

The following algorithm was developed by Cooper (1984) and is known as Cooper's Algorithm:

Algorithm 6.4   Cooper's Best-First Search with Branch-and-Bound Pruning Algorithm for Abductive Inference

Problem: Determine a most probable set of diseases (explanation) given a set of symptoms. It is assumed that if a set of diseases D is a subset of a set of diseases D', then

$$p(D') \leq p(D).$$

Inputs: positive integer n, a belief network *BN* that represents the probabilistic relationships among n diseases and their symptoms, and a set of symptoms S.

Outputs: a set *best* that contains the indices of the diseases in a most probable set (conditional on S), and a variable *pbest* that is the probability of *best* given S.

```
void cooper (int n,
             belief_network_of_n_diseases BN,
             set_of_symptoms S,
             set_of_indices& best,
             float& pbest)
{
   priority_queue_of_node PQ;
   node u, v;
```

```
v.level = 0;                           // Set v to the root.
v.D = ∅;                               // Store empty set at root.
best = ∅;
pbest = p(∅|S);
v.bound = bound(v);
insert(PQ, v);
while (! empty(PQ)) {
  remove(PQ, v);                       // Remove node with best bound.
  if (v.bound > pbest) {
    u.level = v.level + 1;             // Set u to a child of v.
    u.D = v.D;                         // Set u to the child that includes the
    put u.level in u.D;                // next disease.
    if (p(u.D|S) > pbest) {
      best = u.D;
      pbest = p(u.D|S);
    }
    u.bound = bound(u);
    if (u.bound > pbest)
      insert(PQ, u);
    u.D = v.D;                         // Set u to the child that does not
    u.bound = bound(u);                // include the next disease.
    if (u.bound > pbest)
      insert(PQ, u);
  }
 }
}

int bound (node u)
{
  if (u.level == n)                    // A leaf is non-promising.
    return 0;
  else
    return p(u.D|p(S);
}
```

The notation $p(D)$ stands for the prior probability of D, $p(S)$ stands for the prior probability of S, and $p(D|S)$ stands for the conditional probability of D given S. These values would be computed from the belief network BN using the algorithms referenced at the beginning of this section.

We have written the algorithm strictly according to our guidelines for writing best-first search algorithms. An improvement is possible. There is no need to call function *bound* for the right child of a node. The reason is that the right child contains the same set of diseases as the node itself, which means that its bound is the same. Therefore, the right child is pruned only if we change *pbest* to this bound at the left child. We can modify our algorithm to prune the right child when this happens, and to expand to the right child when it does not happen.

Like the other problems described in this chapter, the Problem of Abductive Inference is in the class of problems discussed in Chapter 9.

If there is more than one solution, the preceding algorithm only produces one of them. It is straightforward to modify the algorithm to produce all the best solutions. It is also possible to modify it to produce the *m* most probable explanations, where *m* is any positive integer. This modification is discussed in Neapolitan (1990). Furthermore, Neapolitan (1990) analyzes the algorithm in detail.

Exercises

Section 6.1

1. Use Algorithm 6.1 (The Breadth-First Search with Branch-and-Bound Pruning Algorithm for the 0-1 Knapsack Problem) to maximize the profit for the following problem instance. Show the actions step by step.

i	p_i	w_i	$\frac{p_i}{w_i}$
1	$20	2	10
2	$30	5	6
3	$35	7	5
4	$12	3	4
5	$ 3	1	3

$$W = 13$$

2. Implement Algorithm 6.1 on your system, and run it on the problem instance of Exercise 1.

3. Modify Algorithm 6.1 to produce an optimal set of items. Compare the performance of your algorithm with that of Algorithm 6.1.

4. Use Algorithm 6.2 (The Best-First Search with Branch-and-Bound Pruning Algorithm for the 0-1 Knapsack Problem) to maximize the profit for the problem instance of Exercise 1. Show the actions step by step.

5. Implement Algorithm 6.2 on your system, and run it on the problem instance of Exercise 1.

6. Compare the performance of Algorithm 6.1 with that of Algorithm 6.2 for large instances of the problem.

Section 6.2

7. Use Algorithm 6.3 (The Best-First Search with Branch-and-Bound Pruning Algorithm for the Traveling Salesperson Problem) to find an optimal tour and the length of the optimal tour for the graph below.

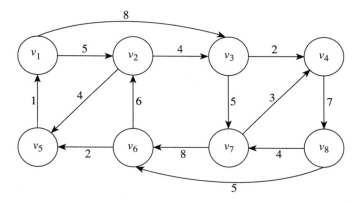

Show the actions step by step.

8. Write functions *length* and *bound* used in Algorithm 6.3.

9. Implement Algorithm 6.3 on your system, and run it on the problem instance of Exercise 7. Use different bounding functions, and study the results.

10. Compare the performance of your dynamic programming algorithm (see Section 3.6, Exercise 27) for the Traveling Salesperson Problem with that of Algorithm 6.3 using large instances of the problem.

Section 6.3

11. Revise Algorithm 6.4 (Cooper's Best-First Search with Branch-and-Bound Pruning Algorithm for Abductive Inference) to produce the *m* most probable explanations, where *m* is any positive integer.

12. Show that if the diseases in Example 6.4 were sorted in nonincreasing order according to their conditional probabilities, the number of nodes checked would be 23 instead of 15. Assume that $p(d_4) = .008$ and $p(d_4, d_1) = .007$.

13. A set of explanations satisfies a comfort measure p if the sum of the probabilities of the explanations is greater than or equal to p. Revise Algorithm 6.4 to produce a set of explanations that satisfies p, where $0 \leq p \leq 1$. Do this with as few explanations as possible.

14. Implement Algorithm 6.4 on your system. The user should be able to enter an integer m, as described in Exercise 11, or a comfort measure p, as described in Exercise 13.

Additional Exercises

15. Can the branch-and-bound design strategy be used to solve the problem discussed in Exercise 34 in Chapter 3? Justify your answer.

16. Write a branch-and-bound algorithm for the problem of scheduling with deadlines discussed in Section 4.3.2.

17. Can the branch-and-bound design strategy be used to solve the problem discussed in Exercise 26 in Chapter 4? Justify your answer.

18. Can the branch-and-bound design strategy be used to solve the Chained Matrix Multiplication Problem discussed in Section 3.4? Justify your answer.

19. List three more applications of the branch-and-bound design strategy.

CHAPTER 7

Introduction to Computational Complexity: The Sorting Problem

*W*e presented a quadratic-time sorting algorithm (Exchange Sort) in Section 1.1. If computer scientists had been content with this sorting algorithm, many applications would now be running significantly slower, and others would not be possible at all. Recall from Table 1.4 that it would take years to sort 1 billion keys using a quadratic-time algorithm. More efficient sorting algorithms have been developed. In particular, in Section 2.2 we saw Mergesort, which is $\Theta(n \lg n)$ in the worst case. Although this algorithm could not sort 1 billion items so quickly that the time would be imperceptible to a human, Table 1.4 shows that it could sort the items in an amount of time that would be tolerable in an off-line application. Suppose someone wanted 1 billion items to be sorted almost immediately in an on-line application. That person might labor for many hours or even many years trying to develop a linear-time or better sorting algorithm. Wouldn't that individual be distraught to learn, after devoting a lifetime of work to this effort, that such an algorithm was not possible? There are two approaches to attacking a problem. One is to try to develop a more efficient algorithm for the problem. The other is to try to prove that a more efficient algorithm is not possible. Once we have such a proof, we know that we should quit trying to obtain a faster algorithm. As we shall see, for a large class of sorting algorithms, we have proven that an algorithm better than $\Theta(n \lg n)$ is not possible.

7.1 COMPUTATIONAL COMPLEXITY

The preceding chapters were concerned with developing and analyzing algorithms for problems. We often used different approaches to solve the same problem with the hope of finding increasingly efficient algorithms for the problem. When we analyze a specific algorithm, we determine its time (or memory) complexity or the order of its time (or memory) complexity. We do not analyze the *problem* that the algorithm solves. For example, when we analyzed Algorithm 1.4 (Matrix Multiplication), we found that its time complexity was n^3. However, this does not mean that the problem of matrix multiplication *requires* a $\Theta(n^3)$ algorithm. The function n^3 is a property of that one algorithm; it is not necessarily a property of the problem of matrix multiplication. In Section 2.5 we developed Strassen's matrix multiplication algorithm with a time complexity in $\Theta(n^{2.81})$. Furthermore, we mentioned that a $\Theta(n^{2.38})$ variation of the algorithm has been developed. An important question is whether it is possible to find an even more efficient algorithm.

Computational complexity, which is a field that runs hand-in-hand with algorithm design and analysis, is the study of all possible algorithms that can solve a given problem. A computational complexity analysis tries to determine a lower bound on the efficiency of all algorithms for a given problem. At the end of Section 2.5, we mentioned that it has been proven that the problem of matrix multiplication requires an algorithm whose time complexity is in $\Omega(n^2)$. It was a computational complexity analysis that determined this. We state this result by saying that a *lower bound* for the problem of matrix multiplication is $\Omega(n^2)$. This does not mean that it must be possible to create a $\Theta(n^2)$ algorithm for matrix multiplication. It means only that is impossible to create one that is better than $\Theta(n^2)$. Because our best algorithm is $\Theta(n^{2.38})$ and our lower bound is $\Omega(n^2)$, it is worthwhile to continue investigating the problem. The investigation can proceed in two directions. On one hand, we can try to find a more efficient algorithm using algorithm design methodology, while on the other hand we can try to obtain a greater lower bound using computational complexity analysis. Perhaps someday we will develop an algorithm that is better than $\Theta(n^{2.38})$, or perhaps someday we will prove that there is a lower bound greater than $\Omega(n^2)$. In general, our goal for a given problem is to determine a lower bound of $\Omega(f(n))$ and develop a $\Theta(f(n))$ algorithm for the problem. Once we have done this, we know that, except for improving the constant, we cannot improve on the algorithm any further.

Some authors use the term "computational complexity analysis" to include both algorithm and problem analysis. Throughout this text, when we refer to computational complexity analysis, we mean just problem analysis.

We introduce computational complexity analysis by studying the Sorting Problem. There are two reasons for choosing this problem. First, quite a few algorithms have been devised that solve the problem. By studying and comparing these algorithms, we can gain insight into how to choose among several algorithms for the same problem and how to improve a given algorithm. Second, the problem of sorting is one of the few problems for which we have been successful in developing algorithms whose time complexities are about as good as our lower bound. That is, for a large class of sorting algorithms, we have determined a lower bound of $\Omega(n \lg n)$ and we have developed $\Theta(n \lg n)$ algorithms. Therefore, we can say that we have solved the Sorting Problem as far as this class of algorithms is concerned.

The class of sorting algorithms for which we have obtained algorithms about as good as our lower bound includes all algorithms that sort only by comparison of keys. As discussed at the beginning of Chapter 1, the word "key" is used because records often contain a unique identifier, called a *key,* that is an element of an ordered set. Given that records are arranged in some arbitrary sequence, the *sorting task* is to rearrange them so that they are in order according to the values of the keys. In our algorithms, the keys are stored in an array, and we do not refer to the nonkey fields. However, it is assumed that these fields are rearranged along with the key. Algorithms that *sort only by comparisons of keys* can compare two keys to determine which is larger, and can copy keys, but cannot do other operations on them. The sorting algorithms we have encountered so far (Algorithms 1.3, 2.4, and 2.6) fall into this class.

In Sections 7.2 through 7.8, we discuss algorithms that sort only by comparisons of keys. Specifically, Section 7.2 discusses Insertion Sort and Selection Sort, two of the most efficient quadratic-time sorting algorithms. In Section 7.3 we show that, as long as we limit ourselves to a restriction in Insertion Sort and Selection Sort, we cannot improve on quadratic time. Sections 7.4 and 7.5 revisit our $\Theta(n \lg n)$ sorting algorithms, Mergesort and Quicksort. Section 7.6 presents another $\Theta(n \lg n)$ sorting algorithm, Heapsort. In Section 7.7 we compare our three $\Theta(n \lg n)$ sorting algorithms. Section 7.8 shows the proof that $\Omega(n \lg n)$ is a lower bound for algorithms that sort by comparing keys. In Section 7.9 we discuss Radix Sort, which is a sorting algorithm that does not sort by comparing keys.

We analyze the algorithms in terms of both the number of comparisons of keys and the number of assignments of records. For example, in Algorithm 1.3 (Exchange Sort), the exchange of $S[i]$ and $S[j]$ can be implemented as follows:

$temp = S[i];$
$S[i] = S[j];$
$S[j] = temp;$

This means that three assignments of records are done to accomplish one exchange. We analyze the number of assignments of records because, when the records are large, the time taken to assign a record is quite costly. We also analyze how much extra space the algorithms require besides the space needed to store the input. When the extra space is a constant (that is, when it does not increase with n, the number of keys to be sorted), the algorithm is called an ***in-place sort.*** Finally, we assume that we are always sorting in nondecreasing order.

7.2 INSERTION SORT AND SELECTION SORT

An ***insertion sort*** algorithm is one that sorts by inserting records in an existing sorted array. An example of a simple insertion sort works as follows. Assume that the keys in the first $i - 1$ array slots are sorted. Let x be the value of the key in the ith slot. Compare x in sequence with the key in the $(i - 1)$st slot, the one in the $(i - 2)$nd slot, etc., until a key is found that is smaller than x. Let j be the slot where that key is located. Move the keys in slots $j + 1$ through $i - 1$ to slots $j + 2$ through i, and insert x in the $(j + 1)$st slot. Repeat this process for $i = 2$ through $i = n$. Figure 7.1 illustrates this sort. An algorithm for this sort follows:

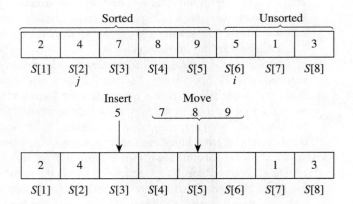

Figure 7.1 An example illustrating what Insertion Sort does when $i = 6$ and $j = 2$. (top) The array before inserting, and (bottom) the insertion step.

Algorithm 7.1

Insertion Sort

Problem: Sort n keys in nondecreasing order.

Inputs: positive integer n; array of keys S indexed from 1 to n.

Outputs: the array S containing the keys in nondecreasing order.

```
void insertionsort (int n, keytype S[ ])
{
   index i, j;
   keytype x;

   for (i = 2; i <= n; i++) {
      x = S[i];
      j = i - 1;
      while (j > 0 && S[j] > x) {
         S[j + 1] = S[j];
         j--;
      }
      S[j + 1] = x;
   }
}
```

Worst-Case Time Complexity Analysis of Number of Comparisons
of Keys in Algorithm 7.1 (Insertion Sort)

Basic operation: the comparison of $S[j]$ with x.

Input size: n, the number of keys to be sorted.

For a given i, the comparison of $S[j]$ with x is done most often when the **while** loop is exited because j becomes equal to 0. Assuming the second condition in an **&&** expression is not evaluated when the first condition is false, the comparison of $S[j]$ with x is not done when j is 0. Therefore, this comparison is done at most $i - 1$ times for a given i. Because i ranges in value from 2 to n, the total number of comparisons is at most

$$\sum_{i=2}^{n} (i - 1) = \frac{n(n - 1)}{2}.$$

It is left as an exercise to show that, if the keys are originally in nonincreasing order in the array, this bound is achieved. Therefore,

$$W(n) = \frac{n(n - 1)}{2}.$$

Average-Case Time Complexity Analysis of Number of Comparisons of Keys in Algorithm 7.1 (Insertion Sort)

For a given i, there are i slots in which x can be inserted. That is, x can stay in the ith slot, go in the $(i - 1)$st slot, go in the $(i - 2)$nd slot, etc. Because we have not previously inspected x or used it in the algorithm, we have no reason to believe that it is more likely to be inserted in any one slot than in any other. Therefore, we assign equal probabilities to each of the first i slots. This means that each slot has the probability $1/i$. The following list shows the number of comparisons done when x is inserted in each slot.

Slot	Number of Comparisons
i	1
$i - 1$	2
$\vdots$	
2	$i - 1$
1	$i - 1$

The reason the number of comparisons is $i - 1$ and not i when x is inserted in the first slot is that the first condition in the expression controlling the **while** loop is false when $j = 0$, which means that the second condition is not evaluated. For a given i, the average number of comparisons needed to insert x is

$$1\left(\frac{1}{i}\right) + 2\left(\frac{1}{i}\right) + \cdots + (i-1)\left(\frac{1}{i}\right) + (i - 1)\left(\frac{1}{i}\right) = \frac{1}{i}\sum_{k=1}^{i-1} k + \frac{i - 1}{i}$$

$$= \frac{(i - 1)(i)}{2i} + \frac{i - 1}{i}$$

$$= \frac{i + 1}{2} - \frac{1}{i}.$$

Therefore, the average number of comparisons needed to sort the array is

$$\sum_{i=2}^{n}\left(\frac{i + 1}{2} - \frac{1}{i}\right) = \sum_{i=2}^{n}\frac{i + 1}{2} - \sum_{i=2}^{n}\frac{1}{i} \approx \frac{(n + 4)(n - 1)}{4} - \ln n.$$

The last equality is obtained using the results of Examples A.1 and A.9 in Appendix A and doing some algebraic manipulations. We have shown that

$$A(n) \approx \frac{(n + 4)(n - 1)}{4} - \ln n \approx \frac{n^2}{4}.$$

Next we analyze the extra space usage.

Analysis of Extra Space Usage for Algorithm 7.1 (Insertion Sort)

The only space usage that increases with n is the size of the input array S. Therefore, the algorithm is an in-place sort, and the extra space is in $\Theta(1)$.

In the exercises, you are asked to show that *the worse-case and average-case time complexities for the number of assignments of records done by Insertion Sort* are given by

$$W(n) = \frac{(n+4)(n-1)}{2} \approx \frac{n^2}{2} \quad \text{and} \quad A(n) = \frac{n(n+7)}{4} - 1 \approx \frac{n^2}{4}.$$

Next we compare Insertion Sort with the other quadratic-time algorithm encountered in this text—namely, Exchange Sort (Algorithm 1.3). Recall that the every-case time complexity of the number of comparisons of keys in Exchange Sort is given by

$$T(n) = \frac{n(n-1)}{2}.$$

In the exercises, you are asked to show that *the worst-case and average-case time complexities for the number of assignments of records done by Exchange Sort* are given by

$$W(n) = \frac{3n(n-1)}{2} \quad \text{and} \quad A(n) = \frac{3n(n-1)}{4}.$$

Clearly, *Exchange Sort is an in-place sort.*

Table 7.1 summarizes our results concerning Exchange Sort and Insertion Sort. We see from this table that in terms of comparisons of keys, Insertion Sort always performs at least as well as Exchange Sort and on the average performs better. In terms of assignments of records, Insertion Sort performs better both in the worst-case and on the average. Because both are in-place sorts, Insertion Sort is the better algorithm. Notice that another algorithm, Selection Sort, is also included in Table 7.1. This algorithm is a slight modification of Exchange Sort and removes one of the disadvantages of Exchange Sort. We present it next.

Table 7.1 Analysis summary for Exchange Sort, Insertion Sort, and Selection Sort*

Algorithm	Comparisons of Keys	Assignments of Records	Extra Space Usage
Exchange Sort	$T(n) = \frac{n^2}{2}$	$W(n) = \frac{3n^2}{2}$ $A(n) = \frac{3n^2}{4}$	In-place
Insertion Sort	$W(n) = \frac{n^2}{2}$ $A(n) = \frac{n^2}{4}$	$W(n) = \frac{n^2}{2}$ $A(n) = \frac{n^2}{4}$	In-place
Selection Sort	$T(n) = \frac{n^2}{2}$	$T(n) = 3n$	In-place

*Entries are approximate.

Algorithm 7.2

Selection Sort

Problem: Sort *n* keys in nondecreasing order.

Inputs: positive integer *n;* array of keys *S* indexed from 1 to *n*.

Outputs: the array *S* containing the keys in nondecreasing order.

```
void selectionsort (int n, keytype S[ ])
{
   index i, j, smallest;

   for (i = 1; i <= n − 1; i++) {
      smallest = i;
      for (j = i + 1; j <= n; j++)
         if (S[j] < S[smallest])
            smallest = j;
      exchange S[i] and S[smallest];
   }
}
```

Clearly, this algorithm has the same time complexity as Exchange Sort in terms of comparisons of keys. However, the assignments of records are significantly different. Instead of exchanging $S[i]$ and $S[j]$ every time $S[j]$ is found to be smaller than $S[i]$, as Exchange Sort does (see Algorithm 1.3), Selection Sort simply keeps track of the index of the current smallest key among the keys in the *i*th through the *n*th slots. After determining that record, it exchanges it with the record in the *i*th slot. In this way, the smallest key is placed in the first slot after the first pass through the **for**-*i* loop, the second smallest key is put in the second slot after the second pass, and so on. The result is the same as that of Exchange Sort. However, by doing only one exchange at the bottom of the **for**-*i* loop, we have made the number of exchanges exactly $n - 1$. Because three assignments are needed to do an exchange, *the every-case time complexity of the number of assignments of records done by Selection Sort* is given by

$$T(n) = 3(n - 1).$$

Recall that the average-case number of assignments of records for Exchange Sort is about $3n^2/4$. Therefore, on the average, we've replaced quadratic time with linear time. Exchange Sort sometimes does better than Selection Sort. For example, if the records are already sorted, Exchange Sort does no assignments of records.

How does Selection Sort compare with Insertion Sort? Look again at Table 7.1. In terms of comparisons of keys, Insertion Sort always performs at least as well as Selection Sort and on the average performs better. However, Selection Sort's time complexity in terms of assignments of records is linear whereas Insertion Sort's is quadratic. Recall that linear time is much faster than quadratic time when n is large. Therefore, if n is large and the records are big (so that the time to assign a record is costly), Selection Sort should perform better.

Any sorting algorithm that selects records in order and puts them in their proper positions is called a ***selection sort***. This means that Exchange Sort is also a selection sort. Another selection sort, called Heapsort, is presented in Section 7.6. Algorithm 7.2, however, has been honored with the name "Selection Sort."

The purpose of comparing Exchange Sort, Insertion Sort, and Selection Sort was to introduce a complete comparison of sorting algorithms as simply as possible. In practice, none of these algorithms is practical for extremely large instances because all of them are quadratic-time in the worst case. Next we show that as long as we limit ourselves to algorithms in the same class as these three algorithms, it is not possible to improve on quadratic time as far as comparisons of keys are concerned.

7.3 LOWER BOUNDS FOR ALGORITHMS THAT REMOVE AT MOST ONE INVERSION PER COMPARISON

After each comparison, Insertion Sort either does nothing or moves the key in the jth slot to the $(j + 1)$st slot. By moving the key in the jth slot up one slot, we have remedied the fact that x should come before that key. However, this is all that we have accomplished. We show that all sorting algorithms that sort only by comparisons of keys, and accomplish such a limited amount of rearranging after each comparison, require at least quadratic time. We obtain our results under the assumption that the keys to be sorted are distinct. Clearly, the worst-case bound still holds true with this restriction removed because a lower bound on the worst-case performance of inputs from some subsets of inputs is also a lower bound when all inputs are considered.

In general, we are concerned with sorting n distinct keys that come from any ordered set. However, without loss of generality, we can assume that the keys to be sorted are simply the positive integers $1, 2, \ldots, n,$ because we can substitute 1 for the smallest key, 2 for the second smallest, and so on. For example, suppose we have the alpha input [Ralph, Clyde, Dave]. We can associate 1 with Clyde, 2 with Dave, and 3 with Ralph to obtain the equivalent input [3, 1, 2]. Any algorithm that sorts these integers only by comparisons of keys would have to do the same number of comparisons to sort the three names.

A ***permutation*** of the first n positive integers can be thought of as an ordering of those integers. Because there are $n!$ permutations of the first n positive integers (see Section A.7), there are $n!$ different orderings of those integers. For example, the following six permutations are all the orderings of the first three positive integers:

   [1, 2, 3]   [1, 3, 2]   [2, 1, 3]   [2, 3, 1]   [3, 1, 2]   [3, 2, 1].

This means that there are $n!$ different inputs (to a sorting algorithm) containing n distinct keys. These six permutations are the different inputs of size 3.

We denote a permutation by $[k_1, k_2, \ldots, k_n]$. That is, k_i is the integer at the ith position. For the permutation $[3, 1, 2]$, for example,

$$k_1 = 3, \; k_2 = 1, \; k_3 = 2.$$

An **inversion** in a permutation is a pair

$$(k_i, k_j) \text{ such that } i < j \text{ and } k_i > k_j.$$

For example, the permutation $[3, 2, 4, 1, 6, 5]$ contains the inversions $(3, 2)$, $(3, 1)$, $(2, 1)$, $(4, 1)$, and $(6, 5)$. Clearly, a permutation contains no inversions if and only if it is the sorted ordering $[1, 2, \ldots, n]$. This means that the task of sorting n distinct keys is the removal of all inversions in a permutation. We now state the main result of this section.

Theorem 7.1 Any algorithm that sorts n distinct keys only by comparisons of keys and removes at most one inversion after each comparison must in the worst case do at least

$$\frac{n(n - 1)}{2} \text{ comparisons of keys}$$

and on the average do at least

$$\frac{n(n - 1)}{4} \text{ comparisons of keys.}$$

Proof: To establish the result for the worst case, we need only show that there is a permutation with $n(n - 1)/2$ inversions, because when that permutation is the input, the algorithm will have to remove that many inversions and therefore do at least that many comparisons. Showing that $[n, n - 1, \ldots, 2, 1]$ is such a permutation is left as an exercise.

To establish the result for the average case, we pair the permutation $[k_n, k_{n-1}, \ldots, k_1]$ with the permutation $[k_1, k_2, \ldots, k_n]$. This permutation is called the **transpose** of the original permutation. For example, the transpose of $[3, 2, 4, 1, 5]$ is $[5, 1, 4, 2, 3]$. It is not hard to see that if $n > 1$, each permutation has a unique transpose that is distinct from the permutation itself. Let

$$r \text{ and } s \text{ be integers between 1 and } n \text{ such that } s > r.$$

Given a permutation, the pair (s, r) is an inversion in either the permutation or its transpose and not in both. Showing that there are $n(n - 1)/2$ such pairs of integers between 1 and n is left as an exercise. This means that a permutation and its transpose have exactly $n(n - 1)/2$ inversions between them. So the average number of inversions in a permutation and its transpose is

$$\frac{1}{2} \times \frac{n(n - 1)}{2} = \frac{n(n - 1)}{4}.$$

Therefore, if we consider all permutations equally probable for the input, the average number of inversions in the input is also $n(n - 1)/4$. Because we assumed that the algorithm removes at most one inversion after each comparison, on the average it must do at least this many comparisons to remove all inversions and thereby sort the input.

Insertion Sort removes at most the inversion consisting of $S[j]$ and x after each comparison, and therefore this algorithm is in the class of algorithms addressed by Theorem 7.1. It is slightly more difficult to see that Exchange Sort and Selection Sort are also in this class. To illustrate that this is the case, we present an example using Exchange Sort. First, recall that the algorithm for Exchange Sort is as follows:

```
void exchangesort (int n, keytype S[ ])
{
   index i, j;
   for (i = 1; i <= n − 1; i++)
      for (j = i + 1; j <= n; j++)
         if (S[j] < S[i])
            exchange S[i] and S[j];
}
```

Suppose that currently the array S contains the permutation [2, 4, 3, 1] and we are comparing 2 with 1. After that comparison, 2 and 1 will be exchanged, thereby removing the inversions (2, 1), (4, 1), and (3, 1). However, the inversions (4, 2) and (3, 2) have been added, and the net reduction in inversions is only one. This example illustrates the general result that Exchange Sort always has a net reduction of at most one inversion after each comparison.

Because Insertion Sort's worst-case time complexity is $n(n − 1)/2$ and its average-case time complexity is about $n^2/4$, it is about as good as we can hope to do (as far as comparisons of keys are concerned) with algorithms that sort only by comparisons of keys and remove at most one inversion after each comparison. Recall that Mergesort (Algorithms 2.2 and 2.4) and Quicksort (Algorithm 2.6) have time complexities that are better than this. Let's reinvestigate these algorithms to see how they differ from ones such as Insertion Sort.

7.4 MERGESORT REVISITED

Mergesort was introduced in Section 2.2. Here we show that it sometimes removes more than one inversion after a comparison. Then, we show how it can be improved.

As mentioned in the proof of Theorem 7.1, algorithms that remove at most one inversion after each comparison will do at least $n(n − 1)/2$ comparisons when the input is in reverse order. Figure 7.2 illustrates how Mergesort 2 (Algorithm 2.4) handles such an input. When the subarrays [3 4] [1 2] are merged, the comparisons remove more than one inversion. After 3 and 1 are compared, 1 is put in the first array slot, thereby removing the inversions (3, 1) and (4, 1).

Figure 7.2 Mergesort sorting an input that is in reverse order.

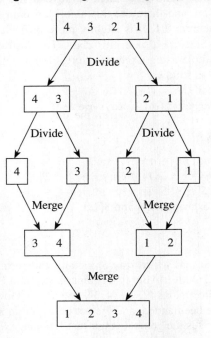

After 3 and 2 are compared, 2 is put in the second array slot, thereby removing the inversions (3, 2) and (4, 2).

Recall that the *worst-case time complexity of Mergesort's number of comparisons of keys* is given by

$$W(n) = n \lg n - (n - 1)$$

when n is a power of 2, and in general, it is in $\Theta(n \lg n)$.

We have gained significantly by developing a sorting algorithm that sometimes removes more than one inversion after a comparison. Recall from Section 1.4.1 that $\Theta(n \lg n)$ algorithms can handle very large inputs, whereas quadratic-time algorithms cannot.

Using the method of "generating functions" for solving recurrences, we can show that the *average-case time complexity of Mergesort's number of comparisons of keys,* when n is a power of 2, is given by

$$A(n) = n \lg n - 2n \sum_{i=1}^{\lg n} \frac{1}{2^i + 2} \approx n \lg n - 1.26n.$$

Although that method is not discussed in Appendix B, it can be found in Sahni (1988). The average case is not much better than the worst case.

It is left as an exercise to show that *the every-case time complexity of*

the number of assignments of records done by Mergesort is given approximately
by

$$T(n) \approx 2n \lg n.$$

Next we analyze the space usage for Mergesort.

Analysis of Extra Space Usage for Algorithm 2.4 (Mergesort 2)

As discussed in Section 2.2, even the improved version of Mergesort given in
Algorithm 2.4 requires an entire additional array of size n. Furthermore, while
the algorithm is sorting the first subarray, the values of *mid, mid*+1, *low,* and
high need to be stored in the stack of activation records. Because the array is
always split in the middle, this stack grows to a depth of $\lceil \lg n \rceil$. The space for
the additional array of records dominates, which means that in every case the
extra space usage is in $\Theta(n)$ records. By ''in $\Theta(n)$ records'' we mean that the
number of records is in $\Theta(n)$.

Improvements of Mergesort

We can improve the basic Mergesort algorithm in three ways. One is a dynamic
programming version of Mergesort, another is a linked version, and the third is
a more complex merge algorithm.

For the first improvement, look again at the example of applying Mergesort
in Figure 2.2. If you were going to do a mergesort by hand, you would not need
to divide the array until singletons were reached. Rather you could simply start
with singletons, merge the singletons into groups of two, then into groups of four,
and so on until the array was sorted. We can write an iterative version of
Mergesort that mimics this method, and thereby avoid the overhead of the stack
operations needed to implement recursion. Notice that this is a dynamic programming approach to Mergesort. The algorithm for this version follows. The loop in
the algorithm treats the array size as a power of 2. Values of n that are not powers
of 2 are handled by going through the loop $2^{\lceil \lg n \rceil}$ times but simply not merging
beyond n.

Algorithm 7.3 Mergesort 3 (Dynamic Programming Version)

Problem: Sort n keys in nondecreasing order.

Inputs: positive integer n; array of keys S indexed from 1 to n.

Outputs: the array S containing the keys in nondecreasing order.

```
void mergesort3 (int n, keytype S[ ])
{
    int m;
    index low, mid, high, size;
```

```
    m = 2^{⌈lg n⌉};              // Treat array size as a
    size = 1;                    // power of 2.
    repeat (lgm times) {         // size is the size of the
                                 // subarrays being merged.
      for (low = 1; low <= m−2*size+1; low = low+2*size) {
        mid = low + size − 1;
        high = minimum(low + 2*size − 1, n);   // Don't merge beyond n.
        merge3(low, mid, high, S);
      }
      size = 2 * size;           // Double the size of the
    }                            // subarrays.
}
```

With this improvement, we can also decrease the number of assignments of records. The array *U*, which is defined locally in procedure *merge2* (Algorithm 2.5), can be defined locally in *mergesort3* as an array indexed from 1 to *n*. After the first pass through the **repeat** loop, *U* will contain the items in *S* with pairs of singletons merged. There is no need to copy these items back to *S*, as is done at the end of *merge2*. Instead, in the next pass through the **repeat** loop, we can simply merge the items in *U* into *S*. That is, we reverse the rolls of the two arrays. In each subsequent pass we keep reversing the rolls. It is left as an exercise to write versions of *mergesort3* and *merge3* that do this. In this way we reduce the number of assignments of records from about $2n \lg n$ to about $n \lg n$. We have established that *the every-case time complexity of the number of assignments of records done by Algorithm 7.3* is given approximately by

$$T(n) \approx n \lg n.$$

The second improvement of Mergesort is a linked version of the algorithm. As discussed in Section 7.1, the Sorting Problem ordinarily involves sorting of records according to the values of their keys. If the records are large, the amount of extra space used by Mergesort can be considerable. We can reduce the extra space by adding a link field to each record. We then sort the records into a sorted linked list by adjusting the links rather than by moving the records. This means that an extra array of records need not be created. Because the space occupied by a link is considerably less than that of a large record, the amount of space saved is significant. Furthermore, there will be a time savings because the time required to adjust links is less than that needed to move large records. Figure 7.3 illustrates how the merging is accomplished using links. The algorithm that follows contains this modification. We present Mergesort and Merge as one algorithm because we need not analyze them further. Mergesort is written recursively for the sake of readability. Of course, the iterative improvement mentioned previously can be implemented along with this improvement. If we used both iteration and links, the improvement of repeatedly reversing the rolls of *U* and

Figure 7.3 Merging using links. Arrows are used to show how the links work. The keys are letters to avoid confusion with indices.

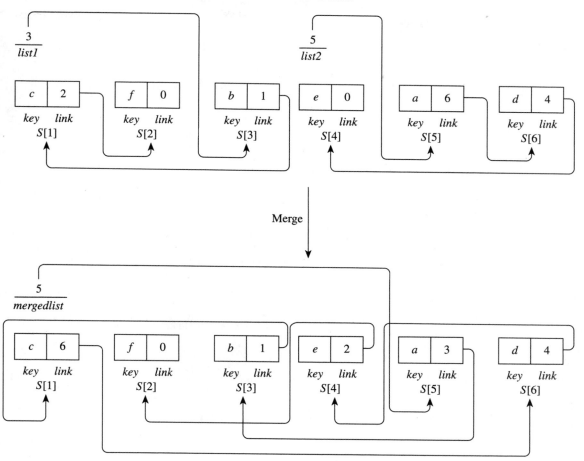

S would not be included because no extra array is needed when linked lists are merged. The data type for the items in the array *S* in this algorithm is as follows:

```
struct node
{
   keytype key;
   index link;
};
```

Algorithm 7.4   Mergesort 4 (Linked Version)

Problem: Sort *n* keys in nondecreasing order.

Inputs: positive integer *n;* array of records, *S*, of the type just given, indexed from 1 to *n*.

Outputs: the array *S* with the values in the *key* field sorted in nondecreasing order. The records are in an ordered linked list using the *link* field.

```
void mergesort4 (index low, index high, index& mergedlist)
{
   index mid, list1, list2;

   if (low == high) {
      mergedlist = low;
      S[mergedlist].link = 0;
   }
   else {
      mid = ⌊(low + high) / 2⌋;
      mergesort4(low, mid, list1);
      mergesort4(mid + 1, high, list2);
      merge4(list1, list2, mergedlist);
   }
}


void merge4 (index list1, index list2, index& mergedlist)
{
   index lastsorted;

   if (S[list1].key < S[list2].key) {            // Find the start of the merged
      mergedlist = list1;                        // list.
      list1 = S[list1].link;
   }
   else {
      mergedlist = list2;
      list2 = S[list2].link;
   }
   lastsorted = mergedlist;
   while (list1 != 0 && list2 != 0)
      if S[list1].key < S[list2].key {           // Attach smaller key to merged
         S[lastsorted].link = list1;             // list.
         lastsorted = list1;
         list1 = S[list1].link;
      }
      else {
         S[lastsorted].link = list2;
         lastsorted = list2;
         list2 = S[list2].link;
      }
```

```
        if (list1 == 0)                    // After one list ends, attach
            S[lastsorted].link = list2;    // remainder of the other.
        else
            S[lastsorted].link = list1;
    }
```

It is not necessary to check whether *list1* or *list2* is 0 on entry to *merge4* because *mergesort4* never passes an empty list to *merge4*. As was the case for Algorithm 2.4 (Mergesort 2), *n* and *S* are not inputs to *mergesort4*. The top level call would be

mergesort4(1,*n*,*listfront*).

After execution, *listfront* would contain the index of the first record in the sorted list.

After sorting, we often want the records to be in sorted sequence in contiguous array slots (that is, sorted in the usual way) so that we can access them quickly by the key field using Binary Search (Algorithm 2.1). Once the records have been sorted according to the links, it is possible to rearrange them so that they are in sorted sequence in contiguous array slots using an in-place, $\Theta(n)$ algorithm. In the exercises you are asked to write such an algorithm.

This improvement of Mergesort accomplishes two things. First, it replaces the need for *n* additional records with the need for only *n* links. That is, we have the following:

Analysis of Extra Space Usage for Algorithm 7.4 (Mergesort 4)

In every case, the extra space usage is in $\Theta(n)$ links. By "in $\Theta(n)$ links" we mean that the number of links is in $\Theta(n)$.

Second, it reduces the time complexity of the number of assignments of records to 0 if we do not need to have the records ordered in contiguous array slots and to $\Theta(n)$ if we do.

The third improvement of Mergesort is a more complex merge algorithm that is presented in Huang and Langston (1988). That merge algorithm is also $\Theta(n)$ but with a small, constant amount of additional space.

7.5 QUICKSORT REVISITED

As a refresher, let's first repeat the algorithm for Quicksort:

```
void quicksort (index low, index high)
{
    index pivotpoint;
```

```
if (high > low) {
    partition(low, high, pivotpoint);
    quicksort(low, pivotpoint − 1);
    quicksort(pivotpoint + 1, high);
}
}
```

Although its worst-case time complexity is quadratic, we saw in Section 2.4 that *the average-case time complexity of Quicksort's number of comparisons of keys* is given by

$$A(n) \approx 1.38(n + 1) \lg n,$$

which is not much worse than Mergesort. Quicksort has the advantage over Mergesort that no extra array is needed. However, it is still not an in-place sort because, while the algorithm is sorting the first subarray, the first and last indices of the other subarray need to be stored in the stack of activation records. Unlike Mergesort, we have no guarantee that the array will always be split in the middle. In the worse case, *partition* may repeatedly split the array into an empty subarray on the left (or right) and a subarray with one less item on the right (or left). In this way, $n − 1$ pairs of indices will end up being stacked, which means that the worst-case extra space usage is in $\Theta(n)$. It is possible to modify Quicksort so that the extra space usage is at most about $\lg n$. Before showing this and other improvements of Quicksort, let's discuss the time complexity of the number of assignments of records by Quicksort.

In the exercises, you are asked to establish that the average number of exchanges performed by Quicksort is about $0.69(n + 1) \lg n$. Assuming that three assignments are done to perform one exchange, *the average-case time complexity of the number of assignments of records done by Quicksort* is given by

$$A(n) \approx 2.07(n + 1) \lg n.$$

Improvements of the Basic Quicksort Algorithm

We can reduce the extra space usage of Quicksort in five different ways. First, in procedure *quicksort,* we determine which subarray is smaller and always stack that one while the other is sorted. The following is an analysis of the space used by this version of *quicksort.*

Analysis of Extra Space Usage for Improved Quicksort

In this version, the worst-case space usage occurs when *partition* splits the array exactly in half each time, resulting in a stack depth about equal to $\lg n$. Therefore, the worst-case space usage is in $\Theta(\lg n)$ indices.

Second, as discussed in the exercises, there is a version of *partition* that cuts the average number of assignments of records significantly. For that version, *the average-case time complexity of the number of assignments of records done by Quicksort* is given by

$$A(n) \approx 0.69(n + 1) \lg n.$$

Third, each of the recursive calls in procedure *quicksort* causes *low, high,* and *pivotpoint* to be stacked. A good deal of the pushing and popping is unnecessary. While the first recursive call to *quicksort* is being processed, only the values of *pivotpoint* and *high* need to be saved on the stack. While the second recursive call is being processed, nothing needs to be saved. We can avoid the unnecessary operations by writing *quicksort* iteratively and manipulating the stack in the procedure. That is, we do explicit stacking instead of stacking by recursion. You are asked to do this in the exercises.

Fourth, as discussed in Section 2.7, recursive algorithms such as Quicksort can be improved by determining a threshold value at which the algorithm calls an iterative algorithm instead of dividing an instance further.

Finally, as mentioned in the worst-case analysis of Algorithm 2.6 (Quicksort), the algorithm is least efficient when the input array is already sorted. The closer the input array is to being sorted, the closer we are to this worst-case performance. Therefore, if there is reason to *believe* that the array may be close to already being sorted, we can improve the performance by not always choosing the first item as the pivot item. One good strategy to use in this case is to choose the median of $S[low]$, $S[\lfloor (low + high)/2 \rfloor]$, and $S[high]$ for the pivot point. Of course, if we have no reason to believe that there is any particular structure in the input array, choosing any item for the pivot item is, on the average, just as good as choosing any other item. In this case, all we really gain by taking the median is the guarantee that one of the subarrays will not be empty (as long as the three values are distinct).

A final point about Quicksort is that it is in the class of algorithms that sort by **transposition.** That is, the sorting is accomplished by exchanging (transposing) adjacent records. A quadratic-time algorithm in this class is Bubblesort. Bubblesort is discussed in the exercises.

7.6 HEAPSORT

Unlike Mergesort and Quicksort, Heapsort is an in-place $\Theta(n \lg n)$ algorithm. First we review heaps and describe basic heap routines needed for sorting using heaps. Then we show how to implement these routines.

7.6.1 Heaps and Basic Heap Routines

Recall that the depth of a node in a tree is the number of edges in the unique path from the root to that node, the depth d of a tree is the maximum depth of all nodes in the tree, and a leaf in a tree is any node with no children (see Section 3.5). An ***internal node*** in a tree is any node that has at least one child. That is, it is any node that is not a leaf. A ***complete binary tree*** is a binary tree that satisfies the following conditions:

• All internal nodes have two children.

• All leaves have depth d.

An ***essentially complete binary tree*** is a binary tree that satisfies the following conditions:

• It is a complete binary tree down to a depth of $d - 1$.

• The nodes with depth d are as far to the left as possible.

Although essentially complete binary trees are difficult to define, it is straightforward to grasp their properties from a picture. Figure 7.4 shows an essentially complete binary tree.

We can now define a heap. A ***heap*** is an essentially complete binary tree such that

• The values stored at the nodes come from an ordered set.

• The value stored at each node is greater than or equal to the values stored at its children. This is called the ***heap property.***

Figure 7.5 shows a heap. Because we are presently interested in sorting, we will refer to the items stored in the heap as keys.

Suppose that somehow we have arranged the keys that are to be sorted in a heap. If we repeatedly remove the key stored at the root while maintaining the heap property, the keys will be removed in nonincreasing sequence. If, while removing them, we place them in an array starting with the nth slot and going down to the first slot, they will be sorted in nondecreasing sequence in the array. After removing the key at the root, we can restore the heap property by replacing the key at the root with the key stored at the bottom node (by ''bottom node'' we mean the far right leaf), deleting the bottom node, and calling a procedure *siftdown* that ''sifts'' the key now at the root down the heap until the heap property is restored. The sifting is accomplished by initially comparing the key at the root

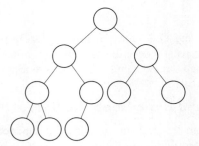

Figure 7.4 An essentially complete binary tree.

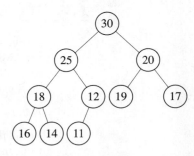

Figure 7.5 A heap.

Figure 7.6 Procedure *siftdown* sifts 6 down until the heap property is restored.

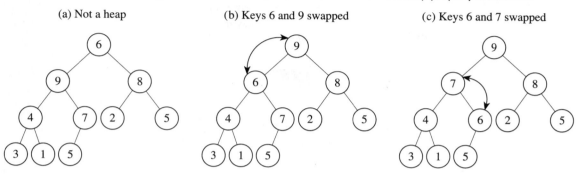

(a) Not a heap   (b) Keys 6 and 9 swapped   (c) Keys 6 and 7 swapped

with the larger of the keys at the children of the root. If the key at the root is smaller, the keys are exchanged. This process is repeated down the tree until the key at a node is not smaller than the larger of the keys at its children. Figure 7.6 illustrates this procedure. High-level pseudocode for it is as follows:

```
void siftdown (heap& H)                  // H starts out having the
{                                         // heap property for all
    node parent, largerchild;             // nodes except the root.
                                          // H ends up a heap.
    parent = root of H;
    largerchild = parent's child containing larger key;
    while (key at parent is smaller than key at largerchild) {
        exchange key at parent and key at largerchild;
        parent = largerchild;
        largerchild = parent's child containing larger key;
    }
}
```

High-level pseudocode for a function that removes the key at the root and restores the heap property is as follows:

```
keytype root (heap& H)
{
    keytype keyout;

    keyout = key at the root;
    move the key at the bottom node to the root;    // Bottom node is far
    delete the bottom node;                          // right leaf.
    siftdown(H);                                     // Restore the heap
    return keyout;                                   // property.
}
```

Given a heap of n keys, the following is high-level pseudocode for a procedure that places the keys in sorted sequence into an array S.

```
void removekeys (int n,
                 heap H,
                 keytype S[ ])
{
   index i;
   for (i = n; i >= 1; i− −)
      S[i] = root(H);
}
```

(a) The initial structure

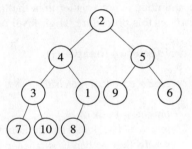

(b) The subtrees, whose roots have depth $d - 1$, are made into heaps

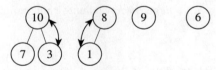

(c) The left subtree, whose root has depth $d - 2$, are made into a heap

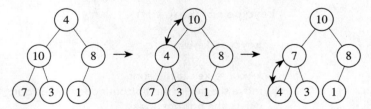

Figure 7.7 Using *siftdown* to make a heap from an essentially complete binary tree. After the steps shown, the right subtree, whose root has depth $d - 2$, must be made into a heap, and finally the entire tree must be made into a heap.

The only task remaining is to arrange the keys in a heap in the first place. Let's assume that they have been arranged in an essentially complete binary tree that does not necessarily have the heap property (we will see how to do this in the next subsection). We can transform the tree into a heap by repeatedly calling *siftdown* to perform the following operations: First, transform all subtrees whose roots have depth $d - 1$ into heaps; second, transform all subtrees whose roots have depth $d - 2$ into heaps; ... finally, transform the entire tree (the only subtree whose root has depth 0) into a heap.

This process is illustrated in Figure 7.7 and is implemented by the procedure outlined in the following high-level pseudocode.

```
void makeheap (int n, heap& H)                    // H ends up a heap.
{
    index i;
    heap Hsub;                                     // Hsub ends up a heap.

    for (i = d - 1; i >= 0; i--)                    // Tree has depth d.
        for (all subtrees Hsub whose roots have depth i)
            siftdown(Hsub);
}
```

Finally, we present high-level pseudocode for Heapsort (it is assumed that the keys are already arranged in an essentially complete binary tree in H):

```
void heapsort (int n,
               heap H,                             // H ends up a heap.
               keytype S[ ])
{
    makeheap(n, H);
    removekeys(n, H, S);
}
```

It may seem that we were not telling the truth earlier because this Heapsort algorithm does not appear to be an in-place sort. That is, we need extra space for the heap. However, next we implement a heap using an array. We show that the same array that stores the input (the keys to be sorted) can be used to implement the heap, and that we never simultaneously need the same array slot for more than one purpose.

7.6.2 An Implementation of Heapsort

We can represent an essentially complete binary tree in an array by storing the root in the first array slot, the root's left and right children in the second and third slots, respectively, the left and right children of the root's left child in the fourth and fifth array slots, and so on. The array representation of the heap in Figure 7.5

Figure 7.8 The array representation of the heap in Figure 7.5.

	Children of key 30		Children of key 25		Children of key 20		Children of key 18		Child of key 12
Root									

30	25	20	18	12	19	17	16	14	11
$S[1]$	$S[2]$	$S[3]$	$S[4]$	$S[5]$	$S[6]$	$S[7]$	$S[8]$	$S[9]$	$S[10]$

is shown in Figure 7.8. Notice that the index of the left child of a node is twice that of the node, and the index of the right child is 1 greater than twice that of the node. Recall that in the high-level pseudocode for Heapsort, we required that the keys initially be in an essentially complete binary tree. If we place the keys in an array in an arbitrary order, they will be structured in some essentially complete binary tree according to the representation just discussed. The following low-level pseudocode uses that representation.

Heap Data Structure

```
struct heap
{
   keytype S[1..n];                    // S is indexed from 1 to n.
   int heapsize;                       // heapsize only takes
};                                     // the values 0 through n.


void siftdown (heap& H, index i)        // To minimize the number
{                                       // of assignment of records,
   index parent, largerchild; keytype siftkey;  // the key initially at the root
   bool spotfound;                      // (siftkey) is not assigned to a
                                        // node until its final position
   siftkey = H.S[i];                    // has been determined.
   parent = i; spotfound = false;
   while (2*parent <= H.heapsize && ! spotfound) {
      if (2*parent < H.heapsize && H.S[2*parent] < H.S.[2*parent+1])
         largerchild = 2*parent + 1;    // Index of right child is 1
      else                              // more than twice that of
         largerchild = 2*parent;        // parent. Index of left child
      if (siftkey < H.S[largerchild]) { // is twice that of parent.
         H.S[parent] = H.S[largerchild];
         parent = largerchild;
      }
      else
         spotfound = true;
   }
   H.S[parent] = siftkey;
}
```

```
keytype root (heap& H)
{
    keytype keyout;

    keyout = H.S[1];                          // Get key at the root.
    H.S[1] = H.S[heapsize];                   // Move bottom key to root.
    H.heapsize = H.heapsize − 1;              // Delete bottom node.
    Siftdown(H, 1);                           // Restore heap property.
    return keyout;
}


void removekeys (int n,                       // H is passed by address
                 heap& H,                     // to save memory.
                 keytype S[ ])                // S is indexed from 1 to n.
{
    index i;

    for (i = n; i >= 1; i− −)
        S[i] = root(H);
}


void makeheap (int n,
               heap& H)                       // H ends up a heap.
{
    index i;                                  // It is assumed that n keys
                                              // are in the array H.S.
    H.heapsize = n;
    for (i = ⌊n / 2⌋; i >= 1; i− −)           // Last node with depth
        siftdown (H, i);                      // d − 1, that has children, is
}                                             // in slot ⌊n / 2⌋ in the array.
```

We can now give an algorithm for Heapsort. The algorithm assumes that the keys to be sorted are already in *H.S.* This automatically structures them in an essentially complete binary tree according to the representation in Figure 7.8. After the essentially complete binary tree is made into a heap, the keys are deleted from the heap starting with the *n*th array slot and going down to the first array slot. Because they are placed in sorted sequence in the output array in that same order, we can use *H.S* as the output array with no possibility of overwriting a key in the heap. This strategy gives us the in-place algorithm that follows.

Algorithm 7.5 Heapsort

Problem: Sort *n* keys in nondecreasing order.

Inputs: positive integer *n*, array of *n* keys stored in an array implementation *H* of a heap.

Outputs: the keys in nondecreasing order in the array *H.S.*

```
void heapsort (int n, heap& H)
{
    makeheap (n, H);
    removekeys (n, H, H.S);
}
```

Worst-Case Time Complexity Analysis of Number of Comparisons of Keys in Algorithm 7.5 (Heapsort)

Basic instruction: the comparisons of keys in procedure *siftdown*.

Input size: *n*, the number of keys to be sorted.

Procedures *makeheap* and *removekeys* both call *siftdown*. We analyze these procedures separately. We do the analysis for *n* a power of 2 and then use Theorem B.4 in Appendix B to extend the result to *n* in general.

Analysis of makeheap

Let *d* be the depth of the essentially complete binary tree that is the input. Figure 7.9 illustrates that when *n* is a power of 2, the depth *d* of the tree is lg *n*, there is exactly one node with that depth, and that node has *d* ancestors. When the heap is constructed, all the keys in ancestors of the node with level *d* will possibly be sifted through one more node (that is, the node with level *d*) than they would be sifted through if that node were not there. All other keys would be sifted through the same number of nodes if that node were not there. We first obtain an upper bound on the total number of nodes through which all keys would be sifted if the node with depth *d* were not there. Because that node has *d* ancestors and the key at each of these ancestors will possibly be sifted through one more node, we can add *d* to this upper bound to obtain our actual upper bound on the total number

Figure 7.9 An illustration using $n = 8$ showing that if an essentially complete binary tree has n nodes and n is a power of 2, then the depth d of the tree is $\lg n$, there is one node with depth d, and that node has d ancestors. The three ancestors of that node are marked "A."

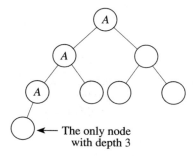

← The only node
with depth 3

of nodes through which all keys are sifted. To that end, if the node with depth d were not there, each key initially at a node with depth $d - 1$ would be sifted through 0 nodes when the heap was constructed; each key initially at a node with depth $d - 2$ would be sifted through at most one node; and so on until finally the key at the root would be sifted through at most $d - 1$ nodes. It is left as an exercise to show that, when n is a power of 2, there are 2^j nodes with depth j for $0 \leq j < d$. For n a power of 2, the following table shows the number of nodes with each depth and at most the number of nodes through which a key at that depth would be sifted (if the node with depth d were not there):

Depth	Number of Nodes with this Depth	Greatest Number of Nodes that a Key Would Be Sifted
0	2^0	$d - 1$
1	2^1	$d - 2$
2	2^2	$d - 3$
⋮	⋮	⋮
j	2^j	$d - j - 1$
⋮	⋮	⋮
$d - 1$	2^{d-1}	0

Therefore, the number of nodes through which all keys would be sifted, if the node with depth d were not there, is at most

$$\sum_{j=0}^{d-1} 2^j(d - j - 1) = (d - 1)\sum_{j=0}^{d-1} 2^j - \sum_{j=0}^{d-1} j(2^j) = 2^d - d - 1.$$

The last equality is obtained by applying results in Examples A.3 and A.5 in Appendix A and doing some algebraic manipulations. Recall that we need to add d to this bound to obtain the actual upper bound on the total number of nodes through which all keys are sifted. Therefore, the actual upper bound is

$$2^d - d - 1 + d = 2^d - 1 = n - 1.$$

The second equality is a result of the fact that $d = \lg n$ when n is a power of 2. Each time a key is sifted through one node, there is one pass through the **while** loop in procedure *siftdown*. Because there are two comparisons of keys in each pass through that loop, the number of comparisons of keys done by *makeheap* is at most

$$2(n - 1).$$

It is a somewhat surprising result that the heap can be constructed in linear time. If we could remove the keys in linear time, we would have a linear-time sorting algorithm. As we shall see, however, this is not the case.

Analysis of removekeys

Figure 7.10 illustrates the case where $n = 8$ and $d = \lg 8 = 3$. As shown in Figure 7.10(a) and (b), when the first and fourth keys are each removed, the key moved to the root sifts through at most $d - 1 = 2$ nodes. Clearly, the same thing happens for the two keys between the first and the fourth. Therefore, when the first four keys are removed, the key moved to the root sifts through at most two nodes. As shown in Figure 7.10(c) and (d), when each of the next two keys is removed, the key moved to the root sifts through at most $d - 2 = 1$ node. Finally, Figure 7.10(e) shows that, when the next key is removed, the key moved to the root sifts through 0 nodes. Clearly, there is also no sifting when the last key is removed. The total number of nodes through which all keys are sifted is at most

$$1(2) + 2(4) = \sum_{j=1}^{3-1} j2^j.$$

It is not hard to see that this result can be extended to n an arbitrary power of 2. Because each time a key is sifted through one node, there is one pass through the **while** loop in procedure *siftdown,* and, because there are two comparisons of keys in each pass through that loop, the number of comparisons of keys done by *removekeys* is at most

$$2 \sum_{j=1}^{d-1} j2^j = 2(d2^d - 2^{d+1} + 2) = 2n \lg n - 4n + 4.$$

The first equality is obtained by applying the result in Example A.5 in Appendix A and doing some algebraic manipulations, whereas the second results from the fact that $d = \lg n$ when n is a power of 2.

Combining the Two Analyses

The combined analyses of *makeheap* and *removekeys* show that the number of comparisons of keys in Heapsort is at most

$$2(n - 1) + 2n \lg n - 4n + 4 = 2(n \lg n - n + 1) \approx 2n \lg n$$

when n is a power of 2. Showing that there is a case in which we have this number of comparisons is left as an exercise. Therefore, for n a power of 2,

Figure 7.10 Removing the keys from a heap with eight nodes. The removal of the first key is depicted in (a); the fourth in (b); the fifth in (c); the sixth in (d); and the seventh in (e). The key moved to the root is sifted through the number of nodes shown on the right.

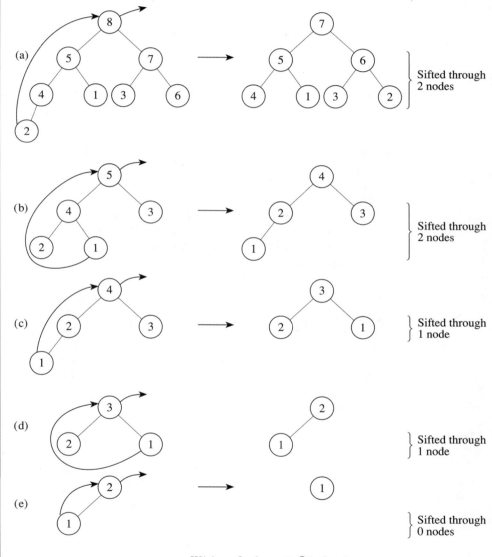

$$W(n) \approx 2n \lg n \in \Theta(n \lg n).$$

It is possible to show that $W(n)$ is eventually nondecreasing. Therefore, Theorem B.4 in Appendix B implies that for n in general

$$W(n) \in \Theta(n \lg n).$$

It appears to be difficult to analyze Heapsort's average-case time complexity analytically. However, empirical studies have shown that its average case is not much better than its worse case. This means that the *average-case time complexity of the number of comparisons of keys done by Heapsort* is approximated by

$$A(n) \approx 2n \lg n.$$

In the exercises, you are asked to establish that the *worst-case time complexity of the number of assignments of records done by Heapsort* is approximated by

$$W(n) \approx n \lg n.$$

As is the case for the comparisons of keys, Heapsort does not do much better than this on the average.

Finally, as already discussed, we have the following space usage.

Analysis of Extra Space Usage for Algorithm 7.5 (Heapsort)

Heapsort is an in-place sort, which means that the extra space is in $\Theta(1)$.

As mentioned in Section 7.2, Heapsort is an example of a selection sort because it sorts by selecting records in order and placing them in their proper sorted positions. It is the call to *removekeys* that places a record in its proper sorted position.

7.7   COMPARISON OF MERGESORT, QUICKSORT, AND HEAPSORT

Table 7.2 summarizes our results concerning the three algorithms. Because Heapsort is, on the average, worse than Quicksort in terms of both comparisons of

Table 7.2 Analysis summary for $\Theta(n \lg n)$ sorting algorithms*

Algorithm	Comparisons of Keys	Assignments of Records	Extra Space Usage
Mergesort (Algorithm 2.4)	$W(n) = n \lg n$ $A(n) = n \lg n$	$T(n) = 2n \lg n$	$\Theta(n)$ records
Mergesort (Algorithm 7.4)	$W(n) = n \lg n$ $A(n) = n \lg n$	$T(n) = 0^\dagger$	$\Theta(n)$ links
Quicksort (with improvements)	$W(n) = n^2/2$ $A(n) = 1.38n \lg n$	$A(n) = 0.69n \lg n$	$\Theta(\lg n)$ indices
Heapsort	$W(n) = 2n \lg n$ $A(n) = 2n \lg n$	$W(n) = n \lg n$ $A(n) = n \lg n$	In-place

*Entries are approximate; the average cases for Mergesort and Heapsort are slightly better than the worst cases.
†If it is required that the records be in sorted sequence in contiguous array slots, the worst case is in $\Theta(n)$.

keys and assignments of records, and because Quicksort's extra space usage is minimal, Quicksort is usually preferred to Heapsort. Because our original implementation of Mergesort (Algorithms 2.2 and 2.4) uses an entire additional array of records, and because Mergesort always does about three times as many assignments of records as Quicksort does on the average, Quicksort is usually preferred to Mergesort even though Quicksort does slightly more comparisons of keys on the average. However, the linked implementation of Mergesort (Algorithm 7.4) eliminates almost all the disadvantages of Mergesort. The only disadvantage remaining is the additional space used for $\Theta(n)$ extra links.

7.8 LOWER BOUNDS FOR SORTING ONLY BY COMPARISONS OF KEYS

We have developed $\Theta(n \lg n)$ sorting algorithms, which represent a substantial improvement over quadratic-time algorithms. A good question is whether we can develop sorting algorithms whose time complexities are of even better order. We show that, as long as we limit ourselves to sorting only by comparisons of keys, such algorithms are not possible.

Although our results still hold if we consider probabilistic sorting algorithms, we obtain the results for deterministic sorting algorithms. (See Section 5.3 for a discussion of probabilistic and deterministic algorithms.) As done in Section 7.3, we obtain our results under the assumption that the n keys are distinct. Furthermore, as discussed in that section, we can assume that the n keys are simply the positive integers $1, 2, \ldots, n$, because we can substitute 1 for the smallest key, 2 for the second smallest, and so on.

7.8.1 Decision Trees for Sorting Algorithms

Consider the following algorithm for sorting three keys.

```
void sortthree (keytype S[ ])      // S is indexed from 1 to 3.
{
   keytype a, b, c;

   a = S[1]; b = S[2]; c = S[3];
   if (a < b)
      if (b < c)
         S = a, b, c;              // This means S[1] = a; S[2] = b; S[3] = c;
      else if (a < c)
         S = a, c, b;
      else
         S = c, a, b;
```

```
    else if (b < c)
      if (a < c)
        S = b, a, c;
      else
        S = b, c, a;
    else
      S = c, b, a;
}
```

We can associate a binary tree with procedure *sortthree* as follows. We place the comparison of *a* and *b* at the root. The left child of the root contains the comparison that is made if $a < b$, whereas the right child contains the comparison that is made if $a \geq b$. We proceed downward, creating nodes in the tree until all possible comparisons done by the algorithm are assigned nodes. The sorted keys are stored at the leaves. Figure 7.11 shows the entire tree. This tree is called a ***decision tree,*** because at each node a decision must be made as to which node to visit next. The action of procedure *sortthree* on a particular input corresponds to following the unique path from the root to a leaf, determined by that input. There is a leaf in the tree for every permutation of three keys, because the algorithm can sort every possible input of size 3.

A decision tree is called ***valid*** for sorting *n* keys if, for each permutation of the *n* keys, there is a path from the root to a leaf that sorts that permutation. That

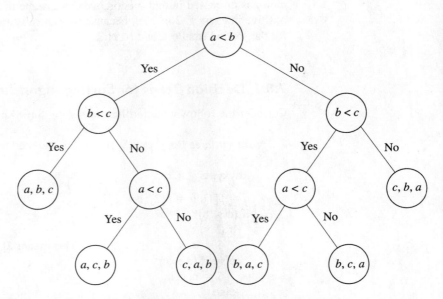

Figure 7.11 The decision tree corresponding to procedure *sortthree.*

is, it can sort every input of size n. For example, the decision tree in Figure 7.11 is valid for sorting three keys, but would no longer be valid if we removed any branch from the tree. To every deterministic algorithm for sorting n keys, there corresponds at least one valid decision tree. The decision tree in Figure 7.11 corresponds to procedure *sortthree,* and the decision tree in Figure 7.12 corresponds to Exchange Sort when sorting three keys (you are encouraged to verify this). In that tree, a, b, and c are again the initial values of $S[1]$, $S[2]$, and $S[3]$. When a node contains, for example, the comparison "$c < b$," this does not mean that Exchange Sort compares $S[3]$ with $S[2]$ at that point; rather, it means that Exchange Sort compares the array item whose current value is c with the one whose current value is b. In the tree in Figure 7.12, notice that the level-2 node containing the comparison "$b < a$" has no right child. The reason that a "no" answer to that comparison contradicts the answers obtained on the path leading to that node, which means that its right child could not be reached by making a consistent sequence of decisions starting at the root. Exchange Sort makes an unnecessary comparison at this point, because Exchange Sort does not "know" that the answer to the question must be "yes." This often happens in suboptimal sorting algorithms. We say that a decision tree is **pruned** if every leaf can be reached from the root by making a consistent sequence of decisions. The decision tree in Figure 7.12 is pruned, whereas it would not be pruned if we added a right child to the node just discussed, even though it would still be valid and would still correspond to Exchange Sort. Clearly, to every deterministic algorithm for sorting n keys there corresponds a pruned, valid decision tree. Therefore, we have the following lemma.

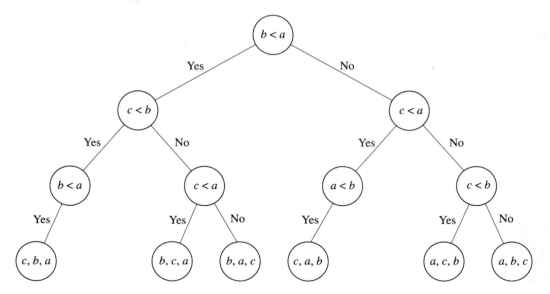

Figure 7.12 The decision tree corresponding to Exchange Sort when sorting three keys.

Lemma 7.1 To every deterministic algorithm for sorting n distinct keys there corresponds a pruned, valid, binary decision tree containing exactly $n!$ leaves.

Proof: As just mentioned, there is a pruned, valid decision tree corresponding to any algorithm for sorting n keys. When all the keys are distinct, the result of a comparison is always "<" or ">." Therefore, each node in that tree has at most two children, which means that it is a binary tree. Next we show that it has $n!$ leaves. Because there are $n!$ different inputs that contain n distinct keys and because a decision tree is valid for sorting n distinct keys only if it has a leaf for every input, the tree has at least $n!$ leaves. Because there is a unique path in the tree for each of the $n!$ different inputs and because every leaf in a pruned decision tree must be reachable, the tree can have no more than $n!$ leaves. Therefore, the tree has exactly $n!$ leaves.

Using Lemma 7.1, we can determine bounds for sorting n distinct keys by investigating binary trees with $n!$ leaves. We do this next.

7.8.2 Lower Bounds for Worst-Case Behavior

To obtain a bound for the worst-case number of comparisons of keys, we need the following lemma.

Lemma 7.2 The worst-case number of comparisons done by a decision tree is equal to its depth.

Proof: Given some input, the number of comparisons done by a decision tree is the number of internal nodes on the path followed for that input. The number of internal nodes is the same as the length of the path. Therefore, the worst-case number of comparisons done by a decision tree is the length of the longest path to a leaf, which is the depth of the decision tree.

By Lemmas 7.1 and 7.2, we need only find a lower bound on the depth of a binary tree containing $n!$ leaves to obtain our lower bound for the worst-case behavior. The required lower bound on depth is found by means of the following lemmas and theorems.

Lemma 7.3 If m is the number of leaves in a binary tree and d is the depth, then

$$d \geq \lceil \lg m \rceil.$$

Proof: Using induction on d, we show first that

$$2^d \geq m. \tag{7.1}$$

Induction base: A binary tree with depth 0 has one node that is both the root and the only leaf. Therefore, for such a tree, the number of leaves m equals 1, and

$$2^0 \geq 1.$$

Induction hypothesis: Assume that, for any binary tree with depth d,

$$2^d \geq m,$$

where m is the number of leaves.

Induction step: We need to show that, for any binary tree with depth $d + 1$,

$$2^{d+1} \geq m',$$

where m' is the number of leaves. If we remove all the leaves from such a tree, we have a tree with depth d whose leaves are the parents of the leaves in our original tree. If m is the number of these parents, then, by the induction hypothesis,

$$2^d \geq m.$$

Because each parent can have at most two children,

$$2m \geq m'.$$

Combining these last two inequalities yields

$$2^{d+1} \geq 2m \geq m',$$

which completes the induction proof.

Taking the lg of both sides of inequality 7.1 yields

$$d \geq \lg m.$$

Because d is an integer, this implies

$$d \geq \lceil \lg m \rceil.$$

Theorem 7.2 Any deterministic algorithm that sorts n distinct keys only by comparisons of keys must in the worst case do at least

$$\lceil \lg(n!) \rceil \text{ comparisons of keys.}$$

Proof: By Lemma 7.1, to any such algorithm there corresponds a pruned, valid, binary decision tree containing $n!$ leaves. By Lemma 7.3, the depth of that tree is greater than or equal to $\lceil \lg(n!) \rceil$. The theorem now follows, because Lemma 7.2 says that any decision tree's worst-case number of comparisons is given by its depth.

How does this bound compare with the worst-case performance of Mergesort—namely, $n \lg n - (n - 1)$? Lemma 7.4 enables us to compare the two.

Lemma 7.4 For any positive integer n,

$$\lg(n!) \geq n \lg n - 1.45n.$$

Proof: The proof requires knowledge of integral calculus. We have

$$\lg(n!) = \lg[n(n-1)(n-2) \cdots (2)1]$$
$$= \sum_{i=2}^{n} \lg i \qquad\qquad \{\text{because } \lg 1 = 0\}$$
$$\geq \int_{1}^{n} \lg x \, dx = \frac{1}{\ln 2}(n \ln n - n + 1) \geq n \lg n - 1.45n.$$

Theorem 7.3 Any deterministic algorithm that sorts n distinct keys only by comparisons of keys must in the worst case do at least

$$\lceil n \lg n - 1.45n \rceil \text{ comparisons of keys.}$$

Proof: The proof follows from Theorem 7.2 and Lemma 7.4.

We see that Mergesort's worst-case performance of $n \lg n - (n-1)$ is close to optimal. Next we show that this also holds for its average-case performance.

7.8.3 Lower Bounds for Average-Case Behavior

We obtain our results under the assumption that all possible permutations are equally likely to be the input.

If the pruned, valid, binary decision tree corresponding to a deterministic sorting algorithm for sorting n distinct keys contains any comparison nodes with only one child (as is the case for the tree in Figure 7.12), we can replace each such node by its child and prune the child to obtain a decision tree that sorts using no more comparisons than did the original tree. Every nonleaf in the new tree will contain exactly two children. A binary tree in which every nonleaf contains exactly two children is called a *2-tree*. We summarize this result with the following lemma.

Lemma 7.5 To every pruned, valid, binary decision tree for sorting n distinct keys, there corresponds a pruned, valid decision 2-tree that is at least as efficient as the original tree.

Proof: The proof follows from the preceding discussion.

The *external path length* (*EPL*) of a tree is the total length of all paths from the root to the leaves. For example, for the tree in Figure 7.11,

$$EPL = 2 + 3 + 3 + 3 + 3 + 2 = 16.$$

Recall that the number of comparisons done by a decision tree to reach a leaf is the length of the path to the leaf. Therefore, the *EPL* of a decision tree is the total number of comparisons done by the decision tree to sort all possible inputs. Because there are $n!$ different inputs of size n (when all keys are distinct) and because we are assuming all inputs to be equally likely, the average number of comparisons done by a decision tree for sorting n distinct keys is given by

$$\frac{EPL}{n!}.$$

This result enables us to prove an important lemma. First we define ***minEPL(m)*** as the minimum of the *EPL* of 2-trees containing *m* leaves. The lemma now follows.

Lemma 7.6 Any deterministic algorithm that sorts *n* distinct keys only by comparisons of keys must on the average do at least

$$\frac{minEPL(n!)}{n!} \text{ comparison of keys.}$$

Proof: Lemma 7.1 says that to every deterministic algorithm for sorting *n* distinct keys there corresponds a pruned, valid, binary decision tree containing *n*! leaves. Lemma 7.5 says that we can convert that decision tree to a 2-tree that is at least as efficient as the original tree. Because the original tree has *n*! leaves, so must the 2-tree we obtain from it. The lemma now follows from the preceding discussion.

By Lemma 7.6, to obtain a lower bound for the average case, we need only find a lower bound for *minEPL(m)*, which is accomplished by means of the following four lemmas.

Lemma 7.7 Any 2-tree that has *m* leaves and whose *EPL* equals *minEPL(m)* must have all of its leaves on at most the bottom two levels.

Proof: Suppose that some 2-tree does not have all of its leaves on the bottom two levels. Let *d* be the depth of the tree, let *A* be a leaf in the tree that is not on one of the bottom two levels, and let *k* be the depth of *A*. Because nodes at the bottom level have depth *d*,

$$k \le d - 2.$$

We show that this tree cannot minimize the *EPL* among trees with the same number of leaves, by developing a 2-tree with the same number of leaves and a lower *EPL*. We can do this by choosing a nonleaf *B* at level $d - 1$ in our original tree, removing its two children, and giving two children to *A*, as illustrated in Figure 7.13. Clearly, the new tree has the same number of leaves as the original tree. In our new tree, neither *A* nor the children of *B* are leaves, but they are leaves in our old tree. Therefore, we have decreased the *EPL* by the length of the path to *A* and by the lengths of the two paths to *B*'s children. That is, we have decreased the *EPL* by

$$k + d + d = k + 2d.$$

In our new tree, *B* and the two new children of *A* are leaves, but they are not leaves in our old tree. Therefore, we have increased the *EPL* by the length of the path to *B* and the lengths of the two paths to *A*'s new children. That is, we have increased the *EPL* by

$$d - 1 + k + 1 + k + 1 = d + 2k + 1.$$

Figure 7.13 The trees in (a) and (b) have the same number of leaves, but the tree in (b) has a smaller *EPL*.

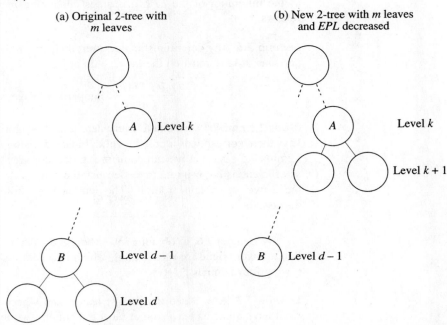

(a) Original 2-tree with
     m leaves

(b) New 2-tree with *m* leaves
     and *EPL* decreased

The net change in the *EPL* is

$$(d + 2k + 1) - (k + 2d) = k - d + 1 \le d - 2 - d + 1 = -1.$$

The inequality occurs because $k \le d - 2$. Because the net change in the *EPL* is negative, the new tree has a smaller *EPL*. This completes the proof that the old tree cannot minimize the *EPL* among trees with the same number of leaves.

Lemma 7.8 Any 2-tree that has *m* leaves and whose *EPL* equals *minEPL(m)* must have

$$2^d - m \text{ leaves at level } d - 1 \quad \text{and} \quad 2m - 2^d \text{ leaves at level } d,$$

and have no other leaves, where *d* is the depth of the tree.

Proof: Because Lemma 7.7 says that all leaves are at the bottom two levels and because nonleaves in a 2-tree must have two children, it is not hard to see that there must be 2^{d-1} nodes at level $d - 1$. Therefore, if *r* is the number of leaves at level $d - 1$, the number of nonleaves at that level is $2^{d-1} - r$. Because nonleaves in a 2-tree have exactly two children, for every nonleaf at level $d - 1$ there are two leaves at level *d*. Because these are the only leaves at level *d*, the number of leaves at level *d* is equal to $2(2^{d-1} - r)$. Because Lemma 7.7 says that all leaves are at level d or $d - 1$,

$$r + 2(2^{d-1} - r) = m.$$

Simplifying yields

$$r = 2^d - m.$$

Therefore, the number of leaves at level d is

$$m - (2^d - m) = 2m - 2^d.$$

Lemma 7.9 For any 2-tree that has m leaves and whose *EPL* equals *minEPL(m)*, the depth d is given by

$$d = \lceil \lg m \rceil.$$

Proof: We prove the case where m is a power of 2. The proof of the general case is left as an exercise. If m is a power of 2, then, for some integer k,

$$m = 2^k.$$

Let d be the depth of a minimizing tree. As in Lemma 7.8, let r be the number of leaves at level $d - 1$. By that lemma,

$$r = 2^d - m = 2^d - 2^k.$$

Because $r \geq 0$, we must have $d \geq k$. We show that assuming $d > k$ leads to a contradiction. If $d > k$, then

$$r = 2^d - 2^k \geq 2^{k+1} - 2^k = 2^k = m.$$

Because $r \leq m$, this means that $r = m$, and all leaves are at level $d - 1$. But there must be some leaves at level d. This contradiction implies that $d = k$, which means that $r = 0$. Because $r = 0$,

$$2^d - m = 0,$$

which means that $d = \lg m$. Because $\lg m = \lceil \lg m \rceil$ when m is a power of 2, this completes the proof.

Lemma 7.10 For all integers $m \geq 1$

$$minEPL(m) \geq m\lfloor \lg m \rfloor.$$

Proof: By Lemma 7.8, any 2-tree that minimizes this *EPL* must have $2^d - m$ leaves at level $d - 1$, have $2m - 2^d$ leaves at level d, and have no other leaves. We therefore have

$$minEPL(m) = (2^d - m)(d - 1) + (2m - 2^d)d = md + m - 2^d.$$

Therefore, by Lemma 7.9,

$$minEPL(m) = m(\lceil \lg m \rceil) + m - 2^{\lceil \lg m \rceil}.$$

If m is a power of 2, this expression clearly equals $m \lg m$, which equals $m\lfloor \lg m \rfloor$ in this case. If m is not a power of 2, then $\lceil \lg m \rceil = \lfloor \lg m \rfloor + 1$. So, in this case,

$$minEPL(m) = m(\lfloor \lg m \rfloor + 1) + m - 2^{\lceil \lg m \rceil}$$
$$= m\lfloor \lg m \rfloor + 2m - 2^{\lceil \lg m \rceil} > m\lfloor \lg m \rfloor.$$

The inequality occurs because, in general, $2m > 2^{\lceil \lg m \rceil}$. This completes the proof.

Now that we have a lower bound for $minEPL(m)$, we can prove our main result.

Theorem 7.4 Any deterministic algorithm that sorts n distinct keys only by comparisons of keys must on the average do at least

$$\lfloor n \lg n - 1.45n \rfloor \text{ comparisons of keys.}$$

Proof: By Lemma 7.6, any such algorithm must on the average do at least

$$\frac{minEPL(n!)}{n!} \text{ comparisons of keys.}$$

By Lemma 7,10, this expression is greater than or equal to

$$\frac{n!\lfloor \lg(n!) \rfloor}{n!} = \lfloor \lg(n!) \rfloor.$$

The proof now follows from Lemma 7.4.

We see that Mergesort's average-case performance of about $n \lg n - 1.26n$ is near optimal for algorithms that sort only by comparisons of keys.

7.9 SORTING BY DISTRIBUTION (RADIX SORT)

In the preceding section, we showed that any algorithm that sorts only by comparisons of keys can be no better than $\Theta(n \lg n)$. If we know nothing about the keys except that they are from an ordered set, we have no choice but to sort by comparing the keys. However, when we have more knowledge we can consider other sorting algorithms. By using additional information about the keys, we next develop one such algorithm.

Suppose we know that the keys are all nonnegative integers represented in base 10. Assuming that they all have the same number of digits, we can first distribute them into distinct piles based on the values of the leftmost digits. That is, keys with the same leftmost digit are placed in the same pile. Each pile can then be distributed into distinct piles based on the values of the second digits from the left. Each new pile can then be distributed into distinct piles based on the values of the third digits from the left, and so on. After we have inspected all the digits, the keys will be sorted. Figure 7.14 illustrates this procedure, which is called "sorting by distribution," because the keys are distributed into piles.

Figure 7.14 Sorting by distribution while inspecting the digits from left to right.

Numbers to
be sorted

Numbers
distributed by
leftmost digit

Numbers
distributed by
second digit
from left

Numbers
distributed
by third digit
from left

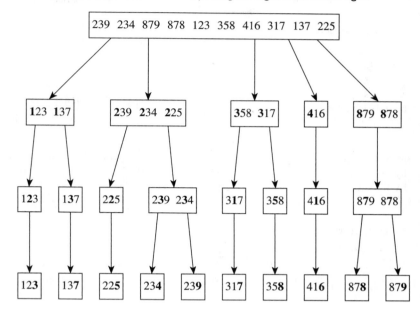

A difficulty with this procedure is that we need a variable number of piles. Suppose instead that we allocate precisely ten piles (one for each decimal digit), we inspect digits from right to left, and we always place a key in the pile corresponding to the digit currently being inspected. If we do this, the keys still end up sorted as long as we obey the following rule: on each pass, if two keys are to be placed in the same pile, the key coming from the leftmost pile (in the previous pass) is placed to the left of the other key. This procedure is illustrated in Figure 7.15. As an example of how keys are placed, notice that after the first pass, key 416 is in a pile to the left of key 317. Therefore, when they are both placed in the first pile in the second pass, key 416 is placed to the left of key 317. In the third pass, however, key 416 ends up to the right of key 317 because it is placed in the fourth pile, whereas key 317 is placed in the third pile. In this way, the keys end up in the right order according to their rightmost digits after the first pass, in the right order according to their two rightmost digits after the second pass, and in the right order according to all three digits after the third pass, which means they are sorted.

This sorting method precedes computers, having been the method used on the old card-sorting machines. It is called ***radix sort*** because the information used to sort the keys is a particular radix (base). The radix could be any number base, or it could be the alphabet. The number of piles is the same as the radix. For

Figure 7.15 Sorting by distribution while inspecting the digits from right to left.

Numbers to be sorted

| 239 | 234 | 879 | 878 | 123 | 358 | 416 | 317 | 137 | 225 |

Numbers distributed
by rightmost digit

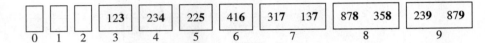

Numbers distributed
by second digit
from right

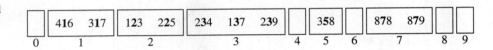

Numbers distributed
by third digit
from right

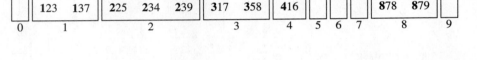

example, if we were sorting numbers represented in hexadecimal, the number of piles would be 16; if we were sorting alpha keys represented in the English alphabet, the number of piles would be 26 because there are 26 letters in that alphabet.

Because the number of keys in a particular pile changes with each pass, a good way to implement the algorithm is to use linked lists. Each pile is represented by a linked list. After each pass, the keys are removed from the lists (piles) by coalescing them into one master linked list. They are ordered in that list according to the lists (piles) from which they were removed. In the next pass, the master list is traversed from the beginning, and each key is placed at the end of the list (pile) to which it belongs in that pass. In this way the rule just given is obeyed. For readability, we present this algorithm under the assumption that the keys are nonnegative integers represented in base 10. It can be readily modified to sort keys in other radix representations without affecting the order of the time complexity. We need the following declarations for the algorithm.

```
struct nodetype
{
    keytype key;
    nodetype* link;
};

typedef nodetype* node_pointer;
```

Algorithm 7.6   Radix Sort

Problem: Sort *n* nonnegative integers, represented in base 10, in nondecreasing order.

Inputs: linked list *masterlist* of *n* nonnegative integers, and an integer *numdigits,* which is the maximum number of decimal digits in each integer.

Outputs: the linked list *masterlist* containing the integers in nondecreasing order.

```
void radixsort (node_pointer& masterlist,
                int numdigits)
{
   index i;
   node_pointer list[0..9];

   for (i = 1; i <= numdigits; i++) {
      distribute(i);
      coalesce;
   }
}
```

```
void distribute (index i)                    // i is index of current
{                                            // digit being inspected.
   index j;
   node_pointer p;

   for (j = 0; j <= 9; j++)                  // Empty current piles.
      list[j] = NULL;
   p = masterlist;                           // Traverse masterlist.
   while (p != NULL) {
      j = value of ith digit (from the right) in p-> key;
      link p to the end of list[j];
      p = p-> link;
   }
}
```

```
void coalesce ( )
{
   index j;
```

```
        masterlist = NULL;                                  // Empty masterlist.
        for (j = 0; j <= 9; j++)
            link the nodes in list[j] to the end of masterlist;
    }
```

Next we analyze the algorithm.

Every-Case Time Complexity Analysis of Algorithm 7.6 (Radix Sort)

Basic operation: Because there are no comparisons of keys in this algorithm, we need to find a different basic operation. In an efficient implementation of *coalesce,* the lists that contain the piles would have pointers to both their beginnings and their ends so that we can readily add each list to the end of the previous one without traversing the list. Therefore, in each pass through the **for** loop in that procedure, a list is added to the end of *masterlist* by simply assigning an address to one pointer variable. We can take that assignment as the basic operation. In procedure *distribute,* we can take any or all of the instructions in the **while** loop as the basic operations. Therefore, to have a unit consistent with *coalesce,* we choose the one that adds a key to the end of a list by assigning an address to a pointer variable.

Input size: n, the number of integers in *masterlist,* and *numdigits,* the maximum number of decimal digits in each integer.

Traversal of the entirety of *masterlist* always requires n passes through the **while** loop in *distribute.* Addition of all the lists to *masterlist* always requires ten passes through the **for** loop in *coalesce.* Each of these procedures is called *numdigits* times from *radixsort.* Therefore,

$$T(n) = numdigits(n + 10) \in \Theta(numdigits, n).$$

This is not a $\Theta(n)$ algorithm because the bound is in terms of *numdigits* and n. We can create arbitrarily large time complexities in terms of n by making *numdigits* arbitrarily large. For example, because 1,000,000,000 has ten digits, it will take $\Theta(n^2)$ time to sort ten numbers if the largest one is 1,000,000,000. In practice, the number of digits is ordinarily much smaller than the number of numbers. For example, if we are sorting 1,000,000 social security numbers, n is 1,000,000 whereas *numdigits* is only 9. It is not hard to see that, when the keys are distinct, the best-case time complexity of Radix Sort is in $\Theta(n \lg n)$, and ordinarily we achieve the best case.

Next we analyze the extra space used by Radix Sort.

Analysis of Extra Space Usage for Algorithm 7.6 (Radix Sort)

No new nodes are ever allocated in the algorithm because a key is never needed simultaneously in *masterlist* and in a list representing a pile. This means that the only extra space is the space needed to represent the keys in a linked list in the first place. Therefore, the extra space is in $\Theta(n)$ links. By "in $\Theta(n)$ links" we mean that the number of links is in $\Theta(n)$.

Exercises

Sections 7.1 and 7.2

1. Implement the Insertion Sort algorithm (Algorithm 7.1), run it on your system, and study its best-case, average-case, and worst-case time complexities using several problem instances.

2. Show that the maximum number of comparisons performed by the Insertion Sort algorithm (Algorithm 7.1) is achieved when the keys are inputted in nonincreasing order.

3. Show that the worst-case and average-case time complexities for the number of assignments of records performed by the Insertion Sort algorithm (Algorithm 7.1) are given by

$$W(n) = \frac{(n+4)(n-1)}{2} \approx \frac{n^2}{2} \quad \text{and} \quad A(n) = \frac{n(n+7)}{4} - 1 \approx \frac{n^2}{4}.$$

4. Show that the worst-case and average-case time complexities for the number of assignments of records performed by the Exchange Sort algorithm (Algorithm 1.3) are given by

$$W(n) = \frac{3n(n-1)}{2} \quad \text{and} \quad A(n) = \frac{3n(n-1)}{4}.$$

5. Compare the best-case time complexities of Exchange Sort (Algorithm 1.3) and Insertion Sort (Algorithm 7.1).

6. Is Exchange Sort (Algorithm 1.3) or Insertion Sort (Algorithm 7.1) more appropriate when we need to find in nonincreasing order the k largest (or in nondecreasing order the k smallest) keys in a list of n keys? Justify your answer.

7. Rewrite the Insertion Sort algorithm (Algorithm 7.1) as follows. Include an extra array slot $S[0]$ that has a value smaller than any key. This eliminates the need to compare j with 0 at the top of the **while** loop. Determine the exact time complexity of this version of the algorithm. Is it better or worse than the time complexity of Algorithm 7.1? Which version should be more efficient? Justify your answer.

8. An algorithm called Shell Sort is inspired by Insertion Sort's ability to take advantage of the order of the elements in the list. In Shell Sort, the entire list is divided into noncontiguous sublists whose elements are a distance h apart for some number h. Each sublist is then sorted using Insertion Sort. During the next pass, the value of h is reduced, increasing the size of each sublist. Usually the value of each h is chosen to be relatively prime to its previous value. The final pass uses the value 1 for h to sort the list. Write an algorithm for Shell Sort, study its performance, and compare the result with the performance of Insertion Sort.

Section 7.3

9. Show that the permutation $[n, n - 1, \ldots, 2, 1]$ has $n(n - 1)/2$ inversions.

10. Give the transpose of the permutation $[2, 5, 1, 6, 3, 4]$, and find the number of inversions in both permutations. What is the total number of inversions?

11. Show that there are $n(n - 1)/2$ inversions in a permutation of n distinct ordered elements with respect to its transpose.

12. Show that the total number of inversions in a permutation and its transpose is $n(n - 1)/2$. Use this to find the total number of inversions in the permutation in Exercise 10 and its transpose.

Section 7.4 (See also exercises for Section 2.2.)

13. Implement the different Mergesort algorithms discussed in Section 2.2 and Section 7.4, run them on your system, and study their best-case, average-case, and worst-case performances using several problem instances.

14. Show that the time complexity for the number of assignments of records for the Mergesort algorithm (Algorithms 2.2 and 2.4) is approximated by $T(n) = 2n \lg n$.

15. Write an in-place, linear-time algorithm that takes as input the linked list constructed by the Mergesort 4 algorithm (Algorithm 7.4) and stores the records in the contiguous array slots in nondecreasing order according to the values of their keys.

16. Use the divide-and-conquer approach to write a nonrecursive Mergesort algorithm. Analyze your algorithm, and show the results using order notation. Note that it will be necessary to explicitly maintain a stack in your algorithm.

17. Implement the nonrecursive Mergesort algorithm of Exercise 16, run it on your system using the problem instances of Exercise 13, and compare the results against the results of the recursive versions of Mergesort in Exercise 13.

18. Write a version of *mergesort3* (Algorithm 7.3), and a corresponding version of *merge3*, that reverses the rolls of two arrays S and U in each pass through the **repeat** loop.

19. Give two instances for which the Mergesort algorithm is the most appropriate choice.

Section 7.5 (See also exercises for Section 2.4.)

20. Implement the Quicksort algorithm (Algorithm 2.6) discussed in Section 2.4, run it on your system, and study its best-case, average-case, and worst-case performances using several problem instances.

21. Show that the time complexity for the average number of exchanges performed by the Quicksort algorithm is approximated by $0.69(n + 1) \lg n$.

22. Write a nonrecursive Quicksort algorithm. Analyze your algorithm, and show the results using order notation. Note that it will be necessary to explicitly maintain a stack in your algorithm.

23. Implement the nonrecursive Quicksort algorithm of Exercise 22, run it on your system using the same problem instances you used in Exercise 20, and compare the results against the results of the recursive version of Quicksort in Exercise 20.

24. The following is a faster version of procedure *partition*, which is called by procedure *quicksort*.

```
void partition (index low, index high, index& pivotpoint)
{
    index i, j;
    keytype pivotitem;

    pivotitem = S[low];
    i = low;
    j = high;
    while (i < j) {
        exchange S[i] and S[j];
        while (S[i] < pivotitem)
            i++;
        while (S[j] >= pivotitem)
            j− −;
    }
    pivotpoint = i;
    exchange S[high] and S[pivotpoint];        // Put pivotitem at pivotpoint.
}
```

Show that with this *partition* procedure, the time complexity for the number of assignments of records performed by Quicksort is given by

$$A(n) \approx 0.69(n + 1) \lg n.$$

Show further that the average-case time complexity for the number of comparisons of keys is about the same as before.

25. Give two instances for which Quicksort algorithm is the most appropriate choice.

26. Another way to sort a list by exchanging out-of-order keys is called Bubble Sort. Bubble Sort scans adjacent pairs of records and exchanges those found to have out-of-order keys. After the first time through the list, the record with the largest key (or the smallest key) is moved to its proper position. This process is done repeatedly on the remaining, unsorted part of the list until the list is completely sorted. Write the Bubble Sort algorithm. Analyze your algorithm, and show the results using order notation. Compare the performance of the Bubble Sort algorithm against those of Insertion Sort, Exchange Sort, and Selection Sort.

Section 7.6

27. Write an algorithm that checks if an essentially complete binary tree is a heap. Analyze your algorithm, and show the results using order notation.

28. Show that there are 2^j nodes with depth j for $j < d$ in a heap having n (a power of 2) nodes. Here d is the depth of the heap.

29. Show that a heap with n nodes has $\lceil n/2 \rceil$ leaves.

30. Implement the Heapsort Algorithm (Algorithm 7.5), run it on your system, and study its best-case, average-case, and worst-case performances using several problem instances.

31. Show that there is a case for Heapsort in which we get the worst-case time complexity of $W(n) \approx 2n \lg n \in \Theta(n \lg n)$.

32. Show that the worst-case time complexity of the number of assignments of records for Heapsort is approximated by $W(n) \approx n \lg n$.

33. Modify Heapsort so that it stops after it finds the k largest keys in nonincreasing order. Analyze your algorithm, and show the results using order notation.

Section 7.7

34. List all the advantages and disadvantages of all the sorting algorithms discussed in this chapter based on the comparisons of keys and the assignments of records.

35. Run the implementations of all the sorting algorithms discussed in this chapter on your system using several problem instances. Use the results, and the

information provided in Exercise 34, to give a detailed comparison of these sorting algorithms.

36. Among Selection Sort, Insertion Sort, Mergesort, Quicksort, and Heapsort, which algorithm would you choose in each list-sorting situation below? Justify your answers.
    (a) The list has several hundred records. The records are quite long, but the keys are very short.
    (b) The list has about 45,000 records. It is necessary that the sort be completed reasonably quickly in all cases. There is barely enough memory to hold the 45,000 records.
    (c) The list has about 45,000 records, but it starts off only slightly out of order.
    (d) The list has about 25,000 records. It is desirable to complete the sort as quickly as possible on the average, but it is not critical that the sort be completed quickly in every single case.

37. Give at least two instances for each of the sorting algorithms (based on the comparisons of keys) discussed in this chapter for which the algorithm is the most appropriate choice.

Section 7.8

38. Write a linear-time sorting algorithm that sorts a permutation of integers 1 through n, inclusive.

39. Write a linear-time sorting algorithm that sorts a list of values of a given ordinal type.

40. Does the linear-time performance of your algorithms in Exercises 38 and 39 violate the lower bound for sorting only by comparisons of keys? Justify your answer.

41. Prove the general case of Lemma 7.9 when the number of leaves m is not a power of 2.

Section 7.9

42. Implement the Radix Sort algorithm (Algorithm 7.6), run it on your system, and study its best-case, average-case, and worst-case performances using several problem instances.

43. Show that when all the keys are distinct the best-case time complexity of Radix Sort (Algorithm 7.6) is in $\Theta(n \lg n)$.

44. In the process of rebuilding the master list, the Radix Sort Algorithm (Algorithm 7.6) wastes a lot of time examining empty sublists when the number of piles (radix) is large. Is it possible to check only the sublists that are not empty?

Additional Exercises

45. Write an algorithm that sorts a list of n elements in nonincreasing order by finding the largest and smallest elements and exchanges those elements with the elements in the first and last positions. Then the size of the list is reduced by 2, excluding the two elements that are already in the proper positions, and the process is repeated on the remaining part of the list until the entire list is sorted. Analyze your algorithm, and show the results using order notation.

46. Implement the Quicksort algorithm using different strategies for choosing a pivot item, run it on your system, and study its best-case, average-case, and worst-case performances for different strategies using several problem instances.

47. Study the idea of designing a sorting algorithm based on a ternary heap. A ternary heap is like an ordinary heap except that each internal node has three children.

48. Suppose we are to find the k smallest elements in a list of n elements, and we are not interested in their relative order. Can a linear-time algorithm be found when k is a constant? Justify your answer.

49. Suppose we have a very large list stored in external memory that needs to be sorted. Assuming that this list is too large for internal memory, what major factor(s) should be considered in designing an external sorting algorithm?

50. Classify the sorting algorithms discussed in this chapter based on the ideas behind the algorithms. For example, Heapsort and Selection Sort find the largest (or smallest) key and exchange it with the last (or first) element according to the desired order.

51. A stable sorting algorithm is one that preserves the original order of equal keys. Which of the sorting algorithms discussed in this chapter are stable? Justify your answer.

52. Which of the sorting algorithms identified as unstable in Exercise 51 can easily be changed to stable sorting algorithms?

CHAPTER 8

More Computational Complexity: The Searching Problem

Recall from the beginning of Chapter 1 that Barney Beagle could find Colleen Collie's phone number quickly using a modified binary search. Barney may now be wondering if he could develop an even faster method for locating Colleen's number. We analyze the Searching Problem next to determine whether this is possible.

Like sorting, searching is one of the most useful applications in computer science. The problem is usually to retrieve an entire record based on the value of some key field. For example, a record may consist of personal information, whereas the key field may be the social security number. Our purpose here is similar to that in the preceding chapter. We want to analyze the problem of searching and show that we have obtained searching algorithms whose time complexities are about as good as our lower bounds. Additionally, we want to discuss the data structures used by the algorithms and when a data structure satisfies the needs of a particular application.

In Section 8.1, we obtain lower bounds for searching for a key in an array only by comparisons of keys (as we did for sorting in the preceding chapter), and we show that the time complexity of Binary Search (Algorithms 1.5 and 2.1) is as good as the bounds. In searching for a phone number, Barney Beagle actually uses a modification of Binary Search called "Interpolation Search," which does more than just compare keys. That is, when looking for Colleen Collie's number, Barney does not start in the middle of the phone book because he know that the names beginning with "C" are near the front. He "interpolates" and starts near the front of the book. We present Interpolation Search in Section 8.2. In Section 8.3, we show that an array does not meet other needs (besides the searching) of certain applications. Therefore, although Binary Search is optimal, the algorithm cannot be used for some applications because it relies on an array implementation. We show that trees do meet these needs, and we discuss tree searching. Section 8.4 concerns searching when it is not important that the data ever be retrieved in sorted sequence. We discuss hashing in Section 8.4. Section 8.5 concerns a different searching problem, the Selection Problem. This problem is to find the kth-smallest (or kth-largest) key in a list of n keys. In Section 8.5 we introduce adversary arguments, which are another means of obtaining bounds for the performance of all algorithms that solve a problem.

8.1 LOWER BOUNDS FOR SEARCHING ONLY BY COMPARISONS OF KEYS

The problem of searching for a key can be described as follows: Given an array S containing n keys and a key x, find an index i such that $x = S[i]$ if x equals one of the keys; if x does not equal one of the keys, report failure.

Binary Search (Algorithms 1.5 and 2.1) is very efficient for solving this problem when the array is sorted. Recall that its worst-case time complexity is $\lfloor \lg n \rfloor + 1$. Can we improve on this performance? We will see that as long as we limit ourselves to algorithms that search only by comparisons of keys, such an improvement is not possible. Algorithms that search for a key x in an array only by comparisons of keys can compare keys with each other or with the search key x, and they can copy keys, but they cannot do other operations on them. To assist their search, however, they can use the knowledge that the array is sorted (as is done in Binary Search). As we did in Chapter 7, we will obtain bounds for deterministic algorithms. Our results still hold if we consider probabilistic algorithms. Furthermore, as in Chapter 7, we assume that the keys in the array are distinct.

As we did for deterministic sorting algorithms, we can associate a decision tree with every deterministic algorithm that searches for a key x in an array of n keys. Figure 8.1 shows a decision tree corresponding to Binary Search when searching seven keys, and Figure 8.2 shows a decision tree corresponding to Sequential Search (Algorithm 1.1). In these trees, each large node represents a comparison of an array item with the search key x, and each small node (leaf) contains a result that is reported. When x is in the array, we report an index of the item that it equals, and when x is not in the array, we report an "F" for failure. In Figures 8.1 and 8.2, s_1 through s_7 are the values such that

$$S[1] = s_1, \qquad S[2] = s_2, \qquad \cdots \qquad S[7] = s_7.$$

We assume that a searching algorithm never changes any array values, so these are still the values after the search is completed.

Each leaf in a decision tree for searching n keys for a key x represents a point at which the algorithm stops and reports an index i such that $x = s_i$ or reports failure. Every internal node represents a comparison. A decision tree is called **valid** for searching n keys for a key x if for each possible outcome there is a path from the root to a leaf that reports that outcome. That is, there must be paths for $x = s_i$ for $1 \leq i \leq n$ and a path that leads to failure. The decision tree is called **pruned** if every leaf is reachable. Every algorithm that searches for a key x in an array of n keys has a corresponding pruned, valid decision tree. In general, a

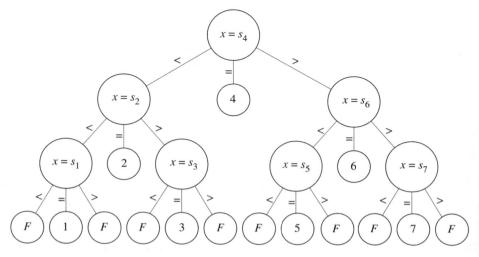

Figure 8.1 The decision tree corresponding to Binary Search when searching seven keys.

Figure 8.2 The decision tree corresponding to Sequential Search when searching seven keys.

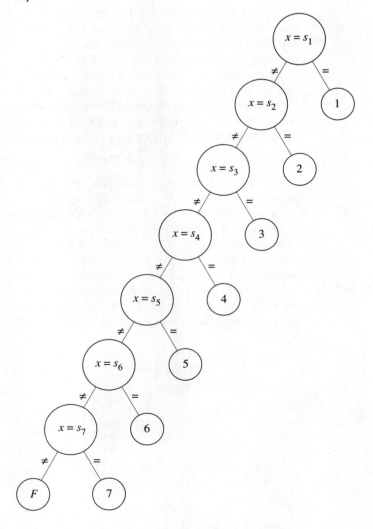

searching algorithm need not always compare x with an array item. That is, it could compare two array items. However, because we are assuming that all keys are distinct, the outcome will be equality only when x is being compared. In the cases of both Binary Search and Sequential Search, when the algorithm determines that x equals an array item, it stops and returns the index of the array item. Some inefficient algorithm may continue to do comparisons when it determines that x equals an array item and return the index later. However, we can replace such an algorithm with one that stops at this point and returns the index. The new algorithm will be at least as efficient as the original one. Therefore, we need only consider pruned, valid decision trees for searching n distinct keys for a key x in which equality leads to a leaf that returns an index. Because there are only three possible results of a comparison, a deterministic algorithm can take at most three different paths after each comparison. This means that each comparison node in the corresponding decision tree can have at most three children. Because equality must lead to a leaf that returns an index, at most two of the children can be comparison nodes. Therefore, the set of comparison nodes in the tree constitutes a binary tree. See the sets of large nodes in Figures 8.1 and 8.2 for examples.

8.1.1 Lower Bounds for Worst-Case Behavior

Because every leaf in a pruned, valid decision tree must be reachable, the worst-case number of comparisons done by such a tree is the number of nodes in the longest path from the root to a leaf in the binary tree consisting of the comparison nodes. This number is the depth of the binary tree plus 1. Therefore, to establish a lower bound on the worst-case number of comparisons, we need only establish a lower bound on the depth of the binary tree consisting of the comparison nodes. Such a bound is established by means of the following lemmas and theorem.

Lemma 8.1 If n is the number of nodes in a binary tree and d is the depth, then

$$d \geq \lfloor \lg(n) \rfloor.$$

Proof: We have

$$n \leq 1 + 2 + 2^2 + 2^3 + \cdots + 2^d,$$

because there can be only one root, at most two nodes with depth 1, 2^2 nodes with depth 2, . . . , and 2^d nodes with depth d. Applying the result in Example A.3 in Appendix A yields

$$n \leq 2^{d+1} - 1,$$

which means that

$$n < 2^{d+1}$$
$$\lg n < d + 1$$
$$\lfloor \lg n \rfloor \leq d.$$

Although the next lemma seems obvious, it is not easy to prove rigorously.

Lemma 8.2 To be a pruned, valid decision tree for searching n distinct keys for a key x, the binary tree consisting of the comparison nodes must contain at least n nodes.

Proof: Let s_i for $1 \leq i \leq n$ be the values of the n keys. First we show that every s_i must be in at least one comparison node (that is, it must be involved in at least one comparison). Suppose that for some i this is not the case. Take two inputs that are identical for all keys except the ith key, and are different for the ith key. Let x have the value of s_i in one of the inputs. Because s_i is not involved in any comparisons and all the other keys are the same in both inputs, the decision tree must behave the same for both inputs. However, it must report i for one of the inputs, and it must not report i for the other. This contradiction shows that every s_i must be in at least one comparison node.

Because every s_i must be in at least one comparison node, the only way we could have less than n comparison nodes would be to have at least one key s_i involved only in comparisons with other keys—that is, one s_i that is never compared with x. Suppose we do have such a key. Take two inputs that are equal everywhere except for s_i, with s_i being the smallest key in both inputs. Let x be the ith key in one of the inputs. A path from a comparison node containing s_i must go in the same direction for both inputs, and all the other keys are the same in both inputs. Therefore, the decision tree must behave the same for the two inputs. However, it must report i for one of them and must not report i for the other. This contradiction proves the lemma.

Theorem 8.1 Any deterministic algorithm that searches for a key x in an array of n distinct keys only by comparisons of keys must in the worst case do at least

$$\lfloor \lg n \rfloor + 1 \text{ comparisons of keys.}$$

Proof: Corresponding to the algorithm, there is a pruned, valid decision tree for searching n distinct keys for a key x. The worst-case number of comparisons is the number of nodes in the longest path from the root to a leaf in the binary tree consisting of the comparison nodes in that decision tree. This number is the depth of the binary tree plus 1. Lemma 8.2 says that this binary tree has at least n nodes. Therefore, by Lemma 8.1, its depth is greater than or equal to $\lfloor \lg n \rfloor$. This proves the theorem.

Recall from Section 2.1 that the worst-case number of comparisons done by Binary Search is $\lfloor \lg n \rfloor + 1$. Therefore, Binary Search is optimal as far as its worst-case performance is concerned.

8.1.2 Lower Bounds for Average-Case Behavior

Before discussing bounds for the average case, let's do an average-case analysis of Binary Search. We have waited until now to do this analysis because the use of the decision tree facilitates the analysis. First we need a definition and a lemma.

A binary tree is called a *nearly complete binary tree* if it is complete down to a depth of $d - 1$. Every essentially complete binary tree is nearly complete, but not every nearly complete binary tree is essentially complete, as illustrated in Figure 8.3. (See Section 7.6 for definitions of complete and essentially complete binary trees.)

Like Lemma 8.2, the following lemma appears to be obvious but is not easy to prove rigorously.

Figure 8.3 (a) An essentially complete binary tree. (b) A nearly complete but not essentially complete binary tree.

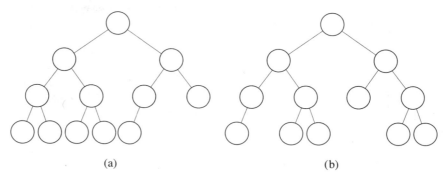

(a)   (b)

Lemma 8.3 The tree consisting of the comparison nodes in the pruned, valid decision tree corresponding to Binary Search is a nearly complete binary tree.

Proof: The proof is done by induction on n, the number of keys. Clearly, the tree consisting of the comparison nodes is a binary tree containing n nodes, one for each key. Therefore, we can do the induction on the number of nodes in this binary tree.

Induction base: A binary tree containing one node is nearly complete.

Induction hypothesis: Assume that for all $k < n$ the binary tree containing k nodes is nearly complete.

Induction step: We need to show that the binary tree containing n nodes is nearly complete. We do this separately for odd and even values of n.

If n is odd, the first split in Binary Search splits the array into two subarrays each of size $(n - 1)/2$. Therefore, both the left and right subtrees are the binary tree corresponding to Binary Search when searching $(n - 1)/2$ keys, which means that, as far as structure is concerned, they are the same tree. They are nearly complete, by the induction hypothesis. Because they are the same nearly complete tree, the tree in which they are the left and right subtrees is nearly complete.

If n is even, the first split in Binary Search splits the array into a subarray of size $n/2$ on the right and a subarray of size $(n/2) - 1$ on the left. To enable us to speak concretely, we will discuss the case in which the odd number of keys is on the left. The proof is analogous when the odd number of keys is on the right. When the odd number is on the left, the left and right subtrees of the left subtree are the same tree (as discussed previously). One subtree of the right subtree is also that same tree (you should verify this). Because the right subtree is nearly complete (by the induction hypothesis) and because one of its subtrees is the same tree as the left and right subtrees of the left subtree, the entire tree must be nearly complete. See Figure 8.4 for an illustration.

Figure 8.4 The binary tree consisting of the comparison nodes in the decision tree corresponding to Binary Search when $n = 12$. Only the values of the keys are shown at the nodes. Subtrees A, B, and C all have the same structure.

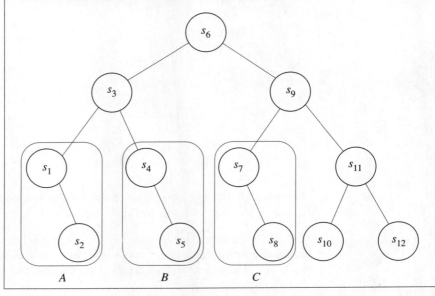

We can now do an average-case analysis of Binary Search.

● **Average-Case Time Complexity Analysis of Algorithm 2.1
(Binary Search, Recursive)**

Basic operation: the comparison of x with $S[mid]$.

Input size: n, the number of items in the array.

First, we analyze the case in which we know that x is in the array. We do this analysis under the assumption that x is equally likely to be in each of the array slots. Let's call the total number of nodes in the path from the root to a node the **node distance** to that node, and the sum of the node distances to all nodes the **total node distance** (*TND*) of a tree. Notice that the distance to a node is one greater than the length of the path from the root to the node. For the binary tree consisting of the comparison nodes in Figure 8.1,

$$TND = 1 + 2 + 2 + 3 + 3 + 3 + 3 = 17.$$

It is not hard to see that the total number of comparisons done by Binary Search's decision tree to locate x at all possible array slots is equal to the *TND* of the binary tree consisting of the comparison nodes in that decision tree. Given the assumption that all slots are equally probable, the average number of comparisons required to locate x is therefore *TND/n*. For simplicity, let's initially assume that $n = 2^k - 1$ for some integer k. Lemma 8.3 says that the binary tree consisting of the comparison nodes in the decision tree corresponding to Binary

Search is nearly complete. It is not hard to see that if a nearly complete binary tree contains $2^k - 1$ nodes, it is a complete binary tree. The binary tree consisting of the comparison nodes in Figure 8.1 illustrates the case where $k = 3$. In a complete binary tree, the *TND* is given by

$$TND = 1 + 2(2) + 3(2^2) + \cdots + k(2^{k-1})$$

$$= \frac{1}{2} [(k - 1)2^{k+1} + 2] = (k - 1)2^k + 1.$$

The second-to-last equality is obtained by applying the result from Example A.5 in Appendix A. Because $2^k = n + 1$, the average number of comparisons is given by

$$A(n) = \frac{TND}{n} = \frac{(k - 1)(n + 1) + 1}{n} \approx k - 1 = \lfloor \lg n \rfloor.$$

For n in general, the average number of comparisons is bounded approximately by

$$\lfloor \lg n \rfloor - 1 \leq A(n) \leq \lfloor \lg n \rfloor.$$

The average is near the lower bound if n is a power of 2 or is slightly greater than a power of 2, and the average is near the upper bound if n is slightly smaller than a power of 2. You are shown how to establish this result in the exercises. Intuitively, Figure 8.1 shows why this is so. If we add just one node so that the total number of nodes is 8, $\lfloor \lg n \rfloor$ jumps from 2 to 3, but the average number of comparisons hardly changes.

Next, we analyze the case in which x may not be in the array. There are $2n + 1$ possibilities: x could be less than all the items, between any two of the items, or greater than all the items. That is, we could have

$$x = s_i \text{ for } i \text{ such that } 1 \leq i \leq n,$$
$$x < s_1,$$
$$s_i < x < s_{i+1} \text{ for some } i \text{ such that } 1 \leq i \leq n - 1,$$
$$x > s_n.$$

We analyze the case in which each of these possibilities is equally likely. For simplicity, we again initially assume that $n = 2^k - 1$ for some integer k. The total number of comparisons for the successful searches is the *TND* of the binary tree consisting of the comparison nodes. Recall that this number equals $(k - 1)2^k + 1$. There are k comparisons for each of the $n + 1$ unsuccessful searches (see Figure 8.1). The average number of comparisons is therefore given by

$$A(n) = \frac{TND + k(n + 1)}{2n + 1} = \frac{(k - 1)2^k + 1 + k(n + 1)}{2n + 1}.$$

Because $2^k = n + 1$, we have

$$A(n) = \frac{(k-1)(n+1) + 1 + k(n+1)}{2n+1}$$

$$= \frac{2k(n+1) + 1 - (n+1)}{2n+1}$$

$$\approx k - \frac{1}{2} = \lfloor \lg n \rfloor + 1 - \frac{1}{2} = \lfloor \lg n \rfloor + \frac{1}{2}.$$

For n in general, the average number of comparisons is bounded approximately by

$$\lfloor \lg n \rfloor - \frac{1}{2} \le A(n) \le \lfloor \lg n \rfloor + \frac{1}{2}.$$

The average is near the lower bound if n is a power of 2 or is slightly greater than a power of 2, and the average is near the upper bound if n is slightly smaller than a power of 2. You are asked to establish this result in the exercises.

Binary Search's average-case performance is not much better than its worst case. We can see why this is so by looking again at Figure 8.1. In that figure, there are more result nodes at the bottom of the tree (where the worst case occurs) than there are in the rest of the tree. This is true even if we don't consider unsuccessful searches. (Notice that all of the unsuccessful searches are at the bottom of the tree.)

Next we prove that Binary Search is optimal in the average case given the assumptions in the previous analysis. First, we define *minTND(n)* as the minimum of the *TND* for binary trees containing n nodes.

Lemma 8.4 The *TND* of a binary tree containing n nodes is equal to *minTND(n)* if and only if the tree is nearly complete.

Proof: First we show that if a tree's *TND* = *minTND(n)*, the tree is nearly complete. To that end, suppose that some binary tree is not nearly complete. Then there must be some node, not at one of the bottom two levels, that has at most one child. We can remove any node *A* from the bottom level and make it a child of that node. The resulting tree will still be a binary tree containing n nodes. The number of nodes in the path to *A* in that tree will be at least 1 less than the number of nodes in the path to *A* in the original tree. The number of nodes in the paths to all other nodes will be the same. Therefore, we have created a binary tree containing n nodes with a *TND* smaller than that of our original tree, which means that our original tree did not have a minimum *TND*.

It is not hard to see that the *TND* is the same for all nearly complete binary trees containing n nodes. Therefore, every such tree must have the minimum *TND*.

Lemma 8.5 Suppose that we are searching n keys, the search key x is in the array, and all array slots are equally probable. Then the average-case time complexity for Binary Search is given by

$$\frac{minTND(n)}{n} .$$

Proof: As discussed in the average-case analysis of Binary Search, the average-case time complexity is obtained by dividing by n the *TND* of the binary tree consisting of the comparison nodes in its corresponding decision tree. The proof follows from Lemmas 8.3 and 8.4.

Lemma 8.6 If we assume that x is in the array and that all array slots are equally probable, the average-case time complexity of any deterministic algorithm that searches for a key x in an array of n distinct keys is bounded below by

$$\frac{minTND(n)}{n} .$$

Proof: As shown in Lemma 8.2, every array item s_i must be compared with x at least once in the decision tree corresponding to the algorithm. Let c_i be the number of nodes in the shortest path to a node containing a comparison of s_i with x. Because each key has the same probability $1/n$ of being the search key x, a lower bound on the average-case time complexity is given by

$$c_1\left(\frac{1}{n}\right) + c_2\left(\frac{1}{n}\right) + \cdots + c_n\left(\frac{1}{n}\right) = \frac{\sum\limits_{i=1}^{n} c_i}{n} .$$

It is left as an exercise to show that the numerator in this last expression is greater than or equal to $minTND(n)$.

Theorem 8.2 Among deterministic algorithms that search for a key x in an array of n distinct keys only by comparison of keys, Binary Search is optimal in its average-case performance if we assume that x is in the array and that all array slots are equally probable. Therefore, under these assumptions, any such algorithm must on the average do at least approximately

$$\lfloor \lg n \rfloor - 1 \text{ comparisons of keys.}$$

Proof: The proof follows from Lemmas 8.5 and 8.6 and the average-case time complexity analysis of Binary Search.

It is also possible to show that Binary Search is optimal in its average-case performance if we assume that all $2n + 1$ possible outcomes (as discussed in the average-case analysis of Binary Search) are equally likely.

We established that Binary Search is optimal in its average-case performance given specific assumptions about the probability distribution. For other probability distributions, it may not be optimal. For example, if the probability was .9999 that x equaled $S[1]$, it would be optimal to compare x with $S[1]$ first. This example is a bit contrived. A more real-life example would be a search for a name picked at random from people in the United States. As discussed in Section 3.5, we would not consider the names "Tom" and "Ursula" to be equally probable. The analysis done here is not applicable, and other considerations are needed. Section 3.5 addresses some of these considerations.

8.2 INTERPOLATION SEARCH

The bounds just obtained are for algorithms that rely only on comparisons of keys. We can improve on these bounds if we use some other information to assist in our search. Recall that Barney Beagle does more than just compare keys to find Colleen Collie's number in the phone book. He does not start in the middle of the phone book because he knows that the C's are near the front. He "interpolates" and starts near the front. We develop an algorithm for this strategy next.

Suppose we are searching 10 integers, and we know that the first integer ranges from 0 to 9, the second from 10 to 19, the third from 20 to 29, . . . , and the tenth from 90 to 99. Then we can immediately report failure if the search key x is less than 0 or greater than 99, and, if neither of these is the case, we need only compare x with $S[1 + \lfloor x/10 \rfloor]$. For example, we would compare $x = 25$ with $S[1 + \lfloor 25/10 \rfloor] = S[3]$. If they were not equal, we would report failure.

We usually do not have this much information. However, in some applications it is reasonable to assume that the keys are close to being evenly distributed between the first one and the last one. In such cases, instead of checking whether x equals the middle key, we can check whether x equals the key that is located about where we would expect to find x. For example, if we think 10 keys are close to being evenly distributed from 0 to 99, we would expect to find $x = 25$ about in the third position, and we would compare x first with $S[3]$ instead of $S[5]$. The algorithm that implements this strategy is called *Interpolation Search*. As in Binary Search, *low* is set initially to 1 and *high* to n. We then use linear interpolation to determine approximately where we feel x should be located. That is, we compute

$$mid = low + \left\lfloor \frac{x - S[low]}{S[high] - S[low]} \times (high - low) \right\rfloor.$$

For example, if $S[1] = 4$ and $S[10] = 97$, and we were searching for $x = 25$, we would compute

$$mid = 1 + \left\lfloor \frac{25 - 4}{97 - 4} \times (10 - 1) \right\rfloor = 1 + \lfloor 2.032 \rfloor = 3.$$

Other than the different way of computing *mid* and some extra bookkeeping, the Interpolation Search algorithm, which follows, proceeds like Binary Search (Algorithm 1.5).

Algorithm 8.1

Interpolation Search

Problem: Determine whether x is in the sorted array S of size n.

Inputs: positive integer n, and sorted (nondecreasing order) array of numbers S indexed from 1 to n.

Outputs: the location i of x in S; 0 if x is not in S.

```
void interpsrch (int n,
                 const number S[ ],
                 number x,
                 index& i)
{
   index low, high, mid;
   number denominator;

   low = 1; high = n;
   i = 0;
   if (S[low] ≤ x ≤ S[high])
      while (low <= high && i == 0) {
         denominator = S[high] − S[low];
         if (denominator == 0)
            mid = low;
         else
            mid = low + ⌊((x − S[low]) * (high − low)) / denominator⌋;
         if (x == S[mid])
            i = mid;
         else if (x < S[mid])
            high = mid − 1;
         else
            low = mid + 1;
      }
}
```

If the keys are close to being evenly spaced, Interpolation Search homes in on the possible location of x more quickly than does Binary Search. For instance, in the preceding example, if $x = 25$ were less than $S[3]$, Interpolation Search would reduce the instance of size 10 to one of size 2, whereas Binary Search would reduce it to one of size 4.

Suppose that the keys are uniformly distributed between $S[1]$ and $S[n]$. By this we mean that the probability of a randomly chosen key being in a particular range equals its probability of being in any other range of the same length. If this were the case, we would expect to find x at approximately the slot determined by Interpolation Search, and therefore we would expect Interpolation Search to outperform Binary Search on the average. Indeed, under the assumptions that the keys are uniformly distributed and that the search key x is equally likely to be in each of the array slots, it is possible to show that the average-case time complexity of Interpolation Search is given by

$$A(n) \approx \lg(\lg n).$$

If n equals one billion, $\lg(\lg n)$ is about 5, whereas $\lg n$ is about 30.

A drawback of Interpolation Search is its worst-case performance. Suppose again that there are 10 keys, and their values are 1, 2, 3, 4, 5, 6, 7, 8, 9, and 100. If x were 10; *mid* would repeatedly be set to *low*, and x would be compared with every key. In the worst case, Interpolation Search degenerates to a sequential search. Notice that the worst case happens when *mid* is repeatedly set to *low*. A variation of Interpolation Search called ***Robust Interpolation Search*** remedies this situation by establishing a variable *gap* such that *mid* − *low* and *high* − *mid* are always greater than *gap*. Initially we set

$$gap = \lfloor (high - low + 1)^{1/2} \rfloor,$$

and we compute *mid* using the previous formula for linear interpolation. After that computation, the value of *mid* is possibly changed with the following computation:

$$mid = minimum(high - gap, maximum(mid, low + gap)).$$

In the example where $x = 10$ and the 10 keys are 1, 2, 3, 4, 5, 6, 7, 8, 9, and 100, *gap* would initially be $\lfloor (10 - 1 + 1)^{1/2} \rfloor = 3$, *mid* would initially be 1, and we would obtain

$$mid = minimum(10 - 3, maximum(1, 1 + 3)) = 4.$$

In this way we guarantee that the index used for the comparison is at least *gap* positions away from *low* and *high*. Whenever the search for x continues in the subarray containing the larger number of array elements, the value of *gap* is doubled, but it is never made greater than half the number of array elements in that subarray. For instance, in the previous example, the search for x continues in the larger subarray (the one from $S[5]$ to $S[10]$). Therefore, we would double *gap,* except that in this case the subarray contains only six array elements, and doubling *gap* would make it exceed half the number of array elements in the subarray. We double *gap* in order to quickly escape from large clusters. When x is found to lie in the subarray containing the smaller number of array elements, we reset *gap* to its initial value.

Under the assumptions that the keys are uniformly distributed and that the search key x is equally likely to be in each of the array slots, the average-case time complexity for Robust Interpolation Search is in $\Theta(\lg(\lg n))$. Its worst-case time complexity is in $\Theta((\lg n)^2)$, which is worse than Binary Search but much better than Interpolation Search.

There are quite a few extra computations in Robust Interpolation Search relative to Interpolation Search and in Interpolation Search relative to Binary Search. In practice, one should analyze whether the savings in comparisons justifies this increase in computations.

The searches described here are also applicable to words, because words can readily be encoded as numbers. We can therefore apply the modified binary search method to searching the phone book.

8.3 SEARCHING IN TREES

We next discuss that even though Binary Search and its variations, Interpolation Search and Robust Interpolation Search, are very efficient, they cannot be used in many applications because an array is not an appropriate structure for storing the data in these applications. Then we show that a tree is appropriate for these applications. Furthermore, we show that we have $\Theta(\lg n)$ algorithms for searching trees.

By *static searching* we mean a process in which the records are all added to the file at one time and there is no need to add or delete records later. An example of a situation in which static searching is appropriate is the searching done by operating systems commands. Many applications, however, require *dynamic searching,* which means that records are frequently added and deleted. An airline reservation system is an application that requires dynamic searching, because customers frequently call to schedule and cancel reservations.

An array structure is inappropriate for dynamic searching, because when we add a record in sequence to a sorted array, we must move all the records following the added record. Binary Search requires that the keys be structured in an array, because there must be an efficient way to find the middle item. This means that Binary Search cannot be used for dynamic searching. Although we can readily add and delete records using a linked list, there is no efficient way to search a linked list. Therefore, linked lists do not satisfy the searching needs of a dynamic searching application. If it is necessary to retrieve the keys quickly in sorted sequence, direct access storage (hashing) will not work (hashing is discussed in the next section). Dynamic searching can be implemented efficiently using a tree structure. First we discuss binary search trees. After that, we discuss B-trees, which are an improvement on binary search trees. B-trees are guaranteed to remain balanced.

Our purpose here is to further analyze the problem of searching. Therefore, we only touch on the algorithms pertaining to binary search trees and B-trees. These algorithms are discussed in detail in many data structures texts, such as Kruse (1994).

8.3.1 Binary Search Trees

Binary search trees were introduced in Section 3.5. However, the purpose there was to discuss a static searching application. That is, we wanted to create an optimal tree based on the probabilities of searching for the keys. The algorithm that builds the tree (Algorithm 3.9) requires that all the keys be added at one time, which means that the application requires static searching. Binary search trees are also appropriate for dynamic searching. Using a binary search tree, we can usually keep the average search time low, while being able to add and delete keys quickly. Furthermore, we can quickly retrieve the keys in sorted sequence by doing an in-order traversal of the tree. Recall that in an ***in-order traversal*** of a binary tree, we traverse the tree by first visiting all the nodes in the left subtree using an in-order traversal, then visiting the root, and finally visiting all the nodes in the right subtree using an in-order traversal.

Figure 8.5 shows a binary search tree containing the first seven integers. The search algorithm (Algorithm 3.8) searches the tree by comparing the search key x with the value at the root. If they are equal, we are done. If x is smaller, the search strategy is applied to the left child. If x is larger, the strategy is applied to the right child. We proceed down the tree in this fashion until x is found or it is determined that x is not in the tree. You may have noticed that when we apply this algorithm to the tree in Figure 8.5, we do the same sequence of comparisons as done by the decision tree (see Figure 8.1) corresponding to Binary Search. This illustrates a fundamental relationship between Binary Search and binary search trees. That is, the comparison nodes in the decision tree, corresponding to Binary Search when searching n keys, also represents a binary search tree in which Algorithm 3.8 does the same comparisons as Binary Search. Therefore, like Binary Search, Algorithm 3.8 is optimal for searching n keys when it is applied to that tree.

We can efficiently add keys to and delete keys from the tree in Figure 8.5. For example, to add the key 5.5 we simply proceed down the tree, going to the right if 5.5 is greater than the key at a given node, and to the left otherwise, until we locate the leaf containing 5. We then add 5.5 as the right child of that leaf. As previously mentioned, the actual algorithms for adding and deleting can be found in Kruse (1994).

The drawback of binary search trees is that when keys are dynamically added and deleted, there is no guarantee that the resulting tree will be balanced. For example, if the keys are all added in increasing sequence, we obtain the tree in Figure 8.6. This tree, which is called a ***skewed tree,*** is simply a linked list. An application of Algorithm 3.8 to this tree results in a sequential search. In this

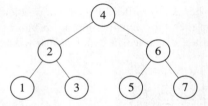

Figure 8.5 A binary search tree containing the first seven integers.

Figure 8.6 A skewed binary search tree containing the first seven integers.

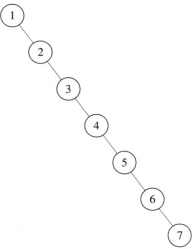

case, we have gained nothing by using a binary search tree instead of a linked list.

If the keys are added at random, intuitively it seems that the resulting tree will be closer to a balanced tree much more often than it will be closer to a linked list. (See Section A.8.1. in Appendix A for a discussion of randomness.) Therefore, on the average, we would expect an efficient search time. Indeed, we have a theorem to that effect. First we explain the result in the theorem. The theorem obtains an average search time for inputs containing n keys under the assumption that all inputs are equally probable. By this we mean that every possible ordering of n keys has the same probability of being the input to the algorithm that builds the tree. For example, if $n = 3$ and $s_1 < s_2 < s_3$ are the three keys, these inputs are all equally probable:

$$[s_1, s_2, s_3] \qquad [s_1, s_3, s_2] \qquad [s_2, s_1, s_3]$$
$$[s_2, s_3, s_1] \qquad [s_3, s_1, s_2] \qquad [s_3, s_2, s_1]$$

Notice that two inputs can result in the same tree. For example, $[s_2, s_3, s_1]$ and $[s_2, s_1, s_3]$ result in the same tree—namely, the one with s_2 at the root, s_1 on the left, and s_3 on the right. These are the only two inputs that produce that tree. Sometimes a tree is produced by only one input. For example, the tree produced by the input $[s_1, s_2, s_3]$ is produced by no other input. It is the inputs, not the trees, that are assumed to be equiprobable. Therefore, each of the inputs listed has probability $\frac{1}{6}$, the tree produced by the inputs $[s_2, s_3, s_1]$ and $[s_2, s_1, s_3]$ has probability $\frac{1}{3}$, and the tree produced by the input $[s_1, s_2, s_3]$ has probability $\frac{1}{6}$. We also assume that the search key x is equally likely to be any of the n keys. The theorem now follows.

Theorem 8.3 Under the assumptions that all inputs are equally probable and that the search key x is equally likely to be any of the n keys, the average search time over all inputs containing n distinct keys, using binary search trees, is given approximately by

$$A(n) \approx 1.38 \lg n$$

Proof: We obtain the proof under the assumption that the search key x is in the tree. In the exercises, we show that the result still holds if we remove this restriction as long as we consider each of the $2n + 1$ possible outcomes to be equally probable. (These outcomes are discussed in the average-case analysis of Binary Search in Section 8.1.2.)

Consider all binary search trees containing n keys that have the kth-smallest key at the root. Each of these trees has $k - 1$ nodes in its left subtree and $n - k$ nodes in its right subtree. The average search time for the inputs that produce these trees is given by the sum of the following three quantities:

- The average search time in the left subtrees of such trees times the probability of x being in the left subtree
- The average search time in the right subtrees of such trees times the probability of x being in the right subtree
- The one comparison at the root

The average search time in the left subtrees of such trees is $A(k - 1)$, and the average search time in the right subtrees is $A(n - k)$. Because we have assumed that the search key x is equally likely to be any of the keys, the probabilities of x being in the left and right subtrees are, respectively,

$$\frac{k - 1}{n} \quad \text{and} \quad \frac{n - k}{n}.$$

If we let $A(n|k)$ denote the average search time over all inputs of size n that produce binary search trees with the kth-smallest key at the root, we have established that

$$A(n|k) = A(k - 1)\frac{k - 1}{n} + A(n - k)\frac{n - k}{n} + 1.$$

Because all inputs are equally likely, every key has the same probability of being the first key in the input and therefore the key at the root. Therefore, the average search time over all inputs of size n is the average of $A(n|k)$ as k goes from 1 to n. We have then

$$A(n) = \frac{1}{n}\sum_{k=1}^{n}\left[\frac{k - 1}{n}A(k - 1) + \frac{n - k}{n}A(n - k) + 1\right].$$

If we set $C(n) = nA(n)$ and substitute $C(n)/n$ in the expression for $A(n)$, we obtain

$$\frac{C(n)}{n} = \frac{1}{n}\left[\sum_{k=1}^{n}\frac{k - 1}{n}\frac{C(k - 1)}{k - 1} + \frac{n - k}{n}\frac{C(n - k)}{n - k} + 1\right]$$

Simplifying yields

$$C(n) = \sum_{k=1}^{n} \left[\frac{C(k-1)}{n} + \frac{C(n-k)}{n} + 1 \right]$$

$$= \sum_{k=1}^{n} \frac{1}{n} [C(k-1) + C(n-k)] + n.$$

The initial condition is

$$C(1) = 1A(1) = 1.$$

This recurrence is almost identical to the one for the average case of Quicksort (Algorithm 2.6). Mimicking the average-case analysis for Quicksort yields

$$C(n) \approx 1.38(n+1) \lg n,$$

which means that

$$A(n) \approx 1.38 \lg n.$$

You must be careful not to misinterpret the result in Theorem 8.3. This theorem does not mean that the average search time for a particular input containing n keys is about $1.38 \lg n$. A particular input could produce a tree that degenerates into the one in Figure 8.6, which means that the average search time is in $\Theta(n)$. Theorem 8.3 is for the average search time over all inputs containing n keys. Therefore, for any given input containing n keys, it is probable that the average search time is in $\Theta(\lg n)$ but it could be in $\Theta(n)$. There is no guarantee of an efficient search.

8.3.2 B-Trees

In many applications, performance can be severely degraded by a linear search time. For example, the keys to records in large databases often cannot all fit in a computer's high-speed memory (called "RAM," for "random access memory") at one time. Therefore, multiple disk accesses are needed to accomplish the search. (Such a search is called an *external search,* whereas when all the keys are simultaneously in memory it is called an *internal search.*) Because disk access involves the mechanical movement of read/write heads and RAM access involves only electronic data transfer, disk access is orders of magnitude slower than RAM access. A linear-time external search could therefore prove to be unacceptable, and we would not want to leave such a possibility to chance.

One solution to this dilemma is to write a balancing program that takes as input an existing binary search tree and outputs a balanced binary search tree containing the same keys. The program is then run periodically. Algorithm 3.9 is an algorithm for such a program. That algorithm is more powerful than a simple balancing algorithm because it is able to consider the probability of each key being the search key.

In a very dynamic environment, it would be better if the tree never became unbalanced in the first place. Algorithms for adding and deleting nodes while maintaining a balanced binary tree were developed in 1962 by two Russian mathematicians, G. M. Adel'son-Velskii and E. M. Landis. (For this reason, balanced binary trees are often called *AVL trees.*) These algorithms can be found in Kruse (1994). The addition and deletion times for these algorithms are guaranteed to be $\Theta(\lg n)$, as is the search time.

In 1972, R. Bayer and E. M. McCreight developed an improvement over binary search trees called *B-trees.* When keys are added to or deleted from a B-tree, all leaves are guaranteed to remain at the same level, which is even better than maintaining balance. The actual algorithms for manipulating B-trees can be found in Kruse (1994). Here we illustrate only how we can add keys while keeping all leaves at the same level.

B-trees actually represent a class of trees, of which the simplest is a 3–2 tree. We illustrate the process of adding nodes to such trees. A *3–2 tree* is a tree with the following properties:

- Each node contains one or two keys.
- If a nonleaf contains one key, it has two children, whereas if it contains two keys, it has three children.
- The keys in the left subtree of a given node are less than or equal to the key stored at that node.
- The keys in the right subtree of a given node are greater than or equal to the key stored at that node.
- If a node contains two keys, the keys in the middle subtree of the node are greater than or equal to the left key and less than or equal to the right key.
- All leaves are at the same level.

Figure 8.7(a) shows a 3–2 tree, and the remainder of that figure shows how a new key is added to the tree. Notice that the tree remains balanced because the tree grows in depth at the root instead of at the leaves. Similarly, when it is necessary to delete a node, the tree shrinks in depth at the root. In this way, all leaves always remain at the same level, and the search, addition, and deletion times are guaranteed to be in $\Theta(\lg n)$. Clearly, an in-order traversal of the tree retrieves the keys in sorted sequence. For these reasons, B-trees are used in most modern database management systems.

8.4 HASHING

Suppose the keys are integers from 1 to 100, and there are about 100 records. An efficient method for storing the records is to create an array S of 100 items and store the record whose key is equal to i in $S[i]$. The retrieval is immediate, with no comparisons of keys being done. This same strategy can be used if there are about 100 records and the keys are nine-digit social security numbers. However, in this case the strategy is very inefficient in terms of memory because an array

Figure 8.7 The way a new key is added to a 3–2 tree.

(a) A 3–2 tree

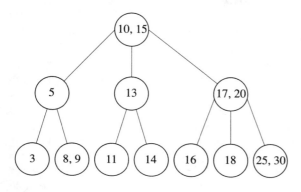

(b) 35 is added to the tree in sorted sequence in a leaf

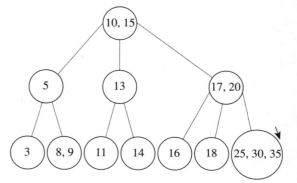

(c) If the leaf contains three keys, it breaks into two nodes and sends the middle key up to its parent

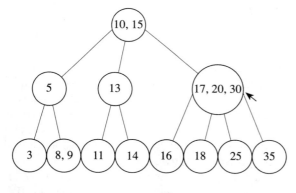

(d) If the parent now contains three keys, the process of breaking open and sending the middle key up repeats

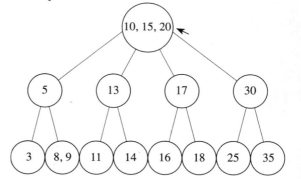

(e) Finally, if the root contains three keys, it breaks open and sends the middle key up to a new root

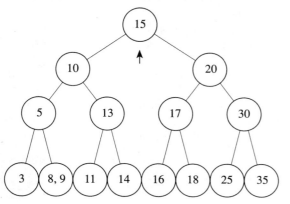

of 1 billion items is needed to store only 100 records. Alternatively, we could create an array of only 100 items indexed from 0 to 99, and "hash" each key to a value from 0 and 99. A **hash function** is a function that transforms a key to an index, and an application of a hash function to a particular key is called "hashing the key." In the case of social security numbers, a possible hash function is

$$h(key) \;=\; key \;\%\; 100.$$

(% returns the remainder when *key* is divided by 100.) This function simply returns the last two digits of the key. If a particular key hashes to *i*, we store the key and its record at $S[i]$. This strategy does not store the keys in sorted sequence, which means that it is applicable only if we never need to retrieve the records efficiently in sorted sequence. If it is necessary to do this, one of the methods discussed previously should be used.

If no two keys hash to the same index, this method works fine. However, this is rarely the case when there are a substantial number of keys. For example, if there are 100 keys and each key is equally likely to hash to each of the 100 indices, the probability of no two keys hashing to the same index is

$$\frac{100!}{100^{100}} \approx 9.3 \times 10^{-43}.$$

We are almost certain that at least two keys will hash to the same index. Such an occurrence is called a **collision** or **hash clash.** There are various ways to resolve a collision. One of the best ways is through the use of **open hashing** (also called **open addressing**). With open hashing we create a bucket for each possible hash value, and place all the keys that hash to a value in the bucket associated with that value. Open hashing is usually implemented with linked lists. For example, if we hash to the last two digits of a number, we create an array of pointers *Bucket* that is indexed from 0 to 99. All of those keys that hash to *i* are placed in a linked list starting at *Bucket*[*i*]. This is illustrated in Figure 8.8.

The number of buckets need not equal the number of keys. For example, if we hash to the last two digits of a number, the number of buckets must be 100. However, we could store 100, 200, 1000, or any number of keys. Of course, the more keys we store, the more likely we are to have collisions. If the number of keys is greater than the number of buckets, we are guaranteed to have collisions. Because a bucket stores only a pointer, not much space is wasted by allocating a bucket. Therefore, it is often reasonable to allocate at least as many buckets as there are keys.

When searching for a key, it is necessary to do a sequential search through the bucket (linked list) containing the key. If all the keys hash to the same bucket, the search degenerates into a sequential search. How likely is this to happen? If there are 100 keys and 100 buckets, and a key is equally likely to hash to each of the buckets, the probability of the keys all ending up in the same bucket is

$$100 \times \left(\frac{1}{100}\right)^{100} \;=\; 10^{-198}.$$

Figure 8.8 An illustration of open hashing. Keys with the same last two digits are in the same bucket.

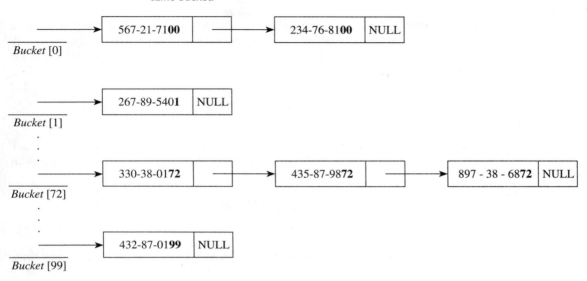

Therefore, it is almost impossible for all the keys to end up in the same bucket. What about the chances of 90, 80, 70, or any other large number of keys ending up in the same bucket? Our real interest should be how likely it is that hashing will yield a better average search than Binary Search. We show that if the file is reasonably large, this too is almost a certainty. But first we show how good things can be with hashing.

Intuitively, it should be clear that the best thing that can happen is for the keys to be uniformly distributed in the buckets. That is, if there are n keys and m buckets, each bucket contains n/m keys. Actually, each bucket will contain exactly n/m keys only when n is a multiple of m. When this is not the case, we have an approximately uniform distribution. The following theorems show what happens when the keys are uniformly distributed. For simplicity, they are stated for an exact uniform distribution (that is, for the case in which n is a multiple of m).

Theorem 8.4 If n keys are uniformly distributed in m buckets, the number of comparisons in an unsuccessful search is given by n/m.

Proof: Because the keys are uniformly distributed, the number of keys in each bucket is n/m, which means that every unsuccessful search requires n/m comparisons.

Theorem 8.5 If n keys are uniformly distributed in m buckets and each key is equally likely to be the search key, the average number of comparisons in a successful search is given by

$$\frac{n}{2m} + \frac{1}{2}.$$

Proof: The average search time in each bucket is equal to the average search time when doing a sequential search of n/m keys. The average-case analysis of Algorithm 1.1 in Section 1.3 shows that this average equals the expression in the statement of the theorem.

The following example applies Theorem 8.5.

Example 8.1 If the keys are uniformly distributed and $n = 2m$, every unsuccessful search requires only $2m/m = 2$ comparisons, and the average number of comparisons for a successful search is

$$\frac{2m}{2m} + \frac{1}{2} = \frac{3}{2}.$$

When the keys are uniformly distributed, we have a very small search time. However, even though hashing has the possibility of yielding such exceptionally good results, one might argue that we should still use Binary Search to guarantee that the search does not degenerate into something close to a sequential search. The following theorem shows that if the file is reasonably large, the chances of hashing being as bad as Binary Search are very small. The theorem assumes that a key is equally likely to hash to each of the buckets. When social security numbers are hashed to their last two digits, this criterion should be satisfied. However, not all hash functions satisfy this criterion. For example, if names are hashed to their last letters, the probability of hashing to "th" is much greater than that of hashing to "qz," because many more names end in "th." A data structures text such as Kruse (1994) discuss methods for choosing a good hash function. Our purpose here is to analyze how well hashing solves the Searching Problem.

Theorem 8.6 If there are n keys and m buckets, the probability that at least one bucket contains at least k keys is less than or equal to

$$\binom{n}{k}\left(\frac{1}{m}\right)^{k-1},$$

given the assumption that a key is equally likely to hash to any bucket.

Proof: For a given bucket, the probability of any specific combination of k keys ending up in that bucket is $(1/m)^k$, which means that the probability that the bucket contains at least the keys in that combination is $(1/m)^k$. In general, for two events S and T,

$$p(S \text{ or } T) \leq p(S) + p(T). \tag{8.1}$$

Therefore, the probability that a given bucket contains at least k keys is less than or equal to the sum of the probabilities that it contains at least the keys in each distinct combination of k keys. Because $\binom{n}{k}$ distinct combinations of k keys can be obtained from n keys (see Section A.7 in Appendix A), the probability that any given bucket contains at least k keys is less than or equal to

$$\binom{n}{k}\left(\frac{1}{m}\right)^{k}.$$

The theorem now follows from Expression 8.1 and the fact that there are m buckets.

Recall that the average search time for Binary Search is about $\lg n$. Table 8.1 shows the bounds on the probabilities of at least one bucket containing at least $\lg n$ keys and $2 \lg n$ keys for several values of n. It is assumed in the table that $n = m$. Even when n is only 128, the chances of the search time ever exceeding $2 \lg n$ are less than 1 in a billion. For $n = 1024$, the chances of the search time ever exceeding $2 \lg n$ are less than 3 in 10 million billion. For $n = 65,536$, the chances of the search time ever exceeding $\lg n$ are about 3 in 1 billion. The probability of dying in a single trip in a jet plane is about 6 in 1 million, and the probability of dying in an auto accident during an average year of driving is about 270 in 1 million. Yet many humans do not take serious measures to avoid these activities. The point is that, to make reasonable decisions, we often neglect exceptionally small probabilities as if they were impossibilities. Because for large n we can be almost certain of obtaining better performance using hashing instead of Binary Search, it is reasonable to do so. We amusingly recall that in the 1970s a certain computer manufacturer routinely talked data-processing managers into buying expensive new hardware by describing a catastrophe that would take place if a contrived scenario of usage occurred. The flaw in their argument, which the data-processing managers often overlooked, was that the probability of this scenario occurring was negligible. Risk aversion is a matter of personal preference. Therefore, an exceedingly risk-averse individual may choose not to take a 1-in-

Table 8.1 Upper Bounds on the Probability That at Least One Bucket Contains at Least k Keys*

n	Bound when $k = \lg n$	Bound when $k = 2 \lg n$
128	.021	7.02×10^{-10}
1,024	.00027	3.49×10^{-16}
8,192	.0000013	1.95×10^{-23}
65,536	3.1×10^{-9}	2.47×10^{-31}

*It is assumed that the number of keys n equals the number of buckets.

a-billion or even a 3-in-10-million-billion chance. However, the individual should not make such a choice without giving serious deliberation to whether such a decision truly models the individual's attitude toward risk. Methods for doing such an analysis are discussed in Clemen (1991).

8.5 THE SELECTION PROBLEM: INTRODUCTION TO ADVERSARY ARGUMENTS

So far we've discussed searching for a key x in a list of n keys. Next we address a different searching problem called the **Selection Problem.** This problem is to find the kth-largest (or kth-smallest) key in a list of n keys. We assume that the keys are in an unsorted array (the problem is trivial for a sorted array). First we discuss the problem for $k = 1$, which means that we are finding the largest (or smallest) key. Next we show that we can simultaneously find the smallest and largest keys with fewer comparisons than would be necessary if each were found separately. Then we discuss the problem for $k = 2$, which means that we are finding the second-largest (or second-smallest) key. Finally, we address the general case.

8.5.1 Finding the Largest Key

The following is a straightforward algorithm for finding the largest key.

Algorithm 8.2   Find Largest Key

Problem: Find the largest key in an array S of size n.

Inputs: positive integer n, array of keys S indexed from 1 to n.

Outputs: variable *large*, whose value is the largest key in S.

```
void find_largest (int n,
                   const keytype S[ ],
                   keytype& large)
{
   index i;

   large = S[1];
   for (i = 2; i <= n; i++)
     if (S[i] > large)
        large = S[i];
}
```

Clearly, the number of comparisons of keys done by the algorithm is given by

$$T(n) = n - 1.$$

Intuitively, it seems impossible to improve on this performance. The next theorem establishes that this is so. We can think of an algorithm that determines the largest key as a tournament among the keys. Each comparison is a match in the tournament, the larger key is the **winner** of the comparison, and the smaller key is the **loser.** The largest key is the winner of the tournament. We use this terminology throughout this section.

Theorem 8.7 Any deterministic algorithm that can find the largest of n keys in every possible input only by comparisons of keys must in every case do at least

$$n - 1 \text{ comparisons of keys.}$$

Proof: The proof is by contradiction. That is, we show that if the algorithm does fewer than $n - 1$ comparisons for some input of size n, the algorithm must give the wrong answer for some other input. To that end, if the algorithm finds the largest key by doing at most $n - 2$ comparisons for some input, at least two keys in that input never lose a comparison. At least one of those two keys cannot be reported as the largest key. We can create a new input by replacing (if necessary) that key by a key that is larger than all keys in the original input. Because the results of all comparisons will be the same as for the original input, the new key will not be reported as the largest, which means that the algorithm will give the wrong answer for the new input. This contradiction proves that the algorithm must do at least $n - 1$ comparisons for every input of size n.

You must be careful to interpret Theorem 8.7 correctly. It does not mean that every algorithm that searches only by comparisons of keys must do at least $n - 1$ comparisons to find the largest key. For example, if an array is sorted, we can find the largest key without doing any comparisons simply by returning the last item in the array. However, an algorithm that returns the last item in an array can find the largest key only when the largest key is the last item. It cannot find the largest key in every possible input. Theorem 8.7 concerns algorithms that can find the largest key in every possible input.

Of course, we can use an analogous version of Algorithm 8.2 to find the smallest key in $n - 1$ comparisons and an analogous version of Theorem 8.7 to show that $n - 1$ is a lower bound for finding the smallest key.

8.5.2 Finding Both the Smallest and Largest Keys

A straightforward way to find the smallest and largest keys simultaneously is to modify Algorithm 8.2 as follows.

Algorithm 8.3   Find Smallest and Largest Keys

Problem: Find the smallest and largest keys in an array S of size n.

Inputs: positive integer n, array of keys S indexed from 1 to n.

Outputs: variables *small* and *large,* whose values are the smallest and largest keys in S.

```
void find_both (int n,
                const keytype S[ ],
                keytype& small,
                keytype& large)
{
   index i;

   small = S[1];
   large = S[1];
   for (i = 2; i <= n; i++)
     if (S[i] < small)
        small = S[i];
     else if (S[i] > large)
        large = S[i];
}
```

Using Algorithm 8.3 is better than finding the smallest and largest keys independently, because for some inputs the comparison of $S[i]$ with *large* is not done for every i. Therefore, we have improved on the every-case performance. But whenever $S[1]$ is the smallest key, that comparison is done for all i. Therefore, the worst-case number of comparisons of keys is given by

$$W(n) = 2(n - 1),$$

which is exactly the number of comparisons done if the smallest and largest keys are found separately. It may seem that we cannot improve on this performance, but we can. The trick is to pair the keys and find which key in each pair is smaller. This can be done with about $n/2$ comparisons. We can then find the smallest of all the smaller keys with about $n/2$ comparisons and the largest of all the larger keys with about $n/2$ comparisons. In this way we find both the smallest and largest keys with only about $3n/2$ total comparisons. An algorithm for this method follows. The algorithm assumes that n is even.

Algorithm 8.4   Find Smallest and Largest Keys by Pairing Keys

Problem: Find the smallest and largest keys in an array S of size n.

Inputs: positive even integer n, array of keys S indexed from 1 to n.

Outputs: variables *small* and *large,* whose values are the smallest and largest keys in *S*.

```
void find_both2 (int n,                          // n is assumed to be even.
                 const keytype S[ ],
                 keytype& small,
                 keytype& large)
{
  index i;
  if (S[1] < S[2]) {
    small = S[1];
    large = S[2];
  }
  else {
    small = S[2];
    large = S[1];
  }
  for (i = 3; i <= n - 1; i = i + 2) {            // Increment i by 2.
    if (S[i] > S[i + 1])
      exchange S[i] and S[i + 1];
    if (S[i] < small)
      small = S[i];
    if (S[i + 1] > large)
      large = S[i + 1];
  }
}
```

It is left as an exercise to modify the algorithm so that it works when n is odd and show that its number of comparison of keys is given by

$$
T(n) = \begin{cases} \dfrac{3n}{2} - 2 & \text{if } n \text{ is even} \\[2ex] \dfrac{3n}{2} - \dfrac{3}{2} & \text{if } n \text{ is odd.} \end{cases}
$$

Can we improve on this performance? We show that the answer is ''no.'' We do not use a decision tree to show this because decision trees do not work well for the Selection Problem. The reason is as follows. We know that a decision tree for the Selection Problem must contain at least n leaves because there are n possible outcomes. Lemma 7.3 says that if a binary tree has n leaves, its depth is greater than or equal to $\lceil \lg n \rceil$. Therefore, our lower bound on the number of leaves gives us a lower bound of $\lceil \lg n \rceil$ comparisons in the worst case. This is not a very good lower bound, because we already know that it takes at least

$n - 1$ comparisons just to find the largest key (Theorem 8.7). Lemma 8.1 is no more useful because we can only readily establish that there must be $n - 1$ comparison nodes in the decision tree. Decision trees do not work well for the Selection Problem because a result can be in more than one leaf. Figure 8.9 shows the decision tree for Algorithm 8.2 (Find Largest Key) when $n = 4$. There are four leaves that report 4 and two that report 3. The number of comparisons done by the algorithm is 3 rather than $\lg n = \lg 4 = 2$. We see that $\lg n$ is a weak lower bound.

We use another method, called an ***adversary argument,*** to establish our lower bound. An ***adversary*** is an opponent or foe. Suppose you are in the local singles bar and an interested stranger asked you the tired question "What's your sign?" This means that the person wants to know your astrological sign. There are 12 such signs, each corresponding to a period of approximately 30 days. If, for example, you were born August 25, your sign would be Virgo. To make this stale encounter more exciting, you decide to spice things up by being an adversary. You tell the stranger to guess your sign by asking yes/no questions. Being an adversary, you have no intention of disclosing your sign—you simply want to force the stranger to ask as many questions as possible. Therefore, you always provide answers that narrow down the search as little as possible. For example, suppose the stranger asks "Were you born in summer?" Because a "no" answer would narrow the search to nine months and a "yes" answer would narrow it to three months, you answer "no." If the stranger then asks "Were you born in a month with 31 days?" you answer "yes," because more than half of the nine possible months remaining have 31 days. The only requirement of your answers is that they be consistent with ones already given. For example, if the stranger forgets that you said you were not born in summer and later asks if you were

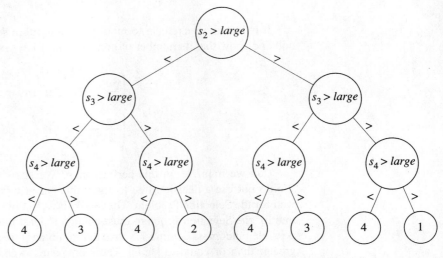

Figure 8.9 The decision tree corresponding to Algorithm 8.2 when $n = 4$.

born in July, you could not answer "yes" because this would not be consistent with your previous answers. Inconsistent answers have no sign (birthday) satisfying them. Because you answer each question so as to leave the maximum number of remaining possibilities and because your answers are consistent, you force the stranger to ask as many questions as possible before reaching a logical conclusion.

Suppose some adversary's goal is to make an algorithm work as hard as possible (as you did with the stranger). At each point where the algorithm must make a decision (for example, after a comparison of keys), the adversary tries to choose a result of the decision that will keep the algorithm going as long as possible. The only restriction is that the adversary must always choose a result that is consistent with those already given. As long as the results are consistent, there must be an input for which this sequence of results occurs. If the adversary forces the algorithm to do the basic instruction $f(n)$ times, then $f(n)$ is a lower bound on the worst-case time complexity of the algorithm.

We use an adversary argument to obtain a lower bound on the worst-case number of comparisons needed to find both the largest and smallest keys. To establish that bound, we can assume that the keys are distinct. We can do this because a lower bound on the worst-case time complexity for a subset of inputs (those with distinct keys) is a lower bound on the worst-case time complexity when all inputs are considered. Before presenting the theorem, we show our adversary's strategy. Suppose we have some algorithm that solves the problem of finding the smallest and largest keys only by comparisons of keys. If all the keys are distinct, at any given time during the execution of the algorithm a given key has one of the following states:

State	Description of State
X	The key has not been involved in a comparison.
L	The key has lost at least one comparison and has never won.
W	The key has won at least one comparison and has never lost.
LW	The key has lost at least one comparison and has won at least one.

We can think of these states as containing units of information. If a key has state X, there are zero units of information. If a key has state L or W, there is one unit of information because we know that the key has either lost or won a comparison. If a key has state LW, there are two units of information because we know that the key has both won and lost comparisons. For the algorithm to establish that one key *small* is smallest and another key *large* is largest, the algorithm must know that every key other than *small* has won a comparison and every key other than *large* has lost a comparison. This means that the algorithm must learn

$$(n - 1) + (n - 1) = 2n - 2$$

units of information.

Because the goal is to make the algorithm work as hard as possible, an

Table 8.2 Our Adversary's Strategy for Foiling an Algorithm That Finds the Smallest and Largest Keys*

Before Comparison		Key Declared Larger by Adversary	After Comparison		Units of Information Learned by Algorithm
s_i	s_j		s_i	s_j	
X	X	s_i	W	L	2
X	L	s_i	W	L	1
X	W	s_j	L	W	1
X	WL	s_i	W	WL	1
L	L	s_i	W	L	1
L	W	s_j	L	W	0
L	WL	s_j	L	WL	0
W	W	s_i	W	WL	1
W	WL	s_i	W	WL	0
WL	WL	Consistent with previous answers	WL	WL	0

*The keys s_i and s_j are being compared.

adversary wants to provide as little information as possible with each comparison. For example, if the algorithm first compares s_2 and s_1, it doesn't matter what an adversary answers, because two units of information are supplied either way. Let's say the adversary answers s_2. The state of s_2 then changes from X to W, and the state of s_1 changes from X to L. Suppose the algorithm next compares s_3 and s_1. If an adversary answers that s_1 is larger, the state of s_1 changes from W to WL and the state of s_3 changes from X to L. This means that two units of information are disclosed. Because only one unit of information is disclosed by answering that s_3 is larger, we have our adversary give this answer. Table 8.2 shows an adversary strategy that always discloses a minimal amount of information. When it doesn't matter which key is answered, we have simply chosen the first one in the comparison. This strategy is all we need to prove our theorem. But first let's show an example of how our adversary would actually use the strategy.

Example 8.2 Table 8.3 shows our adversary's strategy for foiling Algorithm 8.3 for an input size of 5. We have assigned values to the keys that are consistent with the answers. This is not really necessary, but the adversary must keep track of the order of the keys imposed by the answers, so that a consistent answer can be given when both keys have state WL. An easy way to do this is to assign values. Furthermore, assigning values illustrates that a consistent set of answers does indeed have an input associated with it. Other than the order determined by the adversary's strategy, the answers are arbitrary. For example, when s_3 is declared larger than s_1, we give s_3 the value 15. We could have given it any value greater than 10.

Notice that after s_3 is compared with s_2, we change the value of s_3 from 15 to 30. Remember that the adversary has no actual input when presented with the algorithm. An answer (and therefore an input value) is constructed dynamically whenever our adversary is given the decision the algorithm is currently making. It is necessary to change the value of s_3 from 15 because s_2 is larger than 15 and our adversary's answer is that s_3 is larger than s_2.

After the algorithm is done, s_1 has lost to all other keys and s_5 has won over all other keys. Therefore, s_1 is smallest and s_5 is largest. The input constructed by our adversary has s_1 as the smallest key because this is an input that makes Algorithm 8.3 work hardest. Notice that eight comparisons are done in Table 8.3, and the worst-case number of comparisons done by Algorithm 8.3 when the input size is 5 is given by

$$W(5) = 2(5 - 1) = 8.$$

This means that our adversary succeeds in making Algorithm 8.3 work as hard as possible when the input size is 5.

Table 8.3 Our Adversary's Answers in Attempting to Foil Algorithm 8.3 for an Input Size of 5

Comparison	Key Declared Larger by Adversary	States/Assigned Values					Units of Information Learned by Algorithm
		s_1	s_2	s_3	s_4	s_5	
$s_2 < s_1$	s_2	L/10	W/20	X	X	X	2
$s_2 > s_1$	s_2	L/10	W/20	X	X	X	0
$s_3 < s_1$	s_3	L/10	W/20	W/15	X	X	1
$s_3 > s_2$	s_3	L/10	WL/20	W/30	X	X	1
$s_4 < s_1$	s_4	L/10	WL/20	W/30	W/15	X	1
$s_4 > s_3$	s_4	L/10	WL/20	WL/30	W/40	X	1
$s_5 < s_1$	s_5	L/10	WL/20	WL/30	W/40	W/15	1
$s_5 > s_4$	s_5	L/10	WL/20	WL/30	WL/40	W/50	1

When presented with a different algorithm for finding the largest and smallest keys, our adversary will provide answers that try to make that algorithm work as hard as possible. You are encouraged to determine the adversary's answers when presented with Algorithm 8.4 (Find Smallest and Largest Keys by Pairing Keys) and some input size.

When developing an adversary strategy, our goal is to make algorithms for solving some problem work as hard as possible. A poor adversary may not actually achieve this goal. However, regardless of whether or not the goal is reached, the strategy can be used to obtain a lower bound on how hard the algorithms must work. Next we do this for the adversary strategy just described.

Theorem 8.8 Any deterministic algorithm that can find both the smallest and the largest of n keys in every possible input only by comparisons of keys must in the worst case do at least the following numbers of comparisons of keys:

$$\frac{3n}{2} - 2 \qquad \text{if } n \text{ is even}$$

$$\frac{3n}{2} - \frac{3}{2} \qquad \text{if } n \text{ is odd}$$

Proof: We show that this is a lower bound on the worst case by showing that the algorithm must do at least this many comparisons when the keys are distinct. As noted previously, the algorithm must learn $2n - 2$ units of information to find both the smallest and largest keys. Suppose we present our adversary with the algorithm. Table 8.2 shows that our adversary provides two units of information in a single comparison only when both keys have not been involved in previous comparisons. If n is even, this can be the case for at most

$$\frac{n}{2} \text{ comparisons,}$$

which means that the algorithm can get at most $2(n/2) = n$ units of information in this way. Because our adversary provides at most one unit of information in the other comparisons, the algorithm must do at least

$$2n - 2 - n = n - 2$$

additional comparisons to get all the information it needs. Our adversary therefore forces the algorithm to do at least

$$\frac{n}{2} + n - 2 = \frac{3n}{2} - 2$$

comparisons of keys. It is left as an exercise to analyze the case in which n is odd.

Because Algorithm 8.4 does the number of comparisons in the bound in Theorem 8.8, that algorithm is optimal in its worst-case performance. We have chosen a worthy adversary because we have found an algorithm that performs as well as the bound it provides. We know therefore that no other adversary could provide a larger bound.

Example 8.2 illustrates why Algorithm 8.3 is suboptimal. In that example, Algorithm 8.3 takes eight comparisons to learn eight units of information, whereas an optimal algorithm would take only six comparisons. Table 8.3 shows that the second comparison is useless because no information is learned.

When adversary arguments are used, the adversary is sometimes called an *oracle*. Among ancient Greeks and Romans, an oracle was an entity with great knowledge that answered questions posed by humans.

8.5.3 Finding the Second-Largest Key

To find the second-largest key, we can use Algorithm 8.2 (Find Largest Key) to find the largest key with $n - 1$ comparisons, eliminate that key, and then use

Algorithm 8.2 again to find the largest remaining key with $n - 2$ comparisons. Therefore, we can find the second-largest key with $2n - 3$ comparisons. We should be able to improve on this, because many of the comparisons done when finding the largest key can be used to eliminate keys from contention for the second largest. That is, any key than loses to a key other than the largest cannot be the second largest. The Tournament Method, described next, uses this fact.

The ***Tournament Method*** is so named because it is patterned after the method used in elimination tournaments. For example, to determine the best college basketball team in the United States, 64 teams compete in the NCAA Tournament. Teams are paired and 32 games are played in the first round. The 32 victors are paired for the second round and 16 games are played. This process continues until only two teams remain for the final round. The winner of the single game in that round is the champion. It takes $\lg 64 = 6$ rounds to determine the champion.

For simplicity, assume that the numbers are distinct and that n is a power of 2. As is done in the NCAA Tournament, we pair the keys and compare the pairs in rounds until only one round remains. If there are eight keys, there are four comparisons in the first round, two in the second, and one in the last. The winner of the last round is the largest key. Figure 8.10 illustrates the method. The Tournament Method directly applies only when n is a power of 2. When this is not the case, we can add enough items to the end of the array to make the array size a power of 2. For example, if the array is an array of 53 integers, we add 11 elements, each with value $-\infty$, to the end of the array to make the array contain 64 elements. In what follows, we will simply assume that n is a power of 2.

Although the winner in the last round is the largest key, the loser in that round is not necessarily the second largest. In Figure 8.10, the second-largest key (16) loses to the largest key (18) in the second round. This is a difficulty with many actual tournaments because the two best teams do not always meet in the championship game. Anyone familiar with the American football Super Bowl for the past several years is well aware of this. To find the second-largest key, we

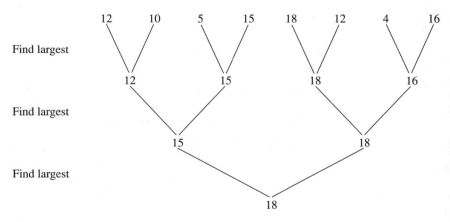

Figure 8.10 The Tournament Method.

can keep track of all the keys that lose to the largest key, and then use Algorithm 8.2 to find the largest of those. But how can we keep track of those keys when we do not know in advance which key is the largest? We can do this by maintaining linked lists of keys, one for each key. After a key loses a match, it is added to the winning key's linked list. It is left as an exercise to write an algorithm for this method. If n is a power of 2, there are $n/2$ comparisons in the first round, $n/2^2$ in the second round, ..., and $n/2^{\lg n} = 1$ in the last round. The total number of comparisons in all the rounds is given by

$$T(n) = n \sum_{i=1}^{\lg n} \left(\frac{1}{2}\right)^i = n\left[\frac{(1/2)^{\lg(n)+1} - 1}{1/2 - 1} - 1\right] = n - 1.$$

The second-to-last equality is obtained by applying the result in Example A.4 in Appendix A. This is the number of comparisons needed to complete the tournament. (Notice that we find the largest key with an optimal number of comparisons.) The largest key will have been involved in $\lg n$ matches, which means that there will be $\lg n$ keys in its linked list. Using Algorithm 8.2, it takes $\lg n - 1$ comparisons to find the largest key in this linked list. That key is the second-largest key. Therefore, the total number of comparisons needed to find the second-largest key is

$$T(n) = n - 1 + \lg n - 1 = n + \lg n - 2.$$

It is left as an exercise to show that, for n in general,

$$T(n) = n + \lceil \lg n \rceil - 2.$$

This performance is a substantial improvement over using Algorithm 8.2 twice to find the second-largest key. Recall that it takes $2n - 3$ comparisons to do it that way. Can we obtain an algorithm that does even fewer comparisons? We use an adversary argument to show that we cannot.

Theorem 8.9 Any deterministic algorithm that can find the second largest of n keys in every possible input only by comparisons of keys must in the worst case do at least

$$n + \lceil \lg n \rceil - 2 \text{ comparisons of keys.}$$

Proof: To determine that a key is second largest, an algorithm must determine that it is the largest of the $n - 1$ keys besides the largest key. Let m be the number of comparisons won by the largest key. None of these comparisons is useful in determining that the second-largest key is the largest of the remaining $n - 1$ keys. Theorem 8.7 says that this determination requires at least $n - 2$ comparisons. Therefore, the total number of comparisons is at least $m + n - 2$. This means that, to prove the theorem, an adversary only needs to force the algorithm to make the largest key compete in at least $\lceil \lg n \rceil$ comparisons. Our adversary's strategy is to associate a node in a tree with each key. Initially, n single-node trees are created, one for each key. Our adversary uses the trees to give the result of the comparison of s_i and s_j as follows:

- If both s_i and s_j are roots of trees containing the same number of nodes, the answer is arbitrary. The trees are combined by making the key that is declared smaller a child of the other key.

- If both s_i and s_j are roots of trees, and one tree contains more nodes than the other, the root of the smaller tree is declared smaller, and the trees are combined by making that root a child of the other root.

- If s_i is a root and s_j is not, s_j is declared smaller and the trees are not changed.

- If neither s_i nor s_j is a root, the answer is consistent with previously assigned values, and the trees are not changed.

Figure 8.11 shows how trees would be combined when our adversary is presented with the Tournament Method and an instance of size 8. When the choice is arbitrary, we make the key with the larger index the winner. Only the comparisons up to completion of the tournament are shown. After that, more comparisons would be done to find the largest of the keys that lost to the largest key, but the tree would be unchanged.

Let $size_k$ be the number of nodes in the tree rooted at the largest key immediately after the kth comparison won by that key. Then

$$size_k \leq 2size_{k-1}$$

because the number of nodes in a defeated key's tree can be no greater than the number of nodes in the victor's tree. The initial condition is $size_0 = 1$. We can solve this recurrence using the techniques in Appendix B to conclude that

$$size_k \leq 2^k.$$

If a key is a root when the algorithm stops, it has never lost a comparison. Therefore, if two trees remain when the algorithm stops, two keys have never lost a comparison. At least one of those keys is not reported as the second-largest key. We can create a new input with all the other values the same, but with the values of the two roots changed so that the key that we know is not reported as the second largest is indeed the second-largest key. The algorithm would give the wrong answer for that input. So when the algorithm stops, all n keys must be in one tree. Clearly, the root of that tree must be the largest key. Therefore, if m is the total number of comparisons won by the largest key,

$$n = size_m \leq 2^m$$
$$\lg n \leq m$$
$$\lceil \lg n \rceil \leq m.$$

The last equality derives from the fact that m is an integer. This proves the theorem.

Figure 8.11 The trees created by our adversary in Theorem 8.9 when presented with the Tournament Method and an input size of 8.

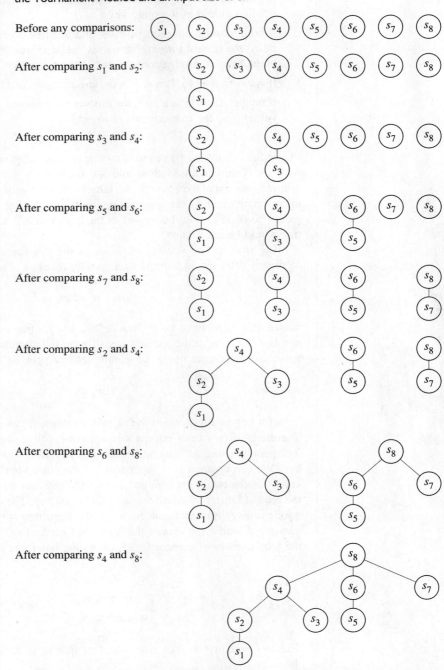

Because the Tournament Method performs as well as our lower bound, it is optimal. We have again found a worthy adversary. No other adversary could produce a greater bound.

In the worst case, it takes at least $n - 1$ comparisons to find the largest key and at least $n + \lceil \lg n \rceil - 2$ comparisons to find the second-largest key. Any algorithm that finds the second-largest key must also find the largest key, because to know that a key is second largest we must know that it has lost one comparison. That loss must be to the largest key. Therefore, it is not surprising that it is harder to find the second-largest key.

8.5.4 Finding the kth-Smallest Key

In general, the Selection Problem entails finding the kth-largest or kth-smallest key. So far, we've discussed finding the largest key, because it has seemed more appropriate for the terms used. That is, it seems appropriate to call the largest key a winner. Here we discuss finding the kth-smallest key because it makes our algorithms more lucid. For simplicity, we assume that the keys are distinct.

An obvious way to find the kth-smallest key in $\Theta(n \lg n)$ time is to sort the keys and return the kth key. We develop a method that requires fewer comparisons.

Recall that procedure *partition* in Algorithm 2.7, which is used in Quicksort (Algorithm 2.6), partitions an array so that all keys smaller than some pivot item come before it in the array and all keys larger than that pivot item come after it. The slot at which the pivot item is located is called the *pivotpoint*. We can solve the Selection Problem by partitioning until the pivot item is at the kth slot. We do this by recursively partitioning the left subarray (the keys smaller than the pivot item) if k is less than *pivotpoint,* and by recursively partitioning the right subarray if k is greater than *pivotpoint.* When $k = pivotpoint,$ we're done. The following divide-and-conquer algorithm solves the problem by this method.

Algorithm 8.5

Selection

Problem: Find the kth-smallest key in array S of n distinct keys.

Inputs: positive integers n and k where $k \le n$, array of distinct keys S indexed from 1 to n.

Outputs: the kth-smallest key in S. It is returned as the value of function *selection.*

```
keytype selection (index low, index high, index k)
{
    index pivotpoint;
```

```
        if (low == high)
          return S[low];
        else {
          partition(low, high, pivotpoint);
          if (k == pivotpoint)
            return S[pivotpoint];
          else if (k < pivotpoint)
            return selection(low, pivotpoint − 1, k);
          else
            return selection(pivotpoint + 1, high, k);
        }
      }

      void partition (index low, index high,      // This is the same routine that
                      index& pivotpoint)          // appears in Algorithm 2.7.
      {
        index i, j;
        keytype pivotitem;

        pivotitem = S[low];                        // Choose first item for pivotitem.
        j = low;
        for (i = low + 1; i <= high; i++)
          if (S[i] < pivotitem) {
            j++;
            exchange S[i] and S[j];
          }
        pivotpoint = j;
        exchange S[low] and S[pivotpoint];         // Put pivotitem at pivotpoint.
      }
```

As with our recursive functions in previous chapters, n and S are not inputs to function *selection*. The top-level call to that function would be

$$kthsmallest = selection(1, n, k).$$

As in Quicksort (Algorithm 2.6), the worst case occurs when the input to each recursive call contains one less item. This happens, for example, when the array is sorted in increasing order and $k = n$. Algorithm 8.5 therefore has the same worst-case time complexity as Algorithm 2.6, which means that the *worst-case time complexity of the number of comparisons of keys done by Algorithm 8.5* is given by

$$W(n) = \frac{n(n-1)}{2}.$$

Although the worst case is the same as that of Quicksort, we show next that Algorithm 8.5 performs much better on the average.

Average-Case Time Complexity Analysis of Algorithm 8.5 (*Selection*)

Basic operation: the comparison of $S[i]$ with *pivotitem* in *partition*.

Input size: n, the number of items in the array.

We assume that all inputs are equally likely. This means that we assume that all values of k are entered with equal frequency and all values of *pivotpoint* are returned with equal frequency. Let p stand for *pivotpoint*. There are n outcomes for which there is no recursive call (that is, if $p = k$ for $k = 1, 2, \ldots, n$). There are two outcomes for which 1 is the input size in the first recursive call (that is, if $p = 2$ with $k = 1$, or $p = n - 1$ with $k = n$). There are $2(2) = 4$ outcomes for which 2 is the input size in the first recursive call (that is, if $p = 3$ with $k = 1$ or 2, or $p = n - 2$ with $k = n - 1$ or n). Listed below are the numbers of outcomes for all the input sizes:

Input Size in First Recursive Call	Number of Outcomes That Yield the Given Size
0	n
1	2
2	2(2)
3	2(3)
⋮	⋮
i	2(i)
⋮	⋮
$n - 1$	2($n - 1$)

It is not hard to see that, for each of these input sizes, all allowable values of k appear with equal frequency. Recall from the every-case analysis of Algorithm 2.7 that the number of comparisons in procedure *partition* is $n - 1$. Therefore, the average is given by the following recurrence:

$$A(n) = \frac{nA(0) + 2[A(1) + 2A(2) + \cdots + iA(i) + \cdots + (n-1)A(n-1)]}{n + 2(1 + 2 + \cdots + i + \cdots + n - 1)} + n - 1.$$

Using the result in Example A.1 in Appendix A and the fact that $A(0) = 0$, and simplifying, we have

$$A(n) = \frac{2[A(1) + 2A(2) + \cdots + iA(i) + \cdots + (n-1)A(n-1)]}{n^2} + n - 1.$$

Next we mimic the technique used in the average-case time complexity analysis of Algorithm 2.6 (Quicksort). That is, we multiply the expression for $A(n)$ by n^2, apply the expression to $n - 1$, subtract the expression for $n - 1$ from the one for n, and simplify to obtain

$$A(n) = \frac{n^2 - 1}{n^2} A(n-1) + \frac{(n-1)(3n-2)}{n^2}$$

$$< A(n-1) + 3.$$

Because $A(0) = 0$, we have the following recurrence:

$$\boxed{\begin{array}{ll} A(n) < A(n-1) + 3 & n > 0 \\ A(0) = 0 \end{array}}$$

This recurrence can be solved using induction, as described in Section B.1 in Appendix B. The solution is

$$A(n) < 3n.$$

In the same way, we can use the recurrence to show that $A(n)$ is bounded below by a linear function. Therefore,

$$A(n) \in \Theta(n).$$

It is straightforward to use the recurrence for $A(n)$ to show that, for large values of n,

$$A(n) \approx 3n.$$

On the average, Algorithm 8.5 (Selection) does only a linear number of comparisons. Of course, the reason that this algorithm performs better on the average than Algorithm 2.6 (Quicksort) is that Quicksort has two calls to *partition,* whereas this algorithm has only one. However, they both degenerate into the same complexity when the input to the recursive call is $n - 1$. (In this case, Quicksort inputs an empty subarray on one side.) That time complexity is quadratic. If we could somehow prevent this from happening in Algorithm 8.5, we should be able to improve on worst-case quadratic time. Next we show how this is done.

The best thing would be if *pivotpoint* were to split the array in the middle, because then the input would be cut in half in each recursive call. Recall that the **median** of n distinct keys is the key such that half the keys are smaller and half are larger. (This is precise only if n is odd.) If we could always choose the median for *pivotitem,* we would have optimal performance. But how can we determine the median? In procedure *partition,* we could try calling function *selection* with

Figure 8.12 Each bar represents a key. We do not know if the boldfaced keys are less than or greater than the median of the medians.

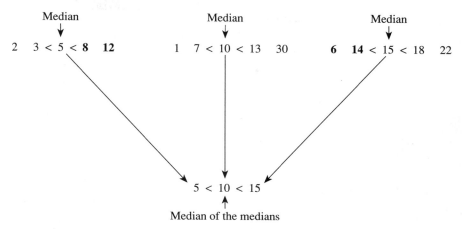

an input consisting of the original array and k equal to about half the size of that array. As just stated, this will not work, because we end up back in *selection* with an instance of the same size as our original instance. However, the following maneuver does work. Assume for the moment that n is an odd multiple of 5. (We need not use 5; this is discussed at the end of the section.) We divide the n keys into $n/5$ groups of keys, each containing five keys. We find the median of each of these groups directly. As you are asked to show in the exercises, this can be done with six comparisons. We then call function *selection* to determine the median of the $n/5$ medians. The median of the medians is not necessarily the median of the n keys, but, as Figure 8.12 shows, it is reasonably close. In that figure, the keys to the left of the smallest median (keys 2 and 3) must be less than the median of the medians, and the keys to the right of the largest median (keys 18 and 22) must be greater than the median of the medians. In general, the keys to the right of the smallest median (keys 8 and 12) and the keys to the left of the largest median (keys 6 and 14) could lie on either side of the median of medians. Notice that there are

$$2\left(\frac{15}{5} - 1\right)$$

keys that could be on either side of the median of the medians. It is not hard to see that, whenever n is an odd multiple of 5, there are

$$2\left(\frac{n}{5} - 1\right)$$

keys that could lie on either side of the median of the medians. Therefore, there are at most

$$\underbrace{\frac{1}{2}\left[n - 1 - 2\left(\frac{n}{5} - 1\right)\right]}_{\substack{\text{Number of keys we} \\ \text{know are on one side}}} + 2\left(\frac{n}{5} - 1\right) = \frac{7n}{10} - \frac{3}{2}$$

keys on one side of the median of the medians. We return to this result when we analyze the algorithm that uses this strategy. First we present the algorithm.

Algorithm 8.6   Selection Using the Median

Problem: Find the kth-smallest key in an array S of n distinct keys.

Inputs: positive integers n and k where $k \leq n$, array of distinct keys S indexed from 1 to n.

Outputs: the kth-smallest key in S. It is returned as the value of function *select*.

```
keytype select (int n,
                keytype S[ ],
                index k)
{
   return selection2(S, 1, n, k);
}


keytype selection2 (keytype S[ ],
                    index low, index high, index k)
{
   if (high == low)
      return S[low];
   else {
      partition2(S, low, high, pivotpoint);
      if (k == pivotpoint)
         return S[pivotpoint];
      else if (k < pivotpoint)
         return selection2(S, low, pivotpoint − 1, k);
      else
         return selection2(S, pivotpoint + 1, high, k);
   }
}
```

```
void partition2 (keytype S[ ],
                  index low, index high,
                  index& pivotpoint)
{
   const arraysize = high − low + 1;
   const r = ⌈arraysize / 5⌉;
   index i, j, mark, first, last;
   keytype pivotitem, T[1..r];

   for (i = 1; i <= r; i++) {
      first = low + 5*i − 5;
      last = minimum(low + 5*i − 1, arraysize);
      T[i] = median of S[first] through S[last];
   }
   pivotitem = select(r, T, ⌊(r + 1) / 2⌋);        // Approximate the medium.
   j = low;
   for (i = low; i <= high; i++)
      if (S[i] == pivotitem) {
         exchange S[i] and S[j];
         mark = j;                                  // Mark where pivotitem
         j++;                                       // placed.
      }
      else if (S[i] < pivotitem) {
         exchange S[i] and S[j];
         j++;
      }
   pivotpoint = j − 1;
   exchange S[mark] and S[pivotpoint];              // Put pivotitem at pivotpoint.
}
```

In Algorithm 8.6, unlike our other recursive algorithms, we show a simple function that calls our recursive function. The reason is that this simple function needs to be called in two places with different inputs. That is, it is called in procedure *partition2* with *T* being the input, and globally as follows:

kthsmallest = *select(n, S, k)*.

We also made the array an input to the recursive function *selection2* because the function is called to process both the global array *S* and the local array *T*.

Next we analyze the algorithm.

Worst-Case Time Complexity Analysis of Algorithm 8.6
(*Selection Using the Median*)

Basic operation: the comparison of $S[i]$ with pivotitem in *partition2*.

Input size: n, the number of items in the array.

For simplicity, we develop a recurrence assuming that n is an odd multiple of 5. The recurrence approximately holds for n in general. The components in the recurrence are as follows.

- The time in function *selection2* when called from function *selection2*. As already discussed, if n is an odd multiple of 5, at most

$$\frac{7n}{10} - \frac{3}{2} \text{ keys}$$

  end up on one side of *pivotpoint*, which means that this is the worst-case number of keys in the input to this call to *selection2*.

- The time in function *selection2* when called from procedure *partition2*. The number of keys in the input to this call to *selection2* is $n/5$.

- The number of comparisons required to find the medians. As mentioned previously, the median of five numbers can be found by making six comparisons. When n is a multiple of 5, the algorithm finds the median of exactly $n/5$ groups of five numbers. Therefore, the total number of comparisons required to find the medians is $6n/5$.

- The number of comparisons required to partition the array. This number is n (assuming an efficient implementation of the comparison).

We have established the following recurrence:

$$W(n) = W\left(\frac{7n}{10} - \frac{3}{2}\right) + W\left(\frac{n}{5}\right) + \frac{6n}{5} + n$$

$$\approx W\left(\frac{7n}{10}\right) + W\left(\frac{n}{5}\right) + \frac{11n}{5}.$$

It is possible to show that the approximate equality holds even when n is not an odd multiple of 5. Of course, $W(n)$ does not really have nonintegral inputs. However, considering such inputs simplifies our analysis. The recurrence does not suggest any obvious solution that can be used in an induction argument. Furthermore, it is not solvable by any of the other techniques in Appendix B. However, we can use a technique called **constructive induction** to obtain a candidate solution that can be used in an induction argument. That is, because we suspect that $W(n)$ is linear, let's assume that $W(m) \leq cm$ for all $m < n$ and for some constant c. Then the recurrence implies that

$$W(n) \approx W\left(\frac{7n}{10}\right) + W\left(\frac{n}{5}\right) + \frac{11n}{5} \leq c\frac{7n}{10} + c\frac{n}{5} + \frac{11n}{5}.$$

Because we want to be able to conclude that $W(n) \leq cn$, we need to solve

$$c\frac{7n}{10} + c\frac{n}{5} + \frac{11n}{5} \leq cn$$

to determine a value of c that would work in an induction argument. The solution is

$$22 \leq c.$$

We then choose the smallest value of c that satisfies the inequality and proceed forward with a formal induction argument to show that when n is not small, the worst-case time complexity is approximately bound as follows:

$$W(n) \leq 22n.$$

Clearly, the inequality holds for $n \leq 5$. It is left as an exercise to complete the induction argument. Theorem 8.7 says that linear time is required just to solve the case where $k = 1$. We can conclude that

$$W(n) \in \Theta(n).$$

We have successfully solved the Selection Problem with an algorithm that is linear-time in the worst case. As mentioned previously, we did not have to divide the array into groups of size 5 to do this. If m is the group size, any odd value of $m \geq 5$ yields a linear-time complexity. We now present the reason. Establishing the results we state is left as exercises. For an arbitrary m, the recurrence for the worst-case time complexity is given by

$$W(n) \approx W\left(\frac{(3m - 1)n}{4m}\right) + W\left(\frac{n}{m}\right) + an, \tag{8.2}$$

where a is a positive constant. The sum of the coefficients of n in the expressions on the right is

$$\frac{3m - 1}{4m} + \frac{1}{m} = \frac{3m + 3}{4m}.$$

It is straightforward that the expression on the right is less than 1 if and only if $m > 3$. It is possible to show that the recurrence

$$W(n) = W(pn) + W(qn) + an$$

describes a linear equation if $p + q < 1$. Therefore, Recurrence 8.2 describes a linear equation for all $m \geq 5$.

When $m = 3$, Recurrence 8.2 is as follows:

$$W(n) \approx W\left(\frac{2n}{3}\right) + W\left(\frac{n}{3}\right) + \frac{5n}{3}.$$

Using induction, it is possible to show that for this recurrence

$$W(n) \in \Omega(n \lg n).$$

Therefore, 5 is the smallest odd value of n that yields linear performance.

When $m = 7, 9$, or 11, the upper bound c on the time complexity is slightly smaller than when $m = 5$. The value of c increases very slowly as m increases beyond 11. For m not small, it is possible to show that c is approximated by $4 \lg m$. For example, if $m = 100$, the constant is about $4 \lg 100 = 26.6$.

Our linear-time algorithm for the Selection Problem is from Blum, Floyd, Pratt, Rivest, and Tarjan (1973). The original version is more complex, but its number of comparisons of keys is only about $5.5n$.

Hyafil (1976) has shown that a lower bound for finding the kth-smallest key in a set of n keys for $k > 1$ is given by

$$n + (k - 1)\left\lceil \lg\left(\frac{n}{k - 1}\right) \right\rceil - k.$$

The proof can also be found in Horowitz and Sahni (1978). Notice that Theorem 8.9 is a special case of this result.

Other selection algorithms and lower bounds can be found in Schonhage, Paterson, and Pippenger (1976) and in Fussenegger and Gabow (1976).

8.5.5 A Probabilistic Algorithm for the Selection Problem

In obtaining lower bounds for algorithms, we have assumed the algorithms to be deterministic, but we mentioned that those bounds also hold for probabilistic algorithms. We close this discussion by presenting a probabilistic algorithm for the Selection Problem to illustrate when such an algorithm is useful.

Section 5.3 presented a probabilistic algorithm—namely, a Monte Carlo algorithm for approximating the efficiency of a backtracking algorithm. Recall that a Monte Carlo algorithm does not necessarily give the correct answer. Rather, it provides an estimate of that answer, and the probability that the estimate is close to the correct answer increases as the time available to the algorithm increases. Here we show a different kind of probabilistic algorithm, called a Sherwood algorithm.

A *Sherwood algorithm* always gives the correct answer. Such an algorithm is useful when some deterministic algorithm runs much faster on the average than it does in the worst case. Recall that this is true of Algorithm 8.5 (Selection). The worst-case quadratic time is achieved in that algorithm when the *pivotpoint* for a particular input is repeatedly close to *low* or *high* in the recursive calls. This happens, for example, when the array is sorted in increasing order and $k = n$. Because this is not the case for most inputs, the algorithm's average performance is linear. Suppose that, for a particular input, we choose the pivot item at random according to a uniform distribution. Then, when the algorithm is run for that input, the *pivotpoint* is more likely to be away from the endpoints than close to them. (Randomness is reviewed in Section A.8 in Appendix A.) Therefore, linear performance is more likely. Because the number of comparisons is linear when averaged over all inputs, intuitively it seems that the ***expected value*** of the number of comparisons of keys done for a particular input should be linear when the pivot item is chosen at random according to a uniform distribution. We prove that this is the case, but first we stress the difference between this expected value and the average value obtained for Algorithm 8.5. Assuming that all possible inputs are presented in equal numbers, the average number of comparisons done by Algorithm 8.5 is linear. For any given input, Algorithm 8.5 always does the same number of comparisons, which is quadratic for some inputs. The Sherwood algorithm we are about to present does not do the same number of comparisons each time it executes on a given input. For any given input, it sometimes does a linear number of comparisons and sometimes does a quadratic number. However, if the algorithm is run many times using the same input, we can expect the average of the running times to be linear.

You may ask why we would want to use such an algorithm when Algorithm 8.6 (Selection Using the Median) guarantees linear performance. The reason is that Algorithm 8.6 has a high constant because of the overhead needed for approximating the median. For a given input, our Sherwood algorithm runs faster on the average than Algorithm 8.6. The decision of whether to use Algorithm 8.6 or the Sherwood algorithm depends on the needs of the particular application. If better average performance is most important, we should use the Sherwood algorithm. If, on the other hand, quadratic performance can never be tolerated, we should use Algorithm 8.6. We stress again the advantage of the Sherwood algorithm over Algorithm 8.5 (Selection). As long as the inputs are uniformly distributed, Algorithm 8.5 also performs better on the average than Algorithm 8.6. However, in some particular application, the inputs may always be ones that approach the worst case in Algorithm 8.5. In such an application, Algorithm 8.5 always exhibits quadratic-time performance. The Sherwood algorithm avoids this difficulty in any application by choosing the pivot item at random according to a uniform distribution.

Next we present the probabilistic (Sherwood) algorithm.

Algorithm 8.7

Probabilistic Selection

Problem: Find the kth-smallest key in array S of n distinct keys.

Inputs: positive integers n and k where $k \leq n$, array of distinct keys S indexed from 1 to n.

Outputs: the kth-smallest key in S. It is returned as the value of function *selection3*.

```
keytype selection3 (index low, index high, index k)
{
   if (low == high)
      return S[low];
   else {
      partition3(low, high, pivotpoint);
      if (k == pivotpoint)
         return S[pivotpoint];
      else if (k < pivotpoint)
         return selection3(low, pivotpoint − 1, k);
      else
         return selection3(pivotpoint + 1, high, k);
   }
}


void partition3 (index low, index high,
                 index& pivotpoint)
{
   index i, j, randspot;
   keytype pivotitem;

   randspot = random index between low and high inclusive;
   pivotitem = S[randspot];                    // Randomly choose pivotitem.
   j = low;
   for (i = low + 1; i <= high; i++)
      if (S[i] < pivotitem) {
         j++;
         exchange S[i] and S[j];
      }
   pivotpoint = j;
   exchange S[low] and S[pivotpoint];          // Put pivotitem at pivotpoint.
}
```

Algorithm 8.7 differs from Algorithm 8.5 only in its random choice of the pivot item. Next we prove that the expected value of the number of comparisons is linear for any input. This analysis must be different from the average-case analysis of Algorithm 8.5 (Selection), because in that analysis we assumed that all values of k are entered with equal frequency. We want to obtain a linear-time expected value for each input. Because each input has a specific value of k, we can't assume that all values of k occur with equal frequency. We show that, independent of k, the expected value is linear.

Expected-Value Time Complexity Analysis of Algorithm 8.7
(*Probabilistic Selection*)

Basic operation: the comparison of $S[i]$ with *pivotitem* in *partition*.

Input size: n, the number of items in the array.

Given that we are looking for the kth-smallest key in an input of size n, the following table shows the size of the input and the new value of k in the first recursive call for each value of *pivotpoint*.

pivotpoint	Input Size	New Value of k
1	$n - 1$	$k - 1$
2	$n - 2$	$k - 2$
⋮	⋮	⋮
$k - 1$	$n - (k - 1)$	1
k	0	
$k + 1$	k	k
$k + 2$	$k + 1$	k
⋮	⋮	⋮
n	$n - 1$	k

Because all values of *pivotpoint* are equally likely, we have the following recurrence for the expected value:

$$E(n, k) = \frac{1}{n} \left[\sum_{p=1}^{k-1} E(n - p, k - p) + \sum_{p=k}^{n-1} E(p, k) \right] + n - 1.$$

We can analyze this recurrence using constructive induction as we did in the worst-case analysis of Algorithm 8.6. That is, because we suspect that the recurrence is linear, we look for a value of c such that an induction argument should prove $E(n, k) \leq cn$. This time, we show the induction argument, but we leave as an exercise the determination that $c = 4$ is the smallest constant that would work.

Induction base: Because no comparisons are done for $n = 1$,

$$E(1, k) = 0 \leq 4(1).$$

Induction hypothesis: Suppose that, for all $m < n$ and all $k \leq m$,

$$E(m, k) \leq 4m.$$

Induction step: We need to show that, for all $k \leq n$,

$$E(n, k) \leq 4n.$$

By the recurrence and the induction hypothesis,

$$E(n, k) \leq \frac{1}{n} \left[\sum_{p=1}^{k-1} 4(n - p) + \sum_{p=k}^{n-1} 4p \right] + n - 1. \qquad (8.3)$$

We have that

$$\sum_{p=1}^{k-1} 4(n - p) + \sum_{p=k}^{n-1} 4p = 4 \left[\sum_{p=1}^{k-1} n - \sum_{p=1}^{k-1} p + \sum_{p=k}^{n-1} p \right]$$

$$= 4 \left[(k - 1)n - \sum_{p=1}^{k-1} p + \sum_{p=1}^{n-1} p \right]$$

$$= 4 \left[(k - 1)n - (k - 1)k + \frac{(n - 1)n}{2} \right]$$

$$= 4 \left[(k - 1)(n - k) + \frac{(n - 1)n}{2} \right]$$

$$< 4 \left[k(n - k) + \frac{n}{2} \right] \leq 4 \left[\frac{n^2}{4} + \frac{n^2}{2} \right] = 3n^2.$$

The third equality is obtained by twice applying the result of Example A.1 in Appendix A. The last inequality derives from the fact that, in general, $k(n - k) \leq n^2/4$. Plugging the result just obtained into Inequality 8.3, we have

$$E(n, k) < \frac{1}{n} (3n^2) + n - 1 = 3n + n - 1 < 4n.$$

We have shown that, independent of the value of k,

$$E(n, k) \leq 4n \in \Theta(n).$$

Exercises

Section 8.1

1. Let us assume that a search does not start at the beginning of a list when the Sequential Search algorithm (Algorithm 1.1) is used, but rather starts wherever the list index was left at the termination of the preceding search. Let us further assume that the item for which we are searching is selected randomly and independently of the destinations of previous searches. Under these assumptions, what would be the average number of comparisons?

2. Let S and T be two arrays of m and n elements, respectively. Write an algorithm that finds all the common elements and stores them in an array U. Show that this can be done in $\Theta(n + m)$ time.

3. Improve the Binary Search algorithm (Algorithm 1.5) assuming a successful search. Analyze your algorithm, and show the results using order notation.

4. Show that, if x is in the array and is equally probable to be in each of the array slots, the average-case time complexity for Binary Search (Algorithm 1.5) is bounded approximately by

$$\lfloor \lg n \rfloor - 1 \leq A(n) \leq \lfloor \lg n \rfloor.$$

Hint: By Lemma 8.4, for some k, $n - (2^k - 1)$ is the number of nodes at the bottom level. The contribution to the *TND* for these nodes is equal to $(n - 2^k - 1)(k + 1)$. Add this expression to $(k - 1)2^k + 1$ (the formula established in the average-case analysis of Binary Search) to obtain the *TND* for the decision tree.

5. Suppose that all of the following $2n + 1$ possibilities are equally probable:

$$x = s_i \qquad \text{for some } i \text{ such that } 1 \leq i \leq n,$$
$$x < s_1,$$
$$s_i < x < s_{i+1} \qquad \text{for some } i \text{ such that } 1 \leq i \leq n - 1,$$
$$x > s_n.$$

Show that the average-case time complexity of the Binary Search algorithm (Algorithm 1.5) is bounded approximately by

$$\lfloor \lg n \rfloor - \frac{1}{2} \leq A(n) \leq \lfloor \lg n \rfloor + \frac{1}{2}.$$

Hint: See the hint for Exercise 4.

6. Complete the proof of Lemma 8.6.

Section 8.2

7. Implement the Binary Search, Interpolation Search, and Robust Interpolation Search algorithms on your system, and study their best-case, average-case, and worst-case performances using several problem instances.

8. Show that the average-case time complexity of Interpolation Search is in $\Theta(\lg(\lg n))$, assuming the keys are uniformly distributed and that search key x is equally probable to be in each of the array slots.

9. Show that the worst-case time complexity of Interpolation Search is in $\Theta(\lg n)^2$, assuming the keys are uniformly distributed and that search key x is equally probable to be in each of the array slots.

Section 8.3

10. Write an algorithm that finds the largest key in a binary search tree. Analyze your algorithm, and show the results using order notation.

11. Theorem 8.3 states that, for a successful search, the average search time over all inputs containing n keys, using binary search trees, is in $\Theta(\lg n)$. Show that this result still holds if we consider an unsuccessful search as well.

12. Write an algorithm that deletes a node from a binary search tree considering all possible cases. Analyze your algorithm, and show the results using order notation.

13. Write an algorithm that creates a 3–2 tree from a list of keys. Analyze your algorithm, and show the results using order notation.

14. Write an algorithm that lists all the keys in a 3–2 tree in their natural order. Analyze your algorithm, and show the results using order notation.

Section 8.4

15. Another clash (collision) resolution strategy is linear probing. In this strategy, all the elements are stored in the array of buckets (hash table). In the case of a clash, the table is searched for the next available (free) bucket. Show how linear probing resolves clashes that occur in the problem instance of Figure 8.8. Linear probing is also known as closed hashing.

16. Discuss the advantages and disadvantages of the two clash resolution strategies open hashing and linear probing (see Exercise 15).

17. Write an algorithm to delete an element from a hash table that uses linear probing as its clash resolution strategy. Analyze your algorithm, and show the results using order notation.

18. A rehashing scheme known as double hashing uses a second hash function in case of a clash. If the first hash function is h and the second hash function is s, the entire sequence of positions of the hash table that will be checked for an available bucket is given by the following equality, where p_i is the ith position in the sequence.

$$p_i(\text{key}) = [(h(\text{key}) + i \times s(\text{key}) - 1) \% \text{ table\_size}] + 1$$

(% returns the remainder when the first operand is divided by the second.) Define a second hash function for the problem instance of Figure 8.8, and show the table after all the keys have been inserted into the hash table.

Section 8.5

19. Modify Algorithm 8.4 (Find Smallest and Largest Keys by Pairing Keys) so that it works when n (the number of keys in the given array) is odd, and show that its time complexity is given by

$$\frac{3n}{2} - 2 \qquad \text{if } n \text{ is even}$$

$$\frac{3n}{2} - \frac{3}{2} \qquad \text{if } n \text{ is odd.}$$

20. Complete the proof of Theorem 8.8. That is, show that a deterministic algorithm that finds the smallest and largest of n keys only by comparisons of keys must in the worst case do at least $(3n - 3)/2$ comparisons if n is odd.

21. Write an algorithm for the method discussed in Section 8.5.3 for finding the second-largest key in a given array.

22. Show that for n in general, the total number of comparisons needed by the method discussed in Section 8.5.3 for finding the second-largest key in a given array is

$$T(n) = n + \lceil \lg n \rceil - 2.$$

23. Show that the median of five numbers can be found by making six comparisons.

24. Use induction to show that the worst-case time complexity of Algorithm 8.6 (Selection Using the Median) is bounded approximately as follows:

$$W(n) \leq 22n.$$

25. Show that for an arbitrary m (group size), the recurrence for the worst-case time complexity of Algorithm 8.6 (Selection Using the Median) is given by

$$W(n) \approx W\left(\frac{(3m - 1)n}{4}\right) + W\left(\frac{n}{m}\right) + an,$$

where a is a constant. This is Recurrence 8.2 in Section 8.5.4.

26. Use induction to show that $W(n) \in \Omega(n \lg n)$ for the following recurrence. This is Recurrence 8.2 in Section 8.5.4 where m (group size) is 3.

$$W(n) = W\left(\frac{2n}{3}\right) + W\left(\frac{n}{3}\right) + \frac{5n}{3}$$

27. Show that the constant c in the inequality

$$E(n, k) \leq cn$$

in the expected-value time complexity analysis of Algorithm 8.7 (Probabilistic Selection) cannot be less than 4.

28. Implement Algorithms 8.5, 8.6, and 8.7 (selection algorithms for finding the kth-smallest key in an array) on your system, and study their best-case, average-case, and worst-case performances using several problem instances.

29. Write a probabilistic algorithm that determines whether an array of n elements has a majority element (the element that appears the most). Analyze your algorithm, and show the results using order notation.

Additional Problems

30. Suppose a very large sorted list is stored in external storage. Assuming that this list cannot be brought into internal memory, develop a searching algorithm that looks for a key in this list. What major factor(s) should be considered when an external search algorithm is developed? Define the major factor(s), analyze your algorithm, and show the results using order notation.

31. Discuss the advantages of using each of the following instead of the other:
    (a) A binary search tree with a balancing mechanism
    (b) A 3–2 tree

32. Give at least two examples of situations in which hashing is not appropriate.

33. Let S and T be two arrays of n numbers that are already in nondecreasing order. Write an algorithm that finds the median of all $2n$ numbers whose time complexity is in $\Theta(\lg n)$.

34. Write a probabilistic algorithm that factorizes any integer using the functions *prime* and *factor*. Function *prime* is a boolean function that returns "true" if a given integer is a prime number and returns "false" if it is not. Function *factor* is a function that returns a nontrivial factor of a given composite integer. Analyze your algorithm, and show the results using order notation.

35. List the advantages and disadvantages of all the searching algorithms discussed in this chapter.

36. For each of the searching algorithms discussed in this chapter, give at least two examples of situations in which the algorithm is the most appropriate.

CHAPTER 9

Computational Complexity and Intractability: An Introduction to the Theory of NP

*C*onsider the following scenario based on a story in Garey and Johnson (1979). Suppose you work in industry, and your boss gives you the task of finding an efficient algorithm for some problem very important to the company. After laboring long hours on the problem for over a month, you make no headway at all toward an efficient algorithm. Giving up, you return to your boss and ashamedly announce that you simply can't find an efficient algorithm. Your boss threatens to fire you and replace you with a smarter algorithm designer. You reply that perhaps it is not that you're stupid, but rather that an efficient algorithm is not possible. Reluctantly, your boss gives you another month to prove that this is the case. After a second month of burning the midnight oil trying to prove this, you are unsuccessful. At this point you've failed to obtain an efficient algorithm and you've failed to prove that such an algorithm is not possible. You are on the verge of being fired, when you recall that some of the greatest computer scientists have worked on creating an efficient algorithm for the Traveling Salesperson Problem, but nobody has ever developed one whose worst-case time complexity is better than exponential. Furthermore, no one has ever proven that such an algorithm is not possible. You see one last glimmer of hope. If you could prove that an efficient algorithm for the company's problem would automatically yield an efficient algorithm for the Traveling Salesperson Problem, it would mean that your boss is asking you to accomplish something that has eluded some of the greatest computer scientists. You ask for a chance to prove this, and your boss reluctantly agrees. After only a week of effort, you do indeed prove that an efficient algorithm for the company's problem would automatically yield an efficient algorithm for the Traveling Salesperson Problem. Rather than being fired, you're given a promotion because you have saved the company a lot of money. Your boss now realizes that it would not be prudent to continue to expend great effort looking for an exact algorithm for the company's problem and that other avenues, such as looking for an approximate solution, should be explored.

What we have just described is exactly what computer scientists have successfully done for the last 25 years. We have shown that the Traveling Salesperson Problem and thousands of other problems are equally hard in the sense that if we had an efficient algorithm for any one of them, we would have efficient algorithms for all of them. Such an algorithm has never been found, but it's never been proven that one is not possible. These interesting problems are called "*NP*-complete" and are the focus of this chapter. A problem for which an efficient algorithm is not possible is said to be "intractable." In Section 9.1 we explain more concretely what it means for a problem to be intractable. Section 9.2 shows that when we are concerned with determining whether or not a problem is intractable, we must be careful about what we call the input size in an algorithm. Section 9.3 discusses three general categories in which problems can be grouped as far as intractability is concerned. The culmination of this chapter, Section 9.4, discusses the theory of *NP* and *NP*-complete problems. Section 9.5 shows ways of handling *NP*-complete problems.

9.1 INTRACTABILITY

The dictionary defines *intractable* as "difficult to treat or work." This means that a problem in computer science is intractable if a computer has difficulty solving it. This definition is too vague to be of much use to us. To make the notion more concrete, we now introduce the concept of a "polynomial-time algorithm."

Definition

A *polynomial-time algorithm* is one whose worst-case time complexity is bounded above by a polynomial function of its input size. That is, if n is the input size, there exists a polynomial $p(n)$ such that

$$W(n) \in O(p(n)).$$

Example 9.1

Algorithms with the following worst-case time complexities are all polynomial-time.

$$2n \qquad 3n^3 + 4n \qquad 5n + n^{10} \qquad n \lg n$$

Algorithms with the following worst-case time complexities are not polynomial-time.

$$2^n \qquad 2^{0.01n} \qquad 2^{\sqrt{n}} \qquad n!$$

Notice that $n \lg n$ is not a polynomial in n. However, because

$$n \lg n < n^2,$$

it is bounded by a polynomial in n, which means that an algorithm with this time complexity satisfies the criterion to be called a polynomial-time algorithm.

In computer science, a problem is called *intractable* if it is impossible to solve it with a polynomial-time algorithm. We stress that intractability is a property of a problem; it is not a property of any one algorithm for that problem. For a problem to be intractable, there must be no polynomial-time algorithm that solves it. Obtaining a nonpolynomial-time algorithm for a problem does not make it intractable. For example, the brute-force algorithm for the Chained Matrix Multiplication Problem (see Section 3.4) is nonpolynomial-time. So is the divide-and-conquer algorithm that uses the recursive property established in Section 3.4. However, the dynamic programming algorithm (Algorithm 3.6) developed in that section is $\Theta(n^3)$. The problem is not intractable, because we can solve it in polynomial time using Algorithm 3.5.

In Chapter 1 we saw that polynomial-time algorithms are usually much better than algorithms that are not polynomial-time. Looking again at Table 1.4, we see that if it takes 1 nanosecond to process the basic instructions, an algorithm with a time complexity of n^3 will process an instance of size 100 in 1 millisecond, whereas an algorithm with a time complexity of 2^n will take billions of years.

We can create extreme examples in which a nonpolynomial-time algorithm is better than a polynomial-time algorithm for practical input sizes. For example, if $n = 1,000,000$,

$$2^{(0.00001n)} = 1024 \qquad \text{whereas} \qquad n^{10} = 10^{60}.$$

Furthermore, many algorithms whose worst-case time complexities are not polynomials have efficient running times for many actual instances. This is the case

for many backtracking and branch-and-bound algorithms. Therefore, our definition of intractable is only a good indication or real intractability. In any particular
case, a problem for which we have found a polynomial-time algorithm could
possibly be more difficult to handle, as far as practical input sizes are concerned,
than one for which we cannot find such an algorithm.

There are three general categories of problems as far as intractability is
concerned:

1. Problems for which polynomial-time algorithms have been found
2. Problems that have been proven to be intractable
3. Problems that have not been proven to be intractable, but for which poly-
    nomial-time algorithms have never been found

It is a surprising phenomenon that most problems in computer science seem to
fall into either the first or third category.

When we are determining whether an algorithm is polynomial-time, it is
necessary to be careful about what we call the input size. Therefore, before proceeding, let's discuss the input size further (see Section 1.3 for our initial discussion of the input size).

9.2 INPUT SIZE REVISITED

So far it has usually sufficed to call n the input size in our algorithms because n
has been a reasonable measure of the amount of data in the input. For example,
in the case of sorting algorithms, n, the number of keys to be sorted, is a good
measure of the amount of data in the input. So we called n the input size. However,
we must not inadvertently call n the input size in an algorithm. Consider the
following algorithm, which determines whether a positive integer n is prime.

```
bool prime (int n)
{
    int i; bool switch;

    switch = true;
    i = 2;
    while (switch && i < n)
        if (n % i == 0)        // % returns the remainder when n is divided by i.
            switch = false;
        else
            i++;
    return switch;
}
```

The time complexity of this prime-checking algorithm is clearly in $\Theta(n)$.
However, is it a polynomial-time algorithm? The parameter n is the input to the

algorithm; it is not the size of the input. That is, each value of n constitutes an instance of the problem. This is unlike a sorting algorithm, for example, in which n is the number of keys and the instance is the n keys. If the value of n is the input and not the size of the input in function *prime,* what is the size of the input? We return to this question after we define input size more concretely than we did in Section 1.3.

Definition   For a given algorithm, the ***input size*** is defined as the number of characters it takes to write the input.

This definition is not different from that given in Section 1.3. It is only more specific about how we measure the size of the input. To count the characters it takes to write the input, we need to know how the input is encoded. Suppose that we encode it in binary, which is used inside computers. Then the characters used for the encoding are binary digits (bits), and the number of characters it takes to encode a positive integer x is $\lfloor \lg x \rfloor + 1$. For example, $31 = 11111_2$ and $\lfloor \lg 31 \rfloor + 1 = 5$. We simply say that it takes about $\lg x$ bits to encode a positive integer x in binary. Suppose that we use binary encoding, and we wish to determine the input size for an algorithm that sorts n positive integers. The integers to be sorted are the inputs to the algorithm. Therefore, the input size is the count of the number of bits it takes to encode them. If the largest integer is L, and we encode each integer in the number of bits needed to encode the largest, then it takes about $\lg L$ bits to encode each of them. The input size for the n integers is therefore about $n \lg L$. Suppose that instead we choose to encode the integers in base 10. Then the characters used for the encoding are decimal digits, it takes about $\log L$ characters to encode the largest, and the input size for the n integers is about $n \log L$. Because

$$n \log L = (\log 2) \, (n \lg L),$$

an algorithm is polynomial-time in terms of one of these input sizes if and only if it is polynomial-time in terms of the other.

If we restrict ourselves to "reasonable" encoding schemes, then the particular encoding scheme used does not affect the determination of whether an algorithm is polynomial-time. There does not seem to be a satisfactory formal definition of "reasonable." However, for most algorithms we usually agree on what is reasonable. For example, for any algorithm in this text, any base other than 1 could be used to encode an integer without affecting whether or not the algorithm is polynomial-time. We would therefore consider any such encoding system to be reasonable. Encoding in base 1, which is called the unary form, would not be considered reasonable.

In the preceding chapters, we simply called $n,$ the number of keys to be sorted, the input size in our sorting algorithms. Using n as the input size, we showed that the algorithms are polynomial-time. Do they remain polynomial-time when we are precise about the input size? Next we illustrate that they do. When we are being precise about input size, we also need to be more precise (than we were in Section 1.3.1) about the definition of worst-case time complexity. The precise definition follows.

Definition   For a given algorithm, $W(s)$ is defined as the maximum number of steps done by the algorithm for an input size of s. $W(s)$ is called the ***worst-case time complexity*** of the algorithm.

A ***step*** can be considered the equivalent of one machine comparison or assignment, or, to keep the analysis machine-independent, one bit comparison or assignment. This definition is not different from that given in Section 1.3. It is only more specific about the basic operation. That is, according to this definition, each step constitutes one execution of the basic operation. We used s instead of n for the input size because (1) the parameter n to our algorithms is not always a measure of the input size (e.g., in the prime-checking algorithm presented at the start of this section) and (2) when n is a measure of the input size, it is not ordinarily a precise measure of it. According to the definition just given, we must count all the steps done by the algorithm. Let's illustrate how we can do this, while still avoiding the details of the implementation, by analyzing Algorithm 1.3 (Exchange Sort). For simplicity, assume that the keys are positive integers and that there are no other fields in the records. Look again at Algorithm 1.3. The number of steps done to increment loops and do branching is bounded by a constant c times n^2. If the integers are sufficiently large, they cannot be compared or assigned in one step by the computer. We saw a similar situation when we discussed large integer arithmetic in Section 2.6. Therefore, we should not consider one key comparison or assignment as one step. To keep our analysis machine-independent, we consider one step to be either one bit comparison or one bit assignment. Therefore, if L is the largest integer, it takes at most $\lg L$ steps to compare one integer or to assign one integer. When we analyzed Algorithm 1.3 in Sections 1.3 and 7.2, we saw that in the worst-case Exchange Sort does $n(n - 1)2$ comparisons of keys and $3n(n - 1)/2$ assignments to sort n positive integers. Therefore, the maximum number of steps done by Exchange Sort is no greater than

$$cn^2 + \underbrace{\frac{n(n - 1)}{2} \lg L}_{\text{Bit comparisons}} + \underbrace{\frac{3n(n - 1)}{2} \lg L}_{\text{Bit assignments}}.$$

Let's use $s = n \lg L$ as the input size. Then

$$W(s) = W(n \lg L) \qquad \{\text{substituting } n \lg L \text{ for } s\}$$

$$\leq cn^2 + \frac{n(n - 1)}{2} \lg L + \frac{3n(n - 1)}{2} \lg L$$

$$< cn^2(\lg L)^2 + n^2(\lg L)^2 + 3n^2(\lg L)^2$$

$$< (c + 4)(n \lg L)^2 = (c + 4)s^2.$$

We have shown that Exchange Sort remains polynomial-time when we are precise about the input size. We can obtain similar results for all the algorithms, which we've shown to be polynomial-time using imprecise input sizes. Furthermore, we can show that the algorithms, which we've shown to be nonpolynomial-time (e.g., Algorithm 3.11), remain nonpolynomial-time when we are precise about the input size. We see that when n is a measure of the amount of data in the input, we obtain correct results concerning whether an algorithm is polynomial-time by simply using n as the input size. Therefore, when this is the case, we continue to use n as the input size.

We return now to the prime-checking algorithm. Because the input to the algorithm is the value of n, the input size is the number of characters it takes to encode n. Recall that if we are using base 10 encoding, it takes $\lfloor \log n \rfloor + 1$ characters to encode n. For example, if the number is 340, it takes 3 decimal digits, not 340, to encode it. In general, if we are using base 10 encoding, and if we set

$$s = \log n,$$

then s is approximately the size of the input. In the worst-case, there are $n - 2$ passes through the loop in the function *prime*. Because $n = 10^s$, the worst-case number of passes through the loop is about 10^s. Because the total number of steps is at least equal to the number of passes through the loop, the time complexity is nonpolynomial. If we use binary encoding, it takes about $\lg n$ characters to encode n. Therefore, if we use binary encoding,

$$r = \lg n$$

is about equal to the input size, and the number of passes through the loop is about equal to 2^r. The time complexity is still nonpolynomial. The result remains unchanged as long as we use a ''reasonable'' encoding scheme. We mentioned previously that we would not consider unary encoding ''reasonable.'' If we used that encoding scheme, it would take n characters to encode the number n. For example, the number 7 would be encoded as 1111111. Using this encoding, the prime-checking algorithm has a linear time complexity. So we see that our results do change if we stray from a ''reasonable'' encoding system.

In algorithms such as the prime-checking algorithm, we call n a ***magnitude*** in the input. We've seen other algorithms whose time complexities are polynomials in terms of magnitude(s) but are not polynomials in terms of size. The time complexity of Algorithm 1.7 for computing the nth Fibonacci term is in $\Theta(n)$. Because n is a magnitude in the input and $\lg n$ measures the size of the input, the time complexity of Algorithm 1.7 is linear in terms of magnitudes but exponential in terms of size. The time complexity of Algorithm 3.2 for computing the binomial coefficient is in $\Theta(n^2)$. Because n is a magnitude in the input and $\lg n$ measures the size of the input, the time complexity of Algorithm 3.2 is quadratic in terms of magnitudes but exponential in terms of size. The time complexity of the dynamic programming algorithm for the 0-1 Knapsack Problem discussed in Section 4.4.4 is in $\Theta(nW)$. In this algorithm, n is a measure of size because it is the number of items in the input. However, W is a magnitude because it is the maximum capacity of the knapsack; $\lg W$ measures the size of W. This algorithm's time complexity is polynomial in terms of magnitudes and size, but it is exponential in terms of size alone.

An algorithm whose worse-case time complexity is bounded above by a polynomial function of its size and magnitudes is called ***pseudopolynomial-time.*** Such an algorithm can often be quite useful because it is inefficient only when confronted with instances containing extremely large numbers. Such instances might not pertain to the application of interest. For example, in the 0-1 Knapsack Problem, we might often be interested in cases where W is not extremely large.

9.3 THE THREE GENERAL CATEGORIES OF PROBLEMS

Next we discuss the three general categories in which problems can be grouped as far as intractability is concerned.

9.3.1 Problems for Which Polynomial-Time Algorithms Have Been Found

Any problem for which we have found a polynomial-time algorithm falls in this first category. We have found $\Theta(n \lg n)$ algorithms for sorting, a $\Theta(\lg n)$ algorithm for searching a sorted array, a $\Theta(n^{2.38})$ algorithm for matrix multiplication, a $\Theta(n^3)$ algorithm for chained matrix multiplication, etc. Because n is a measure of the amounts of data in the inputs to these algorithms, they are all polynomial-time. The list goes on and on. There are algorithms that are not polynomial-time for many of these problems. We've already mentioned that this is the case for the Chained Matrix Multiplication algorithm. Other problems for which we have developed polynomial-time algorithms, but for which the obvious brute-force algorithms are nonpolynomial, include the Shortest Paths Problem, the Optimal Binary Search Tree Problem, and the Minimum Spanning Tree Problem.

9.3.2 Problems That Have Been Proven to Be Intractable

There are two types of problems in this category. The first type is problems that require a nonpolynomial amount of output. Recall from Section 5.6 the problem of determining all Hamiltonian Circuits. If there was an edge from every vertex to every other vertex, there would be $(n - 1)!$ such circuits. To solve the problem, an algorithm would have to output all of these circuits, which means that our request is not reasonable. We noted in Chapter 5 that we were stating the problems so as to ask for all solutions because we could then present less-cluttered algorithms, but that each algorithm could easily be modified to solve the problem that asks for only one solution. The Hamiltonian Circuits Problem that asks for only one circuit clearly is not a problem of this type. Although it is important to recognize this type of intractability, problems such as these ordinarily pose no difficulty. It is usually straightforward to recognize that a nonpolynomial amount of output is being requested, and once we recognize this, we realize that we are simply asking for more information than we could possibly use. That is, the problem is not defined realistically.

The second type of intractability occurs when our requests are reasonable (that is, when we are not asking for a nonpolynomial amount of output) and we can prove that the problem cannot be solved in polynomial time. Oddly enough, we have found relatively few such problems. The first ones were undecidable problems. These problems are called ''undecidable'' because it can be proven that algorithms that solve them cannot exist. The most well-known of these is the Halting Problem. In this problem we take as input any algorithm and any input to that algorithm, and decide whether or not the algorithm will halt when applied to that input. In 1936, Alan Turing showed that this problem is undecidable. In 1953, A. Grzegorczyk developed a decidable problem that is intractable. Similar results are discussed in Hartmanis and Stearns (1965). However, these problems were ''artificially'' constructed to have certain properties. In the early 1970s, some natural decidable decision problems were proven to be intractable. The output for a decision problem is a simple ''yes'' or ''no'' answer. Therefore, the amount of output requested is certainly reasonable. One of the most well-known of these problems is Presburger Arithmetic, which was proven intractable by Fischer and Rabin in 1974. This problem, along with the proof of intractability, can be found in Hopcroft and Ullman (1979).

All problems that to this date have been proven intractable have also been proven not to be in the set *NP*, which is discussed in Section 9.4. However, most problems that *appear* to be intractable are in the set *NP*. We discuss these problems next. As noted earlier, it is a somewhat surprising phenomenon that relatively few problems have been proven to be intractable, and it was not until the early 1970s that a natural decidable problem was proven intractable.

9.3.3 Problems That Have Not Been Proven to Be Intractable but for Which Polynomial-Time Algorithms Have Never Been Found

This category includes any problem for which a polynomial-time algorithm has never been found but yet no one has ever proven that such an algorithm is not possible. As already discussed, there are many such problems. For example, if we state the problems so as to require one solution, the 0-1 Knapsack Problem, the Traveling Salesperson Problem, the Sum-of-Subjects Problem, the *m*-Coloring Problem for $m \geq 3$, the Hamiltonian Circuits Problem, and the problem of abductive inference in a belief network all fall into this category. We have found branch-and-bound algorithms, backtracking algorithms, and other algorithms for these problems that are efficient for many large instances. That is, there is a polynomial in *n* that bounds the number of times the basic operation is done when the instances are taken from some restricted subset. However, no such polynomial exists for the set of all instances. To show this, we need only find some infinite sequence of instances for which no polynomial in *n* bounds the number of times the basic operation is done. Recall that we did this for the backtracking algorithms in Chapter 5.

There is a close and interesting relationship among many of the problems in this category. The development of this relationship is the purpose of the next section.

9.4 THE THEORY OF *NP*

It is more convenient to develop the theory if we originally restrict ourselves to decision problems. Recall that the output of a decision problem is a simple "yes" or "no" answer. Yet when we introduced (in Chapters 3, 4, 5, and 6) some of the problems mentioned previously, we presented them as optimization problems, which means that the output is an optimal solution. Each optimization problem, however, has a corresponding decision problem, as the examples that follow illustrate.

Example 9.2   Traveling Salesperson Problem

Let a weighted, directed graph be given. Recall that a tour in such a graph is a path that starts at one vertex, ends at that vertex, and visits all the other vertices in the graph exactly once, and that the ***Traveling Salesperson Optimization Problem*** is to determine a tour with minimal total weight on its edges.

The ***Traveling Salesperson Decision Problem*** is to determine for a given positive number d whether there is a tour having total weight no greater than d. This problem has the same parameters as the Traveling Salesperson Optimization Problem plus the additional parameter d.

Example 9.3   0-1 Knapsack Problem

Recall that the ***0-1 Knapsack Optimization Problem*** is to determine the maximum total profit of the items that can be placed in a knapsack given that each item has a weight and a profit, and that there is a maximum total weight W that can be carried in the sack.

The ***0-1 Knapsack Decision Problem*** is to determine, for a given profit P, whether it is possible to load the knapsack so as to keep the total weight no greater than W, while making the total profit at least equal to P. This problem has the same parameters as the 0-1 Knapsack Optimization Problem plus the additional parameter P.

Example 9.4   Graph-Coloring Problem

The ***Graph-Coloring Optimization Problem*** is to determine the minimum number of colors needed to color a graph so that no two adjacent vertices are colored the same color. That number is called the ***chromatic number*** of the graph.

The *Graph-Coloring Decision Problem* is to determine, for an integer m, whether there is a coloring that uses at most m colors and colors no two adjacent vertices the same color. This problem has the same parameters as the Graph-Coloring Optimization Problem plus the additional parameter m.

Example 9.5 Clique Problem

A *clique* in an undirected graph $G = (V, E)$ is a subset W of V such that each vertex in W is adjacent to all the other vertices in W. For the graph in Figure 9.1, $\{v_2, v_3, v_4\}$ is a clique, whereas $\{v_1, v_2, v_3\}$ is not a clique because v_1 is not adjacent to v_3. A *maximal clique* is a clique of maximal size. The only maximal clique in the graph in Figure 9.1 is $\{v_1, v_2, v_4, v_5\}$.

The *Clique Optimization Problem* is to determine the size of a maximal clique for a given graph.

The *Clique Decision Problem* is to determine, for a positive integer k, whether there is a clique containing at least k vertices. This problem has the same parameters as the Clique Optimization Problem plus the additional parameter k.

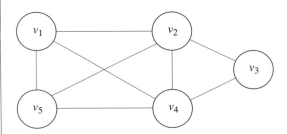

Figure 9.1 The maximal clique is $\{v_1, v_2, v_4, v_5\}$.

We have not found polynomial-time algorithms for either the decision problem or the optimization problem in any of these examples. However, if we could find a polynomial-time algorithm for the optimization problem in any one of them, we would also have a polynomial-time algorithm for the corresponding decision problem. This is so because *a solution to an optimization problem produces a solution to the corresponding decision problem.* For example, if we learned that the total weight of an optimal tour for a particular instance of the Traveling Salesperson Optimization Problem was 120, the answer to the corresponding decision problem would be "yes" for

$$d \geq 120$$

and "no" otherwise. Similarly, if we learned that the optimal profit for an instance of the 0-1 Knapsack Optimization Problem was \$230, the answer to the corresponding decision problem would be "yes" for

$$P \leq \$230$$

and "no" otherwise.

Because a polynomial-time algorithm for an optimization problem automatically produces a polynomial-time algorithm for the corresponding decision problem, we can initially develop our theory considering only decision problems. We do this next, after which we return to optimization problems. At that time, we will see that usually we can show that an optimization problem is even more closely related to its corresponding decision problem. That is, for many decision problems (including the problems in the previous examples), it's been shown that a polynomial-time algorithm for the decision problem would yield a polynomial-time algorithm for the corresponding optimization problem.

9.4.1 The Sets P and NP

First we consider the set of decision problems that can be solved by polynomial-time algorithms. We have the following definition.

Definition P is the set of all decision problems that can be solved by polynomial-time algorithms.

What problems are in P? All decision problems for which we have found polynomial-time algorithms are certainly in P. For example, the problem of determining whether a key is present in an array, the problem of determining whether a key is present in a sorted array, and the decision problems corresponding to the optimization problems in Chapters 3 and 4 for which we have found polynomial-time algorithms, are all in P. However, could some decision problem for which we have not found a polynomial-time algorithm also be in P? For example, could the Traveling Salesperson Decision Problem be in P? Even though no one has ever created a polynomial-time algorithm that solves this problem, no one has ever proven that it cannot be solved with a polynomial-time algorithm. Therefore, it could *possibly* be in P. To know that a decision problem is not in P, we have to *prove* that it is not possible to develop a polynomial-time algorithm for it. This has not been done for the Traveling Salesperson Decision Problem. These same considerations hold for the other decision problems in Examples 9.2 to 9.5.

What decision problems are not in P? Because we do not know whether the decision problems in Examples 9.2 to 9.5 are in P, each of these may not be in P. We simply do not know. Furthermore, there are thousands of decision problems in this same category. That is, we do not know whether they are in P. Garey and Johnson (1979) discuss many of them. There are actually relatively few decision problems that we know for certain are not in P. These problems are decision problems for which we have proven that polynomial-time algorithms are not possible. We discussed such problems in Section 9.3.2. As noted there, Presburger Arithmetic is one of the most well-known.

Next we define a possibly broader set of decision problems that includes the problems in Examples 9.2 to 9.5. To motivate this definition, let's first discuss the Traveling Salesperson Decision Problem further. Suppose someone claimed to know that the answer to some instance of this problem was "yes." That is, the person said that, for some graph and number d, a tour existed in which the total weight was no greater than d. It would be reasonable for us to ask the person to "prove" this claim by actually producing a tour with a total weight no greater than d. If the person then produced something, we could write the algorithm that follows to *verify* whether what they produced was a tour with weight no greater than d. The input to the algorithm is the graph G, the distance d, and the string S that is claimed to be a tour with weight no greater than d.

```
bool verify (weighted_digraph G,
             number d,
             claimed_tour S)
{
    if (S is a tour && the total weight of the edges in S is <= d)
        return true;
    else
        return false;
}
```

This algorithm first checks to see whether S is indeed a tour. If it is, the algorithm then adds the weights on the tour. If the sum of the weights is no greater than d, it returns "true." This means that is has verified that yes, there is a tour with total weight no greater than d, and we know that the answer to the decision problem is "yes." If S is not a tour or the sum of the weights exceeds d, the algorithm returns "false." Returning false means only that this claimed tour is not a tour with total weight no greater than d. It does not mean that such a tour does not exist, because there might be a different tour with total weight no greater than d.

It is left as an exercise to implement the algorithm more concretely and show that it is polynomial-time. This means that, given a candidate tour, we can verify in polynomial time whether this candidate proves that the answer to our decision problem is "yes." If the proposed tour turns out not to be a tour or to have total length greater than d (perhaps the person was bluffing), we have not proven that the answer must be "no" to our decision problem. Therefore, we are not talking about being able to verity that the answer to our decision problem is "no" in polynomial time.

It is this property of polynomial-time verifiability that is possessed by the problems in the set *NP*, which we define next. This does not mean that these problems can necessarily be solved in polynomial time. When we verify that a candidate tour has total weight no greater than d, we are not including the time it took to find that tour. We are only saying that the verification part takes polynomial time. To state the notion of polynomial-time verifiability more concretely, we introduce the concept of a ***nondeterministic algorithm.*** We can think of such an algorithm as being composed of the following two separate stages:

1. **Guessing (Nondeterministic) Stage:**   Given an instance of a problem, this stage simply produces some string *S*. The string can be thought of as a guess at a solution to the instance. However, it could just be a string of nonsense.

2. **Verification (Deterministic) Stage:**   The instance and the string *S* are the input to this stage. This stage then proceeds in an ordinary deterministic manner either (1) eventually halting with an output of "true," which means that it has been verified that the answer for this instance is "yes," (2) halting with an output of "false" or (3) not halting at all (that is, going into an infinite loop). In these letter two cases, it has not been verified that the answer for this instance is "yes." As we shall see, for our purposes these two cases are indistinguishable.

Function *verify* does the verification stage for the Traveling Salesperson Decision Problem. Notice that it is an ordinary deterministic algorithm. It is the guessing stage that is nondeterministic. This stage is called ***nondeterministic*** because unique step-by-step instructions are not specified for it. Rather, in this stage, the machine is allowed to produce any string in an arbitrary matter. A "nondeterministic stage" is simply a definitional device for the purpose of obtaining the notion of polynomial-time verifiability. It is not a realistic method for solving a decision problem.

Even though we never actually use a nondetermiistic algorithm to solve a problem, we say that a nondeterministic algorithm *"solves"* a decision problem if:

1. For any instance for which the answer is "yes" there is some string *S* for which the verification stage returns "true."

2. For any instance for which the answer is "no" there is no string for which the verification stage returns "true."

The following table shows the results of some input strings *S* to function *verify* when the instance is the graph in Figure 9.2 and *d* is 15.

S	Output	Reason
$[v_1, v_2, v_3, v_4, v_1]$	False	Total weight is greater than 15
$[v_1, v_4, v_2, v_3, v_1]$	False	S is not a tour
#@12*&%a₁\	False	S is not a tour
$[v_1, v_3, v_2, v_4, v_1]$	True	S is a tour with total weight no greater than 15

The third input illustrates that *S* can just be a string of nonsense (as discussed previously).

In general, if the answer for a particular instance is "yes," function *verify* returns "true" when one of the tours with total weight no greater than *d* is the input. Therefore, Criterion 1 for a nondeterministic algorithm is satisfied. On the other hand, function *verify* only returns "true" when a tour with total weight no greater than *d* is the input. Therefore, if the answer for an instance is "no,"

Figure 9.2 The tour $[v_1, v_3, v_2, v_4, v_1]$ has total weight no greater than 15.

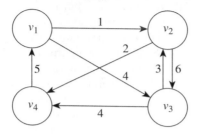

function *verify* does not return "true" for any value of *S*, which means that Criterion 2 is satisfied. A nondeterministic algorithm that simply generates strings in the guessing state and calls function *verify* in the verification stage therefore "solves" the Traveling Salesperson Decision Problem. Next we define what is meant by a polynomial-time nondeterministic algorithm.

Definition

A *polynomial-time nondeterministic algorithm* is a nondeterministic algorithm whose verification stage is a polynomial-time algorithm.

Now we can define the set *NP*.

Definition

NP is the set of all decision problems that can be solved by polynomial-time nondeterministic algorithms.

Note that *NP* stands for "nondeterministic polynomial." For a decision problem to be in *NP*, there must be an algorithm that does the verification in polynomial time. Because this is the case for the Traveling Salesperson Decision Problem, that problem is in *NP*. It must be stressed that this does not mean that we necessarily have a polynomial-time algorithm that solves the problem. Indeed, we do not presently have one for the Traveling Salesperson Decision Problem. If the answer for a particular instance of that problem were "yes," we might try all tours in the nondeterministic stage before trying one for which *verify* returns "true." If there were an edge from every vertex to every other vertex, there would be $(n - 1)!$ tours. Therefore, if all tours were tried, the answer would not be found in polynomial time. Furthermore, if the answer for an instance were "no," solving the problem using this technique would absolutely require that all tours be tried. The purpose of introducing the concepts of nondeterministic algorithms and *NP* is to classify algorithms. There are usually better algorithms for actually solving a problem than an algorithm that generates and verifies strings. For example, the branch-and-bound algorithm for the Traveling Salesperson Problem (Algorithm 6.3) does generate tours, but it avoids generating many of the tours by using a bounding function. Therefore, it is much better than an algorithm that blindly generates tours.

What other decision problems are in *NP?* In the exercises you are asked to establish that the other decision problems in Examples 9.2 to 9.5 are all in *NP*.

Furthermore, there are thousands of other problems that no one has been able to solve with polynomial-time algorithms but that have been proven to be in *NP* because polynomial-time nondeterministic algorithms have been developed for them. (Many of these problems appear in Garey and Johnson, 1979.) Finally, there is a large number of problems that are trivially in *NP*. That is, *every problem in P is also in NP*. This is trivially true because any problem in *P* can be solved by a polynomial-time algorithm. Therefore, we can merely generate any nonsense in the nondeterministic stage and run that polynomial-time algorithm in the deterministic stage. Because the algorithm solves the problem by answering "yes" or "no," it verifies that the answer is "yes" (for an instance where it is "yes") given any input string *S*.

What decision problems are not in *NP?* Curiously, the only decision problems that have been proven not to be in *NP* are the same ones that have been proven to be intractable. That is, the Halting Problem, Presburger Arithmetic, and the other problems discussed in Section 9.3.2 have been proven not to be in *NP*. Again, we have found relatively few such problems.

Figure 9.3 shows the set of all decision problems. Notice that in this figure *NP* contains *P* as a proper subset. However, this may not be the case. That is, *no one has ever proven that there is a problem in NP that is not in P*. Therefore, *NP − P* may be empty. Indeed, the question of whether *P* equals *NP* is one of the most intriguing and important questions in computer science. This question is important, because, as we have already mentioned, most decision problems we have developed are in *NP*. Therefore, if *P* = *NP,* we would have polynomial-time algorithms for most known decision problems.

To show that *P* ≠ *NP* we would have to find a problem in *NP* that is not in *P,* whereas to show that *P* = *NP* we would have to find a polynomial-time algorithm for each problem in *NP*. Next we see that this latter task can be greatly simplified. That is, we show that it is necessary to find a polynomial-time algorithm for only one of a large class of problems. In spite of this great simplification, many researchers doubt that *P* equals *NP*.

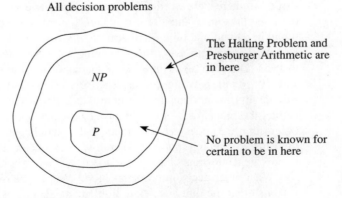

Figure 9.3 The set of all decision problems.

9.4.2 NP-Complete Problems

The problems in Examples 9.2 to 9.5 may not all appear to have the same difficulty. For example, our dynamic programming algorithm (Algorithm 3.11) for the Traveling Salesperson Problem is worst-case $\Theta(n^2 2^n)$. On the other hand, our dynamic programming algorithm (in Section 4.4) for the 0-1 Knapsack Problem is worst-case $\Theta(2^n)$. Furthermore, the state space tree in the branch-and-bound algorithm (Algorithm 6.3) for the Traveling Salesperson Problem has $(n - 1)!$ leaves, whereas the one in the branch-and-bound algorithm (Algorithm 6.2) for the 0-1 Knapsack Problem has only about 2^{n+1} nodes. Finally, our dynamic programming algorithm for the 0-1 Knapsack Problem is $\Theta(nW)$, which means that it is efficient as long as the capacity W of the sack is not extremely large. In light of all this, it seems that perhaps the 0-1 Knapsack Problem is inherently easier than the Traveling Salesperson Problem. We show that in spite of this, these two problems, the other problems in Examples 9.2 to 9.5, and thousands of other problems are all equivalent in the sense that if any one is in P, they all must be in P. Such problems are called *NP*-complete. To develop this result, we first describe a problem that is fundamental to the theory of *NP*-completeness—the problem of CNF-Satisfiability.

Example 9.6 CNF-Satisfiability Problem

A *logical (Boolean) variable* is a variable that can have one of two values: true or false. If x is a logical variable, $\bar{x}$ is the negation of x. That is, x is true if and only if $\bar{x}$ is false. A *literal* is a logical variable or the negation of a logical variable. A *clause* is a sequence of literals separated by the logical **or** operator ($\vee$). A logical expression in *conjunctive normal form (CNF)* is a sequence of clauses separated by the logical **and** operator ($\wedge$). The following is an example of a logical expression in CNF:

$$(\bar{x}_1 \vee x_2 \vee \bar{x}_3) \wedge (x_1 \vee \bar{x}_4) \wedge (\bar{x}_2 \vee x_3 \vee x_4).$$

The *CNF-Satisfiability Decision Problem* is to determine, for a given logical expression in CNF, whether there is some truth assignment (some set of assignments of true and false to the variables) that makes the expression true.

Example 9.7 For the instance

$$(x_1 \vee x_2) \wedge (x_2 \vee \bar{x}_3) \wedge \bar{x}_2,$$

the answer to CNF-Satisfiability is "yes," because the assignments $x_1 = $ true, $x_2 = $ false, and $x_3 = $ false make the expression true. For the instance

$$(x_1 \vee x_2) \wedge \bar{x}_1 \wedge \bar{x}_2,$$

the answer to CNF-Satisfiability is "no," because no assignment of truth values makes the expression true.

Figure 9.4 Algorithm *tran* is a transformation algorithm that maps each instance *x* of decision problem *A* to an instance *y* of decision problem *B*. Together with the algorithm for decision problem *B*, it yields an algorithm for decision problem *A*.

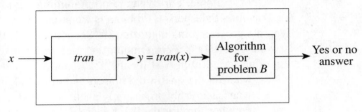

Algorithm for problem *A*

It is easy to write a polynomial-time algorithm that takes as input a logical expression in CNF and a set of truth assignments to the variables and verifies whether the expression is true for that assignment. Therefore, the problem is in *NP*. No one has ever found a polynomial-time algorithm for this problem, and no one has ever proven that it cannot be solved in polynomial time. So we do not know if it is in *P*. The remarkable thing about this problem is that in 1971, Stephen Cook published a paper proving that if CNF-Satisfiability is in *P*, then $P = NP$. (A variation of this theorem was published independently by L. A. Levin in 1973.) Before we can state the theorem rigorously, we need to develop a new concept—namely, the concept of "polynomial-time reducibility."

Suppose we want to solve decision problem *A* and we have an algorithm that solves decision problem *B*. Suppose further that we can write an algorithm that creates an instance *y* of problem *B* from every instance *x* of problem *A* such that an algorithm for problem *B* answers "yes" for *y* if and only if the answer to problem *A* is "yes" for *x*. Such an algorithm is called a ***transformation algorithm*** and is actually a function that maps every instance of problem *A* to an instance of problem *B*. We can denote it as follows:

$$y = tran(x).$$

The transformation algorithm combined with an algorithm for problem *B* yields an algorithm for problem *A*. Figure 9.4 illustrates this.

The following example has nothing to do with the theory of *NP*-completeness. We present it because it is a simple example of a transformation algorithm.

Example 9.8　　A Transformation Algorithm

Let our first decision problem be: Given *n* logical variables, does at least one of them have the value "true"? Let our second decision problem be: Given *n* integers, is the largest of them positive? Let our transformation be:

$$k_1, k_2, \ldots, k_n = tran(x_1, x_2, \ldots, x_n),$$

where k_i is 1 if x_i is true and k_i is 0 if x_i is false. An algorithm for our second problem returns "yes" if and only if at least one k_i is 1, which is the case if and only if at least one x_i is true. Therefore, an algorithm for the second problem returns "yes" if and only if at least one x_i is true, which means that our transformation is successful, and we can solve the first problem using an algorithm for the second problem.

We have the following definition pertaining to the concepts just developed.

Definition

If there exists a polynomial-time transformation algorithm from decision problem A to decision problem B, problem A is ***polynomial-time many-one reducible*** to problem B. (Usually we just say that problem A reduces to problem B.) In symbols, we write

$$A \propto B.$$

We say "many-one" because a transformation algorithm is a function that may map many instances of problem A to one instance of problem B. That is, it is a many-one function.

If the transformation algorithm is polynomial-time and we have a polynomial-time algorithm for problem B, intuitively it seems that the algorithm for problem A that results from combining the transformation algorithm and the algorithm for problem B must be a polynomial-time algorithm. For example, it is clear that the transformation algorithm in Example 9.8 is polynomial-time. Therefore, it seems that if we run that algorithm followed by some polynomial-time algorithm for the second problem, we are solving the first problem in polynomial time. The following theorem proves that this is so.

Theorem 9.1 If decision problem B is in P and

$$A \propto B,$$

then decision problem A is in P.

Proof: Let p be a polynomial that bounds the time complexity of the polynomial-time transformation algorithm from problem A to problem B, and let q be a polynomial that bounds the time complexity of a polynomial-time algorithm for B. Suppose we have an instance of problem A that is of size n. Because at most there are $p(n)$ steps in the transformation algorithm, and at worst that algorithm outputs a symbol at each step, the size of the instance of problem B produced by the transformation algorithm is at most $p(n)$. When that instance is the input to the algorithm for problem B, this means that there are at most $q(p(n))$ steps. Therefore, the total amount of work required to transform the instance of problem A to an instance of problem B and then solve problem B to get the correct answer for problem A is at most

$$p(n) + q(p(n)),$$

which is a polynomial in n.

Next we define *NP*-complete.

Definition   A problem *B* is called ***NP-complete*** if

1. it is in *NP* and
2. for every other problem *A* in *NP*,

$$A \propto B.$$

By Theorem 9.1, *if we could show that any NP-complete problem is in P, we could conclude that P = NP.* In 1971 Stephen Cook managed to find a problem that is *NP*-complete. The following theorem states his result.

Theorem 9.2 (Cook's Theorem) CNF-Satisfiability is *NP*-complete.

Proof: The proof can be found in Cook (1971) and in Garey and Johnson (1979).

Although we do not prove Cook's Theorem here, we mention that the proof does not consist of reducing every problem in *NP* individually to CNF-Satisfiability. If this were the case, whenever a new problem in *NP* was discovered, it would be necessary to add its reduction to the proof. Rather, the proof exploits common properties of problems in *NP* to show that any problem in this set must reduce to CNF-Satisfiability.

Once this ground-breaking theorem was proven, many other problems were proven to be *NP*-complete. These proofs rely on the following theorem.

Theorem 9.3 A problem *C* is *NP*-complete if

1. it is in *NP* and
2. for some other *NP*-complete problem *B*,

$$B \propto C.$$

Proof: Because *B* is *NP*-complete, for any problem *A* in *NP*, *A* $\propto$ *B*. It is not hard to see that reducibility is transitive. Therefore, *A* $\propto$ *C*. Because *C* is in *NP*, we can conclude that *C* is *NP*-complete.

By Cook's Theorem and Theorem 9.3, we can show that a problem is *NP*-complete by showing that it is in *NP* and that CNF-Satisfiability reduces to it. These reductions are typically much more complex than the one given in Example 9.7. We give one such reduction next.

Example 9.9 We show that the Clique Decision Problem is *NP*-complete. It is left as an exercise to show it is in *NP* by writing a polynomial-time verification algorithm for this problem. Therefore, we need only show that

CNF-Satisfiability $\propto$ Clique Decision Problem

to conclude that the problem is *NP*-complete. First recall that a clique in an undirected graph is a subset of vertices such that each vertex in the subset is adjacent to all the other vertices in the subset, and that the Clique Decision Prob-

Figure 9.5 The graph G in Example 9.9 when $B = (x_1 \vee x_2 \vee \bar{x}_3) \wedge (x_1 \vee \bar{x}_2 \vee x_3)$.

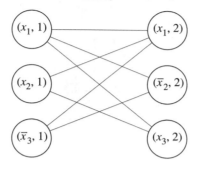

lem is to determine for a graph and a positive integer k whether the graph has a clique containing at least k vertices. Let

$$B = C_1 \wedge C_2 \wedge \cdots \wedge C_k$$

be a logical expression in CNF, where each C_i is a clause of B, and let $x_1, x_2, \ldots,$ x_n be the variables in B. Transform B to a graph $G = (V, E)$, as follows:

$$V = \{(y, i) \text{ such that } y \text{ is a literal in clause } C_i\}$$
$$E = \{((y, i), (z, j)) \text{ such that } i \neq j \text{ and } \bar{z} \neq y\}$$

A sample construction of G is shown in Figure 9.5. It is left as an exercise to show that this transformation is polynomial-time. Therefore, we need only show that B is CNF-Satisfiable if and only if G has a clique of size at least k. We do this next.

1. Show that if B is CNF-Satisfiable, G has a clique of size at least k: if B is CNF-Satisfiable, there are truth assignments for $x_1, x_2, \ldots, x_n$ such that each clause is true with these assignments. This means that with these assignments there is at least one literal in each C_i that is true. Pick one such literal from each C_i. Then let

    $$V' = \{(y, i) \text{ such that } y \text{ is the true literal picked from } C_i\}.$$

    Clearly, V' forms a clique in G of size k.

2. Show that if G has a clique of size at least k, B is CNF-Satisfiable: Because there cannot be an edge from a vertex (y, i) to a vertex (z, i), the indices in the vertices in a clique must all be different. Because there are only k different indices, this means that a clique can have at most k vertices. So if G has a clique (V', E') of size at least k, the number of vertices in V' must be exactly k. Therefore, if we set

    $$S = \{y \text{ such that } (y, i) \in V'\},$$

    S contains k literals. Furthermore, S contains a literal from each of the k clauses, because there is no edge connecting (y, i) and (z, i) for any literals

y and z and index i. Finally, S cannot contain both a literal y and its complement $\bar{y}$, because there is no edge connecting (y, i) and $(\bar{y}, j)$ for any i and j. Therefore, if we set

$$x_i = \begin{cases} \text{true} & \text{if } x_i \in S \\ \text{false} & \text{if } \bar{x}_i \in S \end{cases}$$

and assign arbitrary truth values to variables not in S, all clauses in B are true. Therefore, B is CNF-Satisfiable.

Recall the Hamiltonian Circuits Problem from Section 5.6. The **Hamiltonian Circuits Decision Problem** is to determine whether a connected, undirected graph has at least one tour (a path that starts at one vertex, visits each vertex in the graph once, and ends up at the starting vertex). It is possible to show that

CNF-Satisfiability $\propto$ Hamiltonian Circuits Decision Problem.

The reduction is even more tedious than the one given in the previous example and can be found in Horowitz and Sahni (1978). It is left as an exercise to write a polynomial-time verification algorithm for this problem. Therefore, we can conclude that the Hamiltonian Circuits Decision Problem is *NP*-complete.

Now that we know that the Clique Decision Problem and the Hamiltonian Circuits Decision Problem are *NP*-complete, we can show that some other problem in *NP* is *NP*-complete by showing that the Clique Decision Problem or the Hamiltonian Circuits Decision Problem reduces to that problem (by Theorem 9.3). That is, we do not need to return to CNF-Satisfiability for each proof of *NP*-completeness. More sample reductions follow.

Example 9.10 Consider a variant of the Traveling Salesperson Decision Problem in which the graph is undirected. That is, given a weighted, undirected graph and a positive number d, determine whether there is an undirected tour having total weight no greater than d. Clearly, the polynomial-time verification algorithm given earlier for the usual Traveling Salesperson Problem also works for this problem. Therefore the problem is in *NP*, and we need only show that some *NP*-complete problem reduces to it to conclude that it is *NP*-complete. We show that

Hamiltonian Circuits Decision Problem
$\propto$ Traveling Salesperson (Undirected) Decision Problem.

Transform an instance (V, E) of the Hamiltonian Circuits Decision Problem to the instance (V, E') of the Traveling Salesperson (Undirected) Decision Problem that has the same set of vertices V, has an edge between every pair of vertices, and has the following weights:

$$\text{Weight of } (u, v) \text{ equal to } \begin{cases} 1 \text{ if } (u, v) \in E \\ 2 \text{ if } (u, v) \notin E. \end{cases}$$

An example of this transformation is shown in Figure 9.6. Clearly, (V, E) has a Hamiltonian Circuit if and only if (V, E') has a tour with total weight no more than n, where n is the number of vertices in V. It is left as an exercise to complete this example by showing that the transformation is polynomial-time.

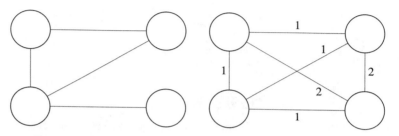

Figure 9.6 The transformation algorithm in Example 9.10 maps the undirected graph on the left to the weighted, undirected graph on the right.

Example 9.11   We have already written a polynomial-time verification algorithm for the usual Traveling Salesperson Decision Problem. Therefore this problem is in *NP*, and we can show that it is *NP*-complete by showing that

Traveling Salesperson (Undirected) Decision Problem
$$\propto \text{Traveling Salesperson Decision Problem.}$$

Transform an instance (V, E) of the Traveling Salesperson (Undirected) Decision Problem to the instance (V, E') of the Traveling Salesperson Problem that has the same set of vertices V and has the edges $<u, v>$ and $<v, u>$ both in E' whenever (u, v) is in E. The directed weights of $<u, v>$ and $<v, u>$ are the same as the undirected weight of (u, v). Clearly, (V, E) has an undirected tour with total weight no greater than d if and only if (V, E') has a directed tour with total weight no greater than d. It is left as an exercise to complete this example by showing that the transformation is polynomial-time.

As mentioned previously, thousands of problems, including the other problems in Examples 9.2 to 9.5, have been shown to be *NP*-complete using reductions like those just given. Garey and Johnson (1979) contains many sample reductions and lists over 300 *NP*-complete problems.

Figure 9.7 The set *NP* is either as depicted on the left or as depicted on the right.

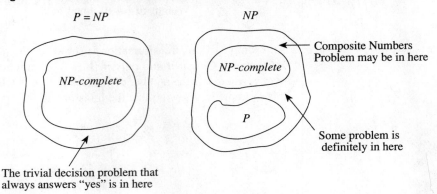

The trivial decision problem that
always answers "yes" is in here

Composite Numbers
Problem may be in here

Some problem is
definitely in here

The State of NP

Figure 9.3 shows *P* as a proper subset of *NP*, but, as mentioned previously, they
may be the same set. How does the set of *NP*-complete problems fit into the
picture? First, by definition, it is a subset of *NP*. Therefore, Presburger Arithmetic,
the Halting Problem, and any other decision problems that are not in *NP* are not
NP-complete.

A decision problem that is in *NP* and is not *NP*-complete is the trivial decision
problem that answers "yes" for all instances (or answers "no" for all instances).
This problem is not *NP*-complete because it is not possible to transform a nontrivial decision problem to it.

If $P = NP$, the situation is as depicted on the left in Figure 9.7. If $P \neq NP$,
the situation is as depicted on the right in that figure. That is, if $P \neq NP$, then

$$P \cap NP\text{-complete} = \varnothing,$$

where ***NP-complete*** denotes the set of all *NP*-complete problems. This is so because if some problem in *P* were *NP*-complete, Theorem 9.1 would imply that
we could solve any problem in *NP* in polynomial time.

Notice that Figure 9.7 (on the right) says that the Composite Numbers Problem may be in

$$NP - (P \cup NP\text{-complete}).$$

That problem is as follows:

Example 9.12 Composite Numbers Problem

Given a positive integer *n*, are there integers $m > 1$ and $k > 1$ such that $n = mk$?

The following algorithm verifies whether the answer to this problem is "yes" in
polynomial time, which means that the problem is in *NP*.

```
bool verify_composite (int n, int m, int k)
{
   if (m and k are both integers > 1 && n == m*k)
      return true;
   else
      return false;
}
```

No one has ever found a polynomial-time algorithm for this problem (notice that n is the input, which means that the input size is about $\lg n$), yet no one has ever proven that the problem is *NP*-complete. Therefore, we do not know whether it is in *P* and we do not know whether it is *NP*-complete. There are more such problems, some of which are discussed in Garey and Johnson (1979).

No one has been able to prove that there is a problem in *NP* that is neither in *P* nor *NP*-complete (such a proof would automatically prove that $P \neq NP$). However, it has been proved that, if $P \neq NP$, such a problem must exist. This result, which is stated on the right in Figure 9.7, is formalized in the following theorem.

Theorem 9.4 If $P \neq NP$, the set

$$NP - (P \cup NP\text{-}complete)$$

is not empty.

Proof: The proof follows from a more general result that can be found in Ladner (1975).

Complementary Problems

Notice the similarity between the Composite Numbers Problem and the following problem.

Example 9.13   Primes Problem

Given a positive integer n, is n a prime number?

The Primes Problem is the one solved by the algorithm at the beginning of Section 9.2. It is the complementary problem to the Composite Numbers Problem. In general, the ***complementary problem*** to a decision problem is the problem that answers "yes" whenever the original problem answers "no" and answers "no" whenever the original problem answers "yes." Another example of a complementary problem follows.

Example 9.14   Complementary Traveling Salesperson Decision Problem

Given a weighted graph and a positive number d, is there *no* tour with total weight no greater than d?

Clearly, if we found an ordinary deterministic polynomial-time algorithm for a problem, we would have a deterministic polynomial-time algorithm for its complementary problem. For example, if we could determine in polynomial time whether a number was composite, we would also be determining whether it was prime. However, finding a polynomial-time nondeterministic algorithm for a problem does not automatically produce a polynomial-time nondeterministic algorithm for its complementary problem. That is, showing that the one is in *NP* does not automatically show that the other is in *NP*. The verification algorithm for the Primes Problem must be able to verify in polynomial time that a number is prime, whereas the verification algorithm for the Composite Numbers Problem must be able to verify that a number is composite. This latter task, which we accomplished with function *verify_composite,* is somewhat simpler. Pratt (1975) has shown that the Primes Problem also is in *NP*. In the case of the Complementary Traveling Salesperson Problem, the algorithm would have to be able to verify in polynomial time that no tour with weight no greater than d exists. This is substantially more complex than verifying that a tour has weight no greater than d. No one has ever found a polynomial-time verification algorithm for the Complementary Traveling Salesperson Decision Problem. Indeed, *no one has ever shown that the complementary problem to any known NP-complete problem is in NP*. On the other hand, no one has ever proven that some problem is in *NP* whereas its complementary problem is not in *NP*. The following result has been obtained.

Theorem 9.5 If the complementary problem to any *NP*-complete problem is in *NP*, the complementary problem to every problem in *NP* is in *NP*.

Proof: The proof can be found in Garey and Johnson (1979).

9.4.3 NP-Hard, NP-Easy, and NP-Equivalent Problems

So far we have discussed only decision problems. Next we extend our results to problems in general. Recall that Theorem 9.1 implies that if decision problem A is polynomial-time many-one reducible to problem B, then we could solve problem A in polynomial time using a polynomial-time algorithm for problem B. We generalize this notion to nondecision problems with the following definition.

Definition   If problem A can be solved in polynomial time using a hypothetical polynomial-time algorithm for problem B, then problem A is ***polynomial-time Turing reducible*** to problem B. (Usually we just say A Turing reduces to B.) In symbols, we write

$$A \propto_T B.$$

This definition does not require that a polynomial-time algorithm for problem B exist. It only says that *if* one did exist, problem A would also be solvable in polynomial time. Clearly, if A and B are both decision problems, then

$$A \propto B \qquad \text{implies} \qquad A \propto_T B.$$

Next we extend the notion of *NP*-completeness to nondecision problems.

Definition   A problem B is called ***NP-hard*** if, for some *NP*-complete problem A,

$$A \propto_T B.$$

It is not hard to see that Turing reductions are transitive. Therefore, all problems in *NP* reduce to any *NP*-hard problem. This means that *if a polynomial-time algorithm exists for any NP-hard problem, then P = NP*.

What problems are *NP*-hard? Clearly, *every NP-complete problem is NP-hard*. Therefore, we ask instead what nondecision problems are *NP*-hard. Earlier we noted that if we could find a polynomial-time algorithm for an optimization problem, we would automatically have a polynomial-time algorithm for the corresponding decision problem. Therefore, *the optimization problem corresponding to any NP-complete problem is NP-hard*. The following example formally uses the definition of Turing reducibility to show this result for the Traveling Salesperson Problem.

Example 9.15   The Traveling Salesperson Optimization Problem is *NP*-hard.

Suppose we had a hypothetical polynomial-time algorithm for the Traveling Salesperson Optimization Problem. Let the instance of the Traveling Salesperson Decision Problem containing the graph G and positive integer d be given. Apply the hypothetical algorithm to the graph G to obtain the optimal solution *mindist*. Then our answer for the instance of the decision problem would be "yes" if $d \leq mindist$ and "no" otherwise. Clearly, the hypothetical polynomial-time algorithm for the optimization problem, along with this extra step, gives the answer to the decision problem in polynomial time. Therefore,

Traveling Salesperson Decision Problem
$$\propto_T \text{Traveling Salesperson Optimization Problem.}$$

What problems are not *NP*-hard? We do not know if there is any such problem. Indeed, *if we were to prove that some problem was not NP-hard, we would be proving that P ≠ NP*. The reason is that if $P = NP$, then each problem in *NP* would be solvable by a polynomial-time algorithm. Therefore, we could solve each problem in *NP*, using a hypothetical polynomial-time algorithm for any problem B, by simply calling the polynomial-time algorithm for each problem. We don't even need the hypothetical algorithm for problem B. Therefore, all problems would be *NP*-hard.

On the other hand, any problem for which we have found a polynomial-time

Figure 9.8 The set of all problems.

All problems

NP-hard

NP-complete

If *P* = *NP*, no problems
are in here. If *P* ≠ *NP*,
all problems in *P* are
in here.

algorithm may not be *NP*-hard. Indeed, *if we were to prove that some problem for which we had a polynomial-time algorithm was NP-hard, we would be proving that P = NP.* The reason is that we would then have an actual rather than a hypothetical polynomial-time algorithm for some *NP*-hard problem. Therefore, we could solve each problem in *NP* in polynomial-time using the Turing reduction from the problem to the *NP*-hard problem.

Figure 9.8 illustrates how the set of *NP*-hard problems fits into the set of all problems.

If a problem is *NP*-hard, it is at least as hard (in terms of our hopes of finding a polynomial-time algorithm) as the *NP*-complete problems. For example, the Traveling Sales Optimization Problem is at least as hard as the *NP*-complete problems. However, is the reverse necessarily true? That is, are the *NP*-complete problems at least as hard as the Traveling Salesperson Optimization Problem? *NP*-hardness does not imply this. We need another definition.

Definition   A problem *A* is called **NP-easy** if, for some problem *B* in *NP*,

$$A \propto_T B.$$

Clearly, if P = NP, then a polynomial-time algorithm exists for all NP-easy problems. Notice that our definition of *NP*-easy is not exactly symmetrical with our definition of *NP*-hard. It is left as an exercise to show that a problem is *NP*-easy if and only if it reduces to an *NP*-complete problem.

What problems are *NP*-easy? Obviously, the problems in *P,* the problems in *NP,* and nondecision problems for which we have found polynomial-time algorithms are all *NP*-easy. The optimization problem, corresponding to an *NP*-complete decision problem, can usually be shown to be *NP*-easy. However, it is not trivial to do this, as the following example illustrates.

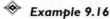

Example 9.16   The Traveling Salesperson Decision Problem is *NP*-easy. To establish this result, we introduce the following problem.

Traveling Salesperson Extension Decision Problem

Let an instance of the Traveling Salesperson Decision Problem be given, where the number of vertices in the graph is n and the integer is d. Furthermore, let a partial tour T consisting of m distinct vertices be given. The problem is to determine whether T can be extended to a complete tour having total weight no greater than d. The parameters for this problem are the same as those for the Traveling Salesperson Decision Problem plus the partial tour T.

It is not hard to show that the Traveling Salesperson Extension Decision Problem is in *NP*. Therefore, in order to obtain our desired result, we need only show that

Traveling Salesperson Optimization Problem

$\propto_T$ Traveling Salesperson Extension Decision Problem.

To that end, let *polyalg* be a hypothetical polynomial-time algorithm for the Traveling Salesperson Extension Decision Problem. The inputs to *polyalg* are a graph, a partial tour, and a distance. Let an instance G of size n of the Traveling Salesperson Optimization Problem be given. Let the vertices in the instance be

$$\{v_1, v_2, \ldots, v_n\}$$

and set

$$dmin = n$$
$$dmax = n \times maximum \text{ (weight on edge from } v_i \text{ to } v_j).$$
$$1 \leq i, j \leq n$$

If *mindist* is the total weight of the edges in an optimal tour, then

$$dmin \leq mindist \leq dmax.$$

Because any vertex can be the first vertex on our tour, we can make v_1 the first vertex. Consider the following call:

$$polyalg(G,[v_1],d).$$

The partial tour that is the input to this call is simply $[v_1]$, which is the partial tour before we ever leave v_1. The smallest value of d for which this call could return "true" is $d = dmin$, and if there is a tour, the call will definitely return "true" if $d = dmax$. If it returns "false" for $d = dmax$, then $mindist = \infty$. Otherwise, using a binary search, we can determine the smallest value of d for which *polyalg* returns "true" when G and $[v_1]$ are the inputs. That value is *mindist*. This means that we can compute *mindist* in at most about $\lg(dmax)$ calls to *polyalg*, which means that we can compute *mindist* in polynomial time.

Once we know the value of *mindist,* we use *polyalg* to construct an optimal tour in polynomial time, as follows. If $mindist = \infty$, there are no tours, and we are done. Otherwise, say that a partial tour is ***extendible*** if it can be extended to a tour having total weight equal to *mindist*. Clearly, $[v_1]$ is extendible. Because

$[v_1]$ is extendible, there must be at least one v_i such that $[v_1, v_i]$ is extendible. We can determine such a v_i by calling *polyalg* at most $n - 2$ times, as follows:

$$polyalg(G,[v_1,v_i],mindist),$$

where $2 \le i \le n - 1$. We stop when we find an extendible tour or when i reaches $n - 1$. We need not check the last vertex, because, if the others all fail, the last vertex must be extendible.

In general, given an extendible partial tour containing m vertices, we can find an extendible partial tour containing $m + 1$ vertices with at most $n - m - 1$ calls to *polyalg*. So we can build an optimal tour with at most the following number of calls to *polyalg*:

$$(n - 2) + \cdots + (n - m - 1) + \cdots + 1 = \frac{(n - 2)(n - 1)}{2}.$$

This means that we can also construct an optimal tour in polynomial time, and we have a polynomial-time Turing reduction.

Similar proofs have been established for the other problems in Examples 9.2 to 9.5 and for the optimization problems corresponding to most *NP*-complete decision problems. We have the following definition concerning such problems.

Definition   A problem is called ***NP-equivalent*** if it is both *NP*-hard and *NP*-easy.

Clearly, *P = NP if and only if polynomial-time algorithms exist for all NP-equivalent problems.*

We see that originally restricting our theory to decision problems causes no substantial loss in generality, because we can usually show that the optimization problem, corresponding to an *NP*-complete decision problem, is *NP*-equivalent. This means that finding a polynomial-time algorithm for the optimization problem is equivalent to finding one for the decision problem.

Our goal has been to provide a facile introduction to the theory of *NP*. For a more thorough introduction, you are referred to the text we have referenced several times—namely, Garey and Johnson (1979). Although that text is quite old, it is still one of the best comprehensive introductions to the *NP* theory. Another good introductory text is Papadimitriou (1994).

9.5 HANDLING *NP*-HARD PROBLEMS

In the absence of polynomial-time algorithms for problems known to be *NP*-hard, what can we do about solving such problems? We presented one way in Chapters 5 and 6. The backtracking and branch-and-bound algorithms for these problems are all worst-case nonpolynomial-time. However, they are often efficient for many large instances. Therefore, for a particular large instance of interest, a backtracking or branch-and-bound algorithm may suffice. Recall from Section 5.3 that the Monte Carlo Technique can be used to estimate whether a given algorithm would be efficient for a particular instance. If the estimate shows that it probably would be, we can try using the algorithm to solve that instance.

Another approach is to find an algorithm that is efficient for a subclass of instances of an NP-hard problem. For example, the problem of probabilistic inference in a belief network, discussed in Section 6.3, is NP-hard. In general, a belief network consists of a directed acyclic graph and a probability distribution. Polynomial-time algorithms have been found for the subclass of instances in which the graph is singly connected. A directed, acyclic graph is **singly connected** if there is no more than one path from any vertex to any other vertex. Pearl (1988) and Neapolitan (1990) discuss these algorithms.

A third approach, investigated here, is to develop approximation algorithms. An **approximation algorithm** for an NP-hard optimization problem is an algorithm that is not guaranteed to give optimal solutions, but rather yields solutions that are reasonably close to optimal. Often we can obtain a bound that gives a guarantee as to how close a solution is to being optimal. For example, we derive an approximation algorithm that gives a solution, which we will call *minapprox,* to a variant of the Traveling Salesperson Optimization Problem. We show that

$$minapprox < 2 \times mindist,$$

where *mindist* is the optimal solution. This does not mean that *minapprox* is always almost twice *mindist*. For many instances, it may be much closer or even equal to *mindist*. Rather, this means that we are guaranteed that *minapprox* will never be as great as twice *mindist*. We develop this algorithm and an improvement on it next. Then we further illustrate approximation algorithms by deriving one for another problem.

9.5.1 An Approximation Algorithm for the Traveling Salesperson Problem

Our algorithm will be for the following variant of the problem.

Example 9.17   Traveling Salesperson Problem with Triangular Inequality

Let a weighted, undirected graph $G = (V, E)$ be given such that

1.   there is an edge connecting every two distinct vertices
2.   if $W(u, v)$ denotes the weight on the edge connecting vertex u to vertex v, then, for every other vertex y,

$$W(u, v) \leq W(u, y) + W(y, v).$$

The second condition, called the **triangular inequality,** is depicted in Figure 9.9. It is satisfied if the weights represent actual distances ("as the crow flies")

Figure 9.9 The triangular inequality implies that the "distance" from *u* to *v* is no greater than the "distance" from *u* to *y* plus the "distance" from *y* to *v*.

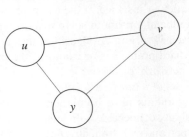

between cities. Recall that weight and distance terminology are used interchangeably for weighted graphs. The first condition implies that there is a two-way road connecting every city to every other city.

The problem is to find the shortest path (optimal tour) starting and ending at the same vertex and visiting each other vertex exactly once. It can be shown that this variant of the problem is also *NP*-hard.

Notice that the graph in this variant of the problem is undirected. If we remove any edge from an optimal tour for such a graph, we have a spanning tree for the graph. Therefore, the total weight of a minimum spanning tree must be less than the total weight of an optimal tour. We can use Algorithm 4.1 or 4.2 to obtain a minimum spanning tree in polynomial time. By going twice around the spanning tree, we can convert it to a path that visits every city. This is illustrated in Figure 9.10. A graph is depicted in Figure 9.10(a), a minimum spanning tree for the graph in Figure 9.10(b), and the path obtained by going twice around the tree in Figure 9.10(c). As the figure shows, the resulting path may visit some vertices more than once. We can convert the path to one that does not do this by taking "shortcuts." That is, we traverse the path, starting at some arbitrary vertex, and visit each unvisited vertex in sequence. When there is more than one unvisited vertex adjacent to the current vertex in the tree, we simply visit the closest one. If the only vertices adjacent to the current vertex have already been visited, we bypass them by means of a shortcut to the next unvisited vertex. The triangular inequality guarantees that the shortcut will not lengthen the path. Figure 9.10(d) shows the tour obtained using this technique. In that figure, we started with the bottom vertex on the left. Notice that the tour obtained is not optimal. However, if we start with the top left vertex, we obtain an optimal tour.

The method just outlined can be summarized in the following steps:

1. Determine a minimum spanning tree.

2. Create a path that visits every city by going twice around the tree.

3. Create a path that does not visit any vertex twice (that is, a tour) by taking shortcuts.

Figure 9.10 Obtaining an approximation to an optimal tour from a minimum spanning tree.

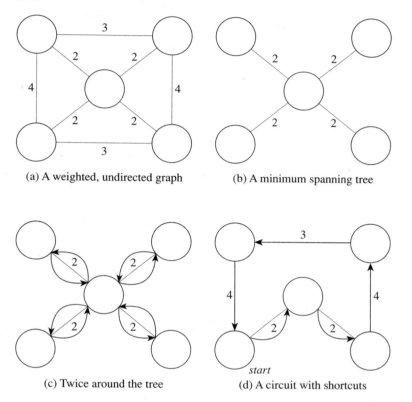

(a) A weighted, undirected graph

(b) A minimum spanning tree

(c) Twice around the tree

(d) A circuit with shortcuts

In general, the tour obtained using this method is not necessarily optimal regardless of the starting vertex. However, the following theorem gives us a guarantee as to how close the tour is to being optimal.

Theorem 9.6 Let *mindist* be the total weight of an optimal tour and *minapprox* be the total weight of the tour obtained using the method just described. Then

$$minapprox < 2 \times mindist.$$

Proof: As we have already discussed, the total weight of a minimum spanning tree is less than *mindist*. Because the total weight of *minapprox* is no more than the total weight of two minimum spanning trees, the theorem follows.

It is possible to create instances that show that *minapprox* can be made arbitrarily close to $2 \times mindist$. Therefore, in general, the bound obtained in Theorem 9.6 is the best we can do.

We can obtain an even better approximation algorithm for this problem as follows. First obtain a minimum spanning tree as done above. Then consider the set V' of all vertices that touch an odd number of edges. It is not hard to show that there must be an even number of such vertices. Pair up the vertices in V' so that each vertex is paired with precisely one other vertex. Such a creation of vertex pairs is called a ***matching*** for V'. Add the edge connecting each vertex pair to the spanning tree. Because each vertex then has an even number of edges touching it, the resultant path visits every city. Furthermore, the total number of edges in this path is no greater than (and often is less than) the total number that would be obtained by simply going twice around the tree. Figure 9.11(a) shows a minimum spanning tree, and Figure 9.11(b) shows the path obtained from that tree with one possible matching. Figure 9.11(c) shows a tour obtained after short-cuts are taken.

A ***minimal weight matching*** for V' is one such that the total weight of the edges obtained from the matching is minimal. Lawler (1976) shows how to obtain a minimal weight matching in polynomial time. We therefore can approximately solve the variant of the Traveling Salesperson Problem given in Example 9.17 in polynomial time using the following steps:

1. Obtain a minimum spanning tree.
2. Obtain a minimal weight matching of the vertices in V', where V' is the set of vertices in the spanning tree that touch an odd number of edges.
3. Create a path that visits every vertex by adding the edges connecting matched vertices to the tree.
4. Obtain a path that does not visit any vertex twice (that is, a tour) by taking shortcuts.

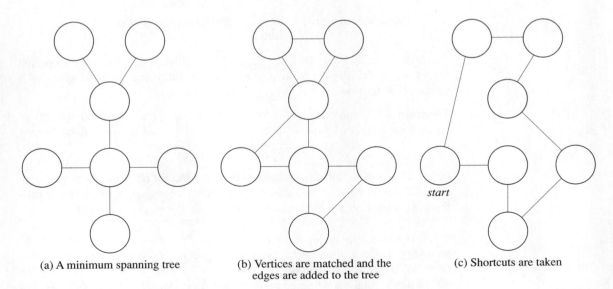

(a) A minimum spanning tree   (b) Vertices are matched and the   (c) Shortcuts are taken
                                        edges are added to the tree

Figure 9.11 A tour obtained using a matching.

Figure 9.11 illustrates these steps without showing any actual weights. The following theorem shows that this method gives a better bound than the first method presented in this section.

Theorem 9.7 Let *mindist* be the total weight of an optimal tour and *minapprox*2 be the total weight of the tour obtained using the method of minimal weight matching. Then

$$minapprox2 < 1.5 \times mindist.$$

Proof: Let V' be the set of all vertices that touch an odd number of edges. Convert an optimal tour to a path connecting only the vertices in V' by bypassing vertices not in V'. By the triangular inequality, the total weight of this path can be no greater than *mindist*. Furthermore, this path provides us with two matchings for the vertices in V', as follows. Choose an arbitrary vertex in V' and match it with the vertex on one side of it in the path. Then continue to match adjacent vertices in pairs going in this same direction. This is one match. Next match the initial vertex with the vertex on the other side of it in the path, and continue to match adjacent vertices going in the other direction. This is a second match. Because the edges in the two matches comprise all the edges in the path, the sum of the total weights of the two matches is equal to the weight of the path. Therefore, at least one of the matches has total weight no greater than half the weight of the path. Because the weight of this path is no greater than *mindist,* and because the weight of any matching is at least as great as the weight of a minimal weight matching, we have

$$minmatch \le 0.5 \times mindist,$$

where *minmatch* is the weight of a minimal weight matching. Recall that the weight of a minimum spanning tree is less than *mindist*. Because the edges obtained in Step 3 of the method of minimal weight matching consist of the edges in a spanning tree and the edges obtained from a minimal matching, the total weight of those edges is less than $1.5 \times mindist$. The theorem now follows, because the total weight of the edges in the final tour obtained in Step 4 is no greater than the weight of those obtained in Step 3.

It is possible to create instances for which the approximation can be made arbitrarily close to $1.5 \times mindist$. Therefore, in general, there is no better bound for this algorithm than the one obtained in Theorem 9.7.

Recall that our salesperson Nancy was last trying to find an optimal tour for her 40-city sales territory using a branch-and-bound algorithm (Algorithm 6.3) for the Traveling Salesperson Problem. Because that algorithm is worst-case non-polynomial-time, it may take many years to solve her particular instance. If the distances between Nancy's cities satisfy the assumptions in the Traveling Salesperson with Triangular Inequality Problem, she finally has an alternative that is sure to work. That is, she can use the method of minimal weight matching to obtain a good approximation to an optimal tour in polynomial time.

9.5.2 An Approximation Algorithm for the Bin Packing Problem

We introduce the following new problem.

Example 9.18 Bin Packing Problem

Let n items with sizes

$$s_1, s_2, \ldots, s_n, \text{ where } 0 < s_i \leq 1,$$

be given, and suppose we are to pack the items in bins, where each bin has a capacity of 1. The problem is to determine the minimum number of bins necessary to pack all the items.

This problem has been shown to be *NP*-hard. A very simple approximation algorithm for this problem is called "first fit." The *first fit* strategy places an item in the first bin in which it fits. If it does not fit in a bin, a new bin is started. Another good idea is to pack the items in nonincreasing order. Therefore, our strategy is called **nonincreasing first fit.** It can be described by the following high-level algorithm:

```
sort the items in nonincreasing order;
while (there are still unpacked items) {
    get next item;
    while (the item is not packed and there are more started bins) {
        get next bin;
        if (the item fits in the bin)
            pack it in the bin;
    }
    if (the item is not packed) {
        start a new bin;
        place the item in the new bin;
    }
}
```

Figure 9.12 shows a result of applying this algorithm. Notice that it consists of a greedy algorithm within a greedy algorithm. That is, we greedily grab items, and for each item we greedily grab bins. It is left as an exercise to write a detailed version of this algorithm and show that it is $\Theta(n^2)$. Notice that the solution in Figure 9.12 is not optimal. We could fit the items in only three bins if we placed the size 0.5 item, the size 0.3 item, and one of the size 0.2 items in the second bin, and placed the two size 0.4 items and one of the size 0.2 items in the third bin.

Figure 9.12 A result of applying nonincreasing first fit.

Sizes: 0.85, 0.5, 0.4, 0.4, 0.3, 0.2, 0.2, 0.1

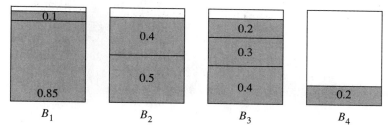

Next we obtain a bound for how close the approximate solution is to an optimal solution. The bound is obtained in Theorem 9.8. The proof of that theorem requires the following two lemmas.

Lemma 9.1 Let *opt* be the optimal number of bins for a given instance of the Bin Packing Problem. Any item that is placed by the nonincreasing first fit strategy in an extra bin (that is, in a bin with index greater than *opt*) has size at most equal to 1/3.

Proof: Let i be the index of the first item placed in bin $opt + 1$. Because the items are sorted in nonincreasing order, it suffices to show that

$$s_i \leq \frac{1}{3}.$$

Suppose by way of contradiction that $s_i > 1/3$. Then

$$s_1, s_2, \ldots, s_{i-1} \text{ are all greater than } \frac{1}{3},$$

which means that all those bins with indices no greater than *opt* contain at most two items each. If every one of those bins contained two items, in an optimal solution there would have to be two of the first $i - 1$ items in every bin. But because their sizes are all greater than $\frac{1}{3}$, there would be no room for s_i in one of the bins. Therefore, at least one bin with index no greater than *opt* contains only one item. If every bin with index no greater than *opt* contained only one item, no two of them could fit in a bin together and the ith item could not fit with any one of them (otherwise, our algorithm would have placed it with one of them). But then an optimal solution would require more than *opt* bins. Therefore, at least one bin with index no greater than *opt* contains two items.

We show that there is some j such that $0 < j < opt$ for which the first j bins contain one item each and the remaining $opt - j$ bins contain two items each. If this were not the case, there would be bins B_k and B_m with $k < m$ such that B_k contained two items and B_m contained one item. However, because the items are packed in nonincreasing order, the item packed in B_m would be no larger than

Figure 9.13 If $s_i > 1/3$, our algorithm would pack the bins like this.

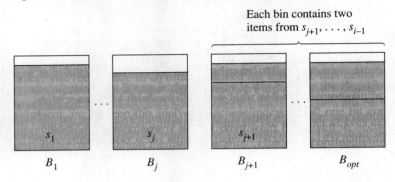

the first item packed in B_k, and s_i would be no larger than the second item packed in B_k. Therefore, the sum of the sizes of the item in B_m and s_i would be no greater than the sum of the sizes of the two items in B_k, which means that s_i would fit in B_m. Therefore, the conjecture above (concerning j) must be true, and the bins appear as depicted in Figure 9.13.

Let an optimal solution be given. In such a solution, the first j items are in j distinct bins, because if any of them could fit together in a bin, our method would have put them together. Furthermore, items

$$s_{j+1}, s_{j+2}, \ldots, s_{i-1}$$

are in the remaining $opt - j$ bins, because none of them can fit with the first j items. Because our algorithm places two of each of these items in $opt - j$ bins, there must be $2 \times (opt - j)$ of these items. Because we assumed that the size of each of these items is greater than $1/3$, there cannot be three of them in any of one of the remaining $opt - j$ bins, which means that there must be exactly two items in each of these bins. Because we assumed that the size of s_i is also greater than $1/3$, it cannot fit in the $opt - j$ bins containing two items each. Furthermore, it cannot fit in one of the bins containing one of the first j items, because if it could fit with one of those items our algorithm would have placed it with that item. Because we assumed that this is an optimal solution, s_i must be in one of the bins, which means that we have a contradiction, and our lemma is proven.

Lemma 9.2 Let opt be the optimal number of bins for an instance of the Bin Packing Problem. The number of items placed by the nonincreasing first fit strategy in extra bins is at most $opt - 1$.

Proof: Because all the objects fit in opt bins,

$$\sum_{i=1}^{n} s_i \leq opt.$$

Suppose by way of contradiction that our approximation algorithm does put opt items into extra bins. Let $z_1, z_2, \ldots, z_{opt}$ be the sizes of those items, and, for

$1 \leq i \leq opt$, let tot_i be the total size that our algorithm puts in bin B_i. It must be true that

$$tot_i + z_i > 1,$$

because otherwise the item of size z_i could have been put in B_i. We therefore have

$$\sum_{i=1}^{n} s_i \geq \sum_{i=1}^{opt} tot_i + \sum_{i=1}^{opt} z_i = \sum_{i=1}^{opt} (tot_i + z_i) > \sum_{i=1}^{opt} 1 = opt,$$

which contradicts what we showed at the beginning of the proof. This contradiction proves the lemma.

Theorem 9.8 Let opt be the optimal number of bins for an instance of the Bin Packing Problem, and let $approx$ be the number of bins used by the nonincreasing first fit algorithm. Then

$$approx \leq 1.5 \times opt.$$

Proof: By Lemmas 9.1 and 9.2, the nonincreasing first fit algorithm puts at most $opt - 1$ items, each of size at most $\frac{1}{3}$, in extra bins. Therefore, the number of extra bins is at most

$$\left\lceil (opt - 1) \times \frac{1}{3} \right\rceil = \left\lceil \frac{opt - 1}{3} \right\rceil = \frac{opt - 1 + k}{3},$$

where $k = 0$, 1, or 2. Taking the largest possible value of k, we conclude that the number of extra bins is less than or equal to $(opt + 1)/3$, which means that

$$approx \leq opt + \frac{opt + 1}{3},$$

and therefore

$$\frac{approx}{opt} \leq \frac{opt + (opt + 1)/3}{opt} = \frac{4}{3} + \frac{1}{3opt}.$$

This ratio is maximized if $opt = 1$. However, when $opt = 1$, our approximation algorithm uses only one bin and therefore is optimal. This means that we can take $opt = 2$ to maximize the ratio and conclude that

$$\frac{approx}{opt} \leq \frac{4}{3} + \frac{1}{3 \times 2} = \frac{3}{2}.$$

It is possible to create instances of arbitrarily large size for which the ratio is exactly 3/2. Therefore, in general, we cannot improve on the bound obtained in Theorem 9.8.

One way to gain further insight into the quality of an approximation algorithm is to run empirical tests comparing the solutions obtained from the approximation algorithm with the optimal solutions. Our approximation algorithm for the Bin Packing Problem has been extensively tested for large values of n. You may wonder how this is possible when we have no polynomial-time algorithm that guarantees an optimal solution, which means that we cannot determine an optimal solution for a large value of n in a tolerable amount of time. Indeed, if we had such an algorithm we would not bother with an approximation algorithm in the first place. The answer to this paradox is that in the case of the Bin Packing Problem we do not need to actually compute optimal solutions to gain insight into the quality of the approximations. Instead, we can compute the amount of unused space (the empty space) in the bins used by the approximation algorithm. The number of extra bins used by that algorithm can be no more than the amount of unused space. This is so because we can rearrange the items in our approximate solution so that they are in an optimal number of bins, leaving the extra bins empty. The amount of unused space in this optimal solution plus the total space in the extra bins is equal to the amount of unused space in our approximate solution. Therefore, because the total space in the extra bins equals the number of extra bins, the number of extra bins can be no greater than the amount of unused space in our approximate solution.

In an empirical study in which the input size was 128,000 and the item sizes were uniformly distributed between 0 and 1, our approximation algorithm used on the average about 64,000 bins, and on the average had about 100 units of unused space. This means that on the average the number of extra bins is bounded by 100 in the instances in this study. Theorem 9.8 implies, for an approximate solution of 64,000, that

$$64,000 \leq 1.5 \times opt,$$

which means $opt \geq 42,666$, and that the number of extra bins is no greater than 21,334. We see that the empirical study indicates that on the average our algorithm performs much better than the upper bound.

For any particular instance of interest, we can compute the amount of unused space in the solution produced by the approximation algorithm. In this way we can determine how well the algorithm performs for that instance.

For more examples of approximation algorithms, you are again referred to Garey and Johnson (1979).

Exercises

Sections 9.1 to 9.3

1. List three problems that have polynomial-time algorithms. Justify your answer.

2. Give a problem and two encoding schemes for its input. Express its performance using your encoding schemes.

3. Show that a graph problem using the number of vertices as the measure of the size of an instance is polynomially equivalent to one using the number of edges as the measure of the size of an instance.

4. In which of the three general categories discussed in Section 9.3 does the problem of computing the nth Fibonacci term belong? Justify your answer.

5. A graph has a Euler Circuit if and only if (a) the graph is connected and (b) the degree of every vertex is even. Find a lower bound for the time complexity of all algorithms that determine if a graph has a Euler Circuit. In which of the three general categories discussed in Section 9.3 does this problem belong? Justify your answer.

6. List at least two problems that belong in each of the three general categories discussed in Section 9.3.

Section 9.4

7. Implement the verification algorithm for the Traveling Salesperson Decision Problem discussed in Section 9.4.1 on your system, and study its polynomial-time performance.

8. Establish that the problems in Examples 9.2 to 9.5 are in *NP*.

9. Write a polynomial-time verification algorithm for the Clique Decision Problem.

10. Show that the reduction of the CNF-Satisfiability Problem to the Clique Decision Problem can be done in polynomial time.

11. Write a polynomial-time verification algorithm for the Hamiltonian Circuits Decision Problem.

12. Show that the reduction of the Hamiltonian Circuits Decision Problem to the Traveling Salesperson (Undirected) Decision Problem can be done in polynomial time.

13. Show that the reduction of the Traveling Salesperson (Undirected) Decision Problem to the Traveling Salesperson Decision Problem can be done in polynomial time.

14. Show that a problem is *NP*-easy if and only if it reduces to an *NP*-complete problem.

15. Suppose that problem A and problem B are two different decision problems. Furthermore, assume that problem A is polynomial-time many-one reducible to problem B. If problem A is *NP*-complete, is problem B *NP*-complete? Justify your answer.

16. When all instances of the CNF-Satisfiability Problem have exactly three literals per clause, it is called the 3-Satisfiability Problem. Knowing that the 3-Satisfiability Problem is *NP*-complete, show that the Graph 3-Coloring Problem is also *NP*-complete.

17. Show that if a problem is not in *NP*, it is not *NP*-easy. Therefore, Presburger Arithmetic and the Halting Problem are not *NP*-easy.

Section 9.5

18. Implement the approximation algorithms for the Traveling Salesperson Problem, run them on your system, and study their performances using several problem instances.

19. Write a detailed algorithm of the approximation algorithm for the Bin Packing Problem given in Section 9.5.2, and show that its time complexity is in $\Theta(n^2)$.

20. For the Sum-of-Subsets Problem discussed in Chapter 5, can you develop an approximation algorithm that runs in polynomial time?

21. Can you develop an approximation algorithm for the CNF-Satisfiability Problem by stating it as an optimization problem—that is, by finding a truth assignment of the literals in the expression that makes the maximum possible number of clauses true?

Additional Problems

22. Can an algorithm be a polynomial-time algorithm for a problem using one encoding scheme, and an exponential-time algorithm for the same problem using another encoding scheme? Justify your answer.

23. Write a more concrete algorithm for function *verify_composite* given in Section 9.4.2, and analyze it to show that it is a polynomial-time algorithm.

24. Write a polynomial-time algorithm that checks if an undirected graph has a Hamiltonian Circuit, assuming that the graph has no vertex with degree exceeding 2.

25. Is the Towers of Hanoi Problem an *NP*-complete problem? Is it an *NP*-easy problem? Is it an *NP*-hard problem? Is it an *NP*-equivalent problem? Justify your answers. This problem is presented in Exercise 17 in Chapter 2.

26. Given a list of *n* positive integers (*n* even), divide the list into two sublists such that the difference between the sums of the integers in the two sublists is minimized. Is this problem an *NP*-complete problem? Is this problem an *NP*-hard problem?

CHAPTER 10

Introduction to Parallel Algorithms

Suppose you want to build a fence in your backyard, and it's necessary to dig 10 deep holes, one for each fence post. Realizing that it would be a laborious and unpleasant task to individually dig the 10 holes in sequence, you look for some alternative. You remember how Mark Twain's famous character Tom Sawyer tricked his friends into helping him whitewash a fence by pretending it was fun. You decide to use the same clever ruse, but you update it a bit. You pass out flyers to your health-conscious neighbors announcing a hole-digging contest in your backyard. Whoever is most fit should be able to dig a hole fastest and therefore win the contest. You offer some insignificant first prize, such as a six-pack of beer, knowing that the prize is not really important to your neighbors. Rather, they just want to prove how fit they are. On contest day, 10 strong neighbors simultaneously dig 10 holes. This is called digging the holes in parallel. You have saved yourself a lot of work and completed the hole digging much faster than you would have done by digging them in sequence by yourself.

Just as you can complete the hole-digging job faster by having friends work in parallel, often a computer could complete a job faster if it had many processors executing instructions in parallel. (A ***processor*** in a computer is a hardware component that processes instructions and data.) So far we have discussed only sequential processing. That is, all of the algorithms we've presented have been designed to be implemented on a traditional sequential computer. Such a computer has one processor executing instructions in sequence, similar to your digging the 10 holes in sequence by yourself. These computers are based on the model introduced by John von Neumann. As Figure 10.1 illustrates, this model consists of a single processor, called the central processing unit (CPU), and memory. The model takes a single sequence of instructions and operates on a single sequence of data. Such a computer is called a ***single instruction stream, single data stream*** (SISD) computer, and is popularly known as a *serial* computer.

Many problems could be solved much faster if a computer had many processors executing instructions simultaneously (in parallel). This would be like having your 10 neighbors dig the 10 holes at the same time. For example, consider the belief network introduced in Section 6.3. Figure 10.2 shows such a network. Each vertex in that network represents a possible condition of a patient. There is an edge from one vertex to another if having the condition at the first vertex could cause one to have the condition at the second vertex. For example, the top right vertex represents the condition of being a smoker, and the edge emanating from that vertex means that smoking can cause lung cancer. A given cause does not always result in its potential effects. Therefore, the probability of each effect given each of its causes also needs to be stored in the network. For example, the probability (.5) of being a smoker is stored at the vertex containing "Smoker." The probability (.1) of having lung cancer given that one is a smoker and the probability (.01) of having lung cancer given that one is not a smoker are stored at the vertex containing "Lung cancer." The probability (.99) of having a positive chest x-ray given that one has both tuberculosis and lung cancer, along with the probabilities of having a positive chest x-ray given the other three combinations of values of its causes, are stored at the vertex containing "Positive chest x-ray." The basic inference problem in a belief network is to determine the probability of having the conditions at all remaining vertices when it is learned that the conditions at certain vertices are present. For example, if a patient was known to be a smoker and to have had a positive

Figure 10.1 A traditional sequential computer.

Figure 10.2 A belief network.

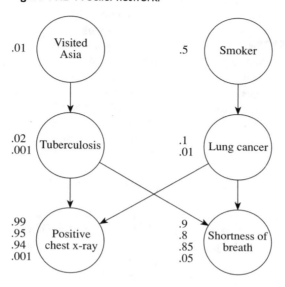

chest x-ray, we might want to know the probabilities that the patient had lung cancer, had tuberculosis, had shortness of breath, and had recently visited Asia. Pearl (1986) developed an inference algorithm for solving this problem. In this algorithm, each vertex sends messages to its parents and children. For example, when it is learned that the patient has a positive chest x-ray, the vertex for "Positive chest x-ray" sends messages to its parents "Tuberculosis" and "Lung cancer." When each of these vertices receives its message, the probability of the condition at the vertex is computed, and the vertex then sends messages to its parents and other children. When these vertices receive messages, the new probabilities of the conditions at the vertices are computed, and the vertices then send messages. The message-passing scheme terminates at roots and leaves. When it is learned that the patient is also a smoker, another message stream begins at that vertex. A traditional sequential computer can compute the value of only one message or one probability at a time. The value of the message to "Tuberculosis" could be computed first, then the new probability of tuberculosis, then the value of the message to "Lung cancer," then its probability, and so on.

If each vertex had its own processor that was capable of sending messages to the processors at the other vertices, we could first compute and send the messages to "Tuberculosis" and "Lung cancer." When each of these vertices received its message, it could independently compute and send messages to its parents and other children. Furthermore, if we also know that the patient was a smoker, the vertex containing "Smoker" could simultaneously be computing and sending a message to its child. Clearly, if all this were taking place simultaneously, the inference could be done much more quickly. A belief network used in actual applications often contains hundreds of vertices, and the inferred probabilities are needed immediately. This means that the time savings could be quite significant.

What we have just described is an architecture for a particular kind of *parallel* computer. Such computers are called "parallel" because each processor can execute instructions simultaneously (in parallel) with all the other processors. The cost of processors has decreased dramatically over the past three decades. Currently, the speed of an off-the-shelf microprocessor is within one order of magnitude of the speed of the fastest serial computer. However, they cost many orders of magnitude less. Therefore, by connecting microprocessors as described in the previous paragraph, it is possible to obtain computing power faster than the fastest serial computer for substantially less money. There are many applications that can benefit significantly from parallel computation. Applications in artificial intelligence include the Belief Network Problem described previously, inference in neural networks, natural language understanding, speech recognition, and machine vision. Other applications include database query processing, weather prediction, pollution monitoring, analysis of protein structures, and many more.

There are many ways to design parallel computers. Section 10.1 discusses some of the considerations necessary in parallel design and some of the most popular parallel architectures. Section 10.2 shows how to write algorithms for one particular kind of parallel computer, called a PRAM (for "parallel random access machine"). As we shall see, this particular kind of computer is not very practical. However, the PRAM model is a straightforward generalization of the sequential model of computation. Furthermore, a PRAM algorithm can be translated into algorithms for many practical machines. So PRAM algorithms serve as a good introduction to parallel algorithms.

10.1 PARALLEL ARCHITECTURES

The construction of parallel computers can vary in each of the following three ways:

1. Control mechanism
2. Address-space organization
3. Interconnection network

10.1.1 *Control Mechanism*

Each processor in a parallel computer can operate either under the control of a centralized control unit or independently under the control of its own control unit. The first kind of architecture is called *single instruction stream, multiple data stream* (SIMD). Figure 10.3(a) illustrates an SIMD architecture. The interconnection network depicted in the figure represents the hardware that enables the processors to communicate with each other. Interconnection networks are discussed in Section 10.1.3. In an SIMD architecture, the same instruction is executed synchronously by all processing units under the control of the central control unit. Not all processors must execute an instruction in each cycle; any given processor can be switched off in any given cycle.

Parallel computers, in which each processor has its own control unit, are called *multiple instruction stream, multiple data stream* (MIMD) computers. Figure 10.3(b) illustrates an MIMD architecture. MIMD computers store both the operating system and the program at each processor.

SMID computers are suited for programs in which the same set of instructions is executed on different elements of a data set. Such programs are called *data-parallel programs.* A drawback of SIMD computers is that they cannot execute different instructions in the same cycle. For example, suppose the following conditional statement is being executed:

```
if (x == y)
    execute instructions A;
else
    execute instructions B;
```

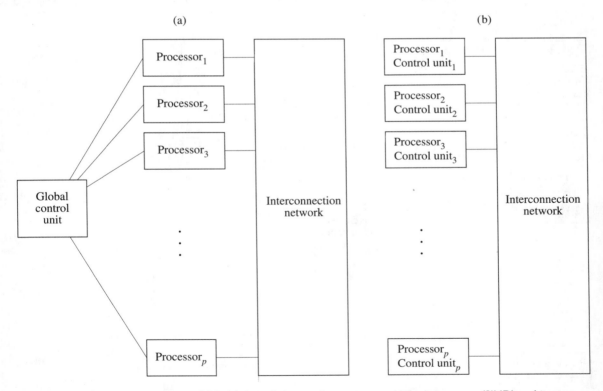

Figure 10.3 (a) A single instruction stream, multiple data stream (SIMD) architecture. (b) A multiple instruction stream, multiple data stream (MIMD) architecture.

Any processor that finds $x \neq y$ (recall that the processors are processing different data elements) must do nothing while the processors that find $x = y$ are executing instructions A. Those that find $x = y$ must then be idle while the others are executing instructions B.

In general, SIMD computers are best suited to parallel algorithms that require synchronization. Many MIMD computers have extra hardware that provides synchronization, which means that they can emulate SIMD computers.

10.1.2 Address-Space Organization

Processors can communicate with each other either by modifying data in a common address space or by passing messages. The address space is organized differently according to the communication method used.

Shared-Address-Space Architecture

In a ***shared-address space-architecture,*** the hardware provides for read and write access by all processors to a shared address space. Processors communicate by modifying data in the shared address space. Figure 10.4(a) depicts a shared-address-space architecture in which the time it takes each processor to access any

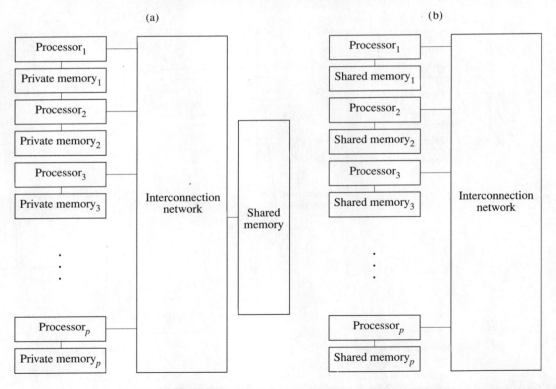

Figure 10.4 (a) A uniform memory access (UMA) computer. (b) A nonuniform memory access (NUMA) computer.

word in memory is the same. Such a computer is called a ***uniform memory access*** (UMA) computer. In a UMA computer, each processor may have its own private memory, as shown in Figure 10.4(a). This private memory is used only to hold local variables necessary for the processor to carry out its computations. None of the actual input to the algorithm is in the private area. A drawback of a UMA computer is that the interconnection network must simultaneously provide access for every processor to the shared memory. This can significantly slow down performance. Another alternative is to provide each processor with a portion of the shared memory. This is illustrated in Figure 10.4(b). This memory is not private, as is the local memory in Figure 10.4(a). That is, each processor has access to the memory stored at another processor. However, it has faster access to its own memory than to memory stored at another processor. If most of a processor's accesses are to its own memory, performance should be good. Such a computer is called a ***nonuniform memory access*** (NUMA) computer.

Message-Passing Architecture

In a ***message-passing architecture,*** each processor has its own private memory that is accessible only to that processor. Processors communicate by passing messages to other processors rather than by modifying data elements. Figure 10.5 shows a message-passing architecture. Notice that Figure 10.5 looks much like Figure 10.4(b). The difference is the way in which the interconnection network is wired. In the case of the NUMA computer, the interconnection network is wired to allow each processor access to the memory stored at the other processors, whereas in the message-passing computer it is wired to allow each processor to send a message directly to each of the other processors.

10.1.3 Interconnection Networks

There are two general categories of interconnection networks: static and dynamic. Static networks are typically used to construct message-passing architectures, whereas dynamic networks are typically used to construct shared-address-space architectures. We discuss each of these types of networks in turn.

Static Interconnection Networks

A ***static interconnection network*** contains direct links between processors and are sometimes called ***direct networks.*** There are several different types of static interconnection networks. Let's discuss some of the most common ones. The most efficient, but also the most costly, is a ***completely connected network,*** which is illustrated in Figure 10.6(a). In such a network, every processor is directly linked to every other processor. Therefore, a processor can send a message to another processor directly on the link to that processor. Because the number of links is quadratic in terms of the number of processors, this type of network is quite costly.

Figure 10.5 A message-passing architecture. Each processor's memory is accessible only to that processor. Processors communicate by passing messages to each other through the interconnection network.

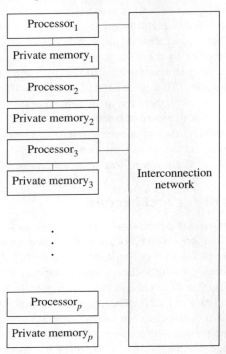

In a ***star-connected network,*** one processor acts as the central processor. That is, every other processor has a link only to that processor. Figure 10.6(b) depicts a star-connected network. In a star-connected network, a processor sends a message to another processor by sending the message to the central processor, which in turn routes the message to the receiving processor.

In a ***bounded-degree network*** of degree d, each processor is linked to at most d other processors. Figure 10.6(c) shows a bounded-degree network of degree 4. In a bounded-degree network of degree 4, a message can be passed by sending it first along one direction and then along the other direction until it reaches its destination.

A slightly more complex, but popular, static network is the hypercube. A zero-dimensional hypercube consists of a single processor. A one-dimensional hypercube is formed by linking the processors in two zero-dimensional hypercubes. A two-dimensional hypercube is formed by linking each processor in a one-dimensional hypercube to one processor in another one-dimensional hypercube. Recursively, a ***(d+1)-dimensional hypercube*** is formed by linking each processor in a d-dimensional hypercube to one processor in another d-dimensional hypercube. A given processor in the first hypercube is linked to the processor

Figure 10.6 (a) A completely connected network. (b) A star-connected network. (c) A bounded-degree network of degree 4.

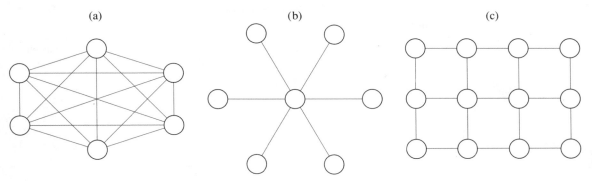

(a)   (b)   (c)

occupying the corresponding position in the second hypercube. Figure 10.7 illustrates hypercube networks.

It should be clear that the reason why static networks are ordinarily used to implement message-passing architectures is that the processors in such networks are directly linked, enabling the flow of messages.

Dynamic Interconnection Networks

In a ***dynamic interconnection network,*** processors are connected to memory through a set of switching elements. One of the most straightforward ways to do this is to use a ***crossbar switching network.*** In such a network, p processors are

Zero-dimensional   One-dimensional   Two-dimensional   Three-dimensional

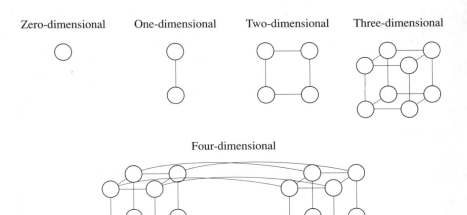

Four-dimensional

Figure 10.7 Hypercube networks.

Figure 10.8 A crossbar switching network. There is a switch at every position on the grid. The circled switch is closed, enabling the flow of information between processor$_3$ and membank$_2$, when the third processor is currently allowed to access the second memory bank.

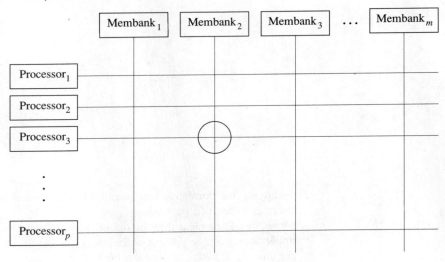

connected to m memory banks using a grid of switching elements, as shown in Figure 10.8. If, for example, processor$_3$ can currently access membank$_2$, the switch at the grid position circled in Figure 10.8 is closed (closing the switch completes the circuit, enabling the flow of electricity). This network is called ''dynamic'' because the connection between a processor and a memory bank is made dynamically when a switch is closed. A crossbar switching network is nonblocking. That is, the connection of one processor to a given memory bank does not block the connection of another processor to another memory bank. Ideally, in a crossbar switching network there should be a bank for every word in memory. However, this is clearly impractical. Ordinarily, the number of banks is at least as large as the number of processors, so that, at a given time, every processor is capable of accessing at least one memory bank. The number of switches in a crossbar switching network is equal to pm. Therefore, if we require that m be greater than or equal to p, the number of switches is greater than or equal to p^2. As a result, crossbar switching networks can become quite costly when the number of processors is large.

Other dynamic interconnection networks, which will not be discussed here, include bus-based networks and multistage interconnection networks.

It should be clear why dynamic interconnection networks are ordinarily used to implement shared-address-space architectures. That is, in such networks each processor is allowed to access every word in memory but cannot send a direct message to any of the other processors.

The introduction to parallel hardware presented here is based largely on the discussion in Kumar, Grama, Gupta, and Karypis (1994). The reader is referred to that text for a more thorough introduction and, in particular, for a discussion of bus-based and multistage interconnection networks.

10.2 THE PRAM MODEL

As discussed in the preceding section, quite a few different parallel architectures are possible, and computers have actually been manufactured with many of these architectures. All sequential computers, on the other hand, have the architecture shown in Figure 10.1, which means that the von Neumann model is a universal model for all sequential computers. The only assumption that was made in designing the algorithms in the previous chapters was that they would run on a computer conforming to the von Neumann model. Therefore, each of these algorithms has the same time complexity regardless of the programming language or computer used to implement the algorithm. This has been a key factor in the impressive growth of the application of sequential computers.

It would be useful to find a universal model for parallel computation. Any such model must first be sufficiently general to capture the key features of a large class of parallel architectures. Second, algorithms designed according to this model must execute efficiently on actual parallel computers. No such model is currently known, and it seems unlikely that one will be found.

Although no universal model is currently known, the ***parallel random access machine (PRAM)*** computer has become widely used as a *theoretical* model for parallel machines. A PRAM computer consists of p processors, all of which have uniform access to a large shared memory. Processors share a common clock but may execute different instructions in each cycle. Therefore, a PRAM computer is a synchronous, MIMD, UMA computer. This means that Figures 10.3(b) and 10.4(a) depict the architecture of a PRAM computer, whereas Figure 10.8 shows a possible interconnection network for such a machine. As already noted, it would be quite costly to actually construct such a computer. However, the PRAM model is a natural extension of the sequential model of computation. This makes the PRAM model conceptually easy to work with when developing algorithms. Furthermore, algorithms developed for the PRAM model can be translated into algorithms for many of the more practical computers. For example, a PRAM instruction can be simulated in $\Theta(\lg p)$ instructions on a bounded-degree network, where p is the number of processors. Additionally, for a large class of problems, PRAM algorithms are asymptotically as fast as algorithms for a hypercube. For these reasons, the PRAM model serves as a good introduction to parallel algorithms.

In a shared-memory computer such as a PRAM, more than one processor can try to read from or write to the same memory location simultaneously. There are four versions of the PRAM model depending on how concurrent memory accesses are handled.

1. *Exclusive-read, exclusive-write (EREW).* In this version, no concurrent reads or writes are allowed. That is, only one processor can access a given memory location at a given time. This is the weakest version of the PRAM computer, because it allows minimal concurrency.

2. *Exclusive-read, concurrent-write (ERCW).* In this version, simultaneous write operations are allowed, but not simultaneous read operations.

3. *Concurrent-read, exclusive-write (CREW).* In this version, simultaneous read operations are allowed, but not simultaneous write operations.

4. *Concurrent-read, concurrent-write (CRCW).* In this version, both simultaneous read and write operations are allowed.

We discuss algorithmic design for the CREW PRAM model and the CRCW PRAM model. First we address the CREW model, then we show how more efficient algorithms can sometimes be developed using the CRCW model. Before proceeding, let's discuss how we present parallel algorithms. Although programming languages for parallel algorithms exist, we will use our standard pseudocode with some additional features, which will be described next.

Just one version of the algorithm is written, and after compilation it is executed by all processors simultaneously. Therefore, each processor needs to know its own index while executing the algorithm. We will assume that the processors are indexed P_1, P_2, P_3, etc, and that the instruction

p = index of this processor;

returns the index of a processor. A variable declared in the algorithm could be a variable in shared memory, which means that it is accessible to all processors, or it could be in private memory (see Figure 10.4a). In this latter case, each processor has its own copy of the variable. We use the key word **local** when declaring a variable of this type.

All our algorithms will be data-parallel algorithms, as discussed in Section 10.1.1. That is, the processors will execute the same set of instructions on different elements of a data set. The data set will be stored in shared memory. If an instruction assigns the value of an element of this data set to a local variable, we call this a read from shared memory, whereas if it assigns the value of a local variable to an element of this data set, we call this a write to shared memory. The only instructions we use for manipulating elements of this data set are reads from and writes into shared memory. For example, we never directly compare the values of two elements of the data set. Rather we read their values into variables in local memory and then compare the values of those variables. We will allow direct comparisons to variables like *n,* the size of the data set. A data-parallel algorithm consists of a sequence of steps, and every processor starts each step at the same time and ends each step at the same time. Furthermore, all processors that read during a given step read at the same time, and all processors that write during a given step write at the same time.

Finally, we assume that as many processors as we want are always available to us. In practice, as already noted, this is often an unrealistic assumption.

The following algorithm illustrates these conventions. We are assuming that there is an array of integers S, indexed from 1 to n, in shared memory and that n processors, indexed from 1 to n, are executing the algorithm in parallel.

```
void example (int n,                    // S is the data set in
              int S[ ])                 // shared memory.
{
    local index p;
    local int temp;

    p = index of this processor;
    read S[p] into temp;                // This is a read form
    if (p < n)                          // shared memory.
        write temp into S[p + 1];       // This is a write to
    else                                // shared memory.
        write temp into S[1];
}
```

All of the values in the array S are read into n different local variables *temp* simultaneously. Then the values in the n variables *temp* are all written back out to S simultaneously. Effectively, every element in S is given the value of its predecessor (with wraparound). Figure 10.9 illustrates the operation of the algorithm. Notice that each processor always has access to the entire array S because S is in shared memory. So the pth processor can write to the $(p + 1)$st array slot.

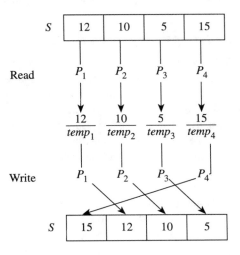

Figure 10.9 Application of procedure *example*.

There is only one step in this simple algorithm. When there is more than one step, we write loops such as the following:

```
for (step = 1; step <= numsteps; step++) {
    // Code to be executed in each step goes here. Every processor starts
    // each step at the same time and ends each step at the same time. All
    // processors that read during a given step read at the same time, and all
    // processors that write during a given step write at the same time.
}
```

There are various ways this loop can be implemented. One way is to have a separate control unit do the incrementing and testing. It would issue instructions telling the other processors when to read, when to execute instructions on local variables, and when to write. Inside the loop, we sometimes do calculations on a variable that always has the same value for all processors. For example, Algorithms 10.1 and 10.3 both execute the instruction

```
size = 2 * size;
```

where *size* has the same value for all processors. To make it clear that each processor does not need its own copy of such a variable, we will declare the variable as a variable in shared memory. The instruction can be implemented by having a separate control unit execute it. We won't discuss implementation further. Rather, we proceed to writing algorithms.

10.2.1 Designing Algorithms for the CREW PRAM Model

We illustrate CREW PRAM algorithms with the following exemplary problems.

Finding the Largest Key in an Array

Theorem 8.7 proves that it takes at least $n - 1$ comparisons to find the largest key only by comparisons of keys, which means that any algorithm for the problem, designed to run on a sequential computer, must be $\Theta(n)$. Using parallel computation, we can improve on this running time. The parallel algorithm still must do at least $n - 1$ comparisons. But by doing many of them in parallel, it finishes sooner. We develop this algorithm next.

Recall that Algorithm 8.2 (Find Largest Key) finds the largest key in optimal time as follows:

```
void find_largest (int n,
                   const keytype S[ ],
                   keytype& large)
{
    index i;
```

```
        large = S[1];
        for (i = 2; i <= n; i++)
           if (S[i] > large)
           large = S[i];
    }
```

This algorithm cannot benefit from using more processors, because the result of each iteration of the loop is needed for the next iteration. Recall from Section 8.5.3 the Tournament Method for finding the largest key. This method pairs the numbers into groups of two and finds the largest (winner) of each pair. Then it pairs the winners and finds the largest of each of these pairs. It continues until only one key remains. Figure 8.10 illustrates this method. A sequential algorithm for the Tournament Method has the same time complexity as Algorithm 8.2. However, this method can benefit from using more processors. For example, suppose you wish to find the largest of eight keys using this method. You have to determine each of four winners in the first round in sequence before proceeding to the second round. If you have the help of three friends, each of you can simultaneously determine one of the winners of the first round. This means that the first round can be completed four times as fast. After that round, two of you can rest while the other two perform the comparisons in the second round. In the final round, only one of you needs to do a comparison.

Figure 10.10 illustrates how a parallel algorithm for this method proceeds. We need only half as many processors as array elements. Each processor reads two array elements into local variables *first* and *second*. It then writes the larger of *first* and *second* into the first of the array slots from which it has read. After three such rounds, the largest key ends up in S[1]. Each round is a step in the algorithm. In the example shown in Figure 10.10, $n = 8$ and there are $\lg 8 = 3$ steps. Algorithm 10.1 is an algorithm for the actions illustrated in Figure 10.10. Notice that this algorithm is written as a function. When a parallel algorithm is written as a function, it is necessary that at least one processor return a value and that all processors that do return values return the same value.

Algorithm 10.1

Parallel Find Largest Key

Problem: Find the largest key in an array S of size n.

Inputs: positive integer n, array of keys S indexed from 1 to n.

Outputs: the value of the largest key in S.

Comment: It is assumed that n is a power of 2 and that we have $n/2$ processors executing the algorithm in parallel. The processors are indexed from 1 to $n/2$ and the command "index of this processor" returns the index of a processor.

```
keytype parlargest (int n, keytype S[ ])
{
   index step, size;
   local index p;
   local keytype first, second;

   p = index of this processor;
   size = 1;                                    // size is the size of the
   for (step = 1; step <= lgn; step++)          // the subarrays.
      if (this processor needs to execute in this step) {
         read S[2*p − 1] into first;
         read S[2*p − 1 + size] into second;
         write maximum(first, second) into S[2*p − 1];
         size = 2 * size;
      }
   return S[1];
}
```

We used the high-level pseudocode "**if** (this processor needs to execute in this step)" in order to keep the algorithm as lucid as possible. In Figure 10.10 we see that the processors used in a given step are the ones for which

$$p = 1 + size*k$$

for some integer k (notice that *size* doubles in value in each step). Therefore, the actual check of whether the processor should execute is

    if ((p − 1) % size == 0)   // % returns the remainder when $p − 1$ is
                                                     // divided by *size*.

Alternatively, we can simply allow all the processors to execute in each step. The ones that need not execute simply do useless comparisons. For example, in the second round, processor P_2 compares the value of $S[3]$ with the value of $S[5]$ and writes the larger value into $S[3]$. Even though this is unnecessary, P_2 may as well be doing it because nothing is gained by keeping P_2 idle. The important things are that the processors that should be executing are executing and that the other processors are not changing the values of memory locations needed by the ones that should be executing. The only problem presented by allowing unneeded processors to execute instructions is that sometimes they end up referring to array elements outside the range of S. For example, in the previous algorithm, P_4 refers to $S[9]$ in the second round. This can be handled by simply padding S with additional slots. We end up wasting space this way, but we save time by eliminating the check of whether the processor should be executing.

When analyzing a parallel algorithm, we do not analyze the total amount of work done by the algorithm. Rather, we analyze the total amount of work done by any one processor, because this gives us a good idea of how fast the computer

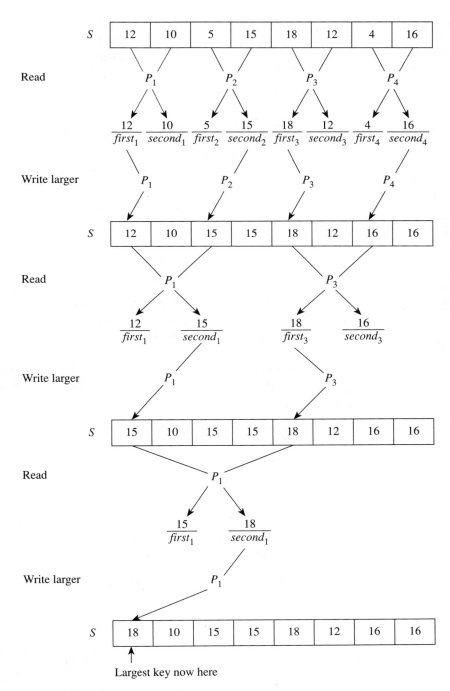

Figure 10.10 Use of parallel processors to implement the Tournament Method for finding the largest key.

will process the input. Because each processor does about lg n passes through the **for**-*step* loop in Algorithm 10.1, we have

$$T(n) \in \Theta(\lg n).$$

This is a substantial improvement over the sequential algorithm.

Applications of Dynamic Programming

Many dynamic programming applications are amenable to parallel design because often the entries in a given row or diagonal can all be computed simultaneously. We illustrate this approach by rewriting the algorithm for the binomial coefficient (Algorithm 3.2) as a parallel algorithm. In this algorithm, the entries in a given row of Pascal's Triangle (see Figure 3.1) are computed in parallel.

Algorithm 10.2

Parallel Binomial Coefficient

Problem: Compute the binomial coefficient.

Inputs: nonnegative integers n and k, where $k \leq n$.

Outputs: the binomial coefficient $\binom{n}{k}$.

Comment: It is assumed that we have $k + 1$ processors executing the algorithm in parallel. The processors are indexed from 0 to k, and the command "index of this processor" returns the index of a processor.

```
int parbin (int n, int k)
{                                      // Use i instead of step to
   index i;                            // control the steps to be
   int B[0..n][0..k];                  // consistent with Algorithm 3.2.
   local index j;                      // Use j instead of p to obtain
   local int first, second;           // index of processor to be
                                       // consistent with Algorithm 3.2.

   j = index of this processor;
   for (i = 0; i <= n; i++)
     if (j <= minimum(i, k))
       if (j == 0 ‖ j == i)
         write 1 into B[i][j];
       else {
         read B[i − 1][j − 1] into first;
         read B[i − 1][j] into second;
         write first + second into B[i][j];
       }
   return B[n][k];
}
```

The control statement in Algorithm 3.2

for ($j = 0$; $j <=$ *minimum*(i, k); $j++$)

is replaced in this algorithm by the control statement

if ($j <=$ *minimum*(i, k))

because all k processors execute in each pass through the **for**-i loop. Instead of sequentially computing the values of $B[i][j]$ with j ranging from 0 to *minimum*(i, k), the parallel algorithm has the processors that are indexed from 0 to *minimum*(i, k) simultaneously computing the values.

Clearly, there are $n + 1$ passes through a loop in our parallel algorithm. Recall that there are $\Theta(nk)$ passes through a loop in the sequential algorithm (Algorithm 3.2).

Recall from Exercise 3.4 that it is possible to implement Algorithm 3.2 using only a one-dimensional array B that is indexed from 0 to k. This modification is very straightforward in the case of the parallel algorithm, because on entry to the ith pass through the **for**-i loop the entire $(i - 1)$st row of Pascal's triangle can be read from B into the k local pairs of variables *first* and *second*. Then, on exit, the entire ith row can be written into B. The pseudocode is as follows:

```
for (i = 0; i <= n; i++)
  if (j <= minimum(i, k))
    if (j == 0 ‖ j == i)
      write I into B[j];
    else {
      read B[j − I] into first;
      read B[j] into second;
      write first + second into [j];
    }
return B[k];
```

Parallel Sorting

Recall the dynamic programming version of Mergesort 3 (Algorithm 7.3). That algorithm simply starts with the keys as singletons, merges pairs of keys into sorted lists containing two keys, merges pairs of those lists into sorted lists containing four keys, and so on. That is, it does the merging depicted in Figure 2.2. This is very similar to using the Tournament Method to find the maximum. That is, we can do the merging at each step in parallel. The following algorithm implements this method. Again, for simplicity, it is assumed that n is a power of 2. When this is not the case, the array size can be treated as a power of 2, but merging is not done beyond n. The dynamic programming version of Mergesort 3 (Algorithm 7.3) shows how to do this.

Algorithm 10.3

Parallel Mergesort

Problem: Sort *n* keys in nondecreasing order.

Inputs: positive integer *n*, array of keys *S* indexed from 1 to *n*.

Outputs: the array *S* containing the keys in nondecreasing order.

Comment: It is assumed that *n* is a power of 2 and that we have $n/2$ processors executing the algorithm in parallel. The processors are indexed from 1 to $n/2$, and the command "index of this processor" returns the index of a processor.

```
void parmergesort (int n, keytype S[ ])
{
    index step, size;
    local index p, low, mid, high;

    p = index of this processor;
    size = 1;                              // size is the size of the subarrays
    for (step = 1; step <= lgn; step++)    // being merged.
        if (this processor needs to execute in this step) {
            low = 2*p - 1;
            mid = low + size - 1;
            high = low + 2*size - 1;
            parmerge(low, mid, high, S);
            size = 2 * size;
        }
}

void parmerge (local index low, local index mid, local index high,
               keytype S[ ])
{
    local index i, j, k;
    local keytype first, second, U[low..high];

    i = low; j = mid + 1; k = low;
    while (i <= mid && j <= high) {
        read S[i] into first;
        read S[j] into second;
        if (first < second) {
            U[k] = first;
            i++;
        }
        else {
            U[k] = second;
            j++;
        }
        k++;
    }
```

```
    if (i > mid)
        read S[j] through S[high] into U[k] through U[high];
    else
        read S[i] through S[mid] into U[k] through U[high];
    write U[low] through U[high] into S[low] through S[high];
}
```

The check of whether a processor should execute in a given step is the same as the check in Algorithm 10.1. That is, we need to do the following check:

if $((p-1)$ % size $== 0)$ // % returns the remainder when $p - 1$ is divided
                              // by size.

Recall that we can reduce the number of assignments of records in the single-processor iterative version of Mergesort (Algorithm 7.3) by reversing the roles of U and S in each pass through the **for** loop. That same improvement can be done here. If this were done, U would have to be an array, indexed from 1 to n, in shared memory. We present the basic version of *parmerge* for the sake of simplicity.

The time complexity of this algorithm is not obvious. Therefore, we do a formal analysis.

Worst-Case Time Complexity Analysis of Algorithm 10.3

Basic operation: the comparison that takes place in *parmerge*.

Input size: n, the number of keys in the array.

This algorithm does exactly the same number of comparisons as does the ordinary sequential Mergesort. The difference is that many of them are done in parallel. In the first pass through the **for**-*step* loop, $n/2$ pairs of arrays, each containing only one key, are merged simultaneously. So the worst-case number of comparisons done by any processor is $2 - 1 = 1$ (see the analysis of Algorithm 2.3 in Section 2.2.) In the second pass, $n/4$ pairs of arrays, each containing two keys, are merged simultaneously. So the worst-case number of comparisons is $4 - 1 = 3$. In the third pass, $n/8$ pairs of arrays, each containing four keys, are merged simultaneously. So the worst-case number of comparisons is $8 - 1 = 7$. In general, in the ith pass, $n/2^i$ pairs of arrays, each containing 2^{i-1} keys, are merged simultaneously, and the worst-case number of comparisons is $2^i - 1$. Finally, in the last pass, two arrays, each containing $n/2$ keys, are merged, which means that the worst-case number of comparisons in this pass is $n - 1$. The total worst-case number of comparisons done by each processor is given by

$$W(n) = 1 + 3 + 7 + \cdots + 2^i - 1 + \cdots + n - 1$$

$$= \sum_{i=1}^{\lg n} (2^i - 1) = 2n - 2 - \lg n \in \Theta(n).$$

The last equality is derived from the result in Example A.3 in Appendix A and some algebraic manipulations.

We have successfully done parallel sorting by comparisons of keys in linear time, which is a significant improvement over the $\Theta(n \lg n)$ required by sequential sorting. It is possible to improve our parallel merging algorithm so that parallel mergesorting is done in $\Theta((\lg n)^2)$ time. This improvement is discussed in the exercises. Even this is not optimal, because parallel sorting can be done in $\Theta(\lg n)$ time. See Kumar, Grama, Gupta, and Karypis (1994) or Akl (1985) for a thorough discussion of parallel sorting.

10.2.2 Designing Algorithms for the CRCW PRAM Model

Recall that CRCW stands for concurrent-read, concurrent-write. Unlike concurrent reads, concurrent writes must somehow be resolved when two processors try to write to the same memory location in the same step. The most frequently used protocols for resolving such conflicts are as follows:

- ***Common.*** This protocol allows concurrent writes only if all the processors are attempting to write the same values.
- ***Arbitrary.*** This protocol picks an arbitrary processor as the one allowed to write to the memory location.
- ***Priority.*** In this protocol, all the processors are organized in a predefined priority list, and only the one with the highest priority is allowed to write.
- ***Sum.*** This protocol writes the sum of the quantities being written by the processors. (This protocol can be extended to any associative operator defined on the quantities being written.)

We write an algorithm for finding the largest key in an array that works with common-write, arbitrary-write, and priority-write protocols and that is faster than the one given previously for the CREW model (Algorithm 10.1). The algorithm proceeds as follows. Let the n keys be in an array S in shared memory. We maintain a second array T of n integers in shared memory, and initialize all elements in T to 1. Next we assume that we have $n(n-1)/2$ processors indexed as follows:

$$P_{ij} \qquad \text{where} \qquad 1 \le i < j \le n.$$

In parallel, we have all the processors compare $S[i]$ with $S[j]$. In this way, every element in S is compared with every other element in S. Each processor writes a 0 into $T[i]$ if $S[i]$ loses the comparison and a 0 into $T[j]$ if $S[j]$ loses. Only the largest key never loses a comparison. Therefore, the only element of T that re-

Figure 10.11 Application of Algorithm 10.4. Only $T[3]$ ends up equal to 1, because $S[3]$ is the largest key and therefore is the only key never to lose a comparison.

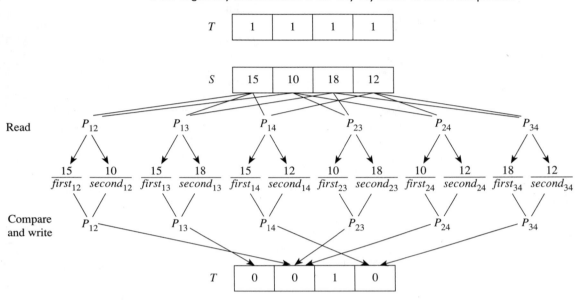

mains equal to 1 is the one that is indexed by k such that $S[k]$ contains the largest key. So the algorithm need only return the value of $S[k]$ such that $T[k] = 1$. Figure 10.11 illustrates these steps, and the algorithm follows. Notice in the algorithm that when more than one processor writes to the same memory location, they all write the same value. This means that the algorithm works with common-write, arbitrary-write, and priority-write protocols.

Algorithm 10.4 Parallel CRCW Find Largest Key

Problem: Find the largest key in an array S of n keys.

Inputs: positive integer n, array of keys S indexed from 1 to n.

Outputs: the value of the largest key in S.

Comment: It is assumed that n is a power of 2 and that we have $n(n - 1)/2$ processors executing the algorithm in parallel. The processors are indexed as

$$P_{ij} \qquad \text{where} \qquad 1 \le i < j \le n,$$

and the command "first index of this processor" returns the value of i, whereas the command "second index of this processor" returns j.

```
keytype parlargest2 (int n, const keytype S[ ])
{
  int T[1..n];
  local index i, j;
  local keytype first, second;
  local int chkfrst, chkscnd;

  i = first index of this processor;
  j = second index of this processor;
  write 1 into T[i];                    // Because 1 ≤ i ≤ n − 1 and
  write 1 into T[j];                    // 2 ≤ j ≤ n, these write
  read S[i] into first;                 // instructions initialize each
  read S[j] into second;                // array element of T to 1.
  if (first < second)
    write 0 into T[i];                  // T[k] ends up 0 if and only
  else                                  // if S[k] loses at least one
    write 0 into T[j];                  // comparison.
  read T[i] into chkfrst;
  read T[j] into chkscnd;
  if (chkfrst == 1)                     // T[k] still equals 1 if and only
    return S[i];                        // if S[k] contains the largest key.
  else if (chkscnd = 1)                 // Need to check T[j] in case
    return S[j];                        // the largest key is S[n]. Recall
}                                       // i ranges in value only from
                                        // 1 to n − 1.
```

There is no loop in this algorithm, which means that it finds the largest key in constant time. This is quite impressive, because it means that we could find the largest of 1,000,000 keys in the same amount of time required to find the largest of only 10 keys. However, this optimal time complexity has been bought at the expense of quadratic-time processor complexity. We would need about $1,000,000^2/2$ processors to find the largest of 1,000,000 keys.

This chapter has served only as a brief introduction to parallel algorithms. A thorough introduction requires a text of its own. One such text is Kumar, Grama, Gupta, and Karypis (1994).

Exercises

Section 10.1

1. Assuming that one person can add two numbers in t_a time, how long will it take that person to add two $n \times n$ matrices considering the operation of addition as the basic operation? Justify your answer.

2. If we have two people to add numbers, and it takes t_a time for one person to add two numbers, how long will the two people take to add two $n \times n$ matrices considering the operation of addition as the basic operation? Justify your answer.

3. Consider the problem of adding two $n \times n$ matrices. If it takes t_a time for one person to add two numbers, how many people do we need to minimize the total time spent to get the final answer? What will be the minimum amount of time needed to find the answer if we have enough people? Justify your answers.

4. Assuming that one person can add two numbers in t_a time, how long will it take that person to add all n numbers of a list considering the operation of addition as the basic operation? Justify your answer.

5. If we have two people to add n numbers of a list, and it takes t_a time for one person to add two numbers, how long will it take the two people to add all n numbers of the list considering the operation of addition as the basic operation and including t_p time for passing the result of an addition from one person to the other? Justify your answer.

6. Consider the problem of adding n numbers of a list. If it takes t_a time for one person to add two numbers, and it takes no time to pass the result of an addition from one person to another, how many people do we need to minimize the total time spent to get the final answer? What will be the minimum amount of time needed to find the answer if we have enough people? Justify your answer.

Section 10.2

7. Write a CREW PRAM algorithm for adding all n numbers of a list in $\Theta(\lg n)$ time.

8. Write a CREW PRAM algorithm for determining for each element of an n-element linked list if it is the middle ($\lceil n/2 \rceil$th) element in $\Theta(\lg n)$ time.

9. Write a CRCW PRAM algorithm that uses n^2 processors to multiply two $n \times n$ matrices. Your algorithm should perform better than the standard $\Theta(n^3)$-time serial algorithm.

10. Write a PRAM algorithm for Quicksort using n processors to sort a list of n elements.

11. Write a sequential algorithm that implements the Tournament Method to find the largest key in an array of n keys. Show that this algorithm is no more efficient than the standard sequential algorithm.

12. Write a PRAM algorithm using n^3 processors to multiply two $n \times n$ matrices. Your algorithm should run in $\Theta(\lg n)$ time.

13. Write a PRAM algorithm for the Shortest Paths Problem of Section 3.2. Compare the performance of your algorithm against the performance of Floyd's Algorithm (Algorithm 3.3).

14. Write a PRAM algorithm for the Chained Matrix Multiplication Problem of Section 3.4. Compare the performance of your algorithm against the performance of the Minimum Multiplications Algorithm (Algorithm 3.6).

15. Write a PRAM algorithm for the Optimal Binary Search Tree Problem of Section 3.5. Compare the performance of your algorithm against the performance of the Optimal Binary Search Tree Algorithm (Algorithm 3.9).

Additional Problems

16. Consider the problem of adding the numbers in a list of n numbers. If it takes $t_a(n - 1)$ time for one person to add all n numbers, is it possible for m people to compute the sum in less than $[t_a(n - 1)]/m$ time? Justify your answer.

17. Can you write a CREW PRAM algorithm for the problem of Exercise 9? Justify your answer.

18. Write a PRAM algorithm that runs in $\Theta((\lg n)^2)$ time for the problem of mergesorting. (*Hint:* Use n processors, and assign each processor to a key to determine the position of the key in the final list by binary searching.)

19. Write a PRAM algorithm for the Traveling Salesperson Problem of Section 3.6. Compare the performance of your algorithm against the performance of the Traveling Salesperson Algorithm (Algorithm 3.11).

APPENDIX A

Review of Necessary Mathematics

Except for the material that is marked ◈ or ◉, this text does not require that you have a strong background in mathematics. In particular, it is not assumed that you have studied calculus. However, a certain amount of mathematics is necessary for the analysis of algorithms. This appendix reviews that necessary mathematics. You may already be familiar with much or all of this material.

A.I NOTATION

Sometimes we need to refer to the smallest integer that is greater than or equal to a real number x. We denote that integer by $\lceil x \rceil$. For example,

$$\lceil 3.3 \rceil = 4 \qquad \left\lceil \frac{9}{2} \right\rceil = 5 \qquad \lceil 6 \rceil = 6$$
$$\lceil -3.3 \rceil = -3 \qquad \lceil -3.7 \rceil = -3 \qquad \lceil -6 \rceil = -6.$$

We call $\lceil x \rceil$ the *ceiling* for x. For any integer n, $\lceil n \rceil = n$. We also sometimes need to refer to the largest integer that is less than or equal to a real number x. We denote that integer by $\lfloor x \rfloor$. For example,

$$\lfloor 3.3 \rfloor = 3 \qquad \left\lfloor \frac{9}{2} \right\rfloor = 4 \qquad \lfloor 6 \rfloor = 6$$
$$\lfloor -3.3 \rfloor = -4 \qquad \lfloor -3.7 \rfloor = -4 \qquad \lfloor -6 \rfloor = -6.$$

We call $\lfloor x \rfloor$ the *floor* for x. For any integer n, $\lfloor n \rfloor = n$.

When we are able to determine only the approximate value of a desired result, we use the symbol $\approx$, which means "equals approximately." For example, you should be familiar with the number π, which is used in the computation of the area and circumference of a circle. The value of π is not given by any finite number of decimal digits, because we could go on generating more digits forever (indeed, there is not even a pattern as there is in $\frac{1}{3} = 0.3333333\ldots$). Because the first six digits of π are 3.14159, we write

$$\pi \approx 3.14159.$$

We use the symbol $\neq$ to mean "does not equal." For example, if we want to state that the values of the variables x and y are not equal, we write

$$x \neq y.$$

Often we need to refer to the sum of like terms. This is straightforward if there are not many terms. For example, if we need to refer to the sum of the first seven positive integers, we simply write

$$1 + 2 + 3 + 4 + 5 + 6 + 7.$$

If we need to refer to the sum of the squares of the first seven positive integers, we simply write

$$1^2 + 2^2 + 3^2 + 4^2 + 5^2 + 6^2 + 7^2.$$

This method works well when there are not many terms. However, it is not satisfactory if, for example, we need to refer to the sum of the first 100 positive integers. One way to do this is to write the first few terms, a general term, and the last term. That is, we write

$$1 + 2 + \cdots + i + \cdots + 100.$$

If we need to refer to the sum of the squares of the first 100 positive integers, we could write

$$1^2 + 2^2 + \cdots + i^2 + \cdots + 100^2.$$

Sometimes when the general term is clear from the first few terms, we do not bother to write that term. For example, for the sum of the first 100 positive integers we could simply write

$$1 + 2 + \cdots + 100.$$

When it is instructive to show some of the terms, we write out some of them. However, a more concise method is to use the greek letter Σ, which is pronounced **sigma.** For example, we use Σ to represent the sum of the first 100 positive integers as follows:

$$\sum_{i=1}^{100} i.$$

This notation means that while the variable i is taking values from 1 to 100, we are summing its values. Similarly, the sum of the squares of the first 100 positive integers can be represented by

$$\sum_{i=1}^{100} i^2.$$

Often we want to denote the case where the last integer in the sum is an arbitrary integer n. Using the methods just illustrated, we can represent the sum of the first n positive integers by

$$1 + 2 + \cdots + i + \cdots + n \quad \text{or} \quad \sum_{i=1}^{n} i.$$

Similarly, the sum of the squares of the first n positive integers can be represented by

$$1^2 + 2^2 + \cdots + i^2 + \cdots + n^2 \quad \text{or} \quad \sum_{i=1}^{n} i^2.$$

Sometimes we need to take the sum of a sum. For example,

$$\sum_{i=1}^{4} \sum_{j=1}^{i} j = \sum_{j=1}^{1} j + \sum_{j=1}^{2} j + \sum_{j=1}^{3} j + \sum_{j=1}^{4} j$$
$$= (1) + (1 + 2) + (1 + 2 + 3) + (1 + 2 + 3 + 4) = 20.$$

Similarly, we can take the sum of a sum of a sum, and so on.

Finally, we sometimes need to refer to an entity that is larger than any real number. We call that entity *infinity* and denote it by ∞. For any real number x, we have

$$x < \infty.$$

A.2 FUNCTIONS

Very simply, a *function* f of one variable is a rule or law that associates with a value x a unique value $f(x)$. For example, the function f that associates the square of a real number with a given real number x is

$$f(x) = x^2.$$

A function determines a set of ordered pairs. For example, the function $f(x) = x^2$ determines all the ordered pairs (x, x^2). A *graph* of a function is the set of all ordered pairs determined by the function. The graph of the function $f(x) = x^2$ appears in Figure A.1.

The function

$$f(x) = \frac{1}{x}$$

is defined only if $x \neq 0$. The *domain* of a function is the set of values for which the function is defined. For example, the domain of $f(x) = 1/x$ is all real numbers other than 0, whereas the domain of $f(x) = x^2$ is all real numbers.

Notice that the function

$$f(x) = x^2$$

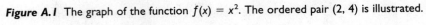

Figure A.1 The graph of the function $f(x) = x^2$. The ordered pair (2, 4) is illustrated.

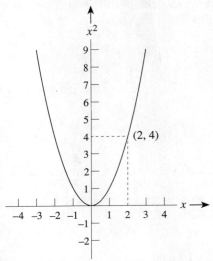

can take only nonnegative values. By "nonnegative values" we mean values greater than or equal to 0, whereas by "positive values" we mean values strictly greater than 0. The **range** of a function is the set of values that the function can take. The range of $f(x) = x^2$ is the nonnegative reals, the range of $f(x) = 1/x$ is all real numbers other than 0, and the range of $f(x) = (1/x)^2$ is all positive reals. We say that a function is from its domain and to its range. For example, the function $f(x) = x^2$ is from the reals to the nonnegative reals.

A.3 MATHEMATICAL INDUCTION

Some sums equal closed-form expressions. For example,

$$1 + 2 + \cdots + n = \frac{n(n + 1)}{2}.$$

We can illustrate this equality by checking it for a few values of n, as follows:

$$1 + 2 + 3 + 4 = 10 = \frac{4(4 + 1)}{2}$$

$$1 + 2 + 3 + 4 + 5 = 15 = \frac{5(5 + 1)}{2}.$$

However, because there are an infinite number of positive integers, we can never become certain that the equality holds for all positive integers n simply by checking individual cases. Checking individual cases can inform us only that the equality appears to be true. A powerful tool for obtaining a result for all positive integers *n* is mathematical induction.

Mathematical induction works in the same way as the domino principle. Figure A.2 illustrates that, if the distance between two dominoes is always less than the height of the dominoes, we can knock down all the dominoes merely by knocking over the first domino. We are able to do this because:

1. We knock over the first domino.
2. By spacing the dominoes so that the distance between any two of them is always less than their height, we guarantee that if the *n*th domino falls, the (*n* + 1)st domino will fall.

If we knock over the first domino, it will knock over the second, the second will knock over the third, and so on. In theory, we can have an arbitrarily large number of dominoes and they all will fall.

An induction proof works in the same way. We first show that what we are trying to prove is true for *n* = 1. Next we show that if it is true for an arbitrary positive integer *n,* it must also be true for *n* + 1. Once we have shown this, we know that because it is true for *n* = 1, it must be true for *n* = 2; because it is true for *n* = 2, it must be true for *n* = 3; and so on, ad infinitum (to infinity). We can therefore conclude that it is true for all positive integers *n*. When using induction to prove that some statement concerning the positive integers is true, we use the following terminology:

> The ***induction base*** is the proof that the statement is true for *n* = 1 (or some other initial value).
> The ***induction hypothesis*** is the assumption that the statement is true for an arbitrary *n* ≥ 1 (or some other initial value).
> The ***induction step*** is the proof that if the statement is true for *n*, it must also be true for *n* + 1.

The induction base amounts to knocking over the first domino, whereas the induction step shows that if the *n*th domino falls, the (*n* + 1)st domino will fall.

Figure A.2 If the first domino is knocked over, all the dominoes will fall.

Example A.1   We show, for all positive integers n, that

$$1 + 2 + \cdots + n = \frac{n(n + 1)}{2}.$$

Induction base: For $n = 1$,

$$1 = \frac{1(1 + 1)}{2}.$$

Induction hypothesis: Assume, for an arbitrary positive integer n, that

$$1 + 2 + \cdots + n = \frac{n(n + 1)}{2}.$$

Induction step: We need to show that

$$1 + 2 + \cdots + (n + 1) = \frac{(n + 1)[(n + 1) + 1]}{2}.$$

To that end,

$$
\begin{aligned}
1 + 2 + \cdots + (n + 1) &= \mathbf{1 + 2 + \cdots + n} + n + 1 \\
&= \frac{\mathbf{n(n + 1)}}{\mathbf{2}} + n + 1 \\
&= \frac{n(n + 1) + 2(n + 1)}{2} \\
&= \frac{(n + 1)(n + 2)}{2} \\
&= \frac{(n + 1)[(n + 1) + 1]}{2}.
\end{aligned}
$$

In the induction step, we highlight the terms that are equal by the induction hypothesis. We often do this to show where the induction hypothesis is being applied. Notice what is accomplished in the induction step. By assuming the induction hypothesis that

$$1 + 2 + \cdots + n = \frac{n(n + 1)}{2}$$

and doing some algebraic manipulations, we arrive at the conclusion that

$$1 + 2 + \cdots + (n + 1) = \frac{(n + 1)[(n + 1) + 1]}{2}.$$

Therefore, if the hypothesis is true for n, it must be true for $n + 1$. Because in the induction base we show that it is true for $n = 1$, we can conclude, using the domino principle, that it is true for all positive integers n.

You may wonder why we thought that the equality in Example A.1 might be true in the first place. This is an important point. We can often derive a possibly true statement by investigating some cases and making an educated guess. This is how the equality in Example A.1 was originally conceived. Induction can then be used to verify that the statement is true. If it is not true, of course, the induction proof fails. It is important to realize that it is never possible to derive a true statement using induction. Induction comes into play only after we have already derived a possibly true statement. In Section 8.5.4, we discuss constructive induction, which is a technique that can help us discover a true statement.

Another important point is that the initial value need not be $n = 1$. That is, the statement may be true only if $n \geq 10$. In this case the induction base would be $n = 10$. In some cases our induction base is $n = 0$. This means we are proving the statement to be true for all nonnegative integers.

More examples of induction proofs follow.

Example A.2 We show, for all positive integers n, that

$$1^2 + 2^2 + \cdots + n^2 = \frac{n(n + 1)(2n + 1)}{6}.$$

Induction base: For $n = 1$,

$$1^2 = 1 = \frac{1(1 + 1)[(2 \times 1) + 1]}{6}.$$

Induction hypothesis: Assume, for an arbitrary positive integer n, that

$$1^2 + 2^2 + \cdots + n^2 = \frac{n(n + 1)(2n + 1)}{6}.$$

Induction step: We need to show that

$$1^2 + 2^2 + \cdots + (n + 1)^2 = \frac{(n + 1)[(n + 1) + 1][2(n + 1) + 1]}{6}.$$

To that end,

$$
\begin{aligned}
1^2 + 2^2 + \cdots + (n + 1)^2 &= \mathbf{1^2 + 2^2 + \cdots + n^2} + (n + 1)^2 \\
&= \frac{\mathbf{n(n + 1)(2n + 1)}}{\mathbf{6}} + (n + 1)^2 \\
&= \frac{n(n + 1)(2n + 1) + 6(n + 1)^2}{6} \\
&= \frac{(n + 1)(2n^2 + n + 6n + 6)}{6} \\
&= \frac{(n + 1)(2n^2 + 7n + 6)}{6}
\end{aligned}
$$

$$= \frac{(n + 1)(n + 2)(2n + 3)}{6}$$

$$= \frac{(n + 1)[(n + 1) + 1][2(n + 1) + 1]}{6}.$$

In the next example, the induction base is $n = 0$.

Example A.3   We show, for all nonnegative integers n, that

$$2^0 + 2^1 + 2^2 + \cdots + 2^n = 2^{n+1} - 1.$$

In summation notation, this equality is

$$\sum_{i=0}^{n} 2^i = 2^{n+1} - 1.$$

Induction base: For $n = 0$,

$$2^0 = 1 = 2^{0+1} - 1.$$

Induction hypothesis: Assume, for an arbitrary nonnegative integer n, that

$$2^0 + 2^1 + 2^2 + \cdots + 2^n = 2^{n+1} - 1.$$

Induction step: We need to show that

$$2^0 + 2^1 + 2^2 + \cdots + 2^{n+1} = 2^{(n+1)+1} - 1.$$

To that end,

$$2^0 + 2^1 + 2^2 + \cdots + 2^{n+1} = \mathbf{2^0 + 2^1 + 2^2 + \cdots + 2^n} + 2^{n+1}$$
$$= \mathbf{2^{n+1} - 1} + 2^{n+1}$$
$$= 2(2^{n+1}) - 1$$
$$= 2^{(n+1)+1} - 1.$$

Example A.3 is a special case of the result in the next example.

Example A.4   We show, for all nonnegative integers n and real numbers $r \neq 1$, that

$$\sum_{i=0}^{n} r^i = \frac{r^{n+1} - 1}{r - 1}.$$

The terms in this sum are called a *geometric progression.*

Induction base: For $n = 0$,

$$r^0 = 1 = \frac{r^{0+1} - 1}{r - 1}.$$

Induction hypothesis: Assume, for an arbitrary nonnegative integer n, that

$$\sum_{i=0}^{n} r^i = \frac{r^{n+1} - 1}{r - 1}.$$

Induction step: We need to show that

$$\sum_{i=0}^{n+1} r^i = \frac{r^{(n+1)+1} - 1}{r - 1}.$$

To that end,

$$\sum_{i=0}^{n+1} r^i = r^{n+1} + \sum_{i=0}^{n} r^i$$

$$= r^{n+1} + \frac{r^{n+1} - 1}{r - 1}$$

$$= \frac{r^{n+1}(r - 1) + r^{n+1} - 1}{r - 1}$$

$$= \frac{r^{n+2} - 1}{r - 1} = \frac{r^{(n+1)+1} - 1}{r - 1}.$$

Sometimes results that can be obtained using induction can be established more readily in another way. For instance, the preceding example showed that

$$\sum_{i=0}^{n} r^i = \frac{r^{n+1} - 1}{r - 1}.$$

Instead of using induction, we can multiply the expression on the left by the denominator on the right and simplify, as follows:

$$(r - 1) \sum_{i=0}^{n} r^i = r \sum_{i=0}^{n} r^i - \sum_{i=0}^{n} r^i$$

$$= (r + r^2 + \cdots + r^{n+1}) - (1 + r + r^2 + \cdots + r^n)$$

$$= r^{n+1} - 1.$$

Dividing both sides of this equality by $r - 1$ gives the desired result.
We present one more example of induction.

Example A.5   We show, for all positive integers n, that

$$\sum_{i=1}^{n} i2^i = (n - 1)2^{n+1} + 2.$$

Induction base: For $n = 1$,

$$1 \times 2^1 = 2 = (1 - 1)2^{1+1} + 2.$$

Induction hypothesis: Assume, for an arbitrary positive integer n, that

$$\sum_{i=1}^{n} i2^i = (n - 1)2^{n+1} + 2.$$

Induction step: We need to show that

$$\sum_{i=1}^{n+1} i2^i = [(n + 1) - 1]2^{(n+1)+1} + 2.$$

To that end,

$$\sum_{i=1}^{n+1} i2^i = \sum_{i=1}^{n} i2^i + (n + 1)2^{n+1}$$
$$= (n - 1)2^{n+1} + 2 + (n + 1)2^{n+1}$$
$$= 2n2^{n+1} + 2$$
$$= [(n + 1) - 1]2^{(n+1)+1} + 2.$$

Another way to make the induction hypothesis is to assume that the statement is true for all k greater than or equal to the initial value and less than n, and then, in the induction step, prove that it is true for n. We do this in the proof of Theorem 1.1 in Section 1.2.2.

Although our examples have all involved the determination of closed-form expressions for sums, there are many other induction applications. We encounter some of them in this text.

A.4 THEOREMS AND LEMMAS

The dictionary defines a ***theorem*** as a proposition that sets forth something to be proved. It has the same meaning in mathematics. Each of the examples in the preceding section could be stated as a theorem, whereas the induction proof constitutes a proof of the theorem. For example, we could state Example A.1 as follows:

Theorem A.1 For all integers $n > 0$, we have

$$1 + 2 + \cdots + n = \frac{n(n + 1)}{2}.$$

Proof: The proof would go here. In this case, it would be the induction proof used in Example A.1.

Usually the purpose of stating and proving a theorem is to obtain a general result that can be applied to many specific cases. For example, we can use Theorem A.1 to quickly calculate the sum of the first n integers for any positive integer n.

Sometimes students have difficulty understanding the difference between a theorem that is an "if" statement and one that is an "if and only if" statement. The following two theorems illustrate this difference.

Theorem A.2 For any real number x, if $x > 0$, then $x^2 > 0$.

Proof: The theorem follows from the fact that the product of two positive numbers is positive.

The reverse of the implication stated in Theorem A.2 is not true. That is, it is not true that if $x^2 > 0$, then $x > 0$. For example,

$$(-3)^2 = 9 > 0,$$

and -3 is not greater than 0. Indeed, the square of any negative number is greater than 0. Therefore, Theorem A.2 is an example of an "if" statement. When the reverse implication is also true, the theorem is an "if and only if" statement and it is necessary to prove both the implication and the reverse implication. The following theorem is an example of an "if and only if" statement.

Theorem A.3 For any real number x, $x > 0$ if and only if $1/x > 0$.

Proof: Prove the implication. Suppose that $x > 0$. Then

$$\frac{1}{x} > 0$$

because the quotient of two positive numbers is greater than 0.

Prove the reverse implication. Suppose that $1/x > 0$. Then

$$x = \frac{1}{1/x} > 0,$$

again because the quotient of two positive numbers is greater than 0.

The dictionary defines a **lemma** as a subsidiary proposition employed to prove another proposition. Like a theorem, a lemma is a proposition that sets forth something to be proved. However, we usually do not care about the proposition in the lemma for its own sake. Rather, when the proof of a theorem relies on the truth of one or more auxiliary propositions, we often state and prove lemmas concerning those propositions. We then employ those lemmas to prove the theorem.

A.5 LOGARITHMS

Logarithms are one of the mathematical tools used most in analysis of algorithms. We briefly review their properties.

A.5.1 Definition and Properties of Logarithms

The **common logarithm** of a number is the power to which 10 must be raised to produce the number. If x is a given number, we denote its common logarithm by $\log x$.

Example A.6   Some common logarithms follow:

$$\log 10 = 1 \qquad \text{because} \qquad 10^1 = 10$$
$$\log 10{,}000 = 4 \qquad \text{because} \qquad 10^4 = 10{,}000$$
$$\log 0.001 = -3 \qquad \text{because} \qquad 10^{-3} = \left(\frac{1}{10}\right)^3 = 0.001$$
$$\log 1 = 0 \qquad \text{because} \qquad 10^0 = 1$$

Recall that the value of any nonzero number raised to the 0th power is 1.

In general, the logarithm of a number x is the power to which another number a, called the base, must be raised to produce x. The number a can be any positive number other than 1, whereas x must be positive. That is, there is no such thing as the logarithm of a negative number or of 0. In symbols, we write $\log_a x$.

Example A.7   Some examples of $\log_a x$ follow:

$$\log_2 8 = 3 \qquad \text{because} \qquad 2^3 = 8$$
$$\log_3 81 = 4 \qquad \text{because} \qquad 3^4 = 81$$
$$\log_2 \frac{1}{16} = -4 \qquad \text{because} \qquad 2^{-4} = \left(\frac{1}{2}\right)^4 = \frac{1}{16}$$
$$\log_2 7 \approx 2.807 \qquad \text{because} \qquad 2^{2.807} \approx 7$$

Notice that the last result in Example A.7 is for a number that is not an integral power of the base. Logarithms exist for all positive numbers, not just for integral powers of the base. A discussion of the meaning of the logarithm when the number is not an integral power of the base is beyond the scope of this appendix. We note here only that the logarithm is an increasing function. That is,

$$\text{if } x < y, \qquad \text{then} \qquad \log_a x < \log_a y.$$

Therefore,

$$2 = \log_2 4 < \log_2 7 < \log_2 8 = 3.$$

We saw in Example A.7 that $\log_2 7$ is about 2.807, which is between 2 and 3.

Listed below are some important properties of logarithms that are useful in the analysis of algorithms.

Some Properties of Logarithms (In all cases, $a > 1$, $b > 1$, $x > 0$, and $y > 0$):

1. $\log_a 1 = 0$
2. $a^{\log_a x} = x$
3. $\log_a(xy) = \log_a x + \log_a y$
4. $\log_a \dfrac{x}{y} = \log_a x - \log_a y$
5. $\log_a x^y = y \log_a x$
6. $x^{\log_a y} = y^{\log_a x}$
7. $\log_a x = \dfrac{\log_b x}{\log_b a}$

Example A.8   Some examples of applying the previous properties follow:

$$2^{\log_2 8} = 8 \qquad\qquad\qquad\qquad\qquad \{\text{by Property 2}\}$$

$$\log_2(4 \times 8) = \log_2 4 + \log_2 8 = 2 + 3 = 5 \quad \{\text{by Property 3}\}$$

$$\log_3 \frac{27}{9} = \log_3 27 - \log_3 9 = 3 - 2 = 1 \quad \{\text{by Property 4}\}$$

$$\log_2 4^3 = 3 \log_2 4 = 3 \times 2 = 6 \qquad\qquad \{\text{by Property 5}\}$$

$$8^{\log_2 4} = 4^{\log_2 8} = 4^3 = 64 \qquad\qquad\qquad \{\text{by Property 6}\}$$

$$\log_4 16 = \frac{\log_2 16}{\log_2 4} = \frac{4}{2} = 2 \qquad\qquad \{\text{by Property 7}\}$$

$$\log_2 128 = \frac{\log 128}{\log 2} \approx \frac{2.10721}{0.30103} = 7 \qquad \{\text{by Property 7}\}$$

$$\log_3 67 = \frac{\log 67}{\log 3} \approx \frac{1.82607}{0.47712} \approx 3.82728 \quad \{\text{by Property 7}\}$$

Because many calculators have a log function (recall that log means $\log_{10}$), the last two results in Example A.8 show how one can use a calculator to compute a logarithm for an arbitrary base. (This is how we computed them.)

We encounter the logarithm to base 2 so often in analysis of algorithms that we give it its own simple symbol. That is, we denote $\log_2 x$ by **lg x.** From now on, we use this notation.

A.5.2 The Natural Logarithm

You may recall the number e, whose value is approximately 2.718281828459. Like π, the number e cannot be expressed exactly by any finite number of decimal digits, and indeed there is not even a repeating pattern of digits in its decimal expansion. We denote $\log_e x$ by **ln *x***, and we call it the ***natural logarithm*** of x. For example,

$$\ln 10 \approx 2.3025851.$$

You may wonder where we got this answer. We simply used a calculator that has an ln function. Without studying calculus, it is not possible to understand how the natural logarithm is computed and why it is called "natural." Indeed, when we merely look at e, the natural logarithm appears most unnatural. Although a discussion of calculus is beyond our present scope (except for some material marked ☯), we do want to explore one property of the natural logarithm that is important to the analysis of algorithms. With calculus it is possible to show that $\ln x$ is the area under the curve $1/x$ that lies between 1 and x. This is illustrated in the top graph in Figure A.3 for $x = 5$. In the bottom graph in that figure, we

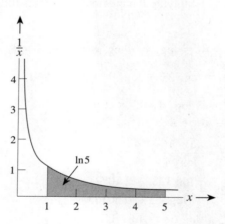

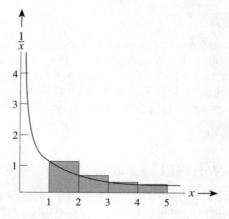

Figure A.3 The shaded area in the top graph is ln 5. The combined area of the shaded rectangles in the bottom graph is an approximation to ln 5.

show how that area can be approximated by summing the areas of rectangles that are each one unit wide. The graph shows that the approximation to ln 5 is

$$(1 \times 1) + \left(1 \times \frac{1}{2}\right) + \left(1 \times \frac{1}{3}\right) + \left(1 \times \frac{1}{4}\right) \approx 2.0833.$$

Notice that this area is always larger than the true area. Using a calculator, we can determine that

$$\ln 5 \approx 1.60944.$$

The area of the rectangles is not a very good approximation to ln 5. However, by the time we get to the last rectangle (the one between the x-values 4 and 5), the area is not much different from the area under the curve between $x = 4$ and $x = 5$. This is not the case for the first rectangle. Each successive rectangle is a better approximation than its predecessor. Therefore, when the number is not small, the sum of the areas of the rectangles is close to the value of the natural logarithm. The following example shows the usefulness of this result.

Example A.9   Suppose we wish to compute

$$1 + \frac{1}{2} + \cdots + \frac{1}{n}.$$

There is no closed-form expression for this sum. However, in accordance with the preceding discussion, if n is not small,

$$(1 \times 1) + \left(1 \times \frac{1}{2}\right) + \cdots + \left(1 \times \frac{1}{n-1}\right) \approx \ln n.$$

When n is not small, the value of $1/n$ is negligible in comparison with the sum. Therefore, we can also add that term to get the result

$$1 + \frac{1}{2} + \cdots + \frac{1}{n} \approx \ln n.$$

We will use this result in some of our analyses. In general, it is possible to show that

$$\frac{1}{2} + \cdots + \frac{1}{n} < \ln n < 1 + \frac{1}{2} + \cdots + \frac{1}{n-1}.$$

A.6 SETS

Informally, a *set* is a collection of objects. We denote sets by capital letters such as S, and, if we enumerate all the objects in a set, we enclose them in braces. For example,

$$S = \{1, 2, 3, 4\}$$

is the set containing the first four positive integers. The order in which we list the objects is irrelevant. This means that

$$\{1, 2, 3, 4\} \quad \text{and} \quad \{3, 1, 4, 2\}$$

are the same set—namely, the set of the first four positive integers. Another example of a set is

$$S = \{\text{Wed, Sat, Tues, Sun, Thurs, Mon, Fri}\}.$$

This is the set of days in the week. When a set is infinite, we can represent the set using a description of the objects in the set. For example, if we want to represent the set of positive integers that are integral multiples of 3, we can write

$$S = \{n \text{ such that } n = 3i \text{ for some positive integer } i\}.$$

Alternatively, we can show some items and a general item, as follows:

$$S = \{3, 6, 9, \ldots, 3i, \ldots \}.$$

The objects in a set are called *elements* or *members* of the set. If x is an element of the set S, we write $x \in S$. If x is not an element of S, we write $x \notin S$. For example,

$$\text{If} \quad S = \{1, 2, 3, 4\}, \quad \text{then} \quad 2 \in S \quad \text{and} \quad 5 \notin S.$$

We say that the sets S and T are equal if they have the same elements, and we write $S = T$. If they are not equal, we write $S \neq T$. For example,

$$\text{If} \quad S = \{1, 2, 3, 4\} \quad \text{and} \quad T = \{2, 1, 4, 3\}, \quad \text{then} \quad S = T.$$

If S and T are two sets such that every element in S is also in T, we say that S is a *subset* of T, and we write $S \subseteq T$. For example,

$$\text{If} \quad S = \{1, 3, 5\} \quad \text{and} \quad T = \{1, 2, 3, 5, 6\}, \quad \text{then} \quad S \subseteq T.$$

Every set is a subset of itself. That is, for any set S, $S \subseteq S$. If S is a subset of T that is not equal to T, we say that S is a *proper subset* of T, and we write $S \subset T$. For example,

$$\text{If} \quad S = \{1, 3, 5\} \quad \text{and} \quad T = \{1, 2, 3, 5, 6\}, \quad \text{then} \quad S \subset T.$$

For two sets S and T, the *intersection* of S and T is defined as the set of all elements that are in both S and T. We write $S \cap T$. For example,

$$\text{If} \quad S = \{1, 4, 5, 6\} \quad \text{and} \quad T = \{1, 3, 5\}, \quad \text{then} \quad S \cap T = \{1, 5\}.$$

For two sets S and T, the *union* of S and T is defined as the set of all elements that are in either S or T. We write $S \cup T$. For example,

$$\text{If} \quad S = \{1, 4, 5, 6\} \quad \text{and} \quad T = \{1, 3, 5\}, \quad \text{then} \quad S \cup T = \{1, 3, 4, 5, 6\}.$$

For two sets S and T, the *difference* between S and T is defined as the set of all elements that are in S but not in T. We write $S - T$. For example,

If $S = \{1, 4, 5, 6\}$ and $T = \{1, 3, 5\}$,

$$\text{then} \quad S - T = \{4, 6\} \quad \text{and} \quad T - S = \{3\}.$$

The ***empty set*** is defined as the set containing no elements. We denote the empty set by $\emptyset$.

If $S = \{1, 4, 6\}$ and $T = \{2, 3, 5\}$,   then $S \cap T = \emptyset$.

The ***universal set*** U is defined as the set consisting of all elements under consideration. This means that if S is any set we are considering, then $S \subseteq U$. For example, if we are considering sets of positive integers, then

$$U = \{1, 2, 3, \ldots, i, \ldots\}.$$

A.7 PERMUTATIONS AND COMBINATIONS

Suppose we have four balls marked A, B, C, and D in an urn or container, and two balls will be drawn from the urn. We must pick the balls in the order in which they are drawn to win a lottery. To gain insight into the likelihood of our winning, we should determine how many outcomes are possible. The possible outcomes are:

AB	AC	AD
BA	BC	BD
CA	CB	CD
DA	DB	DC.

The outcomes AB and BA, for example, are different because we must pick the balls in the correct order. We have listed 12 different outcomes. However, can we be sure that these are all the outcomes? Notice that we arranged the outcomes in four rows and three columns. Each row corresponds to a distinct choice for the first ball; there are four such choices. Once we have made that choice, the second letters in the entries in a row correspond to the remaining distinct choices for the second ball; there are three such choices. The total number of outcomes is therefore

$$(4)(3) = 12.$$

This result can be generalized. For example, if we have four balls and three are drawn, the first ball can be any one of four; once the first ball is drawn, the second ball can be any of three; and once the second ball is drawn, the third ball can be any of two. The number of outcomes is therefore

$$(4)(3)(2) = 24.$$

In general, if we have n balls, and we are picking k of them, the number of possible outcomes is

$$(n)(n - 1) \cdots (n - k + 1).$$

This is called the number of **permutations** of n objects taken k at a time. If $n = 4$ and $k = 3$, this formula yields

$$(4)(3) \cdots (4 - 3 + 1) = (4)(3)(2) = 24,$$

which is the result already obtained. If $n = 10$ and $k = 5$, the formula yields

$$(10)(9) \cdots (10 - 5 + 1) = (10)(9)(8)(7)(6) = 30{,}240.$$

If $k = n$, we are picking all the balls. This is simply called the number of **permutations** of n objects. The previous formula shows that it is given by

$$n(n - 1) \cdots (n - n + 1) = n!.$$

Recall that for a positive integer n, $n!$ is defined as the integer times all the positive integers less than it, the value of $0!$ is defined to be 1, and $n!$ is not defined for negative integers.

Next consider a lottery that we can win by merely picking the correct balls. That is, we do not have to get the order right. Suppose again that there are four balls and two are drawn. Each outcome in this lottery corresponds to two outcomes in the previous lottery. For example, the outcomes AB and BA in the other lottery are both the same for the purposes of this lottery. We will call this outcome

A and B.

Because two outcomes in the previous lottery correspond to one outcome in this lottery, we can determine how many outcomes there are in this lottery by dividing the number of outcomes in the previous lottery by 2. This means that there are

$$\frac{(4)(3)}{2} = 6$$

outcomes in this lottery. The six distinct outcomes are

A and B   A and C   A and D   B and C   B and D   C and D.

Suppose now that three balls are drawn and we do not have to get the order right. Then the following outcomes are all the same for the purposes of this lottery:

ABC   ACB   BAC   BCA   CAB   CBA.

These outcomes are simply the permutations of three objects. Recall that the number of such permutations is given by $3! = 6$. To determine how many distinct outcomes there are in this lottery, we need to divide by $3!$ the number of distinct outcomes in the lottery where the order does matter. That is, there are

$$\frac{(4)(3)(2)}{3!} = 4$$

outcomes in this lottery. They are

A and B and C   A and B and D   A and C and D   A and C and D.

In general, if there are n balls and k balls are drawn, and the order does not matter, the number of distinct outcomes is given by

$$\frac{(n)(n-1)\cdots(n-k+1)}{k!}.$$

This is called the number of ***combinations*** of n objects taken k at a time. Because

$$(n)(n-1)\cdots(n-k+1) = (n)(n-1)\cdots(n-k+1) \times \frac{(n-k)!}{(n-k)!}$$

$$= \frac{n!}{(n-k)!},$$

the formula for the number of combinations of n objects taken k at a time is usually shown as

$$\frac{n!}{k!(n-k)!}.$$

Using this formula, the number of combinations of eight objects taken three at a time is given by

$$\frac{8!}{3!(8-3)!} = 56.$$

The ***Binomial Theorem,*** which is proven in algebra texts, states that for any nonnegative integer n and real numbers a and b,

$$(a+b)^n = \sum_{k=0}^{n} \frac{n!}{k!(n-k)!} a^k b^{n-k}.$$

Because the number of combinations of n objects taken k at a time is the coefficient of $a^k b^{n-k}$ in this expression, that number is called the ***binomial coefficient.*** We will denote it $\binom{n}{k}$.

Example A.10 We show that the number of subsets, including the empty set, of a set containing n items is 2^n. For $0 \le k \le n$, the number of subsets of size k is the number of combinations of n objects taken k at a time, which is $\binom{n}{k}$. This means that the total number of subsets is

$$\sum_{k=0}^{n} \binom{n}{k} = \sum_{k=0}^{n} \binom{n}{k} 1^k 1^{n-k} = (1+1)^n = 2^n.$$

The second-to-last equality is by the Binomial Theorem.

A.8 PROBABILITY

You may recall using probability theory in situations such as drawing a ball from an urn, drawing the top card from a deck of playing cards, and tossing a coin. We call the act of drawing a ball, drawing the top card, or tossing a coin an *experiment*. In general, probability theory is applicable when we have an experiment that has a set of distinct outcomes that we can describe. The set of all possible outcomes is called a ***sample space*** or ***population***. Mathematicians usually say "sample space," whereas social scientists usually say "population" (because they study people). We use these terms interchangeably. Any subset of a sample space is called an ***event***. A subset containing only one element is called an ***elementary event***.

Example A.11

In the experiment of drawing the top card from an ordinary deck of playing cards, the sample space contains the 52 different cards. The set

$$S = \{\text{king of hearts, king of clubs, king of spades, king of diamonds}\}$$

is an event, and the set

$$E = \{\text{king of hearts}\}$$

is an elementary event. There are 52 elementary events in the sample space.

The meaning of an event (subset) is that one of the elements in the subset is the outcome of the experiment. In Example A.11, the meaning of the event S is that the card drawn is any one of the four kings, and the meaning of the elementary event E is that the card drawn is the king of hearts.

We measure our certainty that an event contains the outcome of the experiment with a real number called the probability of the event. The following is a general definition of probability when the sample space is finite.

Definition

Suppose we have a sample space containing n distinct outcomes:

$$\text{Sample space} = \{e_1, e_2, \ldots, e_n\}.$$

A function that assigns a real number $p(S)$ to each event S is called a ***probability function*** if it satisfies the following conditions:

1. $0 \le p(e_i) \le 1$ for $1 \le i \le n$
2. $p(e_1) + p(e_2) + \cdots + p(e_n) = 1$
3. For each event S that is not an elementary event, $p(S)$ is the sum of the probabilities of the elementary events whose outcomes are in S. For example, if

$$S = \{e_1, e_2, e_7\},$$
$$p(S) = p(e_1) + p(e_2) + p(e_7).$$

The sample space along with the function p is called a ***probability space.***

Because we define probability as a function of a set, we should write $p(\{e_i\})$ instead of $p(e_i)$ when referring to the probability of an elementary event. However, to avoid clutter, we do not do this. In the same way, we do not use the braces when referring to the probability of an event that is not elementary. For example, we write $p(e_1, e_2, e_7)$ for the probability of the event $\{e_1, e_2, e_7\}$.

We can associate an outcome with the elementary event containing that outcome, and therefore we can speak of the probability of an outcome. Clearly, this means the probability of the elementary event containing the outcome.

The simplest way to assign probabilities is to use the ***Principle of Indifference.*** This principle says that outcomes are to be considered equiprobable if we have no reason to expect or prefer one over the other. According to this principle, when there are n distinct outcomes, the probability of each of them is the ratio $1/n$.

Example A.12 Suppose we have four balls marked A, B, C, and D in an urn, and the experiment is to draw one ball. The sample space is $\{A, B, C, D\}$, and, according to the Principle of Indifference,

$$p(A) = p(B) = p(C) = p(D) = \frac{1}{4}.$$

The event $\{A, B\}$ means that either ball A or ball B is drawn. Its probability is given by

$$p(A, B) = p(A) + p(B) = \frac{1}{4} + \frac{1}{4} = \frac{1}{2}.$$

Example A.13 Suppose we have the experiment of drawing the top card from an ordinary deck of playing cards. Because there are 52 cards, according to the Principle of Indifference, the probability of each card is $\frac{1}{52}$. For example,

$$p(\text{king of hearts}) = \frac{1}{52}.$$

The event

$$S = \{\text{king of hearts, king of clubs, king of spades, king of diamonds}\}$$

means that the card drawn is a king. Its probability is given by

$$p(S) = p(\text{king of hearts}) + p(\text{king of clubs}) + p(\text{king of spades})$$
$$+ \ p(\text{king of diamonds})$$
$$= \frac{1}{52} + \frac{1}{52} + \frac{1}{52} + \frac{1}{52} = \frac{1}{13}.$$

Sometimes we can compute probabilities using the formulas for permutations and combinations given in the preceding section. The following example shows how this is done.

Example A.14

Suppose there are five balls marked A, B, C, D, and E in an urn, and the experiment is to draw three balls where the order does not matter. We will compute $p(A \text{ and } B \text{ and } C)$. Recall that by "A and B and C" we mean the outcome that A, B, and C are picked in any order. To determine the probability using the Principle of Indifference, we need to compute the number of distinct outcomes. That is, we need the number of combinations of five objects taken three at a time. Using the formula in the preceding section, that number is given by

$$\frac{5!}{3!(5-3)!} = 10.$$

Therefore, according to the Principle of Indifference,

$$p(A \text{ and } B \text{ and } C) = \frac{1}{10},$$

which is the same as the probabilities of the other nine outcomes.

Too often, students, who do not have the opportunity to study probability theory in depth, are left with the impression that probability is simply about ratios. It would be unfair, even in this cursory overview, to give this impression. In fact, most important applications of probability have nothing to do with ratios. To illustrate, we give two simple examples.

A classic textbook example of probability involves tossing a coin. Because of the symmetry of a coin, we ordinarily use the Principle of Indifference to assign probabilities. Therefore, we assign

$$p(\text{heads}) = p(\text{tails}) = \frac{1}{2}.$$

Figure A.4 The two ways a thumbtack can land. Because of the asymmetry of a thumbtack, these two ways do not necessarily have the same probability.

On the other hand, we could toss a thumbtack. Like a coin, a thumbtack can land in two ways. It can land on its flat end (head) or it can land with the edge of the flat end (and the point) touching the ground. We assume that it cannot land only on its point. These two ways of landing are illustrated in Figure A.4. Using coin terminology, we will call the flat end "heads" and the other outcome "tails." Because the thumbtack lacks symmetry, there is no reason to use the Principle of Indifference and assign the same probability to heads and tails. How then do we assign probabilities? In the case of a coin, when we say $p(\text{heads}) = \frac{1}{2}$, we are implicitly assuming that if we tossed the coin 1000 times it should land on its head about 500 times. Indeed, if it only landed on its head 100 times, we would become suspicious that it was unevenly weighted and that the probability was not $\frac{1}{2}$. This notion of repeatedly performing the same experiment gives us a way of actually computing a probability. That is, if we repeat an experiment many times, we can be fairly certain that the probability of an outcome is about equal to the fraction of times the outcome actually occurs. (Some philosophers actually define probability as the limit of this fraction as the number of trials approaches infinity.) For example, one of our students tossed a thumbtack 10,000 times and it landed on its flat end (heads) 3761 times. Therefore, for that tack,

$$p(\text{heads}) \approx \frac{3761}{10,000} = .3761 \qquad p(\text{tails}) \approx \frac{6239}{10,000} = .6239.$$

We see that the probabilities of the two events need not be the same, but that the probabilities still sum to 1. This way of determining probabilities is called the **Relative Frequency Approach** to probability. When probabilities are computed from the relative frequency, we use the $\approx$ symbol because we cannot be certain that the relative frequency is exactly equal to the probability regardless of how many trials are performed. For example, suppose we have two balls marked A and B in an urn, and we repeat the experiment of picking one ball 10,000 times. We cannot be certain that the ball marked A will be picked exactly 5000 times. It may be picked only 4967 times. Using the Principle of Indifference, we would have

$$p(A) = .5,$$

whereas using the Relative Frequency Approach we would have

$$p(A) \approx .4967.$$

The Relative Frequency Approach is not limited to experiments with only two possible outcomes. For example, if we had a six-sided die that was not a perfect cube, the probabilities of the six elementary events could all be different. However, they would still sum to 1. The following example illustrates this situation.

Example A.15   Suppose we have an asymmetrical six-sided die, and in 1000 throws we determine that the six sides come up the following numbers of times:

Side	Number of Times
1	200
2	150
3	100
4	250
5	120
6	180

Then

$$p(1) \approx .2$$
$$p(2) \approx .15$$
$$p(3) \approx .1$$
$$p(4) \approx .25$$
$$p(5) \approx .12$$
$$p(6) \approx .18.$$

By Condition 3 in the definition of a probability space,

$$p(2, 3) = p(2) + p(3) \approx .15 + .1 = .25.$$

This is the probability that either a 2 or a 3 comes up in a throw of the die.

There are other approaches to probability, not the least of which is the notion of probability as a degree of *belief* in an outcome. For example, suppose the Chicago Bears were going to play the Dallas Cowboys in a football game. At the time this text is being written, one of its authors has little reason to believe that the Bears would win. Therefore, he would not assign equal probabilities to each team winning. Because the game could not be repeated many times, he could not obtain the probabilities using the Relative Frequency Approach. However, if he was going to bet on the game, he would want to access the probability of the Bears winning. He could do so using the ***Subjectivistic Approach*** to probability. One way to access probabilities using this approach is as follows: If a lottery ticket for the Bears winning cost $1, an individual would determine how much he or she felt the ticket should be worth if the Bears did win. One of the authors feels that it would have to be worth $5. This means that he would be willing to pay $1 for the ticket only if it would be worth at least $5 in the event that the Bears won. For him, the probability of the Bears winning is given by

$$p(\text{Bears win}) = \frac{\$1}{\$5} = .2.$$

That is, the probability is computed from what he believes would be a fair bet. This approach is called "subjective" because someone else might say that the ticket would need to be worth only $4. For that person, $p(\text{Bears win}) = .25$. Neither person would be logically incorrect. When a probability simply represents an individual's belief, there is no unique correct probability. A probability is a function of the individual's beliefs, which means it is subjective. If someone believed that the amount won should be the same as the amount bet (that is, that the ticket should be worth \$2), then for that person

$$p(\text{Bears win}) = \frac{\$1}{\$2} = .5.$$

We see that probability is much more than ratios. You should read Fine (1973) for a thorough coverage of the meaning and philosophy of probability. The Relative Frequency Approach to probability is discussed in Neapolitan (1992). The expression ''Principle of Indifference'' first appeared in Keynes (1948) (originally published in 1921). Neapolitan (1990) discusses paradoxes resulting from use of the Principle of Indifference.

A.8.1 Randomness

Although the term ''random'' is used freely in conversation, it is quite difficult to define rigorously. Randomness involves a process. Intuitively, by a random process we mean the following. First, the process must be capable of generating an arbitrarily long sequence of outcomes. For example, the process of repeatedly tossing the same coin can generate an arbitrarily long sequence of outcomes that are either heads or tails. Second, the outcomes must be unpredictable. What it means to be ''unpredictable,'' however, is somewhat vague. It seems we are back where we started; we have simply replaced ''random'' with ''unpredictable.''

In the early part of the 20th century, Richard von Mises made the concept of randomness more concrete. He said that an ''unpredictable'' process should not allow a successful gambling strategy. That is, if we chose to bet on an outcome of such a process, we could not improve our chances of winning by betting on some subsequence of the outcomes instead of betting on every outcome. For example, suppose we decided to bet on heads in the repeated tossing of a coin. Most of us feel that we could not improve our chances by betting on every other toss instead of on every toss. Furthermore, most of us feel that there is no other ''special'' subsequence that could improve our chances. If indeed we could not improve our chances by betting on some subsequence, then the repeated tossing of the coin would be a random process. As another example, suppose that we repeatedly sampled individuals from a population that contained individuals with and without cancer, and that we put each sampled individual back into the population before sampling the next individual. (This is called sampling with replacement.) Let's say we chose to bet on cancer. If we sampled in such a way as to never give preference to any particular individual, most of us feel that we would not improve our chances by betting only on some subsequence instead of betting every time. If indeed we could not improve our chances by betting on some subsequence, then the process of sampling would be random. However, if we sometimes gave preference to individuals who smoked by sampling every fourth time only from smokers, and we sampled the other times from the entire population, the process would no longer be random because we could improve our chances by betting every fourth time instead of every time.

Intuitively, when we say that "we sample in such a way as to never give preference to any particular individual," we mean that there is no pattern in the way the sampling is done. For example, if we were sampling balls with replacement from an urn, we would never give any ball preference if we shook the urn vigorously to thoroughly mix the balls before each sample. You may have noticed how thoroughly the balls are mixed before they are drawn in state lotteries. When sampling is done from a human population, it is not as easy to ensure that preference is not given. The discussion of sampling methods is beyond the scope of this appendix.

Von Mises' requirement of not allowing a successful gambling strategy gives us a better grasp of the meaning of randomness. A predictable or nonrandom process does allow a successful gambling strategy. One example of a nonrandom process is the one mentioned above in which we sampled every fourth time from smokers. A less obvious example concerns the exercise pattern of one of the authors. He prefers to exercise at his health club on Tuesday, Thursday, and Sunday, but if he misses a day he makes up for it on one of the other days. If we were going to bet on whether he exercises on a given day, we could do much better by betting every Tuesday, Thursday, and Sunday than by betting every day. This process is not random.

Even though Von Mises was able to give us a better understanding of randomness, he was not able to create a rigorous, mathematical definition. Andrei Kolmogorov eventually did so with the concept of compressible sequences. Briefly, a finite sequence is defined as ***compressible*** if it can be encoded in fewer bits than it takes to encode every item in the sequence. For example, the sequence

$$1\ 0\ 1\ 0\ 1\ 0\ 1\ 0\ 1\ 0\ 1\ 0\ 1\ 0\ 1\ 0\ 1\ 0\ 1\ 0\ 1\ 0\ 1\ 0\ 1\ 0\ 1\ 0\ 1\ 0\ 1\ 0,$$

which is simply "1 0" repeated 16 times, can be represented by

$$16\ 1\ 0.$$

Because it takes fewer bits to encode this representation than it does to encode every item in the sequence, the sequence is compressible. A finite sequence that is not compressible is called a ***random sequence.*** For example, the sequence

$$1\ 0\ 0\ 1\ 1\ 0\ 1\ 0\ 0\ 0\ 1\ 0\ 1\ 1\ 0\ 1$$

is random because it does not have a more efficient representation. Intuitively, a random sequence is one that shows no regularity or pattern.

According to the Kolmogorov theory, a ***random process*** is a process that generates a random sequence when the process is continued long enough. For example, suppose we repeatedly toss a coin, and associate 1 with heads and 0 with tails. After six tosses we may see the sequence

$$1\ 0\ 1\ 0\ 1\ 0,$$

but, according to the Kolmogorov theory, eventually the entire sequence will show no such regularity. There is some philosophical difficulty with defining a random process as one that *definitely* generates a random sequence. Many probabilists feel that it is only highly probable that the sequence will be random, and that the possibility exists that the sequence will not be random. For example, in the repeated tossing of a coin, they believe that, although it is very unlikely, the coin could come up heads forever. As mentioned previously, randomness is a difficult concept. Even today there is controversy over its properties.

Let's discuss how randomness relates to probability. A random process determines a probability space (see definition given at the beginning of this section), and the experiment in the space is performed each time the process generates an outcome. This is illustrated by the following examples.

Example A.16

Suppose we have an urn containing one black ball and one white ball, and we repeatedly draw a ball and replace it. This random process determines a probability space in which

$$p(\text{black}) = p(\text{white}) = .5.$$

We perform the experiment in the space each time we draw a ball.

Example A.17

The repeated throwing of the asymmetrical six-sided die in Example A.15 is a random process that determines a probability space in which

$$p(1) \approx .2$$
$$p(2) \approx .15$$
$$p(3) \approx .1$$
$$p(4) \approx .25$$
$$p(5) \approx .12$$
$$p(6) \approx .18.$$

We perform the experiment in the space each time we throw the die.

Example A.18

Suppose we have a population of n people, some of whom have cancer, we sample people with replacement, and we sample in such a way as to never give preference to any particular individual. This random process determines a probability space in which the population is the sample space (recall that ''sample space'' and ''population'' can be used interchangeably) and the probability of each person being sampled (elementary event) is $1/n$. The probability of a person with cancer being sampled is

$$\frac{\text{Number with cancer}}{n}.$$

Each time we perform the experiment, we say that we sample (pick) a person *at random* from the population. The set of outcomes in all repetitions of the experiment is called a *random sample* of the population. Using statistical techniques, it can be shown that if a random sample is large, then it is highly probable that the sample is representative of the population. For example if the random sample is large, and $\frac{1}{3}$ of the people sampled have cancer, it is highly probable that the fraction of people in the population with cancer is close to $\frac{1}{3}$.

Example A.19

Suppose we have an ordinary deck of playing cards, and we turn over the cards in sequence. This process is not random, and the cards are not picked at random. This nonrandom process determines a different probability space each time an outcome is generated. On the first trial, each card has a probability of $\frac{1}{52}$. On the second trial, the card turned over in the first trial has a probability of 0 and each of the other cards has a probability of $\frac{1}{51}$, and so on.

Suppose we repeatedly draw the top card, replace it, and shuffle once. Is this a random process and are the cards picked at random? The answer is no. The magician and Harvard statistician Persi Diaconis has shown that the cards must be shuffled seven times to thoroughly mix them and make the process random (see Aldous and Diaconis, 1986).

Although von Mises' notion of randomness is intuitively very appealing today, his views were not widely held at the time he developed his theory (in the early part of the 20th century). His strongest opponent was the philosopher K. Marbe. Marbe held that nature is endowed with a memory. According to his theory, if tails comes up 15 consecutive times in repeated tosses of a fair coin—that is, a coin for which the relative frequency of heads is .5—the probability of heads coming up on the next toss is increased because nature will compensate for all the previous tails. If this theory were correct, we could improve our chances of winning by betting on heads only after a long sequence of tails. Iverson et al. (1971) conducted experiments that substantiated the views of von Mises and Kolmogorov. Specifically, their experiments showed that coin tosses and dice throws do generate random sequences. Today few scientists subscribe to Marbe's theory, although quite a few gamblers seem to.

Von Mises' original theory appeared in von Mises (1919) and is discussed more accessibly in von Mises (1957). A detailed coverage of compressible sequences and random sequences can be found in Van Lambalgen (1987). Neapolitan (1992) and Van Lambalgen (1987) both address the difficulties in defining a random process as one that definitely generates a random sequence.

A.8.2 The Expected Value

We introduce the expected value (average) with an example.

Example A.20

Suppose we have four students with heights of 68, 72, 67, and 74 inches. Their average height is given by

$$\text{Average height} = \frac{68 + 72 + 67 + 74}{4} \text{ inches} = 70.25 \text{ inches.}$$

Suppose now that we have 1000 students whose heights are distributed according to the following percentages:

Percentage of Students	Height in Inches
20	66
25	68
30	71
10	72
15	74

To compute the average height, we could first determine the height of each student and proceed as before. However, it is much more efficient to simply obtain the average as follows:

$$\text{Average height} = 66(.2) + 68(.25) + 71(.3) + 72(.1) + 74(.15) \text{ inches}$$
$$= 69.8 \text{ inches}$$

Notice that the percentages in this example are simply probabilities obtained using the Principle of Indifference. That is, the fact that 20% of the students are 66 inches tall means that 200 students are 66 inches tall, and if we pick a student at random from the 1000 students, then

$$p(\text{height} = 66 \text{ inches}) = \frac{200}{1000} = .2.$$

In general, the expected value is defined as follows.

Definition

Suppose we have a probability space with the sample space

$$\{e_1, e_2, \ldots, e_n\}$$

and each outcome e_i has a real number $f(e_i)$ associated with it. Then $f(e_i)$ is called a **random variable** on the sample space, and the **expected value**, or average, of $f(e_i)$ is given by

$$f(e_1)p(e_1) + f(e_2)p(e_2) + \cdots + f(e_n)p(e_n).$$

Random variables are called ''random'' because random processes can determine the values of random variables. The terms ''chance variable'' and ''stochastic variable'' are also used. We use ''random variable'' because it is the most popular.

Example A.21

Suppose we have the asymmetrical six-sided die in Example A.15. That is,

$$p(1) \approx .2 \qquad p(4) \approx .25$$
$$p(2) \approx .15 \qquad p(5) \approx .12$$
$$p(3) \approx .1 \qquad p(6) \approx .18.$$

Our sample space consists of the six different sides that can come up, a random variable on this sample space is the number written on the side, and the expected value of this random variable is

$$1p(1) + 2p(2) + 3p(3) + 4p(4) + 5p(5) + 6p(6)$$
$$\approx 1(.2) + 2(.15) + 3(.1) + 4(.25) + 5(.12) + 6(.18) = 3.48.$$

If we threw the die many times, we would expect the average of the numbers showing up to equal about 3.48.

A sample space does not have a unique random variable defined on it. Another random variable on this sample space would be the function that assigns 0 if an odd number comes up and 1 if an even number comes up. The expected value of this random variable is

$$0p(1) + 1p(2) + 0p(3) + 1p(4) + 0p(5) + 1p(6)$$
$$\approx 0(.2) + 1(.15) + 0(.1) + 1(.25) + 0(.12) + 1(.18) = .58.$$

Example A.22   Suppose the 1000 students in Example A.20 are our sample space. The height, as computed in Example A.20, is one random variable on this sample space. Another one is the weight. If the weights are distributed according to the following percentages:

Percentage of Students	Weight in Pounds
15	130
35	145
30	160
10	170
10	185

the expected value of this random variable is

$$130(.15) + 145(.35) + 160(.30) + 170(.10) + 185(.10) \text{ pounds}$$
$$= 153.75 \text{ pounds.}$$

Exercises

Section A.1

1. Determine each of the following.
   (a) $\lfloor 2.8 \rfloor$ (d) $\lceil -34.92 \rceil$
   (b) $\lfloor -10.42 \rfloor$ (e) $\lfloor 5.2 - 4.7 \rfloor$
   (c) $\lceil 4.2 \rceil$ (f) $\lceil 2\pi \rceil$

2. Show that $\lceil n \rceil = -\lfloor -n \rfloor$.

3. Show that, for any real x,

$$\lfloor 2x \rfloor = \lfloor x \rfloor + \left\lfloor x + \frac{1}{2} \right\rfloor.$$

4. Show that for any integers $a > 0$, $b > 0$, and n,

(a) $\left\lfloor \dfrac{n}{2} \right\rfloor + \left\lceil \dfrac{n}{2} \right\rceil = n$

(b) $\left\lfloor \dfrac{\lfloor n/a \rfloor}{b} \right\rfloor = \left\lfloor \dfrac{n}{ab} \right\rfloor$

5. Write each of the following using summation (sigma) notation.
   (a) $2 + 4 + 6 + \cdots + 2(99) + 2(100)$
   (b) $2 + 4 + 6 + \cdots + 2(n - 1) + 2n$
   (c) $3 + 12 + 27 + \cdots + 1200$

6. Evaluate each of the following sums.

(a) $\displaystyle\sum_{i=1}^{5} (2i + 4)$

(b) $\displaystyle\sum_{i=1}^{10} (i^2 - 4i)$

(c) $\displaystyle\sum_{i=1}^{200} \left(\frac{i}{i + 1} - \frac{i - 1}{i} \right)$

(*Hint:* You should see a pattern if you write the first two or three terms without simplification.)

(d) $\displaystyle\sum_{i=0}^{5} (2^i n^{5-i})$, when $n = 4$

(e) $\displaystyle\sum_{i=1}^{4} \sum_{j=1}^{i} (j + 5)$

Section A.2

7. Graph the function $f(x) = \sqrt{x - 4}$. What are the domain and range of this function?

8. Graph the function $f(x) = (x - 2)/(x + 5)$. What are the domain and range of this function?

9. Graph the function $f(x) = \lfloor x \rfloor$. What are the domain and range of this function?

10. Graph the function $f(x) = \lceil x \rceil$. What are the domain and range of this function?

Section A.3

11. Use mathematical induction to show that, for all integers $n > 0$,

$$\sum_{k=1}^{n} k(k!) = (n + 1)! - 1.$$

12. Use mathematical induction to show that $n^2 - n$ is even for any positive integer n.

13. Use mathematical induction to show that, for all integers $n > 4$,

$$2^n > n^2.$$

14. Use mathematical induction to show that, for all integers $n > 0$,

$$\left(\sum_{i=1}^{n} i\right)^2 = \sum_{i=1}^{n} i^3.$$

Section A.4

15. Prove that if a and b are both odd integers, $a + b$ is an even integer. Is the reverse implication true?

16. Prove that $a + b$ is an odd integer if and only if a and b are not both odd or both even integers.

Section A.5

17. Determine each of the following.
    (a) $\log 1000$ (d) $\lg \frac{1}{16}$ (g) $\lg(16 \times 8)$
    (b) $\log 100{,}000$ (e) $\log_5 125$ (h) $\log(1000/100{,}000)$
    (c) $\log_4 64$ (f) $\log 23$ (i) $2^{\lg 125}$

18. Graph $f(x) = 2^x$ and $g(x) = \lg x$ on the same coordinate system.

19. Give the values of x for which $x^2 + 6x + 12 > 8x + 20$.

20. Give the values of x for which $x > 500 \lg x$.

21. Show that $f(x) = 2^{3 \lg x}$ is not an exponential function.

22. Show that, for any positive integer n,

$$\lfloor \lg n \rfloor + 1 = \lceil \lg(n + 1) \rceil$$

23. Find a formula for $\lg(n!)$ using Stirling's approximation for $n!$,

$$n! \approx \sqrt{2\pi n}\left(\frac{n}{e}\right)^n,$$

for relatively large n.

Section A.6

24. Let $U = \{2, 4, 5, 6, 8, 10, 12\}$, $S = \{2, 4, 5, 10\}$, and $T = \{2, 6, 8, 10\}$. (U is the universal set.) Determine each of the following.
    (a) $S \cup T$ (d) $T - S$
    (b) $S \cap T$ (e) $((S \cap T) \cup S)$
    (c) $S - T$ (f) $U - S$ (called the complement of S)

25. Given that the set S contains n elements, show that S has 2^n subsets.

26. Let $|S|$ stand for the number of elements in S. Show the validity of

$$|S \cup T| = |S| + |T| - |S \cap T|.$$

27. Show that the following are equivalent.
    (a) $S \subset T$ (b) $S \cap T = S$ (c) $S \cup T = T$

Section A.7

28. Determine the number of permutations of 10 objects taken six at a time.

29. Determine the number of combinations of 10 objects taken six at a time. That is, determine $\binom{10}{6}$.

30. Suppose there is a lottery in which four balls are drawn from a bin containing 10 balls. A winning ticket must show the balls in the order in which they are drawn. How many distinct winning tickets are there?

31. Suppose there is a lottery in which four balls are drawn from a bin containing 10 balls. A winning ticket must merely show the correct balls without regard for the order in which they are drawn. How many distinct winning tickets are there?

32. Use mathematical induction to prove the Binomial Theorem, given in Section A.7.

33. Show the validity of the following identity.

$$\binom{2n}{2} = 2\binom{n}{2} + n^2$$

34. Assume that we have k_1 objects of the first kind, k_2 objects of the second kind, . . . , and k_m objects of the mth kind, where $k_1 + k_2 + \cdots + k_m = n$. Show that the number of distinct permutations of these n objects is equal to

$$\frac{n!}{(k_1!)(k_2!) \cdots (k_m!)}.$$

35. Show that the number of ways to distribute n identical objects into m distinct groups is equal to

$$\binom{n + m - 1}{n} = \binom{n + m - 1}{m - 1}.$$

36. Show the validity of the following identity.

$$\binom{n}{k+1} = \frac{n-k}{k+1}\binom{n}{k}$$

Section A.8

37. Suppose we have the lottery in Exercise 30.
    (a) Compute the probability of winning if one ticket is purchased.
    (b) Compute the probability of winning if seven tickets are purchased.

38. Suppose a poker hand (five cards) is dealt from an ordinary deck (52 cards).
    (a) Compute the probability of the hand containing four aces.
    (b) Compute the probability of the hand containing four of a kind.

39. Suppose a fair six-sided die (that is, the probability of each side turning up is $\frac{1}{6}$) is to be rolled. The player will receive an amount of dollars equal to the number of dots that turn up, except when five or six dots turn up, in which case the player will lose \$5 or \$6, respectively.
    (a) Compute the expected value of the amount of money the player will win or lose.
    (b) If the game is repeated 100 times, compute the most money the player will lose, the most money the player will win, and the amount the player can expect to win or lose.

40. Assume we are searching for an element in a list of n distinct elements. What is the average (expected) number of comparisons required when the Sequential Search algorithm (linear search) is used?

41. What is the expected number of movements of elements in a delete operation on an array of n elements?

APPENDIX B

Solving Recurrence Equations: With Applications to Analysis of Recursive Algorithms

The analysis of recursive algorithms is not as straightforward as it is for iterative algorithms. Ordinarily, however, it is not difficult to represent the time complexity of a recursive algorithm by a recurrence equation. The recurrence equation must then be solved to determine the time complexity. We discuss techniques for solving such equations and for using the solutions in the analysis of recursive algorithms.

B.1 SOLVING RECURRENCES USING INDUCTION

Mathematical induction is reviewed in Appendix A. Here we show how it can be used to analyze some recursive algorithms. We consider first a recursive algorithm that computes $n!$.

Algorithm B.1

Factorial

Problem: Determine $n! = n(n-1)(n-2) \cdots (3)(2)(1)$ when $n \geq 1$.
$$0! = 1$$

Inputs: a nonnegative integer n.

Outputs: $n!$.

```
int fact (int n)
{
    if (n == 0)
        return 1;
    else
        return n * fact(n − 1);
}
```

To gain insight into the efficiency of this algorithm, let's determine how many times this function does the multiplication instruction for each value of n. For a given n, the number of multiplications done is the number done when $fact(n − 1)$ is computed plus the one multiplication done when n is multiplied by $fact(n − 1)$. If we represent the number of multiplications done for a given value of n by t_n, we have established that

$$t_n = \underbrace{t_{n-1}}_{\substack{\text{Multiplications} \\ \text{in recursive call}}} + \underbrace{1.}_{\substack{\text{Multiplication} \\ \text{at top level}}}$$

An equation such as this is called a ***recurrence equation*** because the value of the function at n is given in terms of the value of the function at a smaller value of n. A recurrence by itself does not represent a unique function. We must also have a starting point, which is called an ***initial condition.*** In this algorithm, no multiplications are done when $n = 0$. Therefore, the initial condition is

$$t_0 = 0.$$

We can compute t_n for larger values of n as follows:

$$t_1 = t_{1-1} + 1 = t_0 + 1 = 0 + 1 = 1$$
$$t_2 = t_{2-1} + 1 = t_1 + 1 = 1 + 1 = 2$$
$$t_3 = t_{3-1} + 1 = t_2 + 1 = 2 + 1 = 3.$$
$$\vdots$$

Continuing in this manner gives us more and more values of t_n, but it does not enable us to compute t_n for an arbitrary n without starting at 0. We need an explicit expression for t_n. Such an expression is called a ***solution*** to the recurrence equation. Recall that it is not possible to find a solution using induction. Induction can only verify that a candidate solution is correct. (Constructive induction, which is discussed in Section 8.5.4, can help us discover a solution.) We can obtain a candidate solution to this recurrence by inspecting the first few values. An inspection of the values just computed indicates that

$$t_n = n$$

is the solution. Now that we have a candidate solution, we can use induction to try to prove that it is correct.

Induction base: For $n = 0$,

$$t_0 = 0.$$

Induction hypothesis: Assume, for an arbitrary positive integer n, that

$$t_n = n.$$

Induction step: We need to show that

$$t_{n+1} = n + 1.$$

If we insert $n + 1$ in the recurrence, we get

$$t_{n+1} = t_{(n+1)-1} + 1 = \boldsymbol{t_n} + 1 = \boldsymbol{n} + 1.$$

This completes the induction proof that our candidate solution t_n is correct. Notice that we highlight the terms that are equal by the induction hypothesis. We often do this in induction proofs to show where the induction hypothesis is being applied.

There are two steps in the analysis of a recursive algorithm. The first step is determining the recurrence; the second step is solving it. Our purpose here is to show how to solve recurrences. Determining the recurrences for the recursive algorithms in this text is done when we discuss the algorithms. Therefore, in the remainder of this appendix we do not discuss algorithms; rather, we simply take the recurrences as given. We now present more examples of solving recurrences using induction.

Example B.1   Consider the recurrence

$$\boxed{\begin{aligned} t_n &= t_{n/2} + 1 \qquad \text{for } n > 1,\ n \text{ a power of 2} \\ t_1 &= 1 \end{aligned}}$$

The first few values are

$$\begin{aligned}
t_2 &= t_{2/2} + 1 = t_1 + 1 = 1 + 1 = 2 \\
t_4 &= t_{4/2} + 1 = t_2 + 1 = 2 + 1 = 3 \\
t_8 &= t_{8/2} + 1 = t_4 + 1 = 3 + 1 = 4 \\
t_{16} &= t_{16/2} + 1 = t_8 + 1 = 4 + 1 = 5.
\end{aligned}$$

It appears that

$$t_n = \lg n + 1.$$

We use induction to prove that this is correct.

468

Appendix B Solving Recurrence Equations

Induction base: For $n = 1$,

$$t_1 = 1 = \lg 1 + 1.$$

Induction hypothesis: Assume, for an arbitrary $n > 0$ and n a power of 2, that

$$t_n = \lg n + 1.$$

Induction step: Because the recurrence is only for powers of 2, the next value to consider after n is $2n$. Therefore, we need to show that

$$t_{2n} = \lg(2n) + 1.$$

If we insert $2n$ in the recurrence, we get

$$t_{2n} = t_{(2n)/2} + 1 = t_n + 1 = \mathbf{\lg n + 1} + 1$$
$$= \lg n + \lg 2 + 1$$
$$= \lg(2n) + 1.$$

Example B.2

Consider the recurrence

$$t_n = 7t_{n/2} \quad \text{for } n > 1, n \text{ a power of 2}$$
$$t_1 = 1$$

The first few values are

$$t_2 = 7t_{2/2} = 7t_1 = 7$$
$$t_4 = 7t_{4/2} = 7t_2 = 7^2$$
$$t_8 = 7t_{8/2} = 7t_4 = 7^3$$
$$t_{16} = 7t_{16/2} = 7t_8 = 7^4$$

It appears that

$$t_n = 7^{\lg n}.$$

We use induction to prove that this is correct.

Induction base: For $n = 1$,

$$t_1 = 1 = 7^0 = 7^{\lg 1}.$$

Induction hypothesis: Assume, for an arbitrary $n > 0$ and n a power of 2, that

$$t_n = 7^{\lg n}.$$

Induction step: We need to show that

$$t_{2n} = 7^{\lg(2n)}.$$

If we insert $2n$ in the recurrence, we get

$$t_{2n} = 7t_{(2n)/2} = 7t_n = 7 \times \mathbf{7^{\lg n}} = 7^{1+\lg n} = 7^{\lg 2 + \lg n} = 7^{\lg(2n)}.$$

This completes the induction proof. Finally, because

$$7^{\lg n} = n^{\lg 7},$$

the solution to this recurrence is usually given as

$$t_n = n^{\lg 7} \approx n^{2.81}.$$

Example B.3   Consider the recurrence

$$
\begin{array}{ll}
t_n = 2t_{n/2} + n - 1 & \text{for } n > 1, n \text{ a power of 2} \\
t_1 = 0
\end{array}
$$

The first few values are

$$t_2 = 2t_{2/2} + 2 - 1 = 2t_1 + 1 = 1$$
$$t_4 = 2t_{4/2} + 4 - 1 = 2t_2 + 3 = 5$$
$$t_8 = 2t_{8/2} + 8 - 1 = 2t_4 + 7 = 17$$
$$t_{16} = 2t_{16/2} + 16 - 1 = 2t_8 + 15 = 49$$

There is no obvious candidate solution suggested by these values. As mentioned earlier, induction can only verify that a solution is correct. Because we have no candidate solution, we cannot use induction to solve this recurrence. However, it can be solved using the technique discussed in the next section.

B.2 SOLVING RECURRENCES USING THE CHARACTERISTIC EQUATION

We develop a technique for determining the solutions to a large class of recurrences.

B.2.1 Homogeneous Linear Recurrences

Definition   A recurrence of the form

$$a_0 t_n + a_1 t_{n-1} + \cdots + a_k t_{n-k} = 0,$$

where k and the a_i terms are constants, is called a *homogeneous linear recurrence equation with constant coefficients.*

Such a recurrence is called "linear" because every term t_i appears only to the first power. That is, there are no terms such as t_{n-i}^2, $t_{n-i}t_{n-j}$, and so on. However, there is the additional requirement that there be no terms $t_{c(n-i)}$, where c is a positive constant other than 1. For example, there may not be terms such as $t_{n/2}$, $t_{3(n-4)}$, etc. Such a recurrence is called "homogeneous" because the linear combination of the terms is equal to 0.

Example B.4   The following are homogeneous linear recurrence equations with constant coefficients:

$$7t_n - 3t_{n-1} = 0$$
$$6t_n - 5t_{n-1} + 8t_{n-2} = 0$$
$$8t_n - 4t_{n-3} = 0$$

Example B.5   The Fibonacci Sequence, which is discussed in Subsection 1.2.2, is defined as follows:

$$t_n = t_{n-1} + t_{n-2}$$
$$t_0 = 0$$
$$t_1 = 1$$

If we subtract t_{n-1} and t_{n-2} from both sides, we get

$$t_n - t_{n-1} - t_{n-2} = 0,$$

which shows that the Fibonacci Sequence is defined by a homogeneous linear recurrence.

Next we show how to solve a homogeneous linear recurrence.

Example B.6   Suppose we have the recurrence

$$t_n - 5t_{n-1} + 6t_{n-2} = 0 \qquad \text{for } n > 1$$
$$t_0 = 0$$
$$t_1 = 1$$

Notice that if we set

$$t_n = r^n,$$

then

$$t_n - 5t_{n-1} + 6t_{n-2} = r^n - 5r^{n-1} + 6r^{n-2}.$$

Therefore, $t_n = r^n$ is a solution to the recurrence if r is a root of

$$r^n - 5r^{n-1} + 6r^{n-2} = 0.$$

Because

$$r^n - 5r^{n-1} + 6r^{n-2} = r^{n-2}(r^2 - 5r + 6),$$

the roots are $r = 0$, and the roots of

$$r^2 - 5r + 6 = 0. \tag{B.1}$$

These roots can be found by factoring:

$$r^2 - 5r + 6 = (r - 3)(r - 2) = 0.$$

The roots are $r = 3$ and $r = 2$. Therefore,

$$t_n = 0, \qquad t_n = 3^n, \qquad \text{and} \qquad t_n = 2^n$$

are all solutions to the recurrence. We verify this for 3^n by substituting it into the left side of the recurrence, as follows:

$$
\begin{array}{ccc}
3^n & 3^{n-1} & 3^{n-2} \\
\downarrow & \downarrow & \downarrow \\
t_n & -\ 5t_{n-1} & +\ 6t_{n-2}
\end{array}
$$

With this substitution, the left side becomes

$$
\begin{aligned}
3^n - 5(3^{n-1}) + 6(3^{n-2}) &= 3^n - 5(3^{n-1}) + 2(3^{n-1}) \\
&= 3^n - 3(3^{n-1}) = 3^n - 3^n = 0,
\end{aligned}
$$

which means that 3^n is a solution to the recurrence.

We have found three solutions to the recurrence, but we have more solutions, because if 3^n and 2^n are solutions, then so is

$$t_n = c_1 3^n + c_2 2^n,$$

where c_1 and c_2 are arbitrary constants. This result is obtained in the exercises. Although we do not show it here, it is possible to show that these are the only solutions. This expression is therefore the general solution to the recurrence. (By taking $c_1 = c_2 = 0$, the trivial solution $t_n = 0$ is included in this general solution.) We have an infinite number of solutions, but which one is the answer to our problem? This is determined by the initial conditions. Recall that we had the initial conditions

$$t_0 = 0 \qquad \text{and} \qquad t_1 = 1.$$

These two conditions determine unique values of c_1 and c_2 as follows. If we apply the general solution to each of them, we get the following two equations in two unknowns:

$$
\begin{aligned}
t_0 &= c_1 3^0 + c_2 2^0 = 0 \\
t_1 &= c_1 3^1 + c_2 2^1 = 1.
\end{aligned}
$$

These two equations simplify to

$$
\begin{aligned}
c_1 + c_2 &= 0 \\
3c_1 + 2c_2 &= 1.
\end{aligned}
$$

The solution to this system of equations is $c_1 = 1$ and $c_2 = -1$. Therefore, the solution to our recurrence is

$$t_n = 1(3^n) - 1(2^n) = 3^n - 2^n.$$

If we had different initial conditions in the preceding example, we would get a different solution. A recurrence actually represents a class of functions, one for each different assignment of initial conditions. Let's see what function we get if we use the initial conditions

$$t_0 = 1 \qquad \text{and} \qquad t_1 = 2$$

with the recurrence given in Example B.6. Applying the general solution in Example B.6 to each of these conditions yields

$$t_0 = c_1 3^0 + c_2 2^0 = 1$$
$$t_1 = c_1 3^1 + c_2 2^1 = 2.$$

These two equations simplify to

$$c_1 + c_2 = 1$$
$$3c_1 + 2c_2 = 2.$$

The solution to this system is $c_1 = 0$ and $c_2 = 1$. Therefore, the solution to the recurrence with these initial conditions is

$$t_n = 0(3^n) + 1(2^n) = 2^n.$$

Equation B.1 in Example B.6 is called the characteristic equation for the recurrence. In general, this equation is defined as follows.

Definition   The *characteristic equation* for the homogeneous linear recurrence equation with constant coefficients

$$a_0 t_n + a_1 t_{n-1} + \cdots + a_k t_{n-k} = 0$$

is defined as

$$a_0 r^k + a_1 r^{k-1} + \cdots + a_k r^0 = 0.$$

The value of r^0 is simply 1. We write the term as r^0 to show the relationship between the characteristic equation and the recurrence.

Example B.7   The characteristic equation for the recurrence appears below it:

$$5t_n - 7t_{n-1} + 6t_{n-2} = 0$$
$$5r^2 - 7r + 6 = 0.$$

We use an arrow to show that the order of the characteristic equation is k (in this case, 2).

The steps used to obtain the solution in Example B.6 can be generalized into a theorem. To solve a homogeneous linear recurrence with constant coefficients, we need only refer to the theorem. The theorem follows, and its proof appears near the end of this appendix.

Theorem B.1 Let the homogeneous linear recurrence equation with constant coefficients

$$a_0 t_n + a_1 t_{n-1} + \cdots + a_k t_{n-k} = 0$$

be given. If its characteristic equation

$$a_0 r^k + a_1 r^{k-1} + \cdots + a_k r^0 = 0$$

has k distinct solutions $r_1, r_2, \ldots, r_k$, then the only solutions to the recurrence are

$$t_n = c_1 r_1^n + c_2 r_2^n + \cdots + c_k r_k^n,$$

where the c_i terms are arbitrary constants.

The values of the k constants c_i are determined by the initial conditions. We need k initial conditions to uniquely determine k constants. The method for determining the values of the constants is demonstrated in the following examples.

Example B.8   We solve the recurrence

$$
\begin{aligned}
&t_n - 3t_{n-1} - 4t_{n-2} = 0 \qquad \text{for } n > 1 \\
&t_0 = 0 \\
&t_1 = 1
\end{aligned}
$$

1. Obtain the characteristic equation:

$$t_n - 3t_{n-1} - 4t_{n-2} = 0$$
$$r^2 - 3r - 4 = 0.$$

2. Solve the characteristic equation:

$$r^2 - 3r - 4 = (r - 4)(r + 1) = 0.$$

   The roots are $r = 4$ and $r = -1$.

3. Apply Theorem B.1 to get the general solution to the recurrence:

$$t_n = c_1 4^n + c_2 (-1)^n.$$

4. Determine the values of the constants by applying the general solution to the initial conditions:

$$t_0 = 0 = c_1 4^0 + c_2 (-1)^0$$
$$t_1 = 1 = c_1 4^1 + c_2 (-1)^1.$$

These values simplify to

$$c_1 + c_2 = 0$$
$$4c_1 - c_2 = 1.$$

The solution to this system is $c_1 = 1/5$ and $c_2 = -1/5$.

5. Substitute the constants into the general solution to obtain the particular solution:

$$t_n = \frac{1}{5}\, 4^n - \frac{1}{5}\, (-1)^n.$$

Example B.9   We solve the recurrence that generates the Fibonacci Sequence:

$$t_n - t_{n-1} - t_{n-2} = 0 \qquad \text{for } n > 1$$
$$t_0 = 0$$
$$t_1 = 1$$

1. Obtain the characteristic equation:

$$t_n - t_{n-1} - t_{n-2} = 0$$
$$r^2 - r - 1 = 0.$$

2. Solve the characteristic equation:
    From the formula for the solution to a quadratic equation, the roots of this characteristic equation are

$$r = \frac{1 + \sqrt{5}}{2} \qquad \text{and} \qquad r = \frac{1 - \sqrt{5}}{2}.$$

3. Apply Theorem B.1 to get the general solution to the recurrence:

$$t_n = c_1\left(\frac{1 + \sqrt{5}}{2}\right)^n + c_2\left(\frac{1 - \sqrt{5}}{2}\right)^n.$$

4. Determine the values of the constants by applying the general solution to the initial conditions:

$$t_0 = c_1\left(\frac{1 + \sqrt{5}}{2}\right)^0 + c_2\left(\frac{1 - \sqrt{5}}{2}\right)^0 = 0$$

$$t_1 = c_1\left(\frac{1 + \sqrt{5}}{2}\right)^1 + c_2\left(\frac{1 - \sqrt{5}}{2}\right)^1 = 1.$$

These equations simplify to

$$c_1 + \qquad\qquad c_2 = 0$$

$$\left(\frac{1 + \sqrt{5}}{2}\right) c_1 + \left(\frac{1 - \sqrt{5}}{2}\right) c_2 = 1.$$

Solving this system yields $c_1 = 1/\sqrt{5}$ and $c_2 = -1/\sqrt{5}$.

5. Substitute the constants into the general solution to obtain the particular solution:

$$t_n = \frac{[(1 + \sqrt{5})/2]^n - [(1 - \sqrt{5})/2]^n}{\sqrt{5}}.$$

Although Example B.9 provides an explicit formula for the nth Fibonacci term, it has little practical value, because the degree of precision necessary to represent $\sqrt{5}$ increases as n increases.

Theorem B.1 requires that all k roots of the characteristic equation be distinct. The theorem does not allow a characteristic equation of the following form:

Multiplicity
$$\downarrow$$
$$(r - 1)(r - 2)^3 = 0.$$

Because the term $r - 2$ is raised to the third power, 2 is called a ***root of multiplicity 3*** of the equation. The following theorem allows for a root to have a multiplicity. The proof of the theorem appears near the end of this appendix.

Theorem B.2 Let r be a root of multiplicity m of the characteristic equation for a homogeneous linear recurrence with constant coefficients. Then

$$t_n = r^n, \quad t_n = nr^n, \quad t_n = n^2 r^n, \quad t_n = n^3 r^n, \quad \cdots, \quad t_n = n^{m-1} r^n$$

are all solutions to the recurrence. Therefore, a term for each of these solutions is included in the general solution (as given in Theorem B.1) to the recurrence.

Example applications of this theorem follow.

Example B.10 We solve the recurrence

$$t_n - 7t_{n-1} + 15_{n-2} - 9t_{n-3} = 0 \qquad \text{for } n > 2$$
$$t_0 = 0$$
$$t_1 = 1 \qquad t_2 = 2$$

1. Obtain the characteristic equation:

$$t_n - 7t_{n-1} + 15t_{n-2} - 9t_{n-3} = 0$$
$$r^3 - 7r^2 + 15r - 9 = 0.$$

2. Solve the characteristic equation:

Multiplicity
↓

$$r^3 - 7r^2 + 15r - 9 = (r - 1)(r - 3)^2 = 0.$$

The roots are $r = 1$ and $r = 3$, and $r = 3$ is a root of multiplicity 2.

3. Apply Theorem B.2 to get the general solution to the recurrence:

$$t_n = c_1 1^n + c_2 3^n + c_3 n 3^n.$$

We have included terms for 3^n and $n3^n$ because 3 is a root of multiplicity 2.

4. Determine the values of the constants by applying the general solution to the initial conditions:

$$t_0 = 0 = c_1 1^0 + c_2 3^0 + c_3 (0)(3^0)$$
$$t_1 = 1 = c_1 1^1 + c_2 3^1 + c_3 (1)(3^1)$$
$$t_2 = 2 = c_1 1^2 + c_2 3^2 + c_3 (2)(3^2).$$

These values simplify to

$$c_1 + c_2 \qquad\qquad = 0$$
$$c_1 + 3c_2 + 3c_3 \ = 1$$
$$c_1 + 9c_2 + 18c_3 = 2.$$

Solving this system yields $c_1 = -1$, $c_2 = 1$, and $c_3 = -\frac{1}{3}$.

5. Substitute the constants into the general solution to obtain the particular solution:

$$t_n = (-1)(1^n) + (1)(3^n) + \left(-\frac{1}{3}\right)(n3^n)$$
$$= -1 + 3^n - n3^{n-1}.$$

Example B.11   We solve the recurrence

$$t_n - 5t_{n-1} + 7t_{n-2} - 3t_{n-3} = 0 \qquad \text{for } n > 2$$
$$t_0 = 1$$
$$t_1 = 2 \qquad t_2 = 3$$

1. Obtain the characteristic equation:

$$t_n - 5t_{n-1} + 7t_{n-2} - 3t_{n-3} = 0$$
$$r^3 - 5r^2 + 7r - 3 = 0.$$

2. Solve the characteristic equation:

Multiplicity
↓
$$r^3 - 5r^2 + 7r - 3 = (r - 3)(r - 1)^2 = 0.$$

The roots are $r = 3$ and $r = 1$, and the root 1 has multiplicity 2.

3. Apply Theorem B.2 to obtain the general solution to the recurrence:

$$t_n = c_1 3^n + c_2 1^n + c_3 n 1^n.$$

4. Determine the values of the constants by applying the general solution to the initial conditions:

$$t_0 = 1 = c_1 3^0 + c_2 1^0 + c_3(0)(1^0)$$
$$t_1 = 2 = c_1 3^1 + c_2 1^1 + c_3(1)(1^1)$$
$$t_2 = 3 = c_1 3^2 + c_2 1^2 + c_3(2)(1^2).$$

These equations simplify to

$$c_1 + c_2 \qquad\quad = 1$$
$$3c_1 + c_2 + c_3 = 2$$
$$9c_1 + c_2 + 2c_3 = 3.$$

Solving this system yields $c_1 = 0$, $c_2 = 1$, and $c_3 = 1$.

5. Substitute the constants into the general solution to obtain the particular solution:

$$t_n = 0(3^n) + 1(1^n) + 1(n1^n)$$
$$= 1 + n.$$

B.2.2 Nonhomogeneous Linear Recurrences

Definition   A recurrence of the form

$$a_0 t_n + a_1 t_{n-1} + \cdots + a_k t_{n-k} = f(n)$$

where k and the a_i terms are constants and $f(n)$ is a function other than the zero function, is called a ***nonhomogeneous linear recurrence equation with constant coefficients.***

By the zero function, we mean the function $f(n) = 0$. If we used the zero function, we would have a homogeneous linear recurrence equation. There is no known general method for solving a nonhomogeneous linear recurrence equation. We develop a method for solving the common special case

$$a_0 t_n + a_1 t_{n-1} + \cdots + a_k t_{n-k} = b^n p(n), \tag{B.2}$$

where b is a constant and $p(n)$ is a polynomial in n.

Example B.12 The recurrence

$$t_n - 3t_{n-1} = 4^n$$

is an example of Recurrence B.2 in which $k = 1$, $b = 4$, and $p(n) = 1$.

Example B.13 The recurrence

$$t_n - 3t_{n-1} = 4^n(8n + 7)$$

is an example of Recurrence B.2 in which $k = 1$, $b = 4$, and $p(n) = 8n + 7$.

The special case shown in Recurrence B.2 can be solved by transforming it into a homogeneous linear recurrence. The next example illustrates how this is done.

Example B.14 We solve the recurrence

$$t_n - 3t_{n-1} = 4^n \quad \text{for } n > 1$$
$$t_0 = 0$$
$$t_1 = 4$$

The recurrence is not homogeneous because of the term 4^n on the right. We can get rid of that term as follows:

1. Replace n with $n - 1$ in the original recurrence so that the recurrence is expressed with 4^{n-1} on the right:

$$t_{n-1} - 3t_{n-2} = 4^{n-1}.$$

2. Divide the original recurrence by 4 so that the recurrence is expressed in another way with 4^{n-1} on the right:

$$\frac{t_n}{4} - \frac{3t_{n-1}}{4} = 4^{n-1}.$$

3. Our original recurrence must have the same solutions as these versions of it. Therefore, it must also have the same solutions as their difference. This means we can get rid of the term 4^{n-1} by subtracting the recurrence obtained in Step 1 from the recurrence obtained in Step 2. The result is

$$\frac{t_n}{4} - \frac{7t_{n-1}}{4} + 3t_{n-2} = 0.$$

We can multiply by 4 to get rid of the fractions:

$$t_n - 7t_{n-1} + 12t_{n-2} = 0.$$

This is a homogeneous linear recurrence equation, which means that it can be solved by applying Theorem B.1. That is, we solve the characteristic equation

$$r^2 - 7r + 12 = (r - 3)(r - 4) = 0,$$

obtain the general solution

$$t_n = c_1 3^n + c_2 4^n,$$

and use the initial conditions $t_0 = 0$ and $t_1 = 4$ to determine the particular solution:

$$t_n = 4^{n+1} - 4(3^n).$$

In Example B.14, the general solution has the terms

$$c_1 3^n \quad \text{and} \quad c_2 4^n.$$

The first term comes from the characteristic equation that would be obtained if the recurrence were homogeneous, whereas the second term comes from the non-homogeneous part of the recurrence—namely, b. The polynomial $p(n)$ in this example equals 1. When this is not the case, the manipulations necessary to transform the recurrence into a homogeneous one are more complex. However, the outcome is simply to give b a multiplicity in the characteristic equation for the resultant homogeneous linear recurrence. This result is given in the theorem that follows. The theorem is stated without proof. The proof would follow steps similar to those in Example B.14.

Theorem B.3 A nonhomogeneous linear recurrence of the form

$$a_0 t_n + a_1 t_{n-1} + \cdots + a_k t_{n-k} = b^n p(n)$$

can be transformed into a homogeneous linear recurrence that has the characteristic equation

$$(a_0 r^k + a_1 r^{k-1} + \cdots + a_k)(r - b)^{d+1} = 0,$$

where d is the degree of $p(n)$. Notice that the characteristic equation is composed of two parts:

1. The characteristic equation for the corresponding homogeneous recurrence
2. A term obtained from the nonhomogeneous part of the recurrence

If there is more than one term like $b^n p(n)$ on the right side, each one contributes a term to the characteristic equation.

Before applying this theorem, we recall that the degree of a polynomial $p(n)$ is the highest power of n. For example,

Polynomial	Degree
$p(n) = 3n^2 + 4n - 2$	2
$p(n) = 5n + 7$	1
$p(n) = 8$	0

Now let's apply Theorem B.3.

Example B.15   We solve the recurrence

$$
\begin{array}{l}
t_n - 3t_{n-1} = 4^n(2n + 1) \qquad \text{for } n > 1 \\
t_0 = 0 \\
t_1 = 12
\end{array}
$$

1. Obtain the characteristic equation for the corresponding homogeneous equation:

$$
t_n - 3t_{n-1} = 0
$$
$$
r^1 - 3 = 0.
$$

2. Obtain a term from the nonhomogeneous part of the recurrence:

$$
\overset{d}{\underset{b}{4^n(2n^1 + 1)}}.
$$

The term from the nonhomogeneous part is

$$
(r - b)^{d+1} = (r - 4)^{1+1}.
$$

3. Apply Theorem B.3 to obtain the characteristic equation for our nonhomogeneous equation from the product of the terms obtained in Steps 1 and 2. The characteristic equation is

$$
(r - 3)(r - 4)^2.
$$

After obtaining the characteristic equation, proceed exactly as in the linear homogeneous case:

4. Solve the characteristic equation:

$$
(r - 3)(r - 4)^2 = 0.
$$

The roots are $r = 3$ and $r = 4$, and the root $r = 4$ has multiplicity 2.

5. Apply Theorem B.2 to get the general solution to the recurrence:

$$
t_n = c_1 3^n + c_2 4^n + c_3 n 4^n.
$$

We have three unknowns, but only two initial conditions. In this case we must find another initial condition by computing the value of the recurrence at the next-largest value of n. In this case, that value is 2. Because

$$t_2 - 3t_1 = 4^2(2 \times 2 + 1).$$

and $t_1 = 12$,

$$t_2 = 3 \times 12 + 80 = 116.$$

In the exercises you are asked to (6) determine the values of the constants and (7) substitute the constants into the general solution to obtain

$$t_n = 20(3^n) - 20(4^n) + 8n4^n.$$

Example B.16   We solve the recurrence

$$\boxed{\begin{aligned} t_n - t_{n-1} &= n - 1 \qquad \text{for } n > 0 \\ t_0 &= 0 \end{aligned}}$$

1.   Obtain the characteristic equation for the corresponding homogeneous recurrence:

$$t_n - t_{n-1} = 0$$
$$r^1 - 1 = 0.$$

2.   Obtain a term from the nonhomogeneous part of the recurrence:

$$n - 1 = \overset{d}{\underset{b}{1^n}}(n^1 - 1).$$

The term is

$$(r - 1)^{1+1}$$

3.   Apply Theorem B.3 to obtain the characteristic equation from the terms obtained in Steps 1 and 2. The characteristic equation is

$$(r - 1)(r - 1)^2.$$

4.   Solve the characteristic equation:

$$(r - 1)^3 = 0.$$

The root is $r = 1$, and it has a multiplicity of 3.

5. Apply Theorem B.2 to get the general solution to the recurrence:

$$t_n = c_1 1^n + c_2 n 1^n + c_3 n^2 1^n$$
$$= c_1 + c_2 n + c_3 n^2.$$

We need two more initial conditions:

$$t_1 = t_0 + 1 - 1 = 0 + 0 = 0$$
$$t_2 = t_1 + 2 - 1 = 0 + 1 = 1.$$

In the exercises you are asked to (6) determine the values of the constants and (7) substitute the constants into the general solution to obtain

$$t_n = \frac{n(n-1)}{2}.$$

Example B.17   We solve the recurrence

$$\boxed{\begin{aligned} t_n - 2t_{n-1} &= n + 2^n \qquad \text{for } n > 1 \\ t_1 &= 0 \end{aligned}}$$

1. Determine the characteristic equation for the corresponding homogeneous recurrence:

$$t_n - 2t_{n-1} = 0$$
$$r^1 - 2 = 0.$$

2. This is a case where there are two terms on the right. As Theorem B.3 states, each term contributes to the characteristic equation, as follows:

$$\begin{array}{cc} d & d \\ \downarrow & \downarrow \\ n = (1^n)n^1 & 2^n = (2^n)n^0. \\ \uparrow & \uparrow \\ b & b \end{array}$$

The two terms are

$$(r - 1)^{1+1} \qquad \text{and} \qquad (r - 2)^{0+1}.$$

3. Apply Theorem B.3 to obtain the characteristic equation from all the terms:

$$(r - 2)(r - 1)^2(r - 2) = (r - 2)^2(r - 1)^2.$$

You are asked to complete this problem in the exercises.

B.2.3 Change of Variables (Domain Transformations)

Sometimes a recurrence that is not in the form that can be solved by applying Theorem B.3 can be solved by performing a change of variables to transform it into a new recurrence that is in that form. The technique is illustrated in the following examples. In these examples, we use $T(n)$ for the original recurrence, because t_k is used for the new recurrence. The notation $T(n)$ means the same things as t_n—namely, that a unique number is associated with each value of n.

Example B.18   We solve the recurrence

$$T(n) = T\left(\frac{n}{2}\right) + 1 \qquad \text{for } n > 1, n \text{ a power of 2}$$
$$T(1) = 1$$

Recall that we already solved this recurrence using induction in Section B.1. We solve it again to illustrate the change of variables technique. The recurrence is not in the form that can be solved by applying Theorem B.3 because of the term $n/2$. We can transform it into a recurrence that is in that form as follows. First, set

$$n = 2^k, \qquad \text{which means} \qquad k = \lg n.$$

Second, substitute 2^k for n in the recurrence to obtain

$$T(2^k) = T\left(\frac{2^k}{2}\right) + 1$$
$$= T(2^{k-1}) + 1. \tag{B.3}$$

Next, set

$$t_k = T(2^k)$$

in Recurrence B.3 to obtain the new recurrence,

$$t_k = t_{k-1} + 1.$$

This new recurrence is in the form that can be solved by applying Theorem B.3. Therefore, applying that theorem, we can determine its general solution to be

$$t_k = c_1 + c_2 k.$$

The general solution to our original recurrence can now be obtained with the following two steps:

1.   Substitute $T(2^k)$ for t_k in the general solution to the new recurrence:

$$T(2^k) = c_1 + c_2 k.$$

2.   Substitute n for 2^k and $\lg n$ for k in the equation obtained in Step 1:

$$T(n) = c_1 + c_2 \lg n.$$

Once we have the general solution to our original recurrence, we proceed as usual. That is, we use the initial condition $T(1) = 1$, determine a second initial condition, and then compute the values of the constants to obtain

$$T(n) = 1 + \lg n.$$

Example B.19   We solve the recurrence

$$T(n) = 2T\left(\frac{n}{2}\right) + n - 1 \qquad \text{for } n > 1, n \text{ a power of 2}$$
$$T(1) = 0$$

Recall that we were unable to solve this recurrence using induction in Example B.3. We solve it here with a change of variables. First, substitute 2^k for n to yield

$$T(2^k) = 2T\left(\frac{2^k}{2}\right) + 2^k - 1$$
$$= 2T(2^{k-1}) + 2^k - 1.$$

Next, set

$$t_k = T(2^k)$$

in this equation to obtain

$$t_k = 2t_{k-1} + 2^k - 1.$$

Apply Theorem B.3 to this new recurrence to obtain

$$t_k = c_1 + c_2 2^k + c_3 k 2^k.$$

Perform the steps that give the general solution to the original recurrence:

1.   Substitute $T(2^k)$ for t_k in the general solution to the new recurrence:

$$T(2^k) = c_1 + c_2 2^k + c_3 k 2^k.$$

2.   Substitute n for 2^k and $\lg n$ for k in the equation obtained in Step 1:

$$T(n) = c_1 + c_2 n + c_3 n \lg n.$$

Now proceed as usual. That is, use the initial condition $T(1) = 0$, determine two more initial conditions, and then compute the values of the constants. The solution is

$$T(n) = n \lg n - (n - 1).$$

Example B.20   We solve the recurrence

$$T(n) = 7T\left(\frac{n}{2}\right) + 18\left(\frac{n}{2}\right)^2 \qquad \text{for } n > 1, n \text{ a power of 2}$$
$$T(1) = 0$$

Substitute 2^k for n in the recurrence to yield

$$T(2^k) = 7T(2^{k-1}) + 18(2^{k-1})^2. \qquad (B.4)$$

Set

$$t_k = T(2^k)$$

in Recurrence (B.4) to obtain

$$t_k = 7t_{k-1} + 18(2^{k-1})^2.$$

This recurrence does not look exactly like the kind required in Theorem B.3, but we can make it look like that as follows:

$$t_k = 7t_{k-1} + 18(2^{k-1})^2$$
$$= 7t_{k-1} + 18(4^{k-1})$$
$$= 7t_{k-1} + 4^k\left(\frac{18}{4}\right).$$

Now apply Theorem B.3 to this new recurrence to obtain

$$t_k = c_1 7^k + c_2 4^k.$$

Perform the steps that give the general solution to the original recurrence:

1. Substitute $T(2^k)$ for t_k in the general solution to t_k:
$$T(2^k) = c_1 7^k + c_2 4^k.$$

2. Substitute n for 2^k and $\lg n$ for k in the equation obtained in Step 1:
$$T(n) = c_1 7^{\lg n} + c_2 4^{\lg n}$$
$$= c_1 n^{\lg 7} + c_2 n^2.$$

Use the initial condition $T(1) = 0$, determine a second initial condition, and then compute the values of the constants. The solution is

$$T(n) = 6n^{\lg 7} - 6n^2 \approx 6n^{2.81} - 6n^2.$$

SOLVING RECURRENCES
B.3 BY SUBSTITUTION

Sometimes a recurrence can be solved using a technique called ***substitution.*** You can try this method if you cannot obtain a solution using the methods in the last two sections. The following examples illustrate the substitution method.

Example B.21   We solve the recurrence

$$\boxed{\begin{aligned} t_n &= t_{n-1} + n \qquad n > 1 \\ t_1 &= 1 \end{aligned}}$$

In a sense, substitution is the opposite of induction. That is, we start at n and work backward:

$$\begin{aligned}
t_n &= t_{n-1} + n \\
t_{n-1} &= t_{n-2} + n - 1 \\
t_{n-2} &= t_{n-3} + n - 2 \\
&\vdots \\
t_2 &= t_1 + 2 \\
t_1 &= 1.
\end{aligned}$$

We then substitute each equation into the previous one, as follows:

$$\begin{aligned}
t_n &= t_{n-1} + n \\
&= t_{n-2} + n - 1 + n \\
&= t_{n-3} + n - 2 + n - 1 + n \\
&\vdots \\
&= t_1 + 2 + \cdots + n - 2 + n - 1 + n \\
&= 1 + 2 + \cdots + n - 2 + n - 1 + n \\
&= \sum_{i=1}^{n} i = \frac{n(n+1)}{2}.
\end{aligned}$$

The last equality is the result in Example A.1 in Appendix A.

The recurrence in Example B.21 could be solved using the characteristic equation. The recurrence in the following example cannot.

Example B.22   We solve the recurrence:

$$
\begin{aligned}
t_n &= t_{n-1} + \frac{2}{n} \qquad n > 1 \\
t_1 &= 0
\end{aligned}
$$

First, work backward from n:

$$
\begin{aligned}
t_n &= t_{n-1} + \frac{2}{n} \\[6pt]
t_{n-1} &= t_{n-2} + \frac{2}{n-1} \\[6pt]
t_{n-2} &= t_{n-3} + \frac{2}{n-2} \\
&\ \ \vdots \\
t_2 &= t_1 + \frac{2}{2} \\[6pt]
t_1 &= 0.
\end{aligned}
$$

Then substitute each equation into the previous one:

$$
\begin{aligned}
t_n &= t_{n-1} + \frac{2}{n} \\[6pt]
&= t_{n-2} + \frac{2}{n-1} + \frac{2}{n} \\[6pt]
&= t_{n-3} + \frac{2}{n-2} + \frac{2}{n-1} + \frac{2}{n} \\
&\ \ \vdots \\
&= t_1 + \frac{2}{2} + \cdots + \frac{2}{n-2} + \frac{2}{n-1} + \frac{2}{n} \\[6pt]
&= 0 + \frac{2}{2} + \cdots + \frac{2}{n-2} + \frac{2}{n-1} + \frac{2}{n} \\[6pt]
&= 2 \sum_{i=2}^{n} \frac{1}{i} \approx 2 \ln n
\end{aligned}
$$

for n not small. The approximate equality is obtained from Example A.9 in Appendix A.

EXTENDING RESULTS FOR n A POWER OF A POSITIVE

B.4 CONSTANT b TO n IN GENERAL

It is assumed in what follows that you are familiar with the material in Chapter 1.

In the case of some recursive algorithms, we can readily determine the exact time complexity only when n is a power of some base b, where b is a positive constant. Often the base b is 2. This is true in particular for many divide-and-conquer algorithms (see Chapter 2). Intuitively, it seems that a result that holds for n a power of b should approximately hold for n in general. For example, if for some algorithm we establish that

$$T(n) = 2n \lg n$$

for n a power of 2, it seems that for n in general we should be able to conclude that

$$T(n) \in \Theta(n \lg n).$$

It turns out that usually we can draw such a conclusion. Next we discuss situations in which this is the case. First we need some definitions. These definitions apply to functions whose domains and ranges are all the real numbers, but we state them for complexity functions (that is, functions from the nonnegative integers to the nonnegative reals) because there are the functions that interest us here.

Definition   A complexity function $f(n)$ is called ***strictly increasing*** if $f(n)$ always gets larger as n gets larger. That is, if $n_1 > n_2$, then

$$f(n_1) > f(n_2).$$

The function shown in Figure B.1(a) is strictly increasing. (For clarity, the domains of the functions in Figure B.1 are all the nonnegative reals.) Many of the functions we encounter in algorithm analysis are strictly increasing for nonnegative values of n. For example, $\lg n$, n, $n \lg n$, n^2, and 2^n are all strictly increasing as long as n is nonnegative.

Definition   A complexity function $f(n)$ is called ***nondecreasing*** if $f(n)$ never gets smaller as n gets larger. That is, if $n_1 > n_2$, then

$$f(n_1) \geq f(n_2).$$

Any strictly increasing function is nondecreasing, but a function that can level out is nondecreasing without being strictly increasing. The function shown in Figure B.1(b) is an example of such a function. The function in Figure B.1(c) is not nondecreasing.

The time (or memory) complexities of most algorithms are ordinarily nondecreasing because the time it takes to process an input usually does not decrease

Figure B.1 Four functions.

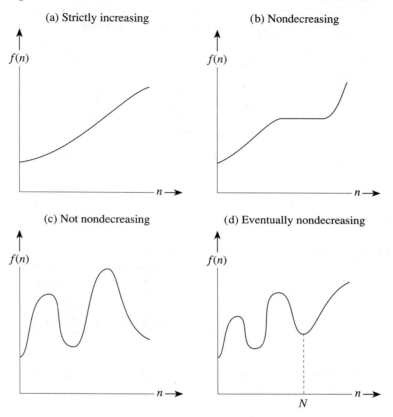

as the input size becomes larger. Looking at Figure B.1, it seems that we should be able to extend an analysis for n a power of b to n in general as long as the function is nondecreasing. For example, suppose we have determined the values of $f(n)$ for n a power of 2. In the case of the function in Figure B.1(c), anything can happen between, say, $2^3 = 8$ and $2^4 = 16$. Therefore, nothing can be concluded about the behavior of the function between 8 and 16 from the values at 8 and 16. However, in the case of a nondecreasing function $f(n)$, if $8 \leq n \leq 16$ then

$$f(8) \leq f(n) \leq f(16).$$

So it seems that we should be able to determine the order of $f(n)$ from the values of $f(n)$ for n a power of 2. What seems to be true intuitively can indeed be proven for a large class of functions. Before giving a theorem stating this, we recall that order has to do only with long-range behavior. Because initial values of a function are unimportant, the theorem requires only that the function be eventually nondecreasing. We have the following definition:

Definition A complexity function $f(n)$ is called ***eventually nondecreasing*** if for all n past some point the function never gets smaller as n gets larger. That is, there exists an N such that if $n_1 > n_2 > N$, then

$$f(n_1) \geq f(n_2).$$

Any nondecreasing function is eventually nondecreasing. The function shown in Figure 3.1(d) is an example of an eventually nondecreasing function that is not nondecreasing. We need the following definition before we give the theorem for extending the results for n a power of b:

Definition A complexity function $f(n)$ is called ***smooth*** if $f(n)$ is eventually nondecreasing and if

$$f(2n) \in \Theta(f(n)).$$

Example B.23 The functions $\lg n$, n, $n \lg n$, and n^k, where $k \geq 0$, are all smooth. We show this for $\lg n$. In the exercises you are asked to show it for the other functions. We have already noted that $\lg n$ is eventually nondecreasing. As to the second condition, we have

$$\lg(2n) = \lg 2 + \lg n \in \Theta(\lg n).$$

Example B.24 The function 2^n is not smooth, because the Properties of Order in Section 1.4.2 in Chapter 1 imply that

$$2^n \in o(4^n).$$

Therefore,

$$2^{2n} = 4^n \text{ is not in } \Theta(2^n).$$

We now state the theorem that enables us to generalize results obtained for n a power of b. The proof appears near the end of this appendix.

Theorem B.4 Let $b \geq 2$ be an integer, let $f(n)$ be a smooth complexity function, and let $T(n)$ be an eventually nondecreasing complexity function. If

$$T(n) \in \Theta(f(n)) \qquad \text{for } n \text{ a power of } b,$$

then

$$T(n) \in \Theta(f(n)).$$

Furthermore, the same implication holds if Θ is replaced by "big O," Ω, or "small o."

By "$T(n) \in \Theta(f(n))$ for n a power of b," we mean that the usual conditions for Θ are known to hold when n is restricted to being a power of b. Notice in Theorem B.4 the additional requirement that $f(n)$ be smooth.

Next we apply Theorem B.4.

◈ **Example B.25**   Suppose for some complexity function we establish that

$$
\boxed{
\begin{aligned}
T(n) &= T\left(\left\lfloor \frac{n}{2} \right\rfloor\right) + 1 \qquad \text{for } n > 1 \\
T(1) &= 1
\end{aligned}
}
$$

When n is a power of 2, we have the recurrence in Example B.18. Therefore, by that example,

$$T(n) = \lg n + 1 \in \Theta(\lg n) \qquad \text{for } n \text{ a power of 2.}$$

Because $\lg n$ is smooth, we need only show that $T(n)$ is eventually nondecreasing in order to apply Theorem B.4 to conclude that

$$T(n) \in \Theta(\lg n).$$

One might be tempted to conclude that $T(n)$ is eventually nondecreasing from the fact that $\lg n + 1$ is eventually nondecreasing. However, we cannot do this because we know only that $T(n) = \lg n + 1$ when n is a power of 2. Given only this fact, $T(n)$ could exhibit any possible behavior in between powers of 2.

We show that $T(n)$ is eventually nondecreasing by using induction to establish for $n \geq 2$ that if $1 \leq k < n$ then

$$T(k) \leq T(n).$$

Induction base: For $n = 2$,

$$T(1) = 1$$

$$T(2) = T\left(\left\lfloor \frac{2}{2} \right\rfloor\right) + 1 = T(1) + 1 = 1 + 1 = 2.$$

Therefore,

$$T(1) \leq T(2).$$

Induction hypothesis: One way to make the induction hypothesis is to assume that the statement is true for all $m \leq n$. Then, as usual, we show that it is true for $n + 1$. This is the way we need it to be stated here. Let n be an arbitrary integer greater than or equal to 2. Assume for all $m \leq n$ that if $k < m$ then

$$T(k) \leq T(m).$$

Induction step: Because in the induction hypothesis we assumed for $k < n$ that

$$T(k) \leq T(n),$$

we need only show that

$$T(n) \le T(n + 1).$$

To that end, it is not hard to see that if $n \ge 1$ then

$$\left\lfloor \frac{n}{2} \right\rfloor \le \left\lfloor \frac{n + 1}{2} \right\rfloor \le n.$$

Therefore, by the induction hypothesis,

$$T\left(\left\lfloor \frac{n}{2} \right\rfloor\right) \le T\left(\left\lfloor \frac{n + 1}{2} \right\rfloor\right).$$

Using the recurrence, we have

$$T(n) = T\left(\left\lfloor \frac{n}{2} \right\rfloor\right) + 1 \le T\left(\left\lfloor \frac{n + 1}{2} \right\rfloor\right) + 1 = T(n + 1),$$

and we are done.

Finally, we develop a general method for determining the order of some common recurrences.

Theorem B.5 Suppose a complexity function $T(n)$ is eventually nondecreasing and satisfies

$$T(n) = aT\left(\frac{n}{b}\right) + cn^k \qquad \text{for } n > 1, \, n \text{ a power of } b$$

$$T(1) = d$$

where $b \ge 2$ and $k \ge 0$ are integers, $a > 0$, $c > 0$, and $d \ge 0$. Then

$$T(n) \in \begin{cases} \Theta(n^k) & \text{if} \quad a < b^k \\ \Theta(n^k \lg n) & \text{if} \quad a = b^k \\ \Theta(n^{\log_b a}) & \text{if} \quad a > b^k. \end{cases} \qquad \text{(B.5)}$$

Furthermore, if, in the statement of the recurrence,

$$T(n) = aT\left(\frac{n}{b}\right) + cn^k$$

is replaced by

$$T(n) \le aT\left(\frac{n}{b}\right) + cn^k \qquad \text{or} \qquad T(n) \ge aT\left(\frac{n}{b}\right) + cn^k,$$

then Result B.5 holds with "big O" or Ω, respectively, replacing Θ.

We can prove this theorem by solving the general recurrence using the characteristic equation and then applying Theorem B.4. Example applications of Theorem B.5 follow.

Example B.26   Suppose that $T(n)$ is eventually nondecreasing and satisfies

$$
\begin{array}{ccc}
a & b & k \\
\downarrow & \downarrow & \downarrow
\end{array}
$$

$$T(n) = 8\,T(n/4) + 5n^2 \qquad \text{for } n > 1,\ n \text{ a power of 2}$$
$$T(1) = 3$$

By Theorem B.5, because $8 < 4^2$,

$$T(n) \in \Theta(n^2).$$

Example B.27   Suppose that $T(n)$ is eventually nondecreasing and satisfies

$$
\begin{array}{ccc}
a & b & k \\
\downarrow & \downarrow & \downarrow
\end{array}
$$

$$T(n) = 9\,T(n/3) + 5n^1 \qquad \text{for } n > 1,\ n \text{ a power of 3}$$
$$T(1) = 7$$

By Theorem B.5, because $9 > 3^1$,

$$T(n) \in \Theta(n^{\log_3 9}) = \Theta(n^2).$$

Theorem B.5 was stated in order to introduce an important theorem as simply as possible. It is actually the special case, in which the constant s equals 1, of the following theorem.

Theorem B.6 Suppose that a complexity function $T(n)$ is eventually nondecreasing and satisfies

$$T(n) = aT\left(\frac{n}{b}\right) + cn^k \qquad \text{for } n > s,\ n \text{ a power of } b$$
$$T(s) = d$$

where s is a power of b, $b \geq 2$ and $k \geq 0$ are integers, $a > 0$, $c > 0$, and $d \geq 0$. The results in Theorem B.5 still hold.

Example B.28   Suppose that $T(n)$ is eventually nondecreasing and satisfies

$$
\begin{array}{ccc}
a & b & k \\
\downarrow & \downarrow & \downarrow \\
\end{array}
$$

$$T(n) = 8\ T(n/2) + 5n^3 \qquad \text{for } n > 64,\ n \text{ a power of } 2$$

$$T(64) = 200$$

By Theorem B.6, because $8 = 2^3$,

$$T(n) \in \Theta(n^3 \lg n).$$

This concludes our discussion of techniques for solving recurrences. Another technique is to use "generating functions" to solve recurrences. This technique is discussed in Sahni (1988). Bentley, Haken, and Sax (1980) provide a general method for solving recurrences arising from the analysis of divide-and-conquer algorithms (see Chapter 2).

B.5 PROOFS OF THEOREMS

The following lemma is needed to prove Theorem B.1.

Lemma B.1 Suppose we have the homogeneous linear recurrence

$$a_0 t_n + a_1 t_{n-1} + \cdots + a_k t_{n-k} = 0.$$

If r_1 is a root of the characteristic equation

$$a_0 r^k + a_1 r^{k-1} + \cdots + a_k = 0,$$

then

$$t_n = r_1^{\,n}$$

is a solution to the recurrence

Proof: If, for $i = n - k, \ldots, n$, we substitute $r_1^{\,i}$ for t_i in the recurrence, we obtain

$$
\begin{aligned}
a_0 r_1^{\,n} + a_1 r_1^{\,n-1} + \cdots + a_k r_1^{\,n-k} &= r_1^{\,n-k}(a_0 r_1^{\,k} + a_1 r_1^{\,k-1} + \cdots + a_k) \\
&= r_1^{\,n-k}(0) \\
&= 0. \qquad \uparrow \\
&\qquad\quad \text{Because } r_1 \text{ is} \\
&\qquad\quad \text{a root of the} \\
&\qquad\quad \text{characteristic equation}
\end{aligned}
$$

Therefore, $r_1^{\,n}$ is a solution to the recurrence.

Proof of Theorem B.1 It is not hard to see that, for a linear homogeneous recurrence, a constant times any solution and the sum of any two solutions are each solutions to the recurrence. We can therefore apply Lemma B.1 to conclude that, if

$$r_1, r_2, \ldots, r_k$$

are the k distinct roots of the characteristic equation, then

$$c_1 r_1{}^n + c_2 r_2{}^n + \cdots + c_k r_k^n,$$

where the c_i terms are arbitrary constants, is a solution to the recurrence. Although we do not show it here, one can prove that these are the only solutions.

Proof of Theorem B.2 We prove the case where the multiplicity m equals 2. The case of a larger m is a straightforward generalization. Let r_1 be a root of multiplicity 2. Set

$$p(r) = a_0 r^k + a_1 r^{k-1} + \cdots + r_k \quad \{\text{the characteristic equation}\}$$
$$q(r) = r^{n-k} p(r) = a_0 r^n + a_1 r^{n-1} + \cdots + a_k r^{n-k}$$
$$u(r) = r q'(r) = a_0 n r^n + a_1 (n-1) r^{n-1} + \cdots + a_k (n-k) r^{n-k},$$

where $q'(r)$ means the first derivative. If we substitute $i r_1^i$ for t_i in the recurrence, we obtain $u(r_1)$. Therefore, if we can show that $u(r_1) = 0$, we can conclude that $t_n = n r_1^n$ is a solution to the recurrence, and we are done. To this end, we have

$$\begin{aligned} u(r) &= r q'(r) \\ &= r[(r^{n-k}) p(r)]' \\ &= r[r^{n-k} p'(r) + p(r)(n-k) r^{n-k-1}]. \end{aligned}$$

Therefore, to show that $u(r_1) = 0$, we need only show that $p(r_1)$ and $p'(r_1)$ both equal 0. We show this as follows. Because r_1 is a solution of multiplicity 2 of the characteristic equation $p(r)$, there exists a $v(r)$ such that

$$p(r) = (r - r_1)^2 v(r).$$

Therefore,

$$p'(r) = (r - r_1)^2 v'(r) + 2v(r)(r - r_1),$$

and $p(r_1)$ and $p'(r_1)$ both equal 0. This completes the proof.

Proof of Theorem B.4 We obtain the proof for "big O." Proofs for Ω and Θ can be established in a similar manner. Because $T(n) \in O(f(n))$ for all n such that n is a power of b, there exist a positive c_1 and a nonnegative integer N_1 such that, for $n > N_1$ and n a power of b,

$$T(n) \le c_1 \times f(n). \tag{B.6}$$

For any positive integer n, there exists a unique k such that

$$b^k \le n < b^{k+1}. \tag{B.7}$$

It is possible to show, in the case of a smooth function, that, if $b \geq 2$, then

$$f(bn) \in \Theta(f(n)).$$

That is, if this condition holds for 2, it holds for any $b > 2$. Therefore, there exist a positive constant c_2 and a nonnegative integer N_2 such that, for $n > N_2$,

$$f(bn) \leq c_2 f(n).$$

Therefore, if $b^k \geq N_2$,

$$f(b^{k+1}) = f(b \times b^k) \leq c_2 f(b^k). \tag{B.8}$$

Because $T(n)$ and $f(n)$ are both eventually nondecreasing, there exists an N_3 such that, for $m > n > N_3$,

$$T(n) \leq T(m) \quad \text{and} \quad f(n) \leq f(m). \tag{B.9}$$

Let r be so large that

$$b^r > \max(N_1, N_2, N_3).$$

If $n > b^r$ and k is the value corresponding to n in Inequality B.7, then

$$b^k \geq b^r.$$

Therefore, by Inequalities B.6, B.7, B.8, and B.9, for $n > b^r$,

$$T(n) \leq T(b^{k+1}) \leq c_1 f(b^{k+1}) \leq c_1 c_2 f(b^k) \leq c_1 c_2 f(n),$$

which means that

$$T(n) \in O(f(n)).$$

Exercises

Section B.1

1. Use induction to verify the candidate solution to each of the following recurrence equations.

   (a) $t_n = 4t_{n-1}$ for $n > 1$
   $t_1 = 3$
   The candidate solution is $t_n = 3(4^{n-1})$.

   (b) $t_n = t_{n-1} + 5$ for $n > 1$
   $t_1 = 2$
   The candidate solution is $t_n = 5n - 3$.

   (c) $t_n = t_{n-1} + n$ for $n > 1$
   $t_1 = 1$
   The candidate solution is $t_n = \dfrac{n(n+1)}{2}$.

(d) $t_n = t_{n-1} + n^2$ for $n > 1$

$t_1 = 1$

The candidate solution is $t_n = \dfrac{n(n+1)(2n+1)}{6}$.

(e) $t_n = t_{n-1} + \dfrac{1}{n(n+1)}$ for $n > 1$

$t_1 = \dfrac{1}{2}$

The candidate solution is $t_n = \dfrac{n}{(n+1)}$.

(f) $t_n = 3t_{n-1} + 2^n$ for $n > 1$

$t_1 = 1$

The candidate solution is $t_n = 5(3^{n-1}) - 2^{n+1}$.

(g) $t_n = 3t_{n/2} + n$ for $n > 1$, n a power of 2

$t_1 = \dfrac{1}{2}$

The candidate solution is $t_n = \dfrac{5}{2}n^{\lg 3} - 2n$.

(h) $t_n = nt_{n-1}$ for $n > 0$

$t_0 = 1$

The candidate solution is $t_n = n!$.

2. Write a recurrence equation for the nth term of the sequence $2, 6, 18, 54, \ldots$, and use induction to verify the candidate solution $s_n = 2(3^{n-1})$.

3. The number of moves (m_n for n rings) needed in the Towers of Hanoi Problem (see Exercise 17 in Chapter 2) is given by the following recurrence equation:

$$m_n = 2m_{n-1} + 1 \quad \text{for } n > 1$$
$$m_n = 1$$

Use induction to show that the solution to this recurrence equation is $m_n = 2^n - 1$.

4. The following algorithm returns the position of the largest element in the array S. Write a recurrence equation for the number of comparisons t_n needed to find the largest element. Use induction to show that the equation has the solution $t_n = n - 1$.

```
index max_position(index low, index high)
{
   index position;

   if (low == high)
      return low;
   else {
      position = max_position(low + 1, high);
      if (S[low] > S[position])
         position = low;
      return position;
   }
}
```

The top-level call is

max_position(1,*n*).

5. The ancient Greeks were very interested in sequences resulting from geometric shapes such as the following triangular numbers:

$$\begin{matrix} & & & & O & & \\ & & & O & & O & \\ & & O & O, & O & O & O, & \ldots \end{matrix} \quad \rightarrow (1, 3, 6, \ldots)$$

O, O O, O O O, ...

Write a recurrence equation for the *n*th term in this sequence, guess a solution, and use induction to verify your solution.

6. Into how many regions do *n* lines divide a plane so that every pair of lines intersect, but no more than two lines intersect at a common point? Write a recurrence equation for the number of regions for *n* lines, guess a solution for your equation, and use induction to verify your solution.

7. Use induction to show that $B(n, k) = \dbinom{n + k}{n}$ is the solution to the following recurrence equation:

$$B(n, k) = B(n - 1, k) + B(n, k - 1) \qquad \text{for } 0 < k < n$$
$$B(n, 0) = 1$$
$$B(n, n) = 1$$

8. Write and implement an algorithm that computes the value of the following recurrence, and run it using different problem instances. Use the results to guess a solution for this recurrence, and use induction to verify your solution.

$$t_n = t_{n-1} + 2n - 1 \qquad \text{for } n > 1$$
$$t_1 = 1$$

Section B.2

9. Indicate which recurrence equations in the problems for Section B.1 fall into each of the following categories.
   (a) Linear equations
   (b) Homogeneous equations
   (c) Equations with constant coefficients

10. Find the characteristic equations for all of the recurrence equations in Section B.1 that are linear with constant coefficients.

11. Show that if $f(n)$ and $g(n)$ are both solutions to a linear homogeneous recurrence equation with constant coefficients, then so is $c \times f(n) + d \times g(n)$, where c and d are constants.

12. Solve the following recurrence equations using the characteristic equation.
   (a) $t_n = 4t_{n-1} - 3t_{n-2}$ for $n > 1$
   $t_0 = 0$
   $t_1 = 1$
   (b) $t_n = 3t_{n-1} - 2t_{n-2} + n^2$ for $n > 1$
   $t_0 = 0$
   $t_1 = 1$
   (c) $t_n = 5t_{n-1} - 6t_{n-2} + 5^n$ for $n > 1$
   $t_0 = 0$
   $t_1 = 1$
   (d) $t_n = 5t_{n-1} - 6t_{n-2} + n^2 - 5n + 7^n$ for $n > 1$
   $t_0 = 0$
   $t_1 = 1$

13. Complete the solution to the recurrence equation given in Example B.15.

14. Complete the solution to the recurrence equation given in Example B.16.

15. Solve the following recurrence equations using the characteristic equation.
   (a) $t_n = 6t_{n-1} - 9t_{n-2}$ for $n > 1$
   $t_0 = 0$
   $t_1 = 1$
   (b) $t_n = 5t_{n-1} - 8t_{n-2} + 4t_{n-3}$ for $n > 2$
   $t_0 = 0$
   $t_1 = 1$
   $t_2 = 1$
   (c) $t_n = 2t_{n-1} - t_{n-2} + n^2 + 5^n$ for $n > 1$
   $t_0 = 0$
   $t_1 = 1$
   (d) $t_n = 6t_{n-1} - 9t_{n-2} + (n^2 - 5n)7^n$ for $n > 1$
   $t_0 = 0$
   $t_1 = 1$

16. Complete the solution to the recurrence equation given in Example B.17.

17. Show that the recurrence equation

$$t_n = (n - 1)t_{n-1} + (n - 1)t_{n-2} \qquad \text{for } n > 2$$
$$t_1 = 0$$
$$t_2 = 1$$

    can be written as

$$t_n = nt_{n-1} + (-1)^n \qquad \text{for } n > 1$$
$$t_1 = 0$$

18. Solve the recurrence equation in Exercise 17. The solution gives the number of derangements (nothing is in its right place) of n objects.

19. Solve the following recurrence equations using the characteristic equation.

    (a) $T(n) = 2T\left(\dfrac{n}{3}\right) + \log_3 n \qquad \text{for } n > 1, n$ a power of 3

    $\quad T(1) = 0$

    (b) $T(n) = 10T\left(\dfrac{n}{5}\right) + n^2 \qquad \text{for } n > 1, n$ a power of 5

    $\quad T(1) = 0$

    (c) $nT(n) = (n - 1)T(n - 1) + 3 \qquad \text{for } n > 1$

    $\quad T(1) = 1$

    (d) $nT(n) = 3(n - 1)T(n - 1) - 2(n - 2)T(n - 2) + 4^n \qquad \text{for } n > 1$

    $\quad T(0) = 0$

    $\quad T(1) = 0$

    (e) $nT^2(n) = 5(n - 1)T^2(n - 1) + n^2 \qquad \text{for } n > 0$

    $\quad T(0) = 6$

Section B.3

20. Solve the recurrence equations in Exercise 1 using the substitution method.

Section B.4

21. Show that
    (a) $f(n) = n^3$ is a strictly increasing function.
    (b) $g(n) = 2n^3 - 6n^2$ is an eventually nondecreasing function.

22. What can we say about a function $f(n)$ that is both nondecreasing and nonincreasing for all values of n?

23. Show that the following functions are smooth.
    (a) $f(n) = n \lg n$
    (b) $g(n) = n^k$, for all $k \geq 0$.

24. Use Theorem B.5 to determine the order of the following recurrence equations.

(a) $T(n) = 2T\left(\dfrac{n}{5}\right) + 6n^3$ for $n > 1$, n a power of 5

    $T(1) = 6$

(b) $T(n) = 40T\left(\dfrac{n}{3}\right) + 2n^3$ for $n > 1$, n a power of 3

    $T(1) = 5$

(c) $T(n) = 16T\left(\dfrac{n}{2}\right) + 7n^4$ for $n > 1$, n a power of 2

    $T(1) = 1$

25. Use Theorem B.6 to determine the order of the following recurrence equations.

(a) $T(n) = 14T\left(\dfrac{n}{5}\right) + 6n$ for $n > 25$, n a power of 5

    $T(25) = 60$

(b) $T(n) = 4T\left(\dfrac{n}{4}\right) + 2n^2$ for $n > 16$, n a power of 4

    $T(16) = 50$

26. We know that the recurrence

$$T(n) = aT\left(\frac{n}{c}\right) + g(n) \qquad \text{for } n > 1, \ n \text{ a power of } c$$

$$T(1) = d$$

has solution

$$T(n) \in \Theta(n^{\log_c a})$$

in the case $a > c$, provided that $g(n) \in \Theta(n)$. Prove that the recurrence has the same solution if we assume that

$$g(n) \in O(n^t), \text{ where } t < \log_c a.$$

APPENDIX C

Data Structures
for Disjoint Sets

*K*ruskal's Algorithm (Algorithm 4.2 in Section 4.1.2) requires that we create disjoint subsets, each containing a distinct vertex in a graph, and repeatedly merge the subsets until all the vertices are in the same set. To implement this algorithm, we need a data structure for disjoint sets. There are many other useful applications of disjoint sets. For example, they can be used in Section 4.3 to improve the time complexity of Algorithm 4.4 (Scheduling with Deadlines).

Recall that an **abstract data type** consists of data objects along with permissible operations on those objects. Before we can implement a disjoint set abstract data type, we need to specify the objects and operations that are needed. We start with a universe U of elements. For example, we could have

$$U = \{A, B, C, D, E\}.$$

We then want a procedure *makeset* that makes a set out of a member of U. The disjoint sets in Figure C.1(a) should be created by the following calls:

> **for** (each $x \in U$)
>   *makeset(x)*;

We need a type set_pointer and a function *find* such that if p and q are of type set_pointer and we have the calls

> p = *find*('B');
> q = *find*('C');

then p should point to the set containing B, and q should point to the set containing C. This is illustrated in Figure C.1(a). We also need a procedure *merge* to merge two sets into one. For example, if we do

> p = *find*('B');
> q = *find*('C');
> *merge(p, q)*;

Figure C.1 An example of a disjoint set data structure.

(a) There are five disjoint sets. We have executed $p := find(B)$ and $q := find(C)$.

{A}   {B}   {C}   {D}   {E}
$\uparrow$ $\uparrow$
p q

(b) There are four disjoint sets after {B} and {C} are merged.

{A}   {B, C}   {D}   {E}

(c) We have executed $p := find(B)$.

{A}   {B, C}   {D}   {E}
$\uparrow$
p

our sets in Figure C.1(a) should become the sets in Figure C.1(b). Given the disjoint sets in Figure C.1(b), if we have the call

$p = find('B');$

we should obtain the result shown in Figure C.1(c). Finally, we need a routine *equal* to check whether two sets are the same set. For example, if we have the sets in Figure C.1(b), and we have the calls

$p = find('B');$
$q = find('C');$
$r = find('A');$

then *equal(p, q)* should return true and *equal(p, r)* should return false.

We have specified an abstract data type whose objects consist of elements in a universe and disjoint sets of those elements, and whose operations are *makeset, find, merge,* and *equal.*

One way to represent disjoint sets is to use trees with inverted pointers. In these trees each nonroot points to its parent, whereas each root points to itself. Figure C.2(a) shows the trees corresponding to the disjoint sets in Figure C.1(a), and Figure C.2(b) shows the trees corresponding to the disjoint sets in Figure C.1(b). To implement these trees as simply as possible, we assume that our universe contains only indices (integers). To extend this implementation to another finite universe we need only index the elements in that universe. We can implement the trees using an array U, where each index to U represents one index in the universe. If an index i represents a nonroot, the value of $U[i]$ is the index representing its parent. If an index i represents a root, the value of $U[i]$ is i. For example, if there are 10 indices in our universe, we store them in an array of indices U indexed from 1 to 10.

Figure C.2 The inverted tree representation of a disjoint set data structure.

(a) Five disjoint sets represented by inverted trees

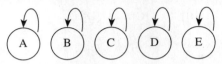

(b) The inverted trees after {B} and {C} are merged

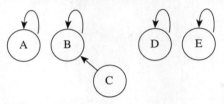

To initially place all the indices in disjoint sets, we set

$U[i] = i;$

for all *i*. The tree representation of 10 disjoint sets and the corresponding array implementation are shown in Figure C.3(a). An example of a merge is illustrated in Figure C.3(b). When the sets {4} and {10} are merged, we make the node containing 10 a child of the node containing 4. This is accomplished by setting $U[10] = 4$. In general, when we merge two sets, we first determine which tree has the larger index stored at its root. We then make that root a child of the root of the other tree. Figure C.3(c) shows the tree representation and corresponding array implementation after several merges have been done. At this point there are only three disjoint sets.

An implementation of the routines follows. For the sake of notational simplicity, both here and in the discussion of Kruskal's Algorithm (see Section 4.1.2), we do not list our universe *U* as a parameter to the routines.

Disjoint Set Data Structure I

```
const n = the number of elements in the universe;

typedef int index;
typedef index set_pointer;
typedef index universe[1..n];          // universe is indexed from 1 to n.

universe U;
```

```
void makeset (index i)
{
   U[i] = i;
}

set_pointer find (index i)
{
   index j;

   j = i;
   while (U[j] != j)
      j = U[j];
   return j;
}

void merge (set_pointer p, set_pointer q)
{
   if (p < q)                    // p points to merged set;
      U[q] = p;                  // q no longer points to a set.
   else
      U[p] = q;                  // q points to merged set;
                                 // p no longer points to a set.
}


bool equal (set_pointer p, set_pointer q)
{
   if (p == q)
      return true;
   else
      return false;
}

void initial (int n)
{
   index i;

   for (i = 1; i <= n; i++)
      makeset(i);
}
```

The value returned by the call *find(i)* is the index stored at the root of the tree containing *i*. We have included a routine *initial* that initializes *n* disjoint sets, because such a routine is often needed in algorithms that use disjoint sets.

Figure C.3 The array implementation of the inverted tree representation of a disjoint set data structure.

(a) The inverted trees and array implementation for 10 disjoint sets.

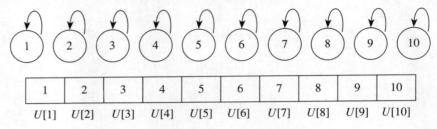

(b) The sets {4} and {10} in part (a) have been merged. The 10th array slot now has value 4.

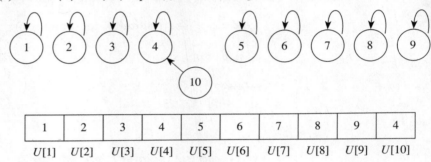

(c) The inverted trees and array implementation after several merges. The order of the merges determines the structure of the trees.

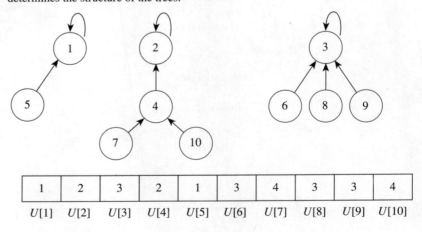

In many algorithms that use disjoint sets, we initialize n disjoint sets, and then do m passes through a loop (the values of n and m are not necessarily equal). Inside the loop there are a constant number of calls to routines *equal, find,* and *merge.* When analyzing the algorithm, we need the time complexities of both the initialization and the loop in terms of n and m. Clearly, the time complexity for routine *initial* is in

$$\Theta(n).$$

Because order is not affected by a multiplicative constant, we can assume that routines *equal, find,* and *merge* are each called just once in each of the m passes through the loop. Clearly, *equal* and *merge* run in constant time. Only function *find* contains a loop. Therefore, the order of the time complexity of all the calls is dominated by function *find.* Let's count the worst-case number of times the comparison in *find* is done. Suppose, for example, that $m = 5$. The worst case happens if we have this sequence of merges:

merge({5}, {6});
merge({4}, {5,6});
merge({3}, (4,5,6});
merge({2}, {3,4,5,6});
merge({1}, {2,3,4,5,6});

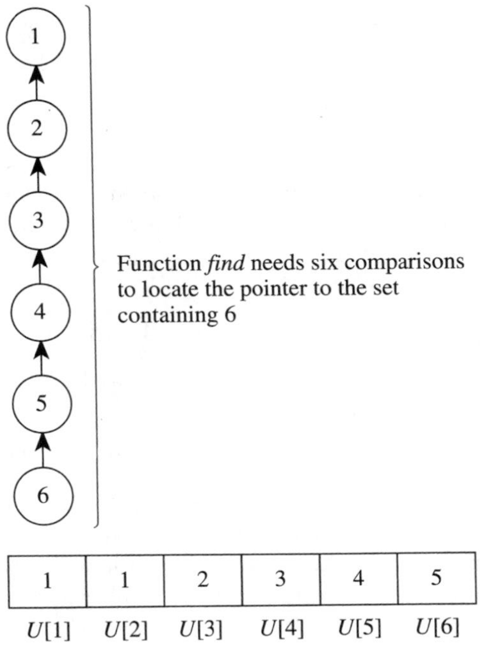

Function *find* needs six comparisons
to locate the pointer to the set
containing 6

1	1	2	3	4	5
$U[1]$	$U[2]$	$U[3]$	$U[4]$	$U[5]$	$U[6]$

Figure C.4 An example of the worst case for Disjoint Data Structure I when $m = 5$.

Figure C.5 In the new way of merging, we make the root of the tree with the smaller depth a child of the root of the other tree.

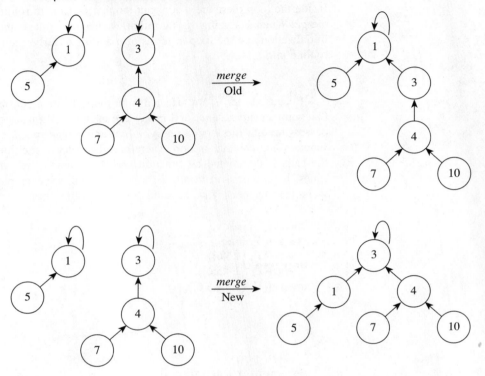

and, after each *merge,* we call *find* looking for index 6. (The actual sets were written as the inputs to *merge* for illustration.) The final tree and array implementation are shown in Figure C.4. The total number of times the comparison in *find* is done is

$$2 + 3 + 4 + 5 + 6.$$

Generalizing this result to an arbitrary *m,* we have that the worst-case number of comparisons is equal to

$$2 + 3 + \cdots + (m + 1) \in \Theta(m^2).$$

We did not consider function *equal* because that function has no effect on the number of times the comparison in function *find* is done.

The worst case occurs when the order in which we do the merging results in a tree whose depth is one less than the number of nodes in the tree. If we modify procedure *merge* so that this cannot happen, we should improve the efficiency. We can do this by keeping track of the depth of each tree, and, when merging, always making the tree with the smaller depth the child. Figure C.5 compares our old way of merging with this new way. Notice that the new way results in a tree with a smaller depth. To implement this method, we need to store the depth of the tree at each root. The following implementation does this.

Disjoint Set Data Structure II

```
const n = the number of elements in the universe;

typedef int index;
typedef index set_pointer;

struct nodetype
{
   index parent;
   int depth;
}

typedef nodetype univere[1..n];        // universe is indexed from 1 to n.

universe U;

void makeset (index i);
{
   U[i].parent = i;
   U[i].depth = 0;
}

set_pointer find (index i)
{
   index j;

   j = i;
   while (U[j].parent != j)
      j = U[j].parent;
   return j;
}

void merge (set_pointer p, set_pointer q)
{
   if (U[p].depth == U[q].depth) {
      U[p].depth = U[p].depth + 1;        // Tree's depth must increase.
      U[q].parent = p;
   }
   else if (U[p].depth < U[q].depth)      // Make tree with lesser depth
      U[p].parent = q;                    // the child.
   else
      U[q].parent = p;
}
```

```
bool equal (set_pointer p, set_pointer q)
{
  if (p == q)
    return true;
  else
    return false;
}

void initial (int n)
{
  index i;

  for (i = 1; i <= n; i++)
    makeset(i);
}
```

It can be shown that the worst-case number of comparisons done in m passes through a loop containing a constant number of calls to routines *equal, find,* and *merge* is in

$$\Theta(m \lg m).$$

In some applications it is necessary to locate efficiently the smallest member of a set. Using our first implementation, this is straightforward, because the smallest member is always at the root of the tree. In our second implementation, however, this is not necessarily so. We can easily modify that implementation to return the smallest member efficiently by storing a variable *smallest* at the root of each tree. This variable contains the smallest index in the tree. The following implementation does this.

Disjoint Set Data Structure III

```
const n = the number of elements in the universe;

typedef int index;
typedef index set_pointer;

struct nodetype
{
  index parent;
  int depth;
  int smallest;
};
```

```
typedef nodetype universe[1..n];        // universe is indexed from 1 to n.

universe U;

void makeset (index i)
{
   U[i].parent = i;
   U[i].depth = 0;
   U[i].smallest = i;                    // The only index i is smallest.
}

void merge (set_pointer p, set_pointer q)
{
   if (U[p].depth == U[q].depth) {
      U[p].depth = U[p].depth + 1;       // Tree's depth must increase.
      U[q].parent = p;
      if (U[q].smallest < U[p].smallest) // q's tree contains smallest
         U[p].smallest = U[q].smallest;  // index.
   }
   else if (U[p].depth < U[q].depth) {   // Make tree with lesser depth
      U[p].parent = q;                   // the child.
      if (U[p].smallest < U[q].smallest) // p's tree contains smallest
         U[q].smallest = U[p].smallest;  // index.
   }
   else {
      U[q].parent = p;
      if (U[q].smallest < U[p].smallest) // q's tree contains smallest
         U[p].smallest = U[q].smallest;  // index.
   }
}

int small (set_pointer p)
{
   return U[p].smallest;
}
```

We have included only the routines that differ from those in Disjoint Set Data Structure II. Function *small* returns the smallest member of a set. Because function *small* has constant running time, the worst-case number of comparisons done in *m* passes through a loop containing a constant number of calls to routines *equal, find, merge,* and *small* is the same as that of Disjoint Set Data Structure II. That is, it is in

$$\Theta(m \lg m).$$

Using a technique called ***path compression,*** it is possible to develop an implementation whose worst-case number of comparisons, in m passes through a loop, is almost linear in m. This implementation is discussed in Brassard and Bratley (1988).

References

Adel'son-Vel'skii, G. M., and E. M. Landis. 1962. An algorithm for the organization of information. *Doklady Akademii Nauk SSSR* 146:263–266.

Akl, S. 1985. *Parallel sorting.* Orlando, Florida: Academic Press.

Aldous, D., and P. Diaconis. 1986. Shuffling cards and stopping times. *The American Mathematical Monthly* 93:333–347.

Bayer, R., and C. McCreight. 1972. Organization and maintenance of large ordered indexes. *Acta Informatica* 1, no. 3:173–189.

Bentley, J. L., D. Haken, and J. B. Saxe. 1980. A general method for solving divide-and-conquer recurrences. *SIGACT News* 12, no. 3:36–44.

Blum, M., R. W. Floyd, V. Pratt, R. L. Rivest, and R. E. Tarjan. 1973. Time bounds for selection. *Journal of Computer and System Sciences* 7, no. 4:448–461.

Borodin, A. B., and J. I. Munro. 1975. *The computational complexity of algebraic and numeric problems.* New York: American Elsevier.

Brassard, G. 1985. Crusade for better notation. *SIGACT News* 17, no. 1:60–64.

Brassard, G., and P. Bratley. 1988. *Algorithmics: Theory and practice.* Englewood Cliffs, N.J.: Prentice Hall.

Brassard, G., S. Monet, and D. Zuffellato. 1986. L'arithmétique des très grands entiers. *TSI: Technique et Science Informatiques* 5, no. 2:89–102.

Clemen, R. T. 1991. *Making hard decisions.* Boston: PWS-Kent.

Cook, S. A. 1971. The complexity of theorem proving procedures. *Proceedings of 3rd annual ACM symposium on the theory of computing,* 151–158. New York: ACM.

Cooper, G. F. 1984. "NESTOR": A computer-based medical diagnostic that integrates causal and probabilistic knowledge. *Technical Report HPP-84-48,* Stanford, Cal.: Stanford University.

Coppersmith, D., and S. Winograd. 1987. Matrix multiplication via arithmetic progressions. *Proceedings of 19th annual ACM symposium on the theory of computing,* 1–6. New York: ACM.

Dijkstra, E. W. 1959. A note on two problems in connexion with graphs. *Numerische Mathematik* 1:269–271.

———. 1976. *A discipline of programming.* Englewood Cliffs, N.J.: Prentice-Hall.

Fine, T. L. 1973. *Theories of probability.* New York: Academic Press.

Fischer, M. J., and M. O. Rabin. 1974. "Super-exponential complexity of Presburger Arithmetic." In *Complexity of computation,* R. M. Karp, ed., 27–41. Providence, R.I.: American Mathematical Society.

Floyd, R. W. 1962. Algorithm 97: Shortest path. *Communications of the ACM* 5, no. 6:345.

Fredman, M. L., and R. E. Tarjan. 1987. Fibonacci heaps and their uses in improved network optimization problems. *Journal of the ACM* 34, no. 3:596–615.

Fussenegger, F., and H. Gabow. 1976. Using comparison trees to derive lower bounds for selection problems. *Proceedings of 17th annual IEEE symposium on the foundations of computer science,* 178–182. Long Beach, Cal.: IEEE Computer Society.

Garey, M. R., and D. S. Johnson. 1979. *Computers and intractability.* New York: W. H. Freeman.

Gilbert, E. N., and E. F. Moore. 1959. Variable length encodings. *Bell System Technical Journal* 38, no. 4:933–968.

Godbole, S. 1973. On efficient computation of matrix chain products. *IEEE Transactions on Computers* C-22, no. 9:864–866.

Graham, R. L., and P. Hell. 1985. On the history of the minimum spanning tree problem. *Annals of the History of Computing* 7, no. 1:43–57.

Gries, D. 1981. *The science of programming*. New York: Springer-Verlag.

Grzegorczyk, A. 1953. Some classes of recursive functions. *Rosprawy Matematyzne* 4. Mathematical Institute of the Polish Academy of Sciences.

Hartmanis, J., and R. E. Stearns. 1965. On the computational complexity of algorithms. *Transactions of the American Mathematical Society* 117:285–306.

Hoare, C. A. R. 1962. Quicksort. *Computer Journal* 5, no. 1:10–15.

Hopcroft, J. E., and J. D. Ullman. 1979. *Introduction to automata theory, languages, and computation*. Reading, Mass.: Addison-Wesley.

Horowitz, E., and S. Sahni. 1974. Computing partitions with applications to the knapsack problem. *Journal of the ACM* 21:277–292.

———. 1978. *Fundamentals of computer algorithms*. Woodland Hills, Cal.: Computer Science Press.

Hu, T. C., and M. R. Shing. 1982. Computations of matrix chain products, Part 1. *SIAM Journal on Computing* 11, no. 2:362–373.

———. 1984. Computations of matrix chain products, Part 2. *SIAM Journal on Computing* 13, no. 2:228–251.

Huang, B. C., and M. A. Langston. 1988. Practical in-place merging. *Communications of the ACM* 31:348–352.

Hyafil, L. 1976. Bounds for selection. *SIAM Journal on Computing* 5, no. 1:109–114.

Iverson, G. R., W. H. Longcor, F. Mosteller, J. P. Gilbert, and C. Youtz. 1971. Bias and runs in dice throwing and recording: A few million throws. *Psychometrika* 36:1–19.

Jarník, V. 1930. O jistém problému minimálnim. *Praca Moravské Prirodovedecké Spolecnosti* 6:57–63.

Johnson, D. B. 1977. Efficient algorithms for shortest paths in sparse networks. *Journal of the ACM* 24, no. 1:1–13.

Keynes, J. M. 1948. *A treatise on probability*. London: Macmillan. (Originally published in 1921.)

Kingston, J. H. 1990. *Algorithms and data structures: Design, correctness, and analysis*. Reading, Mass.: Addison-Wesley.

Knuth, D. E. 1973. *The art of programming, Volume III: Sorting and searching*. Reading, Mass.: Addison-Wesley.

———. 1976. Big omicron and big omega and big theta. *SIGACT News* 8, no. 2:18–24.

Kruskal, J. B., Jr. 1956. On the shortest spanning subtree of a graph and the traveling salesman problem. *Proceedings of the American Mathematical Society* 7, no. 1:48–50.

Kruse, R. L. 1994. *Data structures and program design*. Englewood Cliffs, N.J.: Prentice Hall.

Kumar, V., A. Grama, A. Gupta, and G. Karypis. 1994. *Introduction to parallel computing*. Redwood City, Cal.: Benjamin Cummings.

Ladner, R. E. 1975. On the structure of polynomial time reducibility. *Journal of the ACM* 22:155–171.

van Lambalgen, M. 1987. Random sequences. Ph.D. diss., University of Amsterdam.

Lawler, E. L. 1976. *Combinatorial optimization: Networks and matroids*. New York: Holt, Rinehart and Winston.

Levin, L. A. 1973. Universal sorting problems. *Problemy Peredaci, Informacii* 9:115–116 (in Russian). English translation in *Problems of Information Transmission* 9:265–266.

von Mises, R. 1919. Grundlagen der Wahrscheinlichkeitsrechnung. *Mathematische Zeitschrift* 5:52–99.

———. 1957. *Probability, statistics, and truth.* London: George, Allen & Unwin. (Originally published in Vienna in 1928.)

Neapolitan, R. E. 1990. *Probabilistic reasoning in expert systems.* New York: Wiley.

———. 1992. A limiting frequency approach to probability based on the weak law of large numbers. *Philosophy of Science* 59, no. 3:389–407.

Papadimitriou, C. H. 1994. *Computational complexity.* Reading, Mass.: Addison-Wesley.

Pearl, J. 1986. Fusion, propagation, and structuring in belief networks. *Artificial Intelligence* 29, no. 3:241–288.

———. 1988. *Probabilistic reasoning in intelligent systems.* San Mateo, Cal.: Morgan Kaufmann.

Pratt, V. 1975. Every prime number has a succinct certificate. *SIAM Journal on Computing* 4, no. 3:214–220.

Prim, R. C. 1957. Shortest connection networks and some generalizations. *Bell System Technical Journal* 36:1389–1401.

Sahni, S. 1988. *Concepts in discrete mathematics.* North Oaks, Minn.: The Camelot Publishing Company.

Schonhage, A., M. Paterson, and N. Pippenger. 1976. Finding the median. *Journal of Computer and System Sciences* 13, no. 2:184–199.

Strassen, V. 1969. Gaussian elimination is not optimal. *Numerische Mathematik* 13:354–356.

Tarjan, R. E. 1983. *Data structures and network algorithms,* Philadelphia: SIAM.

Turing, A. 1936. On computable numbers, with an application to the Entscheidungsproblem. *Proceeding of the London Mathematical Society* 2, no. 42:230–265.

———. 1937. On computable numbers, with an application to the Entscheidungsproblem. *Proceedings of the London Mathematical Society* 2, no. 43:544–546.

Yao, A. C. 1975. An $O(|E|\log \log|V|)$ algorithm for finding minimum spanning trees. *Information Processing Letters* 4, no. 1:21–23.

Yao, F. 1982. Speed-up in dynamic programming. *SIAM Journal on Algebraic and Discrete Methods* 3, no. 4:532–540.

Index